REIMAGINING
America
A SURVEY OF AMERICAN HISTORY

Kendall Hunt
publishing company

Solomon K. Smith
DEPARTMENT OF HISTORY
GEORGIA SOUTHERN UNIVERSITY

Kendall Hunt
publishing company

www.kendallhunt.com
Send all inquiries to:
4050 Westmark Drive
Dubuque, IA 52004-1840

Copyright © 2012 by Kendall Hunt Publishing Company

ISBN 978-0-7575-9881-4

Printed in the United States of America

10   9   8   7   6   5   4   3   2

Author's Note

I assembled this manual as an instructional aid to help students enhance their understanding of the lectures and readings for this course, A Survey of American History. These aids go beyond the lectures in some areas, and fall short of them in others. Therefore, it is important to note that each chapter has a corresponding lecture, but this is not to be used as a substitute for attending class. Rather, this should be used as a means of augmenting the lectures presented in class. These aids include vignettes that are usually statements by important figures or commentary of critical events and episodes in the history of the United States. They are not properly documented, although they are exact representations. If you would like proper citations, you can get them from me or track them down yourself.

I also include a list of important terms introduced and emphasized during the lectures or discussed in assigned readings. These terms reflect some critical event or development for a particular period of American history or refer to a concept that will help you better understand the historical process and our contemporary nation. Since I randomly choose some of the terms for your exams, you should learn the definition and historical significance of each, but also understand that they are not the only testable items. Those items not specifically discussed in class are explained by your books, so it is particularly important that you do all the assigned reading. All the instructional materials are arranged in the approximate order in which they are discussed during the semester, but it is sometimes necessary to re-arrange the order so you will need to keep abreast of any changes by actively attending classes.

One final note: You should view the materials in this manual not simply as additional information you will have to learn for exams but as data that will help you better comprehend and assimilate the varied issues addressed in lectures and reading assignments. If you have any questions about any information presented in this manual, please contact me during my office hours, which are listed on your course syllabus.

Solomon K. Smith
Department of History
Georgia Southern University

Table of Contents

Chapters

Lecture Notes

CHAPTER 1

A World of Villages, Part 1: The Americas

North America is one of the most ancient places in the entire world. When we study American history, we too often concentrate on the idea that America was a virgin land, waiting for European conquest. Even when we try to address that shortcoming by concentrating much of our time and energy on the Native American populations, it still too often seems like the role of native peoples in "American" history is to provide a counterbalance to European conquest, one that seems sometimes to exist only to be overcome by the overwhelming tide of American progress, technology, cultural power, and westward expansion.

But North American history has a long past that dates long before 1492, back to a time when both the Americas, North and South, were populated by an extensive series of civilizations, spanning from decentralized hunter-gatherer people and farming communities in the Northeast, to massive and powerful civilizations in Central America—which at the time rivaled any others found on the Earth—to the wealthy and resource rich tribes of the Pacific Northwest. In between was a trading network that linked these peoples together. One ancient grave in modern-day Nebraska, for example, housed trade goods from both the east and west coasts. But wait, there is a story within that story. How did Europeans come to conquer North America? Why, if indeed there was a continent-wide trading network, did Native populations fail to communicate to each other about the initial invasions and push the Europeans back into the sea? Why, indeed, did the Inca not conquer King Charles of Spain? Those questions are answered as we go along. First, we should spend some time describing the situation in the Americas before Europeans arrived.

North America is a land of immigrants, some old, some new. According to the Cherokee myth of creation, the world is an island floating in a great sea, held up by cords at each of the four points of the compass, hanging from the sky. The earth began when a water beetle, tired of being crowded out by the animals above and those swimming, dove into the water. It swam down and down, but always it encountered more animals. Finally it reached the bottom, where it dug into the sand. But even there, it encountered more creatures and, discouraged, the beetle decided to return to the surface where it began hauling mud on its back. As the mud dried, the "Great Buzzard" saw a tiny resting place and flew in for a landing. Where his wings struck the mud-covered back of the beetle, it created mountains and valleys. Other animals saw the new formations, and decided to populate the back of the beetle. When the world grows old, however, the people will die and the cords that hold the earth suspended will break and sink into the ocean.

This creation myth, and the many others like it, tells us a great deal about the beliefs and values of the culture in North America that created it—most importantly, they were valid cultures with as much importance as those of Western Europe. The Cherokees are but one of many groups living in the Americas in the centuries before the arrival of Europeans.

But other cultures, ones in Africa and Europe, experienced tremendous social, political, and economic upheaval in the years before contact, as well. Changes in Europe and Africa placed Native cultures on a collision course with those across the Atlantic. All these groups of cultures had different sets of beliefs and values, different manners of living, different ways of structuring families, working, and worshipping. When these cultures were forced into contact with each another, it drastically changed all three cultures. In the following chapters, we will attempt to answer three questions:

1. What were the cultures and histories of these three populations?
2. How did their first contacts change their cultures?
3. What role did each culture play in the warfare and disease?

To truly understand these questions, we must start at the beginning and follow the story until its final outcome: the modern-day United States of America.

Though the time line usually lists 30,000 BCE (Before Common Era) as the starting point for populating North America, that date is misleading. The ancient quality of that date puts on a few airs, and remains somewhat controversial. Undoubtedly small numbers of Asians crossed into North America during those centuries. J. Leitch Wright in his pivotal work, *The Only Land They Knew*, demonstrated that there was evidence of a Native presence in modern Tampa, Florida as early as 13,000 BCE.

Small bands crossed the Bering Strait, which was then (because of the ice age) a narrow bridge to North America known as Beringia. Large amounts of the world's water were locked in glacial ice, exposing land bridges (like ones also found in southwest Asia and stretching out to the islands of Java and Bali, or the ones in Europe, where the English channel was then dry land). These small bands probably were hunters who came to America following mastodons, bison, woolly rhinos, and other game animals. By 10,500 BCE, they had spread rapidly out from eastern Montana to Tierra del Fuego, the southern tip of South America.

A better starting date for comparing cultures though, is 11,000 BCE. This date corresponds to the rise of village life worldwide, the end of the last Ice Age, and marked the end of the Pleistocene era as it gave way to the modern era. It is interesting to note that human history and the pace of change had increased rapidly over the last 100,000 years. Those humans who lived 100,000 years ago greatly resembled the declining Neanderthal population rather than modern humans. They made the same crude stone tools without standardized shapes, they had no preserved art to speak of, and they did not seem especially skilled at killing large or dangerous prey animals.

Evidence suggests they couldn't even catch fish. Seacoast archaeological sites from the period are devoid of fish bones and fish hooks. Then, about 50,000 years ago, human history shows a sudden change. With the advent of standard stone tools, art, and jewelry, we find fully modern humans. Their garbage dumps included stone and bone tools, needles, scrapers, and eventually bows and arrows. The reason for this change remains unresolved. Some claim it was due to the advent of language, others claim it was the product of more a modern brain structure. In larger cultures, others have offered religious interpretations.

In his book *The Origin of Consciousness in the Breakdown of the Bicameral Mind* (1976), Julian Jayne goes so far as to suggest that modern humans developed only after the evolution of a two-lobed brain. Prior to that biological development, our ancestors were not conscious as we are today. Of course, the biological development of a bicameral mind made for some curious misunderstandings. According to Jayne, as each newly developed lobe struggled for control of our consciousness, they began to speak to each other and thus to us, creating a schizophrenic condition misinterpreted as the voice of god by our ancestors. Rather than making conscious evaluations in novel or unexpected situations, the person would hallucinate a voice or "god" giving admonitory advice or commands, and obey these voices without question. Thus, in Jayne's estimation, Moses did not hear and follow the voice of God, but his own thoughts.

Jayne theorized that a shift from bicameralism marked the beginning of introspection and consciousness as we know it today. According to Jayne, this bicameral mentality began malfunctioning or "breaking down" during the second millennium BCE. He speculates that primitive ancient societies tended to collapse periodically (as in Egypt's Old Kingdom and the periodically vanishing cities of the Mayas) due to increased societal complexity that could not be sustained by this bicameral mindset. The mass migrations of the second millennium BCE created a rash of unexpected situations and stresses that required ancient minds to become more flexible and creative. Self-awareness, or consciousness, was the culturally evolved solution to this problem. Thus, cultural necessity (of interacting with migrating tribes or surviving as a member of one) forced humans to either become self-aware or perish. Thus consciousness, like bicamerality, emerged as a neurological adaptation to social complexity.

Whatever the cause, the fantastic developmental leap led to the worldwide expansion of modern humans, and coincides closely with their expansion into North America. Still, the first major archeological sites in North America that can be definitely identified as a culture date only to about 11,000 BCE. These are the Clovis sites, named after the New Mexico town where they were first discovered. Clovis sites and Clovis culture are characterized by large stone spear points, which are always found among artifacts from the period.

When the first migrants poured out of Alaska, trekked down the ice corridor in Canada, and emerged into the far northern plains near modern-day Edmonton, they must have found a world teeming with game and abundant food sources. Until about 15,000 years ago, North America had pretty much the same kind of wildlife as Africa and Australia. There were saber tooth tigers, giant sloths, armadillo-like glyptodonts, mammoths, camels, cheetahs, and mastodons. But a massive die-off of megafauna ensued at about the same moment that modern humans showed up (the same situation happened in Australia with the arrival of aboriginals). There were herds of elephants and horses, with great predators like lions and cheetahs. There were even animals such as camels and giant sloths. The North American megafauna died out between 15,000 and 11,000 BCE, and for the animals associated with kill site evidence, most died out within a century or two of 11,000 BCE. Some scientists suggest that human hunters moving south slaughtered the great megafauna of North America; others think it the work of climate change or a catastrophic event.

About 8,000 BCE, the climate warmed and the great food sources of the megafauna clearly had gone. So the nature of life changed in North America. Small groups of Native hunters were forced to pursue smaller game in smaller numbers, and hunter populations probably declined. Such drastic change forced some Natives to adapt to small agriculture and begin to cultivate a select group of naturally occurring, easily domesticated crops. In the far south of central Mexico, Natives cultivated corn, beans, squash, sunflowers, and herbs. In turn, the work required to produce those crops in large quantities and the high yields allowed for the rise of highly structured political organizations and a thriving village culture. This sounds like the natural product of a logical decision. In reality, food production on a large scale was a complex phenomenon and one that would eventually lead to massive technological growth and the centralization of strong political power in some parts of the world, and less so in others.

Most species of plants, for example, are useless as sources of food. Some can't be digested. Others, like certain mushrooms, are poisonous. Most have next to no nutritional value for humans. Still other highly nutritious items can't be easily adapted to large populations (like nuts). Some sources of food are too difficult to gather (like insect larva, or even honey on a large scale). So you begin to see the problem. When you look outside your window, you may see an amazing diversity of biomass: mostly grass, trees, leaves, bark—but these things cannot be consumed by humans. Yet, by selecting certain consumable plants, producing large numbers of them on small amounts of land, humans can produce tremendous amounts of necessary calories. One acre of plants cultivated by one person can feed between 10 and 100 times the number of people that one acre of land can produce (in terms of game animals) for a hunter-gatherer society. That is a tremendous advantage for agricultural societies. The domestication of certain animals, like sheep, cows, pigs, and chickens (worldwide) also allowed these early agricultural societies to drastically increase their caloric production in a number of ways. Domestic animals pulled plows, furnished meat, produced milk, and provided fertilizer for the soil.

Food surpluses changed the way human societies were structured. Surpluses allowed some people, a relative handful, not to work in the traditional sense of food production. These first specialists mostly filled the niche of monarchy and bureaucrats, whose sole responsibility was to oversee food production on an increasingly larger scale (in the case of the major Central American empires). Later, these positions would take on a religious context as the society began to invoke the power of a higher entity to boost production or ensure a yield. Crops and domesticated animals provided not only foodstuffs, but items that could be made into manufactured goods, like blankets, nets, tools, and ropes made from cotton, flax, hemp, wool, hide, and bone. So agricultural communities soon began to produce and support much larger populations than hunter-gatherers. North of the Rio Grande, most Native populations practiced agriculture only in limited ways at the moment of contact with Europeans. But south of that river, there were several large agriculturally based cultures.

Mexico and Central America

Though we can't spend too much time on this topic, agricultural production in Mexico grew so rapidly that by 2,000 BCE, cities with permanent bureaucracies existed in Mexico, with great temples and complicated social structures. By 650 CE (Common Era), productive agricultural practices supported an urban environment of 200,000 in the area where Mexico City exists today. That old city was the capital of the Toltec people. There an elite group of religious and political leaders controlled a trading network that spanned from South America to modern-day Arizona. Around 900 CE, the Toltecs conquered Monte Alban and Teotihuacan, and the Mayan centers in the Yucatan. The Maya had, since 300 CE, existed as an agricultural society that supported a leisure class, created fantastic art and jewelry, writing, and a mathematical system, and possessed more accurate calendars than Europe would have for centuries (as late as the 1917 Russian Revolution, for example, the old unreformed Orthodox calendar was nine days off, causing the October Revolution of 1917 to actually take place in November). But around 1200 CE, the Toltec retreated and withdrew toward the central highlands. For the next century, the Aztecs migrated to the area and, by 1325 CE, they had founded Tenochtitlan (now Mexico City). By the time the Spanish arrived in 1519, Tenochtitlan supported a population of 300,000 people, was producing a wealth of manufactured goods, and had built great pyramids to the moon and sun gods, where they sacrificed thousands of captives of war each year (a scene all too familiar to anyone who has seen the movie *Apocalypto*). The Aztecs had an irrigation system that brought fresh water into the city, and their markets filled the streets with food and household goods. By 1500 CE, the Aztec empire controlled over 5 million Native peoples, making it one of the largest empires of its time.

Far to the South in the Andes Mountains of modern Peru another agricultural society flourished between 900 and 200 BCE. They irrigated soil, produced magnificent potatoes, and built great temples—all at more than 6,000 feet above sea level. Though the earlier group (called the Chavins) fell to a drought, the subsequent Inkan People (you may know them as the Inca, but they referred to themselves as Inkan) peaked between 1200 and 1400 CE, aggressively extending their borders to span much of the western coast of South America. Their warrior class forced their subjects to mine great quantities of silver and gold. They domesticated the llama (North American Natives had no domesticated animals but dogs [this is a significant point given the relationship between the domestication of animals, the growth of technology, and the spread of contagions]). The Inkans domesticated corn, lima beans, peanuts, cotton, potatoes, and squash. The Inka demonstrated an ecological understanding we still can't seem to grasp. By 1500, the Inkan capital of Cuzco had a population of 250,000 people, and was located at more than 9,000 feet above sea level. Their empire in total probably included some 8 to 12 million subjects.

Native American Cultures Before European Contact

It is difficult to know how many Native Americans lived in the western hemisphere before the arrival of the Spanish in 1492. Estimates of that population vary greatly and are hotly debated—invested not only with science but contemporary politics. In the 1980s, for example, Kirkpatrick Sale, in his book *The Conquest of Paradise*, wrote of the horrors of European colonization, indicting Europe and especially the Spanish for a sixteenth-century genocide of native Americans. Most scholars agree now that in 1492 the Americas had the potential for a Native population of between 80 to 100 million people. Of that total, somewhere between 4 and 10 million people lived north of the Rio Grande River. This is significant because, in the 1950s, the entire native population of North America was believed to be only about 1 million people. That small number is often used to justify the European colonization of the Americas along the grounds that the land was fundamentally empty when Europeans arrived.

But such a small number is entirely misleading. We know that in the complex cultures of Central American and Peru, there were as many as 25 million living under the empires of the Aztecs, Maya, and the Inka. We know there was also somewhere on the order of 600 to 800 languages spoken in the western hemisphere before the arrival of Europeans. By comparison to Europe, the American continents were places of remarkable cultural diversity. So the real question is: Where did all the people go? They died. Within 15 years of European contact, estimates suggest that nearly 60 percent of the pre-contact populations of the Americas died from exposure to disease. Possibly as much as 40 percent of the population died from the first exposure alone. Native Americans represented a virgin population, with no natural resistance or immunity to European diseases and ailments. In such a situation, even the common cold could be fatal.

The situation was slightly different in North America. In the eastern part of what is today the United States, around the Ohio and Mississippi rivers, large numbers of tribes lived in what is often referred to as Woodland societies. From 1,000 BCE, hunting and gathering populations were actively cultivating certain crops, like tobacco and corn, to supplement their foraging. On the upper banks of the Ohio River, the Adena culture, among the first mound-building and sedentary tribes in North America, flourished until 200 CE. As they declined for unknown reasons, they were replaced by the Hopewell culture that emerged in the Ohio and Mississippi river valleys. The Hopewell, too, built enormous ceremonial burial mounds and took advantage of the few food crops that could be easily cultivated, though those were limited in nature and scope by the eastern woodland environment (intensive agriculture there, for example, developed 9,000 years after it did in the fertile crescent of the Middle East). Hopewell graves contain materials from a myriad of locations, ranging from the Gulf Coast to the South, the Great Lakes to the north, and the Rockies to the West. After 900 CE, when Central American corn was successfully brought to the North America in great amounts, Mississippian culture replaced the Hopewell and the population began to increase. Centered near modern-day St. Louis, their capital, called Cahokia, supported a population that might have reached 40,000, more than any European-inhabited North American city until after the American Revolution. Cahokia suddenly collapsed in the early 1400s. Although we are not certain, we believe it was possibly because the natural resources of the region had reached their limit and were no longer able to support such a large population—making the collapse of Cahokia an ancient warning of environmental overload. Others suggest that Cahokia declined as a result of nutritional deficiencies or diseases. Despite their collapse, the Natchez people to the south would continue to preserve Mississippian culture for nearly a century after Cahokia fell, before succumbing to a French military invasion.

As we have seen, Columbus didn't discover a new world. Rather, he established a connection between two worlds that were both already very old. North America had a rich history prior to the arrival of Europeans, one made by hundreds of culturally distinct groups. The Europeans who came to the Americas never completely understood this situation, nor did the Americans who followed them. They failed to recognize that cultural vitality and, too often, they saw Native populations as uncivilized occupants of what was otherwise a virgin land—nothing more than another barrier to be surpassed.

Items to Consider

Ice Age, Clovis Culture, Beringia, First Americans, Megafauna extinction, Agriculture, Central American Empires, Population Decline, Southwestern Civilizations, Kirkpatrick Sale

CHAPTER 2

Introduction, Part II: The Nature of Africa and Western Europe: 1350–1550

Africa

Though there is not much time to spend on African civilizations and their relationship to American colonization, there are some things that must be discussed before we can continue. Africa was on the verge of a major change by 1400. Much like the societies in the new world, Africans had reached a level of highly productive agriculture; they had stratified societies and complex political hierarchies. By 1400, sub-Saharan Africa probably had a population of about 20 million. They had contacts with Arab traders to the east, with Europe through Bedouin traders crossing the desert, and with Portuguese traders coming south around the bulge of west Africa.

Like the Americas, Africa had hundreds of distinct cultures and languages. Yet, most of Africa's population shared some fundamental qualities. Agricultural practices, especially slash and burn techniques used to produce rice, millet, and sorghum, were similar up and down the coast of West Africa. Strongly bonded extended families served as the basis of identity for both the individual and the community. Many families were matrilineally structured, with property and authority passing along female kinship lines. These complex relationships also determined basic decisions about crop production, community punishment, and the distribution of goods and services in a community. Most West African cultures believed in a polytheistic universe. Their gods inhabit everything, and can be represented in multiple forms. Since the gods inhabited everyday items, every action is an act of religious devotion. This means that the acts of hunting and planting served both secular and spiritual functions. In such a religious tradition, there is no need for a specialized class of religious people to intercede for the practitioner. Every single act of life, each and every day the person is alive, is an intentional act of devotion, so that compromises and agreements are worked out between human and god on a continuous basis.

Western Africa was home to two important civilizations. Ghana, which flourished from the sixth to the fourteenth centuries, was a vast agricultural, herding, and trading power. Ghana was the main supplier of gold and salt to Western Europe, a position that made it one of the wealthiest regions of the period. But prosperity has its dangers. Invading armies from the north, mainly Muslims, would eventually defeat the Ghana Empire at the end of the fourteenth century. Out of the ashes of Ghana would arise the Muslim empire of Songhai (often called Mali). The Songhai began small, conquering agricultural villages from the grasslands to the Sahara. During the height of its power from 1450 to 1590, the Songhai traded extensively with Europe, India, and China. Centered at Timbuktu, Songhai was founded by Sundiata, who led the city (and his empire) to become a major administrative and scholastic center for the Islamic world. At one time, historians estimate that more than 100,000 people lived in Timbuktu, but today it remains a shadow of its former self, a mud-built town of 20,000 people on the edge of the Sahara Desert.

Songhai had an advanced agricultural system, maintained and harvested a fishery on the Niger River and in the Atlantic Ocean, and maintained immense cattle herds roaming the inland grasslands of the region. Songhai would capture the attention of world when its ruler, Mansa Musa, made a pilgrimage to Mecca in 1324. Unlike his grandfather Sundiata, Mansa Musa was a devout Muslim. Islamic law requires that all faithful Muslims make a *hajj*, or holy visit, to the city on the Arabian Peninsula where the faith was started. Mansa Musa was a very rich king. He was said to have taken more than 500 people with him on the hajj, each carrying a staff of solid gold. When Mansa Musa passed through Cairo, legends say he gave away so much gold that the price of it fell and the economy was affected for more than twenty years. The appearance of a wealthy king from a faraway land made a deep impression on the people he encountered, causing Mali to appear on maps throughout the Middle East and Europe. For the first time, sub-Saharan Africa became well known north of the Sahara Desert.

Songhai was destroyed after a bloody war with Morocco. Morocco's sultan wanted West African gold, so in 1590 he sent an army of 3,000 men south across the Sahara Desert. The spears and lances of the Songhai warriors were no match for the cannons and muskets of the Moroccan army, but the fighting continued long after the Songhai government had been destroyed. After ten years, the Sultan lost interest and abandoned his army in Songhai. The Moroccan soldiers were either killed or absorbed into the local population. The Moroccan invasion destroyed Songhai, and with it the trade routes that had brought prosperity to the region for hundreds of years.

The capital city of Timbuktu remained a symbol of the splendor ancient Africa. A great city that flourished on a bend in the Niger River for more than four hundred years, Timbuktu was at the end of the camel caravan route that linked sub-Saharan Africa to North Africa and Arabia. Gold, ivory, and kola nuts passed through Timbuktu, but the most important commodity was salt. Timbuktu is located near several salt mines. Caravans hauled salt from nearby mines to be traded for gold. When the Portuguese showed that it was easier to sail around the coast of Africa than travel through the desert, Timbuktu began to decline in influence and was destroyed at the end of the sixteenth century during the war between Morocco and Songhai.

Western Europe Before the 'Discovery'

Western Europe was a relative back water in the world in the period just before Columbus' voyage. It was not technologically advanced, it did not have a strong economy, and there were few consolidated political systems. What the Western Europeans did have was a definitive idea about themselves. Western Europeans saw their place in the world as part of an intense competition with itself and with the other great civilizations of the world, particularly that of Constantinople and the realms controlled by Islam. (China remained on the political and intellectual margins of European thought.) The competition played out along political, social, and economic lines. And, indeed, even this competition was not taking place in a vacuum, but in the context of a rapid series of changes in Europe dating back to 1300.

1. The Black Death

Plague first came to Europe in 1348 with arrival of the bubonic plague, or Black Death. Developing first in Italian city states, the contagion quickly swept across the European continent killing between 40 and 45 percent of the European population in the first wave. Several more waves would follow, each time wreaking havoc on the population. The European economic and political systems broke down entirely and when they were rebuilt, they changed in important ways. The old feudal system—a European political system comprising a set of reciprocal legal and military obligations among the warrior nobility, revolving around the three key concepts of lords, vassals, and serfs—was gone. Labor was scarce, so the lower classes gained more political power. Rebellions of workers were scattered throughout Europe—Wat Tyler's rebellion in 1381, the Jacqueries in 1358—in the years following the plague, as the lower classes asserted themselves in new ways within society.

2. Warfare

On the heel of this disaster came the so called Hundred Years War of 1337–1453, which brought devastation to Europe and lasted longer than 100 years though less than half the time was actually spent fighting. The war, between the English and the French, began because the King Edward III of England (1327–1377), claimed the French throne as his own when the French king died without heirs. All the battles were fought in France, and the western part of that country was ravaged. England suffered little beyond some serious political unrest (Richard II deposed in 1399, which eventually resulted in the War of the Roses). Although the Hundred Years War led to the political consolidation in France at the expense of colonization, its real importance diminished due to the spread of the plague and the advancement of European military technology.

3. Religious Turmoil

The glue of Europe itself, the Christian church, centered in Rome, was in serious trouble as a result of the plague. Church practice was beleaguered by corrupt church leaders and inflexibility, as well as losing touch with the people. Despite these problems the Church saw great triumphs in the thirteenth century: the beginnings and success of the Crusades to conquer the Holy Lands; the success of missionaries to Christianize all of eastern and northern Europe, and the removal of the Moors from Spain. But the church fell into decline during the fourteenth century. The plague's destruction led to a competition between kings and the popes, which created a crisis in western Christianity. In 1378, the College of Cardinals elected two popes (one centered in Rome and one in Avignon, France), and for a short time there were even three popes. This left Christians with a conundrum: which pope held the keys to salvation? If you followed the wrong man, you were damned for all eternity. All of this came at the worst possible time, in the midst of the Black Death. People handled their uncertainty in different ways. A few people rejected Christianity and turned to cults of death, devil worshiping, and witchcraft. Some rejected religion altogether and began to turn to new sources of knowledge and explanation: the sciences. But my personal favorite is the Order of Flagellants, whose deeply religious members believed that the plague was a punishment from God as a result of European Christianity's irreligious behavior. To correct the problem and restore God's love in the land, the flagellants went through the streets beating each other bloody with whips and chains, all the while spreading the plague further.

The Rise Secularism

It is hardly surprising, then, that as people began to doubt the utility of Christianity that the Renaissance in Florence and other Italian states came to pass. The word *renaissance* is a French word meaning rebirth, and that was exactly what it was, a renewed interest in the ideas and institutions of the classical world, of the Greeks and Romans. Many people see the Renaissance as the origins of modern Europe, but that's really been overdone. All the major institutions that made modern Europe modern, from government to natural science, date back to the Middle Ages, or the "Dark Ages," as Renaissance thinkers called them.

What was really important about the Renaissance was that it brought about a change in attitude and thinking in Europe. The most important question a person asks in the course of their life is what they ought to do with themselves; ultimately, why are we here and what is the purpose of living? These questions have been asked by humanity for eons, but often remained the preoccupation of religious thinkers. But in Renaissance Italy a new group of people began to address this issue, and so we begin to see a secular character emerging in Europe. Life is no longer seen by the intellectuals as a brief preparation for the next world. The old way of thinking was dominated by human frailty and the dangers of life. The power of humanity characterized the new way of thinking. Now don't think of this in linear fashion. One did not replace the other. Instead, they interacted with one another, changing and evolving into one mindset.

These two ways of thought were extremely important in the development of a modern European, or Western culture. The new way of thinking changed everything. Now education was necessary for everyone. The idea of dividing people into grades or levels, of teaching language skills, of encouraging social etiquette emerged. Before this time, adult Europeans acted like big children, they spat, belched, grabbed food, they lacked any sense of decorum or etiquette. Now the elite were encouraged to be polite and to be educated. Most importantly, it gave people the idea that they had the ability to change their situation. Older Christian thought was fatalistic. God's plan dictated how history should go, and it could not be changed. But Europeans began to move beyond that line of thinking, especially the elites. Europeans began to think they had the ability to create lasting changes in this world. And that becomes the most important heritage of the Renaissance: how it changed politics. A new generation of leaders emerged in Europe who tried to make their countries stronger, more centralized, more powerful. One of the most famous pieces of Renaissance literature encouraging these leaders to do so was Niccolo Machiavelli's *The Prince* (1513). Machiavelli encouraged Western leaders to act like the old Romans, to be as ruthless as necessary to make their states powerful. They were also encouraged to make themselves the state, so that it could not exist without them. The success of the state depended on the success of the monarch. Several European leaders would answer Machiavelli's challenge: Henry VII of England, Louis XI of France, and Ferdinand of Aragon and his wife Isabella of Castile. The Renaissance itself came to an end around 1528 when a French army annihilated Rome; but the influence of that culture lived on throughout Europe.

The Protestant Reformation

Before 1517, all of Western Europe's religious life was essentially led by a single religious tradition, Christianity, with the church headed by the pope in Rome. Supporting the Catholic Church was the Holy Roman Empire (HRE), a union of European medieval states during the Middle Ages and the early modern period. The HRE's territorial extent varied over its history, but at its peak it encompassed the territories of present-day Germany, Austria, Switzerland, Liechtenstein, Luxembourg, the Slovak Republic, Slovenia, Belgium, and the Netherlands as well as large parts of modern Poland, France, and Italy. For much of its history the HRE consisted of hundreds of smaller kingdoms, principalities, duchies, counties, Free Imperial Cities, and other domains. After 1517, the Christian religion split into two major camps: Catholics (the old church headed by the pope) and Protestants (the new churches, that eventually split into hundreds of branches, and rejected the authority of the pope in Rome). This split, known as the Protestant Reformation, would tear Christianity and the Holy Roman Empire asunder.

Three things caused the Protestant Reformation. First, there was a general belief in Western Europe, held particularly by the poor, that the church and its leadership only cared about the ruling classes. As a result, the church helped keep elites in power. It allowed them to be oppressive and abuse their power: They taxed too much, they sold church offices, and they freely sold indulgences (the purchasing of relief from punishment in the afterlife). A second source of the rebellion lay in the middle classes of the northern European cities. The European middle class emerged from the ranks of bankers and merchants, who had been growing in wealth and power for about 200 years. They had a stubborn, independent streak and they despised the old feudal systems, old systems of king and pope. They wanted the same type of freedom of religion as they enjoyed in their businesses. The last source of rebellion leading to the reformation resided in a number of kings and princes, again especially in northern Europe, who were fed up with the power of the popes, of following Roman orders, and the showing of fealty on bended knee. Discontent seemed to be everywhere in Europe.

In 1517 something remarkable happened. For more than a millennium, the peoples of western and central Europe had been united in a common faith and their allegiance to the pope in Rome. Then the Protestant Reformation shattered that bond and sparked a century of warfare and social change. At first, reformers only wanted to change the way the Catholic Church was run. Over the centuries, through gifts, fees, and taxes, the church had grown wealthy. Some bishops and cardinals used that wealth to live extravagantly. Corruption became commonplace. Pope Leo X (1513–21), a member of the powerful Italian Medici family, received half a million ducats a year from the sale of religious offices. In England, Cardinal Thomas Wolsey set an equally bad example by giving religious offices to his family. Ordinary priests and monks gathered in their share of the spoils, too, using their religious authority to extract economic (and sometimes sexual) favors from their parishioners. These abuses and many more ignited a smoldering anticlericalism in northern Europe.

Until 1517, those raising their voices had either been ignored or condemned as heretics and executed. Martin Luther, a German monk and a professor at the University of Wittenberg publicly challenged the church by nailing his 95 Theses to the door of the town cathedral. This document, which was widely reprinted, condemned the church for the selling of indulgences. Luther said forgiveness could only come from God, through His grace, not from the church, for a fee. Pope Leo X excommunicated him, and King Charles I of Spain (who was also head of the Holy Roman Empire) threatened him with arrest and punishment. So strong was the sentiment for reform in the northern German states that the German princes protected Luther from arrest, even under the threat of invasion. Soon all of Europe was at war as Charles I dispatched his armies to reestablish Catholicism and his authority in the Holy Roman Empire.

In response to Charles I, Luther broadened his attack on the church. In essence, Luther rejected four major Catholic doctrines.

1. The ability to win salvation by good deeds
2. The spiritual authority of the pope

3. The role of priests as mediators between God and the people
4. The bible as the main source of churchly authority (Luther considered the bible itself as the sole authority in matters of faith)

Of these four, the last was the most important. It created a possibility of numerous interpretations of the Bible, in contrast to the single Roman interpretation.

Europe became a crucible of change. Luther's challenge sparked a number of Protestant religions. The most important, after Lutheranism, was Calvinism, which was created by the French theologian John Calvin in the 1530s. Calvinism was similar to the religion of Luther but departed from it in two important ways. First, it depended much more on the doctrine of predestination—the idea God had selected only a few elect Christians to go to heaven. Second, Calvinists were not as friendly with the government as were Lutherans. In fact, they viewed the role of the government to be a tool of the Catholic Church, a position that did not win them many friends among European leaders, as you can imagine.

The English Reformation

We also have a strange situation in England, in that it broke away from the Roman Church before it was really Protestant. The origins of the English break lay with Henry VIII (1509–47), a man who was called the "Defender of the Faith" by the pope for his scholarly attacks on Martin Luther and the foundations of the Protestant faith. But Henry was most concerned with building a dynasty for the Tudor family and to do that he needed a son. His wife, Catherine of Aragon, could not conceive due to medical complications after the birth of Princess Mary. So Henry asked the pope to annul his marriage in order for him to marry Anne Boleyn, a girl who promised that she could give him a child. The pope loved Henry, but he could not grant a divorce because he already gave Henry a special dispensation to marry Catherine (she was previously married to Arthur, Henry's older brother) and she was a daughter of Charles V, the Holy Roman Emperor. To grant a divorce would require the pope to admit he had been in error when he issued the dispensation and it would anger the Holy Roman Emperor, so the pope had no choice but to say no. At that point, Henry broke with the church in Rome and created the Church of England with himself at the head. Thus, England became technically, but not at heart, a Protestant country. Henry, who remained at heart a Catholic, did not want to change the church's doctrine but he was pressed hard by some members of Parliament to do so. Even worse, the new marriage did not result in a son. In fact, Henry would go through several wives before the birth of his son, Edward. As a result, the religious situation in England wavered back and forth for the next twenty years as one monarch after another came to power. King Henry VIII died a Protestant in 1547, his son, Edward VI, died a Protestant in 1553 (son of Jane Seymour), then Henry's daughter Mary (daughter of Catherine of Aragon) died a Catholic in 1558, and finally Henry's daughter Elizabeth (daughter of Anne Boleyn) took the throne in 1558. By the time of Elizabeth, the Anglican Church was essentially Protestant (although not radically so), but it retained much of Catholic symbolism. Under Elizabeth, England became, somewhat ironically, the defender of the Protestant religion, although almost by default.

The Church Fights Back

While most of the religious turmoil in Europe looks decided by 1560, little was actually settled. The Catholic Church, though wounded and splintered, was not about to accept the Protestant split. The period from 1560 to 1648 was essentially one of constant religious warfare throughout Europe. After 1560, Catholics launched what came to be known as the Counter-Reformation, an effort to reform the problems of the church and eliminate Protestantism. The Catholic Church rededicated itself to God. It founded new organizations like the Jesuit Order (Ignatius of Loyola 1540) dedicated to teaching Catholic beliefs and conducting missionary work (along with trying to suppress Protestantism). In an effort to reaffirm Catholic doctrine, the church gathered its leadership at the Council of Trent in northern Italy in 1545.

The meeting of Catholic leaders continued sporadically until after 1563. The leaders who met at Trent began by reasserting Catholic doctrine against the challenges of Protestantism. As the Catholic response became more assertive, the conflict between Catholics and Protestants intensified. Books were banned; Ecclesiastical courts were created to counter one side or the other. The most-feared of these courts was the Inquisition. There were really two inquisitions, the Spanish, dating back to 1480, and the Roman, created in 1542. These two boards of inquisitors rooted out heretics, or Protestants, sometimes through torture, and turned the unrepentant over to secular authorities for sentencing. The sentences were often harsh, including the practice of burning heretics alive. In the end, neither the Inquisitions nor the Counter-Reformation had little long term affect.

Political units were more important in determining religion. If your king or prince became a Protestant, then you as his subject were Protestant. If he remained Catholic, then you remained a Catholic. By 1560 the division was mostly complete. The most powerful countries, France, Spain, and Austria were all Catholic. The Protestants' most powerful country was England, but they were nothing compared to the powerful nations aligned against them. Had the Catholics ever put together a dedicated attempt to destroy Protestantism, it should have worked. The wars of religion that followed, however, failed to achieve that goal. And the consequences of Spain's failure were immense, but that is addressed in another Chapter.

Items to Consider

Social configuration of West African societies, West African religions, Mali, Black Death, Renaissance, *The Prince*, Protestant Reformation, Martin Luther, English Reformation, Catholic Counter-Reformation

CHAPTER 3

The Spanish Century and The Great Biological Exchange

Right now you might be wondering just what exactly I am up to—you are supposed to be in a class about American history, and yet I have spent all my time talking about stuff that does not seem to relate to the United States. What you have to understand is that the discovery and conquest of the Americas (and thus, the founding of the U. S.), depends on a series of unexpected events outside the two American continents. If there had not been advanced and resource-rich civilizations in the Americas, no one would of cared about Columbus' so-called discovery. Similarly, if there had not been long contact between Europe and Africa before the discovery of the Americas, then Europeans would not have known about the long history of slavery in the region and political turmoil that made it ripe for Europeans' to take advantage of the situation. The same must be said about circumstances in Europe. If Europe had not experienced a series of unusual and catastrophic changes, it might have remained the relative backwater it was after the fall of the Roman Empire. And yet such, was not the case.

The changes in Europe discussed in the last chapter gradually led to a greater desire to extend European influence around the world; however, these changes did not immediately lead to the colonization. Several decades were required to consolidate changes and gains made during those periods, and to set the course of empire. Neither did all the European nations begin the process of exploration and expansion at the same moment; nor did they all concentrate the same amount of resources on those goals.

Portugal, for example, led European exploration during the 1400s, visited much of the known world, and started the trans-Atlantic slave trade, but they would not discover the American continents. Portugal was a nation of only 1.5 million people. It seems ironic that one of Europe's smaller, less powerful nations would begin the process of overseas exploration and conquest. In other ways, it seems obvious that they would. Portugal proved politically stable before any other European nation, it enjoyed a long history of seafaring, and it owned an impressive fleet of merchant vessels. It was also positioned strategically for exploration, at the intersection of two major bodies of water: the Atlantic Ocean and the Mediterranean Sea. But more important than all of that, Portugal had a ruler interested in the world beyond his national borders. In the 1420s, Portuguese was under the control of Prince Henry. Often called the Navigator, Henry dreamed of finding a way to open up water trade routes with Asia to break the Arab States' hold over the Asian trade.

Henry's fleets began by exploring the West African coast. There they acquired commodities in high demand in Europe, but they would also initiate the international slave trade by paying Africans to capture other West Africans in exchange for trade goods. Slavery had a long history in Africa. Coastal empires had long held human beings as chattel slaves, and some were sold overland in the caravan routes to the Middle East. But the kinds of slavery that developed after 1400, as practiced by Europeans, were unlike anything in Africa. In the 14th century, merchants from Italy brought sugar cane from western Asia and created sugar plantations farmed by slave labor on Mediterranean islands. Some Mediterranean

12

sugar planters worked slaves to death, because they were so cheap. Thus the demand for new slaves remained high, but the value of sugar produced in slavery grew higher. When the Spanish eventually arrived in the Caribbean, they brought this sugar-slave system to the new world.

The Portuguese, meanwhile, expanded their exploration and trading routes down the coast of Africa. By 1487, Portuguese sailors would open a sea route to India. Blown off course by storm, Bartholomeu Diaz and his men would sail aimlessly for thirteen days before finally seeing land. Realizing he was at southern tip of Africa in February 1488, Diaz convinced his men to round the Cape of Good Hope. Although Diaz dreamed of traveling all the way to India, his men were exhausted and their food supplies were low so he decided to return to Portugal. Picking up where Diaz left off, Vasco da Gama would go all the way to India in 1497. Da Gama was born in Portugal in 1469. His father held an important position at Court, which gave him an advantage over other explorers. Seeking to expand on the work of Diaz, da Gama left Lisbon for India on July 8, 1497. By December of 1497, he had passed around the Cape of Good Hope. By January of 1498, he was at mouth of Zambezi River. On May 20, 1498, da Gama reached Calcutta. When he returned to Portugal in 1499, he brought with him the most valuable cargo ever acquired in trade by a European power. Each of these explorers planted the Portuguese flag at every spot they visited to claim the land for their native land and create European trading ports along the way, setting the stage for future exploration and conquest.

Once the Moorish invaders were driven from the Iberian peninsula, Spain consolidated under the power of one throne and then they too began to expand from its base. Experienced seafaring populations believed at the time that most of the Earth's surface was covered by land and that the Atlantic (they believed the world was round, just not nearly as big as it turned out to be) covered only a narrow strip of water between Asia and Europe. A young captain from Genoa named Cristobal Colon (you probably know him as Christopher Columbus, but we will refer to him here by his given name) had bold plan of finding a faster route to Asia than traveling south along the African coast. He believed that by heading west one could reach Asia in half the time, a theory he attempted to sell to every major European monarch and government, only to have it dismissed. Colon would eventually get funding from the Spanish crown. Colon left Spain in August 1492 with ninety men in three small ships. He found land on October 12, 1492—the island of San Salvador (called Samana Cay by the people who lived there) in the Caribbean. Colon named the Arawak people he found there "Indians," because he believed he had reached an island off the coast of Asia, which he was certain must be just over the horizon. From there he went to Cuba (thinking it was Japan) and then on to Hispaniola. Colon returned home to great acclaim. He would return to the Americas three times, looking for treasures of gold and silver, and went to his grave believing he had found a new route to Asia.

Recognizing they had something of importance, Spain asked the Church to legitimize the areas Columbus "discovered" as their own territory. The church responded with the Treaty of Tordesillas, which drew a north-south line about 1,100 miles west of the Cape Verde Islands, giving Spain everything west of the line (which amounted to most of the territory in the Americas and positioning them to challenge Portugal's domination of its New World empire) and everything east of the line to Portugal (they were included because they were the only other Catholic state involved in exploration at the time).

The Spanish Century

The Treaty of Tordesillas signaled the dawning of a new era. The sixteenth Century was dominated by the Spanish colonization of America. Spanish conquistadors invaded the Western Hemisphere in search of glory, treasure, and souls. Generally they were hard men, raised during the wars of the *reconquista* (the war waged to drive the Moors from the Iberian peninsula) and determined to find wealth in the New World. Spanish raids into the Caribbean proved both cruel and successful, as native populations had little means to resist their attackers. More than anything else, the native people of America were conquered by the deadly germs the Spanish brought with them. By 1511, most of the Caribbean was under Spanish control and plans were made to explore the mainland to the west. By 1513, Vasco Balboa crossed the thin spit of the isthmus of Panama and reached the Pacific Ocean. In 1519, Hernando Cortés, with a small force of about 400 men, landed in Vera Cruz and marched inland, 200 miles, toward the Aztec capital of Tenochtitlan. Cortés used the technical advantages of Spanish steel and horses, and the powerful effect of cannon fire, to keep the Aztec warriors on the defensive. He exploited discontent among native populations and benefited from the initial misconception that he was the Toltec god Quetzalcoatl who was returning to free the tribute-weary populations from Aztec rule (as local myth predicted). Once they arrived in the capital, Cortés captured the Aztec emperor, Montezuma, seized control of the state, and plundered the treasury.

Technology and Biology in the Spanish Conquest

Students often place too much emphasis on technology in the Spanish conquest of the Meso-American empires. Though it certainly had its role, it was not the main reason for the Spanish success. It is important to note that the Spanish did have some guns, but their most powerful advantage came in their steel and horses. These items allowed the Spanish conquistadors to overwhelm the thinly clad Indians with little armor and no mobility. It would also give rise to a belief in Spanish invincibility, since Spanish steel swords could cleave a man in two while native flint swords shattered on Spanish armor. Time after time, the Spanish slaughtered native armies that so vastly outnumbered them it seems impossible. Disease also played a major role in conquest. It is estimated that small pox and other, less deadly European diseases reduced the Aztec Empire from 20–25 million down to only 2.5 million by the 1570s, and down to only 1.6 million by 1618.

In the 1520s, another conquistador named Francisco Pizarro launched an attack against the massive Inkan empire farther south. This time the Spanish took less than 200 men. Pizarro conquered the Inkan capital of Cuzco, executed the Inkan emperor, and plundered their rich silver mines. But here, too, disease played just as important a role. By the time Pizarro arrived, nearly half the Inkan population lay dead and their empire was in disarray.

Spain North of the Rio Grande

The Spanish had less success settling North America. In 1513, Ponce de León explored the southern Atlantic coast of Florida, but his exploration came to little, and León himself was killed by a Calusa arrow in 1521. Rumors of cities of gold encouraged other explorations. Narváez explored the Texas Gulf Coast in 1528. In 1539 Hernando de Soto launched a massive invasion of what is today the southern United States, fighting his way into the interior. As he went along he found towns abandoned (presumably by epidemics of European diseases) that preceded the Spanish as they moved into the interior. Soto's expedition was nearly destroyed on a number of occasions. He fought off assaults by the Alibamu (Alabama) and the native populations, who eventually became the Chickasaws, before reaching the Mississippi River in 1542. In the 1540s, Spain launched another attempt at exploration of North America, trying again to find Cibola, the mythical city of gold. Francisco Coronado and a party of 300 Spanish (plus 700 Native Americans) pressed up into Arizona and eventually out onto the Great Plains, with no luck at finding the city of gold. Thus the Spanish believed that the New World's wealth lay in Central America and mostly gave up on North America for the near future.

Consequences of Contact

Why were the native populations so open to infection? The answer to that question is elusive, but there are some obvious suggestions. First, the lack of domesticated animals played an important role. The Americas offered relatively few options for domesticated animals, with the exception of llamas, dogs, turkeys, ducks, and guinea pigs. Since most of the worst European diseases were initially crossovers from concentrated interaction with domesticated animal populations, Europe (with a large number of domesticated species) had far better epidemic disease immunity while North America had virtually none. The Americas remained in relative isolation from initial settlement to the arrival of Colon, so the native peoples were a virgin population in terms of disease resistance. As a result, epidemic disease would decimate the American population. Central America would drop from 20–25 million to only 1.6 million by 1630. The Inkas would go from 9 million in 1533 to only 500,000 by 1630. Estimates of population decline in North America remain elusive, but it is reasonable to conclude that similar death rates probably occurred.

The European "invasion" of America changed life radically on three continents, and extended European conflicts to the western hemisphere. The primary legacy of that exchange is often called the "Great Biological Exchange," the transfer of peoples, plants, contagions, and animals from the Old World to the New, and from the New to the Old. Part of that exchange was the arrival of epidemic disease, which devastated so much of the Native American population. Native peoples who survived were forced to work in the Spanish *encomienda* system, where Spanish authorities forced local Indians to work in mines and fields. Europe brought new plants to North America, like a number of grasses, grains, and a major animal in the horse. New World food crops, especially corn and tomatoes increased agricultural yields and stimulated a population explosion in Europe. The vast resources of gold and silver that made their way across the Atlantic filled the treasury of the Spanish monarchy, inflated European currency in general, and made Spain the most powerful nation in the world until 1650.

Items to Consider

Rise of Portugal, West African slavery before contact, Cristobal Colon, Spanish Century, Cortés, Technology and conquest, De León, Great Biological Exchange, Treaty of Tordesillas

CHAPTER 4

Inflation and Persecution

England remained one of the slowest nations in the race to colonize the Americas. Though it did establish a handful of trading outposts in North America, mostly temporary fishing bases, it made little effort to colonize America until the end of the fifteenth century. In 1497, the English sent John Cabot across the Atlantic to what he claimed as Newfoundland (either present Newfoundland or Cape Breton Island) for England. After that, little encouragement could be found for establishing colonies in North America because the English state had its own problems to deal with. Still, substantial changes were apace in England, changes which would eventually encourage an out-migration, peopling what would become British North America.

Luther's assault on Catholicism came two short years before Cortés conquered the Aztec empire and those two events—the Conquest and Reformation—are indelibly linked. Spain became, as a result of its conquest of Inkan and Aztec gold and silver, the most powerful and wealthy nation on Earth, especially since the monarch received over one-fifth of all wealth brought into Spain. Philip II, the grandson of Ferdinand and Isabella, held an empire that included parts of Italy, the wealthy banking and manufacturing centers in the Spanish Netherlands (today mostly Belgium and Holland) in addition to its territories in the New World. Such a vast landholding made him the largest landowner in history. Philip, however, remained an ardent Catholic and was determined to wipe out Protestantism and reestablish the Catholic faith in all of Europe. Unfortunately for Spain, that meant Philip chose to use a good deal of the wealth acquired in the New World in fighting wars on the continent to achieve that end. As for the Spanish north, the people in Holland and parts of Northern Europe felt especially afraid for their Calvinist faith and believed Philip might be successful in reestablishing Catholicism in the north.

Over the course of the 16th and seventeenth centuries, Spain fought a series of wars to put down a revolt in Holland. Since England had become the de facto champion of Protestantism, Queen Elizabeth continued to support the faith by sending troops to the continent to fight in Holland and by harassing the Spanish colonies around the world by secretly authorized pirating. Philip was convinced that nothing short of an invasion of England would overturn the revolt against Catholicism, but his efforts at invasion were dashed when the Spanish Armada was defeated by England in 1588. Eventually the Dutch would win their independence in 1609, and the Thirty Years War that followed, concluding in 1648, ended the last of the great religious wars. Spain's empire would soon be divided, and the Dutch and English profited from the Spanish defeat, claiming European domination in the next century. The vast amounts of money spent in Europe by the Spanish on the wars of religion had an unexpected affect: They contributed to a general inflation which changed social conditions in England, and eventually fueled the English fires of colonization.

Though Cabot made some claim to the New World in 1497, England remained far too weak to exploit any gains in America. Yet the fortunes of the English were on the rise. The incidence of plague in England declined dramatically in the early sixteenth century, as did the death rate in general. The total population grew about 40 percent to 5 million, which triggered a general inflation already being fueled by the price revolution.

Price Revolution

Economic changes greatly altered the nature of life for many classes in England. The English nobility, who had lived off fixed rents on their estates for generations, saw their relative status decline compared to the middle class. Though the prices for goods tripled during the sixteenth century, the rent income on their great estates remained the same for hundreds of years. It can be difficult being wealthy. To be wealthy means you have to show your wealth, which means you have to have the biggest house, the nicest clothes, the most extravagant carriage, and other ostentatious displays of wealth. All these things cost a great deal of money, which the nobility did not have and could not earn from their meager fixed rents. At the same time, the fate of the gentry (landowners without legal titles) generally improved. They were mostly merchants and bankers, so their wealth grew as inflation and the economy expanded. Once they had enough money, the gentry purchased land, the ultimate display of wealth in England due to its limited availability. While their estates were smaller than the nobility, they were often better managed and the gentry was not overwhelmed by inflation. Small family farmers (often called yeoman) profited from the price revolution as well. Their labor costs remained mostly the same (since they worked the land themselves), but the prices they were paid for the grain they produced increased greatly.

The political impact of this economic change was significant. The middle classes, especially the gentry and yeomen, gained more political power while the power of the aristocracy (nobility) declined. In England the House of Lords became less important while the House of Commons grew in importance. Thus the Price Revolution created conditions that encouraged a political development where average property owners had an important voice in the political process. That development had major implications in the early course of American political history.

While we have discussed the three major classes of England in some detail, 75 percent of the English population were peasants and farmworkers. This class of England suffered greatly from the Price Revolution. As prices increased, and especially the demand for wool, more and more aristocrats forced them off the land by using their influence in Parliament to pass the Enclosure Acts. Such laws allowed landowners to fence in their lands so that sheep could graze, and in turn forced peasants off the land. Dispossessed peasants moved away from the villages and into the woods, where they lived as cotters (spinners of wool) and in poverty.

These changes encouraged immigration to America, where land meant freedom from poverty, freedom from debt, and control over one's life. Thus, the Price Revolution helped to push many English out of England. But there were other forces that acted on the system from the outside, ones that also encouraged migration.

Mercantilism

In the 16th century, it was widely believed that there was a fixed amount of wealth in the world. The goal of any nation should be to pull as much of that limited wealth into their borders as possible. This was done by maximizing exports (what the nation sells in return for gold) and minimizing imports (what the nation can't produce and thus must bring in from other nations through trade). England, like other nations, followed a mercantilist policy designed to enhance their manufacturing base and make much of the rest of the world dependent on their products. It was that contest for markets that finally led the English to consider colonizing North America. To export products, a nation must manufacture goods that other countries desire. But the manufacture of goods requires raw materials, many of which cannot be found within a nation's borders. Thus, manufacturing nations had a choice: They could trade for raw materials or they could locate them in their colonies and ship them back to the homeland for manufacturing. In the mercantilist system, colonies did more than provide raw materials. Manufacturing fuels expansion of production through re-investment in more manufacturing facilities, but it also creates a dependency on the laws of supply and demand. Colonies can relieve that dependency, because they supply raw materials and provide an outlet for overproduction.

English colonization existed as an outgrowth of market investment. Building manufacturing and industrial enterprises was expensive and risky. The first manufacturing ventures in England were funded by joint stock companies, where the company acquires money to build and maintain the institution by selling shares or stock in the company. As England turned to colonization, joint stock companies sold shares of stock to investors to raise money for expeditions. The first permanent English settlement was such a company undertaking at Jamestown in 1607.

Religion and America

While some merchants sought wealth in Virginia and other colonies of the new world, other Englishmen wanted to leave England for religious reasons. The origins of religious persecution in England date to the reign of Henry VIII, who first fought against the Protestant faith as a loyal Catholic but eventually converted and became one of its primary defenders when he broke with the Church in Rome over the matter of his divorce. The debate over the future of Catholicism and Protestantism in England fueled a great deal of conflict and eventually led to a civil war in the 1640s.

Though the Church of England was technically Protestant, it originally retained many of its Catholic functions, in various forms. Then English religious reformers, especially those who had some contact with Calvinist thought, encouraged the Church of England to rid itself of older Catholic influences by dropping bishops and adopting congregational forms of church structure (local control). While these reformers wanted church structure changed, others wanted church practice updated and made more Protestant.

One group, which called itself the "unspotted lambs of the lord," or as its critics suggested, the "Puritans," condemned the Church of England for its "false teachings" and practices. The Puritans wanted a number of basic changes that can be broken down into the following categories:

    A. Congregational control: Spiritual and financial control should reside in the hands of the local churches.

    B. Priesthood of the individual: Older Lutheran point about not needing priests as intermediaries.

    C. Condemnation of most religious rites: According to the Puritans, God does not speak through the senses, but through the mind. Thus they place much importance on reading the Bible and concentrating on the sermon.

The older Tudor line ended with Elizabeth. This meant the English had to find a new ruler, so they turned to Elizabeth's cousin King James I of Scotland (1603–25), who became the first Stuart King of England in 1603. James believed in Divine Right Monarchy and had a long history of fighting both Puritans and Presbyterians in his own country, whom he saw as too radical and too democratic. It was his intent to run them out of England. Some did leave to avoid such persecution. The Pilgrims were separatists who fled the Church of England and settled in Holland, before eventually migrating to North America. In 1620, William Bradford and 95 other Pilgrims migrated to North America and founded Plymouth Colony.

Other groups, like the Puritans, wanted not to break from the Church of England but only reform it. Yet they struggled under the repressive policies of James I and his successor Charles I (1625–49). Eventually thousands of Puritans fled England to establish colonies in the New World. Massachusetts Bay was the first such colony. There Puritans wanted to create a new English society, one transplanted directly from Europe, a New England. But these folks were mostly non-separatist Congregationalists. They did not want to break from the Church of England and fully expected that one day the English church would reform itself, by looking at the example of their lives, so they could return to a reformed Church of England. Yet, they were also strong Calvinists, and their religious thought represented some of the most radical of the Reformation. Religious intolerance in England would also eventually drive Catholics to North America. They began settling in America in 1634, with the establishment of the colony of Maryland.

These economic and religious issues in England gave its North American settlements their distinctive character. In England, the power of the aristocracy declined, so most of its settlements in the New World were not dominated by a noble class. The growth of the English merchant class, moreover, quickly created a trans-Atlantic economy that further encouraged the settlement of America, as did the Price Revolution and Enclosure Acts which forced the impoverished English working class to choose emigration. And, as a result of the Calvinist influence in England, many of those who came to the New World from England carried with them some of the most radical brands of Christianity in existence. Thus the societies planted in North America resembled England in many ways, but because of the conditions in which the population arrived in the New World, older English society and tradition remained largely unchanged.

The Irish Experiment, fifteenth to seventeenth Centuries

Although Ireland had been under the jurisdiction of the English crown since the twelfth century, the English people tended to perceive Irish society as one that was culturally different and, indeed, culturally inferior to their own. Partly a creation of those guiding the original Anglo-Norman invasion of the island, Ireland became entrenched and polarized in the sixteenth and seventeenth centuries, when the British government tried to firmly assert control over the Catholic population of Ireland. It was this insistence of the Gaelic elements of Ireland on remaining Catholic that led to problems.

When the English began to colonize Ireland, the Gaelic population remained aloof from Anglicizing influences, which led to the decision that they were an obdurate people who could only be tamed by a comprehensive reform of the population through educational and persuasive means.

Thus Reform, from the English (and by extension American) point of view from the sixteenth onward, has always meant religious as well as social improvement. It became the stated aim of the English government to bring all elements of the Irish population to an acceptance of the Protestant faith and English culture. For Protestant evangelicalism to work, it was necessary to forcefully restructure Irish society. English-born or English-related officials were assigned to control Ireland. Protestantism was made the official religion, forceful conversion was instituted across the island, and those who stubbornly chose to remain Catholic were heavily taxed. Conscripts were raised from among the Irish population and sent to Scotland to assist in the removal of Scottish peasants associated with the enclosure movement and also to keep the peace in Scotland. Landowners of Irish (Gaelic) descent had two-thirds of their land taken away, so it could be given to the swarm of Scottish peasants transplanted from their homelands because of the enclosure movement. Thus we have the formation of Northern Ireland, and the origins of the Scotch Irish.

Whenever the Irish revolted, they were subjugated and sent to the New World as indentured servants. Those who remained in Ireland were isolated on plantations or in urban areas, restricted in their levels of property ownership and removed from participation in the government; essentially limited in wealth to positions of laborer or low-level skilled workers, effectively reduced to second-class members of society within their own land.

Early Attempts at Colonization in the Americas

The first experience of the English in the New World came from the exploits of Sir Francis Drake. Drake was an English privateer, navigator, slave trader, and politician of the Elizabethan era. He was knighted by Queen Elizabeth in 1581 and was second-in-command of the English fleet against the Spanish Armada in 1588. His exploits were semi legendary and made him a hero to the English, but to the Spaniards he was a simple pirate. For his actions, he was known as *El Draque* (from old Spanish meaning The Dragon, derived from the Latin *draco*, an obvious play on his family name which in archaic English has the same etymological root). King Philip II offered a reward of 20,000 ducats (about $10 million by 2007 standards) for his life. Many a city in the 16th century was ransomed to Drake for less.

In 1577 Drake was sent by Queen Elizabeth on an expedition against the Spanish along the Pacific coast of the Americas. Drake crossed from the Atlantic to the Pacific through the Strait of Magellan. During this passage, a storm blew his ship so far south that he realized Tierra del Fuego was not part of a southern continent, as was believed at that time. This voyage established Drake as the first Antarctic explorer, because the southernmost point of his voyage was at least 56 degrees south according to astronomical data quoted in Hakluyt's *The Principall Navigators* of 1589. A few weeks later Drake made it to the Pacific, but violent storms destroyed one of the ships and caused another to return to England. He pushed onward in his lone flagship, now renamed the Golden Hind, and Drake sailed north alone along the Pacific coast of South America, attacking Spanish ports and rifling towns as he went. Some Spanish ships were captured, and Drake made good use of their more accurate charts.

In one of his most notable seizures, Drake captured a Spanish ship, laden with riches from Peru, which held 25,000 pesos of pure, fine gold, amounting in value to 37,000 ducats of Spanish money. Near Lima, they heard news of a ship sailing toward Panama, *The Cacafuego*. They gave chase and eventually captured her, which proved to be their most profitable capture. They found 800 pounds of gold and a golden crucifix, countless jewels, thirteen chests full of royals of plate (coins) and twenty-six tons of silver.

Back in Europe, in a pre-emptive strike against the Spanish, Drake "singed the beard of the King of Spain" by sailing a fleet into Cádiz and also A Coruña, two of Spain's main ports, and occupied the harbors, destroying the thirty-seven naval and merchant ships he found there. The attack delayed the Spanish invasion of England by a year. Over the next month, Drake patrolled the Iberian coasts between Lisbon and Cape St. Vincent, intercepting and destroying Spanish supply lines. Drake estimated that he captured around 1,600–1,700 tons of barrel staves, which is enough to make 25,000–30,000 barrels to carry sea provisions. The most celebrated of Drake's adventures along the Spanish Main in the New World was his capture of the Spanish Silver Train at Nombre de Dios in March 1573. With a crew including many French privateers and Maroons—African slaves who had escaped the Spanish—Drake raided the waters around Darien (in modern Panama) and tracked the Silver Train to the nearby port of Nombre de Dios. He made off with a fortune in gold, but had to leave behind another fortune in silver because it was too heavy to carry back to England.

When Drake returned to Plymouth on August 9, 1573, a mere thirty Englishmen returned with him, every one of them rich for life. However, Queen Elizabeth, who had up to this point sponsored and encouraged Drake's raids, signed a temporary truce with King Philip II of Spain, and so was unable to officially acknowledge Drake's accomplishment. He died of dysentery after unsuccessfully attacking San Juan, Puerto Rico in 1596.

Like his more famous cousin, Walter Raleigh was a soldier and knave of the most extraordinary kind. Enjoying the favor of Queen Elizabeth I, which was unmatched by others, Raleigh secured an unofficial commission to harass and interdict Spanish shipping to and from the New World. But Raleigh never saw himself as a pirate, so he transferred his position as an unofficial pirate into forced mercantile expeditions to several Spanish settlements in the Caribbean. This allowed him to secure the depredatory acquisition of exotic goods, which he then traded in Europe for massive profits. Although his early ventures to the New World were relative failures in comparison to Francis Drake's lucrative and devastating raids on Spanish ports in the Caribbean (particularly the destruction of St. Augustine, Florida or his capture of the Spanish treasure fleet, and his circumnavigation of the Straits of Magellan in 1577–80), Raleigh and the English would learn three important things:

1. how to organize oceanic voyages
2. how to navigate the open seas
3. how to develop new markets for exotic products

Such knowledge would be useful in Raleigh's next undertaking.

Items to Consider

John Cabot, Queen Elizabeth I, Spanish Armada, Price Revolution, English social structure, gentry, mercantilism, Puritan protest, England's first colony

CHAPTER 5

The English Invasion of the Chesapeake

In the years 1584 to 1590, Sir Walter Raleigh undertook a series of voyages and colonizing experiments to bring the first English settlers to North America. Although his colony at Roanoke failed, it lay at root of the English experience in North America and the beginnings of what were to become of the thirteen British colonies in North America and the United States. There is a lot of firsthand documentation for these colonizing attempts, especially the narratives collected by the cartographer Richard Hakluyt and the drawings of John White. These accounts created a mythical aspect around the Americas that remains to today.

The first English settlement was planted in the barrier islands off North Carolina in 1585, but many of the settlers fled back to England when supplies arrived in 1586. The 1585–86 colony was planted as a military outpost in the maritime and colonial struggle with Spain. The struggle with Spain was entering an acute stage, so the colony was needed to provide a maritime supply base for the ships Drake used to plunder Spanish vessels in the Caribbean and along the Gulf Stream, which was the homeward route of the great annual fleets and which the Carolina Outer Banks were conveniently near. Consequently, most of the members of the colony were soldiers—many of them gentlemen—and its governor, Ralph Lane, was an experienced military man and an expert in planning fortifications. The colonists' job was to look out for, prepare for, and repel Spanish invaders. The Spanish were no empty threat, since from late in 1585 their vessels were indeed searching for the English base. Mostly though, these settler-soldiers spent their time wandering the countryside in search of food and wealth.

Early English writers when discussing North Carolina and colonial America tend to depict the peoples who inhabited the areas first touched by European settlers as background material as if they are merely part of the landscape—a difficulty to be overcome. Yet the native peoples owned and occupied the lands the Europeans invaded. Native peoples had highly developed societies, which existed long before Europeans arrived and persist to today. The inroads that Native peoples made into the wilderness enabled Europeans to follow in their tracks, to learn the ways of growing crops, and to discover new ways of catching fish and game—all of which were new to the English settlers.

The languages of the Native peoples, too, were different from anything existing in Europe. With just a few words, Native speakers could convey a vast amount of knowledge and complicated concepts, which made their languages hard to learn and difficult to understand. As such, Europeans rarely learned Native tongues, choosing instead to make Native people learn European languages or to rely on a standard trade language of gestures and grunts. Despite the language barriers, it was easy to establish short-term relationships based on mutual curiosity of two different cultural groups along with the natural desire to learn through the exchange of gifts and by the admiration conveyed in simple, nonlinguistic terms. But long-term contacts, the continued occupation of Native peoples' lands by the English—even though they had been accepted—inevitably brought tensions, while the assumption by the settlers that they could go anywhere and take anything imposed strains on accustomed patterns of life and thought for the Native peoples.

The biggest problem was that each society expected too much from the other. The English anticipated that the Native Americans could go on producing food—corn, fish, and game—throughout the year for their support without any deep understanding of the fragile and cyclical nature of the Native economy. In the Englishmen's view Native peoples were there to provide food as it was needed by the Englishman, like some sort of free Native grocery market. If Native peoples refused to provide food, or ambushed settlers, or resisted English incursions, they were to be repressed as a matter of course, not with any deep-seated hostility but as a recurrent nuisance that must be kept in check. The best example of this mindset can be found in the execution of Wingina, the leader of the local tribe who provided the English settlement with more food and support than any other in the region. As the year passed and his people's food dwindled to almost nothing, Wingina refused to feed the Englishman, indicating to them that he barely had enough food for his own people. Since Wingina stood as an impediment to the settlers, Ralph Lane sought him out and killed him, even though Wingina had supported his settlement without question for more than nine months and was a friend of Lane. Although Lane's act was unconscionable, he did stop his men from wiping out the tribe as they could have. Bored and with no supplies coming from the Native peoples, the entire expedition was abandoned when Drake arrived on June 11, 1586 and offered passage back to England.

The second expedition arrived shortly thereafter-in 1587. A combined group of settlers (mostly in family groups) and soldiers, the second group arrived under different premises. They desired to make their own life near Native friends, but as far as possible they wanted to be self-supporting in their family units and not impose themselves economically on their Native hosts. Their leader, John White, having been a part of the first expedition, had many Native friends both on the island of Croatoan and also in the area to the north near the southern shores of Chesapeake Bay. The attitudes of the Native people near Roanoke Island were decidedly hostile rather than friendly. Although the majority of the settlers wanted to move on to the Chesapeake, the sailors refused to take them there because they hoped to find and attack the Spanish treasure fleet instead. White reluctantly left the settlers, expecting to return with supplies in six months and believing that the settlers would be moving inland 50 miles before his return.

White did not return in 1588. With the Spanish Armada posing a major threat of invasion of England, no ships could be sent to America that year. In fact, the English would not return to Roanoke until August 1590, nearly three years after the settlers had been dropped off. White clearly expected to find the settlers in the vicinity of Roanoke, but instead they were never heard from again. The main body of colonists, all of them family groups and most of the single men undoubtedly went north to the Chesapeake. We are obliged to assume that the small party of soldiers, after ferrying the colonists northward, returned to the island to await White. They certainly took down the flimsy cottages from the first settlement, dismantled the remains of the old fort perimeter, and nearby built themselves a stout palisade enclosure where they could protect themselves and stand guard over the personal goods of White as well as some cannon and bars of iron too heavy to travel with the settlers. Although White did not return in 1588, a Spanish ship passed through the region and examined the disemboweled fort. They saw no Englishmen, but they probably would not have revealed themselves to their sworn enemies.

The settlers were probably unfazed by the Spanish incursion, but the small group had to know the Spanish would return to the area. Consequently, we can envisage them hurriedly evacuating Roanoke Island, burying the baggage and heavy goods, and inscribing "Croatoan" on a tree to indicate their destination (which was later found by White in 1590). Since they did not include crosses (the arranged distress signal), it is doubtful they were in distress. They would also have been welcomed at the villages at Croatoan, but what would they do when White failed to return for three years? Perhaps they tried to reunite with the settlers, or even decided to remain in the villages. Most likely the majority died in some way, and a few were incorporated into the Croatoan tribe. We have no idea what happened to the lost colony of Roanoke.

When White returned in 1590 he found no signs of the colonists, only the dismantled fort and the Croatoan inscription. Autumnal storms wrecked a boat in his fleet and drowned its crew. As a result, the remaining sailors refused to go to Croatoan to see if any settlers were there, while getting them to winter in the western Atlantic was completely out of the question. The outcome for the colony remains a mystery. Another mystery revolves around how these early settlements were financed. The Crown had neither the money nor inclination; neither did Raleigh or any of the other notables involved in his ventures. It is possible that they sold stocks to pay for the colonies, as would be done with Virginia, but no evidence remains to suggest this. More likely, the settlements were funded by booty taken during one of Drake's successful raids, although no evidence supports this either.

Jamestown

James VI of Scotland became King James I of England in 1603. Four years later, he granted charters for the colonization of what became Virginia. That charter was given to companies that raised money for the colony by selling shares.

Then, in 1607, a London group known as the Virginia Company sent an expedition to the Chesapeake Bay area, where they built a fort named Jamestown. The Chesapeake was already inhabited by Algonquian Indians numbering about 20,000, a confederation led by Chief Powhatan. Powhatan proved willing to trade with the English and hoped for their support against competing tribes. The English who first came to Jamestown saw themselves as conquerors and explorers, not farmers. The strenuous labor needed to prepare to survive the first winter was in short supply. They depended on the charity of neighboring tribes to survive, and when that failed they raided them for supplies. The first ten years were little more than one catastrophe after another for the colony. The winter of 1609–10, for example, nearly destroyed it. That year winter started well enough. The settlers had plenty of corn, guns, a truce with the local Native groups, supplies from England, and game in the woods; yet the 500 people in Jamestown would be starving in less than two months. Within three months, they resorted to cannibalism. One man chopped up his wife and ate her. Others dug up graves and cannibalized them. By spring of 1610, only 60 of the recent 500, and 60 of the 900 original settlers remained alive.

The stupidity of the English settlers at times was overwhelming. To begin with, Jamestown was built in the middle of a swamp, which meant the land was unsuitable for growing crops and the water was undrinkable. Although the choice for their settlement was bad, it was at least explainable, as they thought it was the most defensible spot on in the area. But their relationship with the local tribes defies common sense. In the summer of 1611, for example, the English were determined to teach Powhatan a lesson for harboring runaway Englishmen. They decided to attack a neighboring Chickahominie village (which happened to be home to the only people in the area still on friendly terms with the settlers), murdering fifteen of the sixteen adult Native people they found there, cutting down their corn and setting it on fire. Having captured the queen of the village and her children, they decided to return with them via the river to Jamestown. Along the way, the children started crying so the Englishmen pitched them into the river and use them as target practice, shooting them in the head as they struggled in the water. Eventually even the queen was executed. So here we have the English, a people who could not or would not feed themselves, who had ruined their relationship with the Native people because they constantly demanded food from them, now they did the best they could to destroy both the Native people and their corn. Yet English determination (and a constant flow of immigrants) outperformed English stupidity. Within ten years, the company would contribute enough manpower and supplies to allow the settlement to take control of all the lands between the York and James rivers from the lower neck of the peninsula almost to the falls at present-day Richmond (an area of roughly 200 square miles).

Tobacco and the Conquest of Virginia

What finally saved Virginia and made colonization profitable turned out to be intensive agriculture. John Rolfe, who had married Pocahontas in 1614 and provided a period of peace with the Powhatan peoples, introduced a hybrid of North American and Caribbean tobacco, one that proved to be a commercially valuable commodity. To encourage tobacco production, the company initiated *headright grants* (plantation grants of fifty to one hundred acres of land for every laborer brought to the new world) in return for an agreement that landowners would bring workers from England at their own expense. Over 4,500 English settlers arrived between 1619 and 1624, but the high mortality rate held the total population to around 1,000 Englishmen. Unlike France and Spain, England populated its colonies with families. So while they did not require a Native population to intermarry with, and they did not have an interest in trading with them, the practice that developed and underscored the idea of exclusion was to push Native populations entirely out of English-controlled territory. Such a policy triggered a decade-long war of attrition with Native groups that began in 1622, when the Powhatans surprised and slaughtered one-third of Virginia's English population in one massive assault. Before the tide was turned, the war stretched to 1632 and forced the Virginia Company into bankruptcy. In 1624, Virginia became a royal colony, governed with the help of a local legislature (called the House of Burgesses) created in 1619. Despite all its problems, Virginia grew at a rapid pace, having a population of 10,000 by 1640, roughly the same number as the Native American population that same year. By the 1670s, there were 40,000 English. In 1647, there were only 2,000 of the original 20,000 Powhatans still living in Virginia.

Early Colonial Virginia

Tobacco controlled the development of Virginia. To meet the production demands of the crop, land was distributed in large tracts called plantations. Plantations were necessary because tobacco was a voracious crop whose production required a lot of land in wooded areas (the best land for tobacco growing). Since tobacco planters lived isolated from each other, their success depended on access to a means of transportation to their market, which in the case of Virginia meant land adjacent to local rivers or the Chesapeake Bay—natural highways to the Atlantic Ocean and Europe. Tobacco also controlled architecture in the region. Plantations, which after 1676 were built by African slaves, were designed like an African village with the big house (planter's residence) at the center of the plantation complex, surrounded in a circular configuration by outbuildings and worker quarters. Tobacco also controlled the development of transportation networks and settlement patterns. Since plantations were dispersed across the countryside and every major planter had their own landings and loading docks to send their goods to European markets, the few towns that existed in the Chesapeake region (only Williamsburg and Norfolk were large enough to take notice of before 1750) serves a function beyond consumerism (Williamsburg was the capitol of Virginia and Norfolk was the last port before departing the Chesapeake for the Atlantic Ocean).

Tobacco is one of the most difficult and labor-intensive crops grown by man. Tobacco production lasts from February through November of each year. Seeds were planted in February in beds prepared in January. From February to March, planters must weed the beds and tend to the seedlings. In March or April, depending on rain, the fields are plowed and sown with grain to provide food for the plantation and its laborers. In June, the tobacco seedlings are transplanted to small, raked, dirt hills in the fields. The transplanted plants must be tended daily, with special attention paid to weeding and removal of tobacco worms. Cutting began in August, with leaves bound into *hands* (bundles) and hung in a tobacco barn to dry until late October or early November, depending on the prevailing winds from America to Europe. When the tobacco had sufficiently dried and conditions for transportation were correct, the tobacco was packed into *hogsheads* (large casks) of 500 pounds and shipped to England for distribution to European markets.

Though the danger of living in Virginia remained high, the lure of land ownership (and thus freedom) and the income generated by tobacco encouraged a significant migration out of England. Between 1640 and 1700, 100,000 new settlers arrived in Virginia and Maryland perhaps as many as 75 percent young males under the age of 25, who came to British North America in search of opportunity not available in England, and a few women. Many of those individuals came to Virginia as indentured servants. Being unable to pay for their passage, they made labor contracts of indentured servitude in return for transportation. In return for passage, and then room and board in America for anywhere from four to seven years, indentured servants were expected to provide their labor, without further charge, to tobacco planters. For the master, this system proved enormously profitable. A typical servant could produce four or five times his purchase price per year. And, under the rules of the headright system, planters could also claim another 50 to 100 acres of land per servant. Masters had to provide food, clothing, and housing for their servants. Work in the tobacco fields was demanding and led many to complain of inadequate care, housing, and treatment. Masters had the legal right to punish servants by beating. Masters could regulate marriages, sell labor contracts, and often abused female servants. Almost half of indentures died before earning freedom, and 25 percent more remained poor after their contracts expired. As a result, many indentured servants tried to escape, but if they were caught, a common punishment was to extend the term of their contracts. Once a servant gained their freedom, it was common for the planter to provide them with basic tools, clothing, and fire power so they could strike out on their own. For most, this meant heading west to the frontier to the only lands available in the colony, and risking confrontation with Native peoples.

In the boom time of the 1620s, tobacco sold for twenty-four pence per pound. By the 1660s, that price had fallen to less than five pence per pound. The reasons lay in overproduction, which led to more tobacco than the market could support and still sustain the prices of the 1620s. Virginia's problems also reflected the changing nature of its political relationship with the mother country. The English, who practiced mercantilism, believed the role of the colonies was to support the economic welfare of the home country. Beginning in the 1650s, England enacted a number of laws designed to ensure that colonial production met the goals and needs of England's economy, which meant they produced staple crops like tobacco or supplied raw materials like iron, but produced almost no manufactured goods.

The Navigation Acts

To control the economic production of the colonies, the British government passed a series of Navigation Acts. The first of these passed in 1651 and allowed trade with foreign merchants in an attempt to keep Dutch shipping and Dutch merchants away from England's valuable overseas possessions. Parliament's first Navigation Act (1651), revised and extended in 1660 and 1663, allowed only English and colonial ships in American ports. Colonists also had to register and ship certain listed items (like tobacco) only to England. Dutch merchants had traditionally paid more than the English, but now trading with them was illegal.

The English monarchy also had its hand in the American pie. It slowly raised the tariff rates of staple crops and used them as a source for the royal treasury. Such taxes kept the price of tobacco high in England and limited the expansion of the tobacco market. By the 1670s, the price of tobacco had fallen to just one penny per pound in the colonies, and yet more tobacco continued to be produced. The tobacco exports—and the population—grew remarkably at the end of the seventeenth century. Profit margins were thus very thin, and only a few of the largest and most efficient planters actually prospered in tobacco production.

Such economic stagnation ended upward social mobility in Virginia by 1700. A typical yeoman family grew about 1,800 pounds of tobacco per year. By the time taxes and basic necessities were met, only 800 of that 1,800 pounds was left to be bartered for supplies and equipment. Smaller farmers quickly fell into debt. Newly freed indentured servants found it next to impossible to save enough money in such a stagnant economy to become property owners. Most of them eventually had to sell their labor again in one form or another (through indenture or as wages). Though their status was unstable, too, large plantation owners managed to cope with the decline in prices and, even on occasion, to profit from it. They leased small plots to tenant farmers and loaned money at high rates of interest, while others became merchants, *factors* (a person who accepts accounts receivable as collateral for a short-term loan), and cotton commissioners. Power shifted away from the middle class and toward the landing-owning planter elite. As the seventeenth century drew to a close, class antagonisms and conflict dominated Virginia's politics.

Rise of the Gentry Class

Tobacco production had inevitable consequences on the development of colonial society in Virginia. While the perceived wealth of tobacco production brought huge populations to the colony, it created just as many problems. To begin with, the production of tobacco created a dispersed settlement pattern in the colony. Since production centered on large tracts of land (the anonymous author of *Animal Husbandry* told readers that even the smallest planter needed 50 acres for each field laborer), people were spread out across the countryside.

The dispersal of settlements had obvious cultural implications. Social relations were less frequent (especially among the colony's elite) and less spontaneous than those found in urban settings. Religious services could bring people together, but churches were often inconveniently located and inclement weather kept many people at home. Militia practice occasionally broke up the work routine, but it also often meant men used the occasion to get roaring drunk. The meeting of county courts also served social as well as legal functions, but that occurred only a few times each year. Most of plantation life was spent at home in the company of family, servants, and slaves.

Beyond the cultural restrictions of dispersed settlement patterns, Virginia's isolation and the need of capital in the success of tobacco production led to the development of a new elite, or gentry class. The gentry class of Virginia came to maturity in the last half of the seventeenth century. Since few English gentlemen migrated to the colony, most gentry arose from commoners who made themselves into gentlemen. Men made and lost fortunes; indentured servants finished their term, married a heiress, and sat at the right hand of governors. Those who made it to the top, however, left their sons to perpetuate their authority, for mortality remained high and fertility low among immigrants.

By the mid eighteenth century, men like Thomas Jefferson and George Washington inhabited a society in which gentlemen with generations of standing dominated the economy and political system and passed that domination on to their sons undiminished. Justices of the peace administered county government and punished miscreants; with the consent but hardly the advice of lesser men, these gentlemen thought it their duty to provide moral guidance and political leadership as stewards of the entire society. Ordinary men usually deferred to their gentry neighbors in political matters, but insisted that gentlemen protect the property of the ordinary class and they asserted their right to select among the gentlemen who stood for election to the provincial assemblies.

When the gentry failed to protect the property and freedom of their lessers, trouble ensued. Such would be the case during Bacon's Rebellion from 1675–76, when the government of Virginia turned its back on frontier settlers. Beset by high taxes and unprotected from the predations of ruffians and Native raiding parties, the frontiersmen organized themselves under the direction of a local notable named Nathaniel Bacon and marched on the capitol at Jamestown. En route to Jamestown, the ranks of the marchers grew in numbers as indentured servants fled their masters to join the ranks of the rebellion. In Jamestown they met with hostility and accusations from the colonial elites who dominated the government.

Angry and misunderstood, Bacon directed the frontiersmen to burn the plantation of the colonial governor and the capital city of Jamestown, driving the governor and his ministers from the colony. What they expected to do beyond that act is uncertain, but Bacon fell ill and died of dysentery, and his movement crumbled. Virginia elites would never forget Nathaniel Bacon and the support he received from the servants. Within ten years they would abandon the system of indentured servitude for a more controllable labor source, African slavery. In 1685, about 20 percent of Chesapeake's population represented the gentry class. That same group owned more than 80 percent of the arable land of the Chesapeake. These are unusual facts, considering the Chesapeake was settled by the English poor and great, but mostly poor.

Although some gentry migrated south into Chesapeake, most of the in the Chesapeake arose from the local population. So the questions are: Why and How? Partly, it was due to hard work and, partly, a great deal of luck. If you could sell your tobacco for the highest price, it was possible to get ahead. Another way people got ahead was through marriage. But most people got ahead through their connections. Connections could bring favorable decisions on tobacco, grants of land, etc. But the seventeenth century was a time of uncertainty, as well, and a true gentry class requires stability to develop and expand. There was a great deal of death. In many ways Virginia was more like a Wild West town in an old black and white movie than a settlement conducive to families. People rarely lived past 40 years old. Sex ratios were unbalanced, so people married, and remarried countless times in their lives. Early deaths of parents left many orphans, who often were turned over to the protection of uncaring relatives or sometimes complete strangers.

Things began to change by the eighteenth century, when most of the population had been born in the New World. Such homegrown origins brought acclimatization to the region. It wasn't that the Chesapeake was no longer dangerous; people were now accustomed to the new environment. As a result, death rates began to drop, the sex ratio began to even out (this is natural when birth rates are the main means of expanding population), people also began to live longer, which expanded the accumulation of wealth and increased the size of inheritances. Because of these factors, a powerful gentry class developed in the Chesapeake by 1750. But there also was a huge wealth gap between gentry and commoners, even though commoners made up the majority of the population.

The large number of gentry in the Chesapeake region created new problems. Active participation in government was limited to white men who owned the largest portions of land, although voting was open to all white landowners. Thus, the gentry dominated politics. They made the laws and enforced them. The gentry were not a hereditary nobility, as in England, since only a handful of nobles came to the colonies. But the gentry did fill the role of a noble class in Virginia. People of the time believed that leadership naturally fell on the shoulders of the wealthy. By being wealthy, they had proven and earned the merit to lead. As a result, boys of the upper class were trained from childhood to be leaders in politics, economics, and society. Their parents hired teachers to instruct them, and when they reached the proper age, they were sent abroad or to one of America's colleges to complete their education. Of all the people within colonial society, they truly were the most prepared to run the government, but being of a certain class they commonly looked after their own interests and that of their class first.

The life of the gentry was often dull. Although they ran everything in the colony, others performed most of the day-to-day work. The government only met once a year for three months, leaving many in the gentry class with little to do to entertain themselves. In the words of William Byrd of Westover Plantation in 1709, "I rose at 7 o'clock and said my prayers. I ate chocolate for breakfast. We walked about till dinner and then ate roast beef. In the afternoon we rode to my Cousin Berkeley's with design to take him and his wife with us but he escaped by being from home. His wife was at home and gave us a good supper. I ate boiled beef. Then we had some cherries which had been scalded in hot water. They were exceedingly good."

While the life of leisure may see alluring, there were many problems associated with prosperity. Being rich was expensive. You must have a big house, lots of land, hundreds of servants, nice clothes, the best furniture. You have to entertain your neighbors, showing your guests the best time: good food, drink, and entertainment. To pay for this, it was necessary for members of the gentry to find ways to support their lifestyle. The easiest way was through tobacco, but by the eighteenth century, overproduction and poor land quality had reduced prices and oversaturated the world market. The gentry class responded by trying to raise prices and control production through legislation. First the burgesses passed limits on tobacco production; then they tried to control quality through the Tobacco Inspection Act of 1732. Besides limiting quality and production, the burgesses also passed laws on how tobacco was collected and shipped. They created public warehouses where all tobacco was to be stored and evaluated, the owner receiving a receipt for his tobacco in storage. Tobacco receipts quickly became the first currency in the Chesapeake. Despite all these efforts, poor prices remained a problem for tobacco producers.

Another problem for the gentry was that they were tied to the land, thus making their life (and the southern colonies) mostly rural, agricultural, and practical. Town life would develop late in the south (not until after 1760), and there were relatively few towns compared to other colonies and England. The few towns that did exist developed around deep-water ports like Annapolis, Williamsburg, and Charles Town. Even trade did not lead to urbanization, as most gentry planters had their own river landings to ship their goods abroad. Under these conditions, it should be no surprise that the gentry remained rural in reality and mind, seeing themselves as increasingly aristocratic (and of a separate nobility). When they went to England, such pretensions were not be appreciated, leading colonials to be viewed as provincials and causing a social antagonism between Americans and Englishmen, an antagonism that portended the American Revolution.

Items to Consider

1585–86 colony, Walter Raleigh, Roanoke, Jamestown, headright system, tobacco economy, growth of the gentry class, indentured servitude, price of staple crop production, problems of prosperity, Bacon's Rebellion

CHAPTER 6

Awash in a Sea of Faith

The histories of Virginia and New England differed from the very beginning. Jamestown was settled by young male adventurers (who quickly became dead male adventurers). Plymouth and Massachusetts Bay, the first permanent communities in New England, were settled by families. These families were English Pilgrims who had settled in Holland and other religious dissenters who wished, as they put it, to advance the true "gospel of the Kingdom of Christ in those remote parts of the world."

The Virginia Company had planned to create a colony in the northern realms of its grant, which extended all the way to present-day Canada, but the company's first effort came to little. In 1614, it hired John Smith to explore the area, but while he found the land to be somewhat nicer than Virginia, he could not recommend a settlement due to the presence of a large Native population and the harshness of the region's winters. Six years later, little had changed in the Virginia Company's interest in the northern section of its land. As the company began to have financial difficulties supporting the Jamestown settlement, it began to consider the prospect of selling off a section of its charter.

In early 1620, a group of religious separatists known as the Pilgrims approached the company with an interest in buying land for a settlement in the new world. The Pilgrim migration to America began in 1608 at the town of Scrooby, England, just a short distance south of London. Although officially part of the Church of England, the Pilgrim forefathers at Scrooby decided the English Church had taken a wrong turn theologically and resolved to separate themselves from it. They cut off all contact with the rest of England by barricading the city and refusing entry to nonresidents and they refused to pay taxes. The English government tried to reform the Pilgrims and show them the error of their ways by marching an army to reopen Scrooby. Rather than reform, the Pilgrims packed up their entire town and fled to Holland. The Pilgrims quickly re-established themselves in Holland, but still refused to conform to local practices or acquiesce to an outside authority. Not surprisingly, they found themselves being persecuted again, this time by the Dutch government. Seeking a place where they could build a new life and practice their faith in isolation, the Pilgrims decided to transplant themselves to the Americas. They sent agents to the English King in the hopes of acquiring a charter for their own colony or at least get permission to settle in one already begun. When the English government showed no interest in the Puritans' desire to establish their own colony (it seems difficult to believe the Pilgrims actually thought the monarchy would give them a colony so far away considering their actions at Scrooby), their agent approached the Virginia Company to buy a portion of its Charter.

A deal between the Pilgrims and the Virginia Company was agreed to before the summer of 1620. By August of 1620, company directors began to help the Pilgrims put together an expedition of 102 colonists, 35 of whom were Pilgrims (Separatist Puritans) from Holland. The expedition departed England on the *Mayflower* in September 1620. Although the trip across the ocean was relatively uneventful, the ship hit a sizable storm off the coast of America and lost direction for a number of weeks. Landing at Plymouth Rock, farther to the north than originally intended, either by accident or otherwise, the group formed the Mayflower Compact as a document of government. There is a great deal of controversy surrounding the decision to write the Mayflower Compact. Some say it was a mutual decision by the entire group of colonists, while others suggest the non-Pilgrims were coerced. Either way, the Mayflower Compact was the first constitution written on American soil.

Once the compact was signed, the settlers chose a spot for their settlement. They eventually selected two small adjacent natural ports at Pawtuxet and Plymouth Rock. The first winter there was harsh. Only half of the original 102 settlers survived the winter. Those who did survive were visited by the local inhabitants (the Wampanoag) in the spring. The Wampanoag leader, Massasoit, brought the Pilgrims food and taught them how to plant corn. After the first winter, unlike the early history of Virginia, the Plymouth colony thrived. Relations with the Indians, however, quickly deteriorated. Plymouth's governor, William Bradford, believed them to be "savage" subhumans. With the help of Minister William Brewster, he convinced the settlers to break contact with the Wampanoag and other neighboring peoples. Another problem for the Pilgrims is their success attracted many settlers from England. As they quickly became a minority in their own colony, the Pilgrims forbade the majority non-Separatist population from voting (but forced them to pay taxes), making their religion nearly inseparable from the region's government in the Calvinist tradition. They would remain a separate colony until 1691.

The Puritan Experiment

Neighboring the Plymouth colony was the Puritan experiment at Massachusetts Bay. The settlers at Massachusetts Bay also came to the new world to escape religious persecution, but unlike the Pilgrims, the Puritans did not want to separate from the Church of England; they wanted to reform or purify it. Calling themselves the Unspotted Lambs of God, the Puritans believed that the Church of England still held too many traditions and practices from the old Catholic Church, which they wanted to strip away or purify out (hence their enemies gave them the name Puritans).

Puritan migrations to America began in the 1620s, when the English monarchy rejected their attempts at church reform and began to heavily persecute them. Led by John Winthrop, the Puritans received a land patent from the Virginia Company to settle New England in 1629 even though patent to the same land had already been sold to the Pilgrims in 1627. The Puritans came to America with a purpose. As Winthrop reminded the first Puritan colonists, their purpose in coming to the New World was to be "as a City upon a Hill," a beacon for all the world to follow. They wanted to create the perfect Christian society as an example for England and the rest of Christianity. The Puritans hoped that when the English saw what the Puritans were able to create, the English would recognized the error of their ways and call the Puritans back to England, where they would take their rightful place of leaders and help England to reform the church. In 1630, the first 400 Puritan migrants created Salem, and another 700 soon settled around Boston. Again, the first winter nearly killed the entire population. Some people dug caves and others lived in tents made out of the ship's sails. Before the winter concluded, almost 200 settlers at Salem died of exposure to the elements or disease, and 100 more quit and went back to England. But those who remained attracted even more colonists. By 1642, 18,000 colonists had arrived in Massachusetts Bay.

Part of the reason for the Puritans' early success lay in the make-up of the immigrants. Unlike the experiment in Virginia, where most of the arrivals were young males, New England was settled with entire families, many of them skilled labor. Their representatives were skilled and experienced in politics, and knew how to manage the needs of a society. At times, entire towns were transplanted from England. Though much of the migration to New England was a result of economic issues, the religious zeal and power of Calvinism shaped much of early life in New England. The intellectual force of Puritan religion encouraged education and the concepts of justice in the larger world. They believed generally in small, localized government that practiced a radical form of democracy by extending political participation to male members of the church. They lived in a relatively strict society, with many social controls and regulations, which kept eccentricities and crime to a minimum.

Town organization followed a simple plan. The center of a town was an open area of grass called the common and about the size of a football field. Houses were built around the edge of the common, usually in a grid pattern if the landscape allowed it. Houses closest to the common generally belonged to the most important people in society, town leaders and the wealthy. The most important building in town, the town hall or meeting hall, was located at the eastern end of the common. The meeting hall acted as both religious center and town government. Citizens gathered several times each year to choose leaders and make decisions for the town. Next to the meeting hall was often the minister's house, a position which was often elected. Across the common from the meeting hall was the courthouse, a *goal* (jail), and a powder *magazine* (storehouse).

The prominence of the church/meeting hall in the Puritan town organization meant religion was central to life in New England. According to Puritan theology, God had chosen a few Elect men and women for salvation—they alone were predestined to go to heaven. It was a harsh doctrine, seemingly, to non-Calvinist Christians, because everyone not of the Elect was condemned to suffer in hell. It also divided church members between the Elect (or Saints as they were called) and the rest of the population. The Saints set high standards for church membership, so high that many people did not even bother to apply. There was also an odd intellectual byproduct of Calvinism and of being a member of Puritan society: It was impossible to know who the Elect really were. That had the effect of making the pious population nervous and prone to intolerance.

Winthrop and his administrators grew alarmed, for example, at the actions of Salem minister Roger Williams who believed in the separation of church and state (something that did not happen in early Massachusetts Bay). Williams further outraged Winthrop when he objected to the colony's policies toward Native peoples, especially the seizing lands without payment. In 1635, the Massachusetts General Court banished Williams from the colony. Williams and his followers migrated south to Providence. Once other towns (Portsmouth, Newport) sprouted up in the same area, Williams sought and acquired a charter from the English Parliament in 1644 to establish the colony of Rhode Island.

Another often-cited example of Puritan intolerance is Anne Hutchinson. A pious woman, mother of seven, and a critic of the official line of salvation, Hutchinson called into question the authority of Congregationalist ministers in Massachusetts. Because of her challenge and her gender, she was tried for heresy in 1637. Found guilty of over eighty offenses, she, too, was banished to Rhode Island. When she was later killed in an Indian raid in New York, Puritan leaders noted it as an example of God's judgment against her and her teachings.

There were other dissenters in Massachusetts, including Baptists (who baptized only adults), Quakers (who believed God inhabited followers with an Inner Light, thus no need for baptism or communion), and many Puritans themselves, especially after the first generation, who lacked the original religious commitment (and experience of persecution) of those from England. The "backsliders" or those in "declension" proved to be a serious problem for the Congregationalist churches, since the backsliders fundamentally undermined the church's ability to control the government. As fewer and fewer people were being presented for baptism (and thus church membership), the number of Puritans in Massachusetts declined within the population to such an extent that they were in danger of becoming an unimportant minority within their own colony. Others colonists disappeared into the countryside in pursuit of new land, thus beyond the daily control of church and state. Thomas Hooker left Massachusetts Bay in 1630, for example, because he disagreed with the restrictive land policies, and ultimately founded, in 1639, the colony of Connecticut.

Theology

Religion created turmoil for New Englanders. Many Puritans had expected that the settlement of New England would begin the Millennium, the predicted 1,000-year rule of Christ on Earth. At first, events in England appeared to bear them out. In 1637, Archbishop William Laud imposed a new prayer book on Presbyterian Scotland and threatened to send bishops there, as well. In response, a Scottish army invaded England in 1639, forcing King Charles I to call Parliament into session to secure funds to fight the war. Parliament refused to give him the money and, instead, demanded changes in the government. Charles resisted. The nation divided into Royalist and Parliamentary (Puritan) factions, resulting in the English Civil War. After four years, the parliamentary forces won. Charles was tried and executed in 1649. Oliver Cromwell, leader of the parliamentary forces, assumed control of England. The Puritans then had control of the English church, but they could not do much with it. Cromwell became a dictator in 1653 and when he died in 1660, Parliament, feeling bad for having chopped their king's head off, called his son, Charles II, back to the throne. For many Puritans in America Charles II was the Antichrist.

Compared to life in England, by 1660 Puritan life in America was equally grim. Many second-generation Puritans were no longer excited about the religiosity of the New England colony. Many, perhaps even most, of them were not church members. The Puritans were about to become a minority in their own colony because of the high standards for church membership and the loss of the first generation's religious commitment. Therefore, the Saints decided to lower the standards for church membership. They devised the Halfway Covenant in 1662, making it easier for their children to become church members. Under the terms of the Covenant, all children of baptized Puritans could be presented for church membership as halfway members. Thus, it made church membership almost hereditary. The Covenant represented the beginning of a new phase in the Puritan experiment. Many of them had planned to return to England in the future. But after the Halfway Covenant, the Puritan churches concentrated on developing a pure society here in America.

In any Puritan town, the most important centers of power were the church congregation and its meeting house. In theory, land ownership was supposed to be universal, so no social distinctions would undermine the community. In practice, it was difficult to keep social distinctions from emerging. Despite their best efforts, the older families got the best lands and larger tracts than newly arriving migrants. Over time those families built up large estates, which passed down to their sons via heredity. The practicing of subdivision, however, only served to increase social conflict and tension over the land issue. As estates were subdivided among sons, and then subdivided among grandsons, it became increasingly difficult for someone to own enough land, by the end of the third generation, to support his family. Nor were the soils of New England producing what its farmers expected. Combined with the land crunch, the situation encouraged the emergence of other forms of economic activity. By the 1660s, New Englanders manufactured cheese and other dairy items, produced lumber for ships and buildings, and found other outlets for their labor. By the 1660s, 20 percent of New England residents earned their living in lumber, fishing, or crafts. Due to this shift, the New England economy flourished.

Improving economic conditions fueled a population explosion, the result of a lower incidence of disease and longer life spans (most were living to their mid 60s). Children married young and produced families ranging from eight to thirteen children (about half of which would survive to their teenage years). Thus, New England, unlike the South, had a labor surplus, one that would make slavery and indentured servitude unnecessary.

The main problem in New England revolved around religion. The nature of Puritan dogma made its members nervous. That fact was compounded by the seventeenth century understanding of the natural world. They believed that God and other spirits took an active role in the day-to-day affairs of humans. Thus, when a star fell from the sky, it was a sign. When lightning struck a house, it was a sign. When anything out of the ordinary happened, it was a sign. This meant that someone had to interpret those signs so that the desires of God could be followed and those of the devil ignored. Ministers were the first choice for understanding the signs, and they wrote countless books on the subject. Cotton Mather, an influential minister, wondered why God seemed to send so many lightning bolts to strike ministers' houses and wrote a 95-page tract explaining what a strike meant, depending on where it hit the house and how much damage it caused. As can be expected, people began to order their lives around natural phenomena. The movement of the planets and stars—astrology—began to take precedence when people made important decisions in life, like when to plant, when to harvest, when to marry their children, etc.

Puritan ministers, however, attacked such beliefs because they undermined ministers' authority. They labeled anyone who claimed special knowledge of the natural world, like folk healers, as a wizards or witches acting at the command of Satan. In this charged atmosphere, authorities in Massachusetts and Connecticut hanged 14 people for witchcraft between 1647 and 1662. But the most dramatic episode of witch hunting took place in Salem in 1692. The causes for the witch hunt are complex—involving the boredom of young girls and group rivalries as much as just plain deception. Poor and resentful Puritan farmers on the outskirts of Salem apparently sought revenge on their wealthy neighbors by bringing charges of witchcraft against their families and friends. Eventually it got out of hand and led Massachusetts to arrest 175 people. Of that total 22 were eventually executed, mostly older women. Only one, Bridget Bishop, actually admitted to practicing witchcraft.

The Salem episode marked a major turning point in the history of New England. The Calvinist experiment in America was over. The intense government-supported (and -controlled) religion of the Puritans had gotten out of control, resulting in backlash against the Salem hysteria, which brought about the final separation of the church from the state. Puritanism was weakened so severely that it finally splintered into separate congregations. Thereafter, New England society would become more liberal, more rational, and more democratic.

Items to Consider

Pilgrims, Puritans, Roger Williams, Anne Hutchinson, Millennium, Halfway Covenant, problems of Puritan economy, Puritan cosmology, Salem witch trials.

CHAPTER 7

An Empire for Slavery: The Origins of American Slavery

Slavery is as old as humanity. In Europe, and especially in Africa and the Middle East, it had been practiced for hundreds of years. But there was something new about the kinds of slavery brought to the New World and the changes it brought altered the futures of three continents. From the earliest days of Portuguese exploration and expansion, one of their goals had been to take advantage of new opportunities for trade in slaves, a commodity that had been monopolized by peoples of the Middle East. Portuguese mariners delivered their first African slaves to Portugal in 1441 and soon afterward became the western world's leader in slave transportation. Because of the climate and diseases on the African interior, the Portuguese mostly left slave catching to West African groups, basing themselves in port cities where they could purchase slaves without exposing themselves to the death that resided in the interior.

The story of the slave economy begins in the West Indies and Brazil. Between 1550 and 1700, European merchants created a new type of agricultural system. Using land they seized from the Native peoples of the Americas and African labor, Europeans raised sugar, tobacco, and other valuable crops which were in turn shipped to Europe to be sold for huge profits. This massive trading system is commonly known today as the South Atlantic System or the Triangular Trade. It is important for three reasons: 1) It sapped human resources out of West Africa, 2) It set off a commercial revolution in Europe, and 3) It stimulated the growth of British North America.

Without slavery and the wide-scale production and profitability of staple crops produced by slave labor, you do not have an industrial revolution, or a European race to settle the Americas and the rest of the world, or an Africa trapped in poverty and subject to European depredations into the present day. All these things depended on the development of the South Atlantic System in order to occur.

What made West African slavery profitable (and thus essential to this historical equation) was its close association with the rise of worldwide sugar production. Though it is difficult to imagine for us to today, sugar was a boom economy in the fifteenth, sixteenth, and seventeenth centuries. In fact, historically speaking, more money was probably made in the production and marketing of sugar than any other commodity. Prior to this boom period, Europe's access to sugar was limited, so most food Europeans consumed had little sugar in it. Their two most prominent sources for sugar came from beets and honey, both of which are problematic: As any kid can tell you, beets taste like dirt and bees sting you when trying to extract their honey. As a result, neither of these sweeteners saw much use and Europeans had little interest in sweet foodstuff. Yet by 1900, sugar was the most consumed item in the European diet, outpacing even original staples in the European diet, including bread and salt. The massive consumption of sugar sparked a decrease in the consumption of starches, simple carbohydrates, and led to a resultant rise in the consumption of fats. By 1900, sugar accounted for some 20 percent of all calories consumed by the world's population. This meant sugar was an extremely valuable commodity, whose market every nation hoped to control. Sugar production required tropical climates and intensive labor, which created a demand for cheap, inexhaustible labor. Columbus introduced sugarcane to the New World and not long after that the first sugar plantations appeared on Hispaniola. At first, the Spanish tried to use Natives as their labor source. But their numbers grew too thin, so the Spanish brought Africans to the New World, to the Caribbean and Brazil, to labor on massive sugar plantations.

In the 1630s, the Dutch took temporary control of Brazil, using their financial and organizational talents to expand the market for sugar across Europe and even to world markets. In combination with stimulants found in tea, coffee, and tobacco, sugar allowed Europeans to work longer and harder days. Recognizing the possibility for huge profits, the Dutch started a war in order to expand their sugar operations with the capture of Barbados. By the mid seventeenth century, the English, too, began to recognize the value of sugar, using war to secure their own sugar colonies sugar colonies in Barbados (which they took from the Dutch) and Jamaica (which they took from the Spanish). Jamaica alone in 1750 had some 700 large sugar plantations in operation that were being worked by more than 105,000 African slaves. Sugar was complicated and expensive to produce. It required fertile land, extensive amounts of manual labor, and heavy equipment to turn the sugar cane into raw sugar and molasses. So, you see, it required a major investment to start a plantation. Not surprisingly, the whole industry was dominated by a wealthy plantation elite; who were able to turn 8–10 percent profits on their investments each year. Noting the great profits, the French followed the Dutch and English examples by starting a war to acquire and develop colonies for sugar plantations in Martinique and St. Domingue (Haiti).

West Africa

The slaves who labored on American plantations came mostly from West Africa, which had a long, complex history and its own great empires. Community and family, as previously discussed, served as the basis for West African society. Typically they had sophisticated agricultural systems and possessed a good number of skills. African slaves were usually incorporated into the family they served. They were free to marry and their children were born free. They had certain rights extended to them and as much freedom as an indentured servant in colonial America. This was unlike the chattel slavery practiced by Europeans.

Before the nineteenth century, Africans were the largest group of immigrants to the Americas, outnumbering Europeans by six to one. Though the numbers remain somewhat open to debate, it is estimated that somewhere between 10 and 11 million Africans were transported to the Americas in the four hundred years of the slave trade. Of that total, 76 percent came in the peak years of 1701 to 1810. Of those numbers, half went to European plantations in the Caribbean, a third to Brazil, and 10 percent to Spanish America. About one in twenty (roughly 600,000) were brought to British North America. In general, only about one-third of those numbers were women. Most slaves were young, between the ages of fifteen and thirty, and they came from nearly every major West African group, including the Wolof, Mandingo, Hausa, and Ibo. By the end of the sixteenth century, the Dutch were in a position to openly challenge the Portuguese for supremacy in the slave trade. The English also played a major role. In the sixteenth century, the Portuguese had almost thirty slave forts along the West African coast. By the early eighteenth century, the English alone had thirty slave forts operating on the West African Coast.

Process of Enslavement

As in the early years of the trade, European traders left most of the slave catching to Africans. This means that most Africans were enslaved through warfare of some sort. Usually small raids were made against villages at night, capturing a good number of slaves and killing many more. The practice of kidnapping unsuspecting members of West African villages was also popular. Countless stories and songs document those who left the village alone and never returned from chores or other normal activities. Raids eventually extended much deeper into the interior, as demand grew in the eighteenth century. Typically slaves captured in raids were marched to the coast under horrid conditions, where many died from heat or exhaustion. Often tied together with forked logs or bark rope, they sometimes had to march hundreds of miles to reach the coast—often at a run since the raiders feared repercussions from those they just attacked. Once at the coast, European traders examined the captives much in the same way they would examine a horse or cow. Nevertheless, they always employed common human based medical practices of the day—clearly dispelling any suggestion that they thought Africans were anything other than human. Those selected for transportation were usually branded on the back or buttocks with a mark, then prepared for the next stage in the journey. Those not selected were quickly disposed of by execution or sold locally.

The Middle Passage

This stage in the voyage was named by English sailors It was the second leg of a long trip that would eventually carry the sailors back to Europe or to the Americas, while their cargos' final destination either resulted in death or a lifetime of human bondage. From the coastal forts, slaves were boarded onto waiting ships and packed into free standing shelves that averaged six feet long and two feet high. Slaves were forced to sleep like spoons. The crowding was so intense; the conditions were so poor; a massive death toll resulted. Among the slaving industry there was a good deal of debate as to how "packing" should be done. One group argued that packing slaves in loosely would allow more room, and thus prevented a large number of deaths. But economics demanded most slavers follow a tight-packing philosophy. There was an expectation that 10 to 20 percent of a ship's cargo would be lost, so it was important to pack as many people into the hold as possible to minimize financial losses. As a result, many ships were dangerously overloaded—sometimes by as many as 150 people.

With good weather the trip across the Atlantic could be made in three weeks; without it, a ship was lucky to make passage in three months. Throughout the voyage, slaves were locked below deck. The experience was for most slavers that slaves if given the opportunity would jump overboard to avoid remaining onboard. In the mornings, the holds were opened, the dead were disposed of overboard (so great was the death that schools of sharks followed the slavers), and some slaves were brought above decks, where they were attached to leg irons and forced to exercise. At night, the screams of the dying and the distraught was intense. Most sailors aboard slave ships described this as the worst aspect of the passage. Sanitation aboard slave ships was non-existent. In fact, most slavers took to the practice of abandoning ships after a few voyages because it was cheaper to buy a new one than to clean up the last. Typically Africans were locked in the dark below decks, forced to lie in their own waste as well as seawater and bilge water which always built up as the voyage progressed. Many in the cargo acquired dysentery, and others died of epidemics of smallpox and fevers. Maybe as many as one in six slaves died during the middle passage.

Slave revolts on ships were not uncommon (thus the chains and being locked away below decks). Others jumped overboard and drowned, choosing death over a return to the hold, and forcing captains to string safety netting along the edge of their ships. Upon arrival, slaves were typically cleaned up and prepared for market. Any signs of disease or defect were covered up with tar. Buyers went through the market as if they were buying cattle. Most slaves were sold at auction, families and tribal friends divided up, and sent to isolated plantations.

Other than the untold human misery slavery produced, which cannot be calculated, the slave trade drained the human resources of Africa away from the continent. At the least, we know as many people were killed in slave raids in the interior as were taken captive. Since most slaves were acquired in war, there is no way of knowing how many casualties accumulated in the acquisition of one slave. More important, participation in the slave trade destroyed the indigenous African economy. The goods exchanged for each slave were only worth about 25 percent of what that slave had been producing in Africa and for Africa. At the start of the sixteenth century, Africa was mostly independent, but by the eighteenth century, a depopulated Africa in chaos was easy pickings for European states desiring to carve up empires on the continent.

Slavery in North America

Africans first arrived in Virginia in 1619 when a Dutch ship unloaded "twenty and odd negroes." For the next forty years, the African population remained small in number and was not legally enslaved. By tradition, British law did not recognize chattel slavery, the owning of another person. Slavery did exist in the colonies, although it remained small because slaves usually cost about twice the going rate as an indentured servant. As a result, the racial situation in early Virginia remained in a state of flux, with a good amount of intermarriage and an ever-growing mulatto population. There were even a handful of black slave owners, the best example being Anthony Johnson, although questions remain concerning the level of bondage in such a situation.

After Bacon's Rebellion, colonial leaders turned away from indentured servitude and toward a system of labor that could be more easily controlled. By 1700, there were 19,000 West Africans in Virginia and Maryland; representing about

22 percent of the population. In South Carolina slave numbers comprised 40 percent of the population. Slowly, then, slavery became codified into colonial law. After the 1660s, laws were enacted that prevented Africans from owning guns, joining the militia, buying labor contracts of white indentured servants, etc. To be black was increasingly becoming the test of freedom, and an inferior legal status. In 1692, Virginia passed a law prohibiting sexual intercourse between English and Africans. And in 1705, a Virginia law made almost all resident Africans slaves, which meant Africans found their status as slaves both permanent and hereditary.

The change in the status of slaves and Africans coincides with a change in the Chesapeake social order. After 1700, life in the Chesapeake grew to resemble, in some aspects, life in Europe. Men lived longer so they began to take back some of the property control they had lost to women as a result of their early deaths (outside of fatalities caused by pregnancy, men died at much higher rates than women in colonial America). Instead of naming their wives as executors of their wills, men began to name other men. This allowed wealthy planters to consolidate their power, but to do so they had to make some concession to the poor western farmers. They reduced the taxes frontiersmen had to pay and passed laws that favored small farmers. In return, small farmers elected their wealthy neighbors to political office without question. So we have an unstated bargain among men to protect the status of males in Virginia. This pattern would be repeated in South Carolina and the other southern colonies. For males the new situation worked well: Poor white male farmers had more political freedom and the plantation elite retained control over the colony and actually grew even wealthier.

Of course, the elites were growing wealthier on the backs of African labor. By 1770, southern slaves numbered 500,000 and made up about one-third of the southern population; 60 percent of southern white farmers owned at least one slave. Although slavery lined the pockets of the big families, the Pinckneys, Gadsdens, and Carters, it was a brutal experience for Africans.

The Practice of Slavery

The American experience of slavery was formed in the West Indies, and that was bad. The waste of human life in the West Indies was staggering. Slaves died at phenomenal rates. They died of disease, overwork, inadequate food, lack of shelter, and myriad other reasons. In fact, with the price of sugar remaining so high and the prices for slaves so low, planters actively chose to work their slaves to death, rather than waste money to keep them alive; it was just too easy and inexpensive to replace a dead slave. The best example for this mindset can be found in Barbados. The black population of Barbados was 42,000 in 1708. The British imported 85,000 Africans between the years 1708 and 1735. But in 1735 there were only 46,000 slaves living in the colony. This means that from 1708 to 1735 as many as 81,000 people of African descent perished from complications arising from slavery.

In Virginia, living conditions for slaves were less severe and many had long lives. Tobacco production was far less demanding than sugar. Since tobacco plantations were dispersed, disease spread less quickly. Tobacco planters also acted as slave breeders. They brought large numbers of women to the colony and encouraged the procreation of large families among their slave population, even going so far as to track and encourage useful genetic compositions (as was done with domestic animals) and to use the practice of studding. By 1720, most slaves in Virginia were born there. The incentive to produce (or breed) wealth led to the establishment of a large African-American population.

Life was more difficult for slaves in South Carolina. It had been settled by whites from Barbados. When they could not get sugar to grow in their new home, they struggled to find a new staple crop of equal value. As a result, South Carolina grew slowly until the rice economy took off. Whites had been unable to produce an efficient way to hull rice, but Africans from rice-producing cultures showed them how to make the crop profitable. By 1730, Charleston was shipping 17 million pounds of rice a year to Europe; 75 million by 1775. As rice production became more profitable, planters imported tens of thousands of African slaves. As early as the 1710s, Africans made up 80 percent of those living in the rice-growing areas of the south. As in Barbados, high death rates from disease and overwork took a great toll.

Surviving Slavery

The general pattern throughout the period of American Negro slavery was one of oppression and resistance. Slave owners were not a forgiving group. They came from a culture in which the poor were oppressed violently, religious conflict ended in death, and more than 100 minor crimes were punishable by death (stealing a loaf of bread was an executable offence). Not surprisingly, masters did not hesitate to impose strong punishments. Slaves were branded, castrated, had their noses slit, and in some cases fingers, toes, and ears amputated for minor offences. Often, violence was dictated by the size of the slave population. In the West Indies and South Carolina, where a few whites were generally in charge of twenty-five to one hundred slaves, they could maintain authority only by inspiring fear. Slaves who disobeyed commands had to be punished brutally as an example to the rest of the population. Slaves dealt with this in a variety of ways. Sometimes they cooperated; sometimes they used low-level resistance like sabotage and stealing. Others rebelled with violence.

A successful rebellion was nearly impossible on the mainland with such large numbers of well-armed whites. The only real alternative was to escape into the interior and establish slave villages or to join the tribes of native peoples. The first major slave revolt in North America was the Stono Rebellion. In the late 1730s, the Spanish governor of Florida promised slaves freedom if they could escape to land under his control. By February of 1739, some sixty-nine slaves were reported escaped to St. Augustine. Many more went unreported. The rumors spread about a black conspiracy to rise up at once and seek freedom. Not surprisingly, that is exactly what happened when Spain and England went to war in 1739. Seventy-five Africans in South Carolina banded together, stole weapons, killed a number of whites, and began the long march south toward Florida. White militiamen found them shortly after their march began, killed many, and dispensed with the rest, thus preventing a general uprising. The remainder of the rebellious slaves were rounded up. The leaders were executed and the rest were sold back into slavery out of the colony. The incident influenced slavery well after the rebellion was over. Southern whites were so terrified by the incident that they tightened plantation discipline, passed a number of laws restricting the freedom of slaves and freedmen, and kept a constant watch over their enslaved population.

The Tie That Binds Them All

It is important to note that every part of British North America was involved in African slavery in some manner or another. The slave population of the West Indies was a major market for New England bread, lumber, fish, and meat. By 1700, the two economies were tightly interwoven. By the 1720s, the farmers of New York and Pennsylvania were shipping more wheat and corn to the West Indies than any other destination. This commerce tied the empire together in a commercial triangle that everyone benefited from equally, except the slaves. Sugar from the West Indies was be traded in England for bills of credit, which in turn were used to pay slave traders for newly arrived Africans. The slave trades then paid mainland merchants for products produced in the colonies. The trade with the West Indies made many of New England's fortunes, but especially those involved in the rum trade, exporting more than a half-million gallons a year as early the 1740s. As a result of the interconnectedness of the African slave trade, no one in America was exempt from responsibility.

Items to Consider

South Atlantic System, the Sugar Economy, demographics of the slave trade, Middle Passage, tight vs. loose packing, slavery in Virginia, Anthony Johnson, slavery in America, slave forts

CHAPTER 8

Salutary Neglect, the Great War for the Empire, and the Road to Revolution

Before we move on, it is important to consider the political history of Europe from 1713–50. Throughout history to that point, Europe had remained constantly at war, but that was about to change. The treaty of the Utrecht ended Queen Anne's war in 1713. For the next forty years, Europe found itself embroiled in a cold war between the British and French. This meant Britain wanted to dominate its colonies, but for various reasons, theory never quite met practice. As a result from 1713 until roughly 1755, the British government was relatively hands off about dealing with the colonies. Content with its profits in the sugar and tobacco trade, the British chose to leave the colonies pretty much to their own devices. Consequently, this era in colonial history is often called the Period of Salutary Neglect. This salutary neglect gave the colonists a significant degree of self-government, ultimately allowing them to challenge the British mercantile system and become self-sufficient enough to seek independence.

One of the first byproducts of salutary neglect was the increased power of the representative assemblies. They became more powerful, ironically, because they were becoming less democratic. The first families of the colonies dominated the colonial legislatures, a situation that can be traced back to the Glorious Revolution in 1688. The glorious revolution, you see, was led by English Whigs who believed in a mixed government; a division of powers among the king, the aristocracy, and the landowners. The English Whigs believed that landowners should retain control over their own destiny, a mind-set that played a major role in the rise of elites in the colonial assemblies. Seeking control of their own destinies, American Whigs demanded that the colonial legislatures have the right to levy taxes and they demanded equality with the royal governors.

Slowly, over time, that is exactly what happened. The colonial assemblies grew in power, taking the over the right of taxation and passing legislation to dictate the lives of their residents. The rise of the assemblies coincided with the decline of the royal governors, who were powerless to keep themselves from losing power. Many of the colonial assemblies refused to follow the orders of their royal governors on certain issues (particularly, in matters of taxation) and when the royal governor tried to force the matter or enforce policies the legislature disliked, the assembly leaders prevented the governors from succeeding by raising mobs in the cities and marching them to the governor's house and government offices. The rise of the mob in the colonial cities was important in the progression to the Revolution, for it meant that no one, neither governor nor legislature, had the power to impose unpopular policies. It also meant power was slowly shifting hands from royal authorities to the people; and especially to the people through their legislatures.

All this coincided with a shift in royal policy toward the colonies. The English monarchy found itself in a conundrum. When Queen Anne died in 1713, she left no heir to take possession of the country. To solve the problem, England turned to her German cousin George to fill the seat of kingship. But this decision brought its own problems, since the German king and his family did not speak English nor did they have much interest in anything other than their Hanoverian homeland. Consequently, George I (1714–27) and George II (1727–60) relaxed enforcement in the colonies. Instead, they turned their attention entirely toward the European continent, leaving the rest of the British Empire to its own government, so much so that the British political philosopher Edmund Burke would later call this strategy of mild rule as one of "salutary neglect." That neglect was a byproduct of a system developed by Sir Robert Walpole, leader of the Whigs in the Commons, and Prime Minister of England under the two Georges. Walpole ruled England at the behest of the distracted crown, which made it difficult for Walpole to get anyone to follow his orders. By dispensing political offices and other gifts from the government's coffers (often identified as *patronage*), Walpole was able to win the support in Parliament for his policies. But in ruling through patronage, Walpole's political strategy weakened imperial rule in three major ways:

1. Walpole created an empire run by merchants, which inhibited strong imperial rule because no one would do anything without receiving the benefits of patronage.
2. Walpole's willingness to rely on patronage made his domestic policies appear corrupt and persuaded many American leaders that British rule posed a threat to their political liberty.
3. Walpole's patronage system weakened the royal bureaucracy in the colonies because they had no offices or government services to distribute as part of patronage.

It is important to remember that salutary neglect did not cause the American Revolution. In fact, in the short run, it strengthened the ties of the American colonies to Britain. Yet, it allowed the rise of the colonial assemblies, which would, in the end, bring about the rebellion.

As the administrator of the Empire, Walpole did his best to strengthen the British colonial system and bind the colonies to the mother country. To do this, Walpole wanted to perfect the mercantile system. He tried to do so in four ways:

1. Walpole supported James Oglethorpe's establishment of Georgia in the early 1730s as a refuge for Britain's poor. Walpole did not care about the poor, but he saw the settlement of Georgia as an opportunity to create a buffer colony to protect South Carolina and its profitable rice economy from the depredations of the Spanish. By right of discovery, Spain claimed Georgia and South Carolina for itself. The Spanish constantly threatened to seize the territories that made up the colonies, and the creation of Georgia would lead, ultimately, to war with Spain in 1739; the so-called War of Jenkins's Ear.
2. Seeing that the economies of the colonies were maturing, Walpole got Parliament to try to undermine independent American manufacturing to ensure the colonies produced only crops and raw materials, and thus remained dependent on the mother country. To do so, Parliament passed a series of Navigation Acts to control American manufacturing. The Navigation Acts began with the Woolens Act of 1699 and the Hat Act of 1732, which prevented the sale of hats and textiles between the colonies. Later Parliament became more direct with the Iron Act of 1750, which banned the construction of new iron forges and mills in the colonies. By 1760, there was legislation within the Navigation Acts restricting the manufacture of every major type of commodity imaginable.
3. While Walpole wanted to limit the development of economic independence in the colonies, he still needed to bind them to the Empire. As a result, one of the loopholes of the Navigation Acts lay in the fact that Americans were allowed to build ships and transport goods. Thus, Americans dominated almost all of the trade between the colonies, the West Indies, and Britain. While it placed the Americans actively within the British Imperial economic system, it also created some difficulties. By the 1720s, the colonies were producing more foodstuffs than they could sell to the West Indies. Seeking more markets, the Americans sold their foodstuffs to the French West Indies in return for cheap sugar. Since French sugar was cheaper than that produced by the British, the distribution of French sugar in the British empire by the Americans so undermined the British sugar industry that it almost collapsed in the 1730s. To protect British sugar, Parliament passed the Molasses Act of 1733 which placed a high tariff on the importation of French sugar. This act so infuriated American merchants that it was virtually ignored.
4. Another way Walpole thought to perfect the mercantile system was to consolidate the currency of the empire by trying to do away with American paper money. Many colonies had taken to printing their own money, much of which wasn't worth the paper it was printed on. Besides creating confusion of what was legal tender in the

colonies and in the Empire at large, there were also a number of embarrassing scandals involving the printing and use of colonial currency which made this a good policy. In 1751, Parliament passed the Currency Act which forbade the colonies from creating land banks and from using public bills of credit (currency) to pay private debts. While this angered the colonies, this policy made economic transactions in the Empire more uniform and made taxation easier.

To summarize the period from 1713 to 1750, what we have is a period of salutary neglect. The period saw the ascendancy of colonial legislatures, a decline in imperial authority, and an attempt at the end to reestablish that authority through Walpole's four reforms of the mercantile system.

During the period between 1740 and 1765, colonial life was changed by the Enlightenment and Pietism (a movement within Protestantism, lasting from the late seventeenth century to the mid eighteenth century, combining an emphasis on Biblical doctrine with the Reformed, and especially Puritan, emphasis on individual piety, and a vigorous Christian life.). But the colonies were also profoundly influenced by war, economic change, and frontier violence. There were three major political-economic events in this period. First, the British began a major war in the colonies called the French and Indian War (it is also known as the Seven Years' War or the Great War for Empire), which soon grew into a world war that profoundly changed the nature of the British Empire. Second, the expansion of transatlantic trade increased prosperity in the colonies but also, in a certain sense, put Americans into debt with British creditors. Finally, the triumph of the British over the French in 1763 ousted the French from North America and stimulated a new generation of expansion, Indian warfare, and conflict between easterners and westerners.

Fire in the West

Prior to 1750, few Europeans had settled in the Mississippi valley. Only a few fur trading centers and forts dotted the interior. By and large, British settlers had not moved across the Appalachian Mountains because there were few natural transportation routes. The interior of North America was also home to the powerful Iroquois, who had been armed by trade with the French and the British. Then in the 1740s, things began to change. Both British and French officials refused to continue to pay the yearly gifts or tributes which Native peoples had come to depend on. This split the Iroquois by factionalism and slowly increased pressure on them to find new ways to secure European goods. Simultaneously, Americans began to looking to the interior for new lands to colonize.

In 1749 Governor Robert Dinwiddie of Virginia and a group of wealthy planters organized the Ohio Company. As governor, Dinwiddie gave the Ohio Company a royal land grant of some 200,000 acres along the upper Ohio River. Dinwiddie, seeking to secure the region for the Ohio Company, sent Colonel George Washington (a young, ambitious planter as eager to curry favor with the governor as he was to speculate in western lands) and some of the Virginia militia to occupy the region and ward off the French. The French saw Washington's incursion as a threat to their territory throughout the Mississippi valley, so they immediately began construction of Fort Duquesne (in what is now Pittsburgh) to project force into the area. In July of 1754, French troops repulsed the Virginia force and captured Washington. Suddenly, France was at war with Virginia in the backcountry of the British North American colonies.

The British, still nearly broke from the last war with the French, tried to contain the fighting. But several war hawks in Parliament, namely William Pitt and Lord Halifax (the head of Board of Trade), wanted war to expand the American colonies. Halifax even had the Board of Trade propose a union of the colonies to better coordinate the war and the subsequent expansion it would create. Some American political leaders agreed, so delegates from the colonies met in Albany in June 1754 to discuss war aims and to adopt a Plan of Union, mostly the work of Benjamin Franklin. Under the Albany Plan, as it came to be known, there would be a Continental Congress, which would be responsible for orchestrating the war and oversee all Western affairs. The Albany Plan never went into effect, though, because the colonies could not get along enough to secure an agreement. Failure at Albany meant there still was no coordinated plan to deal with war in the West. Finally in 1755, the British sent troops to America under the command of Sir Edward Braddock. In May 1755, Braddock led 1,800 men from Fort Pitt (also near present-day Pittsburgh) west toward Fort Duquesne. They never made it. The French and their Delaware and Shawnee allies knew about the expedition before it even departed. At an isolated location ripe for ambush, the French and their Native allies fell on the English, killing Braddock and half his men. They would have destroyed the expedition altogether if not for the courageous retreat led by George Washington, an act surely meant to redeem himself for past military failures. After this battle, the war expanded from a colonial matter to a world war. Fighting quickly broke out between the English and French in Europe, India, West Africa, and other sections of North America.

In 1757, William Pitt became prime minister of England. Unlike his predecessor, Pitt had a plan to bring about the end of the war and he was determined that England should finish the French and dominate North America, whatever the cost. Pitt's plan was simple. He used the British fleet, the largest navy of the day, to bottle up the French navy in its home ports. With no chance for re-supply or reinforcements from Europe, Pitt initiated a systematic attack against France's over-seas possessions. He sent tons of money to America to fight the war, paying for both the colonial armies and their supplies. He also sent some of his best military leaders to the New World to coordinate the actions of the separate colonial militia (since each colony refused to let its militia fall under the control of other colonial leaders). For a century, the wars between Britain and France ended in stalemate. This time, by following Pitt's leadership and with the colonial militias coordinat-ing their effort, Britain won a brilliant victory. Beginning in 1758, they won one battle after another. Louisburg fell at the end of 1758, Quebec fell in early 1759, Montreal in 1760, thus completing the conquest of Canada in just over a year.

Though most of the North American fighting ended on September 8, 1760 after the Marquis de Vaudreuil sur-rendered Montreal—and essentially all of Canada—to Britain, the war did not officially end until the signing of the Treaty of Paris on February 10, 1763. When the French came to the peace table, they did so with very little to bargain with. Along with Canada, the British had seized Senegal in West Africa, the French sugar islands of Guadeloupe and Martinique, and the Spanish colonies of Cuba and the Philippines. The Treaty of Paris, which ended the war, is indicative of just how great a victory the British had won. Britain got to keep Canada, all of France's territory east of the Mississippi River, and Spanish Florida. In return, Spain got all of Louisiana west of the Mississippi River; which they would hold for the next 40 years, in addition to the return of Cuba and the Philippines. France's once-mighty North American empire had been reduced to a few sugar islands in the West Indies, two rocky islands off the coast of Newfoundland, and the right to fish the Grand Bank off the coast of Canada.

Pontiac's Rebellion

Beyond the interests of the Europeans, the war had one last act to play in America. Early in 1763, an Ottawa chief named Pontiac led a group of loosely aligned tribes stretching from New York to Michigan into an uprising. During the war, the Native tribes suffered a great deal at the hands of the British. American soldiers burned Native villages, often without even bothering to see if it belonged to a friend or foe. British military leaders refused to supply their Native allies, yet implor-ing them for help. British rum traders traveled through Indian territories and actively defrauded Native peoples. General Jeffrey Amherst's decided to cut the number of gifts and gunpowder doled out to British allies after the war, even though Native people had been promised certain allotments for their help. This is also the occasion where Amherst freely distrib-uted blankets taken from a smallpox hospital to the families of some native allies of the British in the hopes they would contract the illness and die, the first documented attempt of a military using biological warfare. With such indiscretions occurring at a time when the British actively needed Native support, the Native people did not relish the idea of a British occupation once the war concluded. As a result, Pontiac's call for all Native peoples of Eastern North America to unify in rebellion was met with fervent support.

Pontiac's forces pounded the daylights out of British garrisons in the West for several months at the start of hostili-ties. Eight forts were destroyed, and hundreds of colonists were killed or captured, with many more fleeing the region. But ultimately the Indians were unable to drive away the British, and so they lost. Pontiac's rebellion did give the British government a new respect of those Indians, at least for a time. To curb future hostilities with Native peoples in the inte-rior, the British committed themselves to stopping white settlement west of the Appalachian Mountains by issuing the Proclamation of 1763 which forbade, for a time, settlement west of those mountains.

By the end of 1763, American support for the British Empire was never higher than it was at the end of the Great War for the Empire. It is remarkable that in only a dozen years that support would fall completely apart. How could such a turnaround have happened? Prior to 1763, the American colonists needed the British Empire to protect them from dep-redations by Native peoples and Europeans (especially the French). When that threat was removed, something remarkable began to happen. A mere dozen years later, the relationship between the American colonies and Britain collapsed into a shooting war. We next look at how such a thing could happen. To begin with, there are two broad sets of causes:

First, the character of the American political and social system created dreams of independence. Unlike most colonial peoples, Americans had long lived in a relatively peaceful and prosperous society with a history of representative government. That experience created a vigorous and confident people, not to mention leaders, who were able to lead their governments and support a revolution.

Still most of them were content under British rule. What sparked their rebellion was the second, and more immediate cause: Britain's much-needed attempt to reform the imperial system.

The British Empire in 1763

The British Empire in 1763 was the strongest in the world. But all was not well. In the process of defeating the French, the British had incurred massive debts (£133 million by 1763). The government honestly felt that since the American colonies had profited to a great degree from the defeat of the French, the colonies should help pay for some of the war's cost. It is important to note that residents in the American colonies were some of the least taxed people in the Empire, while those in England gave nearly half their yearly income to taxation. If the war debt was to be retired, many in the British government believed the Americans had to pay their fair share. Thus the leaders of the British Empire embarked on a policy designed to reform colonial administration in light of the Empire's new financial needs.

At the end of the Great War for Empire, England issued the Proclamation of 1763, which prevented colonial settlement west of the Appalachian Mountains. That decision alone provoked anger in the colonies, but there were other changes that also awakened Americans to the idea that they were being treated as a separate and distinct population. In the process of fighting on the frontier between 1754 and 1763, the American militia was often unnerved by the profane behavior of the British regulars (it is important to note that the ranks of the British Army were filled with criminals and the poor, both of which joined to avoid jail). Americans in contrast were a particularly religious sort in the 1760s, volunteering to serve in the colonial militia. The Americans simply could not appreciate the rough character of the British soldier, and the coercive nature of service in the British army ran counter to their identity and sense of decency. Nor were they particularly happy with the treatment of the common American soldiers by the British military leadership. Officers in the British Army came from the aristocracy, purchasing their position and promotion through the ranks while leading their rabble of an army with violence and intimidation. Instead of the aristocratic military organization of the British, the colonists exhibited a remarkable level of democracy. The American militia was an all-volunteer force. Discipline in these forces was, by British standards, far too relaxed. As a result, the British constantly derided the quality of the American solider, often speaking of them with disgust. These early minor conflicts made it plain to the Americans that there were some distinctions between English and American.

Forming an American Identity

While the Great War for Empire caused tension between the Americans and England, it gave birth to a sense of intercolonial identity in America. The conflict brought Americans together from all over the colonies to fight in areas outside their home regions, and created for the first time a sense of unity among the colonials. Such a sense of unity was accentuated by the growth of highly independent newspapers up and down the colonies. Since most of these newspapers were established with the support of Benjamin Franklin, the editors of the papers published many of the same stories and had the same tone. It was typical of these newspapers to increasingly consider the "continental (American) perspective" and compare that to the aims and purposes of the British in North America. The newspapers took great pains to tell Americans what was happening in each of the colonies, giving them a perspective beyond the individual boundaries of separate colonies. It was during these years that the British colonists in North America first began to use the term American to describe themselves.

Many of the editors of those papers were eighteenth-century Whigs, people who believed in mixed government and who drew heavily on the political theories of John Locke and other British essayists. Like Locke, the editors constantly warned of the threats to liberty, especially those presented by the growth of political power and economic centralization. Instead of submission, they advocated the creation of a larger voting public and the end of rotten boroughs in England, and sought a more responsive form of representative government. The greatest minds of the age feared the power of government, and sought ways to keep it in check and protect liberty from the despotic actions of government. These ideas coalesced into a political philosophy which is best described as republicanism.

Republican thought suggested that the best societies gave as much freedom and liberty to the individual as possible. To do that, they had to limit the power of the state, because governments only exist to limit individual liberty. Like Locke before them, the republicans argued that absolute power was conditional, and that it was the basic right of individuals to create a government that best addressed their needs. Therefore, the best insurance against tyranny was a divided government, divided among the most divergent interests possible. A broad distribution of power would serve as a guarantee, a protection against tyranny.

No system better fit the American experience than that suggested by republican thought. Easy land ownership, a history of representative government in the form of colonial legislatures, and a tradition of fighting imperial rule all came together to make republicanism the most popular system of government in the colonies. But the commitment to independent thought and action (as well as republicanism) was in direct conflict with the British desire to reform the political system in the colonies.

British Troops in America

As insurance against a French uprising in Canada and to quell Native American troubles on the frontier, the British government decided that a large force of 10,000 British regulars would remain in the colonies after the war's end in 1763. That proved an expensive army to support. Some in Parliament demanded that the colonies pay for part of the force that lived there to protect them. Most members of the English Parliament back in London were unwilling to raise taxes in England because they were already high and the population there grew angrier with such taxes each day.

The reasons for keeping regular troops in America were complex, but we can reduce them to three main arguments.

1. There were some 60,000 French Canadians who chose to remain in Canada under British rule. Britain wanted to keep troops in America to discourage any future rebellion.
2. Britain feared another war with Native Americans on the frontier. If British soldiers occupied a string of forts stretching along the frontier, they could effectively stop white westward migration and prevent clashes between whites and Native Americans.
3. Some British politicians genuinely believed that there was a growing independence movement. While this concern was only a conspiracy theory in the 1760s, fear of such a movement had been growing in the British government since the 1740s. Now the danger of a French invasion was gone, what need of British protection did the colonies have? Of course the presence of such a small force could not directly discourage an independence movement, but it was evidence that Britain was prepared, if necessary, to use military force to keep the American colonies in the Empire.

Paying the British Debt

During the war, the British national debt almost doubled from £75 million in 1754 to £133M in 1763. William Pitt retired after winning the war, and was replaced as prime minister by Lord Bute in 1761. The only task before Bute's ministry was to find ways to pay off the national debt. The government increased the import duties on tobacco and sugar, and increased sales taxes on things like salt, beer, and distilled spirits. In effect, they passed the cost on to the consumer in the form of higher prices. To collect all the new sales taxes, they had to double the size of their customs service, roughly increasing it from 5,000 employees in 1750 to 11,000 in 1775. They gave those officials broad powers for collection and provided stiff fines to punish smugglers, including death or being sold into indentured servitude in America.

In the eyes of much of Parliament and the rest of the government, the colonies were the key to Britain's commercial success. Yet the colonials had not lived up to their end of the bargain. They had defied the Navigation Acts by widespread smuggling; they traded with the French during the war; and, they refused to raise their own taxes to pay their fair share of the war costs. Something had to change.

George Grenville

After negotiating the Treaty of Paris in 1763, Bute resigned and George III, who had become king in 1760, replaced him, somewhat reluctantly, with George Grenville. Like Bute, Greenville was tasked with finding a way to reduce the national debt. In such an effort, Grenville introduced the Sugar Act of 1764. It is important to note that the Molasses Act of 1733, as stated earlier, had been designed to cut off trade with the French sugar islands. It seemed to work at first, but became less and less enforced as the decades wore on. By the 1760s, some large colonial merchants, like John Hancock of Boston, had made vast fortunes smuggling sugar. To end the practice once and for all, the Sugar Act of 1764 dropped the duty from 6 pence per gallon to 3 pence. But most important, the rate would be enforced and smugglers punished. Hancock, who had grown rich illegally by not paying any tax, was furious, as were other New England merchants. They began a protest that eventually reached the Massachusetts legislature.

The argument Hancock and his supporter made against the new taxes was ingenious. Rather than address the essence of tax itself, they focused their attack on the Constitutional legality of Parliament passing taxes which would affect the rest of the Empire. They argued that Parliament had the constitutional right to create taxes to regulate trade within the Empire, but that taxes designed to raise revenue had to originate in the colonial legislatures, not in Britain. Their reasoning depended on representation. The English Constitution clearly outlawed the passage of taxes without full representation. Parliament was elected by voters in England. Thus parliament could tax its constituents since they elected the body to office and it could pass laws to regulate the empire because it was the main legislative body for the mother country. But since no American voted for a Member of Parliament and each colony had a duly elected legislative body, then taxes to raise revenue within the empire could only come from the legislative body elected by the constituents being taxed. The terms of the debate, you see, had shifted from what was proper for the British Empire to what was legally constitutional for the English Parliament.

What really angered the colonials was not the actual taxes, for they were relatively small, but the Sugar Act also created vice-admiralty courts to enforce the trade laws. These courts operated without a trial by jury, a right guaranteed in the English Constitution. Thus, a judge, probably with British sympathies, would decide all matters concerning the Sugar Act. Previously colonial legislatures had given themselves the authority to try such cases, which meant Americans were rarely found guilty of smuggling. The new Sugar Act ended all of that. By passing this law, Parliament revived old fears and raised new constitutional issues. Violators would not be tried by juries of their peers, but by a government that was beginning to look like a tyrannical foreign power. In a certain sense, the Americans were right. The colonists' rights as Englishmen were being abridged. There was a general sense in England that the colonists, like all members of the Empire outside of England, were second-class citizens within the Empire and not subject to all the same protections as subjects in England. But England did need to raise money to pay the national debt. Parliament asked the colonial legislatures to raise taxes for that purpose, and the Americans ignored the request. What else could the British do?

The Stamp Act

When Grenville announced the Sugar Act, he also announced his intention to seek a colonial stamp tax the following year to pay part of the £200,000 needed per year to keep 10,000 troops stationed in North America. A similar tax had been in place in England since 1694 on such things as court documents, playing cards, diplomas, and land titles; almost anything that was printed. Grenville knew there would be an objection on constitutional grounds and told the American assemblies that unless they would willingly pay a portion of the bill, a stamp tax would have to be passed in 1765.

Benjamin Franklin, who happened to be in England as a representative the Pennsylvania assembly, said the measure would fail because Americans would never agree to being taxed until they were given representation in Parliament. This supposition on Franklin's part was actually not true, as would become apparent to the English in a few years. Americans did not want representation in Parliament; they wanted their legislative bodies to have equality with Parliament—a move they probably did not realize was one step removed from outright independence. With the exception of William Pitt, Franklin's idea was rejected by British politicians, who argued that the colonists were already virtually represented in Parliament.

In 1765, the House of Commons passed the Stamp Tax by a vote of 205 to 49. Violations of the new act would be tried in the vice-admiralty courts. Parliament also passed the Quartering Act, which forced the colonial governments to provide barracks and food for British troops stationed in America. This was one more slap in the face of the colonists. During the past war, both Massachusetts and New York had refused to pay the billeting for British troops in America. Now they were being compelled to do so by force of law. Grenville's plan was brilliant and complete. He provided for the efficient collection of import duties, he provided for the collection of American revenue to help pay the national debt, he stationed British troops in America, he had forced the colonies to pay for those troops, and any violation of those laws would be tried in his special courts. But something Greeneville never considered or prepared for was about to happen.

The American Response

The Americans responded with outrage. The power of the mobs roiled through the cities of colonial America and terrorized British officials. The composition of the Stamp Act (SA) mobs resembled other colonial mobs in that many participants were poor ruffians looking for fun, but there were a number of other groups participating in the mobs as well. For one, a large number property-less artisans joined the ruffians. These men had economic motivations for joining the mobs, as they feared cheap British imports were about to put them out of business. Another group joining the mob was evangelical Protestants These pious men remembered the fervor of the Great Awakening and resented the immoral and greedy behavior of British officials. And lastly, another group to join the mob was a small group of men who still adhered to the anti-monarchy sentiment of the English Civil War. Often signing many of their anonymous letters with the initials O.C. (for Oliver Cromwell), these radicals saw the mobs as an opportunity to institute a new era in America—one decidedly absent of an Imperial government. Thus the traditional fear of tyrannical power combined with economic self-interest to produce these mobs, and they were effective. Royal tax collectors were too afraid to enforce the law, and the British Government did not know what to do next. This popular revolt of 1765 was important in that it not only rejected British authority, but gave a democratic appearance to the growing American identity.

While the mobs rioted in the streets, opposition began to take shape within the Colonial assemblies. The Massachusetts House called for a meeting of the colonies in New York in October 1766 to consider the issue. Nine of the Colonial assemblies sent representatives to the Stamp Act Congress. The participants did not threaten to rebel against the crown, but instead issued a statement called the Stamp Act Resolves. Therein, they contested the constitutionality of the Stamp and Sugar acts by demanding that only their own colonial assemblies had the power to tax colonial residents under the English Constitution. On these grounds, they asked for the repeal of the Stamp Act.

Parliament was in turmoil when Stamp Act Resolves arrived. King George III had replaced Grenville with Lord Rockingham, who took a more moderate stance toward the colonies. Whigs in Parliament and British merchants feared the Americans would institute an embargo of British goods, so they favored repeal. Other factions in Parliament were outraged by the American protest. Rockingham compromised; he pushed Parliament to repeal the Stamp Act, and changed the Sugar Act by reducing the duty from 3 pence per pound to 1 pence per pound on English molasses. Simultaneously, Rockingham sharpened the constitutional debate by giving in to the hardliners with the passage of the Declaratory Act of 1766, which reaffirmed the full power and authority of Parliament to do whatever it liked in America.

Charles Townshend

Often the course of history can be changed by a small, apparently insignificant event—an illness, a personal grudge, or even a chance comment. That is what happened in 1767, when Rockingham's ministry collapsed and George III named William Pitt prime minister for the second time. Pitt, who had won the Great War for Empire, had been sitting in the House of Lords (as the representative for Chatham), but he was very ill. Pitt was a supporter of American rights, but his illness forced him to miss many of the cabinet meetings and crucial debates in Parliament. So the man who emerged as the leading policy maker for the American colonies was Charles Townshend, Chancellor of the Exchequer. While Pitt had been sympathetic to the problems in the colonies, Townshend was not. In 1767, while Townshend was presenting his military budget to Parliament, George Grenville, Townshend's long-time political rival, rose from his seat and demanded that the colonists be made to pay all the costs of British troops in the colonies. Angered by such a blatant and open challenge, Townshend became defensive and made an unplanned, fateful policy decision. Townshend promised he would find a new source of revenue in America.

The tax legislation that came from that promise, known as the Townshend Act of 1767, was not much different from any that came before. It imposed taxes on paper, paint, glass, and tea imported into the colonies. The tax was expected to raise £35,000–40,000 a year—a pretty small amount. Townshend planned to set aside a small portion of the tax to pay for the British troops, but the major part of it went to pay the salaries of governors, judges, and other colonial officials. Townshend also wanted to make sure that the customs agents in America were able to do their job, so he asked Parliament for the Revenue Act of 1767, which reorganized the customs service and created a board of customs commissioners in Boston and four vice-admiralty courts—in Halifax, Boston, Philadelphia, and Charleston. These were substantial administrative reforms, and they posed a threat to what limited independence the colonies had.

In fact, Townshend had planned to do just that—he intentionally was seeking to bait the Americans into a foolish act in order to diminish the powers of the American legislatures. He immediately had chance to move against colonial legislatures. The New York Assembly had refused to comply with the Quartering Act of 1765, claiming they could not afford it. To many in the British Parliament, New York's refusal to pay was the last straw. A number of British ministers of Parliament wanted to send a military governor to New York to establish martial law and seize the money from New York's treasury. In the end, Townshend decided on a less provocative measure. He pushed through the Restraining Act of 1767, which suspended New York's Assembly until such time as it could produce the money it owed. In the face of such pressure, New York gave in and came up with the money. The Restraining Act was an important step. Prior to its passage, all colonial laws had been subject to approval in Britain. But now Britain had threatened not to just invalidate a law, but to ban an American assembly duly elected by the people of the colonies.

The Embargo

The American reaction to the action against New York was predictable. The Massachusetts Legislature in February 1768 sent a letter to the other American assemblies asking them to condemn Britain's actions. The rest of the colonies were not sure what to do about the matter. Merchants in Boston, however, were not going to wait. In April 1768 they initiated a boycott, or embargo, of all British imports and then pressured the other colonies to follow their lead. New York followed Massachusetts in August. Merchants and dock workers in Philadelphia, the largest city in America, refused to join believing the boycott would hurt them more than the British.

The embargo of 1768, unlike that of 1765, was controversial in America. A few people in the colonies supported the British move against New York, while others feared the embargo would hurt America more than the British. As a result, public support was slow to spread, even in New England. To gain support for the embargo, a decision was made to pressure those dragging their feet into action. A small group of elite patriots, who stretched across the colonies and called themselves the Sons of Liberty, published the names of merchants in each colony who refused to comply with the boycotts. If public humiliation failed to garner support, the Sons of Liberty broke store windows, harassed employees and families, set fires, and destroyed property. Finally in March 1769, merchants holding out in Philadelphia and several other sections of the colonies relented and stopped importing British goods. Two months later, Virginia also joined the boycott, although they called it the Non-Importation Movement. The members of the Virginia House of Burgesses promised not to buy imported goods, including slaves. By the summer of 1769, support for the embargo was solid throughout the colonies. Benjamin Franklin, still in England as Pennsylvania's representative, carefully summarized the American position when he was called before Parliament, stating that the only one way to end the problem was to "repeal the laws, renounce the right, recall the troops, refund the money, and return to the old method of requisition."

The authorities in Britain, however, had something else in mind. When a copy of the Massachusetts Houses' letter to the other colonies reached Parliament in 1768, there were elements (like Lord Hillsborough, the Under Secretary of State for American Affairs) who wanted to dissolve the Massachusetts Legislature if they did not repudiate the embargo. Britain's first response was to send four regiments of troops to Boston, mostly in anticipation of a showdown with the patriots. By the end of that year, 1768, the British military was encamped in Boston and General Gage was accusing the colony's leaders of treason. There were also rumors in Britain that some of the patriot leaders might be rounded up and tried for treason. In Parliament, the government formulated a plan to take care of these pesky patriots once and for all. They decided to repeal the Townshend duties in every colony except Massachusetts (thus isolating them from their colonial counterparts) and then use military force to crush the rebels of Massachusetts if necessary. Once again, fate intervened.

Britain in 1768 was having a critical food shortage. The English poor found it impossible to find food. Starvation was widespread. Food riots swept through the countryside (the worst being the Massacre of Saint George Fields in London). The food crisis combined with the effectiveness of the embargo put pressure on the British government to repeal the Townshend duties. Townshend died suddenly on September 4, 1767. Frederick North, known by the courtesy title of Lord North, became the new chancellor of the exchequer and then prime minister in 1770. Hoping to defuse the situation and get American foodstuffs back in England, Lord North arranged a compromise whereby all the Townshend taxes on everything were repealed, except one, the tax on tea.

Lord North's gesture of goodwill worked. Most American merchants dropped the embargo (save those radicals up in Boston who begged the rest of the colonies to continue). Though there were sporadic outbreaks of violence, like the Golden Hill riots in New York in January 1770 and the Boston Massacre in March 1770, the next few years were relatively peaceful. But all was not well in the British Empire. After five years of intense debate over these issues, there was ill will on both sides of the Atlantic. Many patriots, namely Benjamin Franklin (Pennsylvania), Patrick Henry (Virginia), and Samuel Adams (Massachusetts) had openly rejected Parliament, claiming that the assemblies of their colonies were, while still under King George III, equal to the body on the other side of the Atlantic (Parliament). While there was peace, a powderkeg hung over the colonies, one that could be set alit by the slightest disturbance. Two times the British had tried to force new taxes on the American colonies and both times they had lost. For the next three years there would be peace. But in 1773, the issue would blow up again with such force that it prevented any possibility of compromise.

Boston

Some residents in Boston were dissatisfied with the repeal of the Townshend duties. They wanted independence. These radicals were skilled at political rhetoric and republican imagery. They used the symbol of the Boston Massacre to convince many colonial residents of the dangers of British aggression. In November 1772, Sam Adams, who was good at getting drunk and inciting pub customers to riot—or burn down customs' officials houses—persuaded the Boston town meeting to establish a Committee of Correspondence as a means to communicate to the people to the colony their rights and to spread the word across America. The other American colonies took note of Boston's act, and soon Committees of Correspondence had arisen throughout Massachusetts to Virginia, Rhode Island, Connecticut, New Hampshire, and even South Carolina. The committees were informal by nature and structure, acting as a means for one revolutionary group to talk to another and combining the American colonies into one informal political entity.

There were some minor disagreements in 1772, which the committees discussed in some detail, but 1773 brought forth a major issue, one that eventually led to war. The Tea Act of 1773 was enacted to provide financial relief to the British East India Company (EIC), which was deeply in debt partly due to poor management but also because it bore the entire cost of military expeditions in India during the French and Indian War. As a reward for its patriotic diligence in prosecuting the war effort, Parliament decided to help the financially strapped company. In effect, the Tea Act gave the EIC a virtual monopoly on the tea trade in the British Empire. Lord North knew that the Tea Act would be unpopular in America, but he could not realize how unpopular. The Townshend Act established a 3-pence per pound tax on tea in 1768. Consequently, American merchants boycotted the product, choosing instead to import illegal tea from the Dutch. As a result, 90 percent of the tea in America was contraband. But the Tea Act was so profitable for the EIC, they could afford to sell tea in America and the rest of the Empire, even with the 3 pence tax, at a substantially cheaper rate than the Americans could buy it from the Dutch. That economic reality infuriated many patriots, who thought the British government's real purpose was to get the American public to accept the principle of taxation. If you accept one tax, they reasoned, then you must pay them all.

The patriot leadership begged New England not to consume the tea. As one anonymous American woman put it: "The use of tea is considered not as a private but a public evil … a handle to introduce a variety of oppressions amongst us." That was exactly what North wanted to do, to demonstrate to the colonials that Parliament had control of the colonies. For a time, the new policy did not go as well as Lord North expected. The Committees of Correspondence prevented EIC ships from unloading tea and forced the captains to return it to Britain, or to store the tea in public warehouses. In essence, the committees effectively nullified the Tea Act.

The Boston Tea Party

It is important to remember that Boston was the home of the American resistance. Its mobs, merchants, and statesmen had questioned British authority for years. The governor of Massachusetts, Thomas Hutchinson, adamantly opposed the patriots. And with good reason: Stamp Act rioters had looted his house, Benjamin Franklin stole his personal papers and published embarrassing private letters, and the Massachusetts Legislature condemned his constant defense of the British Parliament. Angered by American obstinacy, Hutchinson was determined to land the tea. His sons, who worked as customs officials, quietly passed a cargo of tea through customs. Once allowed in port and through customs, the tax had to be paid before the ship could leave. But Hutchinson's devious act did not end as he expected. In retaliation, the Boston Committee of Correspondence sent Paul Revere, William Molineaux, and Thomas Young to board the ship in question with a group of patriots. Once aboard the *Dartmouth,* the patriots dumped 342 chests of tea (about £10,000 or roughly $8 million by today's standards) into the harbor.

New England Under the Yoke

The King and Parliament were outraged. The time for concession was over, George III said. In the spring of 1774, Parliament enacted four Coercive Acts to force Massachusetts into submission.

1. The Port bill closed Boston Harbor until the EIC was paid for the loss of their tea.
2. The Government Act annulled the Massachusetts charter and outlawed town meetings.
3. The new Quartering Act required Massachusetts to build barracks or put soldiers into private homes.
4. The Administration of Justice Act allowed royal officials accused of capital crimes to be tried only in Britain.

The last of what was known as the Coercive Acts was the Quebec Act of 1774. The act extended the boundaries of Quebec to the Ohio River, thus threatening to end any future western settlement. The act also recognized Catholicism in Quebec as the state religion, a decision that outraged the religious folks in New England. Essentially, Parliament was attempting to employ the divide-and-conquer strategy that had been proposed back in 1769. It might have worked, but the Committees of Correspondence and the boycotts had generated a sense, small at first, of American unity. The colonies to the south were now willing to aid Massachusetts if necessary. In part, the main reason for American unity was because Parliament had made it painfully clear to the Americans that this was no longer only an issue of New England.

A Continental Congress

To respond to these challenges, American leaders called for the meeting of a colony-wide assembly, which they called the Continental Congress. The newer colonies (Florida, Quebec, Nova Scotia, and Newfoundland) did not attend. But representatives from the 13 mainland colonies, except Georgia, met in Philadelphia in September 1774. That congress passed a Declaration of Rights and Grievances, demanding the repeal of the Coercive Acts and the Declaratory Act of 1766. They also demanded that if these "intolerable acts," as the patriots called them, were not repealed within one year, all colonial exports to the rest of the empire would stop.

Lord North would not be bullied and, with the support of George III, he ordered General Gage to suppress dissent in Massachusetts. Immediately, both the patriots and the British began preparations for armed conflict. In September 1774, Gage ordered troops to march out of Boston and seize patriot armories and supplies at nearby Charlestown and Cambridge. This symbolic invasion of the countryside led to the mobilization of some 20,000 militiamen to protect the other centers of military supply. Thus, by that December, Gage was in control of Boston, mostly at bayonet point of his 3,500 troops, while the patriots controlled the surrounding countryside. Since the British did not intend to leave the city and the American militias were unwilling to dislodge them, a stalemate lasted for six months. Then the British government declared Massachusetts in a state of rebellion, and King George ordered Gage to put it down by force of arms.

On April 19, 1775 Gage followed his orders. He sent troops to capture colonial leaders and supplies twenty miles from Boston at Concord. The American militiamen met them at Lexington, where the first shots of the war were fired. The British easily drove the militiamen out of the Lexington. Pressing on to Concord, the British force of 700 met 400 militiamen on the edge of town. This time the British took the heavier losses, yet won the engagement. Feeling isolated at Concord, the British commanders decided to retreat to Boston, even though Gage knew it meant marching his tired, bloody troops back the way they had come. Along the route, local militias fired at the British time and time again. By the end of the day, 73 British soldiers were dead, 174 wounded so severely that they had to be carried, and the rest were wounded but capable of walking. Casualties among the militias of New England were only 49 killed and 39 wounded. Although the death toll did not even reach 200, too much blood had been spilled to allow a peaceful compromise. The American Revolution had begun.

Items to Consider

French & Indian War, Proclamation of 1763, republicanism, British justifications for staging troops on American soil, George Grenville, Sugar Act, Stamp Act, Stamp Act Congress, Charles Townshend, Coercive Acts

CHAPTER 9

The American Revolution

The Battle of Concord was fought on April 19, 1775, but it would take another 14 months before the rebels made a final break with Britain. In the time between Concord and the Declaration of Independence, most of the patriots, who had only wanted their "rights as Englishmen," decided that that was no longer enough. What they wanted now was independence. After Concord, in colony after colony, patriot forces threw out royal governors. Once gone, the patriot leadership took control of the colonies and realized they needed to create the two essential things for independence: a government and an army.

The Second Continental Congress met in May 1775 at Philadelphia. Georgia again did not appear at first, but later chose to join the debate. John Adams took control of the Second Congressional gathering, exhorting the members to rise to the defense of American liberty. He and his supporters called for the creation of a Continental Army. They also wanted to give control of the New England forces, which had the British surrounded at Boston, to George Washington. The debate over the nature of the army demonstrated some of the fundamental political limitations of the colonies in 1775. Most Americans had a traditional distrust of large standing armies. Instead, they wanted to rely exclusively on the colonial militias, a course of action that would have led to certain defeat. Adams and Washington argued successfully for the necessity of a professional army, however, and such a force was created. Most of the people assembled in Philadelphia were friendly to the Patriot cause, though voting for independence, and thus treason, was not any easy thing to do. As a result, the decision to write a Declaration of Independence and the creation of a Revolutionary government were much slower to come about. The more cautious members of the Second Continental Congress vehemently opposed the creation of a Declaration as proposed by Adams, and would not even discuss the formation of a government incorporating the continental colonies, warning that such a radical response would only commit the colonies to a revolution. It was only with the barest majority that John Adams got his way. After weeks of argument, the Second Continental Congress finally began to organize the framework for a new government and formed a special five-man committee to consider a Declaration of Independence.

Peace or War?

While Congress debated in Philadelphia, war continued to rage in Massachusetts. On June 17, the British generals trapped in Boston realized that their position was untenable. The city was surrounded by high hills, all of which were occupied by American forces. If the Americans secured cannons, they could force a British evacuation. As a remedy to their predicament, more than 3,000 British troops launched an assault against the American fortifications on Breed's Hill and Bunker Hill, the two highest hills overlooking Boston. The British were contemptuous of the American militia, and thus believed the assault would be an easy chore. Three assaults, and the loss of 1,000 men killed or wounded, however, were required to push the Patriots from their fortifications.

Despite even this loss of life, a majority in Congress hoped for reconciliation with the British government. Led by John Dickinson of Pennsylvania, they sent to the King an Olive Branch Petition that expressed American loyalty to King

George III. The petition asked him to repeal the oppressive parliamentary legislation of 1774 so the colonies could return to a peaceful existence within the Empire. George III refused to accept the petition. Instead he issued an order calling for the suppression of the rebellion. In response to that order, Congress decided in June 1775 to invade Canada, hoping to unleash a rebellion there and add a fourteenth colony to the revolt. Colonial forces easily took Montreal, but they failed to capture the fortress city of Quebec before winter set in. While American armies were invading Canada, American merchants cut off all exports to Britain and the British islands in the West Indies. Hoping to disrupt the tobacco and sugar trade, they thought an embargo would force the British to give in to their demands as they had in the past. Parliament, in response to the American embargo, issued the Prohibitory Act of 1775, which outlawed all trade with the rebellious colonies. Thus, for most of 1775, both sides chose to escalate the crisis rather than sue for peace.

Becoming a Revolutionary People?

Though angry, the majority of people living in the colonies still believed themselves to be British. Consequently, the process toward writing a declaration was slow and cautious. It is important to remember that there were three main groups of colonists in 1775:

1. Patriots—they wanted independence from Britain, by war if necessary. They made up roughly one-third of the population in the mainland colonies, but came mostly from the elite class of colonial society.
2. Loyalists—they wanted to remain loyal to Britain. They were a little more than one-sixth of the population, and came from all levels of colonial society.
3. The Middle Third—actually about half the population, but essentially the people in the middle who did not really care about what was going on nor did they have any formed ideas about what should happen, wanted to be left alone so they could live their lives.

The decision for or against revolution was a hard one, full of passion and uncertainty. Not surprisingly then, the Patriots and Loyalists had taken to fighting one another in the southern colonies by 1775. In June, the Patriot-dominated Legislature of Virginia ran the royal governor, Lord Dunmore, out of the colony. Dunmore, reluctant to abandon his post, took refuge aboard a British warship *Fowey* in the Chesapeake Bay. Safely ensconced on the *Fowey*, he branded the Patriots traitors and declared martial law. Then, in November, Dunmore issued his most controversial proclamation. Known today as Dunmore's Proclamation, he tried to dissuade the Virginians from rebellion by offering freedom to slaves who would rebel against their masters and join the loyalist cause. Not only did the Patriots have to face the possibility of a military attack now, but a slave uprising as well. For Virginians, Dunmore's Proclamation was the final straw. The conservative, foot-dragging Middle Third rapidly moved to the Patriot faction.

Still, the break with Britain did not come easily. It was not difficult for Americans to thumb their nose at Parliament, but most colonials held a deep loyalty to King George III. By 1775, that loyalty had begun to erode. The Patriots began to accuse George III of being behind the recent tyrannical acts of Parliament. Agitation against the king became most intense in Philadelphia. The largest American city, Philadelphia was the one place in America with a "continental atmosphere." But Philadelphia had not, however, been a place all that welcoming to the Patriot movement. If you remember, Philadelphia merchants refused to cooperate at first with the boycott of 1768. But now Philadelphia artisans took the lead. They owned nearly 40 percent of the city's wealth and made up roughly 50 percent of the city's male population. Despite that wealth, they were afraid for their future, especially an increase of cheap British imports flooding into America. When fighting broke out, they organized themselves into a Mechanics Association and became a powerful force in the Patriot movement. It is important to recognize that there was more than economic self-interest at work here. Many of those artisans were Scot-Irish, people who had left Northern Ireland to escape oppressive British rule, while others were New Light Christians who despised the unchristian behavior they saw in the exorbitant taxes.

Common Sense

Into that explosive atmosphere, a single revolutionary pamphlet tipped the balance. Enlightenment thinkers in Philadelphia began to question the legitimacy of the monarchy. Up to this moment, revolution was not inevitable. It did not have to take the form it finally did. The southern colonies might not have joined with New England. But in January 1776, Thomas Paine, who had been a failed corset maker in England and had been fired from his job in the English Customs Service for demanding more money than he was allowed, published a pamphlet entitled *Common Sense*—one of the most important documents of the American Revolution. The value of *Common Sense* was not so much what Paine said, as it was the way he said it. By mixing strong biblical themes with the absurdity of an island on the other side of the ocean ruling an entire continent, he framed the argument in ways that colonists could understand. It was a brilliant piece of propaganda, openly encouraging colonists to reject the power of King and Parliament and to create an independent republic. By July, over 100,000 copies of *Common Sense* were sold. It was circulated throughout the colonies and read publicly at every gathering place: in churches, on town hall steps, in front of the courthouse, in market places, and even in taverns. This document single handedly turned the tide of American support against the Loyalist factions.

Faced with almost certain defeat, the Loyalists in the Continental Congress withdrew and left the legislative field open to the Patriots. On July 4, 1776, the Continental Congress took the final step. It approved the Declaration of Independence by a margin of 12 to 1. Only New York, in the end, refused to cast a vote, although its representatives did sign the Declaration of Independence once it passed. John Dickinson, a Quaker pacifist from Pennsylvania, who had done so much to defuse the crisis, was the only representative to refuse to sign the document.

Thomas Jefferson

Thomas Jefferson was the main author of the Declaration of Independence. A young Virginia planter, Jefferson was part of the committee tasked by Congress with writing a Declaration. Although he was well known in Congress for writing the "Summary View of the Rights of British America," which had mobilized Colonial opposition to the Coercive Acts, he was the least famous of the five men on the committee. The committee was composed of John Adams, Benjamin Franklin, Thomas Jefferson, Robert R. Livingston, and Roger Sherman. The other men, busy with other matters in Congress, instructed Jefferson to write the declaration for two reasons: He was the junior member of the committee and he had previously demonstrated his eloquence with the "Summary View."

Regardless of why he was selected, in writing the Declaration of Independence, Jefferson mostly wanted to justify what Congress had been doing both to their critics at home and across the water in England and Europe. He did so, blaming George III for all the current turmoil. He listed all the acts we have talked about so far and a number not mentioned to show that the King had become a tyrant in his dealings with the colonies. He even suggested that such a powerful and centralized government as England's was inherently dangerous to liberty. The document drew on a great deal of Enlightenment thought.

Between them, Jefferson's and Paine's pens pushed many of the remaining half-hearted and undecided Americans into becoming revolutionaries. In both villages and seaport cities, George III was burned in effigy. These acts were significant because they represented the point at which the Patriots finally broke the American psychological ties with the British monarchy. They no longer identified themselves with England; they were Americans. Once the declaration was issued, much remained undone. If the war was lost, most of the authors would be considered criminals in the British system. The standard punishment for rebellion in English was to be drawn and quartered. The Declaration of Independence finally concluded all of the petty squabbling and political skirmishing between the American colonies. All Americans were now in the same boat, and could expect to face the same future. For the next two years, Britain decided to use overwhelming force to crush the revolution. In 1776, it looked like to be an easy task.

Comparing the Two Sides

Great Britain had a population of 11 million people compared to only 2.5 million who resided in the 13 rebel colonies. The American number is misleading, since out of the total 20 percent were slaves who would not be called on to fight for the American cause. The British were rich and about to become even richer. Militarily, Britain had a standing army of some 48,000 men (and plenty of money to hire mercenaries if needed). And, of course, they had the most powerful navy in the world. In contrast, the rebels had no navy. Their small army was primarily made up of militiamen whose terms of enlistment were set to expire at the end of 1776. The cards were clearly stacked against the colonies.

Conquering the Colonies

Lord North, remember, who was still the prime minister, moved quickly to put down the rebellion. He replaced Gage with a new commander, General William Howe. Howe was one of England's best military leaders and had served with distinction in the last war. North ordered Howe to capture New York City and to take control of Hudson River in order to isolate the Patriots of New England at Boston. In July 1776, Howe landed 10,000 troops in New York, with the intention of putting the conquest of the colony into action. Once on land, the British forces were quickly joined by many more thousands of British troops and mercenaries from Germany. By August, that British army in America had swollen to some 32,000 soldiers while being supported by a fleet of 30 warships and 10,000 sailors.

Facing that force was George Washington's newly formed, poorly trained army of about 18,000 troops. The first major engagement in New York was a stunning victory for the British. At the Battle of Long Island in August 1776, Howe cut down more than 1,500 American troops and drove Washington back from his battlements toward Harlem Heights where he was again dislodged and driven all the way to Pennsylvania. Expecting the war to be over before it had begun, Congress abandoned its capital at Philadelphia and headed to Baltimore, where many considered finding ships to escape the continent altogether and the inevitable punishment which seemed only a short time away.

The 1776 campaign was a military disaster for the Patriots. They suffered one defeat after another. Winter came just in time. During the 18th century, it was customary to halt military operations in cold and snowy weather. The British did just that. The British commanders, who had grown overconfident, and rightfully so, let down their guard during the winter that followed, and thus gave the Colonials a chance to score a few victories. Taking advantage of British laxity and benefiting from an unusually harsh winter storm, Washington secretly crossed over the Delaware River and marched toward the British encampments in New Jersey. On Christmas night of 1776, Washington surprised and routed a group of Hessians garrisoned at Trenton, New Jersey. Having captured the Germans so easily and suffering only a few casualties, Washington followed up that victory with an assault on another garrison at Princeton before retreating into Pennsylvania. These two victories proved to be a much-needed boost to American confidence, and convinced the British that their lines were overextended. In the spring, the British fell back to New York and Congress was able to return to Philadelphia.

The British could have won the war that first year. Howe was too cautious and did not follow up on his victories as he should have. The small victories the Americans won encouraged them. Washington's strategy of employing a defensive war had worked well. His main goal was to draw the British deeper into the American countryside, away from their supplies and, above all, to keep his army intact. In that plan, he was successful. But to win an ultimate victory against the British, Washington was fighting more than the British Army. Congress had promised to find him 75,000 men. Yet Washington's army would never reach half that number. He had problems keeping recruits, training them, paying them, equipping them, etc. Given everything Washington was fighting against, it is nothing short of miraculous that he was not crushed in 1776, or the years that followed.

The British Problem

The Americans were not the only ones having trouble fighting the war. Back in Britain, Lord North was beside himself. He could not understand why Howe had failed to crush the Americans in 1776. Only slowly did he begin to realize that it would require a long-term military commitment to win back the colonies. With the war dragging on, Britain had no choice but to increase taxes at home to raise more money to fight the war. Their first goal for the following year would be to isolate New England, which Lord North believed was the home of the rebellion. Lord North devised a three-pronged attack converging on Albany, New York. General John Burgoyne was to lead a large force of British regulars from Quebec down the St. Johns River to Albany. A second, smaller force composed of Loyalists and Native peoples allied with the British would attack Albany from the west, moving through the Mohawk River valley. Those latter troops were mostly Iroquois warriors from central New York. Howe would provide the hammer to smash American resistance by taking the largest force north from New York City.

General Howe, however, was not in favor of this plan. He wanted to attack Philadelphia, the home of the American Congress and end the war as quickly as possible. By attacking the "capital," Howe hoped to force Washington into a battle to destroy him. Rather than march north to Albany, Howe sent his troops toward Philadelphia from the southwest through the Chesapeake Bay. They met Washington at Brandywine Creek, outflanked him, and forced him to withdraw. On September 26, 1777 the British army marched into Philadelphia. Its commanders assumed that capturing the American capital would end the revolution. Congress, though, fled deeper into Pennsylvania (first to Lancaster, then York). So while the British captured the American capital, the government carried on in absentia.

The price for this victory for Britain was high. Howe had marched on Philadelphia at a leisurely pace. Burgoyne, meanwhile, continued to move south from Quebec, overrunning American positions at Fort Ticonderoga and driving down the Hudson River. But then his force stalled. Burgoyne, "Gentleman Johnny" as they called him, fought with style, not speed. His heavy baggage train moved slowly, weighed down with comfortable tents and lots of food and wine. Their progress was also slowed by the forces of Horatio Gates, who kept cutting trees down along the British path and attacking their long supply lines back to Canada. By the end of the summer, Burgoyne's forces were in deep trouble. His 6,600 men were bogged down in the wilderness near Saratoga, New York.

The patriot militia delivered the final blow. On August 16, 1777, Burgoyne's men fought and lost a pitched battle near Bennington, Vermont, which kept the British raiders from acquiring much-needed supplies of food and horses. Burgoyne then got more bad news. The force coming east had been forced to retreat and Howe was in New York City. Burgoyne had no choice but to wait for Howe, hoping he was still marching north and could relieve his forces.

He waited in vain. While Burgoyne did nothing, thousands of militiamen poured in from the countryside. On October 17, 1777, Burgoyne was forced to surrender at Saratoga. The victory at Saratoga proved to be a major turning point in the war. First, the Americans captured 5,000 British troops and their equipment—which provided much more value to Washington than capturing Philadelphia had to Howe. More important, the victory assured the success of American diplomats in Paris, who were trying to secure a military alliance with the French.

American Problems

Despite the great victory at Saratoga, all was far from rosy for the Americans. The average American suffered cruelly during the war. New Jersey was particularly hard hit, as American and British armies marched back and forth across the state. Patriots had to flee their homes as the British advanced, as did Loyalists when the Patriots advanced. Whole towns would switch sides depending on who was there that day. Soldiers looted farms. Crops were destroyed. Drunk and disorderly troops harassed civilians. Wherever the two armies went, families lived in fear. Such an atmosphere created severe anxiety, and with good cause. Mobs of Patriots farmer in New England beat suspected Loyalists and destroyed their property. Patriots in most communities organized Committees of Safety to collect taxes, funnel food and clothing to the Continental Army, or imposed fines and jail sentences on those who did not support the Patriot cause. In some communities, there was no such thing as remaining neutral.

The Americans faced one major problem early in the conflict that they were never able to resolve: how to finance the war. They could not tax, especially since the revolution was, to some degree, a tax revolt. So Congress borrowed and relied on donations from private individuals and foreign nations. Those funds ran out quickly. To pay their part of the debt, the colonies, now states, created a new currency, the dollar, and issued $260 million in currency to pay their soldiers and purchase supplies. In theory, the new notes could be redeemed in gold or silver, but in practice they issued too much of it and never backed it with anything. In fact, North Carolina eventually refused to accept its own money for debts late in the war. Congress tried to issue paper money, as well, with little success. All the paper currency being issued by the various government entities led to the worst inflation in American history. In Maryland, for example, a bag of salt that had cost one British Pound Sterling in 1776 cost 3,900 Maryland dollars a few years later. There were even food riots in many places on the continent. So bad were the economic troubles, some of the leaders of the revolution doubted, privately, that the war could be won.

The French Alliance

The Patriots' prospects improved dramatically in 1778. Out of the American victory at Saratoga came a military alliance with France, the most powerful nation on the European continent. The alliance not only brought the Americans money, troops, and supplies, but it changed the conflict from a colonial rebellion to an international war. In 1777, Benjamin Franklin and two other diplomats, Arthur Lee and Silas Deane, initiated negotiations for a treaty with France. Since 1763, France had been seeking revenge against the British for its defeat in the Great War for the Empire and its loss of Canada. The French foreign minister Pierre de Beaumarchais (Comte de Vergennes) was determined to grind the British nose in the mud and, therefore, he supported American independence. In 1776, he persuaded King Louis XVI to extend a secret loan to the colonies and supply them with gunpowder. When news of the American victory at Saratoga reached Paris in December of 1777, Franklin and the foreign minister persuaded the king to approve a formal alliance with the Continental Congress.

The Treaty of Alliance was signed on February 6, 1778. For their part in the Alliance, France entered the war on the American side and promised to fight until American independence was secured. In return, American diplomats promised to recognize any French conquests in the Caribbean. Both sides specified that after France entered the war, neither would stop fighting until American independence was won.

France and America were unlikely partners. France was Catholic. America was Protestant. France had a divine right king. America was a loose confederation of independent states. They did not speak the same language and had fought one another was only twelve years before. But now they were united against a common enemy.

The value of the French Alliance cannot be understated; at the very least, it isolated the British diplomatically and put the British militarily on the defensive since the war was immediately expanded outside the American colonies to the entire Empire. Not only did the British have to fight in America but also in Europe, the West Indies, and even in India. American independence had become a world war. But the Alliance had important implications for the new nation, as well. It legitimized the independence movement and provided much-needed benefits: supplies, money, and troops.

France and America versus Britain

The British response to the alliance was much like the American response to the Vietnam War during the 1960s and 1970s. The war quickly became unpopular in Britain. Many radical elements in British politics supported the American cause. Neither the gentry nor the aristocracy liked the rising taxes needed to pay for the war. Yet, George III continued to demand that the rebellion be crushed at any cost. If the Americans won independence, George told Lord North, then the West Indies would follow, then Ireland, and the rest of the British empire: It was an eighteenth-century version of the Domino Theory. But North began to take a more practical view. In February of 1778, he tried to seek a negotiated settlement with the Americans. He asked Parliament to repeal the Tea and Prohibitory acts, and renounced the right to tax the American colonies. He then appointed a commission headed by Lord Carlisle to begin peace negotiations with the Continental Congress. The Carlisle Commission was told to offer the Americans a return to the system which was in place in 1763, before the Sugar and Stamp acts. But it was too late.

By early 1778, when the military alliance with France was signed, a majority of Americans favored independence. The Alliance had given new life to the Patriot cause. With access to European money and supplies, the American army and its performance in the field improved. Even Congress, which was about to throw in the towel before the victory at Saratoga, happily paid out more money and pensions to the soldiers and officers of the Army.

The French alliance made the war a world war, but it did not bring about a quick conclusion. France was not interested in pounding the British in North America first. Instead, they wanted to win back some of the rich sugar islands they had lost in the West Indies. Following the French lead, Spain entered the war against Britain as well in 1779. But they, too, had their own goals. The Spanish wanted to win back Florida and Gibraltar, an island they had lost to the English in the last war. Consequently, despite having two major allies, the Americans had to rely on themselves to defeat the British for a time, while the Spanish and French were pursuing their own interests.

Despite the odds against them, Britain did have a bit of hope. The loss at Saratoga almost ensured they could not recapture New England, nor would they be able to hold on to all their mainland colonies. Yet in many ways, New England was the least valuable part of the British Empire. Far more important to the South Atlantic System were the southern colonies, with their rich crops of rice and tobacco. So the British, facing war on many fronts, decided to put all their marbles into a campaign to secure the American south.

The Southern Strategy

Britain's Southern Strategy, as it is called, was designed to recapture Virginia, the Carolinas, and Georgia. There was strong Loyalist sentiment in the South, and the British were going to rely heavily on the help of the Loyalists. Britain actively began to recruit those who might be sympathetic to their cause. They began with the backcountry farmers, a group that traditionally hated the government run by Low Country planters. They also began to recruit the Scottish Highlanders of North Carolina, who only recently came to the colonies and still had strong ties to the mother country.

The British also hoped to take advantage of the racial situation in the south. Lord Dunmore's Proclamation, you will remember, offered freedom to slaves who were willing to fight for the King. In 1776 alone, more than 1,000 Virginia slaves had run away to fight for Lord Dunmore. Recognizing the possibilities, the British hoped that thousands more might join the cause. From a military standpoint, the slaves were a valuable commodity for the British. Not only did they offer a potential source of manpower, but the large population of black slaves in the region forced plantation owners to keep their sons and overseers at home and out of the American army in order to prevent any slave uprisings.

The man responsible for implementing the southern strategy was Sir Henry Clinton, who had replaced Howe early in 1778. In June 1778, Clinton ordered the British army to evacuate Philadelphia and fall back to New York. Then in December, he initiated his southern campaign by landing a force of 3,500 men near Savannah, Georgia. By the end of 1779, the British had retaken all of Georgia and had some 10,000 troops ready to invade South Carolina. The Continental Congress was worried about the possibility that South Carolina might be invaded and captured. Realizing the immediate need for troops, the Continental Congress asked the South Carolina legislature to raise as many as 3,500 black troops from their slave population. South Carolina declined.

During most of the following year, 1780, the British moved from one victory after another in South Carolina. By May, Clinton had taken Charleston, before having to resign from duty after suffering a nervous breakdown. With Clinton gone, Lord Cornwallis assumed control of the British forces in the summer of 1780 and sent out expeditions to secure the South Carolina countryside. In August Cornwallis routed an American force commanded by Horatio Gates, the hero of Saratoga, at Camden. That victory gave the British complete control of South Carolina.

The British southern strategy seemed to be working. Thousands of African slaves had fled to Florida and hundreds more fled to the British lines in Georgia and South Carolina. There, the newly freed men proved to be an important source of labor for the British army. The Southern Loyalists, as predicted, rallied to the King's cause. By contrast, the Patriots in the South proved little help to Horatio Gates' army at Camden. Only about 1,200 southerners came to help him when he asked for their support, and many of those who did come panicked, dropped their guns, fleeing the battlefield without firing a shot.

The Road to Yorktown

Just when it seemed like the British were about to re-conquer the South, another blow befell the British cause. The Dutch joined the war against England. The British were now at war with the Americans, French, Spanish, and Dutch. But more important, after two years, the French finally sent troops to North America. At long last, the Marquis de Lafayette had persuaded Louis XVI to commit French troops on the American mainland. In July 1780, a French army of 5,500, commanded by General Comte de Rochambeau, arrived in Newport, Rhode Island. At the same moment, Washington replaced Gates with Nathanael Greene as the American commander in the South.

Greene immediately made better use of the few Patriots to be found. He divided them into small groups and sent them to harass Loyalists. It was here that American guerilla fighters like Francis Marion, the Swamp Fox, won a series of small battles in South Carolina. Eventually, the guerrilla forces harassed the British enough to lure them out of the security of Charleston. In January 1781, Daniel Greene defeated a regiment of British regulars at Cowpens, North Carolina. The tide was turning in the South. The British juggernaut that had marched up the coast from Georgia to South Carolina no longer was winning.

In the spring of 1781, Cornwallis decided to give up the Carolinas and Georgia and make a last-ditch effort to secure Virginia. Aided by reinforcements from General Clinton in New York, Cornwallis moved north toward the Tidewater area of Virginia with Nathanael Greene hot on his trail. Cornwallis' forces, led by the turncoat Benedict Arnold, met little resistance at first as they moved north. As they reached the James River, Arnold took part of the force up the James to the Virginia capitol at Richmond. Nearly catching Governor Thomas Jefferson in his bed, Arnold chased him all the way to Albemarle County before turning south to meet up with Cornwallis at Yorktown at the southern tip of the York peninsula. Meanwhile, Washington slipped out of the north and began marching south toward Virginia. Washington's forces and Rochambeau's forces (who were simultaneously marching south from Rhode Island) met north of the York peninsula. At the same time, a large French fleet secretly positioned itself just off the Virginia coast, preventing a possible British evacuation.

By the time Cornwallis knew what was going on, it was too late. His army of 9,500 men was outnumbered two-to-one and was cut off by land and sea. Surrounded, Cornwallis surrendered at Yorktown on October 19, 1781. That victory broke the back of the British war effort. Lord North was heard to say, "Oh God! It is all over!" He and the British no longer had the will or the resources to raise a new army to continue the long war in America. Besides, they had bigger problems than losing America. The combined fleets of the Spanish and French were threatening to take Britain's valuable sugar islands. Britain found no sympathy in Europe; they were defeated on the field of battle, and they had almost no political support at home. The war effort collapsed around them. The only military action in the thirteen colonies after Yorktown was a few isolated attacks against the Loyalists and the Cherokees, a southern tribe that sided with the British.

The Fallout

Parliament, of course, was furious. How could Britain, victorious over the French only fifteen years ago and possessing the greatest financial resources in Europe, lose to a motley crew like the Americans? The government blamed the military: Howe failed to go after the Americans in 1776 and he was responsible for the bungling at Saratoga. They also blamed Cornwallis for marching his army into a sea of rebels in 1781.

Well, perhaps the case against the British military has been overstated. Although only one-third of the American population could be called true Patriots, the middle third was supportive enough to pay their taxes. But the Patriots had the home field advantage, and when the French intervened, the odds favored the Patriots even more than the British army. Lastly, Lord North was no William Pitt. He was not charismatic and he could not move the masses to sacrifice as Pitt had been able to do in the last war.

The Americans, by contrast, were blessed with great leadership. George Washington had a conviction and presence that were well suited to motivating others. He recruited good officers and turned the Continental Army into a decent fighting force. He learned how to use the militia effectively and recognized that all he had to do to keep the revolution alive was to keep his army alive, which he did.

In the end, it appears that the assumed British advantage was not as great as it appeared on paper. Given the way events transpired, the Patriots had a decided advantage after 1778. The British won many battles but, like the Americans in Vietnam 200 years later, they failed to win anything in the end. By contrast the two major British defeats, Yorktown and Saratoga, proved to be catastrophic.

The Peace

After Yorktown, it took the diplomats two years to conclude the war. Peace talks began in Paris in April 1782, but the French and Spanish were stalling for time. Remember the Americans had promised not to make peace with the English until the French did as well. But with the French and Spanish hoping for a major naval victory or territorial conquest, there was no chance for peace as the war dragged on and on. Those delays infuriated the American diplomats (Benjamin Franklin, John Adams, and John Jay) at Paris who feared that drawn-out negotiations would tempt the French to sacrifice American interests for their own. So the Americans secretly opened negotiations with the British. If necessary, they were prepared to cut the French loose and sign a separate peace.

The British were eager to get the mattered settled before the French won any other victories. As a result, Franklin was able to exploit that desire to end the war quickly, while winning a major victory for America at the negotiating table. The Treaty of Paris, signed on September 3, 1783, formally recognized the independence of the United States. Britain would keep Canada, but only the part north and west of the Great Lakes. All the land between the Appalachian Mountains and the Mississippi River which Britain had taken from France twenty years before was ceded to the United States. The only concession the Americans gave up was the promise to return Loyalist property and to treat them as equal citizens if they returned to their homes.

France, realizing its chance of a great victory had slipped away, made peace with Britain at the same time. Despite their great plan, France had only gained the Caribbean island of Tobago. But in doing so, France's national debt had increased by 400 percent, a financial crisis that would spark the French Revolution in six years. Spain managed to retake Florida and then they, too, made peace with Britain.

Items to Consider

Second Continental Congress, Bunker Hill, Thomas Paine, Saratoga, Committees of Safety, Treaty of Alliance, Carlisle Commission, Southern Strategy, Lord Dunmore's Proclamation, Peace of Paris (1783)

Chapter 10

The Early Republic: Confederation, Constitution, and the Federalist Nation

The Revolution of 1776 began as a struggle to determine who would rule the colonies. But there was another struggle of the Revolutionary era, a conflict over who should rule the newly independent colonies. This struggle was one over both the character of the state constitutions and governments as well as the nation as a whole. It involved a debate over all these political theories we have already discussed, along with practical politics, to decide who would control the new republican governments: the old elite or ordinary citizens.

After fighting broke out at the start of the Revolution, Patriot leaders moved quickly to shift from colonial governments to create state and national governments based on popular rule, on what the people wanted. The Declaration of Independence argued that the power of governments was based on the consent of the governed. But in reality, no one was quite sure what that meant. Did it mean that slaves, women, and the working urban poor would rule alongside the planters and merchants? No, not really. Politics was the realm of white men who owned property, for in the eighteenth-century mind only they had a stake in the future. Women, blacks, Indians, and poor white males who did not own property were excluded from political participation. More conservative elements of the Patriot cause went even further: They wanted to exclude those who owned only a little bit of property, since they had little to lose if things turned sour. The theory behind that position was that only the white males who owned property had a stake in a system. And since they had a stake in the system, they were the people best able to judge which direction the new nation should take.

A small but growing group of radical Patriots, however, believed just the opposite. They embraced a truly democratic outlook. Every citizen, they felt, who had supported the Revolution, whether they were a property owner or not, should be able to participate in the government. This inclusive theory—that everyone should participate—is called *democratic-republicanism*. Some states, mostly those in New England and the Middle Atlantic, were more inclined to take such a view. Pennsylvania, for example, abolished property owning as a qualification for voting or holding office in 1776. All you had to do in Pennsylvania to vote or hold office was to pay your taxes. The Pennsylvania constitution also mandated basic elementary education for its citizens and protected them from imprisonment for debt. These reforms were seen at the time as very progressive and very democratic. Some embraced the idea, while others looked with on trepidation.

In fact, Pennsylvania's constitution was seen as radical and it alarmed Patriots in other states, most of whom did not believe in that kind of democracy. For the most part, you must remember, the main cadre of the Patriot leadership came from the top of colonial society. If they were to hand over control to the underclasses, they feared ordinary citizens would use their numerical advantage to heavily tax the rich. John Adams of Boston was one of the Patriots who denounced the Pennsylvania system as being too democratic. Adams wanted to make sure that other states did not adopt such constitutions, so he wrote *Thoughts on Government* and sent it to friends at constitutional conventions in other states. In his *Thoughts on Government,* Adams created a new form of government which adapted the traditional English system of mixed government (monarch, House of Lords, House of Commons, and independent judicial system) to a republican system. Instead of dividing each state along social lines though, he divided the state into three functions (or branches) of government—lawmaking, administering, and judging. Adams said his scheme was republican because people would elect the chief executive and members of the legislature. The legislature, by the way, would be divided into two houses: the common people would sit in the lower house and gentlemen of property and standing in the upper house. The judiciary would be appointed with the purpose of reviewing laws and, as a further check on democracy, the executive would have veto power over the legislature.

Obviously, most Patriots preferred Adams's mixed system. They did so in part because it was less democratic than the Pennsylvania system and it seemed more familiar; in many ways like the English system. As a result, when most of the state constitutions were created, Adams' system was the one most commonly employed. The only noticeable difference from Adams' system was that only three states gave their governor the veto power. New York's system was typical. New York's constitution, mostly written by John Jay, had a *bicameral* (two houses) legislature, a governor, an appointed judiciary, and property qualifications that prevented 60 percent of white males from voting. The most flagrant use of property qualifications to protect the power elite occurred in South Carolina, whose constitution, written in 1778, required candidates for governor to have a net worth about $450,000, senators $90,000, and assemblymen $45,000. South Carolina's property qualifications prevented 90 percent of the white adult population of the state from holding office.

Despite the obvious intent to create political systems dominated by the elite, the character of American politics slowly became more democratic after the Revolution. It did so for two reasons:

1. Most of the state constitutions allotted seats in the lower houses on the basis of population, which gave poor western farmers, the yeomen, the representation they had always wanted.
2. The revolution raised the political consciousness of ordinary people. Militiamen during the revolution, for example, often demanded the right to elect their own officers. When they laid down their weapons, they still felt they should have the right to elect their own government representatives.

These two things changed the nature of the American assemblies. Before the war, 85 percent of assemblymen were wealthy, averaging over $90,000 in wealth. By 1784, though, ordinary farmers controlled the lower houses of New York, New Hampshire, and New Jersey. They even had large numbers in the lower houses of Virginia, Massachusetts, and South Carolina. Their growing power was reflected in the movement of many of the state capitals away from the seaports and into the interior: New York City to Albany, Philadelphia to Harrisburg, and Charleston to Columbia. Conservative Patriots, like John Adams, were able to maintain control, but just for the moment Only in Pennsylvania and in Vermont were the radicals able to take power. While men of property and wealth dominated America's early political life, gradually the average people and even women were able to chip away at elite superiority. White male elites would dominate politics until at least 1828, longer than that for African-Americans and for women, but their control could not last forever.

As the Patriots moved toward independence in 1776, one of their biggest challenges was the need to confront the problem of what to do for a national government. Most Patriots wanted a Continental Congress of limited power. They wanted Congress to deal with things like war, peace, trade, and treaties. Thus, most power would remain with the states. The Patriots were firm believers in decentralized government, of home rule. The first national Constitution reflected those views. On November 15, 1777, the Second Continental Congress passed the Articles of Confederation. Mostly the work of John Dickinson of Pennsylvania, the Articles of Confederation provided for a loose confederation of the states. Each state retained its freedom and all powers not given to the United States. The Confederation government had the authority to declare war and peace, make treaties with foreign nations, resolve disputes between states, and borrow or print money. The Continental Congress was charged with taking care of these matters. Each state had one vote in the Confederation Congress. There was no president. There was no Supreme Court. All powers not delegated to the Articles of Confederation government were retained by the states.

Despite even this limited form of national government, the Articles were not ratified by all the states until 1781. The problem was western land claims. The Articles gave Congress authority over land disputes between states, but did not give authority to the Congress to hold western lands under a national domain. As a result, states with no western land claims, like Maryland and Pennsylvania, would not ratify the Articles until the states with large claims, some of which extended all the way to the Pacific Ocean, gave those areas over to the national government. But states with large claims, like Virginia, were not about to do that. So for a long time, there was deadlock on the issue, and there was no national government until the pressures of the war finally broke the deadlock.

Formal ratification of the Articles, though, was a dead issue. Congress had been operating as a de facto national government for four years. It had raised an army, negotiated a treaty with France, and financed the war effort. Despite these successes, Congress was a failure under the Articles. The main problem was that the Continental Congress could not tax, only ask the states for money and hope they paid. Faced with the prospect of bankruptcy in 1780, George Washington warned Patriot leaders that the war would soon be lost unless Congress was soon given the powers to tax.

In response, some members of Congress tried to expand the powers of Congress. It was a difficult undertaking. To amend the Articles of Confederation; all the states had to agree. For example, there was an attempt to create a 5 percent national tariff on foreign goods to pay for the war, but Rhode Island vetoed that in 1781. Two years later New York vetoed a similar bill. The underlying message is that the government under the Articles of Confederation was weak. It is a wonder that the Revolution did not fall apart under the ineptness of the government established under the Articles of Confederation.

After the war, the Articles of Confederation government did succeed in one crucial area. It was able to create a plan for the settling the lands contained in the trans-Appalachian west which the United States received in the Treaty of Paris. Congress had two goals with respect to the new western lands.

1. It needed to assert its title so that it could sell most of the lands to pay the government's war expenses and debts. Standing in the way of that plan, of course, was who/what? The western land claims of the states as well as a myriad of white squatters who were pouring into the region.
2. Congress was determined to bind western settlements to the United States. To ensure they remained closely tied to the eastern U.S., Congress created a system for orderly settlement of the region and established a plan for the eventual admission of states from the territories into the Union.

Given the Appalachian Mountains barrier, Congress was afraid Westerners might try to create their own nations or align themselves with Spanish Louisiana. That danger was very real as thousands of settlers in what is now eastern Tennessee tried to create a new state, the state of Franklin, and to apply for admission to the Confederation in 1784. Congress, wanting to preserve its authority over the West, refused to recognize Franklin or consider the application.

To prevent similar, unauthorized actions as the State of Franklin, Congress pursued a dual policy. First, it directed Virginia, North Carolina, and Georgia to take temporary control of the western lands south of the Ohio River. North of the Ohio River, Congress created the Northwest Territory, an area owned by the United States, and issued three ordinances for the settlement and administration of that region. The Ordinance of 1784, written by Thomas Jefferson, called for the admission of several states carved out of the territory as soon as their populations equaled the current size of the smallest state (Delaware had 59,000 people in 1790). The Land Ordinance of 1785 created a rectangular grid system for surveying land and a set of rules that dictated the pattern of settlement. For example, the rules said that western lands had to be surveyed before they could be settled. The Northwest Ordinance of 1787 said that, eventually, there would be three to five states carved out of the Northwest territory (eventually those would become the states of Ohio, Indiana, Illinois, Michigan, and Wisconsin). The Ordinance of 1787 also prohibited slavery in the territories. Once the population of an area grew to 60,000 residents, they could write a constitution and apply for admission to the union.

It is almost impossible to overestimate the value of these ordinances. They provided for the orderly settlement of the West and reduced the possibility that the residents of the region might try to create a nation of their own. Just as important, the sale of lands gave Congress a needed source of revenue. But most important, the Ordinance began the push of the United States across the continent. Problems remained—the Spanish, Native Americans, and illegal British forts in the west, for instance—but the Land Ordinances slowly pulled the United States away from the eastern seaboard and laid the foundation for a continental nation.

Well, I've made it seem pretty rosy, but there were plenty of problems in the new republic. Prosperity did not return with peace. American trade had been totally disrupted. Many American merchant ships had been burned. Consequently, the economy in many regions underwent serious transformations (particularly South Carolina, which switched from rice production to cotton). Most of the state governments emerged from the war ridden with debt and paper money that was worthless. North Carolina alone owed $1.7 million dollars to various sources. Virginia owed $2.7 million. Many Americans, and especially the western yeoman farmers, were in bad economic shape as a result of the recession and taxes. Some states passed debtor relief laws, which helped, but other states refused to do so.

The lack of debtor relief in Massachusetts provoked the first armed uprising in the new nation. When the war ended, merchants and creditors in eastern Massachusetts lobbied their state government to increase taxes and to stop printing paper money. Strangely, they got what they wanted. Creditors and sheriffs hauled farmers into court, fined them for not paying their debts and taxes, threatened to imprison them for debt, and took away their lands as compensation. In 1786, angry bands of farmers forced the closing of the courts and began to release debtors from jails. Resistance gradually grew into a full-scale revolt in western and central Massachusetts, where hundreds of farmers organized a revolt led by Daniel Shays, a former captain in the continental army.

The Shays' Rebellion looked much like the protests between colonies and British officials just a few years prior. The governor of Massachusetts and his eastern merchant supporters put together an army to put down the rebellion. Shays army fell apart during the winter of 1786–87, when the states' military force easily dispersed the rioters. Although it ended quickly, the rebellion had major aftershocks. The governor was turned out of office by the voters in the next election, and similar farmers' movements in other states closed courts. The situation in New England became so serious that British officials in Canada predicted that America would soon collapse. The lesson, though, at least for the various Patriot leaders, was the need for a stronger and more centralized government whose size and strength could deal effectively with such problems in the future.

The U. S. Constitution

Shays' Rebellion demonstrated to Nationalist interests within the country that the Articles of Confederation government was far too weak to handle the problems it would face in the future. The Nationalists believed the new nation needed a stronger national government to deal with foreign and domestic problems. Among the most serious of their concerns was the great level of democracy being practiced in many of the state legislatures. The Nationalists worried about the rights of the minority, especially a minority of rich landowners like themselves, and so they wanted to check unlimited democracy as best they could.

The most important of these early nationalists were George Washington, and one of his closest advisors, Alexander Hamilton. Hamilton had acquired wealth by working hard. Born illegitimately in the West Indies to a merchant of modest means, he was a self-made man. Hamilton served well at Washington's side during the Revolution, went on to a legal career in New York, and married into one of the most powerful families in colonial America. But Washington and Hamilton were only two of a growing group of nationalists in the republic. Many of these nationalists were merchants, who were greatly concerned about the financial crisis of the postwar period and wanted some relief from debts. Others were concerned about Shays' Rebellion, and the possibility of future turmoil. These two crises gave the Nationalists a reason to organize and, in the spring of 1787, the Confederation Congress suggested the calling of a convention to revise the Articles of Confederation.

After the call went out, every state except Rhode Island sent delegates to Philadelphia. Fifty-five men gathered there in May 1787. The convention was conspicuous by those individuals not in attendance. Thomas Jefferson and John Adams were in Europe as American ambassadors. Patrick Henry, an ardent anti-Federalist, chose to stay home. But George Washington, Benjamin Franklin, Alexander Hamilton, James Madison, George Mason, and others were there. A typical delegate was college educated, often trained in the legal profession. They had all served in the war either in Congress or the military. About one-third of the representatives owned slaves. Clearly, the Constitutional Convention was a meeting of America's elite. There were no commoners there. No workers. No women, Native Americans, or African-Americans. As their first act, George Washington was elected chair, and in a key decision, the body chose to keep its deliberations secret.

One of the key players at the convention was a young representative from Virginia named James Madison. He and others authored the Virginia Plan as a basis for discussion in the development of a new government. Madison wanted to do away with the Articles of Confederation. In its place, Madison wanted to create an entirely new government. Instead of being a confederation with only the powers given to it by the states, the new national government under Madison's plan would be a true, powerful federal government, one that could create laws for an entire nation. This limited the power of the state governments to only what was not held by the federal government.

Madison also sought to alter the configuration of the new government. He called for a bicameral legislature. The lower house would be apportioned on the basis of population and its members would be elected by popular vote. The upper house, or Senate as he called it, would be elected by the members of the lower house, not by the people. The president under Madison's plan was to be appointed by Congress, as were the members of the national judiciary. Thus

Madison's government differed from that of the Confederation in three important ways. First, it created a government based on popular sovereignty (the will of all the people) instead of the will of the individual states. Second, it created a republic whose authority came directly from the people, not from the states. And third, its three-branch government differed greatly from the one house parliamentary system employed by the Articles of Confederation.

Madison's plan, however, had little chance for success. It gave too much power to the lower house, which was elected on the basis of population. To large states, like Virginia, Massachusetts, and New York, that was a good thing. But to small states like New Jersey, Delaware, and Connecticut, it effectively undermined the power they enjoyed in the Confederation Congress. Each state under the current state had an equal number of votes—one—although a state could send as many representatives as it wanted. As a result, every state was equal regardless of its size.

After struggling to find a common ground among the representatives, an alternative to the Virginia plan emerged from one of the New Jersey representatives, William Paterson. This New Jersey Plan had many national aspects: it would transform the confederation by giving it the power to raise revenue, control commerce, and make binding requisitions on the states. But it also would preserve the equality among the states by limiting each state to one vote in a unicameral legislature; as in the Articles of Confederation. Of course, the larger states rejected this plan. After a month of intense debate back and forth between the plans, a bare majority of the states voted to accept the Virginia plan as the basis for further discussion. That decision changed the course of American history because it kept the possibility of a new Constitutional structure alive. The New Jersey plan was, in essence, a revision of the old Articles of Confederation. The Virginia plan was something entirely new. The delegates were authorized to rework the Articles of Confederation, but what was now about to occur was the creation of an entirely new government. As a resultant, two delegates from New York walked out in protest. The remaining representatives worked six days a week through the summer of 1787; a long hot and humid one, working out the details. They knew what they were doing was beyond their commission, that they were creating a new form of government without the true consent of the governed, but they thought it was in the best interest of the nation. If their action was to be ratified, they realized they would also have to create a system that would make everyone happy.

The biggest sticking point throughout the discussions was how the states should be represented in Congress. To satisfy the interests all of states, both large and small, the Connecticut delegates suggested changing the Virginia Plan so that the upper house, the Senate, would have two members from each state, regardless of a state's size. The lower chamber, the House of Representatives, would give seats on the basis of population. To ensure accurate representation, population would be determined every ten years by a national census. This change in the Virginia Plan is often called the Great Compromise.

The delegates from the larger states accepted that compromise with reservations. To them, it felt like less of a compromise than a defeat. Having settled that larger issue, the delegates at the Convention moved on to smaller issues. They agreed on the structure of the Supreme Court: nine justices, with federal courts reviewing laws and the Supreme Court getting the final decision in terms of the Constitutionality of laws. The delegates also found ways to make the states important parts of the new Constitutional structure. For example, they placed the selection of the president in the hands of an electoral college, a group of representatives chosen from the states legislatures. They gave the state legislatures the power to elect their state's senators, which meant the various state assemblies would elect the senators, not the people. The election of senators would remain with the state legislatures until the Seventeenth Amendment was ratified in 1913. Both of these examples, the president and senators, were trade-offs with the state governments; hoping they would accept a reduction of their power.

The last crucial problem for the delegates at the Convention was the issue of slavery. Most conflicts at the convention were about large states versus small states. Slavery was the first North versus South issue. Surprisingly, no one called for the abolition of slavery, but there was sentiment among the northern delegates to abolish the slave trade. Delegates from the Carolinas and Virginia, however, insisted the trade had to continue. Without some formal recognition of slavery, there is no doubt as to what the South would have done. They would not have joined the new union. So to keep them in the fold, the delegates compromised once again. Consequently, the U.S. Constitution indirectly legalized and thus protected the institution of slavery in three major ways.

1. It contained a fugitive slave clause, which ensured that the power of the federal government would be used to return runaway slaves to their master.
2. It had a clause prohibiting Congress from abolishing the international slave trade for twenty years, although it should be noted that Congress did abolish the trade when it had its first opportunity in 1808.

3. It possessed a clause that allowed each slave to be counted as three-fifths of a person for the purpose of determining how many representatives a state would send to Congress. It is a remarkable turn of events that Southerners got the convention to agree on the three-fifths clause, since it gave them a decided advantage in votes within the lower house of Congress.

Despite these concessions to the slave owners, at no time did the Constitution use the word slave or slavery. Instead, it used phrases like bondage or persons of servitude, which clearly reflected the contradictions that existed between the principles embodied in the Constitution and the institution of slavery.

The finished document was far different than the Articles of Confederation. The U.S. Constitution was the supreme law of the land and it gave the national government broad powers over taxation, defense, and trade. It also drastically restricted the authority of the individual states. Benjamin Franklin admitted that it was not perfect, yet he confessed that he knew of no other system which so closely approached perfection as did this one. His colleagues agreed. All but three of the remaining forty-one delegates signed the document. The choice was then sent to the states. The delegates decided to use a bit of trickery to ensure the Constitution was ratified. Instead of the old system requiring all the states to agree before a law became legal, the delegates said the Constitution would go into effect when nine of the thirteen states had ratified it. This bit of trickery was designed to work around Rhode Island, which many believed would probably reject the Constitution. Technically, the change in ratification was illegal under the terms of the Confederation Congress. But in fact, the delegates had no right to write the Constitution in the first place, so the technicality really did not matter. Because they were Nationalists, they winked at the law and sent the Constitution to the states.

Then the greatest debate in American history began: those who favored ratification versus those who did not. The people who did not favor ratification were known as the Antifederalists. They came from diverse backgrounds and were less organized then their opposition. Some, like Governor George Clinton of New York, had great power in the state and feared losing it under the new system. Others were farmers, whose primary ideological objection to the new Constitution rested on the premise that a republic could only function properly when it remained small, like at the local and state level. They worried that a strong national government would prove as bothersome as had the British. George Mason of Virginia, one of three who had refused to sign on to the new Constitution, argued that it was not democratic and that it would destroy the state governments. He feared, as did Patrick Henry of Virginia, the new national government could take away the property of citizens as it pleased or suspend state laws whenever it desired. In essence, these people saw the new republic not as the United States but as the States United. It is an important play on words, one which would come to a head in the struggle over ratification.

New York was the first place where ratification was hotly contested. The Federalists—James Madison, John Jay, and Alexander Hamilton—countered the arguments against the new Constitution with a series of newspaper articles later collected as *The Federalist Papers*. In New York, the Federalists stressed the need for a strong government. They reassuringly said the authority of the national government would not turn tyrannical because they believed the three branches would serve as a system of checks and balances to ensure that power could not be concentrated in the hands of a few. Madison denied that a republic was only suited to small states, pointing out that it actually gave them more power in the Senate (both in terms of representation and outright voting power) than they possessed under the Articles of Confederation. In "The Federalist #10," Madison maintained that the great size of the republic would be its best insurance against tyranny.

The Constitution was discussed by the various states between December 1787 and June 1788. Massachusetts was the first real test. There was a strong Antifederalist sentiment in Massachusetts, mostly among the backcountry yeomen. Sam Adams and Gov. John Hancock publicly opposed the new Constitution, as did many of the people who had supported Daniel Shays in the west. Facing such strong opposition, the Federalists pointed at the Shaysites and used scare tactics to secure a narrow victory of 187 to 168. When New Hampshire ratified the Constitution in June, the required nine states had approved it but the outcome was still in doubt.

The two largest and most powerful states—New York and Virginia—had not yet acted. Facing sizable opposition in those states, the Federalists barely secured enough votes to make sure it passed by promising that the first act of the new government would be the enactment of a new Bill of Rights. The inclusion of a Bill of Rights undermined the Antifederalist position that individual liberty would not be protected by the new government. In the end, the Federalists won in both Virginia (89 to 79) and New York (30 to 27). As expected, Rhode Island was the last of the thirteen colonies to ratify the Constitution on May 29, 1790. It was a remarkable triumph for the Federalists. The United States Constitution of 1787 officially ended the revolutionary period. It represented the triumph of the power elite and the decline of the yeomen. It also created a new national political system—one unlike anything that had existed before.

The Federalist Nation

The ratification of the Constitution led to the first national federal elections for both Congress and the presidency in the fall of 1788. The next spring, in 1789, the new government took power in its temporary capital of New York City. The Federalists who wrote the Constitution dominated the elections of 1788 and the first government. Forty-four of the ninety-one members of the first United States Congress, which met in 1789, either helped to ratify or write the Constitution. The Federalists dominated the electors from the states who chose a member of their party to be the first president: George Washington of Virginia. John Adams received the second-highest number of electoral votes and became vice president. Washington, at the age of 57, selected one of the best cabinets in history (Thomas Jefferson was Secretary of State; Alexander Hamilton Secretary of the Treasury; Henry Knox, Secretary of War; and Edmund Randolph, Attorney General).

Congress set out immediately to do its part in the creation of the new national government. Its first act was to keep its promise to amend the Constitution with a bill of rights. The ten amendments received legislative approval and eventually came to be known as the Bill of Rights. Those ten amendments cover a wide variety of issues and have been interpreted differently through time. Moreover, in the case of *Barron v. Baltimore* (1833), the Supreme Court declared that the Bill of Rights protected only citizens from infringements by the national government. It was not until the 1920s that the Supreme Court would use the Fourteenth Amendment to rule that the Bill of Rights protected everyone from every level of government. Not only did the Bill of Rights prove to be, perhaps, the most important part of the Constitution but in the 1790s, it quieted the protests of the Antifederalists and ensured that the new Constitution would enjoy broad support. Next, Congress created a federal court system. One of the most important parts of the Constitution was the establishment of a free and independent federal court system. Congress followed through on the constitutional language by enacting the Judiciary Act of 1789. The Judiciary Act set up a system of federal courts and created a Supreme Court (first of six, then later of nine justices). Though there was some effort to limit the power of these courts—they were usually only given the power of review over appealed state cases—the act established the principle of federal judicial review of state law. The Supreme Court proved mostly inactive during its first decade, although it did manage to generate considerable debate. In the case of *Chisholm v. Georgia* (1793), for example, the Supreme Court ruled in favor of two South Carolina men who had sued Georgia over property loss. The case helped undermine the clause that states could not be sued without their consent, and was the first time the Supreme Court had sided with citizens against state power. In a second case, *Hylton v. United States,* the Supreme Court upheld the constitutionality of an act of Congress for the first time—an important part of the Court's current role.

The next decade of American history, perhaps one of the most overlooked times in all of American history, was a period of crisis. The basic framework of the American political scene was established over the next ten years. The Federalists who carried the day in 1788 eventually split into two factions over financial policy and the French Revolution. The wars sparked by the 1789 French Revolution revived the sluggish American economy and produced a flush time for farmers and merchants. Yet those wars also divided public opinion sharply into pro-British and pro-French camps. The resulting confrontation in America led to an undeclared war against France by the end of the 1790s, and the suppression of free speech at home.

The Washington Government

Washington's initial cabinet contained significant thinkers and doers, including Alexander Hamilton as Secretary of the Treasury. Hamilton was an ambitious and self-made man. His father had been a Scottish merchant in the West Indies. Young Hamilton was raised by his mother, Rachel Faucett, after his father abandoned the family. His mother ran a store, and Hamilton delighted in the affairs of business. He moved to the mainland in 1772 and enrolled at King's College in New York. His talents secured him a position as Washington's aide during the Revolution. In the 1780s, he married Elizabeth Schuyler, the daughter of a wealthy Hudson River landowner, and became one of the leading lawyers in New York City. At the Philadelphia Constitutional Convention, he condemned democracy and lobbied for a president with near-dictatorial powers. He was one of the fourteen who left the convention early, yet Hamilton fought long and hard for ratification of the Constitution.

Though some prosperity returned to the nation by 1790, Hamilton was convinced the American economy needed a sounder financial footing. The government itself still suffered under massive debt and the United States seemed near bankruptcy. In 1789, Congress passed the Tariff of 1789, the first federal tariff designed to produce revenue. That pattern would continue, with tariffs being the most important revenue-producing source for the federal government until the twentieth century. In response to the debt problems, Hamilton delivered a *Report on Public Credit* in January 1790, wherein he recommended that the federal government take over the debts accumulated by the states during the last fifteen years and begin to pay off all the federal debt through the sale of interest-bearing bonds. One of his recommendations encouraged the creation of an excise tax (an internal fee for the production of something for domestic sale) on liquor.

Hamilton hoped to encourage domestic and foreign interests to have confidence in the American economy and thus invest in American interests. He also wanted to solve the nation's financial problems by redeeming all the securities (stocks) issued by the Confederation government at face value. While this plan would bolster the credit of the national Treasury, it would also make rich all those speculators who had purchased the securities at very low prices. He wanted to redeem the old notes with new government securities which would pay interest at about four percent. Hamilton's scheme, as some called it, reawakened fears of British monopolies and corruption. Republican ideology warned that wealth undermined virtue and liberty. Hamilton created and presented to Congress his "Assumption Plan," in which the national government would take on all the states' outstanding war debts. Of course, one fact he seemed to have overlooked was that speculators had purchased many of the old southern war bonds. In actuality Hamilton was deliberately ignoring the issue concerning speculators as he and many of his friends were among their ranks. These speculators stood to profit from the federal government's buyout of the old debt. James Madison was outraged at the Assumption Plan. Nevertheless, Hamilton was able to get it through Congress by cutting a deal with the representatives of Virginia and Maryland to place the new federal capital on the banks of the Potomac.

In Hamilton's second address to Congress in December 1790, "The Bank Address," he recommended creation of a national central banking authority: the Bank of the United States. The bank would be a public institution, but financed by private capital. The government's funds would be deposited there and it would become the Treasury's major arm of economic policy. The bank would make loans, issue notes, and handle the nation's accounts. The service was one in great demand. The nation needed a central bank to cope with the market revolution taking place. Yet other interests, like James Madison, believed the bank to be unconstitutional. Madison was, like Jefferson, a strict constructionist. Unless the Constitution specifically allocated a power to the federal government, they believed it was a power reserved to the states. Jefferson joined Madison against Hamilton and encouraged Washington to dismiss the bank as unconstitutional. Hamilton responded to his opposition by saying that he favored a loose interpretation of the Constitution. He pointed to Article I, Section 8, which empowered Congress to make all laws necessary and proper to carry out the Constitution. It was his view that as long as the Constitution did not specifically say "don't do this" then it was constitutional. Washington agreed with Hamilton and signed the bank bill into law. The bank was situated in Philadelphia, which was at the time the financial capital of the United States.

Hamilton's third congressional report, "The Report on Manufactures," was submitted to Congress in December 1791. Hamilton believed the nation's future depended on becoming an industrial nation, and he wanted to use the power of the national government to promote the development of American industry. Hamilton wanted state support as well, but he did not want to recreate the old British mercantilist system. Embracing Adam Smith's theories about a new economic order replacing mercantilism as laid out in *The Wealth of Nations* (1776), Hamilton was a staunch supporter of laissez-faire capitalism—free trade without government intervention—and he wanted to position America so it could take advantage of the economic change. As a result, he called for government to assist in the development of the nascent American industry and manufacturing by using tariffs protect them from foreign competitors. Over the course of the decade, Hamilton's programs did restore American credit, and financial conditions improved markedly.

By the time Washington began his second term in 1793, both Congress and his cabinet were split by factions. Madison and Jefferson had turned against Hamilton and Washington. In the 1794 elections, these factions coalesced and became more organized, even acquiring names. The Federalists supported Washington and Hamilton, while the Democratic-Republicans supported Madison and Jefferson. The Federalists controlled the government. The forces of Madison and Jefferson were in the minority. Hamilton, therefore, was able to push for the final element of his financial system, a national revenue. He convinced Congress to impose a variety of domestic taxes, including a tax on whiskey. Congress also created several tariffs, ranging from 5 to 15 percent on the value of imported goods. Hamilton's plan was complete. He had bolstered public credit, created a national bank, and initiated taxes that provided the government with revenue. It was a bold plan, one that was pro-business from which the economic future of the nation benefited fully.

The Wars of the French Revolution

The disagreements between Jefferson and Hamilton grew more intense over matters of international policy. The single most important development in the world during the 1790s was the revolution in France. It began in 1789 and quickly enveloped all of Europe in one way or another. The collapse of the French monarchy in 1789 was welcomed by most Americans, but the initial enthusiasm was blunted by the violence and terror that followed. The execution of the king and the war with Great Britain in 1793 turned many conservatives in America against the French. Americans began to ask themselves important questions: Should Washington and the United States continue to support the French, according to the treaty of alliance? Or should the United States remain neutral? Washington and most of his advisors preferred to remain neutral. It was good for business. Hamilton especially favored siding with the British, our most important trading partner. Hamilton foresaw a future Atlantic world of trade centered on the vast navies of Britain and America. But Madison and Jefferson looked to a future for the U.S. that was fixed on the interior, an America empire in the West.

In April 1793, the French sent an ambassador, Edmond Genet, to the United States to urge support for France in the wars. Genet was a popular speaker and stirred the passions of the pro-French and pro-Republican elements in America. Many in America still hated the British and admired the Republic of France. Most conservatives felt a pro-French policy would jeopardize American profits, however, at the very time the economy seemed to be recovering. While Genet rounded up support for the French and its war effort, Washington issued a declaration of neutrality in April 1793, angering Jefferson and many of the Democratic Societies created to support the Republican cause in France. These clubs were modeled on the Jacobin clubs in Paris. In Philadelphia, the societies held a dinner to celebrate the beheading of Louis XVI. At that dinner the head of a roasted pig was separated from its body and then carried around to each of the guests, who placed the cap of liberty on its head and pronounced the word *tyrant*. In some cities, they even began to adopt the French practice of calling each other *citizen*, a symbol of equality. Such actions only stirred conservative concerns.

Washington's Problems—The United States and the Western Tribes

After the Revolution was won in 1783, the United States tried to impose its will on the unconquered tribes of the Mississippi and Ohio valleys. That policy led to a generation of warfare in the West. The Constitution said nothing about Native policy. Congress claimed early on that the Indian nations to the west were independent tribes, but independent tribes who lived on the soil of the United States. In 1790, Congress passed the Indian Intercourse Act, which became the basis for regulating trade and diplomacy to those tribes. Part of the act created a federal licensing system to prevent trade wars from turning into real wars (over trade abuses). The act also declared that the only way Native peoples could be removed from their land was through a formal treaty with the U.S. national government. Despite attempts to avoid trouble, conflicts between Native Americans and settlers led to a great deal of violence during Washington's presidency. In 1790, Little Turtle led a collection of Shawnees, Delawares, and Miamis to victory over an American expedition, and in 1791 the Western Confederacy of tribes nearly destroyed the forces of Gen. Arthur St. Clair, who suffered more than 900 casualties. In August 1794 Gen. Anthony Wayne and a larger American army defeated the Western Confederacy at the Battle of Fallen Timbers. The defeat there forced the Confederacy to sign the Treaty of Greenville in 1795, which ceded a massive amount of land to American settlers, including most of modern Ohio and Indiana.

Washington's Problems—The Whiskey Rebellion

This popular uprising broke out in 1794, in the midst of Washington's difficulties with Europe and the Western Confederacy. Upset at Hamilton's excise taxes, farmers in western Pennsylvania staged a riot. Many in western Pennsylvania were living in poverty. Landlords there towered over the poor population like great barons. One such landowner was Washington himself, who regarded squatters on his land as nearly subhuman. Many farmers in that region depended on whiskey for their livelihood, so the tax on that product was burdensome on them. Washington rounded up 13,000 troops and marched at their head to put down the minor insurrection. Twenty were arrested and charged with treason, though all were eventually released.

Washington's Problems—The British Blockade

In 1793, Great Britain declared an international blockade of all goods traded in the French West Indies, and in 1793 and 1794 more than 250 American ships were stopped by the British navy and their cargos seized. Washington sent John Jay to negotiate with the British and in the fall of 1794 Jay signed a document that provided for the withdrawal of British forces from American soil by 1796 and granted the United States most-favored-nation status in matters of trade. Though it did not prevent the British practice of seizing ships, it still proved to be a substantial victory for Jay and Hamilton. The Jay Treaty, however, alienated some sections of the American public. Jefferson was furious that the government was aligning the country with Britain rather than France, as were many of his supporters in the South and West. By 1795, the issue of the Spanish claims to eastern American had been resolved as well, mostly a result of Spain's defeat in Europe at the hands of the French. Thomas Pinckney negotiated a treaty whereby Spain agreed to a boundary with the U.S. at the thirty-first parallel. Spain also agreed to open up the Mississippi River to American shipping. In combination with the defeat of the Western Confederacy, Jay's and Pinckney's treaties gave the U.S. firm control over the Northwest as well as the area between the Appalachian Mountains and the Mississippi River.

The Adams Presidency

Having served his nation for two terms, Washington decided not to run for a third term, setting a precedent which remains to this day with the exception of Franklin Delano Roosevelt. In the election of 1796, John Adams became the second U.S. president. Jefferson had the second highest number of electoral votes and became vice president. This meant the nation had a split administration for the first time. As president, Adams upheld Washington's pro-British foreign policy. He condemned French seizures of American ships and accused them of meddling in American domestic affairs. For months, Adams had been trying to open negotiations with Talleyrand, the French foreign minister, but his agents demanded a bribe of $250,000 before they would begin negotiations. The French agents, whom Adams called X, Y, and Z, had insulted American honor, so President Adams said. The Federalists controlled Congress and they cut off trade with France and began seizing French shipping. Between 1798 and 1800, the U.S. became an unofficial ally of Great Britain—a monarchy and recent enemy—and fought an undeclared war against France, a republic and the major U.S. supporter during the American Revolution.

Angry at the turnaround in American foreign policy, pro-French immigrants from Ireland began attacking Adam's foreign policy in newspapers and pamphlets. To quiet them, the administration pushed through the Alien Act of 1798, which authorized the deportation of foreigners. They also passed a Naturalization Act, which increased the residency requirement for citizenship from five to fourteen years. Also in 1798, the Federalist Congress enacted a harsh Sedition Act, making it illegal to publish malicious attacks against the U.S. government, whether it was against the President or Congress. Using the powers of that act, Federalist prosecutors arrested and charged more than twenty Republican newspaper editors and politicians, sending some of them to prison. Among the imprisoned was Matthew Lyon, a Republican House member from Vermont. He was convicted in July 1798 of libelous statements about Adams and thrown into jail; he would later be reelected to Congress from his cell.

The Republicans said the Alien and Sedition acts violated the Bill of Rights, namely the First Amendment. (Most constitutional scholars today say the acts were probably unconstitutional.) Republican leaders could not turn to the Supreme Court for help. The Court's powers were still too ill defined and the principle of judicial review, though established, remained vague. Moreover, the Supreme Court was packed with Federalists who would have probably upheld the law. Madison and Jefferson instead took the issue to the states. In November of 1798, Kentucky, which had been admitted to the union in 1792, passed a resolution declaring the Alien and Sedition acts to be null and void, thus making them unenforceable within its borders. Virginia joined Kentucky shortly afterward, issuing a resolution that the states had the right to nullify a federal law that exceeded the Constitution. The Virginia and Kentucky Resolves became the basis for the subsequent states' rights interpretations of the constitution.

The Election of 1800

The debate over the Sedition Act set the stage for the presidential election of 1800. The Republicans supported Jefferson's bid for the presidency by pointing to the wrongful imprisonment of the newspaper editors and by championing the rights of states. Adams, who at times was quite vain, could have stepped up the war against France and rallied more political support. Instead he decided to begin negotiations that ultimately brought an end to the war with France. The Federalists tried to win the election by depicting Jefferson as an irresponsible pro-French radical. They did not succeed. The Republicans won a great victory in both the House and Senate. In the first round Jefferson and Aaron Burr of New York tied with seventy-three electoral votes each. John Adams got sixty-five, Charles Cotesworth Pinckney got sixty-four, and John Jay got only one. Since the first round ended in a tie, the decision was sent to the House of Representatives. For 35 rounds of voting, the Federalists blocked Jefferson's election. Then, Hamilton, the head of the Federalist Party, gave a speech calling Aaron Burr an embryonic Caesar and the most unfit man in the United States for the office of president. Hamilton's condemnation of Burr persuaded the Federalists to allow Jefferson his victory. Jefferson called the election the Revolution of 1800, and so it was. It signaled the virtual end of the Federalist Party in national politics. Never again would they win a presidential election and by 1816 they would virtually disappear. The election was also the first occasion in which political power changed hands from one party to another. It was the bloodless transition of power that made the American democracy so unique.

Items to Consider

Articles of Confederation, "the theory of government," Northwest Ordinance of 1787, Shays' Rebellion, Philadelphia Convention, Virginia Plan, New Jersey Plan, Great Compromise, Hamilton's Three Reports, loose construction, strict construction

CHAPTER 11

The Agrarian Republic

Thomas Jefferson (1743–1826) was an Enlightenment thinker and one of the most controversial and enigmatic figures in American history. He was a seasoned diplomat, politician, and political philosopher. When he became president in 1801, Jefferson quickly tried to win over his Federalist opponents by naming three Federalists to his cabinet. Jefferson was the first president to be inaugurated in Washington D.C., the new national capital. But despite moving into a new city, Jefferson could not begin his presidency with a clean slate.

After a dozen years of Federalist presidents, Jefferson inherited a government filled with political opponents. Not only was the administration full of Federalists, but the Supreme Court was as well. Among the men on that court was John Marshall, who had been appointed chief justice of the Supreme Court in 1801 by John Adams. In some sense, Marshall would become the most influential American of the country's first fifty years.

The composition of the judicial branch of the national government was a major point of contention in the early years of Thomas Jefferson's presidency. Presidents did not take office in January until the Twentieth Amendment was ratified in 1933. In 1801, they took office in March. Between December 12, 1800, when it became clear that he would not win reelection, and the day of Jefferson's inauguration on March 4, 1801, John Adams took advantage of his extra time in office to appoint a significant number of federal judges. These midnight appointments consisted exclusively of Federalists, most of who had previous political or familial ties to prominent party members. When Jefferson took office, not a single Republican held a federal judgeship. Republicans were further infuriated by the Federalists' Judiciary Act of 1801, passed on February 27, just five days before Jefferson's inauguration. While the main thrust of the act was the creation of sixteen new federal judgeships to ease the load on the Supreme Court, the most distressing clause to Republicans was that which cut the number of Supreme Court Justices from six to five. This would deny Jefferson his first opportunity to appoint a Supreme Court justice, and ensured the court system remained in Federalist control for years to come.

The Republican-dominated Congress repealed the Judiciary Act and dismissed Adams' appointed judges. Jefferson's Republicans also brought impeachment charges against one federal judge and tried to remove Samuel Chase from the Supreme Court. This clearly partisan attempt failed. Jefferson, disturbed by the radical policies of his own Republican Congress, decided to pursue a more moderate course. While many radical Republicans insisted that judges should be elected and not appointed, Jefferson was not radical enough to agree, and he did not challenge the powers of the courts. He did, however, challenge Federalist control of the courts. He originally declared that he would not dismiss any Federalist appointees, but he later revised this statement to protect only the appointees who did not fall into the category of midnight appointments. Although he believed that the party in power should control somewhere between one-half and two-thirds of the appointed offices in government, he only removed 109 of 433 Federalist office holders during his eight years. And almost half those had been Adams' midnight appointees.

One major reason the election of 1800 has been called a Revolution was that Jefferson had a different vision of America's future and he was determined to change the character of the national government. He though the government was too large and too powerful. The Republicans refused to renew the Alien and Sedition acts when they expired in 1801 and they amended the Naturalization Act, reducing from the number of years a noncitizen had to wait to become an

American citizen from fourteen back to five. Jefferson next turned his attention to the size of the government. He reduced the size of the bureaucracy by cutting federal jobs by one-third, and then dropped the size of the military by nearly one-half; which many Republicans saw as becoming dangerously large.

For his part, Jefferson changed many Federalist policies, as well. The Federalists during the 1790s had been paying tribute to the Barbary States of North Africa—meaning they bribed those pirates not to attack American merchant ships in the Mediterranean. Jefferson refused to pay. When the city-states of Tunis, Morocco, Tripoli, and Algiers renewed their attacks, he ordered the U.S. Navy and Marine units to retaliate. Jefferson also set his own course in domestic affairs. He abolished all internal taxes, including the tax that had ignited the Whiskey Rebellion of 1794. Despite his Republican efforts to put the smaller, limited-government philosophy in force, Jefferson was not a complete ideologue. He accepted the Bank of the United States, the same bank he had condemned as unconstitutional in 1791, as necessary to the health and development of the U.S. economy. Still, Jefferson's vision was much different from that of Adams and Hamilton. He redirected the nation's political identity away from the eastern bankers and markets of Europe and toward the West. This is another reason why the election of 1800 is often referred to as the Revolution of 1800. Not only was it a change in the political power in the United States, but it redirected the attention of the nation away from the Atlantic world toward the frontier.

Agrarianism

Jefferson was trying to create a new identity for the nation, but what would that new identity be? Jefferson's dream was to create and preserve an agricultural nation. He quickly moved to help western settlers in any way he could. Despite the Northwest Ordinance of 1787, the land in Ohio had fallen into the hands of wealthy speculators. Part of the problem lay in the ordinance itself. The ordinance created a minimum price of $1 per acre but also said that at least half the townships had to be sold in blocks of 23,000 acres. That requirement made it virtually impossible for all but the wealthiest to buy land. The other half had to be sold in blocks of 640 acres. Even at $640 a block, this was beyond the means of most yeomen. The Federalist Congress had meant to keep it that way. In fact, the Federalists' Land Act of 1796 doubled the minimum price to $2 per acre. So, in effect, much of the land fell into the hands of land speculators, not cash-poor Americans.

Jefferson and his Republican Congress changed that situation. They passed new laws to help the cash-poor yeoman. First in 1800 and then in 1804, the new laws reduced the minimum purchase size to 320 acres, then to 160, and allowed payments in installments extending as long as four years. Eventually, the Land Act of 1820 reduced the minimum purchase to 80 acres and set the price at $1.25 per acre, which meant a farmer needed only $100 cash to buy a farm in the West.

Foreign Affairs

Despite his attempts to disengage from the affairs of Europe, Jefferson had troubles abroad. In 1799 Napoleon Bonaparte, a daring thirty-year-old general, seized power in France and immediately began to create a French empire in both Europe and North America. In 1800, he persuaded Spain to sign a secret treaty that returned Louisiana to France, and two years later Spain began to restrict American access to New Orleans. In the meantime, Napoleon sent an army to restore French rule in what is today Haiti, then a rich sugar island. These actions forced Jefferson to reconsider the traditional pro-French foreign policy of the Republican Party. Trade through New Orleans was crucial to American development in the West. Thus, Jefferson concluded, any nation that tried to restrict American traffic in the Mississippi River Valley was America's enemy. Jefferson did not know exactly what to do about the problem, but he did take two immediate steps: First, he instructed Robert Livingston, the U.S. minister in Paris, to see if he could buy New Orleans from Napoleon. Second, he sent James Monroe, a former congressman and governor of Virginia, to Britain to ask for help in case France and the United States went to war.

Indeed, war was a possibility. But Jefferson's efforts yielded a magnificent and unexpected prize: all of Louisiana. The planned French invasion of Haiti faltered in 1802, due to a spirited black resistance led by Toussaint L'Ouverture and a yellow fever epidemic that decimated what remained of the French invasion force. Napoleon was militarily stretched thin. He was afraid that he might have to fight the British in Europe again, and that the Americans would invade Louisiana, so, he gave up his dream of an American empire. In April 1803, he offered to sell not only New Orleans but the entire territory of Louisiana for only $15 million (about $180 million today), one of the biggest land bargains in history. Livingstone and Monroe (who had joined Livingstone in Paris) jumped at the offer and, thus, doubled the size of the United States.

The sheer magnitude of the Louisiana Purchase overwhelmed Jefferson's reservations about loose construction of the Constitution and implied powers. Jefferson had always advocated a strict construction. The Constitution said nothing about the acquisition of new territory. Thus there would seem to be some contradiction between what he believed and what he practiced. Yet, given his dream of a Western empire, Jefferson was pragmatic enough to realize the value of the deal. The Federalists harshly criticized him for violating his own principles while at the same moment applauding his diplomatic triumph. The Senate ratified the purchase by a vote of 26 to 6.

Jefferson, therefore, single-handedly doubled the size of the country. But in 1803, the American government knew more about the moon than it did about the Louisiana territory. Jefferson wanted detailed information about the physical features of the region, including its plant and animal life, as well as knowledge about a about possible passage to the pacific ocean. To explore the region, Jefferson sent his personal secretary, Meriwether Lewis. Aided by native guides (like Sacagawea) and army officer William Clark, the expedition traveled up the Missouri River, across the Rocky Mountains, and down the Columbia River to the Pacific Ocean. When they returned to the home, the explorers brought back detailed reports of everything they encountered—drastically increasing our knowledge of the West.

The Louisiana Purchase was a great triumph, but it led to another threat to the union among the states. Federalists in New England had long feared that western expansion would diminish their region's political power. They called a gathering of Federalists at the Hartford Convention in 1814, to discuss the future of New England. There some Federalists began to talk openly of the possible secession of the northeastern states. They even approached Alexander Hamilton and asked him to be their first president, but the New York Federalist would not support their plan of a northern confederacy. That plan would remain alive until the Hartford Convention of 1814, however, and would continue to resurface as a political issue until the 1840s. After Hamilton rejected the secessionists, they turned to Aaron Burr, the Republican vice president and a man whose ambitions knew few bounds. Burr was running for governor of New York in 1804. The secessionists offered him their help. When he accepted, his opponent in that election, Alexander Hamilton, accused Burr of trying to break up the union. Burr challenged him to a duel and killed Hamilton in July of 1804. Burr was then indicted for murder in both New York and New Jersey.

The murder of Alexander Hamilton led Burr to yet another secessionist scheme. In early 1805 he completed his term as vice president and moved west to avoid prosecution. There he conspired with Gen. James Wilkinson, the American military governor of the Louisiana Territory. It is not clear what the two men conspired to do, but apparently they planned to foment a rebellion in Louisiana and establish a separate country with Burr as its leader. In any event, Wilkinson got cold feet and arrested Burr on a charge of treason. Chief Justice Marshall presided over Burr's trial. Jefferson tried to get Burr convicted using a loose Constitutional construction of the definition of treason, but Marshall would not allow him to do so, insisting on a strict interpretation. Burr was acquitted. In the scheme of things, this decision was unimportant. What is important is what it revealed about this period. The Republicans wanted to increase the size of America in order to create their vision of an agrarian Republic. Yet those same policies fueled a backlash that led to a renewed interest in states' rights.

The Crisis of the 1805–11

When the Napoleonic wars broke out again in Europe in 1802 (they would last until 1815), they distracted American attention from the West. Despite American efforts to stay out of the European war, America was soon caught in the middle. Neither side, Britain or France, would accept American neutrality. Both countries, as they had in the 1790s, claimed the right to board American merchant ships and seize their cargo if they were heading toward the enemy.

The problem over neutrality rights reached a climax in the years after 1805. In 1805, the British Admiral Horatio Nelson defeated the French Navy at the Battle of Trafalgar, and thus the British were able to tighten their blockade of the European continent. The British promptly seized the American freighter *Essex* for carrying sugar and molasses from the West Indies to France. As the British began to seize more ships, their actions threatened the profits of American merchants and revived a strong anti-British sentiment in the U.S.

Both the Federalists and the Republicans resented what Britain was doing. What they found most objectionable was the British policy of *impressment,* of stopping American ships to search for deserting British sailors and, if found, forcing them back into military service. Between 1802 and 1811, Britain impressed nearly 8,000 American sailors into the British Navy. Some of these cases were legitimate, some were cases of mistaken identity. Later the British would take sailors as they needed them. The situation simmered for a time and then boiled over in 1807, when the British warship *Leopard* attacked the U.S. frigate *Chesapeake,* killing or wounding twenty-one men and seizing four alleged deserters. Tantamount to an act of warfare, war was close. Jefferson, however, kept his head and demanded an apology and monetary damages, both of which the British offered. Despite that, the British continued both their blockade and their policy of impressment.

At home, Jefferson was still faced with hundreds of merchants who were up in arms over the British Navy seizing their ships. Jefferson and Secretary of State James Madison tried to put economic pressure on the British in 1807 by securing passage of the Embargo Act. This act prohibited American ships from leaving their home ports until both the British and French recognized American neutrality rights, but the act was largely ineffective, as neither the British nor French depended much on American trade, and the Federalist merchants found ways around the embargo to trade with Canada. What the embargo did succeed in doing was to reduce the number of exports out of America. They dropped from $108 million in 1806 to $22 million in 1808. Jefferson soon found himself under attack from all sides. The Federalists argued that he was trying to destroy the economy. Those same Federalists became even more alarmed when the Republican Congress passed the Force Act to prevent smuggling between New England and Canada. The Force Act gave American customs officials extraordinary powers to seize illegal goods. New England merchants had been smuggling goods to Canada and placing them on ships bound for Britain. It was one way the Federalist merchants got around the embargo. Now those actions would be stopped.

Jefferson's second term ended in 1809. James Madison, Jefferson's Secretary of State and one of the chief architects of the embargo, won the presidency in 1808. Madison had been a major player in the writing of the Constitution, an advocate of the Bill of Rights, and a congressman and party leader. He was the obvious choice to succeed Jefferson, but he was not a great diplomat. He acknowledged that the embargo was not working and secured its repeal in 1809. He replaced it with the Nonintercourse Act. This new act allowed American merchants to trade with everyone except the British and French. If they finally respected American neutrality rights, the act offered a return to normal commerce. Of course, Britain and France took little notice, and Madison was forced to bow under congressional pressure and accept what was known as Macon's Bill, which reopened legal trade with both Britain and France in 1810.

The War of 1812

As the relationship between the Americans, French, and British grew tenser after 1810, the United States grew more uneasy. Clearly the best option was to resist a war with European powers. But how far should the U.S. go to avoid war? Indeed, if war was necessary, with which nation should the U.S. side? The Republicans became convinced that the British were the greater evil of the two. In 1810, Republican congressmen from the West—who become known as War Hawks in 1812—accused Britain of arming the Native tribes in the trans-Appalachian region. It was not a false charge to incite a war. The British had been supplying the Shawnee chief Tecumseh for some time. Tecumseh and others were trying to revive the old western Confederacy of the 1790s and even began recruiting southern tribes to join.

Thus, the threat on the frontier brought home the dangers of European entanglements on the American continent in a powerful way. Tecumseh and his followers claimed all territory north of the Ohio River. He was determined to keep white settlers out of those lands. Tecumseh and his brother, Tenskwatawa, who had mixed the Christian religion with what was essentially a Native American cultural nationalism, then called for a holy war against the Western white settlements. That threat on the frontier pushed Congress to act. Republicans in Congress condemned British support of the new Western Confederacy. In a rush of war fever and nationalism, the Republications pushed the reluctant Madison toward war. The War Hawks, led by Henry Clay of Kentucky and a rising young South Carolinian congressman named John C. Calhoun, urged the invasion of Spanish Florida and British Canada. When sporadic fighting between western settlers and the Shawnee broke out in 1811, war seemed imminent. In the Northwest, Governor William Henry Harrison, a future U.S. president, defeated the Shawnee at the Battle of Tippecanoe in 1811.

With fighting on the frontier and the War Hawks breathing down his neck, Madison abandoned the economic strategy that had clearly failed (it is difficult to know if it would have worked, given more time). Madison publicly demanded the British respect American sovereignty in the West and its neutral rights in the Atlantic. When the British did not respond, Madison asked Congress to declare war. In June 1812, a sharply divided Senate voted nineteen to thirteen for war. The House concurred by a vote of seventy-nine to forty-nine.

The causes of this war are complex. Traditionally, historians have interpreted it as a war over the violation of American neutrality rights on the high seas. But recently, the focus has shifted to the West. Some historians believe it was a war fought over who would control this more important region, instead of a war fought over the British seizure of American ships. In any case, New England opposed the war as unnecessary and undesirable. The Federalist merchants there condemned it. After all, Britain was the source of their wealth and had been for many years. From their perspective, the war did not make sense. Most importantly, the war furthered regional tensions. De Witt Clinton, the Federalist candidate for president in 1812, for example, received most of his electoral votes from New England. Madison, in winning his second term, won most of his support from the South and West, areas where the demand for war was high.

Regardless of the origins, the War of 1812 was a near disaster for the United States. Republican congressmen predicted an easy victory, and the War Hawks predicted that Canada was ripe for the taking. There were some impressive military victories; the American Navy dominated the Great Lakes region. Gen. William Henry Harrison launched an attack on British and Indian forces near Detroit, forcing the British to withdraw, and killing Tecumseh, who had become a British general, at the Battle of the Thames in October 1813. Another American force captured and burned what is now Toronto. Still, the planned invasion of Canada stumbled. A serious lack of manpower, along with political problems at home, allowed the Canadians to remain independent. New England governors, furthermore, opposed the war and would not let their militiamen fight in it. Boston merchants and banks refused to lend money to the national government—some even investing in British interests instead—making it difficult to finance the war. In Congress, a talented young Federalist from New Hampshire, Daniel Webster, led his party to oppose higher taxes to pay for the war effort. He also discouraged people from enlisting in the Army and prevented the drafting of state militiamen into the national Army. Obviously, the Federalists wanted nothing to do with this war. Madison, who had erred in leading a divided nation into war, was unable to seize British Canada, despite the overwhelming military advantage the United States had in this theater.

American success was no more impressive at sea. By 1814, the British enjoyed superiority in the waters off the American coast. Once they controlled the oceans, the British fleet sailed into Chesapeake Bay where British army units stormed ashore and soon overran Washington, D.C. The president and his wife were forced to flee the white house (this is where the stories about Dolley Madison saving paintings from a fire come from) and British officers dined on the dinner the Madisons had to leave behind. The British burned Washington, D.C. and then moved toward Baltimore where they were finally turned back at Fort McHenry.

In the South, the war was mostly between a group of Native Americans allied with the British and an American Army led by Andrew Jackson. The Creeks, who had been stirred by the rhetoric of Tecumseh and his brother, were divided over what to do about white encroachment. When the war broke out, a group of Creeks, known as the Red Sticks, aligned themselves with the British and Spanish and, in 1813, attacked Fort Mims on the Alabama River, slaughtering more than 500 Americans and mixed-race Creeks who had gathered there for safety. Jackson and troops from Kentucky and Tennessee combined with the traditional foes of the Creeks—the Cherokees, Choctaws, and Chickasaws. Together the forces under Jackson fought back with some of the most brutal tactics of the war. Jackson waged a campaign of attrition, attacking and burning Red Stick villages.

Still, the grand strategy of the War Hawks did not come to fruition even here. Although Jackson's armies won several battles, he was unable to take Florida. Jackson did capture Mobile and then Pensacola in 1814, but he was unable to hold either port. Jackson's best-known victory came at the Battle of New Orleans in 1815, a full two weeks after the war was over. It was, in any case, a major victory. There was no guarantee, without full possession of New Orleans, that the British would have followed their treaty and returned that land to the U.S. Jackson's victory, moreover, made him a national hero and set the stage for his own political rise a decade later. The war ended with the treaty of Ghent signed on Christmas Eve 1814. The treaty restored the prewar borders.

Jackson's victory at New Orleans made him a western hero and thrust the slave-owning planter from Tennessee onto the national stage. That victory was also important in that it allowed the U.S. to salvage some honor from what was by and large a poorly conceived and miserably executed war. Indeed, it almost led to the direct breakup of the American union when New England Federalists met in Hartford, Connecticut in late 1814. Representatives from the five New England states aired their grievances and, after some talk about leaving the union, they reasserted the doctrine of *nullification*, which stated that a state had the right to nullify an unconstitutional law or policy of the federal government. Those principles were not new, having first appeared in the Kentucky and Virginia Resolves.

The atmosphere created by this antipatriotic meeting, the refusal of Federalists to participate in the war, and the refusal of New England to support the war in combination with the patriotic symbolism of New Orleans, destroyed the

Federalist Party. The Federalists were thereafter associated with disloyalty. Indeed many Republicans suggested that they were guilty of treason. The Federalists quickly collapsed as a national party. By 1820, they could not even field a candidate for president.

Items to Consider

midnight appointees, Barbary States, Louisiana Purchase, impressment, embargo, John Marshall, War Hawks, Tecumseh, Hartford Convention, Battle of New Orleans

CHAPTER 12

An Empire of Slavery in the Old Southwest: Race and Slavery in the U.S.

We have already seen how slavery developed in the West Indies, and how slavery spread to the continental United States. Now we track the development of slavery in the Deep South and see what it was like to be a slave in the South in 1840. The Old Southwest was the area that became Alabama, Mississippi, and Louisiana. The Constitution of 1787 ensured that twenty years would pass before the international slave trade would end, which it did on the first vote in 1808. By that time, 250,000 new slaves had entered the United States. That influx, plus natural population growth, produced 1.8 million African-Americans slaves living in the U.S. by 1820. Many of those slaves still labored on rice and tobacco plantations. But after 1820, the rice economy went downhill. Sugar became the chief product in Louisiana, and after 1820 cotton became king in the rest of the old Southwest. Technological change allowed the mass production of cotton clothing. All of Europe, and indeed the world, demanded cotton cloth. Great demand fueled the expansion of the American cotton industry. Slowly, thousands of white planters moved away from the coasts of South Carolina and Georgia into the interior where they created vast cotton plantations. After the War of 1812, production spread to Alabama (which joined the union in 1817) and Mississippi (1819).

The expansion of cotton meant great social upheaval for African slaves. They were either forced to move west with their masters or, in thousands of cases, were sold west away from their families. What was slavery like? It depends on whom you ask. I have identified four aspects that I want you to consider as we answer this question:

1. Acculturation
2. Slave culture
3. The slave family
4. Plantation life

Were slaves acculturated into Anglo society? The answer is extraordinarily difficult to answer and yet simple at the same time. There is little information on what average slaves thought. There are many travel accounts, but most of these people saw slavery through a filter of their race, class, and region. There are also many slave narratives, but there are certain problems there, too. Another possibility is to look at cross-cultural comparisons—to see what slave life was like in areas like Brazil. Still, there are limitations even there. There seems to be something different about the experience of slavery in the United States, so let's look at each point individually:

Acculturation

West African language, music, folk tales, religion, art all remained part of the African-American experience with slavery. West African slaves were never fully acculturated, at least not completely. It is important to remember that cultural exchange is never a one-way street. In fact, the white south became more Africanized by the experience of slavery than vice versa. White Southerners adopted African agricultural practices (the growing of rice and the use of the task system to organize labor), architecture, and food (hoe cakes, corn bread, and dumplings come directly from the African tradition) to their own culture. In important ways, slavery led to a mixing of two worlds.

Slave Culture

Antebellum African slaves created several unique cultural forms that lightened their burdens, promoted group solidarity, built self-esteem, and sustained hope. Let's look at four specific examples: an emotional religion, folk songs and tales, dances, and superstitions. These things set them apart from their masters, made them distinct. These things are extraordinarily important because they created a group identity on the plantation and acted as a social glue for slaves. All four require leisure time, which the slaves had, especially on Sunday. Some slaves did set aside time on Sunday to take care of their gardens and washing clothes, but Sundays were usually days of rest. They spent Sundays visiting, fishing, singing, playing marbles, telling stories, gambling, or even drinking whiskey. All of these were ways to escape from the difficult reality of their situation. Another way of psychologically distancing themselves from their masters was the belief in witches, fortune tellers, magic, and conjurers. Conjurers were often the most powerful of the plantation slaves. They claimed the ability to avoid punishment, to make harsh masters kind, to prevent flogging, to make someone fall in love, and to cure illness. The belief in such supernatural powers was a way to circumvent the total control of the masters.

Stories about conjurors were so pervasive in the South that often the white masters believed them, as well. On one Alabama plantation, for example, a conjurer named Dinkie exerted a good amount of magical influence. Dinkie had only one eye, he was supposedly frightful in appearance, he wore a snake skin around his neck, and he carried a petrified frog in one pocket and a dried lizard in the other. Dinkie never worked, he never was beaten, and the slave patrols would not even stop him. He was a master at telling the future, at reading signs of everyday life, at healing, and curing.

Interestingly, everything Dinkie and others like him claimed to understand came directly from knowledge brought over from Africa. The signs and omens they followed had direct correlation with similar ones in Africa; and they seemed to have quite a long life. For example, they believed that if someone stole from another slave, lied about it, and drank a bottle of water mixed with dust from the grave of a recently departed slave, the individual would die. That tale has direct links to older African proverbs. It is estimated that some 30 percent of slave proverbs by the time of the Civil War still incorporated an African element. Their songs also reflected a strong African influence. Much of their music maintained the complex West African rhythms, instead of adopting the much simpler European forms.

Folk tales were also important in slave culture. They served two purposes. They worked both as a form of entertainment and as a way to instruct young slaves on proper behavior. They also show something else. They show rebellion. Take the tales of Brer Rabbit, where the smaller and weaker animal is always tricking and defeating the larger, stronger animals, in some cases even killing them. Another example can be found in the Jack or John tales. John was an irascible slave who makes a fool of the white folks, longs for freedom, runs away, is caught and beaten, often defies his master, and expresses desires for revenge. These stories can be interpreted in many ways, but the mere existence of them is proof that the creative energies of slaves were not crushed by slavery. Such stories were also therapeutic. They gave the slave a life away from his master and served an important psychological need: repressing anger.

Another factor of slave culture to consider was slave religion. Religion, too, was a form of escape. Although the slave religion was nominally Christian, it was a radically different version than that taught in white churches. Many of these black churches had to meet in secret to escape punishment; especially after 1850 because it was illegal for slaves to be able to read or gather without their master's consent. The center of the black church was the preacher, who was often the only one in the crowd who could read. The preacher had the ability to not only deliver powerful sermons but to act as the glue in the slave community. Such churches usually ignored the traditional Christian theological questions, instead envisioning God as a warrior who would someday liberate his chosen people. Slaves especially identified with the story of the Israelites. Such messages stressed resistance against one's oppressors. Still other slaves identified with Christ because he died in this world so that his followers might find peace in the next. Others practiced the folk religion of voodoo, especially in places like Louisiana. The point being made here is that the slaves' culture bolstered the self-esteem, courage, and confidence of slaves despite the dehumanizing conditions they endured each day.

The Slave Family

It was often argued that slavery was so destructive that traditional family systems broke down. As recently as the early 1970s, Daniel Patrick Moynihan maintained that the problems within African-American families in that generation were directly tied to the destruction of the slave family during slavery. On closer examination, it appears that this assertion was untrue. The slave family was the core of slave society. It thrived despite the horrible conditions. One historian has even remarked that the family remained the center of existence for slaves, no matter how many times it was broken by sell or displacement, and allowed the slave to survive on the plantation without being totally dependent on the master.

Many slave owners even encouraged stable, monogamous unions because they thought it lessened the possibility of rebellion. Families made life more stable. Masters thought that if a slave loved his wife and children, he would be less inclined to rebel or run away. Some slave owners would even whip a slave who had relations outside of marriage. Hugh Davis of Alabama, for example, would give ten to fifty lashes for such an offense. Of course, it is important to remember that this family model was always more true in the nineteenth century South than it had been in the eighteenth-century slavery, where slaves on some Virginia and Maryland plantations struggled in vain to establish normal West African family structures.

Still, most planters did not bother to enforce morality within the slave community. In many cases, they violated it with impunity. The white planters' or overseers' lust was a constant impediment to slave morality. Few slave parents could protect their daughters from the sexual advances of white men, and even wives were under regular threat of attack. That was particularly true when a slave belonged to an unmarried white man or lived in proximity to unmarried white men. Sometimes they were offered gifts for their service, but usually these women were violated by force. Resistance often meant a beating. In some occasions, beautiful black women were purchased as concubines and became permanent mistresses of slave owners. Of course, such behavior led to numerous divorces in slave owning families, but more often the situation was publicly ignored by the plantation wife while privately she plotted her revenge against the slave. On a rare occasion, they might even engaged in an affair with slave men, but more often they abused the slaves in question.

Slave courtship was an complex exercise, and I don't have as much time to go into it in as much detail as I would like, but I will say that white masters had the final word as to who married whom. Many owners demanded that their slaves marry someone on their own estate. After all, marrying the slave of another man did not bring a slave owner any profit if they had children since they remained with the mother. Sometimes there were agreements allowing slaves from different plantations to marry, but more often than not they were encouraged to look for unions on their own plantations. Such encouragement was easier on larger plantations. It often became a depressing reality on smaller ones. Regardless of where your mate lived, one of the most difficult things for a male slave to accept was the sexual or physical abuse of his own wife or children. No matter what, he was expected to say nothing. Most white masters probably were hesitant, however, about raping a married slave. Occasionally, slaves killed white men for such things. While forming a family could give the master a level of control over the slave population, it also limited his ability to fully dominate his slaves.

Care of Children

It was masters, also, who determined how much care and attention slave women received when they were pregnant as well as what kind of treatment infants received. The overwhelming majority of pregnant women were forced to work until a few weeks before the child was born. After the birth, women were given a few days off, sometimes more, but the longer they were kept away from work the less money the master made from them, so most masters tried to get female slaves back to work as quickly as possible. If the master was especially interested in rearing slave children, and most were, a routine would be established for nursing the child. Either the child would be carried to the field, or the mother would return to the cabin at regular intervals during the day to feed the child. Otherwise, there was not a great deal of nurturing for slave children. Those types of activities usually fell to older women or children too young to work. This general lack of care led, of course, to high mortality rates.

The children who did survive led mixed childhoods. On one hand, they often remarked about the carefree and idyllic childhood of the plantation. Yet, they were constantly reminded that they were inferior. They watched horrible punishments to black males and saw the crimes committed against women. They also saw two very different versions of their parents. At home, the father and mother ruled supreme, acting as a leader and protector. Yet at work they were docile and submissive. Such examples taught young slaves how to survive, but it also had important implications with regard to psychological development. Clearly, you can see just how important the family was.

Field Work

It is hard, in many ways, to characterize plantation life. It varied from place to place, but it is possible to make certain generalizations. Seventy-five percent of all slaves worked in the fields in some fashion. Fifty-five percent worked in cotton, ten percent in tobacco, and ten percent in the areas of rice, sugar, and hemp. The other twenty percent was split evenly between some form of industry and domestic work. Most field workers rose before dawn, made their meals, fed the livestock, and the rushed to the fields before sunrise—failure to get to the fields in time resulted in punishment, like being whipped. Depending on the season or crop, the worker might hoe the field, pick worms off the plants, build fences, cut down trees, construct dikes, clear new land, or plant and harvest. Often after working to sunset, slaves had to feed the livestock, put away tools, and cook their meals before the horn sounded bedtime in the quarters. During cotton-picking season, men sometimes ginned cotton until nine at night. For the slaves on the sugar plantation, the work of boiling the sugar cane continued well after dark. The work, in fact, seemed almost endless. Cotton planting started at the end of March, while picking lasted from August to December or longer. After the cotton was in, the corn was harvested. A slave had to pick cotton at the rate of 150 pounds or more per day. During slack periods in the growing season, they were engaged in a variety of tasks from building fences to repairing cabins. Never did they get time to themselves. Life expectancy was short. In 1850 the life expectancy was 25.5 years for whites, but only 21.4 for African-Americans. Those statistics reflected the high infant mortality rate.

Food and Housing

The quality, quantity, and variety of food, clothing, housing, and medical care rarely satisfied the slave, in part due to their dependence on white owners and in part due to shortages in the South. Most slaves lived in one-room log cabins with dirt floors. Their houses had too many cracks in them to keep them warm in the winter. John Brown complained of them: "The wind and rain will come in and the smoke will not go out." Most cabins contained two families. On one large plantation 260 slaves shared only 38 cabins, an average of 6.8 people per cabin. They often had to make the most of their furniture—building their own tables, beds, benches, etc. The beds, if they had them, were usually made of straw-covered boards.

A common food ration for a week was three pounds of meat, a quart of corn meal, and some molasses for each person. That varied depending on age and time of the year. Slaves were able to supplement their food supply by farming their own gardens and by hunting—though not with guns. Slaves were also provided with clothes, usually of rough homemade cloth. Each year they received two shirts, two pairs of pants, and one pair of shoes for men and enough cloth for women to make an equal number of smocks for themselves and their children.

The last question to consider was how cruel the average plantation owner or overseer could be. In the East, where the plantations were run more professionally, it appears that there were fewer cruel masters. But in the West, where there were large numbers of young overseers and many plantation owners who did not live on the plantation, the nature of plantation life could be much harsher. There were many benign owners, but there were far too many cruel ones, as well. Frequently even the more benign planters were so quick to punish that they thought little about the punishments they meted out. Flogging of fifty to seventy-five lashes was not uncommon. On some occasions planters branded, stabbed, tarred and feathered, burned, shackled, tortured, maimed, crippled, mutilated, or castrated their slaves. Despite the southern defenders of slavery who argued that their African slaves were better treated than the workers who labored in northern factories, it is clear—crystal clear—that slavery was and remains the greatest moral crime in American history. No matter how kind a master might be, slaves lived under the constant threat of violence or being sold or separated from their families and the community. They had virtually no control over their own destiny.

The South's White Folks

Look at the white population of the South. The white South could generally be broken down into three classes: poor whites, yeomen, and planters. Sixty-four percent of all southerners did not own slaves. The yeomen were small farmers and ranchers who owned their own land. They grew enough vegetables to feed their families, including corn that they ate and fed to their hogs. They also produced crops for sale. Generally, they could live off what they were able to produce. They often sold excess goods and products to plantation owners, as well. The poor whites were mostly tenet farmers and renters. It is hard to say just what percentage of southern society they comprised, but a good guess would place them somewhere between 30 and 50 percent. They lived in abject poverty. Even the plantation slaves, who were often better fed and better dressed, dismissed them as poor white trash. The last group was the planters. They were far and away a minority in the Old South. While they comprised about 36 percent of the population, only 2.5 percent owned more than fifty slaves. But those planter elite, that 2.5 percent, dominated southern politics. They had money, thus, they had power.

The best example of the life of southern elites can be found in Natchez County, Mississippi. One such man who resided there was Frederick Stanton, who, at the time of his death, owned 444 slaves and 15,000 acres of land. Another family, the Surgets, owned some 93,000 acres in Mississippi, Arkansas, and Louisiana. The extraordinary wealth in Natchez—which in 1850 was the richest county in the nation—created a distinct southern elite. Yet, the southern elite was not an elite in the European sense—they were not educated or cultured. Thomas Taylor, a Pennsylvania Quaker who visited Natchez in 1847, noted: "[T]he men of the gentry who I have been permitted to see dashing about here on highbred horses, seem to find their greatest enjoyment in recounting their bear hunts, great fights, their occasional exploits with revolvers and Bowie Knives—swearing terribly and sucking mint juleps and cherry cobblers with straws." In a number of cases, the plantation elite came to Natchez by following the Mississippi River from Virginia, North Carolina, and Kentucky to establish plantations in Louisiana, Mississippi, and Arkansas. Isaac Henry Hilliard and Miriam Hilliard of Chicot County, Arkansas traveled the river extensively, going from parties at the Mississippi capital to visits with wealthy friends in Louisiana to trips back home to Kentucky.

Slavery as a Political Issue

The people who thought slavery would die a natural death were mistaken. Slavery expanded rapidly between 1790 and 1820, spreading out to the Old Southwest when the tobacco trade shifted to the cotton boom. As early as 1800, though, Abolitionists in the North had been hard at work to pass personal liberty laws to protect free blacks from kidnapping or seizure under the Fugitive Slave Act of 1793. They also opposed the extension of slavery into the West. At first, they failed. Alabama, Louisiana, and Mississippi all joined the union as slave states. But when Missouri applied for admission in 1819, the antislavery forces rallied together to stop its admission. Congressman James Tallmadge of New York proposed a ban on the importation of slaves into Missouri, and called for the gradual emancipation of its black inhabitants. Missouri whites rejected those conditions and, in response, the House of Representatives, which northerners dominated, blocked the admission of Missouri into the union. In retaliation, southerners in the Senate (where free states and slave states were split eleven to eleven) blocked the admission of Maine, which was seeking to separate itself from Massachusetts. Tempers flared and Senator Thomas W. Cobb of Georgia accused Tallmadge of kindling "a fire which all the water of the ocean cannot put out and which seas of blood can only extinguish." A two-year stalemate followed.

Finally, Henry Clay of Kentucky put together what became known as the Missouri Compromise. As a result Maine entered the union as a Free State in 1820, Missouri as a slave state in 1821. That bargain preserved the existing sectional balance and set the precedent that in the future all states would be admitted on a one-by-one basis. In the rest of the Louisiana territory, slavery was confined to the region south of the 36 parallel, 30 degree boundary, the southern boundary of Missouri. This decision held major implications for the South because it tied Western expansion to the question of slavery. It also raised the prospect of civil war. Thomas Jefferson said of the decision, "[T]his momentous question, like a fire-bell in the night, awakened and filled me with terror."

Items to Consider

English experience with chattel slavery, slave resistance, Virginia Slave Laws, slave culture, conjuring, child care, field work, three classes of white southerners, Compromise of 1820, Brer Rabbit

CHAPTER 13

The Age of Jackson

The Age of Jackson spanned the years from 1820 to 1844. While the Industrial Revolution changed American society, it also sparked a revolution in politics, known as the Democratic Revolution. In the first forty years of the United States, there was a lot of discussion about republicanism. In a republic, the nation is governed for the good of the whole. In a republic, every man is public property. The good of the nation is absolute, the individual citizen's duty is to protect, defend, and extend the nation. A democracy is much different. A democracy implies social equality and respect for the individual. It was in the years between 1820 and 1844 when there was a slow shift from a republic to a democracy.

During this period, democracy became the byword of those who wanted to increase political participation in the early nineteenth century. At the head of the movement were Andrew Jackson and his new Democratic party. Jackson was born in the Carolina backcountry to Irish immigrants; he fought in the Revolution, and was captured and imprisoned by the British. By the end of the war, all but one of his immediate family members had died in connection with that war. He was a teenager, alone, so he moved to Tennessee. He had a minor political career in the late 1790s, serving briefly in the Tennessee Legislature, Senate, and on the Tennessee Supreme Court. He also set himself up as a slaveholder on a small plantation that would later grow into a major cotton plantation called the Hermitage.

Jackson won national fame in the War of 1812; becoming the hero of the American victory at New Orleans in January 1815. His huge following grew after the war. He served as the military governor of the Florida Territory in 1821 before winning a U.S. Senate seat in 1823. At the urging of his friends, Jackson decided to run for president in 1824. Jackson was not part of the old republican system of American politics. Every American president from Washington to Monroe had been part of the Eastern old guard. But now things were beginning to change. The generation that had won the Revolution was now aging and it was time for a new generation of Americans to step forward to lead the nation. In many ways, Jackson typified the new generation. Jackson and his party were the protectors of farmers and workers—the common man. They were a committed to attacking monopolies and special privileges, to remove Indians from the path of Western settlement, and to protect American democratic government from the power and influence of the elite.

Jackson was not, however, without opposition. The Whigs, as they eventually came to be known, defined themselves as the party of economic improvement and prosperity. And they had no qualms about using government power to ensure those goals. The Whig challenge to the Jacksonians began what historians have called the Second Party System—a system that remained in place until the 1850s with the rise of the new Republican Party. This established a competitive two-party system. In its scope and significance, the new two party system completed a democratic revolution that matched the Industrial Revolution in importance.

But how did this occur? The best place to begin is with the changing nature of politics in the 1820s. There were two political parties in 1800 the Democratic-Republicans (or just Republicans) and the Federalists. Over the next 20 years, the Federalists would collapse as a political entity, especially after the war of 1812, and they would be unable to field a presidential candidate by 1820. That left only one political party: the Republicans. For a while they dominated the nation, but they would be unable to stand their own success.

Two key democratic shifts occurred in the period between 1820 and 1829. First, the right to vote was being expanded; more people would be enfranchised. Many of the states had had property qualifications to limit the right of the vote to those who best "deserved" it. The elites who started the Revolution wanted to restrict the electorate to white elite men like themselves as much as possible. Approaching the 1820s and the next two decades thereafter, more and more people were being brought into the political system of the nation. Eventually even the poorest wage earner would be given the right to vote. By 1840, the electorate included more than 90 percent of the adult white male population. It took almost sixty years after the Revolution for the idea that all adult white men should vote to finally triumph. To ensure fuller participation, states established direct election of governors, presidential electors, and even some judges. Of course, more than half of the American population was still excluded: minorities and women. Nonetheless, it was an important development.

The second key democratic shift was the emergence of new political parties in every state during the 1820s and 1830s. Question: The Constitution mentions political parties in which part? It does not mention them at all. The founding fathers hated political parties, which they believed were inherently corrupt and self-serving. They would not have been happy to see political parties emerge, but unlike the political parties they were familiar with, those of the 1820s tended to be more democratic and interactive with their constituents. The reason for this difference is that party identity became one of the most important aspects of a person's identity, partly because politics in this period was entertainment. The noise of television, the theater, and the sports world did not exist then. So along with an individual's religious denomination, party membership was a crucial part of one's identity.

It was not long before astute politicians, like Martin Van Buren, were able to manipulate and shape party loyalty for their own purposes. In New York, Van Buren and his friends took over the old Republican Party and turned it into an effective tool for governing. Van Buren's political skills were so renowned that they earned him the nickname The Little Magician. People joked that he could get anyone elected to public office, if he only set his mind to it. Essentially, what Van Buren and company did was to implement more effective organizational techniques. The Republican Party can be compared to the Industrial Revolution, in that Van Buren and his supporters took what businessmen had learned about labor organization and applied it to politics. The Republicans introduced collective leadership and built a strong, bureaucratic party organization, which made political parties look a lot like a company. They used party newspapers to circulate the party line and to maintain party discipline; the most famous party newspaper was the *Albany Argus*. They also employed modern democratic tools, such as a caucus—which is, in essence, a bunch of party members, say, from a county, come together make decision about a question at hand. And finally, they embraced political platforms, or programs of action, they would enact if elected. This meant that for the first time in American history, a politician running for office in Georgia stood for the same principles as one from the same party in New York. Once they created this first organized political party, the foremost man to weave together these new techniques of a modern political organization to reach across sectional and class lines was Andrew Jackson in 1828.

Before Jackson became president, he would first lose a close political race for that position. As the state parties were gaining strength, the national parties were on the verge of collapse by 1824. The Federalists had all but vanished, and the Republicans had broken into factions. In the election of 1824, five candidates, all calling themselves Republicans, would run for president. Three of them were veterans of James Monroe's cabinet: Secretary of State John Quincy Adams of Massachusetts and the son of John Adams; Secretary of War John C. Calhoun of South Carolina; and Secretary of the Treasury William H. Crawford of Georgia. The fourth was Henry Clay of Kentucky, the Speaker of the House of Representatives. The last candidate was Gen. Andrew Jackson, a U.S. senator from Tennessee.

The election of 1824 was seen at the time as a contest of personalities, although today we can see it was more than that. Andrew Jackson represented the West, strong currency, and internal developments (although he would move away from that final position). Clay also represented the West, but lacked Jackson's appeal. Clay was a different kind of Westerner than Jackson. Clay's platform was called the American System—high tariffs to protect American industries and generate revenue for the federal government; high public land rates to generate revenue for the government; the preservation of the Bank of the United States to stabilize the currency and rein in risky state and local banks; and the development of a system of internal improvements (such as roads and canals) that would knit the nation together and be financed by the tariff and land sales revenues—a plan to strengthen and unify the nation. John C. Calhoun represented Southern interests. Although he was still a Nationalist, having been as Clay a war hawk in 1812, he was in the process of becoming a champion of states' rights. Adams represented the Northeast; banking and financial interests. Crawford, really only represented the Southern planter elite; however, he was the most famous politician in the race and most people expected him to win.

Jackson did not actively campaign for the presidency. It was the tradition of the day not to do so, but his supporters campaigned for him vigorously as a man of integrity who would root out corruption (Jackson's supporters felt that corruption was rampant in the national government). The election of 1824 was the first election in which the majority of presidential electors were selected by the voters. Six of the twenty-four states retained the practice of having the state legislature choose the electors, while only three still had property qualifications: Virginia, Louisiana, and Rhode Island.

The results of the election were a complete surprise. Jackson, who was dismissed by most informed observers, won 99 electoral votes, Adams 84, Crawford 41, and Clay 37. Crawford, who had been the favorite to win, was paralyzed by a stroke just weeks before the election and won only his home state of Georgia and Virginia where he was born. Adams had broad support but was because the American public saw him as New England's candidate. Clay's support was limited largely to the Ohio Valley. Calhoun, reading the writing on the wall, decided to bow out and switched over to the vice presidential race, which he won easily with the support of Jackson's forces. Jackson, however, did not have a majority with his 99 electors (44 percent of the popular vote to Adams' 31 percent). Without a clear winner, the election had to be decided in the House of Representatives. The House took the top three candidates, eliminating Clay, which left a vote among Jackson, Adams, and Crawford. Each of the twenty-four states got one vote.

With the election shifting to the House, Henry Clay was now in an important position. As the speaker of the House, he would be able to manipulate the vote to some extent. He controlled the votes of Kentucky, Missouri, Illinois, and Ohio. In Clay's mind, Crawford was immediately eliminated because of his health and the fact that Clay did not like him. But he had a problem, because he did not like the other two candidates either. Clay and Jackson were bitter enemies, having battled over the issue of what to do with Florida (Spain had given it up in 1819). Clay and Adams had their differences as well, having fought at Ghent where they negotiated to end the war of 1812. For Clay though, the decision was really one concerning the future, and he made up his mind to block Jackson's election. Clay wanted to remain the leader of the West and he, as an established politician, feared Jackson's election. At the time, it was not clear publicly whom Clay would support. Before Clay could make up his mind, an advertisement appeared in the pages of the *National Intelligencer*, the Republican Party newspaper, saying that a corrupt bargain had been struck between Adams and Clay. In return for the position as Secretary of State in the new administration, Clay would support Adams. Clay denied the accusation and challenged whoever published it to a duel. The author was a congressman from Pennsylvania as it turns out, but no duel took place. The charge, interestingly, seemed validated when Clay supported Adams for the presidency and then was made the Secretary of State in the new administration.

The election of 1824 is significant because it 1) It destroyed the old Republican Party and 2) it laid the foundation for the emergence of the two-party system. The two new parties were the Democrats (the supporters of Andrew Jackson, Martin Van Buren, and John C. Calhoun) and the National Republicans (later known as the Whigs; the supporters of Henry Clay, Daniel Webster, and John Quincy Adams).

As president, John Quincy Adams tried to institute a bold and sweeping program to promote the nation's economic and social development. He fully embraced the basic features of Clay's American system: a protective tariff to stimulate manufacturing, internal improvements to simulate commerce, and a national bank to provide a uniform currency and to expand the economy. As a result, John Quincy Adams had a new, different vision of the national government than any president before him. He wanted to expand its power and influence. He wanted to build a national university in Washington, finance more explorations to the West, adopt a uniform standard of weights and measures; and build a national observatory.

Many of his critics, however, felt he was overstepping his bounds. Thomas Jefferson, for example, said on his death-bed that John Quincy Adams was trying to establish a government of aristocracy, that he had rewarded too many of his friends. Others felt his plans exceeded the constitutional powers granted to the presidency. In the end, Adams was able to accomplish little more than to regionalize the nation. His tariff policies (1824, 1827) and his support for Native American rights alienated the South.

John Quincy Adams decided to run again in 1828, but following the tradition of the day he refused to campaign. He said, "If my country wants my services, she must ask for them." Things did not bode well for his re-election. As Adams floundered, Jackson gained momentum. He put together a brilliant political coalition: his friends in the Old Southwest; the supporters of John C. Calhoun in South Carolina, who was his semi-official running mate; the Crawford support-ers; the old Republican politicians in Virginia; and Martin Van Buren's New York organization. Each group had a large state organization with newspapers and means for making the election of 1828 a truly national campaign, the first in American history.

Jackson's message was the same in 1828 as it had been in 1824, but it was delivered more thoroughly and with greater emotion. Jackson claimed the nation had been corrupted by special interests, and only he could root them out. He talked a great deal about his hero, too, Thomas Jefferson. Only through forceful democratic measures, he said, could the republic be made pure again. There is a lot of sexual imagery implicit in this argument, but take that for what it is worth. Adams made a perfect target. Had he and Clay not stolen the last election from Jackson despite 44 percent of the people naming

Jackson as their choice? Jackson even made the charge, which appears untrue, that John Quincy Adams had tried to find an American girl to marry the tsar of Russia. By contrast, Jackson's virtues, the purity of his frontier existence, and his rise from poverty to power typified all that his supporters wanted the country to believe. His supporters, who had been calling themselves Democratic-Republicans, dropped the Republican prefix so that their name might better reflect the ideas of the new nation. In particular, Jackson's hostility toward banking (Jackson himself had once been swindled) made him popular outside the South and West to wage-earners in the Northeast. That issue made him a national candidate. In the South, he was able to promise to do something about the tariffs and Indian removal.

It is important to note that Jackson, however, was no paragon of piety. He was accused of once killing a man in a duel, which he had done. And—the most sensational charge—he lived with his wife Rachel while she was married to another man. This act alone made him adulterer, and she a bigamist. Of course, the story was more complicated than that. Rachel was married to an abusive husband in Kentucky, so she wrote to her childhood sweetheart, Andrew Jackson, about her predicament. Being the dashing hero, Jackson rushed to Kentucky to rescue her. Rachel's husband sued her for divorce, although he did not complete that action. Deciding they wanted to be married, Jackson and Rachel went to Natchez to get married under Spanish law, and later would be remarried when the first divorce was finally granted. Technically, Rachel was guilty of wrongdoing. Anyway, Henry Clay uncovered the story and told Charles Hammond, publisher of the Cincinnati newspaper. Hammond went public with the story during the 1828 campaign. Jackson was furious and tried to shield Rachel from the criticism. To his credit, she did not learn of the charges until after the election of 1828. But she died unexpectedly on December 22, 1828. Jackson believed she had died from heartbreak, and he held Clay personally responsible.

With such shenanigans on both sides, it should be no surprise that the election of 1828 was contentious. In the end, Jackson received 178 of the 261 electoral votes available. His only area of weakness was New England, which John Quincy Adams swept. Nevertheless, Jackson won 56 percent of the popular vote and 68 percent of the electoral vote, winning the South, West, and Northwest. Only New England remained loyal to Adams. Jackson became the nation's first Western president, and his election struck fear into the heart of the establishment. Daniel Webster, the old Federalist, said Jackson would "bring a breeze with him. Which way it will blow, I cannot tell ... my fear is stronger than my hope."

The Age of the Common Man

Jackson's election ushered in a new era in American politics, an era that historians have called the Age of the Common Man. America under Jackson has even been called the Coonskin Democracy, referring to the western frontier and the egalitarian aspects of American democracy. Jackson was not a common man. He was a slave owner, a military hero, and had almost an imperial personality. It was his way or the highway, so to speak. "Old Hickory," as he was called, was inflexible, tough, and unbending, like hickory itself, one of the hardest of all woods. Yet he had a mass appeal to ordinary people that was unmatched by previous presidents.

While Jackson was at first denied the presidency in 1824, he won a great victory in 1828. Jackson began his new term by rewarding party loyalists with positions in the national government. While he spoke highly of democratizing the holding of public office, other Democrats put the matter more bluntly. William Marcy of New York said there was "nothing wrong in the rule, that to the victor belong the spoils of the enemy." Hence, the expression "spoils system" was used to describe the practice of awarding government jobs to one's political friends. Many historians have wrongly credited Jackson with beginning this system. In fact, Thomas Jefferson believed that the victorious party had the right to the majority of public jobs. But Jackson took what had been a small state practice and took it to the national level. Future presidents would follow his precedent until the practice was eliminated by the Pendleton Civil Service Act of 1883, which reformed the civil service system. Jackson opened up every job in the government to his party loyalists, some of whom were corrupt, inefficient, or both. His opponents would complain long and hard about this practice but, truth be known, the number of officeholders Jackson replaced was small—only about 10 percent. It was his heavy-handed way of doing things that really upset people. For example, Jackson had talked about all the corruption in the Treasury Department during the John Quincy Adams administration, yet when he became president he made his close friend Amos Kendell the fourth auditor of the Treasury and instructed him to go over the books and root out corruption.

For all of his western origins, Jackson was the first genuinely national figure since George Washington. He was more interested in asserting strong national leadership than promoting sectional compromise. He believed that the president, who symbolized the popular will of the people, must dominate the government. As he put it in his first annual message:

"[T]he first principle of our system is that the majority is to govern." This was new. Voters, and politicians for that matter, were more accustomed to thinking of politics in sectional terms. Jackson faced a Congress full of strong, popular sectional figures. Three stood out: Southerner John C. Calhoun, Northerner Daniel Webster, and Westerner Henry Clay.

Intense, dogmatic, and uncompromising, John C. Calhoun of South Carolina began his political career as an ardent nationalist and expansionist in his early days as a War Hawk before the War of 1812. Since the debate over the Missouri Compromise in 1820, however, Calhoun had wholeheartedly identified himself with the southern cause, which was first and foremost the expansion and preservation of the institution of slavery. As the South's minority position in Congress became clear over the years, Calhoun's defense of southern economic interests and slavery become increasingly more rigid. Not for nothing did he earn his nickname, "The Cast-Iron Man."

Senator Daniel Webster of Massachusetts was one of two outstanding orators of the age. A large, dark, and stern man, Webster delivered his speeches in a deep, booming voice that listeners said "shook the world." He was capable of subtle speech, as well, bringing tears to the eyes of those who heard him say, while defending Dartmouth College before the Supreme Court, "[I]t is a small college, sir, but there are those of us who love [it]." Webster, a lawyer for business interests, became the main spokesman of the new northern commercial interests, supporting a high protective tariff, a national bank, and a strong federal government. Webster's fondness for comfortable living, and especially brandy, made him less effective as he grew older. A contemporary of his remarked, "No man could be as great as Daniel Webster looked."

And finally, Henry Clay, like Webster, was a skilled orator. He was also a great parliamentarian—he never met a compromise he did not like; so to speak. Clay held the powerful position of speaker of the House of Representatives from 1811 until 1825, and he later served several terms in the Senate. A spellbinding storyteller, Clay worked to incorporate western desires for cheap and good transportation into national politics. His system to improve the country was the American system—a national bank, a protective tariff, and internal improvements—all financed by the federal government. Clay always wanted to be president, but Jackson, his greatest political rival, prevented him from being so. For no other reason, he would oppose Jackson on every issue.

While each of the three sectional leaders had their own interests, Jackson's style led many people to oppose him. He was far different than previous presidents. Jackson played rough and he relished controversy. His administration, spanning the years from 1829 to 1837, had plenty of it. Jackson thoroughly dominated his administration. He ignored his cabinet most of the time, with the exception of Secretary of State Martin Van Buren. Instead, he consulted with an informal group, dubbed the "Kitchen Cabinet," made up of Van Buren and a select group of old western friends. It did not include Calhoun, the vice president.

The reason Jackson did not include Calhoun in his decisions and did include Van Buren is rather … petty. Both men, Calhoun and Van Buren, were vying to be the next U.S. president. Slowly, the three men began to grow apart. In truth, Jackson only tolerated Calhoun because he felt he owed him a favor. When Jackson invaded Spanish Florida without authorization in 1818, there was talk of both a censure and a court martial. Jackson grew to believe that Calhoun, as Secretary of War, and stood up during a cabinet meeting and defended and protected him. Calhoun let Jackson believe that for a number of years. The person who actually defended Jackson then, however, was none other than John Quincy Adams, Secretary of State, who was in negotiations at the time with Spain to acquire the territory.

Despite their connection, events quickly pushed Jackson and Calhoun apart. Jackson's Secretary of War was an old friend by the name of John Eaton. Eaton had been in Congress prior to becoming a member of Jackson's cabinet. In those days it was the habit of congressmen not to move their families to Washington, which was more of a frontier town on the edge of a swamp than an actual city. Instead, politicians stayed in hotels and boarding houses while the government was in session, and then went home when the government closed. Eaton had stayed at a popular Washington, D.C. tavern, the home of Peggy O'Neal, the daughter of the tavern owner and wife of a purser in the United States Navy, John B. Timberlake, who committed suicide while on service in the Mediterranean in 1828. It was rumored that Peggy and John had had an affair. Whether that is true is uncertain, but John fell in love Peggy, who was acknowledged as the most beautiful woman of her day. Recognizing that they were breaking social mores of the time, Eaton asked Jackson for permission to marry her, which he gave.

The sudden elevation of Mrs. Eaton into the cabinet social circle was resented by the wives of several of Jackson's secretaries, and charges were made against her of improper sexual conduct with Eaton prior to her marriage to him. Believing she had broken the moral code of the day, they snubbed her socially. They would not talk to her at dinners and would not return her calls. Eventually, even members of his own cabinet and their wives snubbed Mrs. Eaton, all except Martin Van Buren. Jackson became unnerved over the whole situation. The refusal of the cabinet wives to recognize the wife of his friend angered Jackson, and he tried in vain to coerce her acceptance in society by launching an investigation into her character. His wife, after all, had had her character impugned as well. After taking depositions, Jackson pronounced her chaste; at least as much as possible and ordered all the snubbers to stop. The ring leader of the whole affair appeared to be Calhoun's wife. Eventually, and partly for this reason, Jackson almost completely reorganized his cabinet. The effect of the incident on the political fortunes of Vice President Calhoun was, perhaps, most important. Partly on this account, Jackson's favor was transferred from Calhoun to Van Buren, the Secretary of State, who had taken Jackson's side in the quarrel and had shown marked attention to Mrs. Eaton. Van Buren's elevation to the vice presidency and presidency through Jackson's favor is no doubt partly attributable to this incident. Jackson could not seem to get along with members of his own political party, nor could he get along with the other great sectional leaders. He never forgave Clay for Mrs. Jackson's death and the corrupt bargain of 1824, and Daniel Webster represented the privileged elite who were Jackson's favorite targets of ridicule.

Jackson freely used the tools of his office to strengthen the executive branch of government at the expense of Congress and the courts. One thing he did that outraged Congress was his practice of vetoing bills. It was seen as the duty of the president to sign any bill passed by Congress unless there was a constitutional objection. The previous six presidents had vetoed a total of six bills. In his first four years in office, Jackson would veto ten bills. One of his more famous vetoes was that of the Maysville Road Bill of 1830. The bill would have provided federal funds to extend the national road some fifty miles along a spur route into Kentucky. All the construction was to take place within the state of Kentucky. Jackson vetoed the bill, claiming such funding should be left to the state. That was not a new idea; Madison and Monroe had believed the same thing. But what was surprising is here is that a Westerner vetoed a bill that would have helped the West. Henry Clay, who had been in retirement, was so angry that he came out of retirement. With the veto, Jackson seemed to be risking the region that had supported him the most. Yet, by shaping his veto in the terms of states' rights, he actually found political support in the West and South. He told the people of Kentucky that he vetoed the bill in their interest, for if people outside the state had to pay for the construction of a road they would not benefit from, how could Kentuckians refuse to accept a bill that hurt them for the benefit of others. (Here, you should begin to think seriously about the future of the institution of slavery, because everyone in the South did the moment he framed his decision in such a manner).

That very question—the balance of power between the state government and the federal government—would prove the most serious test of the Jacksonian presidency. The Constitution had been ambiguous as to the correct balance between the national government and the state governments. It had to be. After all, that was an issue the founders were trying to avoid because every time two sections of the country disagreed, thereafter, it automatically produced arguments over the meaning of the Constitution, which seemed to threaten the existence of the Union.

During Jackson's administration, the issue that came to symbolize the differences between North and South was the protective tariff. The first major protective tariff was enacted in 1816. It was passed because northern manufacturing interests demanded protection from the British at the end of the War of 1812. As a group, wealthy southern planters opposed tariffs, both because they raised the cost of the luxury goods the planters imported from Europe and because they believed in the principle of free trade; fearing that American tariffs would cause other countries to retaliate with tariffs against southern cotton. Most southern congressmen were assured in 1816 that that tariff was a temporary measure to address an emergency; thus, they voted for it. It turned out not to be temporary. As northern industry grew, it demanded higher and higher protective tariffs. This resulted in the tariff bills of 1824 and 1828, which raised rates still higher and covered more items. Southerners tried to stop them, of course, but they were outvoted in Congress by the North and the West.

The 1828 tariff, nicknamed "the Tariff of Abominations," became a special target of southern anger, because Jackson supporters in Congress passed it in order to increase northern support for him in the presidential election that year. The tariffs on iron and textiles were especially high, ranging from one-third to one-half of their value. Lacking the votes to block the tariff, Southerners in Congress faced the bleak prospect that their economic interests would always be ignored by the majority. Southern opponents of the tariff insisted that the tariff was not a truly national measure, but a sectional one that helped only some groups while harming others. The tariff was unconstitutional, in their opinion, because it violated the rights of some of the states.

South Carolina, Calhoun's home state, reacted the most forcefully to the Tariff of 1828. Of the older southern states, South Carolina had been hit hardest by the opening of new cotton lands in the Southwest (Alabama, Mississippi, and Louisiana). South Carolina's population was declining and there was a growing fear that the future of slavery was in doubt. This created a concern that if South Carolina did not stand up to the federal government now over tariff issues, how could it possibly protect the legality of the institution of slavery in the future?

The result of these concerns was a renewed interest in *nullification*, the doctrine that a state had the right to nullify a federal law or act on the grounds that particular state felt it was unconstitutional. Nullification was not new. Thomas Jefferson and James Madison had used it in the Virginia and Kentucky resolves in opposing the Alien and Sedition acts, and the Hartford Convention used it to protest the War of 1812. Now it came up again in order to protect, at bottom, South Carolina's institution of slavery. South Carolina, moreover, had an important supporter of nullification in the person of John C. Calhoun, who wrote a widely circulated defense of the doctrine in 1828 entitled *The Exposition and Protest*. Because Calhoun was soon to serve as Jackson's Vice President, he wrote *The Exposition and Protest* anonymously; hoping to gain Jackson's support before going public as its author. He failed, of course.

Jackson saw nullification as a threat to the union, not as a safeguard against federal tyranny. In 1830, at the annual Jefferson Day dinner, he proclaimed to all in attendance that "our federal union—It must be preserved at all costs" for only "the union—next to our liberty—I hold most dear." That event marked the beginning of the public split between Calhoun and Jackson. Calhoun quickly lost Jackson's favor, and Van Buren would become Vice President for Jackson's second term. Calhoun, having lost his chance at the presidency, moved to the Senate.

In 1832, the nullification controversy became a full-blown crisis. By passing the Tariff of 1832, Congress retained high taxes on woolens, iron, and hemp, although it reduced duties on other items. South Carolina responded by calling a special convention, whose participants passed an Ordinance of Nullification, in which they rejected the tariff, and the state refused to collect the required taxes. The state further issued a call for a volunteer militia, and threatened to secede from the Union if Jackson used force against the state. Jackson responded with a public denunciation, stating that armed resistance was treason. He immediately began preparing steps to make war against South Carolina. He obtained from Congress a Force Bill authorizing the federal government to collect the tariff in South Carolina at gunpoint, if necessary. That was enough to intimidate the other southern states from following South Carolina into secession.

Jackson was smart enough to find a way out of the crisis with South Carolina. He quietly asked Congress to revise the tariff. Henry Clay, along with Calhoun, soon pushed through the Compromise Tariff of 1833. This measure appeared to meet southern demands by pledging a return to the tariff rate of 1816 (much lower) by the year 1842 through a series of small, annual decreases over the next nine years. As it would work out, Congress did all of that but also passed a new, higher tariff in 1842. In the meantime, South Carolina was isolated and quickly decided to accept the compromise. The state repealed the nullification of the 1832 tariff and, in a final act of defiance, nullified the Force Bill, an act that was ignored by Jackson and Congress as an empty gesture. This crisis was the most serious threat to the Union up to that point in time. Jackson had managed to avoid a civil war thirty years earlier by providing effective leadership. Nevertheless, had force been used against South Carolina, it is a safe assumption that the rest of the South would have come to its aid and the Union would have been shattered.

Jackson's most vigorous political offensive was his attack on the Second Bank of the United States; one of the key elements of Clay's American System. Jackson began to dismantle the American system in May 1830 when he issued the Maysville Road Veto. The Bank of the United States was a far more serious opponent.

The Second Bank was a large commercial institution that the federal government had chartered in 1816 and owned 20 percent of its stock. Its federal charter was set to expire in 1836. The Bank's most import role was to stabilize the nation's money supply. Most American money consisted of notes—in effect, paper money—that the state-chartered banks had issued with the promise to redeem the notes in hard money—gold or silver—on demand. The Second Bank insured the stability of this system by only doing business with banks that engaged in sound financial practices. At least, that was the way the system worked in theory. But the state banks continued to issue more notes than they could redeem at any one time; thereby expanding the money supply and destabilizing the entire system. As long as citizens wanted to do business with the Second Bank, they had to do so cautiously. During the 1820s, under the leadership of its president, Nicholas Biddle, the Second Bank performed well, maintaining steady, predicable increases in the money supply. Thus, the Bank served its purpose. It created confidence.

Unfortunately, most Americans neither understood nor appreciated the role of the Bank of the United States. Many, especially in the West, believed banks to be little more than parasites, calling them the undemocratic tools of special privilege. Jackson himself blamed banks for the loss of large sums of money he had lost during the 1790s. Wage-earners in New England distrusted banks because their employers sometimes paid them in highly depreciated notes from financially unsound banks. Jackson and others wanted an end to banking uncertainty; hoping there would be no money but gold and silver.

In 1832, Jackson's opponents in Congress, led by Clay and Webster, hatched a plan to embarrass him. They knew the president opposed the Second Bank and, knowing that many Democrats in Congress supported the Bank, they tried to lure Jackson into a trap that would divide the Democratic Party just prior to the fall elections of that year. Carrying out their plan, Clay and Webster persuaded Biddle to request an early re-charter of the Second Bank, which he did. Biddle favored Clay and Webster, but probably wanted to stay out of the scheme. Clay and Webster pressured him into the decision and then pushed a bill through Congress that would re-charter the bank for another 20 years.

As expected, Jackson publicly vetoed the bill. He denounced the Second Bank as a net of special privilege and monopoly power that promoted "the advancement of the few at the expense of the many." He even called on American patriotism, saying the Second Bank of the United States was dominated by heavy investment from British aristocrats, so it must be destroyed to end undue foreign influence on the nation's finances. Surprisingly for Clay and Webster, Jackson's veto of the bank re-charter proved popular. The move backfired on Clay and Webster.

Even worse, Jackson rode the momentum of that veto into that fall's election, the election of 1832. Jackson and his new running mate, Martin Van Buren, faced Henry Clay, who headed the National Republican ticket in the presidential election of 1832. Clay attacked Jackson for abusing patronage and the veto power. Clay ran on his American System and called for another charter for the Second Bank of the United States. In the election that followed, Jackson and Van Buren destroyed Clay 219 to 49 in the Electoral College, while winning 54 percent of the popular vote. William Wirt, the Anti-Masonic candidate, received 8 percent of the vote.

Immediately after his reelection, Jackson launched a new attack on the Second Bank of the United States, which became known as the "Bank War." The Second Bank still had four years left on its original charter, but Jackson, thinking he had a popular mandate, decided to destroy it immediately by withdrawing the federal government's deposits. The trouble was that his Secretary of the Treasury refused to cooperate. Louis McLane opposed withdrawing the deposits. What could Jackson do? His Secretary of State, Edward Livingston, was about to retire, so Jackson promoted McLane to the position of Secretary of State and, without much thought, replaced him with William Duane. It backfired. Duane also refused to withdraw the deposits. Furious, Jackson fired him and replaced him with Roger B. Taney, a member of his Kitchen Cabinet and a man who would, in 1836, become Chief Justice of the Supreme Court when John Marshall died. Taney did as Jackson wanted, removing the government's cash to the state banks—called "pet banks" by Jackson opponents.

Both Congress and the Second Bank retaliated. In March 1834, the Senate censured Jackson. Henry Clay wrote it himself. He declared, "We are in the midst of a revolution, hitherto bloodless, but rapidly descending towards a total change or the pure republican character of the Government, and the concentration of all power in the hands of one man." Biddle also spoke out against the action. He sharply reduced the number of loans given out by the National Treasury, which had a ripple effect on other banks and brought about a brief recession in 1834. Jackson and Taney would not be moved. In 1836, the Second Bank of the United States closed its doors, becoming a state-chartered bank under the laws of Pennsylvannia.

While Jackson today is most famous for strengthening the power of the presidency, he is most notorious for the policy of Indian removal. By the 1820s, the pressure for western lands was intense. The problem revolved around the fact that many Indian tribes remaining in the old South occupied some of the best land. Most American believed that the federal government must remove the tribes from the path of American expansion. Clearly, it was not enough to conquer those tribes; they had to be moved west of the Mississippi. By the time Jackson became president, the federal government had nearly broken the resistance of Native Americans in the Old Northwest. In 1832, Jackson finished the assault. He sent Regular Army troops to the frontier area of Illinois in 1832 to remove Chief Black Hawk, a leader of the Sauk and Fox tribes, who occupyied rich farmland in western Illinois. Black Hawk, reduced to maybe 1,000 people because of disease, tried to surrender but the troops refused and chased him into the Wisconsin territory. On August 3, the Army ended its pursuit with the eight-hour-long Bad Axe Massacre, leaving alive only 150 of the 1,000 warriors who had followed Black Hawk. That defeat ended the last significant Indian resistance in the Old Northwest.

In the South, however, there were still large numbers of Indians living in large enclaves. The Five Civilized Tribes, as they were called, the Cherokee and Creek in Georgia, Tennessee, and Alabama; the Chickasaw and Choctaw in Mississippi, Alabama, and Tennessee; and the Seminole in Florida remained in control of quite a bit of territory. Of these tribes, the Cherokee in particular were becoming acculturated in American society: building plantations, growing cotton, and owning slaves. While it was alright with many whites in the region that the Native peoples were fitting in to western society, what they owned—high quality cotton land—and what made acculturation possible was exactly what white settlers wanted the most. The tribes were plagued by land-hungry white settlers who continually harassed them by stealing their livestock, burning their towns, and squatting on their land.

Jackson publicly committed himself to Indian removal. From 1814 to 1824, Jackson was instrumental in negotiating nine of the eleven treaties that divested the southern tribes of their eastern lands in exchange for lands in the West. The tribes agreed to the treaties for strategic reasons. They wanted to appease the government in the hopes of retaining some of their land and they wanted to protect themselves from white harassment. As a result of the treaties, the United States gained control over three-quarters of Alabama and Florida, as well as parts of Georgia, Tennessee, Mississippi, Kentucky, and North Carolina. This was a period of voluntary Indian migration, however, and only a small number of Creeks, Cherokee, and Choctaws actually moved to the new lands. Jackson's first move as president in Indian removal was to withdraw federal troops protecting the tribal enclaves that had been created after the War of 1812. He realized this would leave those Indians subject to state laws which were almost exclusively anti-Indian. In 1828, Georgia declared that the Cherokee were not an Indian nation but a collection of individuals who were tenants on state-owned land. Other states followed Georgia's example. This step obviously made it easier to swindle Indians out of their lands.

Jackson's next act toward Indian removal was to push through the Indian Removal Act of 1830, which offered southern Indians land west of the Mississippi in exchange for what they had in the East. Jackson sent agents to negotiate with the Indians and nearly one hundred removal treaties were signed to exchange lands. Jackson carried out his Indian policy despite two rulings by the Supreme Court that tended to uphold Indian rights. In 1827, the Cherokees had adopted a Constitution and proclaimed themselves a separate nation within the U.S. After Georgia's 1828 declaration denied their claim of an independent nation, the Cherokee appealed to the Supreme Court, arguing that Georgia's action was a violation of the U.S. Constitution. In *Cherokee Nation v. Georgia* (1831) John Marshal denied the Cherokee claim of independence but argued that the Indians were "domestic dependent nations." In another case *Worcester v. Georgia* (1832), Marshall held that the Indian nations were "distinct political communities, having territorial boundaries, within which their authority is exclusive." Jackson responded to Marshall's ruling by stating, "John Marshall has made his decision; now let him enforce it." Jackson refused to oppose Georgia, and since the policy of removal was so popular, the court found no support.

The Cherokee, however, refuse to budge. They repudiated the treaty, forced on them in 1835, that required them to leave by May 23, 1838. By the deadline only 2,000 of the 17,000 Cherokee had left. In 1838, Van Buren ordered Gen, Winfield Scott, with an army of some 7,000 men, to enforce the treaty. Scott rounded up 15,000 Cherokee and concentrated them in government camps, where many died. Some escaped to isolated villages in the mountains of North Carolina. In the fall and winter the rest were forced to undertake a 1,200 mile march to what is now Oklahoma—a route that is remembered as The Trail of Tears. Only 11,000 reached Oklahoma, and as many as 4,000 died of starvation and exposure on the journey. By the 1840, only the Seminole remained in the Southeast.

The success of Jackson's party and policies represented the first real challenge to the northern business class. To check the growing power of the Democratic Party, northern leaders organized a new national party—the Whig party—to contest Jackson. These two parties would dominate national politics until the Whigs fell apart and were replaced by the Republican Party in the mid 1850s.

How did the Whig party come about? During Jackson's first term in office, his opponents in Congress began to call themselves "Whigs" and referred to Jackson as King Andrew I. Those names conjured images of American and British politicians, also called Whigs, who had opposed the tyrannical policies of George III. The Whigs charged that Jackson had violated the Constitution through the abuse of executive power. In the beginning, they were united only by their opposition to Jackson. That was the litmus test of being a Whig. The party Webster, Clay, and Calhoun (although Calhoun remained a Democrat in name).

Jackson's victory over Clay in 1832 deeply troubled his opponents. At the most basic level the Democrats represented the elite, the American aristocracy. The Whigs were disturbed by what they considered to be rampant democracy that Jackson was bringing about. They believed it was natural for a few individuals to acquire a large share of the nation's wealth, to represent the people in a republican government, and to use government power as they thought necessary for the welfare of all.

There we have a conflict between elitism and republican ideals, particularly given their respective definitions of a proper government. Those supporting American elitism (The Whigs) attempted to resolve that conflict in three ways. First, they asserted that American society was really classless. People were not trapped in any permanent condition, and it was possible to be upwardly mobile. Second, they argued that in a republic it was natural for wealthy individuals to represent other citizens. A combination of the Constitution and morality would force the wealthy elite to rule in the best interest of the majority. Third, they claimed that a strong ruling elite promoted economic growth, thereby strengthening the country.

The Whigs criticized Jackson and the Democrats for underestimating the possibilities for upward mobility, for pitting the poor against the rich, the haves against the have-nots. They also berated Jackson for abusing the office of the presidency. They feared he was gaining too much power. Instead, they wanted to create a system in which Congress would take the lead and the federal government would play a major role in the economy. The Whigs were strongest in New England and New York; they also appealed to some western farmers in the Ohio and Mississippi river valleys and to whites in the southern backcountry, places like western Virginia and among capitalists in the South.

The struggle between the Whigs and Jackson's Democrats comes to a head during the election of 1836. On one side we have Martin Van Buren of New York, Jackson's vice president and hand-picked successor. Van Buren campaigned on Jackson's record; offering freedom from elite oppression. The Whigs did not hold a national nominating convention that year. Instead, they ran three candidates, hoping to throw the election into the House of Representatives. Those three were William Henry Harrison of Ohio (Old Tippecanoe himself), Hugh Lawson White of Tennessee, and Daniel Webster of Massachusetts. Although they almost succeeded in throwing the election into the House, Van Buren won the electoral contest with 170 votes. Harrison had 73 votes, White 26, and Webster 14. South Carolina threw away its votes on Senator W. P. Mangum of North Carolina. Van Buren, who was popular in the South, used his strong base in New York and Pennsylvania to ensure his election.

Van Buren won. The anti-Jackson factions had lost three elections in a row. But the victory would be short lived; Martin Van Buren had to reap the whirlwind of Jackson's Bank War and the major depression it ignited. The years between 1820 and 1837 had been good years. They lulled people into comfort; people began to think that panics and depressions could not happen after periods of rapid growth. They did not realize how the American economy heavily depended on events in Europe. Much of American industry and commerce depended on long-term British financing, which meant any European problem was likely to quickly cause one in America, as well.

That is exactly what happened in 1837. The Panic of 1837 began in Britain. In late 1836 the Bank of England, convinced that it was sending too much specie to the U.S., reduced the amount it was investing. What followed immediately thereafter was a sharp decline in agricultural prices and demand in Europe, notably for American cotton. The decline set in motion a series of bankruptcies and bank failures in the United States, beginning in New York on May 10, 1837.

The depression dragged on until 1843, becoming the most severe American depression until the 1870s. By 1843, average price for goods had fallen by 50 percent, and overall investment in the American economy had declined by almost 25 percent. Canal building dropped by 90 percent. Unemployment rose as high as 10 percent in 1838 and in some seaport cities it reached almost 20 percent. The emerging labor movement was completely crushed.

The election of 1840, held in the middle of the depression, created a political crisis for the Democrats in which, ironically, Jackson's great success proved to be a liability. Jackson had made the office of the presidency so strong that people genuinely believed the president could make a difference in maintaining prosperity. They did not understand the invisible forces of an international economy. What they could see, what was visible, was Jackson's destruction of the Bank of the U.S., and for that they held him and, more to the point, President Van Buren responsible. Van Buren's presidency is a bit of an enigma. The only two pieces of meaningful legislation he sponsored were a Ten Hour Day Act (limiting the work day to ten hours for federal employees) and the Independent Treasury Act (designed to remove the national government from involvement with all banks by placing the government's money in vaults).

The Whigs made the most of the Democrats' problems. The depression helped to discredit the Democrats and made Whig task for the elections of 1840 much easier. After the debacle of 1836, the Whigs decided to hold a national convention. There were three candidates at that convention: Henry Clay, the favorite; William Henry Harrison, the Whig candidate who had the broadest support in 1836; and Gen. Winfield Scott, a popular military figure. After the first ballot, Clay led with slightly less than 50 percent of the votes. Scott and Harrison split the rest. At that moment, someone gave a letter written by Scott to the Virginia delegation, which had supported him. The letter expressed some sympathy for abolition, causing the southern Whigs to drop their support of Scott and switch to Harrison, who now had enough votes to capture the nomination. Clay was furious. He said, "[M]y friends are not worth the shot it would take to kill them. They nominate me when I cannot win but refuse to do so when I cannot lose."

Harrison was a perfect candidate for the Whigs. They did not want a strong chief executive. Rather they wanted someone who would rubber stamp their congressional policies. Moreover, Harrison's military record, Virginia roots, and strong identification with the West made him a Whig version of Andrew Jackson. It is hard to imagine better conditions for the Whigs. Van Buren, by contrast, was in trouble. He was unable to distance himself from the depression, mostly because he lacked charisma and was seen as a manipulative party politician.

The election of 1840 was perhaps the first modern political campaign. The issues were ignored. Instead, it turned into an election of slogans and symbols. The most important symbol was provided by a democratic newspaper editor who wrote that Harrison would be happy to retire to a log cabin if he had a pension and an ample supply of hard cider. Thus, the Harrison campaign of 1840 became the Log Cabin Campaign. Harrison broke with tradition, and actively participated in the campaigning. The Whig strategy worked. They narrowly won the popular vote, but they won an overwhelming electoral victory, 234–60, and gained control of Congress. Popular interest in an American election had never been higher. More than 80 percent of eligible voters voted in 1840.

Just when it appeared that the Whig program, the American System of Henry Clay, was about to triumph, fate conspired to punish the Whigs. Clay had control of Congress and, he felt, control over Harrison. If Clay could not be president himself, perhaps this was the next best thing. Harrison would not cooperate, however, because he caught pneumonia, possibly from one of the longest inauguration speeches in American history conducted in terrible weather, and died one month later. Succeeding him was John Tyler of Virginia.

John Tyler had been placed on the ticket as an afterthought. The office was believed to be beneath the upper political crust. consequently, most vice presidents after Burr were political nobodies, with the exception of Calhoun. No president had ever died in office so the vice presidential nomination was not carefully considered. That turned out to be a mistake for the Whigs.

John Tyler was not a typical southern Whig. He opposed the urban commercial interests that dominated the Whig party and he opposed the Second Bank of the U.S. He had joined the Whig party out of disgust with Jackson's nationalism and out of an enthusiasm for states' rights. Since Tyler came to power on a fluke, Clay thought that Tyler should be only an acting president, a rubber stamp for whatever Congress sent to him. Clay was in for a surprise. Tyler betrayed the Whigs as president. He took it upon himself to block their economic programs. He vetoed two bills sponsored by Clay to reestablish the national bank and blocked major protective tariffs. Clay openly broke with Tyler in disgust and then, probably, orchestrated the resignation of all of Tyler's cabinet with the exception of Secretary of State Daniel Webster.

Because of the tension between Clay and Tyler, Whig success during Tyler's administration was limited. They only managed to repeal the independent treasury in 1841 and got a modest increase in tariffs in 1842. Probably the most important piece of legislation to come out of Tyler's administration was the Preemption Act of 1841, which gave American citizens and immigrants the right to stake a claim to 160 acres of land in the western territories and purchase it later at the standard price of $1.25 an acre, as long as they built a house on the land and made other improvements. This Preemption Act funneled more of the western lands into the hands of settlers instead of land speculators and, of course, increased the pace of westward expansion. Tyler, obviously, was not going to get the Whig nomination in 1844, which led him to change political parties and try, unsuccessfully, to secure the democratic nomination in 1844.

Items to Consider

Era of the Common Man, Whigs, Corrupt Bargain, Election of 1828, Henry Clay, John C. Calhoun, the American System, Daniel Webster, Peggy Eaton, Maysville Road Veto, nullification crisis

CHAPTER 14

An Empire of Reform: Urbanization, Reform Movements, and Abolition

When the United States declared its independence in 1776, the nation was overwhelmingly agrarian. Its more complicated financial needs were largely met by the former mother country, Great Britain, on which it depended for markets, credit, and manufactured goods. Over the next fifty years, however, the American financial, industrial, and commercial sectors expanded and matured. Between 1775 and 1825, a pre-capitalist infrastructure developed in the United States.

We should begin with a definition. What is *capitalism?* There are many ways to answer that question, but if we look at a narrow economic definition it would go something like this: Capitalism is a political economy in which the investment in and ownership of the means of production are primarily controlled by private citizens and corporations. Merchants had long dominated American economic life of the port cities. In the relative peace from 1775 to 1825, they prospered, especially between 1792 and 1815. These merchants were not a social class, though. There was a great deal of mobility among the merchant ranks, and it was possible to find yourself in it and out of it with shocking speed.

The United States experienced a period of remarkable growth in these decades. That growth is sometimes called the Market Revolution. Though the Market Revolution played a role in the countryside, especially with the development of the putting out system, the greatest and most visible changes in the economic sphere manifested themselves in the cities of the East. In 1820, only a handful of Americans lived in cities. Then between 1820 and 1860, American cities grew rapidly. By 1860, the urban population nearly tripled to almost 20 percent of the U.S. population. Among the fastest-growing areas were the Atlantic seaports of Boston, Philadelphia, New York, and Boston, and Gulf seaport of New Orleans, each of which grew at a rate of about 25 percent per decade. New York alone grew 64 percent between 1820 and 1830, and quickly became the home of American commerce.

Growth also occurred in personal wealth. Individual incomes doubled between 1800 and 1850, but the gap between rich and poor widened greatly. In the late 1840s, the top 1 percent of the U.S. population owned 40 percent of the nation's wealth, while the bottom one-third of the population owned nearly nothing. The poor, often immigrant families from Ireland or Germany, worked in unskilled jobs with next to no financial security. They lived in poor housing, moving constantly in search of better conditions or wages. The cities they lived in were unsanitary: There were no city water supplies, garbage collection, or even sewers. People often drank from wells contaminated by run-off sewer water. Every American city, thus, was plagued by epidemic diseases related to sanitation, such as yellow fever, cholera, and typhus. Though some basic urban sanitation programs were developed, they were almost all fee based, and few in the poor parts of town could afford to pay for them.

Differences in wealth distribution led to communities laid out on a class basis. The middle class began to escape the cities to suburbs in the 1850s, leaving neighborhoods that quickly became slums. The worst nineteenth-century slum in New York was the infamous Five Points—populated mostly by free blacks and recent immigrants. As popularized in the movie *Gangs of New York*, the neighborhood was plagued by gangs and thieves of all sorts.

Within the cities, working-class leisure reflected the growing rough nature of life in the neighborhoods. Taverns were plagued by drunken brawls. As the trades became populated with young toughs, they, too, were often notorious for starting fights in bars. Theaters, as well, were noted not only for their theatrical presentations but for their violence and vice. Mostly attended by men, save for the few prostitutes who waited in and near them, theater riots by young, poor, often intoxicated patrons against unpopular actors were common. By the 1830s, most middle and upper class men no longer attended downtown theaters, instead going to suburban locations where they could bring their wives and children. Other popular forms of working-class culture included the blackface minstrel shows, where dances, skits, and anti-black comedy were the order of the day. Among the most popular characters were Zip Coon (an irresponsible free black) and the now-famous Jim Crow. Such shows represented not only racism, but probably, a desire for a return to the pre-industrial world. Another increasingly common urban feature were the so-called penny papers, including the *New York Sun*. These tabloids resembled the *National Enquirer* of our day, but focused on sex, violence, and political scandals rather than alien abductions and Bigfoot babies.

Such a common and increasingly crass popular culture led the middle class to concerns for civic order. As the urban crowds grew more violent and difficult to control, cities began to create professional police forces. By 1845, New York City had a permanent police force created primarily to keep the poor in line. Traditionally, the middle classes had wanted nothing to do with an organized police force, but as the "dangerous classes" grew more dangerous, concerns for civil liberties were replaced with the desire for order.

The Changing Nature of Work

With the commercial explosion and the rise of banks came the growth of domestic manufacturing. Traditionally, artisans had made furniture, tools, wagons, shoes, and dozens of other items. In the New England and Mid Atlantic states, artisans had made a comfortable living exchanging what they made for other items. As the 1790s wore on, those domestically manufactured goods began to increase in number and the market area increased. Cordwainers in Boston were selling shoes throughout New England. Over time, these artisans began to create their own version of the European *putting-out system*. Merchant-capitalists recruited and organized households in rural areas to manufacture specific goods. They paid the households to increase their output and hired young men to market the products throughout the country. The earliest source of this putting-out system was in the shoe and boot trade. In the 1780s, merchants and master craftsmen in Lynn, Massachusetts began buying large quantities of leather, thread, and tools and soon put thousands of families in the New England countryside to work. Farm women and children stitched together the thin leather and canvas uppers of the shoes, and the half-finished shoes were taken by wagon to Lynn for assembly by journeymen shoemakers.

What is interesting about this explosion is that their success did not stem from developments in technology but from efficient organization. The first American Industrial Revolution was dependent on the organization of labor, and had nothing to do with technology. The technology being used was pre-industrial handicraft technology. The use of power-driven machines—the product of the Industrial Revolution in Britain—came only slowly to America, beginning first in the textile industry. In the 1780s, merchants built hundreds of small mills along the creeks and rivers of New England and the Mid Atlantic states. They installed water-powered machines and hired workers to comb wool—and later cotton—into long strands of thread. For several decades the next step in the system was accomplished under the *outwork system*. Farm women and children spun the strands into yarn, receiving wages for their work, while men, usually in other households, wove the yard into cloth.

With so many people beginning to work in the piece industry, American gradually saw a cash system replace the barter-exchange system of the earlier agricultural society. As farm families joined the outwork system, they stopped producing all their own food and making their own clothing. Instead of bartering their surplus crops for household necessities, they supplied merchants with specialized goods in return for cash or credit at the local store. However, the emergence of the cash economy had its drawbacks. Rural people had to work longer and harder, making shoes or hats during the winter as well as planting, weeding, and harvesting crops when that time of year rolled around. In a very real way, they lost some of their independence. They became dependent on the part-time wages instead of working for themselves. So at the same time it made workers more productive; it also made them less self-sufficient.

The loss of self-sufficiency and identity was one of the major byproducts of the commercial changes taking place. America's growing democracy also led to a decline of the elite in urban politics. By 1845, most of the elite leadership in New York politics had been replaced by professional politicians who were more responsive to working-class needs. Among the most vocal of these new working-class political elements were the labor unions. In the past, work in the United States—skilled labor that is—had been divided along the lines of craft associations or guilds. By the 1830s, the financial status of skilled workers had declined sharply. The older system of artisans was gradually giving way to unskilled workers, and increasingly, unskilled workers working with machines. Skilled workers were expensive. Shop owners sought ways to cut them out of the business and replace them with unskilled labor. The first developments along those lines was the putting-out system, where work was sent out to the countryside. The unskilled workers, targeted as they were, proved easy targets for manipulation. Soon they were protesting for better wages, hours, and working conditions. As worker protests spilled into the streets, increasingly a working-class identity was being fashioned that would fuel the demand for unions.

The first American labor unions grew out of the old craft and guild systems. They organized around their individuals trades—carpenters, shipbuilders, etc. The skilled shoemakers in Philadelphia were representative. In 1794, they formed the Federated Society of Journeymen Cordwainers (the name comes from the cordovan leather they worked) to press for a uniform wage for their members. The shoemakers struck against wage cuts and had some success until 1806, when leaders were convicted of criminal conspiracy under the common law in *Commonwealth v. Pullis*. It was illegal, the court said, to form a union. The decision in Massachusetts hampered the union movement for some years. As the Industrial Revolution developed in the 1820s and 1830s, the artisans began to grow conscious of themselves as a class. They had always seen themselves as Americans, and in a certain sense elite Americans. They played a big role in the American Revolution, especially in Boston and Philadelphia. Some felt they were the chosen people of the nation, but the economic changes began to undermine their livelihoods.

Changes in working hours, wages, and conditions brought about by the Industrial Revolution made artisans realize they had distinct interests as a class. The traditional workday, for example, went from sunrise to sunset, but nobody really worked all those hours. As economic conditions changed, their employers began to expect their laborers to work every hour they were being paid. As the demand for labor increased, so did a worker's power. In 1825, about six hundred carpenters in Boston struck against their employers and demanded a ten-hour work day; from 8 a.m. to 6 p.m. This was the first strike in what became known as the Ten Hour Work Day Movement. It failed, of course, but two years later a group of journeymen carpenters in Philadelphia did not. After a brief strike, several hundred workers there won a ten-hour day.

The Ten Hour Work Day Movement succeeded in Philadelphia because the Mechanics' Union of Trade Associations (MUTA) recruited the members of most of the trades of Philadelphia, forming the first effective citywide organization of wage earners in America. The members of the Building Trades in Philadelphia went even further. They formed the Working Men's Party in 1828, a political party. Unfortunately, it fell apart because members could not concentrate on wages, hours, and working conditions. Instead, the party's platform included things like equal taxation, the abolition of banks, universal education, and separate cemeteries for working men. They did hold enough seats for a time to control Philadelphia's city council, and they played an important role in the decision to expand public schools in Philadelphia and the decision by the Pennsylvania Legislature to authorize free, universal, tax-supported schools in 1834.

Many laborers did all right financially in the late 1820s early 1830s, but artisans were increasingly dissatisfied. They faced declining incomes, unemployment, and a loss of status as machines took over their jobs. Workers like hatters, printers, and weavers were among the most threatened and they began to band together to form craft unions. They advanced what is known as the Labor Theory of Value, arguing that the price of a product should reflect the labor required to make it and that most of the income from its sale should go to the person who made it. They condemned the accumulation of wealth by capitalists who were, as they saw it, trying to reduce them to slavery. These new unions quickly turned to politics. Union members supported the Jacksonian movement, which, in turn, energized the workers' political efforts. They joined the Democratic Party, becoming that party's most radical element. They agitated against banks, demanded universal white male suffrage, and abolition of imprisonment for debt. They even wanted to destroy monopolies.

As the 1830s wore on though, laborers turned their attention from politics and back to economics. They formed city-wide unions, sometimes even crossing craft lines. In 1834, federations from Boston to Philadelphia joined to form the National Trades Union, the first national union of different trades. By 1836, the National Trades Union included federations from as far south as Washington, D.C., and as far west as Cincinnati. In the early 1830s, the federations came together in a series of strikes against employers for ten-hour work days. Philadelphia, once again, was the scene of the most dramatic victories. In 1835, the Philadelphia city council set ten hours as the standard work day and the following year President Jackson established a ten-hour work day at the Philadelphia Naval Yard. After winning such concessions, workers turned their attentions to increasing wages and again won great victories. In 1836 and 1837, there were more than fifty strikes by unions. They succeeded in part because of organization and financial support from other unions. For example, when the journeymen bookbinders in Philadelphia struck for higher wages in 1836, thirty-seven trade unions from New York to Washington, D.C. provided financial support that enabled workers to hold out for over two months.

The success of the artisans inspired yet another group of workers—the factory laborers. They were a new group without a history of organization or any craft identity. They were also poorer than the artisans. Nevertheless, they managed to resist the demand that they do more work for less pay. There were about 20,000 cotton mill workers in the U.S. by 1830; with most being women or girls. To protest pay cuts or work rules, many of them engaged in sporadic strikes. In 1828, women mill workers in Dover, New Hampshire struck against two new rules—one that levied fines for being late and another that said only faithful workers would be given discharge papers. Sadly, they lost. Then in 1834, some 2,000 women in Lowell, Massachusetts struck. But, again, they lost. The employers fired the leaders and the rest went back to work. Finally in 1836, the Lowell mill women were able to successfully force the owners to reduce an increase in the boarding house rate.

Employers always resisted the demands of workers but rarely had they acted together to combat labor organization. In response to the wave of strikes in 1836 and 1837, however, employers all over the country mobilized against the unions. Among the most effective anti-union tactics they developed was the blacklist. For example, in 1836, employers in New York City agreed not to hire workers belonging to the Union Trade Society of Journeymen Tailors and they circulated a list—a blacklist—of its members. Employers also used the court system. They filed lawsuits to open up *closed shops*— agreements by which employers promised to hire only union workers. During the 1830s, employers sued the carpet weavers union in Thompsonville, Connecticut, the shoemakers union in Geneva and Hudson, New York, the tailors union in New York City, the plasterers union in Philadelphia, and the union of journeymen Cordwainers in Boston—arguing that the closed shop violated common law. In several of these cases, the employers won, slowly beginning to break the power of the first union movement.

Unfortunately for the labor movement, the unions collapsed dramatically with the Panic of 1837, a stunning defeat from which the labor movement did not recover until after the Civil War. There is a great deal of debate over the nature and character of the early union movement. Traditional labor history shows it as a utopian response to the changes in the industrial order. They point out that the labor movement in the 1830s excluded far more than it represented, such as African-Americans and women. Others see it as the training ground for early unions, and try to bridge the gap between antebellum and the postwar unionism of the 1870s. Regardless of how one views it, the first labor movement was an important step and marked a unique response to the growing urbanization and industrialization of America, but workers were not alone in their uncertainty toward the rapid changes affecting America.

The Age of Reform

Rising in response to many of the challenges produced by industrial society, the reform movements of the 1840s sought a way to deal with the dislocations caused by the market and industrial revolutions. One typical response for the American middle class was to join community-based associations and groups that sought to reform what they believed to be fundamental ills in American society. The reform movements of the 1840s should be seen as a reflection of the duality of American character: an impulse to help ones self, yet also one to help others. Often, those two basic elements of American identity conflict, and prove impossible to reconcile.

Crucial to understanding the forces behind reform, was the rise of American evangelical religion in the nineteenth century. Evangelicals were those who took it upon themselves not only to better their own lives, but also the lives of those around them. Among religious folks of the 1840s, there was a general impulse toward perfectionism, a doctrine outlined by the revivalist Charles G. Finney, who claimed it was possible that all mankind could live under God's plan and be "as perfect as God" Himself. It was a hopeful, demanding, and challenging outlook for America, and unrealistic. The evangelicalism produced by the Second Great Awakening of the 1830s, tailored well the demands of self-discipline and achievement among the middle and business classes, who quickly became the heart of the movement.

Women and Families

In combination with the market revolution, evangelicalism encouraged middle-class women to believe their world was private, not public. It stressed that their duties were to raise good children; trained in character to meet the demands of the new business and religious world. Marriages were changing, though, and moved away from the older financial and economic arrangements to a compassionate marriage wherein love became the deciding factor in marriage considerations. Since children were no longer needed for the middle class (economically), couples had fewer children. By 1900 the number of children born to American women fell to only four, when it had been seven in 1800. The reason for the drop in children was the increased employment of new birth control methods, including *coitus interruptus*, condoms, and the rhythm method. But shockingly, abstinence or near abstinence began to characterize the sexual relationships of middle class families (and as working class families imitated the middle class in order to win respectability, their numbers of children fell off, as well). Some medical and sexual manuals of the period suggested that married couples end their sex lives after their children were born. And finally, when birth control failed, married women often had surgical abortions, which were widely advertised after 1830. Some estimates suggests that 25 percent of pregnancies between 1840 and 1860 were aborted (about the same number as 1990). Surgical abortions were used as a form of birth control until it was banned after 1860, though illegal abortions remained very high.

Social Control

Reflecting the middle class' belief in restraint, a wave of moral reforms swept America in the 1840s and 1850s. Given their general religious background, most of these reformers believed in the basic goodness of society and its institutions. They believed that, with effort, crime could be done away with, and that even the problems of poverty could be addressed. Only the proper environment was necessary; so insane asylums were built in rural areas away from the noise and stress of the cities, and prisoners were isolated from each other in new penitentiaries. Dorothea Dix shocked the state of Massachusetts in 1843 when she told the state legislature of the crimes being committed against the insane, who were commonly chained together naked, beaten, or caged. Nineteenth-century prisons were constructed not only to punish, but to reform. Since the belief that environment dictated action was common, prisoners were usually isolated from each other. "Sing Sing" in New York was constructed along this model, and quickly proved to be a place where order, discipline, and isolation were the chief characteristics.

It was a short step, however, to go from social reform to social control, and many of these efforts spiraled out of hand. The great Protestant evangelical sentiment of the reform movement led to anti-Catholicism, anti-immigration, and Nativism. Others tried to establish a moral government. Thus, they tried to outlaw prostitution, alcohol consumption, and even enforce prohibitions against work on the Sabbath. Such efforts underscored the basic secularity of American civilization, however. Immigrants refused to follow the reformers call for Sabbath temperance, and were especially angered when reformers tried to close down some of the most important elements of working-class entertainment: bars and taverns.

Given that they were isolated, increasingly, from the public and political world, women often took positions of leadership among the reform efforts. They raised most of the funds, dispatched missionaries around the world, and established schools (increasingly stocked by women teachers). The largest reform effort of the period was the American Society for the Promotion of Temperance, founded in 1826, which had more than 200,000 members by 1835. Comprised mostly of evangelicals, the tracts they distributed described the horrors and dangers of alcohol abuse. Excessive drinking was a national problem, and one mostly centered on men. Respectable women did not drink, at least in public. Men usually drank hard liquor in large quantities and were especially given to drunkenness—twice as much then as today. There were also elements of social control in the temperance movement. The reformers tended to be middle-class women from Anglo backgrounds, often Whig by politics. Their targets were often German and Irish immigrants, who were Catholics and often favored Democrat politicians. Although the Temperance movement never secured full prohibition as they wanted, so successful were they that alcohol consumption was reduced by half by the mid 1840s.

Moral Reforms

Among the evils targeted by the reformers was prostitution. Though not common in the West, prostitution was a major enterprise in the larger urban areas like Boston, Philadelphia, and New York, and other towns of the East. Reformers usually tried to entice women out of the profession by offering them temporary shelter, money, and religion. But because assistance came with an imposition of spirituality, the success rate was not high. When that failed, reformers usually offered prostitutes low-paying domestic work, which again was unsuccessful. Nevertheless, they continued to try to end the profession.

Among the most famous of the antiprostitution leagues was the Female Moral Reform Society created in New York in 1834. By 1840, it had more than five hundred branches nationwide. What is surprising about its success is that middle-class Victorian women admitted the existence of prostitution, and having spent time with prostitutes, they learned that this was more often an economic ill rather than a moral one. To fight the need for women to sell themselves as prostitutes, reformers rounded up jobs and child care for former prostitutes. They also went after the clients, often printing the names in newspapers of men who frequented prostitutes and demanding criminal charges not only against prostitutes, but those who solicited them.

Escape for the Ills of the World

Some reformers looked beyond what they considered superficial social ills and formed utopian communities to isolate themselves from the general wickedness of the world. In part, these developments can be traced to the fervour of evangelical religion in New England. So strong was the moral reform sentiment in western New York, for example, that it became known as the "burned over district," the home to most of America's reform movements in the nineteenth century, including abolition, women's rights, and the Mormon religion. Hard times and evangelical religion produced an apocalyptic world view among some in western New York. The Millerites (founded by William Miller) emerged here. They believed that the second coming of Christ would happen on October 22, 1843, so they sell everything they owned and waited. When the prophecy failed most left the movement, but a few remained. "The Great Disappointment" (as it began to be called) spawned two religious groups, the Seventh-Day Adventists (who argued that Jesus returned in spirit on that day, but not the flesh) and the Jehovah's Witnesses (who went on to set nine new dates between 1874 and 1984).

Another interesting group was the Shakers, founded by Anne Lee in 1774. Coming out of the Quaker movement, the Shakers called for the end of the traditional family to be replaced with a spiritual one of fellowship and celibacy. By 1830, there were twenty Shaker communities with a total population of about 6,000. While the Shakers disavowed sexuality, the Oneida Community embraced a radical form of sexual freedom. Created by John Humphrey Noyes in 1848, the Oneida Community of New York resembled the Shaker family structure. But within that family, members practiced "complex marriage," a system of group sexual activity. Technically each man was married to each woman—and sexual interaction was highly regulated. But the number of childbirths remained small, because Oneida members also practiced male continence in order to discourage unwanted pregnancies. Noyes was highly criticized outside the movement, as you can imagine, not only for "complex marriage," but also for the doctrine of "Ascending Fellowship," in which older members of the church selected virgins (male and female) for initiation into the fellowship. This type of free-love socialism remained small in numbers, but other socialist communities tried to create utopian societies. The Scottish industrialist Robert Owen created a manufacturing community at New Harmony, Indiana in 1825. Other organizations followed the "phalanx" model of Charles Fourier, who believed that communities should be divided into 1,620 members, with each person doing the job that best fit his personality.

The most successful of the religiously inspired reform movements that came out of New York was Mormonism, a new religion that blended a radical form of Protestantism with communitarianism. Mormonism required a close, tight-knit community that worked hard for their mutual benefit. Sadly, their secrecy and prosperity quickly antagonized their neighbors (as did a number of their practices), and Mormons were forced to flee New York to Ohio and, eventually, to Illinois where they set up a model community in 1839. Then the leader of the movement, Joseph Smith, created a new doctrine that stressed polygamy. Outrage against Smith and the Mormon's eventually led to Smith's murder in 1844. In 1846 the Mormon community fled west to Mexican Utah. Unfortunately for them, the Mexican war brought them back into the United States, and western land and gold rushes ended the isolation they sought.

The Transcendentalists

Abolitionism did not have to take a strong hold in the North and the events that led to the Civil War need not have happened. But it did, obviously. The question is, How? Among the reformers who most vigorously championed freedom were the Transcendentalists, a group of intellectuals who emerged in New England in the very heart of the Industrial Revolution. At first, the Transcendentalists only wanted to loosen the stringent restrictions imposed on them by the Puritan religion, but later they would expand their protest to include industrial society. Many of the Transcendentalists would later withdraw to utopian communities where they would offer examples of an alternative America.

The first Transcendentalists were young men—often Unitarian ministers—generally from wealthy New England families. They were romantics—people who believed that beyond the concrete world of the senses was another ideal order of realty that transcended, or went beyond, the usual ways by which people know the world. According to the Transcendentalists, if an individual could somehow harness this greater truth, they could travel past the limits of ordinary experience and gain mystical knowledge about the nature of life, the universe, and everything. The intellectual leader of all the Transcendentalists, and the most popular of all of them was a Unitarian minister named Ralph Waldo Emerson. Emerson resigned his Boston pulpit in 1832 at the age of 29, after a crisis of conscience led him to choose individual moral insight over organized religion.

Emerson moved to Concord, Massachusetts and turned to writing essays and lecturing, but mostly he lived off the wealth of his first wife. His message centered on the radical freedom of the individual. People, Emerson believed, were trapped by tradition. They were trapped by their religion. They were trapped by political traditions. They were trapped by social structure. These ideas that caged humanity really were not their ideas, Emerson said. Rather they were ideas from the past—ideas forced on them by their fathers and mothers. America needed to break free, he said, of these old ideas; the boundaries of custom and tradition. The only way to do that, Emerson believed, was for each person to discover their relation to nature. He celebrated individuality, self-reliance, dissent, and nonconformity as the only means by which a person could be free to discover their true selves. But the best way to do this, he believed, was to go back to nature, to ponder life amid the trees and the rocks.

Emerson's message reached hundreds of thousands of people, mostly through his lectures, but Emerson's radicalism went far beyond middle class tradition. He emphasized nature as the only true route to knowing God—a route that stood outside of Christian doctrine. He was also disturbed by consumerism and the quest for factory-made goods. "Things," he wrote, "are in the saddle and they ride mankind." Emerson's genius lay in his capacity to translate radical but vague ideas into examples that made sense to ordinary middle-class Americans. As a result, he soft-peddled his more radical ideas on the lecture circuit; instead of saying nature was the only true way to God, he would say things like God, who was presumed to be everywhere, should be visible even in the most routine signs of everyday life; like a tree or railroad crossing. Emerson hoped to expand the influence of his movement by changing the nature of American literature. In 1837, he delivered an address at Harvard entitled *The American Scholar*. Emerson intended for his *American Scholar* address to act as an American literary Declaration of Independence from the style of European writing. He urged American writers to celebrate democracy and individual freedom and to find inspiration in the "familiar, the low … the milk in the pan; the glance of the eye, the form and gait of the body."

His call to arms was immediately met. Among those who responded to Emerson's call was Walt Whitman. Whitman's *Leaves of Grass* was a radical attack on the older American-British style. At the center of *Leaves* is the poet himself. "I Walt," he writes, "I celebrate myself and sing myself." Whitman was celebrating democracy as well as himself. For both Emerson and Thoreau, the individual had a divine spark. For Whitman, however, the individual had become the divine spark. The individual was the essence of life and truth. Do not think that Whitman, Thoreau, and Emerson were completely optimistic. They were not. Whitman wrote of human suffering with as much passion as he wrote of everything else. Thoreau could be gloomy. But for the most part, that pessimism was hidden by the promise of individual freedom.

Emerson's influence also reached two great American novelists, Nathaniel Hawthorne and Herman Melville. Hawthorne, who for a time was a member of Emerson's circle, and Melville both had more pessimistic visions. They dwelt on the vanity, corruption, and excesses of individualism rather than on its positive potential. Both acted as warnings against unrestrained individualism. While they embraced the idea of freedom, they believed freedom had to accept an inner discipline. Hawthorne's most brilliant exploration of the excessiveness of individuals appeared in his novel *The Scarlet Letter* (1850). The two main characters, Hester Prynne and Arthur Dimmesdale, challenge their seventeenth-century New England community in the most blatant way—by committing adultery, producing a child, and refusing to bend to the community's condemnation. The result of their assertion of individual freedom against communal discipline is not exaltation but tragedy. Wrecked by guilt and unable to confess, Dimmesdale dies in anguish. Prynne learned from her experience that the way to a truly virtuous life can be only be had by a person who is willing to do good within the social order.

Melville, strongly influenced by Hawthorne, explored the same problem in even more extreme and tragic terms and emerged as a scathing critic of Transcendentalism. He made his most powerful statement in *Moby Dick* (1851). The novel begins as a whaling captain, Ahab, embarks on an obsessive hunt for a white whale, Moby Dick, that severed his leg during an earlier whaling expedition. Ahab is a version of Emerson's liberated individual with an intuitive grasp of hidden meanings in nature. He believes that the whale is pure, demonic evil. Ahab's form of self-reliance is to hunt down the whale, no matter what the cost. The trouble, as Melville writes, is that Ahab can hunt the whale only in a social way; i.e., with others. Ahab's transcendental adventure subverts the legitimate purposes of the whaling voyage. As a result, not only Ahab but the crew dies; only one person, Ishmael, is left to tell the tale. Moby Dick was a commercial disaster. No one bought it. They did not want to hear a dark tale of individualism gone mad. They wanted to hear about the triumph of individualism—of personal freedom. Logically, Americans would ignore Edgar Alan Poe as well. A southern-born admirer of Hawthorne, Poe created *The Raven* in 1845 and other dark poems and short stories in which he questioned individuality. Poe could not find a middle-class audience. Emily Dickinson, another poet whose work expressed doubts about individualism, did not even try to find readers. During the 1850s, she kept private the poetry she had begun to write in isolation in Amherst, Massachusetts. While many of the Transcendentalists struggled to be heard, their message would be absorbed into American society and come to affect change in the questioning of human bondage and America's institution of slavery.

The Anti-Slavery Movement Through 1850

By 1820 opponents of slavery had made headway. They had not yet won over the middle class, but they still had made important gains. Congress outlawed the importation of slaves in 1808, the earliest possible date permitted by the Constitution. Most northern states abolished slavery by that time, and the Missouri Compromise prohibited slavery in most of the Louisiana Purchase. Yet the most vocal of opponents wanted to go much further. After 1840, the antislavery forces took two steps to achieve their goal of ending the institution. First, they adopted a specific political program and began to push it into national politics. Second, they tried to keep slavery from expanding into the new territories.

There were three approaches to ending slavery that were contemplated between 1820 and 1844.

1. The gradual emancipation of the nation's slaves—1.5 million of them in 1820—and return the freed slaves to Africa with payment to their owners
2. Emancipation through slave flight or rebellion
3. Emancipation through direct appeals to the conscience of slave owners

The first solution to end slavery in the period between 1820 and 1850 was the recolonization movement. Those who supported the first plan created the American Colonization Society in 1817. People who supported it seemed to have their own reasons for supporting recolonization. For the most part, the American Colonization Society was led by prominent people from the Upper South who wanted to eradicate slavery to make sure the south developed along the lines of the North—as an industrial power. Members of the society from the North, however, were mostly interested in getting free blacks out of the North because of prejudice and anger over job competition; the same people in the North had also tried to keep free blacks from voting. By 1860, only five northern states allowed free blacks to vote (Maine, Massachusetts, New Hampshire, Rhode Island, and Vermont). Of course those places had almost no African-Americans. Southern supporters of recolonization believed that African-Americans lacked the capacity to succeed in white American society. Recolonization, they thought, was necessary to prevent a destructive race war, which they felt had to occur at some point in America's future since slaves made up almost 40 percent of the southern population in 1820. Henry Clay, for example, wanted full emancipation, but declared that emancipation without recolonization would be followed by a race war. By 1830, the American Colonization Society had raised enough money to transport 1,400 African-American's to the west coast of African, to a colony society they called Liberia. The colonists who arrived in Liberia declared it an independent republic in 1847 and adopted a Constitution much liked that of the U.S. Most free blacks in America, however, rejected recolonization. They loved America, and been integral in its creation, so why would they leave?

Instead, Northern free blacks were more inclined to believe that it would take a slave rebellion to free southern slaves and, thus, were the main supporters of the second method for ending slavery. The Constitution mentioned slavery in three places, and it was widely believed that Congress could not abolish slavery; only the individual states could do that. William Lloyd Garrison, for example, denounced the Constitution as a deal with the devil and would, now and then, burn it before he spoke at rallies—a dangerous thing to do. In 1827, John Russwurm and Samuel Cornish began publishing the first African American newspaper, *Freedom's Journal*, in New York. A Boston correspondent for that newspaper, a man by the name of David Walker, who was a free black from North Carolina and supported himself selling secondhand clothes, published a stirring pamphlet called *An Appeal … to the Colored Citizens of the United States*. Arguably the most radical of all antislavery documents, it caused a stir when it was published in September 1829 with its call for slaves to revolt against their masters. In essence, Walker's *Appeal* justified slave rebellions, claiming that slavery was the greatest of all moral crimes. Within a year, his *Appeal* had gone through three printings and was actively circulated in the South. In 1830, Walker called a national convention of Abolitionists to Philadelphia where they condemned slavery and colonization and demanded abolition. Walker died under mysterious circumstances later that year but thereafter the convention became a regular event. The first major violence was Nat Turner's slave revolt in 1831.

The radical alternative, race war and slave rebellion, frightened some Abolitionists to the point that they chose the third path to end slavery: Evangelical Abolitionism. Many young New England evangelical ministers tried to appeal to the Christian conscience of the slave owners for immediate emancipation. The issue, as they saw it, was absolute. Slave owners and their supporters were sinning by depriving slaves of their God-given right to be free, moral agents. If they did not repent, the master faced revolution in this world and eternal damnation in the next.

The two most influential leaders in the antislavery movement during the 1830s were William Lloyd Garrison and Theodore Dwight Weld. Garrison was an early antislavery advocate and was less influenced by religion than Weld. A Massachusetts-born printer, Garrison began an antislavery newspaper with Benjamin Lundy, a Quaker, in the 1820s. In 1830, Garrison went to jail, convicted of libeling a New England merchant engaged in the slave trade. After seven weeks, he was released, largely because of Lundy's intervention. Garrison later split with Lundy and founded his own antislavery paper, *The Liberator*, in Boston in 1831. In 1832, he helped to create the New England Anti-Slavery Society. *The Liberator* was not moderate. It demanded immediate emancipation without reimbursement to slaveholders. He also condemned the American Colonization Society for trying to subvert free blacks in the North. Garrison would cut no corners. He criticized ministers and even the authenticity of the Bible whenever he felt slavery was sanctioned. His style attracted a large number of followers, and he became a cultural hero on the scale of Emerson. Garrison, like the Transcendentalists, framed the argument in his own personal terms. In the first edition of his *Liberator* he declared: "I will be harsh as truth and as uncompromising as justice … I am in earnest—I will not equivocate—I will not excuse—I will not retreat a single inch—And I will be Heard."

In contrast to Garrison, Theodore Dwight Weld came to abolitionism from the religious revivals of the 1830s and he was more restrained. He worked in the churches of the Burned-Over District, where he preached the moral responsibility of all Americans for slavery. Weld married Angelina Grimke in 1838—Angelina and her sister Sarah were two South Carolinian Abolitionists and women's rights advocates. In 1839 Weld published a massive book, *American Slavery as it is: Testimony of a Thousand Witnesses*. To write the book, he researched some 20,000 editions of southern newspapers for evidence for the harsh nature of slavery in order to present the question of slavery's morality to the northern population. One of the first-hand accounts he cited was Angelina Grimke who recalled an incident from her childhood in Charleston. She told of a treadmill that Charleston slave owners used for punishment, and of a prominent white woman who sent her slaves there regularly. "One poor girl," she wrote, "who she sent there to be flogged, and who was according[ly] stripped naked and whipped, showed me the deep gashes on her back—I might have laid my whole finger in them—large pieces of flesh had actually been cut out by the torturing lash."

Weld's book sold over 100,000 copies during its first year alone. In 1833, Weld, Garrison, and others met in Philadelphia to establish the American Anti-Slavery Society. Led by this society, Abolitionists gradually developed two approaches: one for the general public and one for the politicians. First, they tried to create a moral climate so intense that slave owners would have to accept programs of abolition. They used revivals, public meetings, and importantly newspapers to get the American population involved. In 1834 they were able to distribute more than 100,000 pieces of mail and in 1835, more than 1 million. Most dramatic was the "great postal campaigning" begun in 1835, which flooded the nation, including the South, with Aabolitionist pamphlets. In July 1835 alone, Abolitionists mailed 175,000 tracts through the New York City post office. Their second strategy was to mobilize public pressure on Congress. In 1835, the Society encouraged local chapters and members to bombard Congress with petitions for specific action: the abolition of slavery in Washington, D.C., the abolition of the domestic slave trade, the removal of the three-fifths clause from the U.S. Constitution, the outlawing of new slave states, etc. By 1838, nearly 500,000 signed petitions arrived in Washington. Congress was so inundated with petitions that Northerners and Southerners joined together to end the onslaught, instituting the Gag Rule, which tabled the issue, keeping all abolitionist petitions from being addressed.

It was these activities that drew increasing numbers of middle-class men and women to the abolitionist movement. During the 1830s, local abolitionist societies grew quickly from about 200 in 1835 to more than 500 in 1836 and nearly 2,000 by 1850. Their members numbered nearly 200,000. It was at that point that the traditional antislavery base of free blacks, Quakers, and evangelical Christians expanded to include many of the Transcendentalists, as well. Emerson spoke out against slavery and, as the Civil War grew closer, he even condoned abolitionist violence. Thoreau protested as well against the Mexican War, which was seen as an exercise to extend slavery, and against the institution of slavery by refusing to pay his taxes and submitting to arrest. He would later publish pamphlets calling for civil disobedience to purge the nation of the crime of slavery.

In the South, there as a great deal of hostility toward abolition. Nat Turner's rebellion, the abolition of slavery by the British in the West Indies, and the beginnings of Garrison's *Liberator* sparked an intense southern effort to defend the institution of slavery. The immediate response was to toughen the slave codes. The codes were various state laws that regulated the institution of slavery. Southern states took further steps to limit the movement of slaves and prohibited anyone from teaching slaves to read, so that they would be unable to read abolitionist literature. Southern legislatures also banned abolitionism and passed resolutions demanding that northern states take similar actions. The Georgia Legislature even offered a $5,000 reward to anyone who would kidnap Garrison and bring him to the South to be tried for inciting slave rebellion. A similar award was offered for the murder of David Walker.

There was increasing public pressure on Abolitionists. Anti-abolition mobs terrorized Abolitionists at their rallies in the North. They even attacked U.S. post offices for delivering Abolitionist mail from the North. Southern leaders—politicians, newspaper editors, and clergymen—developed a new intellectual defense of the institution of slavery. It was new in that they moved beyond the defense of slavery as a necessary evil to a defense of slavery as a positive good. They argued that slavery protected slaves against the evils of the industrial system; that it promoted "harmony" in relations between the races; that it provided for a more efficient and orderly labor supply; and that it had a basis in the Bible. That last argument was crucial to the southern defenders who needed a rationalization for enslaving an entire population that had become Christian. Defenders of slavery, like Thornton Stringfellow, a Baptist minister from Virginia, claimed that St. Paul had recognized Christian churches that contained both masters and servants. Stringfellow cited Paul's words: "Servants, obey your masters." As this argument developed, it was clear that only one person in the South deserved freedom, the planter. He was seen as being surrounded by people who were incompetent and incapable of dealing with their problems. The planter was burdened with the task of taking care of those people.

Surprisingly, those southern arguments won a wide following in the North. Some wealthy Northerners sympathized with the South's appeal for unity among social elites and feared that the abolitionist attack on the ownership of slaves as property could turn into a general assault on property rights. The tactics of the Abolitionists troubled many northern elites. They were worried about their own social status. The Abolitionists were too radical, too democratic. Northern wage-earners did not support abolition either, fearing that free blacks would take their jobs.

Opponents of slavery could be as violent as those in the South. Mobs, sometimes led by influential people, intimidated free blacks and Abolitionists. Mobs also disrupted abolitionist meetings and routinely destroyed abolitionist printing presses. Fifteen hundred New Yorkers stormed a church in 1833 in search of William Lloyd Garrison and Arthur Tappan. The next year prominent New Yorkers cheered as a mob of workers set fire to the home of abolitionist Lewis Tappan. That same year, a white mob swept thorough Philadelphia African-American neighborhoods, clubbing and stoning residents while destroying homes and churches. In 1835, William Lloyd Garrison was dragged through the streets of Boston. In 1837 a mob shot and killed abolitionist editor Elija P. Lovejoy in Alton, Illinois.

The reaction against abolitionism was so strong that Andrew Jackson privately approved of a policy that South Carolina had adopted to censure the mail service. He publicly called on northern states in 1835 to suppress abolitionism and asked Congress to restrict the use of the mails by abolitionist groups. Congress did not give him that, but in 1836 the House of Representatives did adopt the Gag Rule. Under the rule, which remained in force until 1844, antislavery petitions were autocratically tabled when they were received so they could not be discussed in the House.

The violent reaction stunned antislavery advocates. It convinced some Abolitionists that the only way to do away with slavery was not through the three approaches already mentioned, but through politics. The more radical elements slowly began to turn to and recruit the moderates; people who were more willing than someone like Garrison to work within the political system, though Garrison remained a radical at heart.

As a result, the Abolitionists started taking their issue to politics. The platform of the American Anti-Slavery Society included political equality for women, pacifism, abolition of prisons and asylums, and in 1843, the expulsion of the slave states from the Union. As Garrison's faction became more radical, the antislavery movement split into several factions. Most of the leaders who split with Garrison began in 1840 to emphasize politics as a way to eliminate slavery. They created the Liberty Party and nominated James G. Birney as their presidential candidate in both 1840 and in 1844. Birney himself was a former slave owner who had lived in Alabama and Kentucky. Educated at Princeton, he came under the influence of Weld and converted to abolitionism. Birney was more moderate than Garrison and was willing to work within the political system. He and the Liberty Party believed that the Constitution did not recognize slavery, regarding it as a state institution; they argued that the Fifth Amendment (which also bars Congress from taking away life, liberty, or property) prevented Congress from sanctioning slavery. They also argued that slaves became automatically free when they entered areas of federal authority, such as Washington, D.C. or the western territories. The Liberty Party was a political failure, by and large. They won less than 3 percent of northern votes for their candidate in 1844. Political abolitionism, by the end of the 1840s, as well as Garrison's more radical approach, appeared to have very little future.

Items to Consider

Market Revolution, Five Points, putting out system, Labor Theory of Value, perfectionism, middle-class women and birth control, Oneida Community, Abolitionism prior to 1844, American Colonization Society, David Walker's Appeal, Biblical defense of slavery

CHAPTER 15

The Impending Crisis

For nearly a generation after the Missouri Compromise, the two major political parties managed to prevent the issue of slavery from dividing the nation. The parties tried to maintain a national appeal and national interests. Both sought to avoid the slavery issue because they knew it had the potential to destroy the Union, thus, the system of two separate Americas remained intact. The North and South both expanded west until the South began to run out of room in the 1830s.

An event was to soon take place that would change everything—The Mexican War. In March 1845, James K. Polk of Tennessee assumed the presidency. A Democrat, he had defeated the Whig Henry Clay in the election of 1844. Polk was elected on a platform of Western expansion, promising voters he would take all of Oregon and annex Texas. When Polk came into office, he did not limit his dreams of empire to only those areas. He decided the American nation should expand into California and New Mexico, as well. The war that followed brought huge new territories into the U.S. and doomed the Missouri Compromise as a means of reconciling the interests of the South and the North.

Shortly after he was inaugurated, Polk told his Secretary of the Navy that he regarded the acquisition of California to be as important as the Oregon question. Diplomacy would come first, and then war if necessary. In April he sent an agent to Mexico to see whether Mexico's government was willing to resume diplomatic relations and negotiate a settlement that would resolve differences over Texas and possibly transfer California to the U.S. On July 4, 1845, Texas formally decided to join the U.S., but claimed that the Rio Grande River was its western and southern boundary rather than the Nueces River as negotiated in its peace treaty with Mexico during its independence movement. Not surprisingly, Polk agreed with Texas and to strengthen his position, he ordered Gen. Zachary Taylor to lead several thousand troops to occupy the territory south of the Nueces River. Taylor camped near the town of Corpus Christi, just south of the Nueces. By October, Taylor had doubled his force. In November, after learning that Mexico would accept an American minister, Polk sent John Slidell to Mexico City. Polk told Slidell to buy New Mexico and California and to secure the Rio Grande boundary in return for as much as $30 million.

Mexico, once they learned what Polk planned to offer, refused to see the U.S. minister because they believed the American annexation of Texas was illegal. Mexico was buying time. They were in political turmoil and trying to hold off the Americans to keep them from gobbling up any Mexican territory. In fact, the Mexicans hoped the U.S. would soon find itself at war with Britain and would forget about the acquiring territory in the Southwest. But the Mexicans were ready to fight if necessary.

Unfortunately for the Mexicans, the same week Slidell was being turned away by the Mexican government, Polk unveiled a new policy toward Britain. Polk claimed that British intentions in the Pacific Northwest violated the Monroe Doctrine, which was a U.S. doctrine, which proclaimed on December 2, 1823 that European powers would no longer be allowed to colonize or interfere with the affairs of the newly independent nations of the Americas. Polk was determined to drive the British from Oregon and discourage them from taking California, which they wanted as compensation for debts owed to them by Mexico. Polk, meanwhile, was planning to take California for the U.S. He was trying to incite a revolution in California that would, as had been the case in Texas, lead to the creation of an independent republic and a request for annexation. But Polk was not about to rely on that hope alone. He sent Captain John C. Fremont and a party of heavily armed soldiers west from St. Louis toward the Sacramento valley in the spring of 1845.

In January 1846, Polk increased the military pressure on Mexico. Trying to provoke a fight, he sent Taylor south to build a fort on the Rio Grande. Secretary of State of James Buchanan simultaneously sent secret orders to Fremont.

Fremont thereafter destroyed the orders. To this day, the content of that letter is unknown but Fremont moved his force into California and made his base near its capital at Sacramento. Freemont later described his arrival as the first step in the conquest of California. News of skirmishes between Mexican and American forces near the Rio Grande River reached Polk in early May. On May 9, he delivered a war message he had written weeks before stating that Mexico has "passed the boundary of the United States, has invaded our territory, and shed American blood upon the American soil." Congress declared war four days later.

With a war with Mexico, Polk knew he had to diffuse the pending war with Britain. He could not fight the Mexicans and the British at the same time, so he chose to accept a British proposal to divide the Oregon country at the forty-ninth parallel. Everything south was American; everything north was British. The Senate agreed with Polk, and ratified the Oregon Treaty on June 15, 1846. This allowed the U.S. to focus on the war with Mexico. An American victory in the Mexican War was anything but certain. Most informed European observers gave the Mexicans the advantage. In fact, the only ones who knew they had no chance was the Mexican government. Unfortunately for the Mexican government, the Mexican people were so anti-American by the time the war started that the government could not seek a compromise, especially since it would result in Mexico giving up half of its territory.

In June 1846, the American citizens living in California, unaware of the formal state of war between the U.S. and Mexico, staged a revolt with the aid of Fremont's forces and captured the town of Sonoma. Fremont did not have formal authority to take California, so he refused to let the American rebels raise the American flag. Instead, Fremont instructed them to make a crude flag of their own displaying a bear, proclaiming themselves as the Bear Flag Republic on July 4, 1846, making California, at least in name, an independent nation. The next day, an American naval commander off the California coast landed 250 American marines in Monterey. He had no objections to running up the American flag. He did so and proclaimed that California was now American territory. Over the next few weeks, American forces solidified control over New Mexico and all of California.

On May 1, prior to Congress' declaration of war, Zachary Taylor's army moved across the Rio Grande River. After two bloody battles in which the outnumbered Americans used their advantage in artillery to subdue the Mexicans, Taylor's forces secured a position south of the Rio Grande. On September 25, 1846, after a fierce six-day battle, Taylor took the town of Monterrey. In December, another American force under Col. Alfred Doniphan set out on a six hundred-mile march south from Santa Fe toward Chihuahua, which it conquered in March of 1847.

American armies were victorious on all fronts. Even by the end of 1846, they controlled a long line across northeastern Mexico. Polk expected the Mexicans to give up. They had no chance of winning after March of 1847 and there was no hope of British intervention. But he had underestimated the Mexican leadership. Under the command of Gen. Antonio Lopez de Santa Anna, who was elected president in December 1846, Mexico refused to agree to a peace or give up any of its territory. Polk was at a loss as to what to do.

Polk and Gen. Winfield Scott, the Army's commanding general, decided to strike deep into the heart of Mexico. In November of 1846, Polk sent Scott to first take Veracruz and then advance 260 miles inland to Mexico City. In March of 1847, Scott captured Veracruz. Leading Scott's 14,000 troops were talented West Point officers who would become famous in the Civil War: Robert E. Lee, George Meade, and P. T. Beauregard. Having secured Veracruz, Scott turned toward Mexico City, marching along the same route that Cortés had taken some three hundred years earlier. Scott seized Mexico City in September 1847. The Mexican government had little choice but to make peace.

The American public was pleased with the war's outcome. They saw it as a war for democracy. A few Whigs, called Conscience Whigs because of their antislavery views, denounced the war from the start as part of a proslavery conspiracy. Most Whigs, however, had participated in or at least tolerated the great enthusiasm for the war. But by the time the news of Scott's victory reached Washington, the Whigs had strengthened their opposition. The biggest problem was that the government, in victory, could not decide what it wanted to do about the new lands it had acquired. The Whig Party by this point in time had reached a crisis. They had won one presidential election, but they were looking for an issue to win future elections. Clay's American System had failed too often. And thus, a group of Whigs began to turn to the antislavery movement, to abolitionism.

When the midterm elections of 1846 rolled around, the Whigs won Congress back, and more and more of them became critical of the Mexican war. New slave states in the West, they felt, would give the South too much political power. As the number of American war dead increased, the Whigs grew increasingly critical, especially during the deadly march on Mexico City. Ninety-two thousand American troops served in the war, but 13,000 were killed or died of disease. These numbers shocked many Americans, who could not believe the Mexicans had put up a spirited resistance, and did not want to see America's boys die for a cause like the expansion of slavery.

Surprisingly, it was a Democrat, however, who came up with the most disruptive way of opposing the war. On a warm August evening in 1846, David Wilmot, a congressman from Pennsylvania, proposed a simple amendment to a military appropriations bill ($100 million total cost). It said that slavery would be prohibited in any territory acquired from Mexico. This provision, known as the Wilmot Proviso, quickly became the rallying point for Northerners who feared the expansion of slavery into the West. In the House, a Democratic minority joined forces with the Whigs to pass the Proviso on several occasions. Each time the Proviso was killed by the Senate, which reflected more proslavery interests. In the meantime, the expansionist Democrats argued that the U.S. should enlarge its war aims because of the high cost of the war. The most important segments of this faction, President Polk, Secretary of State Buchanan, senators Stephen Douglas of Illinois and Jefferson Davis of Mississippi, all wanted the U.S. to take all or at least part of Mexico south of the Rio Grande. That goal put them in the path of the small number of antislavery northern Democrats who were still upset that Polk had not taken more of Oregon. Many began to think Polk had intentionally added more lands in the South where slavery could expand as a means of increasing slave state representation in the future.

Polk had to make a decision. In the end, he decided to put the interests of the Democratic Party first. He backed a plan by John C. Calhoun whereby the U.S. would take only California and New Mexico, thus, Polk backed away from his earlier support of the all-Mexico policy. As a result, Polk endorsed the Treaty of Guadalupe Hidalgo, signed February 2, 1848. The U.S. promised to pay Mexico $15 million in return for more than one-third of what belonged to Mexico before the war. Texas north of the Rio Grand, New Mexico, and California became American soil. Congress also agreed to pay $3.2 million in damage claims as a result of the war by U.S. citizens against the Mexican government. The Senate quickly ratified the treaty in March 1848. As he promised when running for president, Polk had gained northern Mexico as well as Texas and Oregon. Those land acquisitions would prove more detrimental than he or anyone else could have imagined.

Election of 1848

While the South resorted to its three programs for protecting and extending slavery in the western territories, the Northern Whigs (and some Democrats) struggled to find a politically viable expression for an abolitionism that sought, primarily, to protect freedom in the West. This issue, and the fate of the lands of the Mexican cession, proved to be the most serious situation since the South Carolina nullification crisis fifteen years before. As the election of 1848 approached, each party struggled to deal with this issue, while preserving not only themselves, but the Union.

When Polk chose not to seek a second term, the Democrats turned to Lewis Cass of Michigan. Cass was a northern Democrat, but one who supported the expansionist foreign policies of southern Democrats. Cass had been one of the primary architects, for example, of the concept of Popular Sovereignty. He wanted to let the residents of the individual territories decide for themselves whether their state should be free or slave. In some ways, he was a strange pick for the Democrats. Though his policies were openly in sympathy with southern Democrats, the Party hoped that he would poll well enough in his northern base to win the election. The Whigs, on the other hand, turned to a tried-and-true model, their only one, and selected a war hero. This time, however, their war hero was a southern slave owner from Louisiana, Zachary Taylor.

Both parties came into the election arguing that Congress did not have the right under the Constitution to address the issue of slavery in the territories. When November elections finally came, many southern Democrats chose to vote for the Whig Taylor, due in large part to their general distrust of the northern Democrat, Cass. Southerners felt that, as a slave owner, Taylor would do a better job of protecting their fundamental social and economic interest: the institution of slavery. Many northern Whigs and some northern Democrats, however, chose to bolt their party and support the new Free Soil Party, which had been built on the ashes of the old Liberty Party. The Free Soilers nominated the disaffected Democrat, Martin Van Buren, and advocated a policy of free labor in the West. In the end, Van Buren polled well, bringing in 10 percent of the overall vote, and contributing to Taylor's victory (he defeated Cass by 1.4 million votes to 1.2 million votes).

As each party came away from the election of 1848, however, there was much to fear. Slavery and the War for Mexico had further polarized North and South from one another. Slavery had become the one issue that found its way into every other discussion as they moved into the 1850s.

California and the Compromise of 1850

The first battleground over slavery would be California. Added as part of the Treaty of 1848, California quickly became a major destination of migrants moving from the East, especially after gold was discovered there in 1849. As the population of California increased, more pressure was put upon Congress and President Taylor to act, to admit California to the union. Taylor openly encouraged California to draft a constitution, and eventually announced that he was determined to admit California as a free state. Settlers there drafted a proposed state Constitution that would have outlawed slavery. When it arrived in Congress, however, southern political leaders saw the admission of a free California as one of the most serious threats to their way of life. Slave and free states were currently balanced at fifteen each in the United States Senate. Additional free states would place the South in the minority, and leave them unable democratically to defend its economic and social investments in the continuation of slavery.

A war could have followed in 1850, but Henry Clay, in his last years, put together a final compromise to save the union. He introduced a package of compromise laws in the Senate. Stephen Douglas and Daniel Webster supported his efforts, although it was condemned by Calhoun. The initial package Clay introduced failed to get enough support for passage, but the bills were reintroduced as individual measures by Douglas, and they eventually passed. There were five major parts to the Compromise of 1850, as the laws were collectively known:

1. The admission of California as a free state
2. The establishment of the Texas boundary at its modern lines
3. The organization of New Mexico and Utah territories on the principle of popular sovereignty
4. The establishment of a new, more powerful Fugitive Slave Law
5. The abolition of the slave trade in Washington, D.C.

The Compromise of 1850 was not a lasting solution to the problems. At best, it avoided the Civil War for ten years. At worst, it made conflict more likely. The Compromise had passed not because a consensus on these matters had been reached, but because of the strategy Douglas employed of getting them through the complex and competing interest blocs in Congress. No one was sure, moreover, how popular sovereignty would work in practice. There was no mechanism in federal law ensure the concept was legally employed in the territories. Could the territories have slavery before they reached the point of admission? Could it be prohibited before admission? Would territories start as "slave territories" or "free lands" before their admission? Would northern states accept the new, invasive Fugitive Slave Law? None of these questions had been adequately answered. Nor had the U.S. Supreme Court had its say on the Compromise, or Popular Sovereignty. Much remained unresolved. Indeed, it can be argued that the Compromise *caused* more problems than it solved, setting up an impending crisis.

The Presidency of Millard Fillmore

As president, Zachary Taylor urged settlers in New Mexico and California to bypass the territorial stage and draft constitutions for statehood, setting the stage for the Compromise of 1850. Only sixteen months into his term, Taylor died of acute gastroenteritis. More specifically, Taylor consumed a hasty snack of iced milk, cold cherries, and pickled cucumbers during a hot Independence Day celebration. The combination of heat and cold shocked his system. By July 9, Taylor was dead. Taylor's death left Millard Fillmore of New York as U.S. president. When Taylor died, his entire cabinet resigned. Daniel Webster came to Fillmore's rescue as he had to Tyler's a decade before. A man no one elected with that intention was no president.

Fillmore immediately ran into trouble. It began when he tried to enforce the new, more stringent Fugitive Slave Act. Fillmore despised the act, but he believed in upholding the law and was determined to do so. The Fugitive Slave Act was unpopular in the North. It created slave courts headed by commissioners appointed by the federal government. Slave owners could capture an African-American in the North and bring him before these courts, which would then determine if the person was, indeed, an escaped slave. The problem was this: The courts were viewed by Northerners as both corrupt and incompetent. The accused could not testify in their own behalf. There was no trial by jury. In many cases the judges did not take great care to make sure they had the right person. Judges also had a financial incentive to convict: $10 to convict the accused compared to $5 to find in favor of the accused.

Abolitionists attacked this system as a violation of the Bill of Rights. Protests soon roiled northern cities in Massachusetts, New York, Pennsylvania, and Ohio. Into this politically charged atmosphere stepped one woman. This woman dramatized the plight of runaway slaves in a way that gripped the northern population. Her name was Harriet Beecher Stowe, and her book was *Uncle Tom's Cabin*. First published in March 1852, *Uncle Tom's Cabin* further polarized the issues and made slavery a major issue in the election of 1852.

The Election of 1852

The election of 1852 rolled around later that year. The Whigs were stumped as to what to do with Millard Fillmore. The southern Whigs liked him and wanted to keep him as president, but the northern Whigs sent Fillmore home over his enforcement of the Fugitive Slave Act. In his place, they selected Gen. Winfield Scott, a war hero. The Whigs had, however, few issues in 1852. They looked like a dying party. The Democrats nominated Franklin Pierce of New Hampshire. They also came up with a catchy slogan, "We Polked you in '44 and now we'll Pierce you in '52."

Pierce was the father of three, had become a senator in 1837, three years after he had married Jane Appleton. Appleton did not like Washington and convinced Pierce to retire and return home, which he did in 1842. When the Mexican War began, he enlisted as a private but was soon promoted to colonel and then brigadier general. He served under Scott on the march to Mexico City and had his leg crushed on that expedition. He really had no interest in becoming president, but he came when called to service.

Pierce won a great victory, getting 254 of 296 electoral votes. His wife, however, was determined that he should not serve. To begin with, they did not get along well, and she took it as a sign from God that her husband should not serve when their third and only surviving son, Benjamin, was crushed in a train wreck two months before the inauguration. After that event, she became a recluse in the White House and avoided all social functions. Pierce, too, never recovered from the death of his last son and it did, perhaps, damage his effectiveness as a president.

Popular Sovereignty

The biggest problem facing Pierce or any other politician in the 1850s was that the future of the nation rested on the success of the Compromise of 1850. Because the Missouri Compromise guaranteed free soil north of 36-30, southerners had blocked the admission of states from this region, allowing only the admission of Iowa in 1846 and the formation of the Minnesota Territory. Finally, though, the weight of the population pouring into this area demanded something be done. Their foremost spokesman was Stephen A. Douglas of Illinois. He wanted to develop the West. He also wanted to be president. Working toward those goals, in 1854 he introduce a bill to organize what he called Nebraska. To win southern support, he made two major concessions. First, he agreed with southerners that the principle of popular sovereignty, embraced in the Compromise of 1850, had voided the Missouri Compromise's prohibition of slavery in the northern part of the Louisiana Purchase. Second, he advocated the formation of two new territories, Nebraska and Kansas, rather than one, giving slaveholders a chance to dominate the settlement of Kansas, the more southern territory. Douglas believed the numbers of nonslaveholders in Kansas, along with a physical environment hostile to plantation agriculture would ensure that Kansas, like California, would remain free.

These concessions attracted the support of almost all Southerners in Congress and the Kansas-Nebraska Act passed in May 1854 despite the opposition of northern Whigs and half the northern Democrats. In the north, the Kansas-Nebraska Act was vehemently denounced. Douglas misread northern opinion. The repeal of the Missouri Compromise seemed to attack freedom in an area that had been secure for more than a generation. Suddenly the idea of a Slave Power Conspiracy seemed real. Free Soilers were convinced that the federal government had been captured by slaveholders and was now firmly in the hands of the southern elite. Northern Whigs, Anti-Nebraska Democrats, and members of the Free Soil Party united under a new party in 1854, calling themselves Republicans. They were dead set against the expansion of slavery into the territories.

Another party—the American Party or Know-Nothings—was already attracting support from former Whigs. The party had its origins in the anti-immigrant, anti-Catholic reaction of the 1840s. In 1850, various secret anti-Catholic societies hand banded together in the Order of the Star-Spangled Banner. In 1851, they formed a new political party, the American Party. Its members sometimes answered outsiders' questions by saying—"I know nothing," which gave the party its nickname. They attempted to unite northern and southern voters in a program of opposition to Catholics— both Irish and German. In the 1854 elections in the North, the Republicans cooperated with the Know-Nothings. The Know-Nothings stressed the "Catholic Conspiracy," while the Republicans focused on the "Slave Power Conspiracy."

The Know-Nothings were racist by contemporary standards, but so were the Republicans, since one of their most important constituents were the Free Soilers. In 1854, these two factions together won a majority in the U.S. House of Representatives—an amazing political feat by any standards.

Bleeding Kansas

In 1854, thousands of settlers began rushing into Kansas. The state became a battleground between proslavery and antislavery sentiment. Missouri Sen. David R. Atchinson organized residents of his state to cross into Kansas and intervene in crucial elections. Antislavery forces fought back. The preference of President Pierce was clear. In March 1855, his administration recognized a Kansas Territorial Legislature that was largely elected by Missourians who had crossed the border just to vote and who then went home. That Legislature declared that it was a felony to even question the institution of slavery in Kansas and that aiding a fugitive slave was a capital offense. Violence broke out. In the summer of 1856, a proslavery gang, seven hundred strong, destroyed the Free Soil town of Lawrence. While Lawrence burned, a New York abolitionist named John Brown headed to Kansas. Brown, born in 1800, had started more than twenty business ventures in six states, had gone through bankruptcy, and had been sued several times. Despite those failures, he had the power and strength of character to convince people of almost anything. The day after Brown heard about the sack of Lawrence, he acted with a vengeance. He and his followers murdered and mutilated five proslavery settlers in Kansas. We must fight fire with fire, he said, and strike terror in the hearts of the proslavery people. The Potawatomie Massacre, as the killings were known, provoked reprisals and started a guerilla war that cost some two hundred lives.

Violence over slavery even reached the halls of Congress. Sen. Charles Sumner of Massachusetts delivered a famous speech in the Senate called "The Crimes Against Kansas." In the speech, Sumner denounced President Pierce, the South, and Sen. Andrew P. Butler of South Carolina, who Sumner said had taken the institution of slavery as his mistress. Butler's nephew, Preston Brooks, a member of the House of Representatives, vowed to defend his uncle's honor and accosted Sumner at his desk when the Senate was not in session. Brooks beat Sumnerhim on the head with a walking cane until it broke in two while another man with a drawn pistol kept people from coming to Sumner's aid. Sumner struggled to his feet, ripped up his desk which was bolted down, and then collapsed on the floor. For his actions, the House censured Brooks and removed him from office. The voters of South Carolina would immediately return him to Congress with over 90 percent of the vote. Sumner would not return to the Senate for two and a half years after the beating.

Election of 1856

The violence in Kansas and in Congress dominated the election of 1856. The Democrats, now advocates of popular sovereignty, insisted that the Kansas-Nebraska Act was the right thing to do. Pierce, however, seemed a liability. He was unpopular with northern Democrats. For the sake of party unity, they dumped him and nominated James Buchanan of Pennsylvania. Buchanan had more than forty years of experience in politics, but he could also be unimaginative and at times timid despite his reputation. The Republicans counted on a northern backlash against the violence in Kansas. They denounced the Kansas-Nebraska Act and demanded that the federal government prohibit slavery in all the western territories. The Republicans nominated John C. Fremont, western explorer and military hero. The Republicans hit the issue of a Slave Power Conspiracy hard. Many southern politicians said that they would consider leaving the union if Fremont won.

In the election that followed, Buchanan won with 45 percent of the vote, Fremont finished with 33 percent, and Fillmore (Know-Nothing) with 22 percent. Despite their loss, the Republicans had a stunning performance. The party, on the presidential ballot for its first time, won several large free states. Buchanan won the electoral vote only by a margin of 174 to 114. That narrow margin surprised the Democrats. No one had really expected the Republicans would make such a strong showing. This election is often identified as one of political realignment. The old second-party system was destroyed and the new second-party system, of Democrats and Republicans, had replaced it.

Dred Scott

One can still make the case that the war was not inevitable. But the Democrats and President Buchanan had made two terrible mistakes leading up to the election of 1860: the Dred Scott Decision and the Lecompton Constitution. The Free

Soil program of the Republican Party had never been subjected to a clear the constitutional test, despite its popularity in the North. The Supreme Court had never reviewed the free soil doctrine (or the position of Calhoun) that slavery was protected by the Constitution in the territories. In 1857, the case of Dred Scott, a slave suing for his freedom, reached the Supreme Court. Scott had lived for a time with his master in the free state of Illinois and in the Wisconsin Territory, two places where the Northwest Ordinance of 1787 and the Missouri Compromise 1820 had prohibited slavery. In his suit, which began in 1846 in the courts of Missouri, Scott claimed that his residence in a free state and a free territory had made him a free man. In March 1857, only two days after Buchanan's inauguration, the Court reached a decision in *Dred Scott v. Sandford*.

There was little agreement among the justices on the issues raised by the case, but seven members of the Court agreed on one critical matter—Scott was to remain a slave. There was no majority opinion. Every justice wrote his own opinion on the case, but Chief Justice Roger B. Taney's was the most influential. Taney ruled that blacks, free or slave, could not be citizens of the United States and that Scott therefore had no right to sue in a federal court. Taney could have stopped there. Instead, he insisted on going further and making two important points. First, he ruled that the Fifth Amendment's prohibition against the federal government taking private property without due process of law meant that Congress could not pass a law depriving persons of their slave "property" in the territories. Thus, the Missouri Compromise, voided three years earlier by the Kansas-Nebraska Act, had always been unconstitutional. Second, Taney said that Congress could not extend to territorial governments any powers that Congress itself did not possess. Since Congress had no power to prohibit slavery in a territory, neither did the government of that territory. Thus, Taney endorsed Calhoun's interpretation of the constitutional protection of slavery.

Immediately, the political composition of the Supreme Court caught everybody's interest. Five of the seven justices, including the chief justice, were southern Democrats. Democrats hoped the Republicans would give in. But the Court's decision did just the opposite of calming the storm. It made exacerbated things. In a single stroke, the Democratic-dominated Supreme Court had declared the Republican's antislavery platform unconstitutional. It was a decision the Republicans could not tolerate. They demanded that Dred Scott was further evidence that a Slave Power Conspiracy was in complete control of the U.S. government. Even many northern Democrats were up in arms by the decision, notably Stephen Douglas, who had worked so hard to protect his party's strength in the north.

The Ordeal of James Buchanan

The more serious mistake came with Buchanan's decision to support the proslavery forces in Kansas. In early 1858 he recommended the admission of Kansas as a slave state under the so-called Lecompton Constitution. Most observers—including Stephen Douglas—believed that the Lecompton Constitution had been obtained by voter fraud. Douglas thought that admitting Kansas under this constitution would be a disaster for the Union. Stephen Douglas broke with Buchanan and the southern Democrats and organized western Democrats and Republicans in the House of Representatives to defeat the Lecompton Constitution. Kansas, by the way, would finally enter the union as a free state in 1861—well after secession was under way. Buchanan's support for the Lecompton Constitution meant that he had firmly sided with the South over the North. That choice was catastrophic for him. In doing so, he lost any chance of making Kansas a slave state, he broke the Democratic Party into factions, and he gave the Republicans even more evidence that there was a Slave Power Conspiracy in control of the government.

That Lincoln Fellow

Bleeding Kansas and the Dred Scott Decision destroyed the Democratic Party. Former northern Democrats and Whigs switched to the new Republican Party in the north. It was during this crisis that Abraham Lincoln emerged as the pivotal figure in American politics. Lincoln's family had moved from Kentucky, where he was born in 1809, to Indiana and then to Illinois. In 1831, at the age of 22, he set out on his own, settling in New Salem, a small town in central Illinois. He decided against farming and began working as a store clerk. He had also taken flatboats loaded with produce down the Mississippi River to New Orleans in 1828 and 1831. The profits from those trips helped him become a partner in a general store in New Salem. In 1831, he was elected captain of the company of men who volunteered for the Black Hawk War. He had little formal education but with the help of a local teacher he mastered English grammar and elementary math. Lincoln was a man of ambition. In 1832 he ran for the state Legislature on a program of business expansion and universal education. He lost the 1832 election, but won most of the votes from his home town and therefore became much more influential.

In 1834, Lincoln ran again and won a seat in the Illinois Legislature. He was admitted to the bar in 1837 and he move to Springfield, the new state capital, where he met Mary Todd. They married in 1842. The two were a picture in contrasts. Her tastes were aristocratic; his were not. She was emotional; he was easygoing. Lincoln served four terms in the Illinois Legislature and became an important man in the Whig party. In 1844 he campaigned for his political hero, Henry Clay. In 1846, Lincoln was elected as Illinois' representative to the U.S. Congress.

Prior to entering Congress, Lincoln had intentionally avoided taking a stand on slavery, but the Mexican War forced him to state his position. At some point in his life, he decided that slavery was unjust, probably on one of his early trips to New Orleans. Since Lincoln lived in an area of southern Illinois known as Little Egypt because it was mostly settled by proslavery Southerners who continued to practice slavery, he avoided the issue as much as possible in order to build Whig support in those towns. The Whigs, he knew, had a problem. They had to reconcile the unpopularity of abolitionism and the growing number of people in his party who were opposed to the expansion of slavery. Lincoln condemned the Polk administration for its war and voted for the Wilmot Proviso. He believed that recolonization was the only practical way to solve the problem. Of course, Abolitionists denounced his approach, but even his limited support of gradual emancipation made him too radical for most of the voters of his district.

Lincoln went into retirement from 1849 till 1854, during which time he served mostly as a corporate lawyer. In a speech he gave to eulogize Henry Clay after his death in 1852, Lincoln condemned both the proslavery fanatics and the Abolitionists. He believed the nation had to find a middle way. After the Kansas-Nebraska Act he re-entered politics. He did not oppose slavery in the South, but he could not sit by and let it take over the West. In 1858, the Illinois Republicans nominated him for the U.S. Senate against the popular Democrat Stephen Douglas. In a series of debates across the state in 1858, Lincoln and Douglas outlined their positions on slavery. Lincoln attacked it; in some places harder than in others. He saw a conspiracy in the Kansas-Nebraska Act, in the Dread Scott Decision, and in Buchanan's endorsement of the Lecompton constitution. Douglas defended popular sovereignty. By a narrow margin, Douglas was reelected. Despite the loss, the debates made Lincoln the most famous Republican in the country, the unnamed spokesman for the party.

Election of 1860

Some Democrats, particularly in the South, feared they would lose the election of 1860, so they increased their demands. The more moderate party members, known as Southern Rights Democrats, insisted the party and the federal government make commitments to protect slavery. One of their leading spokesmen was Jefferson Davis, a Mississippi planter and Mexican War hero. More radical Southern Democrats like Robert B. Rhett of South Carolina and William L. Yancy of Alabama demanded that Stephen Douglas and his followers restore the international slave trade. Those radicals are better known as Fire-Eaters, secessionist radicals who hoped to drive a wedge between the North and South. Douglas was unmoved.

In the meantime one of the most shocking events in American history came to pass. On a night in October 1859, John Brown led eighteen heavily armed followers on a raid that seized the federal arsenal at Harper's Ferry, Virginia. Brown's purpose was to arm a slave rebellion and help create an African-American state in the South. The local militia and the U.S. Marines, under the command of Robert E Lee, quickly reclaimed the arsenal, capturing Brown and killing ten of his party. Republicans dismissed Brown as a criminal. The Democrats called his plot a result of the teachings of the Republican Party. The Virginia governor charged Brown with treason, a state court sentenced him to death, and Brown was hanged from the neck until dead—making him a martyr of the antislavery movement.

Just a few months later, the Democratic convention met Charleston, South Carolina in April 1860. The southern Democrats were determined to force the party to embrace the program of Jefferson Davis and his followers: ensuring national protection of slavery in the territories. Northern Democrats refused. They wanted the decision in the region left to popular sovereignty and the Supreme Court. When the convention adopted the northern platform, the delegates from eight southern states walked out. Buchanan, in whom the Northern Democrats had lost confidence, was not re-nominated. Instead, Stephen Douglas was the leading candidate but his opponents denied him the necessary two thirds majority. The Democratic convention adjourned and reconvened in Baltimore in June. There, they nominated Douglas for president. The bolting Southerners convened separately in Baltimore and nominated Buchanan's vice president, John C. Breckinridge of Kentucky. The Democratic Party had finally broken into two factions.

The Republicans, meanwhile, sensed victory and nominated Abraham Lincoln. Their platform was free soil in the West, but ruled out interference with slavery in the South. It also denied the right of states to secede from the union. Douglas campaigned nationally but in the later months shifted his attention to the South. He was fighting a losing battle. Lincoln won the election without getting a single vote outside the North. He won 40 percent of the popular vote, and 180 electoral votes compared to Breckinridge's 72, Bell's 39, and Douglas' 12. Douglas won only two states—Missouri and New Jersey, despite finishing second with 21 percent of the popular vote. The political fracturing of the Democratic Party spoke to a fracturing of the nation that would be complete before Lincoln could even take office.

Items to Consider

James K. Polk, manifest destiny, Bear Flag Republic, Mexican-American War, Wilmot Proviso, Treaty of Guadeloupe Hidalgo, Compromise of 1850, Fugitive Slave Act, *Uncle Tom's Cabin*, popular sovereignty, Bleeding Kansas

CHAPTER 16

The Road to Disunion

For the leaders of the South, Abraham Lincoln's election to the American presidency in 1860 presented them with a clear and present danger to the institution of slavery. They knew he regarded it as morally wrong. They knew that Lincoln had united the North in opposing the "Slave Power" and the extension of slavery into the territories. Lincoln had been elected without a single southern electoral vote; the first time that had happened, and Southerners knew he owed them nothing, nor could they expect anything from him. They feared he would reopen southern post offices to abolitionist mail, that he would appoint Abolitionists to federal jobs in the South, and they were certain the result would be a wave of bloody slave revolts across the South. They were outraged. They felt they had been loyal American citizens, and that the Constitution protected their right to slavery. And it did. They decided collectively that only way they could save slavery was to leave the Union: to create their own nation.

If Lincoln refused to recognize their right to do so, they would fight. Thus came the American Civil War, the greatest test of the American nation and, without doubt, a watershed moment in American history. Before the final shot was fired, the American Civil War would cost more lives than Vietnam, Korea, World War II, World War I, and the Spanish-American War put together. Nothing would be the same thereafter. There was a slim chance in early 1861 for another compromise; to give the Union new life. That had happened in 1820, 1833, and in 1850. But it would not happen this time.

The movement toward secession was most rapid in South Carolina—the home of John C. Calhoun and the state with the largest concentration of slaves. The Fire-Eaters took the lead there in organizing a convention to consider secession. On December 20, 1860, only six weeks after Lincoln was elected, the convention unanimously enacted an ordinance dissolving the union between South Carolina and the other states. During the next six weeks, Fire-Eaters in six other cotton states called conventions. They moved quickly, while public opinion was in their favor and before the southern unionists could mobilize an opposition. In the meantime, southern militias began to organize and make sure the southern unionists had little effect on the outcome. In early January, Mississippi left the Union. In less than a month, Florida, Alabama, Georgia, Louisiana, and Texas also left the Union. In early February, representatives from each of those states met in Montgomery, Alabama where they adopted a temporary constitution and named Jefferson Davis acting president. Together, in an atmosphere of great celebration, they proclaimed a new nation: the Confederate States of America.

So fast did this proceed that it was all over before Buchanan handed the reins of government over to Lincoln. The panic that produced this crisis was less severe in the upper South where concentrations of slaves were not as large. Nevertheless, secessionist fervor had been gathering there since Lincoln's election and many political leaders in the upper South, in the states of Arkansas, Delaware, Kentucky, Maryland, Missouri, North Carolina, Tennessee, and Virginia demanded that a state had the right to leave the Union. While this was happening Buchanan did little. He did not support secession but his cabinet persuaded him to take a soft approach, to keep from driving the upper South out of the Union. In his last message to Congress, he declared secession illegal but also stated that the federal government lacked the authority to force a state to return to the Union.

South Carolina grabbed on to this statement, claiming it was an official recognition of its independence and it demanded the U.S. turn over Fort Sumter, a federal garrison in Charleston harbor. Buchanan would not do so, however. He decided to test South Carolina's resolve. In January 1861, he ordered an unarmed merchant ship to reinforce Ft. Sumter. South Carolina fired on the ship as it entered the harbor, and Buchanan backed off; declining to send in the Navy. As the situation in the South worsened, Buchanan urged Congress to find a solution.

The proposal that received the most support was submitted by Senator John J. Crittenden of Kentucky, an old follower of Henry Clay. Crittenden proposed amending the Constitution with a set of provisions that could never be changed. Congress would be prohibited from abolishing slavery in the states, and the Missouri Compromise line would be extended westward to the California border. South of the line, slavery would be protected by the Constitution. Congressional leaders consulted with President-Elect Abraham Lincoln, then rejected the plan. Lincoln feared that extending the Missouri Compromise line would merely encourage the South to conquer new territory for slavery in Mexico, the Caribbean, and Latin America. If adopted, Lincoln said, Crittenden's plan would be an everlasting declaration of war against every person owning a foot of land between here and Tierra del Fuego—the southern tip of South America. He would not sacrifice his most sacred position; free soil in the territories.

Lincoln took the oath of office on March 4, 1861. His address was carefully balanced between the possibility of compromise and a determination to protect the Union. He promised to let the southern states back into the Union and to protect slavery where it already existed in the South, but he refused to compromise on the territories. Most important, he said that secession was illegal and that acts of violence in support of it were insurrection. He announced his attention to enforce the law and hold on to federal property in the South. If force was necessary, so be it. The choice for the South was clear: return to the Union or face war.

Fort Sumter was in drastic need of re-supply. Lincoln wanted to move slowly, but he needed food and other supplies to be delivered. He decided to send an armed expedition and informed South Carolina of his intentions. Jefferson Davis and the Confederate government received word of Lincoln's intention on April 8. They welcomed the news. They knew that Lincoln's show of force would set the wavering southern states against the North and win foreign support for the Confederate cause. Immediately, they decided to take Fort Sumter before the Union reinforcements could arrive. Davis authorized General P. T. Beauregard, the Confederate commander in Charleston, to take the fort. The Union commander there was Major Robert Anderson. He refused to surrender and the Confederates opened fire on April 12, 1861. Two days later, Anderson surrendered. The Confederate cannon had destroyed large segments of the fort; miraculously no one was killed.

The day after Fort Sumter's surrender, Lincoln called 75,000 state militiamen into federal service for ninety days to put down the rebellion. The war was under way. In the North, Fort Sumter became a symbol of national unity, and Major Anderson became a national hero. Northern states responded to Lincoln's call to arms. Governor Dennison of Ohio, when asked to provide thirteen regiments of volunteers, sent twenty regiments instead. Many northern Democrats were equally as angry. Stephen Douglas proclaimed just six weeks before his death: "There are only two sides to the question. Every man must be for the United States or against it. There can be no neutrals in this war, only patriots or traitors."

After Fort Sumter fell, Lincoln hoped to hold as many of the eight states of the upper South as possible. If he could keep them from leaving, the war would not last long. Lose them all, and the war might be lost as well. Those eight states contained two-thirds of the southern population, more than 75 percent of its industrial production, and well over half of its food and fuel. They were also home to many of the nation's very best military commanders. Among them was Robert E. Lee of Virginia; a man who would have had command of the Union Army had he not sided with his home state.

Those eight states of the upper South also held key geographical advantages. Kentucky, with its five hundred-mile border along the Ohio River, was essential to the movement of supplies and troops. Maryland was vital to national security because it bordered the nation's capital on the north, in addition to having the major port of Baltimore. Virginia was important psychologically, because it was the home of Washington, Jefferson, Madison, Monroe, Patrick Henry, and others. The best way to understand the necessity of the upper South to the outcome of the war is to divide the region into two parts. Part A has Virginia, North Carolina, Tennessee, and Arkansas. Lincoln never had a chance to hold Virginia. He had even threatened to invade Virginia in his inaugural address. When Lincoln issued his call to arms, it pushed Virginia into southern hands. On April 17, 1861 Virginia voted eighty-eight to fifty-five to leave the Union. The dissenters came mainly from the mountainous areas of western Virginia; men who resented the Tidewater planters and were closely aligned with Ohio and Pennsylvania. On April 18, Gen. Winfield Scott offered Lee command of the Union army. Lee declined and resigned from the Army, stating, "[S]ave in defense of my native state, I never desire again to draw my sword."

At the same time, the Virginia militia seized the federal encampments at Harpers Ferry and the Navy Yard at Newport News. The upper South states of North Carolina, Tennessee, and Arkansas quickly joined Virginia in the Confederacy and sent their militias to that state's defense. Part B has Maryland, Kentucky, Missouri, Delaware, and the western third of Virginia. Lincoln moved aggressively to hold these areas. In May, he order Gen. George McClellan, often called Little Napoleon and a man who was prone to outbursts and melodrama, to cross the Ohio River into Virginia. By

June his army had secured the rout of the Baltimore & Ohio Railroad. In October the voters in fifty western Virginia counties overwhelmingly approved the creation of a new state: West Virginia was admitted to the Union in 1863.

Lincoln had to deal with the other states quite differently. Maryland almost left the Union, as well, but Lincoln made it clear he would hold it at any cost. A week after Fort Sumter fell, pro-Confederate mobs attacked Massachusetts troops marching through Baltimore, while others destroyed railroad bridges and telegraph lines. Lincoln immediately sent troops to secure the transportation and communication lines. Then he suspended the Constitution in the state and had the army arrest several suspected secessionists, including the police chief of Baltimore and several members of the State Legislature. Unlike Maryland and West Virginia, Kentucky was evenly balanced between Union and Confederate interests. Lincoln was careful not to do anything that would tip the balance against him. He took no immediate military action there. After the Unionists won control of the Kentucky Legislature that August, Lincoln shut off the flow of horses, mules, food, and whiskey to the lower South. The Confederacy then made a stupid mistake of sending troops into Kentucky, seizing Bowling Green and Columbus. Outraged, Kentucky asked for federal protection from southern aggression in the form of troops. Ulysses S. Grant's first action during the war was in Kentucky as a brigadier general. He drove out the Confederates in September of that year. In Missouri, Lincoln was bolder. He moved quickly to control communications and trade on the upper Mississippi and Missouri rivers. By July he had troops in St. Louis and defeated Confederate sympathizers commanded by Missouri Gov. Claiborne Fox Jackson. Small bands of Confederate raiders led by William Quantrill and Jessie and Frank James—known as bushwhackers by the Unionists—waged violent guerrilla campaigns throughout the war. Nevertheless, the Union maintained control of the state. Of the eight states of the upper South, Lincoln had kept four, and part of a fifth. It would prove to be a decisive victory as the war progressed.

On July 4, 1861, Lincoln made his first major statement of war aims. He said that the war was a noble crusade to see if any democracy could uphold the rule of law against its domestic opponents. Only by crushing the rebellion, he said, would the nation survive. Lincoln had no idea in 1861 what an effort that would take. A military victory was not enough. They had to destroy the will of the southern people, and that was no easy task. To win, the Union had to fight a total war—war against an entire society, not only its armies. Confederate leaders also called on their people to fight for democracy. At his inauguration in February of 1861, Jefferson Davis identified the Confederate cause with the principles of the American Revolution. He claimed that Southerners were fighting against tyranny and on behalf of the sacred right of self-government. A month later, shortly after his election as vice president, Alexander Stephens of Georgia defined more explicitly what Confederate democracy meant: The Confederacy's "cornerstone rests upon the great truth that the Negro is not equal to the white man, that slavery—subordination to the superior race—is his natural or normal condition."

Specifically, Davis' strategy was to preserve the independence of the Confederacy. This strategy gave Confederate leaders a major advantage. Although they might dream of a battlefield victory that would force formal recognition, they were willing to settle for the Union's giving up the fight and accepting Confederate independence. If they could make the cost of the war high enough, the North might quit. In either case, they would have won.

The Home Front

Despite the euphoria that accompanied the initial victory at the first Battle of Bull Run, Southerners quickly settled down to face the harsh realities of a bloody war, a war fought almost entirely on Southern soil. Even more than the fighting itself, changes in civilian life robbed Southerners of their gaiety and nonchalance. The war altered southern society beyond all expectations and with astonishing speed. One of the first traditions to fall was the southern preference for local government. The South had been an area of little government. States' Rights had been its motto, but even the state governments were weak and sketchy affairs by modern standards. To withstand the massive power of the North, however, the South had to centralize. No one saw the necessity of centralization more clearly than Jefferson Davis. If the states insisted on fighting separately, said Davis, "we had better make terms as soon as we can."

From the outset, Davis pressed to bring all arms, supplies, and troops under his control. He advocated conscription when the states failed to enroll enough new soldiers and he took a strong leadership role toward the Confederate Congress, which raised taxes and later passed a tax-in-kind—a levy not on money but on wheat, corn, oats, rye, cotton, peas, and other farm products. Almost three thousand agents dispersed to collect the tax, assisted by almost fifteen hundred appraisers. Where opposition arose, the Confederate government suspended the writ of habeas corpus and imposed martial law. In the face of a political opposition that cherished states' rights, Davis proved unyielding. To replace the food that soldiers would have grown, Davis exhorted farmers to switch from cash crops to food crops; he encouraged the states to require that they do so.

But the Army was still short of food and labor. In emergencies, the Confederate War Department resorted to impressing slaves to labor on fortifications, or took meat and grain in lieu of forced labor. After 1861, the Confederate government relied heavily on food impressments to feed the armies. Officers swooped down on farms in the line of march and carted away grain, meat, and other food, plus wagons and draft animals to carry it. Shortly after the war began, the Richmond administration took nearly complete direction of the southern economy. Because it controlled the supply of labor through conscription, the administration could regulate industry, compelling factories to work on government contracts to supply government needs. In addition, the Confederate Congress passed laws giving the central government almost full control of the railroads; later shipping also came under extensive regulation.

A large Confederate bureaucracy sprang up to administer these operations: over seventy thousand civilians were needed to run the Confederate war machine. By the war's end, the southern bureaucracy was proportionally larger than its northern counterpart. The mushrooming Confederate bureaucracy expanded southern cities. Clerks and subordinate officials, many of them women, crowded the towns and cities where Confederate departments had their offices. These sudden population booms stretched the existing housing supply and stimulated new construction. The pressure was especially great in Richmond, whose population increased two and a half times. Before the war's end, Confederate officials were planning the relocation of entire departments to diminish crowding in that city. Mobile's population jumped from 29,000 to 41,900. Another prime cause of urban growth was industrialization. The Union blockade interrupted imports of manufactured products, so the traditionally agricultural South became interested in industry. Davis exulted that Southerners were manufacturing their own goods, thus "becoming more and more independent of the rest of the world."

Many planters shared Davis' expectations, remembering their battles against tariffs and hoping that their agrarian nation would industrialize enough to win "deliverance, full and unrestricted, from all commercial dependence" on the North. Indeed, though the Confederacy started from scratch, it achieved tremendous feats of industrial development. Chief of ordnance Josiah Gorgas was able to increase the capacity of the Tredegar Iron Works and other factories to the point that his Ordinance Bureau was supplying all Confederate small arms and ammunition by 1865. In spite of the industrial achievements, mass poverty descended on the South during the war, afflicting for the first time a large minority of the white population.

The crux of the problem for the Confederacy was that many yeoman families had lost their breadwinners to the Army. The poor sought help from relatives, neighbors, friends—anyone really. Sometimes they took their cases to the Confederate government, sometimes directly to Jefferson Davis. Other factors aggravated the effect of the labor shortage. The South was in many places so sparsely populated that the conscription of one skilled craftsman could work a hardship on the peoples of an entire county. Often they begged in unison for the exemption or discharge of the local miller or the neighborhood tanner, wheelwright, or potter. Physicians were also in short supply. Most serious, however, was the loss of a blacksmith.

The blockade created further shortages of common but important items—salt, sugar, coffee, nails—and speculation and hoarding aggravated these shortages. Avaricious businessmen moved to corner the supply of some commodities; prosperous citizens tried to stock up on food. Inflation raged out of control, and many of the poor could not afford to feed themselves. Some concerned citizens tried to help, but the need was so vast that it overwhelmed private charity. A rudimentary relief program organized by the Confederacy offered some hope, but was soon curtailed to avoid conflict with the task of supplying the armies.

Millions of southern yeomen sank into poverty and suffering. Class antagonism began to rise. As their fortunes declined, people of once modest means looked around and found abundant evidence that all classes were not sacrificing equally. They saw that the wealthy curtailed only their luxuries, while many poor families went without necessities. They saw the Confederate government contribute to these inequities through policies that favored the upper class. Until the last year of the war, for example, prosperous Southerners could avoid military service by furnishing a hired substitute. Prices for substitutes skyrocketed in the Confederate states; it was common for a man of means to pay $5,000–6,000 to send someone to the front in his place. Well over fifty thousand upper-class Southerners purchased such substitutes. The rich also traded on their social connections to avoid danger. They could get positions in the Confederate government or serve as a courier for a behind-the-scenes general.

Anger at such discrimination exploded when in October 1862 the Confederate Congress exempted from military duty anyone who was supervising at least twenty slaves. The law became notorious. Protests arose from every corner of the Confederacy, and North Carolina's legislators formally condemned the law. Its defenders argued, however, that the exemption preserved order and aided food production, and the statute remained on the books. Dissension spread as growing numbers of citizens concluded that the struggle was a "rich man's war and a poor man's fight." Alert politicians and newspaper editors warned that class resentment was building to a dangerous level. Letters to Confederate officials during this period contained a bitterness that suggested the depth of the people's anger. "If I and my little children suffer and die while there father is in service," threatened one woman, "I invoke God Almighty that our blood rest upon the conscious of the South." Food riots spread across southern cities in the spring of 1863. Atlanta, Macon, Columbus, and Augusta in Georgia saw riots as did Salisburg and High Point in North Carolina. Even Richmond was not exempt. At one point during the war, President Davis himself was compelled to quell a riot there.

The northern economy also had to cope with war. With the onset of war, a tidal wave of change rolled over the North, just as it had over the South. Factories and citizens' associations geared up to support the war, and the federal government and its executive branch gained power they had never had before. Civil liberties were restricted. Idealism and greed flourished side by side. But there was an important difference between the North and South: War did not destroy the North's prosperity. Northern factories ran overtime, and unemployment was low. Furthermore, northern farms and factories came through the war unscathed, whereas most areas of the South suffered extensive destruction. To Union soldiers on the battlefield, sacrifice was a grim reality; but northern civilians experienced only the bustle and energy of wartime production.

Initially, the war was a shock to northern business. With the sudden closing of the southern market, firms could no longer predict the demand for their goods; many companies had to redirect their activities to remain open. Even worse, southern debts became uncollectible, jeopardizing not only merchants but many western banks. In farming regions, families struggled with an aggravated shortage of labor. For reasons such as these, the war initially caused an economic slump for the North. A few enterprises never pulled out of the tailspin: Cotton mills lacked cotton; construction declined; shoe manufacturers sold fewer of the cheap shoes planters had bought for their slaves. Overall, the war slowed industrialization in the North. Yet historians have shown that the war's economic impact was not all negative. Certain entrepreneurs, such as wool producers, benefited from shortages of competing products, and soaring demand for war-related goods swept some businesses to new heights of production. To feed the voracious war machine, the federal government pumped unprecedented amounts of money into the economy. The Treasury issued $3.2 billion in bonds and paper money called greenbacks, while the War Department spent over $360 million in tax revenues. Government contracts soon totaled more than $1 billion. War-related spending rivaled business in many northern states.

In every department, the government became, directly or indirectly, the chief employer and paymaster. Government contracts had a particularly beneficial impact on the states' wool, metal, and shipbuilding industries, and saved many shoe manufacturers from ruin. War production also promoted the development of heavy industry in the North. The output of coal rose substantially. Iron makers improved the quality of their product while boosting the production of pig iron from 920,000 tons in 1860 to 1,136,000 tons in 1864. Although new railroad construction slowed, the manufacture of rails increased. Of considerable significance for the future was the railroad industry's adoption of a standard gauge for track. Another crucial step came when foundries developed new and less expensive ways to make steel. A final strength of the northern economy was the complementary relationship between agriculture and industry. The mechanization of agriculture had begun well before the war. Now though, wartime recruitment and conscription gave western farmers an added incentive to purchase labor-saving machinery like mowers and reapers. The shift from human labor to machines had a doubly beneficial effect, creating new markets for industry and expanding the food supply for the urban industrial workforce. The boom in the sale of agricultural tools was tremendous. As a result, farm families whose breadwinners had gone to war did not suffer as they did in the South.

Some in the North did suffer, though. The northern workers who suffered most during the war were wage-earners, particularly industrial and urban workers. While jobs were plentiful following the initial slump, inflation took much of a worker's paycheck. By 1863, beef that sold for nine cents a pound was selling for as much as eighteen cents. The price of coffee tripled; rice and sugar doubled; and clothing, fuel, and rent all climbed. Studies of the cost of living indicate that between 1860 and 1864 consumer prices rose at least 76 percent; meanwhile, daily wages rose only 42 percent. To make up the difference, workers' families had to do without. As their real wages shrank, industrial workers also lost job security. To increase production, some employers were replacing workers with labor-saving machines. Other employers urged the government to liberalize immigration procedures so they could import cheap labor. Workers responded by forming unions and sometimes by striking. As troublesome as unions were, they did not prevent many employers from making a profit.

The biggest fortunes were made in profiteering on government contracts. Unscrupulous businessmen took advantage of the sudden, immense demand for goods for the Army by selling clothing and blankets made of "shoddy" wool fiber reclaimed from rags or worn cloth. The clothes often came apart in the rain; most of the shoes purchased in the early months of the war were worthless, too. Contractors sold inferior guns for double the usual price and tainted meat for the price of good. Corruption was so widespread that it led to a year-long investigation by the House of Representatives.

Legitimate enterprises also turned a neat profit. The output of woolen mills increased so dramatically that dividends in the industry nearly tripled. Some cotton mills, though they reduced their output, made record profits on what they sold. Brokerage houses worked until midnight and earned unheard-of commissions. Railroads carried immense quantities of freight and passengers. Other businessmen benefited handsomely from the Morrill Land Grant Act of 1862. To promote education in agriculture, engineering, and military science, Congress granted each state 30,000 acres of public land for each of its congressional representatives. The states were free to sell the land as they saw fit, as long as they used the income for the purposes Congress had intended. Though the law eventually fostered sixty-nine colleges and universities, one of its immediate effects was to enrich a few prominent speculators. Hard pressed to meet wartime expenses, some states sold their land cheaply to wealthy entrepreneurs. Another measure that brought joy to the business community was the tariff. Northern businesses did not uniformly favor high import duties; some manufacturers desired cheap imported raw materials more than they feared foreign competition. But northeastern congressmen traditionally supported higher tariffs, and after southern lawmakers left Washington, they had their way; the Tariff Act of 1864 raised tariffs generously.

Wartime Powers of the U.S. Executive

As long as the war lasted, the powers of the federal government and the president continued to grow. Abraham Lincoln found, as had Jefferson Davis, that war required active presidential leadership. At the beginning of the conflict, Lincoln launched a major ship-building program without waiting for Congress to assemble. The lawmakers later approved his decision, and Lincoln continued to act in advance of Congress when he deemed it necessary. In one striking exercise of executive power, Lincoln suspended the writ of habeas corpus for all people living between Washington and Philadelphia. The justification for this action was practical rather than legal; Lincoln was ensuring the loyalty of Maryland. Later during the war, with congressional approval, Lincoln repeatedly suspended the writ of habeas corpus and invoked martial law. Roughly ten to twenty thousand U.S. citizens were arrested on suspicion of disloyal acts.

On occasion Lincoln used his wartime authority to bolster his political power. He and his generals proved adept at arranging furloughs for soldiers who could vote in close elections. Needless to say, the citizens in arms who Lincoln helped to vote usually voted Republican. Among the clearest examples of the wartime expansion of federal authority were the National Banking acts of 1863, 1864, and 1865. Prior to the Civil War, the nation lacked a uniform currency. Banks operating under a variety of state charters issued no fewer than seven thousand kinds of bank notes, which had to be distinguished from a variety of forgeries. Acting on the recommendations of the Secretary of the Treasury Salmon Chase, Congress established a national banking system empowered to issue a maximum number of national bank notes.

At the close of the war in 1865, Congress laid a prohibitive tax on state bank notes and forced most major institutions to join the system. This process led to a sounder currency and a simpler monetary system, but also to inflexibility in the money supply and an eastern-oriented financial structure. The frantic wartime activity, the booming economy, and the Republican alliance with business combined to create a new atmosphere in Washington. The balance of opinion shifted against consumers and wage-earners and toward large corporations; the notion spread that government should aid businessmen but not interfere with them. This was the golden hour of untrammeled capitalism, and railroad builders and industrialists like Leland Stanford, Collis P. Huntington, John D. Rockefeller, John M. Forbes, and Jay Gould took advantage of it. Their enterprises grew with the aid of government loans, grants, and tariffs.

While the economy was growing, there was considerable dissension in the North concerning the war. The "Peace" Democrats influenced politics in New York State and won majorities in the Legislatures of Illinois and Indiana. Led by outspoken men like Clement L. Vallandigham of Ohio, the Peace Democrats were highly visible. Vallandigham criticized Lincoln as a dictator and condemned both conscription and emancipation. Although Vallandigham stayed carefully within legal bounds, his attacks were so damaging to the war effort that military authorities arrested him after Lincoln suspended habeas corpus. Fearing that Vallandigham might gain the stature of a martyr, the president decided against a jail term and exiled him to the Confederacy instead. More violent opposition to the government and to the war came from ordinary citizens facing the draft, especially the urban poor.

As happened in the South, there was a class dimension to opposition to the war and/or war policies. In the North conscription was a massive but poorly organized affair. Federal enrolling officers made up the list of eligible men, a procedure open to personal favoritism and ethnic or class prejudice. Lists of those conscripted reveal that poor men were called more often than rich, and that disproportionate numbers of immigrants were called. As with the South, rich men could furnish substitutes or pay a commutation to avoid service. As a resultant, there were scores of disturbances and melees. Enrolling officers received tough treatment in many parts of the North, and riots occurred in Ohio, Indiana, Pennsylvania, Illinois, and Wisconsin.

By far the most serious outbreak of violence, however, occurred in New York City in July 1863. The war was unpopular in that Democratic stronghold, and ethnic and class tensions ran high. Shippers had recently broken a longshoremen's strike by hiring black strikebreakers who worked under police protection. Working-class New Yorkers feared an influx of black labor from the South and regarded blacks as the cause of the unpopular war. Irish workers, often recently arrived and poor themselves, resented being forced to serve in the Army in the place of others. And indeed, an examination of local draft lists certifies that the poor foreign-born disproportionately bore the burden of service. The riot began with an attack on the provost marshal's office. Then mobs crying "down with the rich" looted wealthy homes and stores.

Yet blacks would prove to be the rioters' special target. Luckless blacks who happened to be in the rioters' path were beaten; soon the mob rampaged through black neighborhoods, destroying an orphans' asylum. At least seventy-four people died during the violence, which raged out of control for three days. Ironically, the troops used to put down the violence were fresh from the battle at Gettysburg. So men who had defeated Robert E. Lee's army were now turning their bayonets on their own citizens.

Discouragement and war-weariness neared their peak during the summer of 1864. At that point, the Democratic Party nominated Gen. George B. McClellan for president and put a qualified peace plank into its platform. Many Democrats were essentially ready to accept disunion or, in the alternative, renounce emancipation and guarantee the rights of Southerners to hold property in slaves as a condition of reunion. Then Lincoln insisted that any terms for peace would absolutely include reunion with the South and the abandonment of slavery. A wave of protest arose in the North in response to Lincoln's insistence on emancipation, and only some shrewd political maneuvering on Lincoln's part won him the election in 1864. In the meantime, the war ground on with a horrifying loss of life on the battlefield.

The Military Side of the War

The Civil War was the most brutal and destructive conflict in American history. Much of the bloodshed resulted from the application of the theories of Henri Jomini, a French military historian, to the battlefield. Jomini's ideas were enshrined in the curriculum of West Point, where most of the Union and Confederate officers had studied the art of war.

Jomini argued that an army seized victory by concentrating its infantry attack at the weakest point of the enemy's defenses. At the time Jomini wrote, this offensive strategy made military sense. The artillery, stationed well outside the range of enemy fire, could prepare the way for the infantry attack by bombarding enemy lines. But the soldiers fighting in the American Civil War were Industrial Age killers. By 1861, however, the range of rifles had increased from 100 yards to 500 yards. It was no longer possible to position the artillery close enough to the enemy to allow it to soften up the opposing line in preparation for the infantry charge. During the Civil War, then, enemy fire mowed down attacking infantry soldiers as they ran the 500 fatal yards to the front lines. Battles based on Jomini's theories produced a ghastly crop of dead men.

It is best to break the military action of the war into three categories, and then deal with them individually.

1. War in the East

The war's brutal character would reveal itself only gradually. The two armies did not meet on the battlefield until July of 1861. The Union commanding general, seventy-year-old Winfield Scott, at first pressed for a cautious, long-term strategy known as the Anaconda Plan. Scott's Anaconda Plan proposed for the weakening of the South gradually through blockades on land and at sea until the northern army was strong enough to move in for the kill. The excited public, however, hungered for action and a quick victory. So did Lincoln, who knew that the longer the war lasted, the more embittered the South and the North would become, making reunion ever more difficult. In July 1861, under the cry of "Forward to Richmond!" and as a result of Lincoln's unyielding prompting, Scott sent 35,000 partially trained men led by Gen. Irvin McDowell south from Washington in a sweltering heat.

Only twenty-five miles from the capital at Manassas Creek, or Bull Run, as it is also called, northern troops confronted 25,000 raw Confederate soldiers commanded by Brigadier Gen. P. G. T. Beauregard, a West Point classmate of McDowell's. Although sightseers, journalists, and politicians had accompanied the Union troops expecting only a Sunday outing, the first encounter at Bull Run was no picnic. The course of battle swayed back and forth before the arrival of 2,300 fresh Confederate troops from the Shenandoah Valley decided the day. Union soldiers fled toward Washington in terror and confusion, most in a frenzy to reach the safety of the capital. The Confederates lost their chance to turn the rout into the quick and decisive victory they sought. Inexperience was the problem. As Gen. Joseph E. Johnston pointed out, his men were disorganized, confused by victory, and not well enough supplied with food to chase the Union army back toward Washington.

In many ways, the Battle of Bull Run was prophetic. For three key reasons, victory would be neither quick nor easy.
1. As the disorganization and confusion of both sides suggested, the armies were unprofessional.
2. Both sides faced problems with short-term enlistments.
3. Logistical problems connected with mass armies plagued both sides.

The Civil War put more men in the field than any previous American engagement. Supplying and moving so many men and ensuring adequate communication, especially during battle, were tasks of an unprecedented kind. It was hardly surprising that the armies floundered trying to meet these logistical challenges.

For the South, the first Battle of Bull Run was regarded as a victory. For the Union, the loss was sobering. Replacing McDowell with thirty-four-year-old Gen. George McClellan, President Lincoln began the long search for a Northern commander capable of winning the war. Seven commanders would serve in the next two years. McClellan, formerly an army engineer, began the task of transforming the Army of the Potomac into a fighting force. Short-term militias were sent home. When Scott retired in the fall of 1861, McClellan became general-in-chief of the Union armies. McClellan had considerable organizational ability but was not a daring battlefield leader. Indeed, he had no wish for boldness. Convinced that the North must combine military victory with efforts to persuade the South to return to the Union, McClellan sought to avoid unnecessary and embittering loss of life and property. He intended to win the war by maneuvering rather than fighting.

In March 1862, pushed by an impatient Lincoln, McClellan finally led his army of 130,000 toward Richmond, now the Confederate capital. Hoping to take the city without excessive casualties, McClellan believed the enemy would be convinced to abandon a war it could never win. By late June, his army was close enough to Richmond to hear its church bells pealing. But just as it seemed that victory was within grasp, Robert E. Lee took control of the Confederate forces and counterattacked, slowly droving the Union forces away from Richmond. Losses were heavy on both sides. Finally, orders came from Washington: Abandon the Peninsula campaign.

Other Union defeats followed in 1862, as commanders came and went. In September, the South abandoned the defensive with a bold invasion of Maryland. After a costly defeat at Antietam, in which more than 5,000 soldiers were slaughtered, Lee withdrew his army to Virginia. Victory eluded both sides. The War in the East fell into stalemated.

2. War in the West

The early struggle in the East focused on Richmond, the Confederacy's capital city and one of the South's most important railroad, industrial, and munitions centers. Yet the East was only one of three theaters of action. Between the Appalachian Mountains and the Mississippi River lay Kentucky, Tennessee, Mississippi, and Alabama. At its edge lay the Mississippi River, with the vital river trade and its great port, New Orleans. Beyond that lay the trans-Mississippi West—Louisiana, Arkansas, Missouri, Texas, and the Great Plains, where Native American tribes joined the conflict on both sides.

In the western theater, the Union had two strategic objectives: 1) the domination of Kentucky and eastern Tennessee, the avenues to the South and the West and 2) maintain control of the Mississippi River. If Union forces managed to dominate the Mississippi River, they would split the South in two. Thus, major campaigns sought strategic points along rivers and railroads. Southern forces were determined to hold the four hundred-mile line stretching from the Appalachian Mountains to the Mississippi River. But the western commander, Albert S. Johnston, was hampered by inadequate supplies (many of his men had flintlock muskets, which would not fire in wet weather) and insufficiently trained troops. The weakness of this southern line reflected Davis' belief that the western theater was not as vital to the Confederacy as the Virginia hills.

In the western theater and for the North, Ulysses S. Grant came to the forefront. Working in his family's leather stores in Illinois when the war broke out, Grant had lackluster military credentials. Although he had attended West Point and served creditably in the Mexican War, his career in the peacetime army was undistinguished. It is rumored that boredom on frontier posts drove the young Grant to drink and he finally resigned from the service. Soon after Fort Sumter, though, Grant re-enlisted as a colonel in an Illinois militia regiment. Within two months, he was a brigadier general.

Of all the leaders, North or South, during the war, Ulysses S. Grant would be the most important. Grant's military genius consisted of an ability to see beyond individual battles to larger goals. In 1862, he realized that the Tennessee and Cumberland rivers could be used as paths for the successful invasion of Tennessee. Assisted by gunboats, Grant was largely responsible for the capture of Fort Henry and Fort Donelson, key points on those rivers, in February 1862. The capture of those forts forced Confederate troops to retreat into northern Mississippi, effectively giving up the state.

The two forces clashed again on a rainy April day in 1862 at Shiloh Church (also called Pittsburg Landing) in Tennessee. There had never before been a battle of this size on American soil. Albert Johnston commanded 40,000 troops; Grant also had 40,000 men and expected reinforcements of 25,000 more. The battle tilted first toward the Confederacy, but during the first day, Gen. Johnston was hit in the leg. The wound need not have been fatal, but Johnston stayed in the saddle and bled to death. The arrival of fresh Union troops won the day for the North, allowing Grant to hold the Confederates in place. Technically a northern victory, the Battle of Shiloh Church proved to be an immensely costly engagement. The Union suffered over 13,000 casualties, while 10,000 Confederates lay dead. Untreated wounds caused many of the deaths. A full day after the battle had ended, nine-tenths of the wounded still lay in the rain. Many died of exposure, others drowned in the downpour. Though more successful than efforts in the East, the devastating Union campaigns in Tennessee failed to bring decisive results. This was largely because western plans were never coordinated with eastern military activities. Unlike the West, victories in the East did not force the South to its knees.

3. The Trans-Mississippi Campaign

The War in the Trans-Mississippi West was a sporadic, far-flung struggle for the control of the manpower and natural resources of this vast area. New Mexico was the scene of an unsuccessful Confederate campaign in early 1862. Missouri and Arkansas saw bitter fighting in 1862 and 1863. The prize both sought was the Missouri River, which flowed into the Mississippi, bordered Illinois, and affected military campaigns in Kentucky and Tennessee. In 1861, Confederate forces in the far West led by Gen. Sterling Price and Gen. Ben McCulloch, a former Texas Ranger, did win a series of bloody victories, but they failed to amount to much. In March 1862, at Pea Ridge in northwestern Arkansas however, the tide finally turned. There a Confederate army of 16,000, which included a brigade of Native Americans from the Five Civilized Nations, fell before the Union Army led by Gen. Samuel Curtis. This defeat kept Missouri in the Union camp, although fierce guerrilla warfare continued in the region.

Throughout the first two years of conflict, both sides achieved victories, but the war remained deadlocked. Although the South was far from being defeated, the North was as far from giving up and accepting southern independence. The costs of war, in manpower and supplies, far exceeded what either side had anticipated. The need to replace lost men and supplies thus loomed ever more serious at the end of 1862.

The Emancipation Proclamation

Hard political realities as well as Lincoln's sense of the public's mood help explain why he delayed an Emancipation Proclamation until 1863. Like congressional Democrats, many Northerners supported a war to preserve the Union but not one for emancipation. Not only did many, if not most, northern whites see blacks as inferior, but they also suspected that emancipation would trigger a massive influx of former slaves who would steal white men's jobs and political rights. Race riots in New York, Brooklyn, Philadelphia, Buffalo, and Cincinnati dramatized white attitudes. If the president moved too quickly on emancipation, he risked several things. First, he risked losing the allegiance of many Northerners; second, he risked offending the border states; and third, he risked increasing the Democrats' chances for political victory.

Lincoln had at first hoped that a pro-Union sentiment would emerge in the South and compel its leaders to abandon their rebellion. But as the war dragged on, Lincoln recognized that if did not move at all on emancipation, he would alienate Abolitionists and lose the support of radical Republicans, which he could ill afford. In this context, Lincoln proceeded cautiously. At first, he hoped the Border States would take the initiative on the emancipation question. In the early spring of 1862, he urged Congress to pass a joint resolution offering federal compensation to states beginning a "gradual abolishment of slavery." Border state opposition killed that idea and suggested their reluctance to believe, as did Lincoln, that the "friction and abrasion" of war would finally end slavery.

Abolitionists and northern blacks, however, greeted Lincoln's proposal with a "thrill of joy." That summer—1862— Lincoln told his cabinet he intended to emancipate the slaves. Secretary of State Seward urged the president to delay any general proclamation until the North won a decisive military victory. Otherwise, Seward warned, Lincoln would appear to be urging racial insurrection behind the Confederate lines to compensate for northern military bungling. Lincoln followed Seward's advice, using that summer and fall to prepare the North for the shift in the war's purpose. To counteract white racial fears of free blacks, he promoted various schemes for establishing free black colonies in Haiti and Panama. Seizing unexpected opportunities, he worked tirelessly to lay the groundwork for the Emancipation Proclamation itself. In August 1862, Horace Greeley, the influential abolitionist editor of the *New York Tribune*, printed an open letter to Lincoln attacking him for failing to act on slavery. In his reply, Lincoln linked the idea of emancipation to military necessity. His primary goal, he said, was to save the Union. He wrote: "If I could save the Union without freeing any slave, I would do it; and if I could save it by freeing all the slaves, I would do it; and if I could do it by freeing some and leaving others alone, I would also do that. What I do about Slavery and the colored race, I do because I believe it helps to save the Union." If Lincoln attacked slavery then, it would only be because emancipation would save white lives, preserve the democratic process, and win the conflict for the Union.

In September 1862, the important Union victory at Antietam in Maryland gave Lincoln the opportunity to issue a preliminary Emancipation Proclamation. It stated that unless rebellious states (or parts of states in rebellion) returned to the Union by January 1, 1863, the president would declare their slaves "forever free." Although supposedly aimed at bringing the southern states back into the Union, Lincoln never expected the South to lay down its arms after two years of bloodshed. Rather, he was preparing Northerners to accept the eventuality of emancipation on the grounds of "war" necessity. Frederick Douglas greeted the president's action with jubilation. "We shout for joy," he wrote, "that we live to record this righteous decree."

Not all Northerners shared Douglas' joy. In fact, the September proclamation probably harmed Lincoln's party in the fall elections. Although the elections of 1862 weakened the Republicans' grasp on the national government, it did not destroy their control over the government. Still, cautious cabinet members begged Lincoln to forget about emancipation. On New Year's Day 1863, Lincoln issued the final Emancipation Proclamation as he promised. He said it was "an act of justice, warranted by the Constitution upon military necessity." Thus, what had started out as a war to save the Union, now also became a struggle that, if victorious, would free the slaves.

The Proclamation had no immediate impact on slavery. It affected only slaves living in the unconquered portions of the Confederacy. It was silent about slaves in the border states and in parts of the South already in northern hands. These limitations led Elizabeth Cady Stanton and Susan B. Anthony to establish the Woman's Loyal National League to lobby Congress to emancipate all southern slaves. Though the Emancipation Proclamation did not immediately liberate southern slaves from their masters, it had a tremendous symbolic importance. On New Year's Day, blacks gathered outside the White House to cheer the president. They realized that the Proclamation had significantly changed the nature of the war. For the first time, the government had committed itself to freeing the slaves. Jubilant blacks could only believe that the president's action heralded a "new era" for their race. More immediately, the Proclamation sanctioned the policy of accepting blacks as soldiers into the Army. Blacks also hoped that the news would reach southern slaves, encouraging them either to flee to Union lines or to subvert the southern war effort by refusing to work for their masters.

More than anything else, diplomatic concerns lay behind the Emancipation Proclamation. Lincoln and his advisers anticipated that the commitment to abolish slavery would favorably impress foreign powers. European statesmen, however, did not at once abandon their cautious stance toward the Union. The English prime minister called the Proclamation "trash," but important segments of the English public who opposed slavery now came to regard any attempt to help the South as "immoral." Foreigners could better understand and sympathize with a war to free the slaves than they could with a war to save the Union. In diplomacy, where image is so important, Lincoln created a more attractive picture of the North. The Emancipation Proclamation became the North's symbolic call for human freedom.

Other Unanticipated Consequences of the War

The Emancipation Proclamation was but one example of the war's surprising consequences. Innovation was necessary for victory. In the final two years of the war, both the North and the South experimented on the battlefields and behind the lines in desperate efforts to conclude the conflict successfully.

One of the Union's experiments involved using black troops for combat duty. Blacks had offered themselves as soldiers at the start of the war and later in 1862, but they had been turned away. They were serving as cooks, laborers, teamsters, and carpenters in the Army, however, and composed as much as a quarter of the Navy. Yet as white casualties mounted, so did the interest in black service on the battlefield. Other forces beyond white self-interest also lay behind the new policy: the promises of the Emancipation Proclamation and the desire of blacks to prove their value to the North. Black leaders like Frederick Douglas pressed for black military service. Douglas believed that service would be key to establishing their citizenship rights (which the Dred Scott Decision had called into question).

By the war's end, 186,000 blacks (10 percent of the army) had served the Union cause. Approximately 134,000 of them had been escapees from slave states. Enrolling blacks in the Union Army was an important step toward citizenship and acceptance of blacks by white society. The black experience in the Army, though, highlighted some of the obstacles to racial acceptance. Black soldiers, usually led by white officers, were treated as second-class soldiers for most of the war, receiving lower pay ($10 a month compared to $13), poorer food, often more menial work, and fewer benefits than whites. The Army racial experiment had mixed results. The faithful and courageous service of black troops did help modify some of the most demeaning white racial stereotypes of blacks. The black soldiers, many of them formers slaves who helped conquer the South, felt a sense of pride and dignity as they performed their duties. They served gallantly, and a far higher percentage of them died on the battlefield. They were sent into the most desperate battles, but they did not shy away from combat, even after Southerners instituted a policy of executing any black soldiers captured.

Another major innovation came in tactics, as faith in the military tactics of Jomini dissipated. The infantry charge, so valued at the war's beginning, resulted in horrible carnage. As skepticism in the value of the charge increased, military leaders realized the importance of strong defensive positions. Although Confederate soldiers criticized Gen. Lee as "King of Spades," early in the war when he first ordered them to construct earthworks, the term evolved into one of affection as it became obvious that earthworks saved lives. Union commanders followed suit. By the end of 1862, both armies dug defensive earthworks and trenches whenever they interrupted their march.

Gone, too, was the courtly idea that war involved only armies. In the first years of war, many officers tried to protect civilians and their property. In his campaign against Richmond, Gen. McClellan actually posted guards to prevent stealing. Such careful concern for rebel property soon vanished, and along with it went chickens, corn, livestock, and even the furnishings of churches. Southern troops, on the few occasions when they came north, also lived off the land. War touched all levels of society, not only battlefield participants.

The End Game

In the early war years, the South's military strategy combined defensive with selective maneuvers. Until the summer of 1863, the strategy seemed to be succeeding, at least in the eastern theater. A most spectacular defeat of the Union occurred in May 1863. At Chancellorsville, Lee and Stonewall Jackson inflicted a bloody defeat on an army more than twice their size. Stonewall Jackson, mistakenly shot by one of his own men, was a casualty of the battle. Despite the loss of Jackson, Chancellorsville was a great Confederate victory. Yet once again, the triumph did not change the course of the war. Realizing this, Lee reviewed his strategy and concluded that unless the South won victories in the North, it could not gain the peace it so desperately needed.

In the summer of 1863, Lee led the Confederate Army of Northern Virginia across the Potomac into Maryland and southern Pennsylvania. His goal was a victory that would threaten both Philadelphia and Washington. He even dreamed of capturing a northern city. He ardently believed such spectacular feats would surely bring diplomatic recognition and might even force the North to sue for peace. Yet he risked much. The fertile Pennsylvania farmlands would allow his army to live off the land, but since long supply lines stretched far back into Virginia, the enemy could just as easily disrupt the flow of military supplies.

At Gettysburg, on a hot and humid July 1, Lee came abruptly face to face with a Union army led by Gen. George Meade. Much depended on the battle's outcome. During the three days of fighting, Lee attacked again and again. The fatal obsession with the infantry charge returned, as the general ordered frontal assaults on Union forces positioned along a series of ridges. These costly assaults probably lost him the battle, and eventually the war. On July 3, Lee sent three divisions, 15,000 men in all, against the Union center. The assault, known as Pickett's Charge, was as gallant as it was futile. At 700 yards, the Union artillery opened a blistering fire on the Confederates. One southern officer described the scene: "Pickett's division just seemed to melt away in the blue musketry smoke which now covered the hill. Nothing but stragglers came back." Lee's dreams of victory died that hot week, with grave consequences for the southern cause. Fighting in the eastern theater dragged on for another year and a half, but Lee's Gettysburg losses were so heavy that he could never mount another southern offensive. Instead, the Confederacy committed itself to a desperate defensive struggle. Gettysburg marked the turn of the military tide in the East.

Despite the Gettysburg victory, Lincoln was dissatisfied with Gen. Meade, who had failed to finish off Lee's demoralized and exhausted army as it retreated. Lincoln's disappointment soon faded with news of a great victory at Vicksburg in the western theater. The commander, Ulysses S. Grant, would soon solve Lincoln's leadership problem. His July 4 triumph at Vicksburg was thus doubly significant. Vicksburg represented the completion of the Union campaign to gain control of the Mississippi River and to divide the South in half. The successful capture of the city illustrated Grant's boldness and flexibility and his ability to think beyond particular engagements to the long-term plans for victory. No northern commander in the East could match him.

By the summer of 1863, the military situation finally looked promising for the North. The Union controlled much of Arkansas, Louisiana, Mississippi, Missouri, Kentucky, and Tennessee. In March 1864, Lincoln recognized Grant as the commander to conclude the war and appointed him general in chief of the Union armies. Grant planned for victory within a year and he came close to doing it within that time frame. Grant's first objective was to destroy the two main Confederate armies: Lee's Army of Northern Virginia and Joe Johnston's Army of Tennessee. Lee, still faithful to some conventional military theories, hoped for one great, decisive victory. Grant, an outsider to the prewar military establishment, had no difficulty in rejecting conventional military wisdom. He sought no one decisive engagement. Rather, he proposed a grim campaign of annihilation, using the North's superior resources of men and supplies to wear down and defeat the South.

Although Grant's plan entailed large casualties on both sides, he justified the strategy by arguing that "now the carnage was to be limited to a single year." A campaign of annihilation involved the destruction not only of enemy armies but also of the resources that fueled the southern war effort. While the idea of cutting the enemy off from needed supplies was implicit in the naval blockade, economic or "total" warfare was a relatively new and shocking idea. Grant, however, "regarded it as humane to both sides to protect the persons of those found at their homes, but to consume everything that could be used to support or supply armies." Grant followed this policy as he set out against Lee's army in Virginia.

Gen. William Tecumseh Sherman, who pursued Gen. Johnston from Tennessee toward Atlanta, further refined this plan. The war, Sherman believed, must also be waged in the minds of civilians. His desire was to make Southerners "fear and dread" their foes. Therefore, Sherman's campaign to Atlanta, and the subsequent march to Savannah, attempted to spread as much destruction as it did terror. Ordered to forage "liberally" from the land, his army left desolation in its wake. In the months after Lincoln's re-election in 1864, Sherman moved north from Atlanta into South Carolina and North Carolina while Grant pummeled Lee's forces in Virginia. The losses Grant was prepared to take were staggering: 18,000 in the Battle of the Wilderness; over 8,000 at Spotsylvania; another 12,000 at Cold Harbor. New recruits stepped forward to replace Grant's immense Union dead, while the Confederates had no such replacements. On April 9, 1865, Grant accepted Lee's surrender at Appomattox. In an unprecedented display of compassion and reconciliation, Grant allowed the southern soldiers and officers to return home with their personal equipment after promising to remain there peaceably. The war was over.

The war was technically won on the battlefield and at sea. Yet it was Grant's military strategy that succeeded, because the Union's manpower and economic resources could survive staggering losses of men and equipment, where the Confederacy's could not. As Union armies pushed back the borders of the Confederacy, the South lost control of territories essential for its war effort. Finally, naval strategy eventually paid off because the North could build enough ships to make its blockade work. By 1863, it was beginning to hurt the South. In 1861, fully 90 percent of the blockade runners were slipping through the naval cordon. However by the war's end, only half made it.

Lee's surrender at Appomattox usually signifies the end of the war, but was it? Today we know it was all but over, but Lee's surrender was not entirely clear then. President Davis had called for guerilla resistance on April 4; Lincoln was assassinated—shot on April 14, dying the next morning, and Seward was wounded in a knife attack as part of the same conspiracy. Johnston did not surrender to Sherman in North Carolina until April 29. Jefferson Davis was not captured until May 10 at Irvinsville, Georgia. Even with complete military defeat, many questions remained unanswered.

Items to Consider

Fire-Eaters, Process of Secession (December 1860–February 1861), Confederate States of America, Crittenden Compromise, Fort Sumter, West Virginia, Bull Run's lesson, Henri Jomini, U.S. Grant, emancipation, total war

CHAPTER 17

Reconstruction: The Unfinished Promise

When Lee surrendered at Appomattox, his act signaled not only an end to the war but the end of the old way of life in the South. The South lay defenseless in 1865, conquered by the superior armies of the North, broken in spirit, and yet full of contempt for their recent conquerors. The price they had paid for their efforts to preserve, protect, and defend slavery was high. Much of the South lay in ruin. Its industry was smashed; its plantations lay idle; its working class (both black and white) was suffering from the trauma of the last four years. More than a generation would pass before the South began to recover from the destruction of the war.

The intellectual consequences of the war required a much longer time. The South, shocked by the violence and destruction, unable to explain its loss, turned against the African-American population and blamed them for the origins of the war and ultimately the defeat. In the end, white southerners grew angrier, and racial distinctions became more rigid. In race, white Southerners found a sort of identity that seemed to transcend their material poverty. As poor as some were, they could still count on racial solidarity as a source of pride and identity. But by excluding African-Americans in this way, the situation in the South grew more complex and more violent.

The planters in the South neither willingly accepted emancipation nor oversaw the process (unlike what happened elsewhere). Southerners lost the war, and thus they lost the initiative in deciding what would happen. What would happen after the war was in Northern hands. There were many questions left unanswered at the end of the war—important questions.

1. One question involved the status of the freedmen. Would they be truly free? And how free is free? Were they to have political freedoms as well as social freedoms? Would they be economically free? Would they be free to choose their own occupations?

2. Another question involved what the South would look like economically in the postwar period. Would it have the same type of economy; that is, a plantation economy dominated by cotton and some form of unfree labor?

3. A question that was present in the minds of most people, North and South, both during and immediately after the war, was, who would govern the South in the future? Who would be the political leaders? Would the old political leadership be deposed?

4. A more generalized question was, would Reconstruction bring great social change to the South or would there be restoration to the basic form as it existed before?

5. Finally, all these questions spoke to a larger question: Who would run the federal government and on what principles would that government be run? Remember that Southerners had dominated the presidency for most of the history of the United States and held their own in the Senate. If the southerners were kept out of political power in the postwar years, Northerners and Westerners could determine the course of the nation's development.

The answers to these questions would define social relations in the South, the economic and political organization of the South, and, indeed, define the South itself.

The process of deciding these questions began during the Civil War when slaves began leaving plantations. As the Union armies moved through the South, the federal government had to decide how to reorganize certain confederate states politically. Lincoln was the first president to begin to deal with these issues. He did not develop a coherent plan, but he did begin moving toward a general Reconstruction policy. Lincoln's policy was essentially "malice toward none and charity for all." He had felt that the war was about restoring the Union and not about ending slavery, however much he personally hated the institution. The Emancipation Proclamation had been a war measure, and a particularly effective one at that. But Lincoln wanted a full restoration of the Union and he wanted it as fast as he could get it. As a result, once Southern states fell under federal control, Lincoln immediately appointed a military governor and began the process of attempting to bring them back into the Union as the war continued. His plan was called the Ten Percent Plan. When one-tenth of all the people who had voted in 1860 in the state took an oath declaring their loyalty to the Constitution, the captured state would be permitted to form a government. By 1864 three states (Tennessee, Arkansas, and Louisiana) had done so.

Lincoln's policy faced opposition from members of his own party. On one hand, many Northerners thought he was being too easy on the rebellious states. On the other hand, they felt he lacked the authority to impose this Ten Percent Plan. Many people argued that the authority was in the hands of Congress. Besides, they felt, whatever policy was established, it should be a much tougher policy. When the delegates from the three states showed up in Congress, the Republicans refused to seat them.

On their own, the Republicans put forward their own plan. The Republican plan was articulated in the Wade-Davis Bill of 1864. According to the Wade- Davis Bill, one-half of the citizens in a state who had voted in 1860 had to take the loyalty oath, though the oath itself was not more stringent than the one offered by Lincoln. Captured Southerners merely had to say that they had never voluntarily aided the Confederacy, which meant they could not have participated in the Confederate fight at all under this plan. Unlike Lincoln, who wanted a quick restoration, Congress did not want to move quickly, and under its plan virtually no state could return to the Union during the war. The Wade-Davis Bill further stated the Confederates who served in any office in the Confederate government or who served in the Confederate Army would be automatically disqualified from voting.

When the Wade-Davis Bill passed Congress, Lincoln did not entirely disagree with it, but he did not want to be tied down to any one plan so he vetoed it. He also claimed that he, the president, should formulate the Reconstruction policy, not Congress. In April of 1865 Lincoln was assassinated, and Vice President Andrew Johnson became president. Johnson was from Eastern Tennessee and had been the military governor of Tennessee under Lincoln's Ten Percent Plan. He was also a Democrat, brought on to the ticket with Lincoln, a Republican, in 1864 because he was a pro-Unionist. It was the only time in American history when there was such a split ticket.

Johnson came from humble origins. Never a slave owner, Johnson had considerable antipathy toward the plantation class. He first served in the House of Representatives and then in the Senate, where he introduced homestead legislation in the 1840s. Although he hated the planter class in the South, he was himself a vehement racist.

When Johnson became president in the spring of 1865, the war had just ended and Congress was out of session. Johnson, therefore, had the initiative in forming Reconstruction policy. He put forward his own plan. He appointed provisional governors in the former Confederate states. Those provisional governors were expected to call for constitutional conventions within their respective states. The task of the constitutional conventions was to write new state constitutions. Johnson was attempting to restore the Union as quickly as possible, and although he had expressly forbidden certain ex-confederates and Southerners with over $20,000 in property from participating in the conventions, he also allowed for a liberal "pardon" policy on an individual basis. As long as a Confederate came to Washington and asked for clemency, it was given. Johnson was so liberal in this policy that many ex-confederates, including the vice president of the Confederacy, Alexander H. Stephens, returned to Washington in the fall of 1865 to retake the seats in Congress they had vacated when their states seceded.

The immediate restoration of former rebels to Congress was unacceptable to many Republicans. For one thing, the Republican Party wanted to maintain its power nationally. It was a sectional party, a party with no constituency in the South, only outside the South. Repubicans knew that if they were to maintain their power they needed to build a constituency in the South. This would not be possible if the leaders of the South before the war were allowed to return to power. Many also feared that Restoration meant southern blacks would not be able to gain political freedom in the region. Because of these problems, many Republicans wanted some guarantees for the protection of black civil liberties and protection for whites who might be sympathetic to the Republican Party.

Unfortunately, the Republicans themselves had problems to deal with. When it came to a Reconstruction policy, the Republicans were divided into two main factions: (1) moderates (the majority) and (2) radicals. The moderate Republican plan for Reconstruction accepted much of the Johnson plan. They wanted to dispossess those Confederates who had held office, but also wanted to allow special pardons, just as the Johnson plan did. The moderate plan differed from Johnson by including some basic guarantees for voting rights and civil rights. While it expressed doubts about whether all black males should be given the vote, the plan indicated that some of them should get the vote. The moderate Republicans, moreover, seemed willing to discuss the possibility of requiring educational or property qualifications for voting. Both of those requirements would have hurt not only the freedmen but many poor whites in the South. Under the moderate plan, the southern states would also have the right of refusal for educational requirements and property qualifications. This was true of the Johnson plan, as well. If the southern states did not accept the measures, however, they would not get back into the Union. The point was that no southern state was going to be forced into accepting the measures of Reconstruction. They would suffer the consequences, but it was their choice.

The Radical Republicans were in complete opposition to the moderate Republicans and Johnson's plan for Reconstruction. A small group, they called for more severe measures. They thought the most important thing was to establish an equitable basis on which the nation could operate in the future. In other words, they wanted a vastly restructured South that essentially deposed much of the old planter class and brought a new class of Southerners to power. To facilitate this, the Radical Republicans wanted to reduce the southern states to territories and federal government would impose martial law. Anyone who would not take an ironclad oath of loyalty to the U.S. would be eliminated from politics. The Radicals felt it was important to weaken (if not completely destroy) the old planter class and build up a constituency of blacks and poor whites for the Republican Party. The Radicals also wanted to confiscate and redistribute plantations, which they felt was the only way to break the hold the plantation elite had over the south.

The radical plan for Reconstruction was not much different than the moderate one. They essentially wanted basic guarantees for universal suffrage, voting rights, and black civil rights generally. They also wanted the federal government to take some role in promoting the education of blacks. Significantly, they did not want to give the South a choice of whether to agree to this. Under the radical plan, the South would have no choice but to accept it. Where the moderates and Johnson wanted things to move quickly, the radicals wanted things to take a long time. This was partly because the Radicals wanted the South to pay for the destruction it had caused, but they also believed that exacting reparations would require an extended timetable.

Regardless of what each group wanted, the situation would be dictated by the moment. Johnson became president while Congress was out of session, and he followed through with his own plan. In September 1865 Congress came back into session and found that the southern states had thumbed their noses at the spirit of Johnson's plan. On both the state and local level, the planter elite who led the South into secession were back in power. On the national level, former Confederates were in Washington ready to re-take their seats. Johnson had pardoned many of them. This incensed the Republicans as well as many Union war veterans. The behavior of the individual states was also a problem. South Carolina refused to repudiate secession in its constitution. Even worse, South Carolina, Mississippi, and Louisiana passed black codes (laws restricting the freedom of blacks) based on the old slave codes. Mississippi would not ratify the Thirteenth Amendment to the U.S. Constitution.

Despite the Civil War, not much seemed to have changed. When the Republicans went back to Congress, they thought this was unacceptable. As a result, they decided to move in a different direction. It is important to note, however, that few Northerners supported the Radical Republicans. The moderates were not in favor of confiscating rebel plantations or giving blacks land. The moderates generally feared radical plans as too extreme for two reasons: (1) They were wary about the implications of the radical plan for property rights and (2) Most Republicans were wary of the power of the federal government because they were not sure the government had the authority the radicals supposed it did.

Moderate fears about the radical approach had to do with the moderate vision of what the South should look like after the war. They thought it would still be a cotton economy. They were afraid blacks would not grow cotton if they got their own land. In spite of the differences between moderates and radicals, both groups wanted something different than Johnson's plan. But what could they do in the fall of 1865 when the former Confederates showed up in Washington to take their seats under Johnson's plan? For a start, Congress refused to seat the southern representatives. Then Congress passed a series of bills in 1866 (including a Civil Rights Bill) designed to guarantee some civil rights for blacks. Johnson vetoed many of the bills, but Congress overrode his vetoes.

Republicans, however, found that there were many people in the North who did not want to go much further than that. Republicans were also afraid the Supreme Court would overrule it if it went too far. To prevent a rollback, they embodied many of the new proposals in an amendment. The Fourteenth Amendment (proposed on June 13, 1866 and ratified on July 9, 1868) was established to re-define citizenship in the United States. The amendment had four tenets: (1) Everyone born in the United States was a citizen; (2) No state may deprive a citizen of the privileges of citizenship or due process of law; (3) In an attempt to encourage the southern states to enfranchise all males, black and white, it allowed for a decrease in representation if states did not enfranchise blacks; and (4) It declared that no person who had held office in the Confederate government could hold office in the United States government.

The Fourteenth Amendment was written, in fact, by moderate Republicans who wanted to keep blacks in the South. They were also concerned about maintaining their own political power nationally. They wanted to sponsor the formation of a Republican party within the South. There was also the question of enforcement. It was not clear how much jurisdiction the federal government had. As a result, the federal government never said a state had to accept the Fourteenth Amendment, but to re-enter the Union, they had to ratify it; otherwise, the state would remain a territory. Johnson felt the Fourteenth Amendment was unconstitutional and told the South not to ratify it. Tennessee did anyway, but Tennessee was the only southern state that did. Thereupon the conflict between the Congress and the president began to heat up, officially ending presidential Reconstruction plans.

In the fall elections of 1866 the Republicans did well at the polls. By March 1867, Republicans in Congress enacted their own Reconstruction policy in a series of reconstruction acts—known as radical or military or congressional Reconstruction. It put the South under military jurisdiction. This was not the same as territorial status, but established three key principles: (1) It divided the South into five military districts under the control of the Union army; (2) It established that all people not excluded by the Fourteenth Amendment were to be immediately enrolled to vote; and (3) It provided for universal manhood suffrage; That is, all males, white or black, would be allowed to vote.

This was as far as the federal government would go. While it has often been referred to as Radical Reconstruction, it had its limits. Enforcement was ambiguous and the legislation had many loopholes. According to the voting statutes, it was not legal to deny the vote to anyone on the basis of color but you might be able to do so for other reasons. By 1869 the Fifteenth Amendment was ratified, enfranchising blacks in the North as well as in the South.

Items to Consider

Emergence of racism, Lincoln's plan for Reconstruction, Wade-Davis Plan, Andrew Johnson, Radical Republicans, Reconstruction bills, Fourteenth Amendment, five military districts, Freedman's Bureau, three major Republican problems

CHAPTER 18

The Failure of Southern Agriculture & the Rise of Populism

The American Civil War was certainly the Second American Revolution. But while the North had done so much so well in winning the war, it did little to ensure that southern blacks enjoyed the fruits of that victory. In fact, once the war was won, the North turned its back on the situation and allowed a century of subjugation of African-Americans in the South.

The labor arrangements that emerged after the Civil War were a direct result of the labor arrangements made during the war. When the Union Army came into contact with southern slaves, it had to come up with a system for dealing with them. The Union Army employed a contract-labor system for blacks who came under their care. Slaves were required to remain on the plantations and were punished if they did not work. If they tried to run off, the Army, when it found them, would return them to serve out their contracts. Though they were required to work, they were guaranteed either a wage or a share of the crop in return.

Freedmen, of course, did not want to return to the situation under slavery and they resisted the reestablishment of the plantation system as it had existed prior to the war. While still working in the plantation system, they exercised a form of freedom by moving around from one plantation to the other, until state laws were enacted in reconstructed states to prevent planters from "enticing" another planter's laborers away. Freedmen also withdrew their women and children from field work. This latter action had a serious consequence for southern agriculture: Productivity declined and labor was in short supply. Thus for a short time, freedmen were able to move around and get better contracts. But we should not overexaggerate those gains. Freedmen were fighting against two facts that were nearly impossible obstacles. First, most of the wealth in the South remained in the hands of whites. Second, northern whites wanted to keep blacks in the South. Neither planter nor freedman was happy with the contract system. Blacks did not want to work in gangs under white overseers. Planters were not happy with the labor shortage. Change had to come, although only one group would lead it.

In the late 1860, a new system of farm tenancy emerged from the discontent of both groups. Under this system blacks no longer lived in the old slave quarters, but were dispersed throughout the plantation. They were generally allotted twenty to thirty acres to farm, and left to their own devices. There were several types of tenancy, depending on the soils and crops. In the plantation belt, or Black Belt, where the soil was suited to plantation agriculture and cotton production, the most common type was sharecropping, followed by share rentals.

- **Cash Rentals:** This was the least common type of tenancy. In this system the renter supervised himself and paid his rent in the form of a fixed dollar amount or a fixed number of bales of cotton, not as a percentage. Since most blacks and landless whites in this region had little cash, this type of tenancy was uncommon.
- **Share Rental:** This was more common in the plantation areas. In this system the renter paid the plantation owner one-fourth of his cotton crop and one-third of his corn crop each year. Profits and losses were shared, despite production. Typically, cash renters came out a bit better than share renters.

- **Sharecropping:** This system was the most common form of tenancy in the plantation areas. Under the two types above, the renter had legal control of the crop. He "paid" the plantation owner. Under sharecropping, however, the renter did not have legal control of the crop. In this system the planter was the supervisor and the renter gave one-half of all crops to the owner. This type emerged because most freed blacks had little to bring to the bargaining table, ony themselves and their clothes. Here the owner provided all tools and materials and supervised the production of the crop. The renter becaome little more, in this system, than a wage laborer, as he had no control over the types of crops being planted, or when and at what price it was sold.

Labor was not the only problem planters faced. Getting their plantations back up and running required cash, something that was, again, in short supply. Prior to the war, planters had borrowed heavily from cotton factors to grow their crops. It worked fine before the war when cotton prices were high and everyone was making money. After the war, those cotton merchants were less willing to provide financing. Planters were losing their labor source, while the price of land and cotton were going down. To the merchants, planters appeared to be poor risks, thus credit came very high. Still, things might have been fine if the southern banks had recovered, but they did not for reasons that include the new uniform national currency (passed by the Union war Congress as banking acts), their inability to extend loans with real estate as collateral, and a high tax (10 percent) on state-issued bank notes.

The result was that the South had few postwar banks, and all those were in major cities. The factor system faced another problem in that now many of them were dealing with black farmers with small amounts of acreage. The merchants who acted as cotton factors considered freedmen even riskier. The persons who stepped in to lend credit then were local merchants, mostly Southerners. They set up shop in small country towns and took advantage of changes in transportation and communications. After the war, southern railroad construction changed. Instead of building lines from the major plantation areas to the ports, they were built to northern markets instead. Railroads, along with the expansion of telegraph lines bringing news of price changes, made it possible for small merchants in rural areas to turn a nice profit. Most merchants bought goods on credit from wholesalers. Then the merchant passed that debt on to mostly black consumers, beginning a two-level pricing system: The consumer paid one price if they bought in cash, a much higher one if they bought on credit. Most transactions for food and clothing were made on credit.

Mark-ups ranged from 40 to 70 percent. To ensure the tenant farmers would pay, merchants took a lien on their share of the crop. Thus, the merchant controlled the crop and would give what was left, if anything, to the black farmer. Since the farmer seldom grew a large enough crop to pay out, he became indebted to the merchant. What begins to happen here is a competition between the merchants and planters over who got the first lien on crops and who controlled black labor. In the short run, the planters won. During the 1870s, the courts issued ruling after ruling that favored the planters and laws that tied debtors to the lands, making them virtual debt peons.

Political Ramifications

The rise of the sharecropping system ensured that planters would retain complete control over the crops produced on their land by other people, their tenants. The planter, as these state laws mandated, received his share first. This crop-lien financing system had a significant impact on tenant farmers: 1) Anyone who invested in merchandising (owning the small stores, be they originally planter or merchant) usually had a monopoly over necessary supplies and credit; 2) States passed laws that made it illegal to leave the employment of a planter if he was owed money. These laws bound the freedmen to the land, making them debts peons; and 3) Small white farmers in the backcountry, where merchants had control, had to make similar agreements. The lack of planter dominance in these back regions encouraged merchants to move there and set up shop.

Most of the southern population before the Civil War was white, and did not own slaves. About two-thirds of southern families owned no slaves and only 2.5 percent owned more than fifty. Thus, the South was populated by small farmers generally engaged in subsistence agriculture, growing a little cotton as a cash crop. In many cases, plantations depended heavily on them for growing foodstuffs. While they tried to produce everything they needed, they could not, and a small, local-level barter economy, the exchange of goods and services as currency, grew up in place of a cash economy. The Civil War changed all that. Despite the fact that the War was fought for the interests of the elite, these yeomen farmers did the actual fighting. Their absence created dire economic hardships for their families at home, compounded by the fact that most of the fighting occurred in these areas, not on the plantations. Thus, there was plenty of property damage, as well.

When the war ended, suffering in the rural South was immense. The people needed to buy things immediately, but cash was scarce and prices were high. Even worse, their debts accrued during the war were substantial. This is one reason the Republican Party had such good success in these backcountry areas: They were willing to pass laws that kept those debts from being collected immediately, keeping farms from being foreclosed. Since these yeoman farmers needed cash and the price of cotton was high just after the war, they started growing more cotton. Unfortunately the price fell and, because of the crop-lien financing system, small farmers found themselves locked into the cotton economy. There lay the trap. Once you began to grow cotton, you were obligated to pay off the debts you incurred. This meant the small farmer had no choice but to grow cotton again the next year, and the next.

What happened, of course, was the transformation of the economy in these backcountry areas. No longer were they local barter economies but, because of the pain of the war, the debts, and the crop-lien system, Southerners began to grow cotton for a wider market. The yeomen had little choice. They need supplies that they can only get on credit from the merchants, who in turn were only willing to give credit for a promise to grow cotton, which the merchant could sell for a profit in northern markets. The merchant was uninterested in the items of the old barter economy: eggs, chickens, and vegetables. He wanted white gold—cotton. There was a slight chance for the farmers to make enough money, of course, to get out of the system. But the merchants charged high interest rates, and the worldwide cotton market was depressed to the extent that prices fell drastically. What happened was that these small farmers found themselves in an ever-tightening cycle of debt.

The results were traumatic. The old barter economy system was gone. The old reliance on subsistence agriculture was gone. And with these went economic independence, as well. Eventually, the majority of small farmers would lose their land and be reduced to tenant farmers on their old lands. Merchants in the backcountry became like the planters in the cotton belt. They controlled the land the laborers wanted to own. From this situation arose agrarian radicalism in the South, which became known as Populism.

The emergence of agrarian radicalism in the South came about for three reasons: First, there was a transformation of the southern economy, which included two particularly important elements: the rise of black tenancy and the absorption of white farmers into the cotton market. The latter meant that by 1890 more people were in cotton than before the Civil War. Second, equally important to understanding the discontent of the mass of farmers in the South, is the need to understand the place of the South in the national economy. By 1890, the South had assumed something of a colonial status in the national economy. It engaged in export agriculture and depended on the North for manufactured articles. It was essentially producing raw materials to be used in the industrialization of the North. What industry that developed in the South was either *extractive* in nature (removal of raw materials) or concentrated on processing of agricultural goods or forest products. The textile industry was the most important of the processing industries that developed in the South. Its labor force was white because planters controlled black labor and feared that the use of black labor in the textile mills would threaten the plantation system. The planters essentially did not want industrialization to develop in the South because that would also threaten the plantation system. Third, another important element to comprehend when considering the causes of agrarian radicalism in the South was the state of the national economy. The national economy was undergoing major stresses. In 1873, a severe depression hit the nation. In fact, it was a worldwide depression—the most serious depression in modern history. It continued until the end of the nineteenth century. The periods of 1873 to 1878 and 1893 to 1897 were the worst.

Rural areas were especially hard hit because the price of agricultural commodities dropped precipitously. What hit the South hardest, of course, was the drop in the price of cotton, especially during the depression. By the early 1890s, the price that cotton fetched on the market was far less than the cost of production. While the depression was hard for planters and plain folk alike throughout the South, it hit poor whites and blacks the hardest. If you were a black tenant farmer, you had to pay off the landlord and the merchant. The point is simple: It would have been hard enough to gain landownership in the best of situations, but in this scenario it was impossible.

Because of the sad state of the economy and because poor southern white farmers were going into serious debt and either lost their farms or were close to losing it, political discontent began to surface. But white southern farmers were in a political bind. Why? Because southern whites would only vote for the Democratic Party, but it was controlled by planters, merchants, and industrialists who were uninterested in reform. The alternative was to align with the Republican Party, but that was almost unthinkable. In the south, the Republican Party was the "black" party, the party of "radical reconstruction." As a result, most southern whites would not align themselves with the Republicans. But what could they do?

In the 1880s some whites began to run as Independents. They rarely won political office, and they never formed a real political organization. Politics in the South remained under the control of the Democratic Party. Then in the late 1880s, a powerful organization formed in the South that would become the backbone of the largest third-party organization in American history. The Southern Farmers Alliance started in Texas in the 1870s. The precipitating factor in Texas were cattle barons who were fencing in land. Small farmers needed access to the land being enclosed, so they formed a Farmers Alliance to stop the fencing. It was a brilliant success, and quickly spread to other states. Between 1886 and 1888 this organization of farmers began to spread to all states in the South. It became known as the Southern Farmers Alliance and had 2 million white members and 1 million black members by 1895.

At first the Southern Farmers Alliance was not a political organization. In fact, it attempted to organize a large spectrum of southern farmers outside of politics. The alliance wanted to address financial remedies, and it even attempted to appeal to some planters. The only people who could not join the organization were merchants, bankers, and speculators. Blacks also could not exactly join. They were allowed to form separate all black cadres, which in 1886 became known as the Colored Farmers Alliance. In short, outside of Texas, the members of the Farmers Alliance tried to work out arrangements to sell their cotton at better prices and buy goods without paying inflated credit prices. They tried to work out deals with merchants to sell them cotton in bulk and then allow the farmers to buy goods in bulk to reduce the cost. When that failed, they formed local cooperatives, which were Alliance-operated stores where farmers could sell cotton to the organization and purchase goods at competitive prices.

Part of the reason the Farmers Alliance did not get involved in politics at first was because it did not want to be sidetracked from its main goal; however, in the end, it did get politically involved. It found that the obstacles its members faced were too substantial to avoid politics forever. What were the obstacles? First, merchants were hostile to the Farmers Alliance and did everything they could to undermine it, especially the cooperatives. These merchants often controlled or heavily influenced the local political machines and made life hard for those who became involved in the Alliance. Second, the farmers discovered they did not have the money to finance the cooperatives. They did develop state cooperatives in many areas, but they were considerably underfunded and vulnerable to attack from the merchants.

Political Involvement

As the southern elite did everything in its power of obstruct the efforts of the Southern Farmers Alliance, the leaders of the Alliance came to realize that the only way they were going to accomplish their goals was to create a national alliance. They convened a huge alliance meeting in 1889 with the Western Farmers Alliance, which had about 2 million members. At the meeting, the Alliance members devised a strategy called the Sub Treasury Plan, and it became the centerpiece of their program. According to this plan, every agricultural county in the U.S. would have a warehouse to which a farmer could bring his cotton crop and get credit on 80 percent of it at an interest rate of 1 percent. The warehouse would sell the crop at the best price on the market. It would hold the cotton off the market rather than sell all cotton produced on the market at once. The entire plan would be financed by the federal government, and later extended to include all crops produced in the nation.

The Sub Treasury Plan immediately became a key political issue for two reasons: First, it challenged the established credit and marketing structure in the American economy. It proposed to reorient the whole way in which exchange relationships were carried on, and it proposed to do so in a "cooperative" way. Planters and merchants were especially hostile because it would end the crop lien system. Second, it unavoidably pushed the Alliance into politics. Alliance men knew they could only bring about the Sub Treasury Plan through political action.

The question that political involvement immediately raised for the Farmers Alliance was how to organize. A meeting of the southern and western branches of the Farmers Alliance in 1889 failed to unite the two because could not agree on some fundamental issues. Each side had its own unique concerns. Southerners were fearful of a party that united blacks and whites. They feared there would be reprisals from southern planters and that, in any case, it flew in the face of southern racism, which would prevent many Southerners from voting with them. Western farmers were fearful of being outnumbered by the southerners. The southerners had 3 million members (counting 1 million blacks), while the western/midwestern farmers made up only 2 million. Another problem involved politics. Westerners and Southerners had different political orientations. Westerners, who were more likely to be Republican, wanted protective tariffs. Southerners, who were almost certainly Democrats, were unilaterally opposed to protective tariffs.

In the end, neither side could come up with a compromise. The dreams of a national Farmers Alliance were set aside in 1889 as was the Sub Treasury Plan. Southern Alliance men went home and tried to work within the Democratic Party. During the 1890 elections, some Democrats seemed to speak to the interests of the Alliance. Those Democrats who did were easily voted into office; however, once in office, they did not fulfill their campaign promises. Too many of the large planters, merchants, bankers, and industrialists in the South were against these policies—and they had more influence with the Democratic Party.

The People's Party

In 1890 most of the Alliance men became discouraged with traditional parties. One group in Kansas formed its own political party, which was called the People's Party. The members were called Populists. They met success locally. The next year western and southern Alliance farmers again met to discuss uniting, but again they failed. It was not until early 1892 that an independent party incorporating both western and southern farmers' alliances was successfully formed. In that year, 1892, they ran a number of candidates. Three things are especially important about their challenge: ideology, political program, and race relations.

Ideology

The populists criticized the concentration of wealth and power in American society. This was the age of the *robber baron*, which was a pejorative term used in the nineteenth century referring to businessmen and bankers who dominated their respective industries and amassed huge personal fortunes, typically as a direct result of pursuing various allegedly anti-competitive or unfair business practices. This may have led to increased productivity, expansion of markets, more jobs, or acts of philanthropy, but it also often depended on the application of unscrupulous practices and bribery of public officials for "sympathetic" interpretations of the law. What rankled Populists and others in the nation was not just that a small number of people were getting rich, but that they were doing it at everyone else's expense. And these "rich" people (bankers, investors, speculators) were not working for a living, they were wheeling and dealing in the marketplace while the people who were doing the manual labor were getting poorer. The Populists came to believe that this was happening because the political system was corrupt. Thus, their criticism of American society was based on economic change and also on the political corruption they witnessed. America was no longer a democracy from their point of view but a *plutocracy*, a system of rule through wealth or by the wealthy. In a plutocracy, the degree of economic inequality is high while the level of social mobility is low; working people have no protection because unions were weak; the average worker was vulnerable to wage cuts, lay-offs, etc., and only wealthy citizens had meaningful rights.

It has been argued by some historians that the Populist critique was informed by two basic principles: 1) the Labor Theory of Value. This is the notion that labor is the source of all wealth, and manual labor in particular. Only those who physically produce something have a right to benefit from its sale. 2) Cooperative Ideal. We think of Americans as being fundamentally committed to individualism, but if you look back to the early colonial period, you will see that the strongest strain was geared to cooperation. The Populists did more than champion cooperation. They criticized competition. They saw competition as leading to excesses in the marketplace. The only reasonable alternative would be a society where basic relations were not governed by the marketplace and where competition held sway. Populists wanted a commonwealth of small producers. They wanted a nation dominated by people who worked and owned small property. They wanted cooperative enterprise and government regulation to protect small holders against the likes of the robber barons.

The Populist Political Program

What was the Populist program asembodied in their political platform? There were three aspects to the Populist political platform. The first was taken from the Farmers Alliance: The Sub Treasury Plan. This was to be financed by the federal government. To finance it by the federal government flew in the face of the "supposed" norm of the day—laissez faire—a period when the government did not involve itself in the economy. At least, that was the ideology espoused by the government and by big business. The trouble with this laissez faire philosophy, however, was that it was not followed. The government had always had its hand in the economy. On one side, it was involved in canal building and railroad building. On the other, it intervened on the side of industrialists to end strikes. What the Populists were asking for was a new role for the government—to come to the aid of farmers, and small farmers at that.

Second, the Populists called for the expansion of the money supply. Populists wanted the free and unlimited coinage of silver. In the 1890s the minting of coin was regulated. Populists essentially wanted silver monetized. The idea was that this would democratize the money supply. They wanted control of the money supply out of the hands of the bankers and speculators and placed under federal control—federal control more sympathetic to farmers, of course.

And finally, the Populists called for government ownership of all railroads and telegraphs (transportation and communication). The U.S. was the only western society where the government did not own the railroads. Instead, the U.S. relied on private ownership, which placed it in the hands of the richest men in the nation. The ownership of railroads by private men (robber barons), with their discriminatory rates, was a special irritant to farmers. It raised the price of goods and made it nearly impossible for farmers to find better markets, placing them squarely in the control of merchants and middlemen. Government ownership would mean control over prices and transportation costs, which would benefit farmers as well as consumers.

Race Relations

In outlining this kind of platform, the Populists were challenging the way the American economy was organized; but they also challenged the established order in another way. The second way they challenged the established order was on the issue of race relations. The Populists tried to build a coalition of poor whites and blacks within the South. This was the most threatening aspect for the planters. What was Populists' racial policy? At their best, they demanded that blacks have full civil and political rights. Populists suggested that they were willing to set a new view of race relations. When the People's Party was organized, blacks were included. They were no longer separated into black and white alliances. Individual state Populist Party leaders denounced lynching and the convict leasing system, which affected blacks mostly.

But racism did not disappear in America. It remained and qualified the commitment that populists were willing to make to blacks. It would have been unusual, in fact, for racism to disappear overnight. In any case, Populists were always careful to say they did not support social equality. Some of them would even continue to support the idea of white supremacy. Blacks found themselves in a predicament. Should they support the Populists? The economic reforms sponsored by the Populists were better for people who actually owned land. All the same, the Populists did offer more political democracy than the Democratic Party. Nonetheless, the persistence of racism among some prominent Populists made many blacks suspicious. In areas where blacks had been able to build up strong Republican organizations, they were reluctant to switch. Many not only did not join populists but denounced them for not coming out in support of black issues. Still, large numbers of blacks did vote for Populist candidates, which offered the beginnings of a biracial coalition.

By 1892 the agrarian radicals who were calling themselves Populists had formally launched their own political party, the People's Party. Their presidential candidate, James B. Weaver of Iowa, received only 8 percent of the popular vote in 1892, but Populism had become a national force. Not since 1856 had a third party, the Republican Party, won so many votes in its first national effort. Since it looked as if they were on the rise, what defeated the Populists? To begin with, the Populists faced wide spread fraud, particularly in the South, as Democrats stole elections and engaged in violence to suppress the party. But the real reason the Populists failed is that they allowed themselves to be sidetracked into two issues that eventually destroyed them. Those issues were fusion and the monetization of silver.

Populist successes in 1894 had come through the tactic of fusing with one of the two major parties by agreeing on a joint ticket. But fusion had already revealed itself to have particular problems. Many Democrats and Republicans who had "fused" with the Populists went their own way once elected. And, in any case, fusion always required the Populists to abandon much of their own platform. Meanwhile, under the influence of silver mine owners, many Populists became convinced that the hope of the party lay in the single-issue commitment to the free and unlimited coinage of silver.

The head of the People's Party, James B. Weaver, expected both major parties to nominate gold candidates for the presidential race in 1896, which would send disappointed silverites to the People's Party standard. The Republicans, holding their convention first, nominated William McKinley on the first ballot. A congressman from 1877 to 1891 and twice governor of Ohio, McKinley was identified with the high protective tariff that bore his name. Republicans argued that prosperity depended on tariff protection and the gold standard. The Republicans' nomination of McKinley was exactly what Weaver expected: a gold candidate.

The Democrats disappointed Weaver. The surprise nominee of the convention was William Jennings Bryan, a thirty-six-year-old congressman from Nebraska. Few people saw Bryan as presidential material, but as a member of the Resolutions Committee of the Democratic Convention, Bryan arranged to give the closing argument for a silver plank to himself. His dramatic speech swept the convention for the silver plank and ensured his nomination. In the final moments of the speech, Bryan stretched out his arms as if on a cross and the convention exploded with applause.

With the nomination of a silver candidate by the Democratic Party, the Populist strategy lay in shambles. Some People's Party leaders favored fusion with the entire Democratic Party ticket. Antifusionists were outraged, in part because the Democratic vice presidential candidate, Arthur Sewall, was an East Coast banker and an ardent hard money (gold) man. An unwise compromise was achieved when the Populist convention nominated Bryan but instead of Sewall chose Populist Tom Watson of Georgia as his running mate.

What essentially occurred was that the Populists were subsumed into the Democratic Party. Bryan ran as a Democrat/Populist. This meant there were two presidential candidates—Bryan as the Democrat/Populist and McKinley as the Republican; and three vice presidential candidates—a New Jersey businessman named Hobart as the Republican, Sewell as the Democrat, and Tom Watson as the Populist. Of course McKinley won the election by a handsome margin, and the Populist ticket crumbled. Although the Populist Party never again competed in a national election, they continued to dominate some sections of the nation while their platform was absorbed by the two dominant parties—finally coming to complete fruition in New Deal of the 1930s.

Items to Consider

Share cropping, problem with Southern politics, Southern Farmers Alliance, cooperatives, Sub-Treasury Plan, People's Party, Populist ideology, Fusion, the Silver Issue, Tom Watson

The Rise of Jim Crow and the African American Experience, From 1877 to the 1920s

Populism began a slow process of bringing poor white and poor black voters together in a political alliance, but it was a slow and painful process. Black voters were mostly in the Republican Party, poor whites in the Democratic Party. Nevertheless, the Populist movement made such an alliance possible. The Populists wanted a biracial alliance and believed in cooperation among poor farmers. This was a threat to the southern social system. It threatened the class advantages of the elite and it threatened the racial caste system of the south.

Populism collapsed in 1896 because the Populists sold out their party to free silver. Sadly, it also collapsed because of violence and intimidation in the South. When Populism had spent its last gasp, members of the Democratic white elite wanted to make sure that they would have no trouble from such an alliance again. To do that, they would try to eliminate as many of these poor voters from voting as possible. The effort to disenfranchise black and white voters was accomplished in four ways.

1. Poll taxes—a tax of a uniform, fixed amount per individual required for voting in parts of the United States that was often designed to disenfranchise poor people, including African-Americans, Native Americans, and whites of non-British descent.
2. Literacy requirements—the practice of testing the literacy of potential voters. Adopted by a number of southern states, the literacy test was applied in a patently unfair manner, as it was used to disfranchise many literate southern blacks and southern whites as it was up to the tester to decide whether the individual had the right to vote.
3. Property requirements—varied by state, but essentially voter had to hold property or hold a certain amount of property, or have taxable property.
4. All-white primaries—limited participation in Democratic primaries to "white citizens," effectively barring blacks from political participation in local and state elections in what was then a one-party state.

Some historians have claimed that these laws were only directed toward blacks and that they had some support from white Populists. According to this view, the Populists were frustrated at voting fraud and saw disfranchisement as a way to clean up southern politics. But this point of view is in error. It was not beneficial for the Populists to eliminate votes coming from people they were trying to attract to their party. The Fifteenth Amendment to the Constitution prohibited explicit disenfranchisement on the basis of race or prior enslavement. But sadly, the amendment did not prevent laws restricting the right to vote for other reasons, which is why the southern elite used these four types of laws to get around the Fifteenth Amendment and eliminate the Populist vote. Nevertheless, the evidence that these laws had white support is based on three escape clauses that, presumably, allowed poor whites to vote.

1. Understanding clause—entitled voters who could not pass the literacy test to vote, provided they could demonstrate their understanding of the meaning of a passage in the Constitution to the satisfaction of the registrar.

2. Grandfather clause—entitled voters who could not pass the literacy test to the satisfaction of the registrar, that they either were or were descended from someone eligible to vote in 1867, the year before blacks attained the franchise.

3. Good character clause—An appointment board in each county could register "all voters under the present [previous] law" who were veterans or the lawful descendants of such, and "all who are of good character and understand the duties and obligations of citizenship."

The key point was that the decision as to whether or not a voter satisfied those requirements rested with the registrar, who was of course a white Democrat. Obviously, the first view was wrong. Rather, most Populists realized the reason behind the laws and were opposed to them; but they lacked the power to stop their passage. These laws were made for and by the elite to keep poor people of both races from voting.

Not that disfranchisement was entirely a southern phenomenon. Northern states were employing similar measures, a number of them making the ability to read English a requirement, thereby eliminating a great number of immigrants. There were two main results of disfranchisement: First, the U.S. experienced a tremendous decline in voter turnout. In 1888, the number of eligible voters voting was about 80 percent. Only two years later, in 1890, that number had fallen to 60 percent. By 1910, only 30 percent were voting. Only five percent of blacks were voting by 1910. The number of white voters dropped, too. By the 1930s, only 20–30 percent of the eligible white voters cast a ballot. And secondly, the Republican Party was completely eliminated in the South. That left a one-party South, led by the Democrats who remained in exclusive power until the passage of the Voting Rights Act in 1965.

Rise of Jim Crow

At the same time poor whites and blacks were being denied the right to vote, they were also being socially segregated from one another. It was part of a larger national, indeed worldwide trend. But it was at its worst in the South. The 1870s and 1880s were the age of racism, of the new imperialism. It was a time when Social Darwinism, and all the racial assumptions that includes, held sway. It even hit the U.S. Supreme Court. In 1896, the Supreme Court issued its famous *Plessey v. Ferguson* decision which legalized the "separate but equal" doctrine. It was not overturned until 1954.

Segregation had a long history in the South. Slavery itself was a form of segregation, yet the segregation of the 1890s was different. During slavery, it did not make sense for slaves not to go along with their owners on train rides or in hotels. While there had been some segregation in cities, the situation before and after the Civil War was fluid; no hardline segregation had developed. The between 1889 and 1915, all southern states enacted Jim Crow laws, which provided for the legal segregation of black and white in schools, railroads, workplaces, hospitals, hotels, taverns, water fountains, even school books. Why had this situation not come about earlier, given racial views in the South? 1) Most of the South was rural, and segregation made no sense in that setting. 2) In the 1870s and 1880s the planters were dominant and they opposed segregation. 3) Black voting power made sure planters and merchants did not support any such laws, but once that voting power was gone, they had no reason not to.

The growth of towns and cities, though, created more situations in which black and white could mingle. Merchants and planters came together in the 1890s and agreed that black voters should be disfranchised and segregated. The Populist movement itself, which the planters and merchants saw as a radical threat, contributed to the impetus among the southern elite to deny blacks and poor whites the right to vote, and to separate them along the lines of race to ensure they would not have the opportunity to mingle and learn who their true enemies were.

By the turn of the twentieth century, the Solid South had emerged. In every election, the Democratic Party received solid support from southern voters. In fact, Republican candidates did not even appear on the ballot in most southern areas. Led by merchants and planters, the Solid South would endure before another major depression and, eventually, the Second World War forced the South to modernize. It also required another reconstruction, this time in the form of the

Civil Rights movement, which rocked the South and forced a change where southern blacks regained the freedoms they lost at the end of the nineteenth century.

African American Life, 1877 to the 1920s

Most Americans like to believe in the idea of progress, that the condition of all peoples improves through time. It is hard for them to accept that that does not always happen. It did not happen for women, blacks, Native Americans, or Loyalists in the aftermath of the American Revolution. Nor did it happen for African-Americans after the Civil War. The failure of the Confederacy sparked a great hope among blacks of finally achieving total equality and a true opportunity for citizenship. Thousands stepped forward to claim that right, only to be steamrolled back in the other direction. The Compromise of 1877, which ended Reconstruction in the South and (in effect) reestablished the dogma of states' rights, marked a death sentence for the hopes of black Americans. The black codes passed in the immediate aftermath of the war had given irrefutable proof that the white South was determined, once and for all, to keep southern blacks in complete and total subjugation. Southerners claimed they were only efforts to resist Republican rule, to prevent a Yankee punishment for having brought on the war. Regardless of the purpose, the facts are crystal clear.

As Reconstruction came to an end, most of the early black leadership in the South was killed, intimidated, or driven out. Keep in mind that the issue of class here is just as important as race. It was the southern elite who had the most to lose. They were determined not to let anyone, white or black, stand in their way. Even white politicians who tried to encourage political activity by southern blacks faced the same treatment. Take the case of "Print" Matthews of Copiah County, Mississippi. Matthews was a powerful man. His father had been a slave owner. His sons went to the University of Mississippi. Matthews owned the biggest general store in his home town of Hazelhurst. The county was evenly divided (at roughly 5,000 population) between black and white. After the war, Matthews worked with Republicans to make the transition to freedom easier for blacks in that county. In the election of 1883, he called together the supporters of his Fusion Independent Party, made up of black Republicans and a few white farmers.

The response by the rest of the white population was a campaign of terror. One hundred fifty armed men roamed the countryside, pulling a cannon with them, firing at any African-Americans they found. Beatings and murders intimidated the black population from voting. Many of those 150 mob members were planters and merchants. Their purpose was to intimidate and eliminate their opposition. The gang visited the cabin of a black farmer named Tom Wallis, a friend of Matthews. When Wallis resisted a beating, they shot him dead and wounded his wife as she ran to his aid. The black church was burned to the ground and much of the black population of the county was force to flee their homes and hide in the woods until the election was over. Matthews was served notice not to go to the polls. He told them to drop dead and went anyway. He was confronted by a Democratic thug named Ras Wheeler who had been given the task of keeping Matthews from voting. The two argued for a moment, then Matthews gave his ballot to an election official. At that moment, Wheeler reached into a wooden box, pulled out a shotgun, and killed Matthews. At this point in the story, you would think I would talk about law and order being established. But such was not the case. The next day the Copiah Democratic Executive Committee met at the county courthouse. They passed a number of resolutions. First, anyone trying to avenge Matthews' death would find swift retribution. Second, no member of the Matthews family was ever to enter politics again. And last, no man, of any color, was allowed to organize blacks against whites again within the county.

Sadly, these kinds of events were repeated throughout the South time after time. In place after place, blacks and poor southern whites were intimidated into following the Democratic Party's lead. By the 1890s, thanks to disenfranchisement laws and the failure of Populism, blacks had lost the right to vote in much of the South. William Sinclair in his *Aftermath of Slavery* (1868) realized how important the vote was to the African-American. With the vote, he wrote, the black man was a man. Without it, he was less than a slave. He was merely a thing. According to Sinclair, such atrocities as what happened to Print Matthews were evident everywhere in the South. Sinclair pointed specifically to Sen. Benjamin Tillman of South Carolina, who had recently advocated the killing of 30,000 black men in that state, even boasting in public lectures before Congress that he had taken part in "shooting niggers." In a lecture in Detroit, Tillman claimed that he took part in the murder of seven blacks. Tillman did not know how many he had killed but, he said, "I got my share." Sinclair noted that "not one of these unfortunate colored people had committed, or even been charged with, any offense." They had simply tried to vote and for this they had been gunned down.

In fact, Tillman became the prototype of these politicians who used "nigger baiting" for public support. One of the things that Tillman hated the most was the South Carolina Constitution of 1868, which he said was drafted by black

Republicans. To destroy it, he called for a new convention in 1895 to adopt a new constitution. Of the 160 delegates, only six were black. One of the most eloquent speakers was Thomas Miller, a graduate of Lincoln University in Pennsylvania and former congressman. Miller knew what the purpose of the convention was, to take away the right of South Carolina blacks to vote. Miller publicly denounced the 1895 Constitution, but was promptly chased out of the state by threats against his life.

Economic discrimination went hand in hand with political discrimination. After the Civil War ended, blacks were excluded from a wide range of jobs. John Mercer Langston, a black lawyer and representative of the Freedmen's Bureau, reported that after the war one-third of the black population in North Carolina were skilled craftsmen. Ten years later, he found after conducting a similar study that the blacks were mostly driven out of those fields and almost all were tenant farmers. It was that way throughout the South. As the words of Mississippi politicians James Vardamen declared, black people had only one role in the south: "That of a menial. That is what God designed him for and the white people [of the south] will see to it that God's design is carried out."

Despite the effort to contain African-Americans, there were a number of individuals who stood against the progression of discrimination. The first man who emerged as leader and spokesman, first of southern blacks then of all blacks, was Booker T. Washington. When he was a student at Hampton Institute, he attracted the attention of the president of the University for his energy and intelligence. The president recommended the twenty-five-year-old man as the head of a newly established teacher training school in Tuskegee, Alabama. With forty students and an abandoned shack, Washington began in 1881 what came to be known as the Alabama Normal and Industrial Institute (later the name would be changed to Tuskegee Normal and Industrial Institute or Tuskegee Institute).

Washington stressed hard work, simple living, healthy diet, cleanliness, and piety at the Tuskegee Institute. Perhaps his best talent though was that of diplomacy in dealing what he called the "other nation"—that of southern whites—and in attracting the attention of northern capitalists like Andrew Carnegie. In Washington's mind, the future of the South lay in entering the Industrial Age and escaping from agriculture. It had been that overdependence on agriculture that caused slavery and the Civil War. To become great, the South had to cast off the bonds of agriculture and create its own industry. Free blacks then had a great opportunity. But to succeed they had to master new industrial skills, making themselves vital parts of the New (industrial) South.

Industrial or practical education then, was to be the most important aspect of the Tuskegee Institute. While science, math, history, and literature were important, they were secondary to training for the new tasks that would make black people wealthy enough to take care of themselves. Black advancement had to be based, Washington argued, on hard work, thrift, saving, and owning property. It was not Washington's goal to keep blacks from succeeding in other areas, but in order to improve the conditions of the race, practical skills were most important. In his words, he wanted industrial education not to "cramp" the black man, but "because I want to free him." Washington was proud that Tuskegee taught thirty trade skills. Of the institute's sixty buildings, fifty-six had been built by the students themselves. In a single year, they had manufactured 2 million bricks.

Despite his work at Tuskegee, Washington gained national fame for his speech at the Cotton States and International Exposition in Atlanta in 1893. It was widely reprinted by white newspapers who agreed with what he was saying. The wisest among "his race," Washington proclaimed during the speech, "understand that the agitation of questions of social equality is the extremist folly, and that progress in the enjoyment of all the privileges will come to us [African-Americans], but must be the result of severe and constant struggle." He assured the white South that they did not need immigration to become an industrial power. "Cast down your bucket among those people who have, without strikes and labor wars, tilled your fields, cleared your forests, built your railroad and cities. ... You can be sure in the future, as in the past, that you and your families will be surrounded by the most patient, faithful, law-abiding and unresentful people that the world has seen ... with a devotion that no foreigner can approach, ready to lay down our lives, if need be, in defense of yours." Yet even then, Washington assured white Southerners that they need not fear blacks would demand social equality. "In all things that are purely social, we can be as separate as the fingers, yet one as the hand in all things essential to [our] mutual progress."

Outrage came quickly from several sectors of the black community. One of the loudest voices was that of John Hope, a graduate of Brown University and a later member of the faculty at Atlanta Baptist College. Hope was offended by Washington's repeated assurances that blacks did not want social equality. "If we are not striving for social equality, in heaven's name for what are we living? I regard it [as] cowardly and dishonest for any of our men to tell white people or colored people that we are not struggling for equality. Why build a wall to keep me out? I am no wild beast, nor am I an unclean thing."

Others criticized Washington for stressing industrial education over true education. The most famous of these was a young man from Massachusetts named William Edward Burghardt Du Bois. W. E. B. Du Bois grew up in Great Barrington, Massachusetts, a classic New England town pervaded by decaying Puritanism. In 1885, at age of 18, Du Bois was awarded a scholarship to Fisk University in Tennessee. His family did not really want him going to the South, but he went anyway. To say his experience there was a culture shock is an understatement. The church services were emotional and passionate. And then, of course, there was racism. Both would shape him in ways he could not imagine.

Du Bois graduated from Fisk and won a scholarship to Harvard, where he entered as a junior in 1888. Even before he left the South, he had become concerned with the "black question." At his graduation, Du Bois spoke about Jefferson Davis. He described Davis as a decent and honorable person misled by Teutonic ideals that suggested it was necessary to conquer other peoples to advance civilization. If only he had understood the turmoil such conquest would cause, Du Bois suggested, Davis would never have led the South into war or supported the institution of slavery. After going to Germany to study for a year, Du Bois returned to Harvard and earned his Ph.D. with a brilliant dissertation on the African Slave Trade. Upon graduation, he was offered a position at Wilberforce University in Ohio, where he began his academic career. Two years later, he moved on to the University of Pennsylvania.

At the University of Pennsylvania, Du Bois was given the task of examining the Seventh Ward, a predominately black area in Philadelphia. Black crime in the Seventh Ward had risen dramatically since the Civil War. It was here that Du Bois had his first great experience at analyzing social problems. Poverty and segregation, he argued, were destroying the black community in America. The rising crime rate there was only a symptom of a larger problem.

Du Bois then went to Atlanta University where he continued to study the problems of black life in urban places. He was still young and idealistic. He thought the problem of race relations was simply one of education. Ignorance and stupidity were the ultimate evils. But then something happened. One particular moment turned Du Bois away from these types of studies. A black farmer named Same Hose killed his landlord in a dispute over wages. Before he could be arrested, a mob lynched him.

Shortly afterward, Hose's knuckles were put on display at a nearby grocery. This made Du Bois realize that complete scientific detachment, for purposes of study, was impossible in the South. More and more after that he turned to journalism to make these problems known. Part of this transformation was that Du Bois had slowly come to realize that black culture had its own "soul"—an inner power and meaning. The fate of that soul was not to be brushed aside or absorbed by white America. It had to be honored for what it was. These ideas came to focus in one of the most remarkable books of the age, *The Souls of Black Folk* (1903). It was a book about what it meant to be black at the turn of the century. To Du Bois, the new man of power in the South was neither the planter or the merchant or the African-American. It was a class of poor whites who had been freed from the dominance of the planters by the war and who had remade the South in their own image, exploiting both planters and blacks.

Just as important, Du Bois believed that the true source of a distinctive African-American culture lay in black religion. There were three distinguishing characteristics to black religion—the Preacher, the Music, and the Frenzy. The preacher was the most unique. He was a leader, a politician, an orator, and an idealist. Du Bois believed the black preacher to be the direct inheritor of the tribal medicine man. During slavery, the preacher was the one who healed the sick, interpreted God's actions, comforted the slaves. He was a doctor, a judge, and a priest. From the black preacher came the first true African-American institution—the Negro church. To Du Bois, blacks should strive to attain the role of the preacher in order to become a leader and teacher of their people.

But Du Bois did not simply advocate the power of religion. To him the most important thing about being black in the U.S. was what he called the Black Consciousness. The black American was downtrodden throughout history. Yet they had been given a great gift according to Du Bois; they were able to see the hope and promise of America in ways no white ever could. African-Americans were constantly, Du Bois wrote, aware of their special place in American history. He was both American and black, struggling to become more American while struggling not to lose that which made him distinct. *The Souls of Black Folk* belongs right there with Harriet Beecher Stowe's *Uncle Tom's Cabin* or Thomas Jefferson's *Declaration of Independence* or Thomas Paine's *Common Sense* or the *U.S. Constitution* as one of the most important pieces of literature in American history. Its genius was that it defined Black Consciousness for black people. It became a creed for black people all around the world.

Yet the part that caused the greatest sensation was Du Bois' attack on Booker T. Washington. Du Bois represented a new generation of northern blacks, who were unwilling to accept the social inequality espoused by Washington. Washington had been the perfect black folk hero for the post-Reconstruction period, Du Bois wrote. But his day was done. Washington's message no longer held meaning for a new generation of black leaders. Indeed, Du Bois thought Washington had sold out, using the Atlanta Compromise speech (as it came to be known) to become the most distinguished southerner since Jefferson Davis. The policy of submission was, Du Bois wrote, a clear failure. It had only led to the stripping away of what few civil rights blacks enjoyed. It was now the duty of the new generation of black leaders to oppose the policy of the most famous black man in America.

Du Bois' attack was a bit unfair. First, Washington was not at all opposed to higher education. There was more to Washington and Tuskegee than accommodation and economic improvement. Washington taught his students how to earn a good living and that they had an important mission in life—to go back into the black community and spend their lives trying to improve the conditions of their fellow man. Washington built community, which was not the case for Du Bois.

As much as I love and respect Du Bois, he called for a selfish form of education which tended to encourage blacks to escape their homes and act in their own self-interest; to leave behind their impoverished brethren. Washington had no alternative, given the racial situation in the South at that time and, at the very least, his system was democratic. Du Bois called for the creation of black elitism, suggesting that leadership of the African-American community be handed over to the "talented tenth" of the black population, those who had a liberal education such as himself, so that the intellectual elite could make the best decisions for black America. Despite these discrepancies, Du Bois was clearly one of the most intelligent men in our nation's history; his call to arms resonates generations after his death.

One final note: It is curious that the South spawned the two most progressive movements in American history, Populism and Civil Rights. In both cases blacks played prominent roles, and yet they still did not achieve the equality they so deserved. Remember the words of Martin Luther King Jr. The true enemy of both black and white was poverty. Until both races were free of that condition, nothing would change. It is the same populist message echoing seventy years later.

Items to Consider

"Print" Matthews, William Sinclair, aftermath of slavery, Booker T. Washington, W. E. B. Du Bois, Atlanta Compromise, John Hope, *The Souls of Black Folk,* talented tenth, Jim Crow

CHAPTER 20
Progressivism and the Progressive Movement

Movements for reform swept America between the 1890s and 1917. Everybody in the country seemed to want change. Farmers wanted better prices, railroad regulation, and an end to the power of bankers, middlemen, and corrupt politicians. Urban residents wanted better city services and better city government. Members of various professions, such as social workers and doctors, wanted to improve the dangerous and unhealthy conditions in which many people lived and worked. Businessmen, too, lobbied for goals that they defined as reform. By 1910, many of these crusaders began to call themselves Progressives. Ever since, historians have used the term Progressivism to describe the many reform movements of the early twentieth century.

Yet in the goals they had and in the reforms they wanted, the reformers varied a lot, and were often contradictory. Some wanted political influence over ordinary people. Others wanted to concentrate all political power in the hands of a few, the technical elite. Some wanted to restrict the growth of large corporations, while others believed that large corporations were good and proper. Some Progressives were concerned about the welfare of the new immigrants from southern and eastern Europe; others wanted to either "Americanize" them or keep them out altogether. In general they all sought to improve America and create social stability, but each group of Progressives had its own definition of what improvement and progress meant. Certainly there was no unified progressive movement. But it was a movement in the sense that so many people wanted to reform what they saw as the evils of nineteenth century America—poverty, lack of education, immigration, big business, etc.

One of the problems with understanding the Progressive Movement is a matter of terminology. Historians have often tried to see many of these reforms as "good" or "enlightened." Progressives liked to think that those reforms were. But truth be known, we should not accept all these reforms as good. Many of them were not. Many of them were antimodern and some were downright evil. Thus, in a broad sense, Progressivism was the way in which a whole generation of Americans defined themselves politically and responded to the nation's problems at the turn of the century.

The Cities

Cities were hotbeds of political, social, and labor unrest. Within the American city you could find the extremes of American society: poverty and wealth. If there was to be a revolution in the U.S., it would start in the cities. Throughout the nineteenth century, the American city had grown rapidly. As industry and immigrants, mostly from southern and eastern Europe, poured into the urban environment, the effect was the creation of a number of contrasts: wealthy and poor, powerful and weak, crime and culture, corruption and reform, the dangerous classes (made up mostly of immigrants living in tenement houses) and the hard-working (or was that just a myth?) middle class, along with a growing faction of intellectuals: writers, journalists, and scholars. New York and Chicago were the two major American cities. By 1877 New York was a filthy, crime-infested hole. American writer John Jay Chapman said the city was not even a civilization but rather a railroad station, a stop on the way to somewhere else. From 1881 to 1895, murders in New York City increased six times faster than the population. Juvenile crime became a major scandal, with many of the young criminals starting as early as six and seven years old.

The American city's greatest failure to deal with the problems of crime and poverty was best embodied in the institution of the tenement house. They were certainly not nice places to live, yet so much of New York's population did live here. Jacob Riis pointed out that 75 percent of New York City's population (about 1.2 million people) lived in some 37,000 tenements. These tenement houses were hotbeds of crime, poverty, and every social problem you can imagine. A typical New York City tenement was four to six stories high and next to a street. The first floor was often some kind of store. Four families occupied the other floors where each had a living room and two or three small dark closets they used as bedrooms. In one of the worst of these tenements, police counted some 101 adults and 91 children. Some tenement houses even had basements, often including a bakery which was a breeding ground for tuberculosis because floor dust makes everyone cough and spit. A number of tenement houses burned down because of fires starting in these hot-grease-filled basements. The tenement house basement was also the center of criminal activity and, after New York City forced prostitution off the streets, centers of prostitution, as well.

The first modest tenement house reforms came in 1869, when New York passed a law requiring a window in every bedroom. To get around the law, most tenement houses put in an air shaft, which often was used as a trash shoot and quickly became the home of every kind of filth you can imagine—worsening the air supply. Death, of course, was common. In 1888, one-third of all Italian babies born in Mulberry Bend, an Italian ghetto in New York City, died. When ninety-four of the worst tenements were seized by New York City in 1888, the death rate in them had been two and one-halfs times higher than the city as a whole. The Society for the Prevention of the Cruelty to Children had come to the aid of 138,891 children that same year and had removed some 25,000 battered children. Infants were left in doorways and on the street every night; the police generally collected some three or four a night. In 1889, of the 508 babies born at Randall's Hospital in New York City, 333 died. Of the 170 picked up off the streets that year, 80 percent died. That same year 72 more babies were found dead in the streets. Of the 82,200 people arrested by New York City police in that same year, 10,505 were under the age of twenty. Chicago was only better in that it had burned to the ground in 1871, and most of the worst parts of the city went up in the fire. When the city was rebuilt, however, it was still ruled with an iron hand by a combination of political bosses, real estate agents, and capitalists. Later, they were forced to compete with crime bosses.

By 1895, you can see the state of the American city. It was an increasingly polarized place. During the Gilded Age (roughly 1878 to 1889), the impetus for reform was undermined by the large numbers of politicians, businessmen, and thinkers who opposed reform: laissez fair businessmen, social Darwinians, and antireform politicians dominated the discourse. Yet in the period of the Progressives, that rigid partisanship and polarization over whether there should actually be reform dissipated. It was replaced by the question of what type of reform there must be. Even the best and the brightest in business, industry, government, and the intellectual elite realized that something had to be done or the growing underclass in the American city would indeed revolt.

The "Progressive Era"

The period of 1895–1920 is called the Progressive Era. Yet, Progressivism was no single political movement. It was a combination of a wide variety of reforms. Historians cannot agree on what Progressivism was or who, in fact, were the Progressives. There are too many paradoxes in the movement itself. Even more perplexing, a good deal of the sentiment for reform was instigated by big businesses who wanted to stabilize the American economy, workforce, and society.

When forced to describe the origins of the movement, most historians believe the roots of Progressivism lay in the Populist movement and emergence of muckraking journalism. Many of the reforms championed by the People's Party were adopted by the progressives. The collapse of the farmer's movement led to the Progressives carrying the Populist movement's plans, or many of them, to the cities. The American city is where Mugwump Republican ideas—Republicans who championed honest government—combined with the ideals of the Populists and put them to the test. The second group that helped bring about Progressivism was the muckraking journalists. These journalists and other literary social critics exposed the evils of tenement life, the corruption of city government, the excesses of industry, and every other problem they could find in the American city and nation. Mugwumps got their name from Teddy Roosevelt, who saw them as a negative influence in American society and compared them to one of the characters in John Bunyan's *Pilgrim's Progress*. Henry D. Lloyd was perhaps the first muckraker. He criticized Standard Oil and other monopolies. Jacob Riis was a Danish immigrant who exposed New York City slums in *How the Other Half Lives* (1890). There were countless other, like Ida Tarbell and Lincoln Steffens, all exposing the unsavory nature of American society during the period.

The Mugwumps and muchrackers were responsible, along with the problems of city and farm life, for instigating the progressive movement. But who were the Progressives? This is a difficult question, because they seemed to represent so many points of view. The first group was represented by political reformers (mainly from the middle class). They believed that science and the scientific method should be employed to help the urban poor. Generally, they disdained partisan politics. The second group was upper-class reformers: they were generally the political and social elite who wanted limited political and economic reform in order to stabilize American society. They would not support wide-scale changes, but rather, they sought stabilization. The third group of progressives was working-class reformers: they were generally from the East and of immigrant stock. They wanted government to alleviate the hardships brought about by industrial growth in the cities. And generally, they were against reforms like prohibition and changes to the civil service system. The fourth and final group was the socialists who included everyone from radical populists, to unionists, to intellectuals. They wanted more than reform. They wanted a revolution. On one hand, they wanted to dismantle large concentrations of wealth so it could be redistributed among the lower classes. On the other, they wanted a new form of government that allowed for equal participation.

The Progressive Movement was a complicated combination of these groups. Yet the most important element was the middle class. While all the groups participated and had a voice in the movement, the voice of the middle class dominated and it is crucial to remember that these people hoped to bring about a conservative reform movement, reform from the center. As a result, change would be widespread and long lasting.

The Five Features of Progressivism

Although the Progressive Movement included a large number of different kinds of reformers, the "movement" had a number of general themes. The first is democracy. Progressives wanted to make government more responsible to the people. Their primary opponent there was the urban political machine, which the Progressives viewed as corrupt and fundamentally antidemocratic. One of the first major changes the Progressives called for was the creation of the direct primary. Prior to 1870 there were few direct primaries in America. But from 1896, when South Carolina was the first to adopt the system, until 1916, virtually every state in the nation adopted a direct primary system, making the electors sent to national conventions legally bound to vote for the candidates the people voted for in the primary on the first ballot. The day of the smoke-filled room was coming to an end. But that is not the only change. Other reforms, like Initiatives and referendums, gave voters the right to enact laws directly. Some twenty states adopted Initiative and referendum during the progressive period. Some states even began to directly elect their senators; by 1912, thirty states had senate primaries and it became a national law when the Seventeenth Amendment was ratified in 1913.

The second theme of the Progressives was efficiency. Progressives liked to preach what they called the Gospel of Efficiency. Frederick Taylor's Theory of Scientific Management laid out the principles of labor efficiency. This became a mainstay of Progressive politicians. In federal and state governments, agencies and departments were reorganized with overlapping and redundant functions discarded. They also worked to get state governments to adopt a budget system where the state created a budget, an annual plan for expected expenditures, for each fiscal year. Two new ideas for making city government more efficient gained support during the progressive period. First was the Commission System, which placed city government in the hands of an elected committee responsible for sub-areas of city government ranging from police power to sanitation to utilities. The second, and more durable idea, was the city-manager plan, where a professional urban planner was hired to direct the efficient functioning of that city's municipal government.

The third characteristic of the progressive period was regulation. Here you can see the heritage of the Populist movement. The concern over the power of large corporations reached a head during this period. Interestingly, the Progressives had the perfect tool to combat monopolies in the Sherman Anti-Trust Act of 1890. The Sherman Act provides that "Every contract, combination in the form of trust or otherwise, or conspiracy, in restraint of trade or commerce among the several States, or with foreign nations, is declared to be illegal." The act further stated that "Every person who shall monopolize, or attempt to monopolize, or combine or conspire with any other person or persons, to monopolize any part of the trade or commerce among the several States, or with foreign nations, shall be deemed guilty of a felony." Thus, the act put responsibility on government attorneys and district courts to pursue and investigate trusts, companies, and organizations suspected of violating the act.

The Progressives wanted to use the Sherman Anti-Trust Act to regulate the excesses of these corporations, but they were at odds as to how to do it. There were four possible routes: 1) Let business work out its own destiny under laissez-faire; 2) Adopt a socialist program of public ownership; 3) Direct the government to engage in a program of trust busting to destroy monopolies; and 4) Use the government to reform the worst abuses of monopolies. The first two solutions proved to be too extreme for most people and were largely put aside. The socialist movement was successful on the municipal level; gas and water socialism, as it was called, allowed cities to own their own utilities. The other two solutions were what most of the fuss was about in the progressive period. Either the government could engage in a program of trust busting to destroy monopolies in the hope that competition would be good for the economy, or they could allow monopolies to go their own way and only reform the worst abuses. There was a period of trust busting, but in the long run the pattern of regulating corporate excesses proved more viable because competition was not restored when the trusts were busted. The same old problem, however, surfaced. Who guards the guards? In every case, the regulatory commissions, one by one, again fell under the influence of big business.

The fourth important theme of the Progressives was that of social justice. This was perhaps the most spirited of progressive reforms. They used this premise to reform liqor laws and child labor abuses, and to create private charities that sought to reform the lives of the urban poor. The quest for social justice also spawned a generation of reformers; many of them women, who remained active in public service throughout their lives. The most significant reform to emerge from this quest for social justice was labor legislation. The National Child Labor Committee effectively lobbied to create state laws in most states, which banned labor by underage children (from age twelve to sixteen). Many other states passed maximum hour laws for women and forbade night labor on the part of women. Sadly, loopholes in these laws kept them from being enforced. The Supreme Court was slow in coming to terms with this issue. In the case of *Lochner v. New York* in 1905, the Court held that a Utah law that created a ten-hour workday was in violation of the freedom to make contracts. Twelve years later, in a case called *Bunting v. Oregon* (1917), the Court finally upheld a ten-hour day law but would hold out for twenty more years before it would uphold a state minimum wage law. Another social justice issue for the Social Progressives was that of Prohibition. The Woman's Christian Temperance Union put a good deal of time and money into campaigning for the prohibition of the manufacture, sale, and importation of alcohol. The Woman's Christian Temperance Union along with the Anti-Saloon League eventually was successful, for a time, in getting a Constitutional Prohibition amendment passed.

The fifth and final theme of the Progressives was that of active government. The Progressives were able to bring the national government into many new areas of public service. They used the resources of the national government to build good roads with the institution of the National Highway System. They expanded public education by extending free education for citizens from primary to secondary school. They instituted a national environmental conservation plan, founding the national park system, which was copied by the individual states. And finally, they used the government to create a public health and welfare system, which included sanitation and social welfare services.

Progressivism (City/State Reform, Social Justice, and the Purity Crusade)

As the United States moved into the new century, some of the short-term causes of social and political unrest in the 1890s began to wane. In 1897, the European wheat crop completely collapsed, causing the price of wheat to rise and initiating an era of economic recovery for western farmers. As new mines opened (along with important technological innovations), the nation's gold supply expanded greatly, bringing with it the inflated currency the Populists had sought. This new money stimulated an era of industrial expansion, finally ending the economic depression of the early 1890s.

But the old concerns about the power of corporations and the declining democracy of America still troubled many Americans. As the importance of farmers waned, the reform crusade fell into the hands of the urban middle class, a diverse group who called themselves Progressives. Many of these Progressives came to believe that the idea of "public interest" should be the guiding principle for organizations and corporations (and even individuals) in America. The idea was that government should intervene in the affairs of society to ensure the public interest was being met. They stressed the role of technology, the need for planning, the social responsibility of corporations, the ability of government to secure social justice, and the desire to impose social controls to make America conform to their values.

Progressives made their first impact in the nation's cities when they began to challenge the power of urban political machines led by powerful bosses. These political bosses had replaced the traditional Anglo-Protestant elite in city government in the years after the Civil War. As the older leaders moved on to other opportunities, ethnically oriented politicians (particularly those of Irish American descent) used a personal form of leadership to win the loyalty of ethnic and working-class voters in urban America. These types of bosses appealed to Catholic and Jewish families who came from different European cultures than the Anglo-Protestants of America. But it is important to note that local bosses did do some good. Since there were few programs to protect workers against accidents, unemployment, or disasters, local bosses like New York's George Washington Plunkitt intervened to offer needed help to workers. They intervened when help was needed most, providing food baskets, picnics, parades, and recreation for laborers. There was as much bad as there was good. Tammany Hall, the headquarters of New York's political machine, controlled a payroll of $12 million and had more jobs to fill than Carnegie Steel, the largest corporation in America. In Chicago, Jane Addams guessed that 20 percent of all voters in her district depended on the goodwill of the ward bosses for employment. While they met the needs of the urban ethnic population, they also won their loyalty which gave them a stranglehold over urban politics and elections.

Since it was nearly impossible to remove a political machine from control, graft and corruption were endemic within the boss rule system that dominated America's urban areas. This was an expensive way to provide city services. The sale of city franchises for public transportation, road construction, and public utilities caused the costs of those projects to rise greatly, placing an even heavier burden on the urban taxpayer. Plunkitt defended his system as "honest graft," but progressive reformers only saw corruption and the ethnic and class rhetoric of the bosses. Thus, the Progressives determined they would change the ways in which city governments worked. As ethnic and working-class interests were forced on the defensive, another section of the progressive movement added fuel to the fire for reform. Lincoln Steffens' published his harrowing book *The Shame of the Cities* (1904), which chronicled organized graft in America's largest cities. Such publicity made possible the election of reform-minded mayors in New York, St. Louis, San Francisco, Detroit, and Cleveland.

Surprisingly, the first Progressive attack on Boss Rule happened in Galveston, Texas in 1900. There the city bosses had proved ineffective in dealing with a devastating tidal wave that devastated the city. Since the city bosses failed to restore order after the unexpected tragedy, the next election led to a change in the city charter. The Galveston Plan, as it came to be known, introduced the city commissioner form of government. Under this system, voters selected at-large commissioners, each of whom administered a different part of the city government. Urban progressives adopted the Galveston Plan because it made city administration more professional (i.e., took city rule out of the hands of the bosses), and made those elected dependent on the entire city, not only certain ethnic sections. But the change was not without its problems. For one, citywide elections diluted the voting strength of ethnic minorities. Even worse, the new system used Civil Service examinations to staff non-elected positions. While it made city services more professional, the tests tended to discriminate against those not from Anglo-Protestant backgrounds or wealthy enough to afford a proper technical education. And finally, the growth of city manager systems further depersonalized urban politics. Loss of interest and tighter voter registration and voting requirements combined to reduce the urban voting by 20 percent between 1890 and 1920.

Cities were not the only targets of reformers. Since many state governments had substantial control over urban politics, the reform crusade led a number of progressives to the state capital, and often they found that corruption at that level of government was just as pervasive. Thus, progressive reform quickly spread to the state level. Robert LaFollette, the Republican governor of Wisconsin, best symbolized the promise of Progressivism at the state level. Elected governor in 1900, LaFollette turned Wisconsin into a social experiment, using university-trained experts to administer his programs. The "Wisconsin Idea" of government, as it came to be known, demanded that the new test of citizenship within the state would be concern with the triumph of the "public interest" over private greed. LaFollette won passage of the direct primary (giving the nomination of candidates to the people, not the party); he adopted initiative and referendum laws to allow citizens to vote directly for the government actions affecting them; he created regulatory boards for railroads to ensure fair fees were charged for shipping and travel; he increased taxes on corporations and inherited wealth, while reducing it on private citizens; and finally, he created a program of workmen's compensation. Iowa, California, Indiana, and New York elected governors with similar programs.

As they gained more power, the Progressives, like the Populists before them, realized that to be successful they needed access to federal power. After 1900, they increasingly looked toward Washington for help. Many of the progressive governors (like LaFollette) moved to the U.S. Senate, there contributing to the national reform impulse.

Social Justice and the Purity Crusade

Washington Gladden was a reform-minded minister who, with the help of other religious figures, contributed heavily to the Progressive Movement. Gladden wrote that "Jesus Christ knew a great deal about organizing society and the application of his law to industrial society will be found to work surprisingly well." There was a strong sense of concern for social justice in America, which manifested itself in a desire that the working-classes should get their fair share. Much of that sentiment for social justice was motivated by strong religious ideals. The 1890s witnessed a vibrant Social Gospel movement, which emerged among liberal Protestants. Under the leadership of ministers like Gladden and Walter Rauschenbush, they began to seek a program of social reform rooted in the New Testament.

Progressive women played an important role in the new urban social justice movement. Smaller families and increased leisure time gave them the opportunity to move into the reform movement. Since men monopolized leadership in politics, economics, and the professions, women tended to take leadership roles in matters involving social justice and public virtue. They saw a crisis of morality facing industrial America. Many of them rejected the admired qualities of capitalism and argued that family values were the proper pursuit of individual lives—that good family character depended on a wholesome environment.

Like the men, progressive women began by forming organizations to work for the restoration of morality in public life. The General Federation of Women's Clubs, for example, grew from a membership of 50,000 in 1898 to over 1 million by 1914. Federation president Sarah Platt Decker worked hard to improve working conditions for women and children. Other women sought to publicize the horrible living conditions of the poor. Jane Addams, a restless college graduate, established Hull House in Chicago in 1889, one of the first settlement houses in America providing a number of services from child care to a library to classes in housekeeping, cooking, and art. Hull House, and others like it, became crucibles of reform. The middle-class women who staffed these settlement houses believed that America's current great wealth was a sin, since so many people in the country were poor. Settlement house leaders formed the National Child Labor Committee to lobby state governments to prohibit children under fourteen from working in factories and to keep those under sixteen out of mines. They also wanted children prevented from working nights or for more than eight hours a day, especially in southern textile mills. By 1916, they succeeded in lobbying Congress to pass the Keating-Owen Child Labor Act, banning the products of child labor from interstate commerce, though the Supreme Court struck down that law two years later in 1918.

The Progressive concern for child labor grew out of a concern for children in general. Education was required for high-status, white collar jobs. Thus, the Progressives pushed to increase education for common people. Their efforts resulted in an immediate expansion of elementary enrollment, which more than doubled between 1898 and 1914. By 1917, thirty-eight states passed laws requiring kids to remain in school until the age of sixteen. Progressive women also played an important role in the struggle against prostitution. Red-light districts were common in urban America in the late nineteenth century, all the way up to 1917. Many young female immigrants found themselves either forced or enticed into prostitution. The draw to prostitution for many women was that it could bring in several times the earnings of working in the factories. In 1900, an unskilled worker usually earned from $5 to $7 per week, while a prostitute could earn $30 to $40 per week. Most women working as prostitutes saw their work as only a temporary remedy until they found a better job or were married.

Reformers like Elizabeth Blackwell and Caroline Wilson, two of the first women medical doctors, and Antoinette Blackwell, the first woman ordained as a Protestant minister, tried to keep women from becoming prostitutes. They created organizations to serve as surrogate families for young women who found themselves alone in the city. They campaigned against the double standard that allowed wealthy married men to have sexual relations with prostitutes without concern of being prosecuted, while the prostitutes themselves were punished. By abolishing prostitution, or white slavery as they called it, the reformers hoped to destroy the sexual marketplace and force men to accept monogamy. By 1900, purity reformers were successful in establishing vice commissions in nearly every major American city. Their work led to the Mann Act of 1910, which made it a federal crime to transport a woman to another state for immoral purposes.

Other Progressive women fought against the dangers of substance abuse. The use of narcotics like opium, morphine, and cocaine had grown steadily throughout the nineteenth century. Doctors often prescribed diluted opium called laudanum, a highly addictive substance that was found in most patent medicines of the day, for a variety of minor ailments. Even the popular soft drink Coca-Cola contained small amounts of cocaine until 1903. By the turn of the century, the U.S. had about 250 million drug addicts. Drug use was also linked to the Chinese and African-American communities, two groups that the dominant white elite were eager to suppress. The developing health professions (which, not surprisingly, were dominated by the white middle-class) moved quickly to regulate narcotics. Eager to establish professional standards of practice, doctors and pharmacists embraced the idea that widespread drug use was harmful. The newly founded American Medical Association (AMA) and the American Pharmaceutical Association (APA) both insisted that only professionals with appropriate credentials should dispense drugs. Other groups, eager to impose middle-class behavioral standards on immigrants and blacks, quickly joined the crusade. In response to this type of pressure, Congress passed the Pure Food and Drug Act in 1906, beginning the first federal regulation of drugs. Three years later, the U.S. outlawed the importation of smoking opium. Then in 1914, the Harrison Narcotics Act restricted the use of narcotics to medical purposes, required federal registration of all drug manufacturers, required a record of all legal narcotic sales, and a required a doctor's prescription before drugs could be dispensed.

Alcohol was the main target of the women's Purity Crusade. The mostly middle-class, Protestant Anti-Saloon League (founded in 1805) wanted to outlaw the sale and manufacture of alcoholic beverages in the U.S. They described alcohol as a socially destructive drug that had to be outlawed. What they were really doing, though, was trying to get control of the new immigrants, many of whom came from cultures that had a tolerant view of alcohol. The middle-class reformers attacked the saloons (which fostered immigrant cultures and served as immigrant political centers for ethnic politicians and labor unions). Prohibition became a rallying cry for middle-class, white Protestant culture in its assault on working-class, ethnic culture, trying to replace the values of the latter with the former. One of the reformers strongest sources of support came from evangelical white Southerners, many of whom were from the working-class but whose religion denounced the consumption of alcohol. Most of the early success for the Purity Crusade came in the South, where Prohibition served as a tool for social control (this time over blacks and poor whites). Using the strong Baptist and Methodist churches as their base, they persuaded some two-thirds of all southern counties to "vote dry" by 1907, winning total prohibition laws in six states by 1909. The Webb-Kenyon Act of 1913 allowed those six to interdict the transportation of alcohol across their state lines. Nevertheless, an underground economy of bootleggers and moonshiners continued to supply alcohol across the South.

Progressivism in National Politics

Theodore Roosevelt, or Teddy as he was fondly called, was the first real president of the twentieth century. The previous president, William McKinley, had died from an assassin's bullet. McKinley represented the last, philosophically, of the Gilded Age presidents. Roosevelt was nominated to be vice president fresh off his fabulous and press-gathering victory in Cuba during the Spanish American War. Although he was a Republican, Roosevelt was an independent, reform-minded individual—typical of conservative Progressives.

Roosevelt had agreed to run on the Republican ticket as vice president in 1900 after having been pushed to the front of national politics by his war hero status and because many prominent New Yorkers who wanted him out of New York. The Republican slogans for that election were "Republican Prosperity" and "The Full Dinner Pail." For the election that year the Socialists nominated Eugene Debs. The Populists, barely holding out as a party, nominated Philadelphia banker Wharton Baker. Mark Hanna, the leader of the Republican Caucus, was set against Roosevelt's position as vice president, but Boss Platt of New York wanted Roosevelt out of his hair, so Roosevelt became the vice president candidate much to the delight of Republican reformers and the *Goo-Goos* (refers to a group of like-minded Progressives who were called the Good Government Club, or Goo-Goos for short). The Democrats once again nominated William Jennings Bryan.

A combination of the end of the depression in 1897 and the victory over the Spanish led to McKinley winning a second term. Then in September of 1901, an anarchist named Leon Czolgosz shot McKinley at a railroad station in Buffalo, New York with a revolver he bought out of a Sears and Roebuck catalog. McKinley died shortly afterward, mostly as a result of the operation to remove the bullet. Supposedly, McKinley died while holding the hand of Mark Hanna and singing the hymn *Nearer My God to Thee*. With McKinley's death, Mark Hanna's worst fears had come true—he is quoted as saying just after McKinley took his last breath, "Now look, that damned cowboy is president of the United States." Such was the sentiment of a lot of political leaders in America. Roosevelt had made a career out of destroying corruption and underhanded politics, and now he was president. Surprisingly, considering his reputation, the Progressivism of Teddy Roosevelt can best be characterized as cautious. He stayed away from political meat grinders like the tariff and banking policy and he was always careful to reassure the business community. His reforms were taken, by and large, as preventive medicine to keep power from the hands of the Democrats and Socialists.

Teddy Roosevelt's first efforts at reform were embodied in a program he called the Square Deal. This essentially meant enforcing existing antitrust laws and tightening controls on big business. He did not believe in widescale trust busting, but thought that regulation was the key to success. He chose his targets carefully. While manufacturing could not be regulated under the Sherman Act due to the Supreme Court decision *U.S. v. E. C. Knight*, the Court had never ruled that railroads could not be regulated. Therefore, Roosevelt went after Northern Securities, a holding company that controlled the Great Northern and Northern Pacific Railroad—one of the largest railroad companies in the country. The move worked. In 1904, the Supreme Court ordered the holding company dissolved despite a massive propaganda war on the part of J.P. Morgan and James J. Hill. (This Supreme Court case was called *Northern Securities Company v. United States*).

While Roosevelt's action against the railroads was popular, he received overwhelming public support for using what the muckrakers referred to as the big stick of government against the mining trusts when he threatened to take over the anthracite coal fields of western Pennsylvania. The situation emerged because the mine operators in the region refused to speak to representatives of the United Mine Workers union at a conference Roosevelt called at the White House. The mine workers were in the midst of a strike for safer working conditions and better wages. The mine owners refused to accept union demands, using violence against the strikers and attempting to bring in scab workers. The situation seemed to be at a stalemate, with the owners refusing to attend the White House meeting because they did not want to be in the same room as the union representatives. Roosevelt became so frustrated with the mine owners the he threatened to throw George Baer out of a White House window by the seat of his pants. Baer was the president of Reading Railroad and the representative for the mine owners. In the end, Roosevelt threatened to nationalize the mines and put the miners back to work at any rate they desired in order to get coal into the marketplace—it was winter and coal was the main heating material in the country. Roosevelt had little authority, or legal basis, to nationalize the mines, but the owners were fearful that he might try to settle the strike. They had no choice but to give in.

Teddy Roosevelt continued to use his executive power to enforce the Sherman Anti-Trust Act. All in all, his administration filed about twenty-five antitrust suits. The most notable victory came against the beef trust in a 1905 Supreme Court case called *Swift and Co. v. U.S.* Here the Supreme Court put out a new "stream of commerce" doctrine, which overturned its previous position that manufacturing was not interstate commerce and thus could not be regulated. Other notable reforms Roosevelt passed in his first term included the Expedition Act of 1903, which gave priority to antitrust suits in state courts; the creation of the Department of Commerce; and the Elkins Act of 1903, which made it illegal to take or give railroad rebates. Eventually Standard Oil was broken up in 1911, as was the American Tobacco Company. This approach fell short of the regulation TR wanted, but there was no backbone in Congress to pass more stringent legislation, so Roosevelt had to rely on executive orders. Roosevelt's policies built a coalition between the Republicans and the Progressives, which led to his overwhelming re-election victory in 1904. Having won the opportunity to begin a second term, Roosevelt believed he had a mandate from the people to become even more aggressive. He pushed through the Hepburn Act of 1906, which gave the Interstate Commerce Commission power, for the first time, to set maximum rates for railroads and expanded the powers of the Interstate Commerce Commission to assert control over pipelines, express companies, sleeping-car companies, bridges, and ferries.

The pure genius of TR's plan of change is evident. He was able to steal the momentum of the Progressive Movement away from the more radical leftist Progressives like Robert La Follette, who saw TR's reforms as only completing half of what needed to be done. Roosevelt co-opted the leftist agenda, and altered it to serve his own needs. It is important to understand that he was not trying to implement progressive change merely for his own political gain. He really wanted to change America, just like the radical Progressives, but he felt they were trying to go too far. If America fell into the hands of the radicals, TR feared there was no telling where the change would end—many dreaded that it could become a revolution like that of the Bolsheviks, which was consuming Russia.

Another important issue that quickly fell upon TR's hit list was meat packing and food processing. After Teddy read the scandalous novel *The Jungle* by Upton Sinclair, which exposed the filthy conditions in Chicago's meat packing industry, TR decided something had to be done. Meat at the factories was stored in dark places and you could sweep off the dried dung of rats from the piles of meat. The supervisors tried to kill the rats with poisoned bread. The rats would die, but no one cleaned them up. Often, the rats, the poisoned bread, the dung, and whatever meat remained at the end of the day would all go into the grinding hopper together to make hamburger and other processed meats. Because of the unsanitary conditions, the factories were a breeding ground for diseases like tuberculosis. Teddy read the novel and sent two inspectors to Chicago to confirm Sinclair's work, which the investigators did. The investigation led to the Meat Inspection Act of 1906 and the Pure Food and Drug Act (enacted on the same day, June 30, 1906).

The final part of Roosevelt's progressive program was conservation. TR was an unabashed naturalist and big game hunter. He was determined to halt the exploitation of timber in the West that had been going on since the Timber and Stone Act of 1878 was passed. This act was designed to stimulate settlement of the West by allowing anyone to buy 160 acres at $2.50 an acre. Instead of spurring settlement, timber and mining companies recruited people to purchase the land, who then turned around and sold it to the companies. TR put a stop to the practice by seizing western lands for protection. In the course of his presidency, he added some fifty federal wildlife refuges, approved five new national parks, and created a system of national monuments such as the Grand Canyon. Working with Gifford Pinchot, who was chief of the forestry service, TR established forty-one state conservation commissions which quickly began to add state protected areas to the nation's conservation plan.

On the night he won the election in 1904, Roosevelt promised not to run for reelection. So when the election of 1908 rolled around, TR said that he had had a great time as president but it was time to move on. Roosevelt had become so strong politically, unlike many presidents before him, that he was able to hand-pick a successor to carry his torch of progressive reform into the future. At the Republican convention of 1908, William Howard Taft was selected on the first ballot. Taft was born in Ohio. A man of large girth and renowned intelligence, he would eventually become the only man ever to serve as both the president of the United States and as a justice on the Supreme Court. Before becoming president, Taft graduated from Yale, served as the solicitor general of Ohio, and was the governor general of the Philippines from 1900–04; even declining a spot on the Supreme Court to remain there. Teddy recalled him from the Philippines in 1904 so he could accept the presidential nomination.

Thus, an unlikely series of events occurred for Taft, and he found himself, a career member of the judiciary, a man who openly disdained politics (in fact, he had once even said "politics make me sick"), and now he was the Republican candidate for president. To run against Taft, the Democrats nominated who again? Yes, you guessed it—William Jennings Bryan, already a two-time loser. The Socialists nominated Eugene Debs who ended up getting 420,000 votes. But, of course, Taft won. Teddy was still a young man, only 50, so he decided to go big game hunting in Africa. When J. P. Morgan heard of Roosevelt's plan, he was heard to say, "Let every lion do his duty."

From the start, Taft's presidency was beset by problems. His wife, Nellie, who was his principal political advisor, suffered a debilitating stroke soon after he entered the White House. He was never able to feel comfortable as president. Taft's first major attempt at reform was his tariff policy. He, unlike most republicans, favored a lower tariff. The bill that he asked for moved through Congress and in the end lowered the tariff rates on some items (coal, boots, shoes) but extended tariff protection to other items. As a result, a group of progressive western Republicans balked, fearful that the party was leaning back toward unquestioning submissiveness to big business. Taft began to side with this renegade group; but later, fearful of a party split, he changed his mind and backed the majority.

In trying to keep the party together, Taft kept pushing adherents farther apart. A decade of successes for the Republicans led to vicious infighting over a number of issues. In 1910, in what came to be called the Ballinger-Pinchot controversy, the image of Taft as the keeper and protector of Teddy's reforms began to fade. Taft's Secretary of the Interior, Richard Ballinger of Seattle, was aware that many Westerners opposed the conservation programs espoused by Roosevelt. Generally, they despised conservation because it kept some of the best areas of the West from being developed, or so they believed. The strongest advocates of western conservation were usually Easterners like Gifford Pinchot, who was the chief of forestry, and Teddy Roosevelt. Therefore, acting in what he thought was the best interest of progress, Ballinger allowed a million acres of water power sites and forest lands in the West to be thrown open to development, the same sites that Roosevelt had ordered protected.

Taft agreed with the reopening. He felt that Roosevelt exceeded the law in protecting those sites. Simultaneously, Ballinger turned over some valuable coal lands in Alaska to a group of developers in Seattle, some of whom he had worked for as a lawyer. An investigator in the land office went to Pinchot with "evidence" of collusion in the land deal: Ballinger received a large kickback from his former employer for opening the lands. Pinchot went to Taft. For his trouble, Taft fired the investigator in the land office. When notified about the situation in early 1910, Pinchot went public with the controversy and was promptly fired by Taft. Ballinger was later investigated by Congress and cleared of all complicity in the matter, but the Progressives' suspicion was so high that Ballinger resigned in 1911. Taft was elected to carry out the plans of Teddy Roosevelt, to take them to completion. "He was carrying them out," one historian noted, "but carrying them out on a stretcher."

The Ballinger-Pinchot controversy created a firestorm in Congress, and a number of progressive Republicans sided with the Democrats in voting to investigate the matter. In the congressional elections of 1910, the public, which was full of progressive sentiment, rebuked the Republicans, and they lost the House to the Democrats. Roosevelt, who had been off shooting lions and bears in Africa, came home and, much like a man who had trusted his house to his children only to find they had burned it down, was more than a little annoyed. He did not openly break with Taft at first, as his supporters encouraged him to do. Instead, TR went on a speaking tour in the West where he outlined his principles under the catchy phrase of New Nationalism. New Nationalism was a program of federal regulatory laws to control big business and it set forth national democratic measures (such as referendums, initiatives, etc.) for the purpose of saving the country from the threat of revolution.

The break between Taft and TR was inevitable. It finally came in 1911, when Taft announced a new antitrust suit against U.S. Steel. TR had acquiesced to U.S. Steel during his presidency, allowing the company to acquire control of the largest coal and iron company in Tennessee. Taft, however, found that the purchase violated antitrust laws and he was intent on breaking it up. TR violently denounced trust-busting as old fashioned and said the only logical solution to monopolies was federal regulation. TR, urged on by a group of progressive Republicans, announced his candidacy for the presidency. In a sense, Taft was more successful than Roosevelt made him appear to be. The Appalachian Forest Reserve Act of 1911 enlarged the national forest. He brought about eighty antitrust suits in his four years, while Teddy only had twenty-five in eight years. Under Taft's supervision, Congress passed the Mann-Elkins Act in 1910, which extended the regulatory powers of the Interstate Commerce Commission; he established the Bureau of Mines; he set the provisions of statehood for Arizona and New Mexico; and he established a territorial government for Alaska. In a similar boost to the government, Taft supported the passage of the Sixteenth Amendment, which established a federal income tax.

As the Republican Party began to select its candidate, Roosevelt won many of the state primaries. But at the national convention, many states did not require Taft supporters to vote as the primaries had mandated. Taft and his factions, securely in control of the Republican convention, steamrolled him to the nomination. TR was outraged. In response, he created his own political party and called for progressive Republicans to meet at a separate convention in Chicago. Most believed TR was a lost cause and stayed home. But some did come, and TR was selected to head a new political party that would become known as the Bull Moose Party, and split the Republican constituency. The split among Republicans allowed two things to happen: 1) It allowed for the first Democratic president since Cleveland to be elected and 2) It passed the torch of Progressivism from the Republicans to the Democrats.

In the election of 1912, the Democrats nominated Woodrow Wilson. Wilson was a native Virginian and the son of a Presbyterian minister. Wilson was tall, slender, with a chiseled face and a stern disposition. He was, first and foremost, a public servant. He was an intellectual, perhaps the smartest man who ever occupied the office of president. Wilson was a historian and political scientist. He believed in a strong president—one who acted for the general welfare of the nation, not for party or personal interests. He was a graduate of Johns Hopkins University and had served as president of Princeton University before becoming governor of New Jersey in 1910. At his best, he was an effective parliamentarian. At his worst, he was a stubborn, bull-headed man. Above all, he was committed to the reform principles embodied by the Progressive movement.

In 1912, there was a solid three-way race for the presidency. It was almost a two-man race after an incident in Milwaukee where TR was shot by a fanatic. The bullet pierced his overcoat, the case he kept his glasses in, and his speech and it broke a rib before lodging below his lung. As the crowd mobbed the would-be assassin, TR jumped up and yelled, "Step back, don't harm the man." Afterward, he insisted that he be allowed to give the speech, which he did, showing the crowd his coat, shirt, and speech with a hole in them. When asked if he should be taken to the hospital, TR proclaimed, "Well, no, I feel as strong as a Bull Moose." And thus, he gave the name for his party. Only after he finished the speech did TR let the doctors operate on him. As to be expected, TR and Taft split the Republican vote nearly in half, which allowed Wilson to win the election.

The election of 1912 is important for several reasons:
1. The election of 1912 was the high watermark for the Progressive movement. All three of the presidential candidates, to differing degrees and with differing means, were devoted to progressive reform.
2. It restored the Democratic Party to the presidency, almost by accident, after years of Republican rule.
3. The election of Wilson brought the South back into national politics. Wilson was from the South, and many of his appointees would be from the South, as well.
4. The election changed the character of the Republican Party. Republican Progressives were discredited within the party. When the party returns to the White House in the 1920s, it would be more conservative in nature, taking its place on the right, a position it has held to this day.

Items to Consider

Tenements, muckraking, themes of Progressivism, who were the Progressives, Sherman Anti-Trust Act, boss rule, Galveston Plan, Wisconsin Idea, Purity Crusade, Pure Food & Drug Act, Teddy Roosevelt, conservation

CHAPTER 21
World War I: The Great War

Woodrow Wilson and Neutrality in Europe

In June 1914, Slavic nationalists murdered the Austrian Archduke Francis Ferdinand and his wife, Sophie, in a dank and dirty small town that no European had even heard of called Sarajevo. Those murders triggered a series of events and crises that plunged all of Europe into war by the end of the summer of 1914. Complying with an endless series of alliance treaties, every nation of consequence in Europe was forced to select a side and begin war preparations. As the Guns of August commenced, most of Europe went off to war with smiles on their faces—all convinced they would be home before Christmas. The conflict pitted the Allies (Great Britain, France, and their less-than-democratic friend Russia) against the Central Powers of Germany and the Hapsburg Empire (Although this sounds like an immense entity, it really just means Austria).

While Europe mobilized, America remained neutral. Woodrow Wilson, as the president, declared that the United States would have nothing to do with the war, calling for the American people to remain neutral in both name and deed. The first Progressive elected with complete and total support for Progressive reforms from the general public found his administration highjacked by war. Sadly, the declaration that the U.S. had no stake in the war was a lie. For the past 25 years, Germany had been seen as our greatest threat, while the British moved closer to the U.S. over the course of that period. Strong ties in religion, culture, language, and law linked the U.S. to Britain and led the mostly Anglo-Protestant officials at the U.S. State Department to frown on the Germans. Complicating the situation, President Wilson admired Britain and its institutions, especially Parliament. While publicly remaining neutral, privately Wilson refused to accept a German victory.

It was money, more than anything else, that drew America into the British camp. The war created an enormous demand for American foodstuffs and war goods. American trade increased with the Allies from $825 million in 1914 to $3.2 billion in 1916, creating something of a miniboom within the American economy. When the Allies ran short of money in 1915, American bankers began to invest heavily in the Allied war effort by giving huge loans to Britain and France. This forced Wilson use the Federal Reserve to guarantee those loans to protect the American economy. By 1917, American bankers had loaned more than $2.5 billion to the Allies. Secretary of State William Jennings Bryan denounced American loans to the Allies as a violation of American neutrality, but his power in the nation had declined. J. P. Morgan's influence, on the other hand, had not. Morgan was the wealthiest man in America and controlled most of the nation's financial institutions. From the start, Morgan said that he and America would do everything possible to contribute to the Allied victory. By contrast, American trade with the Central Powers had virtually vanished; U.S. loans amounted to only $300 million over the course of the entire war. Clearly, America was following its own definition of neutrality.

While American business was assisting in the Allied war effort, the nation itself remained relatively idle in terms of war preparations. Theodore Roosevelt and the Republicans pressed Wilson to begin a military build-up, but he hoped instead that the U.S. could maintain enough prestige by remaining neutral, so he could thereby shape the peace to follow. Wilson saw the war as a way to end European imperialism and open the world to free trade (and here, he means American-dominated trade). A great moralist, Wilson hoped the massive numbers of deaths would teach Europe an essential lesson: that only liberal politics and economic cooperation could prevent these types of disasters in the future.

While Wilson wanted to remain neutral, the Allies and the Central Powers tried to force his hand. Britain blockaded the North Sea to keep the U.S. from trading with Germany. Wilson did not protest this action. But when German U-boats sank ships supplying the Allies, Wilson protested long and loud, proclaiming that the Germans were "violating the rights of neutrals to free trade." The German reliance on submarine warfare was the most serious problem between Berlin and Washington. British blockade methods depended on surface ships practicing the rules of "Cruiser Warfare," whereby warships stopped merchant vessels, boarded them to search for contraband, and seized the ship when contraband items were discovered. This practice seldom led to deaths. Germany, however, had a Navy that was far inferior to the British on the open sea. They had no surface ships to patrol with, relying instead on submarines, which by their very nature could not practice the rules of Cruiser Warfare. Submarines had to force ships to turn back by firing warning shots and threatening them with imminent destruction if the captain did not turn back. Sadly, weapons technology had not advanced far enough for submarine captains to differentiate between a warning shot and one right on target. For this reason, the use of submarines to intercept merchant ships led to many neutral deaths.

Unfortunately for Germany, to win the war, they had to cut the steady flow of supplies to the Allies from the West. But, doing so played right into the hands of Allied propagandists. Britain controlled the only surviving telegraph cable connecting Europe to the U.S., which meant Britain provided the U.S. with all its war news. Astonishingly, the American media accepted every British war report without challenge. American media broadcast countless stories of German atrocities, and portraying Germans as "Huns," barbaric and savage monsters that murdered babies and raped women. Those stories along with neutral deaths on ships outraged the American public, moving them closer toward war.

Considering the details of the situation, Wilson's neutrality was unrealistic. He insisted that American merchant ships had the right to sail into the European war zone and trade without restriction. While he did not challenge the British blockade of Germany, he demanded that American ships traveling to Britain not be subject to attacks by German submarines. The Germans tried to avoid attacking American vessels, but such considerations became more difficult as time progressed. The tragic fate of the *Lusitania* demonstrated more than any other event how unrealistic Wilson's assumptions were. In May 1915, a British passenger liner departed Ireland with a mixed cargo of war materials and passengers—a human shield. Within sight of the Irish coast, the ship was fired on by a German submarine, which accidentally scored a direct hit with its first salvo. The *Lusitania* sank within minutes of being hit, killing 1,198 passengers, including 128 Americans. Theodore Roosevelt immediately denounced the attack as an act of piracy and called for Wilson to take military action. While the *Lusitania* was carrying small numbers of rifle cartridges and ammunition, it did not have any high explosives on board. Germany maintained they were right to sink the ship, despite the accident, because they had evidence that there was important military cargo on board. Regardless of the truth, the British were using the passengers as human shields.

After *Lusitania* was destroyed, Wilson sent a strongly worded letter to the German government. He chastised them for the attack and threatened to enter the war on the side of the British unless the Germans immediately stopped using submarines. Nothing was said to the British. William Jennings Bryan, apparently the only truly neutral figure in the U.S. government, was so outraged by Wilson's stance that he resigned. Surprisingly, the Germans decided to give in to Wilson's demand and promised not to sink any more passenger liners, though they did increase strikes on merchant vessels. The issue boiled over again in 1916, when the Allies decided to arm merchant ships. Germany countered by issuing a "fire without warning" policy on all merchant vessels that its submarines discovered passing through or within the war zone. Wilson responded by declaring that either Germany had to stop sinking merchant and passenger ships, or the U.S. would enter the war on the side of the Allies. Again, strangely, the Germans gave in.

Though Wilson had long pledged himself to nonviolence, in practice he realized his neutrality stance was becoming impracticable and began urging for an increase in the size of the American military. More than anything, Wilson wanted to build a Navy larger than that of the British. He also wanted to expand the size of the American Army in case war was declared. Wilson toured the country to drum up support for the National Defense Act of 1916, a $500 million program of military spending. He also made sure that the funding for the National Defense Act was secured with the passage of the Revenue Act to 1916, the first major income and inheritance taxes in American history.

Despite his best efforts to remain neutral, by 1916 Wilson found himself being pushed toward war by the State Department, the defense community, bankers, and British sympathizers. Wilson felt as if the majority of Americans wanted war, but there were a surprising number who supported his neutrality stance. German-Americans, for one, did not want to fight against their homeland, and many Irish-Americans were against the war because they hated the British. Westerners and Midwestern farmers also opposed the war, not having the same strength of ties as the Southerners and Easterners.

Not surprisingly then, the question of whether the U.S. should choose war or peace dominated the election of 1916. The Republican Party nominated Charles Evans Hughes, a Supreme Court justice and former governor of New York. Unlike 1912, the Republican Party was united and thus offered a serious threat to Woodrow Wilson and the Democrats. Wilson managed, though, to take advantage of the war by calling himself a "Peace Candidate" and his supporters adopted the slogan: He kept us out of war. Wilson and his vice presidential candidate, Thomas R. Marshall, won a close victory. Wilson won the election by the tiny margin of 277 to 254 in the Electoral College, the smallest advantage since 1876.

Having been reelected, Wilson decided it was his responsibility to make an effort to end the war. Twice he had made efforts to end the war in the past, and twice he had failed. The first came early in 1914, when Wilson sent his close friend Col. Edward House to Europe as an informal representative of the United States. Wilson had hoped that House could relieve the mounting war tensions in Europe before the continent plunged headlong into war. Both the Allies and the Central Powers tried to force House (and thus the United States) to choose sides in the conflict. With U.S. neutrality in jeopardy, House told Wilson to prepare the American home front for the coming war. Wilson next tried to broker an end to the war in mid 1915, when Col. House was again sent to Europe to find some way to mediate a peace agreement. Wilson hoped House could broker a peace without victory, but he again failed. By 1915, so many soldiers had died that both sides felt they had to win to justify their human losses. Frustrated by their stubbornness, Wilson decided to ignore the Europeans and, in January 1917, issued an address to Congress calling for an immediate "peace without victory." The Germans and the Allies refused to listen, and the stalemate and destruction continued.

With the war deadlocked on land, the German generals persuaded the Kaiser to resume unrestricted submarine warfare. "Let the U.S. come in," they said. German U-boats began to attack neutral shipping wherever it could be found. Wilson severed relations with Germany, and released to the American public the Zimmerman Telegraph, a secret German dispatch to Mexico that had been intercepted by the British. The Zimmerman Telegraph encouraged Mexico to attack the U.S. in the event America came into the war on the side of the Allies. In return for Mexican support, Germany would help Mexico recover its "lost provinces" of Texas, New Mexico, and Arizona. While the sentiment of the Zimmerman Telegraph is clear, it is important to note that the note came from the British (who had a clear reason to give it to the U.S.) and there was a chance the offer would not be taken by Mexico.

In combination with the Zimmerman Telegraph, the collapse of Russia into the Bolshevik Revolution (1917) and the sinking of American merchant ships by German submarines, Wilson believed he had no option but to ride down Pennsylvania Avenue to ask Congress for a declaration of war that April. "The U.S. must," he said, "make the world safe for democracy." On April 6, 1917, Congress gave him what he wanted.

Organizing for Victory

The first task of the U.S. once the declaration was made was to determine how to finance the war, one that ultimately cost $32 billion. In Europe, the situation was desperate. Russia collapsed into Revolution in the East; the British and French troops were broken and depleted. Britain had barely six weeks of food remaining within the nation, and German U-boats were sending 900,000 tons of supplies to the floor of the Atlantic each month. Despite the apparent necessity, the U.S. would take its time entering the war.

It started with the need to figure out how to pay for the war. The U.S. government began by launching a series of Liberty Bond drives, netting $23 billion in small loans. To make the economy run more smoothly and produce what was needed to win the war, the government created the War Industries Board (WIB). The WIB was headed by Bernard Baruch, who set new production goals for American industry and manufacturing and controlled the allocation of raw materials. In short, the government fixed prices in the economy and conspired to constrain free trade in return for national security. On the premise that it would be good for the American war effort, Baruch and the WIB actually encouraged the growth of large corporations through an emerging idea they called Corporatism, a joint government- and business-sponsored program of central planning and social responsibility. With Corporatism, the government allowed big business any control it needed in the economy and actually trusted it to act fairly—a huge shift from the Progressive position.

To ensure America had enough foodstuffs to fight the war, Herbert Hoover was put in charge of the Food Administration. The Food Administration took control of the nation's agricultural production. It set prices for crops and established new records for production. The Food Administration also encouraged private citizens to make sacrifices for the good of the war effort It set aside certain days when no one was allowed to eat meat, eggs, milk, and wheat products. It also issued food stamps to individual citizens, limiting the amount of foodstuffs they could use.

And finally, the government used the emergency to create a working relationship among labor, business, and industry. Wilson encouraged Samuel Gompers and the American Federation of Labor (AFL) to support the nation's war programs. Gompers, president of the AFL, was enlisted to help increase wages, curb unemployment, and reduce working hours through his role on the newly established War Labor Board, which was a national planning body created by Wilson to ensure there would be no strikes in America's time of need. This was the first time the national government offered support to the organized labor movement, doubling union membership to more than 5 million during the war years.

The War Against Dissent

Most Progressives were afraid America was moving away from its traditional Anglo-Protestant culture. Mostly this was because of the substantial growth in America's immigrant population after 1890. The war only heightened these concerns. By 1917, one American in three was either an immigrant or the child of an immigrant. Even worse in the minds of most Americans, the new immigrants came mostly from Central, eastern, and southern Europe—the nations that comprised the Central Powers.

To counter a possible draw to the wrong motherland, the Wilson administration created a large propaganda machine to rally national support for the war. The centerpiece in that effort was the Committee of Public Information (CPI). Headed by journalist George Creel, the CPI employed 150,000 people and distributed over 75 million pieces of prowar propaganda. The passions the CPI created in the nation would soon consume Americans. Their attacks on the enemy sound, today, harsh and xenophobic. Creel's CPI actually encouraged people to turn in their neighbors, creating a paranoia that eventually led to the postwar Red Scare.

The government was not alone its desire to protect the home front. Private citizens and civic groups were also enlisted in the cause. Across the nation, concerned citizens became members of the American Protective League (APL), which issued them identification cards that celebrated private citizens as agents of the Justice Department and implored them to stamp out antiwar activities. In the name of freedom, APL members spied on their neighbors and harassed antiwar activists. Their primary targets were German-Americans. Concerned by a newly materialized fear of all things German, hysteria swept the American nation and led to a flurry of name changes and accusations. German measles were renamed "liberty measles," dachshunds became "liberty pups," and sauerkraut was turned into "liberty cabbage." German-language publications were prohibited, as was the teaching of the German language in schools, and there were numerous attacks on German-Americans in general. In Indiana, a jury actually dismissed charges against a man who shot a persecuted man of German descent for supposedly shouting: "To hell with the United States."

Not all Americans would be bullied, though. Socialist party leader Eugene Debs joined up with anticorporation Progressives like Robert La Follette and tried to show Americans the war was being fought to protect the interests of the eastern elite. The Socialist Party called American involvement in the war a "crime against humanity" and won more than 30 percent of the votes from working-class Americans in cities like Chicago and Buffalo. La Follette, Idaho Sen. William E. Borah, and other dissenters attacked the draft when it was passed in June 1917. For his trouble, La Follette was condemned by the faculty of the University of Wisconsin for giving aid and comfort to the enemy. There was even a failed attempt to oust La Follette from the Senate.

In response to America's entrance into the war, Randolph Bourne, one of the few vocal critics of the war among American intellectuals, wrote a stirring attack on America's involvement in the war in his brilliant book *The State* published in 1918. Bourne declared that "war represents the health of the state" and due to our participation in the Great War, America might just have mounted its deathbed. Wilson agreed with Bourne, at least in the short term, but his administration actively moved to repress dissent wherever they could. New laws were passed to let Wilson deport Socialist immigrants without trials. The Espionage Act of 1917 prohibited the perpetration of any action that might be considered giving aid or comfort to the enemy. It also stated that no publications deemed "treasonable" by the government could be sent via the U.S. mail. Under this law, the government imprisoned Debs and prevented the circulation of Socialist and other dissenter materials. They even gave movie producer Robert Goldstein a ten-year prison term because his film *The Spirit of '76* showed British soldiers attacking American civilians during the Revolutionary War.

Adding to the prosecutorial power of the government, Congress passed the Sedition Act in 1918. This act made it a crime to "utter, print, write, or publish any disloyal, profane, scurrilous, or abusive language" about the Armed Forces. While the government rarely used this law during the war, Wilson did invoke it when he sent the Army to quash the Green Corn Rebellion, a small uprising of farmers protesting American involvement in the war. It also acted as a counterpoint to any war dissenters, since they could face serious repercussions if they spoke out against the war.

While keeping a firm grasp on basic dissent was important, the favorite targets for government persecution were radicals and pacifists. One such famous example is the government's botched handling of the case of a misunderstood labor union called Industrial Workers of the World (IWW). Under the leadership of Big Bill Haywood, the IWW actually rejected both the American Socialist Party and the American Federation of Labor because Haywood felt the two groups were led by and harbored individuals who were both Communist and un-American. Yet, Wilson decided that the IWW had to be a subversive group, and, thus, they deserved what was coming to them. When the IWW called for strikes for safer working conditions in Washington and Montana, Wilson sent troops to end IWW-led strikes and arrested 165 IWW men. Haywood was especially singled out for persecution. Government agents relentlessly hunted Haywood, eventually forcing him to flee the U.S. for Bolshevik Russia. Essentially, Wilson's plan to give Haywood exactly what he deserved seemed to mean driving him into the arms of Communism, the very group Haywood despised. In his efforts to give dissenters exactly what they deserved, Wilson also went after pacifists and conscientious objectors, imprisoning more than 400 people during the war for refusing to support the nation in a time of war.

Surprisingly, the Supreme Court upheld Wilson's move to build national unity. In the case *Schenck v. U.S.* in 1919, the Supreme Court ruled that the constitutional right to free speech did not apply in times of war. The case hinged on the conviction of an American Socialist Party member who attempted to mail antiwar materials to draft-age men. In the decision, Justice Oliver Wendell Holmes wrote that the Court could deny free speech when a "clear and present danger" existed for either public safety or national security. In a similar case, the *U.S. v. Debs*, the Supreme Court upheld the conviction of Eugene Debs under the auspices of the Espionage Act because he was caught telling an audience that elites caused wars throughout the world, but let the working class fight them. For this comment, Debs received eighteen months in jail.

The Military Victory and Wilson's Fourteen Points

While men like Theodore Roosevelt wanted to raise a volunteer military force, Wilson chose to run the war under the principles of "progressive" government. He created a Selective Service System, a system that drafted some 3 million "doughboys" (a term that probably came from the big buttons on military uniforms) while another 2 million volunteered for service. The commander of the American Expeditionary Force (AEF) was to be Gen. John J. Pershing, a professional military man who believed in West Point, harsh training, and the "professional" army. He insisted on a separate military command for the U.S. Forces. The Americans fought together as an associated power, not as a member of the Allies (who wanted to use fresh American troops to plug their depleted reserves). The first Americans arrived in Europe on July 4, 1917, building a large force by winter/spring of 1918.

The arrival of the AEF came at a crucial juncture in the war. The AEF helped turn back a massive German spring offensive. The Germans, looking to win the war before the Americans entered the battle, launched a massive assault against the Allied powers. Across the line, the Germans pushed back the Allies, but that could not achieve a total victory. That summer, the AEF launched a counterattack and pushed the Germans back through the Argonne Forest, 1 million Americans fighting along a 200-mile front for forty-seven days. The Germans for the first time in the war were driven back into their own territory. Facing an invasion of their homeland, Germany asked for a ceasefire while the German monarchy fell apart. The fighting ended at 11 a.m. on November 11, 1918. Only 112,432 Americans died, half of them from disease. The French lost 1.38 million soldiers, Russia 1.7 million soldiers, Great Britain 947,000 soldiers (60,000 of those died on the first day of the Battle of the Somme). Germany lost 1.8 million, Austria 1.2 million. Another 20 million soldiers from the two sides were wounded. In keeping with the times, no records were kept concerning civilian casualties.

With an end to World War I, Woodrow Wilson's greatest desire was to broker an effective and lasting peace. With the help of aides like Col. Edward House, Wilson established a think tank in 1915 called the "Inquiry." The Inquiry was a collection of like-minded intellectuals and diplomats who were tasked with the purpose of establishing an effective end to the war. When the war concluded, the members of the Inquiry enumerated Wilson's goals and warnings within his now-famous Fourteen Points Speech and the creation of the League of Nations. The combatants met in 1919 to convene the Paris Peace Conference. The ultimate outcome of the conference was the Treaty of Versailles, which effectively ended the war. The treaty blamed everything on Germany, who was deemed responsible for starting the war and all destruction it caused. As part of recognizing responsibility, Germany was forced to pay a huge reparations to the Allied nations. At the Paris Peace Conference in 1919, Wilson fought hard, but was not able to incorporate his Fourteen Points in the Treaty of Versailles. He did, however, make sure the League of Nations was inextricable part of a final agreement. He hoped that once the League was established, it could rectify the treaty's many shortcomings.

Of the treaties 440 articles, the first 26 comprise the covenant of the League of Nations. This covenant describes the operational workings of the League. Article 1 returned all captured territories to their prewar owners. Article 2 opened international diplomacy to public view. Article 3 guaranteed the absolute freedom of navigation on the seas for neutrals outside the territorial waters of the neutral nation in peace and war. Article 4 removed all economic barriers and established free trade among all nations who consent for peace. Article 5 called for the reduction of national armaments to the lowest point necessary to ensure domestic safety within a nation. Article 6 called for all colonial claims to be given the right to consider their own sovereignty by a legislative process which would include the interest of their own populations. And article 10 obliged signatories to guarantee the political independence and territorial integrity of all member nations against outside aggression, and to consult together to oppose aggression when it occurs. This article became the critical point in America, and the one that ultimately prevented the treaty from being ratified by the U.S. Senate.

Sen. Henry Cabot Lodge led the opposition to passage of the treaty. Lodge and Wilson were bitter political foes, but they also had legitimate differences on the League and on the covenant's tenth article. Lodge believed that the league, under Article 10, could require the United States to commit economic or military forces to maintain the collective security of member nations. Wilson did not share this interpretation of Article 10—an article that Wilson had written himself. Wilson stated that the veto power enjoyed by the United States in the League Council would prevent any League sanctions the United States did not want. But if they unanimously voted for sanctions against the will of the United States—that vote only amounted to advice, in any case. The United States would not be, therefore, legally bound to follow the League's dictates. However, Wilson did declare that the United States was to be morally bound to adhere to League resolutions. A moral bond was, for Wilson, infinitely superior to a mere legal one. Thus, Article 10 was, for Wilson "a grave and solemn obligation."

Wilson and Lodge surely could have found a middle ground. Some sort of compromise language could have been drafted. There were pro-treaty Republicans who could have formed a coalition with the Democrats to win the necessary two-thirds majority in the Senate. But Wilson blocked the compromise after he suffered a massive stroke in October 1919. No accommodation with the opposition could be found on either side. The Treaty was voted down.

The United States remained officially at war with the Central Powers until June of 1921, when President Warren Harding approved a joint congressional resolution proclaiming the war had ended, and later signed a separate peace treaty with them. The resolution in the treaty specified that although the United States was not a party to the Versailles Treaty, it retained all rights and advantages accorded to it under the Treaty's terms, excluding the League Covenant. The United States never joined the League of Nations.

In the words of historian David M. Kennedy, "Woodrow Wilson was asking for not only a major change in the international system itself, but for no less major change in the way the United States would conduct its own international business in partnership with other nations." He simply asked for too much.

The War Lives On—The Red Scare

While the war came to an end, the passions brought on by the war continued to grow. Massive waves of black immigrants to northern cities triggered a racist backlash. Race riots exploded in some twenty-five U.S. cities in the summer of 1919, killing seventy-eight African-American's.

Inflation continued to grow though wages were mostly stable, leading to some thirty-six hundred strikes from 1919 to 1920 and including more than 4 million workers. In the aftermath of the war and the Russian Revolution, many middle-class Americans felt that the U.S. was on the verge of a revolution. In the spring of 1919, a series of terrorist incidents fed those fears. The U.S. Postal Service found several mail bombs addressed to John D. Rockefeller, Oliver W. Holmes, and other prominent Americans. In May, undiscovered bombs exploded in eight American cities. One of them rocked the home of Attorney General A. Mitchell Palmer. Almost all the middle class believed these bombings were a result of the labor unrest and labor unions.

To fight the "red" threat, Wilson ordered Palmer into action. Palmer named a government lawyer, J. Edgar Hoover, to head an antiradical division of the Justice Department. Hoover began to round up labor leaders, peaceniks, Communists, and other dissenters. In January 1920, Palmer's men arrested 6,000 alleged radicals, holding many without charges and giving them no access to lawyers. Hoover defended this by saying that it "defeats the ends of justice" to let them see a lawyer. When family members inquired about arrested loved ones, they were also arrested. The raid, known as the Palmer Raid, was designed to capture a huge arsenal that the Reds were suspected of gathering to use to overthrow the government. Instead, government agents found only three pistols.

As the Red Scare grew, the persecution of radicals and the attempt to enforce Anglo–middle class hegemony grew, as well. Tennessee Sen. Kenneth McKellar proposed that any American with radical ideas should be sent to a penal colony in Guam. The New York state Legislature expelled five elected Socialists. The U.S. House of Representatives twice refused to seat Milwaukee Socialist Victor Berger. Twenty-eight states enacted sedition laws. Others states forced school teachers to sign loyalty oaths. In some cases, persecution boiled over into violence. In Centralia, Washington, IWW organizer Wesley Everest was castrated and then lynched from a railroad bridge after a shoot-out between IWW members and the American Legion. The coroner there wrote that Everest had "jumped off with a rope around his neck and shot himself full of holes."

The Red Scare, though, had run its course by the summer of 1920. Palmer looked silly after his arrests turned up nothing and he mistakenly identified a design for an improved record player as a plan for a bomb. As the labor unrest quieted down, the middle class felt more secure. The old fears and xenophobic attitudes, however, would remain an integral, if dormant, part of American society. They would resurface again during the next Great War, as would the fear of Communists after it.

Items to Consider

Central Powers, U-boats and Cruiser Warfare, loans to the Allies, *Lusitania*, Zimmerman note, Liberty drives, War Industries Board, Committee on Public Information, Randolph Bourne, Espionage Act of 1917, Fourteen Points, Henry Cabot Lodge

CHAPTER 22
The Roaring Twenties

While the twentieth century is dominated by individuals working sometimes together and sometimes at odds with each other to change American society, nothing changed the nation like Materialism. Even at the level of the working class, there seems to have been a relaxation of the traditional American values of thrift and sobriety during the 1920s. To a certain extent, Americans were growing more attached to the acquisition of things. There was still plenty of poverty and social injustice in the country, but the middle class, especially, seems to have been caught up in the present; believing that the future could only get better. And it seemed as if they were correct. From 1919 to 1929, the Gross National Product—the total value of all goods and services produced in the U.S.—increased by 40 percent. Wages and salaries also increased but not by nearly as much; while the cost of living remained stable. Thus, people had more purchasing power and they spent like Americans had never spent before. Most people did not really care about the shift in values. They were content to pay more for better services and goods. The benefits of technology were finally reaching more people. By 1929, two-thirds of the population had electricity. In 1912 that number had been only one-sixth of the population. By 1929, 25 percent of all families owned electric vacuum cleaners and one-fifth had electric toasters. Many could afford those items in addition to things like radios and washing machines. These goods had been luxury items just one year before, but now they were available, for the first time, to the majority of the population.

Perhaps the most significant change was the widespread availability of the automobile. During the 1920s, auto registrations went from 8 million to 23 million as mass production and competition kept driving the cost of car production down. By 1926, it was possible to buy a Model T Ford for less than $300. A Chevrolet sold for $700. All of this was during in a time when most industrial workers made about $1,300 a year, and most clerical workers about $2,300, which meant most people could not afford to buy a car outright until a new kind of buying was made available—the loan purchase. The automobile changed American society in a way few things ever had. It gave kids, for example, the opportunity to escape their parents. In fact, many conservative critics called the automobile a potential house of prostitution on wheels. As the 1920s wore on, the number of car models increased to 108 in 1923 and they were available in a variety of colors, as well. Of course, the increase in cars created all kinds of real problems: from safety legislation to the need for the construction of new roads. In 1921, the federal government passed the Federal Highway Act, which gave federal aid for state roads; and in 1923, the Bureau of Public Roads planned a national highway system. The auto industry also became a boon to the oil industry, which shifted its production from lubrication and illumination to propulsion in order to feed America's appetite for gas.

The 1920s was the first great decade of advertising. Mainstream materialism, business found, could be influenced by advertising. So advertising and salesmanship became the gospel of the 1920s. One book by an advertising executive named Bruce Barton called Jesus the founder of modern business because he took twelve men from the bottom ranks of society and forged an organization that conquered the world. Barton advocated modern executives to follow the example. Packaging and product display also became sciences during the 1920s. This trend toward advertising was aided by the widespread use of radios, which could carry thousands upon thousands of commercials to the entire country. By 1922 there were 508 commercial radio stations in the nation. And by 1929, Americans were spending $850 million a year on radio equipment. NBC was charging advertisers $10,000 to sponsor an hour-long show.

While many people in the country could not afford many of the new products and services being offered, some new trends did touch the working classes, especially those living in cities. Indoor plumbing and electricity became common, and canned foods and massed produced clothing became the norm. If you had a little cash and a lot of credit, you could even get a car.

The pattern of increasing urbanization that we saw before the turn of the century continued in the 1920s. In 1920, for the first time a majority of Americans, 51 percent lived in urban areas (places with more than 2,500 people). Cities like Detroit, Houston, and Birmingham grew into major industrial centers, while growth in Atlanta, Minneapolis, and Seattle was sparked by major service and retail trades. Part of this growth was due to a large-scale migration by African-Americans into the cities. About 1.5 million blacks moved to urban areas in the 1920s. Unfortunately, they quickly became squeezed into ghettos in the central cities because of economics; as most rural immigrants could only afford substandard housing. Even in the inner city, they faced discrimination and racism as some landlords tried to keep them out.

Because of the population shift of blacks from rural areas to urban, the 1920s marked the first real racial conflict to emerge in America. The first real urban conflict between whites and blacks appeared as African-Americans spilled into nearby, nonblack, neighborhoods in search of new housing opportunities. Racial tension was not limited to black and white. Puerto Ricans poured into New York City looking for work in the 1920s. In the West, Mexican immigrants began to move north into the U.S. to look for work in agriculture. A large number flowed into the growing cities of Los Angeles, Denver, Tucson, and San Antonio. Again, the same pattern prevailed: Latinos were crowded into substandard inner-city housing and faced the same types of discrimination that African-Americans did; often being deprived of basic city services such as sanitation, schools, and police protection.

The general white response to this influx of minorities was to pack up and flee the city. So it is during the 1920s that the origins of whites moving outside the city to suburbs began to take shape. In the 1950s, this trend would increase greatly. Some major suburbs, like Oak Park and Evanston, Illinois or Burbank and Inglewood, California, grew at rates of five to ten times as fast as the central cities. Most of these suburbs became bedroom communities with their own city services and they generally fought annexation efforts. Suburban residents wanted to stay away from city crime, dirt, and taxes. But this situation left the city with a major tax problem: with the taxable base fleeing to the suburbs, it became increasingly difficult for city leaders to pay for city services.

The urban and suburban environments created a mass culture that gave the 1920s its character. Most people of the time were going to specialized shops, movie houses, and sporting arenas. These people of the city and suburbs embraced the fads of the 1920s, like crossword puzzles, miniature golf, and marathon dancing. It was in the cities and suburbs where people were breaking the law by going to speakeasies, wearing outlandish clothing, and listening to jazz. And yet, ironically, these city folk retained many of their small-town values. City and suburban residents often longed for the days when things were simpler and their choices were clearer. That past became their moral anchor. Even if it was, at times, not a very firm moral anchor.

Amid all this change, Americans were developing new social values and new ways of using their time. Increasingly they were dividing their time into three phases: work, family, and leisure. Each phase of time was altered during the 1920s. Time at work, for most people, actually began to decline. Work days for industrial workers dropped to 5.5 days per week. Many clerical workers were only working forty hours a week. Family time also changed. Less time at work meant more time at home. Surprisingly, birth rates dropped noticeably in the 1920s. It was not because people were having sex less often though, birth control became more widely practiced (especially new forms of control, like diaphragms, cervical caps, and condoms). Thus, family size continued to fall. In 1880, over half of the women who lived to age fifty had five children. By the 1920s, that number had fallen to only 20 percent. Divorce rates rose from one in every 7.5 in 1920 to one in 6 by 1929, and reached as high as 2 in 7 in many large cities.

Life for women changed drastically. Some machines, along with prefabricated items like clothes and preserved foods, lightened the work load for the housewife. Electric irons and washing machines, hot water heaters and central heating, all saved women from having to haul in wood, coal, and water into their household. While the wife was spending less time on domestic chores, she was spending more time on things like shopping for the family and making sure the family spent its money wisely. Women were also cleaning more than ever before. The 1920s really saw a new standard of cleanliness being introduced in society. The companies that made products created the trend: advocating healthy foods full of vitamins, strong soaps, and new personal hygiene items like mouth wash and deodorant.

Leisure time was also increasing in the 1920s. Young people began to spend more time in school, to the point that by 1929 one-third of all high school graduates went on to college. As the use of electricity spread, people stayed up later at night, reading for fun and listening to ball games on the radio. Some people even went riding in the car or out to the movies. The effect of an increase in rest and a better diet, along with new advances in medicine, was a significantly increase in the life expectancy for the average American—going from the age of fifty-four in 1920 to sixty in 1930. Medical progress was not egalitarian, however. Among African-Americans, the stillborn and infant mortality rates were 50 to 100 percent higher than whites. Tuberculosis was rampant in urban settings. Automobile accidents rose 150 percent. Yet despite those problems, most Americans were living longer. In fact, the total number of people over the age of sixty-five grew by 35 percent between 1920 and 1930. As a result of the increase in the aged population, the first efforts to take care of the elderly living in poverty emerged during the 1920s. By 1933, almost every state would at least provide minimal assistance to the aged.

While the demographics of the population were changing, social values were changing, as well. The middle class, especially, became more liberal socially during the 1920s. The style of clothing became increasingly gaudy and colorful. There seemed to be more smoking, swearing, and sex in general. Many of the quasi-intellectual youth believed, based on Sigmund Freud's work which most of them had never read, that the key to happiness was an uninhibited sex life. Birth control became increasingly popular as people like Margaret Sanger advocated the use of birth control devices, which led to a drastic increase in sexual activity. Another trend was the theme of generational conflict. As kids stopped working with adult family members and increasingly found themselves in school with people of their own age, they increasingly bonded together into new social units (such as through school and sports) and became intellectually distinct from older generations. This distinctiveness caused a generational tension that was not part of American society prior to this period.

Another example of the breakdown of traditional values can be seen with more and more women taking jobs outside the home. The First World War really brought women into the work place. By 1930, 10.8 million women held paying jobs. Sex segregation did continue, however. Women were mostly limited to jobs like teachers, nurses, typists, bookkeepers, and office clerks. Wages, moreover, were seldom more than half that of what men earned for the same work. Part of the reason these women entered the workforce was that it was a way in which to support the broad-based consumerism most of the country was involved in. So it was really in support of the family that most of these women went to work. Feminist groups of the period, however, felt that women were going to work to gain their independence. And for this reason, feminist groups opposed laws restricting the hours women could work because, they felt these laws tended to limit the types of jobs women could do and preserved the system of sexual separation.

Another aspect of mass culture that manifested during the 1920s was the emergence of what is called the Age of Play. Americans developed a thirst for recreation. In 1919, Americans spent $2.5 billion on leisure activities. By 1929, that figure topped $4.3 billion. And this thirst manifested itself in a variety of forms. Movies, the theater, and sports accounted for about 21 percent of that figure for 1929. The remainder was taken up by individual recreations ranging from participatory sports to hobbies to music and travel. By 1930, nearly every community had at least one movie theater. Movie viewers increased from 40 million per week in 1922 to over 100 million per week by 1930—pretty impressive for a time when the total population of the country was only 120 million and the total weekly church attendance was under 60 million. When color and sound were added, it only reinforced the realism movies offered. The most popular of films were either mass spectacles like Cecil B. DeMille's *The Ten Commandments* (1923) or slapstick comedies with such stars as Charlie Chaplin and Fatty Arbuckle.

Spectator sports also boomed during the 1920s. Millions packed into arenas to watch college and professional sports. The gate receipts for college football alone surpassed $21 million in the late 1920s. Baseball, in particular, drew a huge following during the period, especially after Judge K. Mountain Landis, the baseball commissioner during the 1920s, rooted out corruption in the game and added a ball redesigned to increase home runs. Boxing, football, and baseball all produced major sports heroes from Jack Dempsey to Red Grange to Babe Ruth. Americans identified with such figures.

Identification could also be found in the movies and the public realm as well. Rudolph Valentino, Gloria Swanson, and Douglas Fairbanks filled a yearning for romance and adventure. The news media also created its own heroes, like Floyd Collins who was trapped in a Kentucky cave and a plethora of flagpole sitters, marathon dancers, and other record seekers. The most notable news hero of the day had to be Charles Lindbergh, who was the first man to fly a nonstop solo flight across the Atlantic in 1927. In part this adulation of heroes could have reflected some of the guilt Americans felt over the relaxation of social standards, or it could represent a yearning for escape from the drudgery of everyday life.

In many ways it seems that during the 1920s, Americans were caught between two competing value systems. One was characterized by the Puritan work ethic, sobriety, and restraint—prevailing in rural areas and some sections of the cities. The other value system was one of personal liberation and self-adulation. These tensions pulled Americans in different directions and seemed to lend a frantic momentum to society, something best reflected in the arts of the period. Artists constantly moved in new directions and prompted experimentation in literature, art, and music. The will to protect the individual from the vices of modern civilization became a consistent theme in their work.

Many of the literary figures of the 1920s were appalled by the materialism of the decade. They became disillusioned, and are often referred to as the Lost Generation. A number of them, like Hemingway and the poets Ezra Pound and T. S. Eliot, moved to Europe. Others, such as William Faulkner and Sinclair Lewis, remained in the U.S., but became bitter critics of the increasing isolation of modern man. Much of their themes revolved around two issues: the materialism of the middle class and the impersonality of the modern society.

Another different intellectual trend occurred in Harlem and is known as the Harlem Renaissance. Here, a young group of black writers rejected assimilation into white culture and militantly asserted their pride in their African heritage. Yet, they also realized that black Americans had to become participants in the American experience. That dichotomy meant they needed to find new ways to express themselves inside what was a polarized society. Harlem of the 1920s fostered a number of gifted writers, such as poet Langston Hughes and a variety of jazz singers including Florence Mills and Josephine Baker. Jazz, especially, brought to Harlem from the Mississippi Delta, was in itself an expression of personal freedom with its emotional rhythms and improvisation.

Screening Out the Past

In some sense, the motion picture presents our customs and daily life more than any other medium of our world. So, if you look back at films made in the 1920s, motion pictures can tell you more about that time than anything else. They are not only descriptive, but prescriptive as well. The best example of this situation can be found in Muncie, Indiana. In the 1920s, the weekly attendance at the nine theaters in Muncie equaled three times the entire population of the city. There were more people in the movies on Sunday than in the churches of Muncie. Moviegoers came from all classes and ethnic groups. Movies were a mass medium. The great figures of the period: D. W. Griffith, Mary Pickford, Douglas Fairbanks, Charlie Chaplin, and Cecil B. DeMille were all here. But the main theme of the movies was just this: the change from Victorian customs to modern mores, the shattering of old values and their replacement with modern values. How did people learn what those new values were? Just as mass production brought about a higher standard of living, it altered visions of success in the country. Now, in order to be successful, you had to acquire "things," whether they were homes, cars, clothes, vacuum cleaners, etc. The movies taught America how to think like this. The values and dreams reflected in the movies became those of the New America, Twentieth Century America. The movies did not cause this change, but they increased its momentum. Movies helped to alter the morality of western culture. And by building movie houses, creating stars, and publishing fan magazines, Hollywood helped to integrate the imagery on the screen into the everyday lives of its audience. That is what made the movies work. They are successful because we can see ourselves as Leonardo DiCaprio in *Titanic*, or Luke Skywalker in *Star Wars*, or as Drew Barrymore in *Charlie's Angels*. The new culture of the 1920s was decidedly suburban. It was sports, leisure, nightclubs, popular music, amusement parks, and the movies. The movies helped screen out that older American identity, replacing it with an exclusively modern one.

In many ways, the 1920s became the most creative decade in American history to that point. Despite a variety of social problems, it was really the cultural climax of modernization: the highpoint of fifty years of industrial, technological advancement, and social change.

Politics & Society

Sadly, the 1920s is one of the most difficult decades in American history to say anything meaningful about. So much was going on, in terms of social and cultural change, and often much of that was contradictory in nature, that the decade sometimes resembled a bottomless black hole, sucking assumptions and generalizations down into destruction. Nevertheless, there are some workable approaches to this topic. One of the most important, I think, is to look at the social and cultural changes created by technology. But first, let's summarize the major political trends of the decade, for context if nothing else.

Conservatives politicians dominated the 1920s. Progressivism did not completely die out; in fact. it would resurface during the Depression, but it became a non-issue during the 1920s. The Republican presidents of the period—Warren Harding, Calvin Coolidge, and Herbert Hoover—are often seen as men who turned back the clock to a simpler era, one that existed before the Progressivism of Theodore Roosevelt. As such, these conservative politicians can be blamed for sticking their head in the sand and ignoring needed reforms, a behavior that eventually led to the Stock Market Crash of 1929 and the Great Depression. There is something to be said for that. The Republicans returned the nation to a high-tariff policy, they paid far less attention to the concentration of power and wealth, they were not sympathetic to the union movement, and there was a general lack of presidential leadership.

Yet for all those shortcomings, there was something inherently new about politics in the 1920s. The innovations were in the sphere of the government's relationship with the business community. And it was mostly the work of Herbert Hoover. Hoover was a brilliant man. He wanted to establish a new mercantilism for America. For Hoover (acting first as the Secretary of Commerce and then later as President of the United States), the role of the government was to help make the American economy work, to provide information to the public, and to make business more efficient and profitable. In this sense, Hoover was probably more like Bill Clinton than any other president of the century. He wanted to create managed competition, which would, he believed, make the national economy profitable and stable.

The Election of 1924

resident Coolidge was nominated by the Republican convention. His vice president was Charles G. Dawes. The Democrats, meeting in New York, had a knock-down drag-out fight for the nomination. In the end, it fell to John W. Davis of West Virginia, a Wall Street lawyer (over Al Smith and William McAdoo). Charles W. Bryan was named as the vice presidential candidate. The Progressives, who had no chance to win, nominated Bob La Follette. Coolidge easily won the general election. The conservative Davis did so poorly that future Democratic candidates would be much more liberal, establishing a precedent for the party that continues to this day.

Prohibition

Perhaps the most important conflict of the period was that of rural versus urban. The nation's rural sections were still caught in the nineteenth century. Life there remained much as it was in 1880. But life in the cities was becoming modern at a frantic pace. In rural areas, children still went to school in one-room school houses; horses and buggies were still common up until 1918. Most rural values were formed in this context, of a stable, unhurried life. Most urban values, however, reflected the symbols of the new age—from cars to airplanes to Hollywood. Caught between these dueling beliefs systems was an increasingly social desire to drink alcohol.

The origins behind the movement to abolish alcohol are complex. Prohibition was embraced by evangelical Protestantism, the belief that social evils could be destroyed: whether they were found in racial tensions, class conflicts, rural distrust of the cities, or a hatred of immigrants. The short-term origins of Prohibition went back to 1917, when Congress prohibited the manufacture of alcohol for the rest of the war (since it consumed grain needed for food). But in December 1917, Congress adopted the Eighteenth Amendment and sent it to the states. As long as three-fourths of the states agreed, there would be no more sale or manufacture of "intoxicating liquors" in the United States. That did not take long, as thirty-six states ratified the Eighteenth Amendment by January of 1919.

Enforcing Prohibition was another matter. Too many people in America wanted to drink. It was cheap and easy to make, and the market was large. Thus a huge black market for illegal booze developed immediately after the Amendment was passed. And it was easy to evade the law. The federal Prohibition Bureau was a joke until 1928. Even at the local level, it was easy to bribe low-paid federal enforcement officers. One in twelve officers was fired for accepting bribes, but those were only the ones who were caught. It was easy to smuggle liquor in via Canada and the Caribbean. Some people even consumed industrial alcohol as a beverage (a dangerous practice since bootleggers often did not remove all the denaturants, leading to blindness and even death). In the long run, the Eighteenth Amendment and the Volstead Act (the enabling legislation) were a disaster. They did little to increase the average person's respect for the law, and led to even more corruption. While it did not lead to an increase in organized crime, organized criminals became more violent as a result. Legal business depends on the law to enforce order, but organized crime can only depend on violence.

So if Prohibition was unenforceable and unpopular, why was it not repealed before 1933? The answer seems to be that while most people disapproved of Prohibition for themselves, they did favor it for others. Whites wanted prohibition for blacks in the South. The urban middle-class wanted Prohibition for immigrants. Elites and religious folks wanted

Prohibition for everyone. It was only after Hoover began to enforce the law in 1928 that there was a strong effort to repeal the Amendment. Congress passed the Twenty-first Amendment in February 1933, repealing the Eighteenth Amendment. By December of that year, the thirty-sixth state ratified the Amendment, returning legalized alcohol consumption to law.

Immigration Restriction

Another major conflict between rural and urban elements of America revolved around immigration reform. Most rural areas were Protestant; most of those coming to America as immigrants were Catholic or Jewish, poorly educated, and stricken with poverty. The habits and culture of the immigrants were unusual compared to mainstream America. The xenophobia unleashed by the First World War triggered a move to restrict the massive immigration to the U.S. during the last twenty years. The motivations to restrict immigration were numerous. To some, it was pure racism. To others, immigrants were radicals who endangered American stability. Still others thought the immigrants were too conservative and would prevent social progress. Even unions did not want immigrants, fearing they would work for cheaper wages than unionized American workers.

In response to the immigrant issue, the government established the Emergency Quota Act—a temporary law signed by Warren Harding in May 1921. The Emergency Quota Act said that the number of aliens of any nationality could not exceed 3 percent of the number of foreign-born of that nationality counted by the U.S. Census of 1910. In a simple example (1,000 Italian-born counted by the 1910 Census—only 3 percent (thirty) Italians could enter the U.S. in any one year). This scheme was designed to discriminate against immigrants from southern and eastern Europe, but it failed because most of the immigrants still coming were from southern and eastern Europe. Thus, while Italy filled its quota, the British did not.

The next piece of legislation focused on limiting immigration was the National Origins Act. Signed by the eager Calvin Coolidge, who stated, "America must be kept American," the National Origins Act was an ugly and complicated piece of legislation. It established that each foreign nation would have an immigration quota equal to 2 percent of the foreign-born of that nation living in the U.S. in 1890. By pushing the census date back from 1910 to 1890, the opposition to immigration was further restricted the numbers of immigrants from southern and eastern Europe. After 1927, the total number of immigrants allowed in per year was reduced to 150,000, again with a sliding percentage scale. The new quota system finally went into effect in 1929. The quota for Britain was set at 65,721; for Germany it was 25,957; for the Scandinavian nations 7,501; Poland only had 6,524; Italy 5,802; and Russia 2,712. The ironies were numerous. The law did not prohibit immigration from Canada or Mexico and, by the time it went into effect, America was about to find itself in the grips of a major depression. Massive European immigration had come to an end.

The Ku Klux Klan

Prohibition, immigration restriction, anti-Catholicism, and religious fundamentalism—all were products of rural and small-town America. One other product of American ruralism was the Ku Klux Klan. From 1922 until 1925, the Klan emerged as a major force in American politics and rural life. It remains the strongest hate organization that ever existed in America. The origins of the 1920s Klan were seemingly innocent. William J. Simmons, a history teacher at Lanier College in Georgia, a romantic who yearned for a return to the Old South, an individual who never got over the Civil War, started the KKK as a new fraternal lodge. Creating fraternal orders was a common action in America of the 1920s. What could be better, Simmons' thought, than a lodge named after the Ku Klux Klan, an organization that had terrorized freedmen and Republicans during Reconstruction. Simmons thus invented all kinds of terminology for the organization. He held the highest office, that of Imperial Wizard. Local chapters were called Klaverns. He also created a lodge costume, a loose white robe with a peaked white hood and mask. Simmons' KKK was founded in 1915, and by 1920 it only had a few chapters in Georgia and Alabama. Then a racist dentist from Texas, Hiram Wesley Evans, became the new Imperial Wizard. Evans hired fundraisers and marketing people who used modern mass media techniques to recruit new members. In something of a pyramid scheme, Klan membership expanded rapidly—each time you recruited a member you got a share of the $10 fee. The KKK grew in the South, and then spread to the Midwest and far West, using first rhetoric against blacks and later Catholics. In general, the KKK was against immigration, was in favor of Prohibition, and frowned on sexual immorality. According to several influential historians, religious fundamentalists played an important role in reviving the Klan, using it as a tool against what they saw as America's growing immorality.

As the KKK expanded across the nation, its members turned to politics. As a political group, the New Klan valued nineteenth-century morality and rural life. They used modern political tactics like bloc voting as well as terror and violence to achieve their goals. Burning a cross was usually as far as they went, but sometimes they turned to violence and even murder. The New Klan was hard to fight because it was a secret organization. When the New Klan turned to politics, it began by endorsing candidates in the 1922 Texas Democratic primary. Then it helped impeach the governor of Oklahoma in 1923, moved into both the Democratic and the Republican parties in Oregon by wining control over both houses and the governorship. One of its strongholds was Indiana, where it had solid support among members of both parties. At its highest point, nearly 10,000 members of the New Klan marched in their regalia down the streets of Washington, D.C.

But it was in Indiana that the New Klan reached its peak, and in turn, began to crumble as a national political movement. D. C. Stephenson, leader of the Midwestern Klan, made his organization a major political force there. But in 1925, he was involved in an episode that discredited the entire organization. At a KKK rally in Indianapolis, Stephenson picked up a secretary who worked for the state, got her drunk on bootleg whiskey, marshaled her aboard a Pullman railroad car bound for Chicago, and sexually assaulted her. The young woman was so sick with what happened that she swallowed poison, becoming dangerously ill. Stephenson, with the help of some associates, moved her from the train to a Chicago hotel, where they denied her medical treatment because they were afraid that she might tell someone what happened. A month later she died. Indiana politicians, who were long tired of Stephenson's influence, had him arrested, indicted, tried, and sentenced for manslaughter. The most famous and influential leader of the New Klan was carted off to the state prison, serving time for a crime that violated the basic principles the organization he was supposed to represent. The New Klan was so discredited that it immediately died as a political force, though it did hang on in local areas and does so even to this day.

Anti-Catholicism

While the New Klan was limited in membership, anti-Catholicism remained a widespread American institution. In 1928, the Democratic Party nominated Al Smith, a Roman Catholic and one of the most popular men in America, for president. When the Democrats met that year, the Republicans had already nominated Herbert Hoover with Charles Curtis of Kansas as vice president. Urban Democrats had been angry since 1924 that the Party refused to nominate Smith sooner. Yet while Smith was one of the most popular politicians in the country, it was clear to the Democratic leadership that his nomination might split the party if they refused again. Therefore, Al Smith received the nomination on the first ballot. To appease the rural-southern-dry-Protestant faction, they also nominated Sen. Joe T. Robinson of Arkansas as vice president.

To much of Protestant America, Al Smith was not only a Catholic but represented the classic big-city politician. His parents were Irish immigrants. He had lived in a tenement as a child. He was against Prohibition. Thus, he proved an easy target for attack. Anti-Catholic and pro-wet (people who supported Prohibition) critics pounded the Democrats for Smith's candidacy. Protestant clergymen constantly asked: "Shall dry America elect a cocktail President?" Some Hoover supporters claimed that if Smith was elected, the pope would be the actual ruler of the United States. Not surprisingly, Hoover won by a large margin: 444 electoral votes to Smith's 87. The Republicans also won easy majorities in both houses of Congress. There was some hope for the Democratic Party. A closer look at the vote showed that Smith had done better in the big cities of the Northeast than any Democratic candidate since the Civil War. Smith won those cities by a slight margin. Smith's candidacy had delivered the big city vote to the Democrats, where it has remained ever since.

Items to Consider

Model T, advertising, rise of the suburb, leisure time, women and work, Harlem Renaissance, movies and the New Values, Eighteenth Amendment, Emergency Quota Act, Ku Klux Klan

CHAPTER 23

The Crash of 1929 & the New Deal

The Depression and then the experience with the Second World War defined an entire generation of Americans. They were born into poverty, at a time when the American economy seemed on the verge of collapse. Their sacrifices during this time of little material wealth, and their efforts to win at first what appeared to be an unwinnable war, gave the "WWII Generation" their character. The origins of that character lay in the great prosperity of the 1920s, and the drudgery of the Great Depression.

When Herbert Hoover was elected president in 1928, the mood of the general public was one of optimism and great confidence in the U.S. economy. In his acceptance speech for his party's nomination, Hoover said: "We in America today are nearer to the final triumph over poverty than ever before in the history of any land. The poorhouse is vanishing from among us." That same year, John Jacob Raskob, chief executive of General Motors and head of the Democratic National Congress, published an article called "Everybody Ought to Be Rich," in *Ladies Home Journal*. Raskob said that every American could be wealthy by investing as little as $15 a week in common stocks, but this was hard to do when the average salary ranged from $17 to $22 per week. Still, the optimism was there and everyone in the nation invested at least a small amount of money in the stock market.

The "Bull Market"

From 1924 to 1929, the stock market grew at a fantastic pace. A *Bull Market* means that stock prices were rising quickly, as opposed to a *Bear Market* when stock prices drop quickly. The stock market of the 1920s grew because of the expansion of credit and the rapid increase in investment. There were essentially six reasons for this growth:

1. Rising Stock Dividends—The market was based on a foundation of fresh growth. For example, a substantial number of new investors were entering the market every day. Many people saw the market as a way to "get rich quickly." While only about 4 million Americans were invested in the market at any one time, thousands were "getting in and getting out" every day, thus ensuring that lots of cash changed hands.

2. An increase in personal savings—As wages increased (slowly) and the cost of living remained stable, more Americans had the money to save or invest in the stock market.

3. A Federal Policy of Easy Money—Credit was widely available to anyone who might want to speculate. Interest rates were low, be it for automobiles or stock investments. Americans took advantage of the situation by taking out loans they could not reasonably expect to pay off in their lifetimes. A risky venture even in the best of circumstances.

4. Over-production—After 1925, American industry was knowingly producing more than American consumers could consume. Instead of scaling back production, business leaders anticipated their surpluses would eventually be sold off, thus they reinvested their earnings in the industry by building new factories, purchasing new machinery, and hiring more workers. The result, of course, was that overproduction increased.

5. A Lack of Federal Regulation—In the probusiness climate of the 1920s, there were few national guidelines on the buying and selling of stocks. Corporations turned stock certificates into essentially worthless paper by printing more and more of it. To compound that problem, many investors practiced "buying on the margin," buying stock on credit. The investor was confident that the price of the stock would rise and he would be able to pay off his balance, plus accumulated interest, and still have a nice profit. This was an attractive practice since it allowed you to make money on other people's money. But if you think about it, the opportunity for disaster is looming. If you borrowed $50,000 to invest, on the assumption that the price would increase, and then it did not, you not only lose your money, but also the bank's. The U.S. stock market was constructed on this house of cards, filled with money that really was not actually there.

6. The Psychology of Consumption—In the 1920s, Americans purchased like they had never consumed before, always believing the future could only get better. The unquestioning faith in prosperity led people to invest more and consider the consequences later. This faith, becoming almost a new Gospel of Wealth, made the Crash far worse when it came.

September 1929

Americans had put too much confidence in the market. Unlike the previous century, the stock market was seen as the best indicator of the health status of the American economy, not the health of banks or sales of real estate or consumer goods. In September 1929 stock prices began to fluctuate. This was seen as only a temporary bump in the road. What most people did not understand was that stock prices were completely out of relation to actual profits. Sales were falling, factory construction had slowed; all the while stock market prices climbed upward. Not many people were worried though; they believed the market would take care of itself.

Black Thursday

October 24, 1929, Black Thursday as it came to be called, was one of the worst days in American economic history. Investors dumped their stocks as quickly as they could. Sell, sell, sell was the order of the day. The bull market had suddenly become a bear market. By nightfall, the market caught its breath, but only because J. P. Morgan and other wealthy financial investors bought up stocks to keep the market alive. The following day the market remained stable. But when business closed for the weekend, people began to worry. They feared the markets would collapse again on Monday and, thus, decided to sell and cut their losses while they still could. When the Exchange opened on Monday, the stage was set for financial disaster. The sell orders resumed and swelled, but the worse had yet to come.

Black Tuesday

October 29, Black Tuesday, was the single most devastating day in the history of the New York Stock Exchange. As it opened that morning, prices fell so far that they erased all the profits made over the last year, destroying what confidence people had left in the market. Between October 29 and November 13 (when prices hit their lowest point), the U.S. economy lost over $30 billion. This was more than the U.S. had spent during all of WWI, and it was lost in just two weeks.

J. P. Morgan and many leaders in America were confident that prosperity would return. But it did not. The GNP fell from $87 billion in 1929 down to $75 billion in 1930. By 1931 it was down to $59 billion, 1932 only $42 billion, and down to just $40 billion by 1933. Former President Coolidge remarked: "This country is not in good condition." Hoover tried not to alarm the public. Traditionally these types of things were called Panics, like the one of 1873 or 1893. They happened periodically, causing great distress within the nation. Instead, Hoover chose to call this one a Depression and the name stuck. America was not alone. All the industrialized nations of the world were suffering. Germany, Britain, and France owed appalling amounts of money to each other and to the U.S. The Allies alone owed the U.S. some $9.5 billion, but were unable to pay after 1928. In fact, most would never repay the U.S.

Social Problems

The first result of the Depression was a drastic increase in social problems. There were a number of social problems triggered by the Depression, including high unemployment, a breakdown of families, large numbers of high school dropouts (2–4 million), hopelessness, and labor protests. Everyone in the nation was suffering. It seemed that the U.S. might be on the verge of revolution. No one understood what went wrong, but they looked to the president. The homeless built cardboard and tar-paper shacks, calling them Hoovervilles. Empty pockets turned inside out became Hoover Flags. Newspapers were Hoover blankets. At the rural level, farmers armed with shotguns and rifles marched on banks to stop foreclosures. And in Washington, D.C., a group of WWI veterans, calling themselves the Bonus Expeditionary Force, came to the capital to ask Congress to give them immediate pensions, rather than being forced to wait another ten years. In 1932, twenty thousand war veterans set up a tent city within the capital, promising to stay until they were paid. Hoover panicked and sent in the Army led by future heroes Douglas MacArthur and Dwight D. Eisenhower to break up the demonstration and destroy the men's tent city. Thus, we have U.S. soldiers being used to break up veteran protesters and driving them from the city.

The Great Depression has come down to us as a stereotyped experience. Popular culture and mass media have imprinted on our imaginations things like soup kitchens, transients wandering from town to town, college graduates working in service jobs, high rates of suicide and mental illness, and the catastrophe of the Dust Bowl as set forth in Steinbeck's *Grapes of Wrath*. But the truth is that those images represented only the experiences of a small percentage of the American population. In short, there were two fundamental problems in America that no one seemed to be able to address. The first was unemployment; second, low consumption. Until those two problems could be addressed, the situation would not improve.

Compounding the market problems, the Depression brought with it a farm crisis. Many farmers were destroyed by the Depression. Large numbers of them had gone into debt to buy machinery and land during the 1920s and now they could not make their payments. Crop prices fell through the floor, and there seemed to be little hope for the future. Making matters worse, one of the greatest ecological disasters in American history chose that moment to appear, the Dust Bowl crisis in the Midwest (and part of the South). The drought of 1931–32 turned much of Plains into an apocalyptic nightmare, turning vast acres of the country's interior into vegetation-less dust and forcing many farmers to leave to look for other work.

As the situation in the nation seemed to spiral further and further out of control, Americans began to ask a single question: Who was to blame? The most common answer for the American people was the so-called Three Bs: Bankers, Businessmen, and Brokers. But the American cultural climate encourages people to be selfish—to worry about themselves first. Some historians have argued that the guilty party was the Federal Reserve, because it refused to tighten credit during the boom and refused to loosen it when things turned to bust. The answer is probably more complicated than that, the result of several interlocking factors. Regardless of who was at fault, the government seemed not to take the right action to fix the problem.

Herbert Hoover believed that no president could ever admit he was wrong. With that in mind, it should be no surprise that the common perception was Hoover did nothing to check the tide of the Crash and Depression. The truth is just the opposite. He did, in fact, try to stem the tide. Unfortunately, Hoover was only willing to go so far, only willing to compromise his laissez faire capitalism to a certain degree. In late 1931, Hoover called for a new public works program of $2.5 billion, the most expensive one in American history to date—it included the construction of the Hoover Dam. He also approved the Federal Home Loan Bank Act of 1932, which encouraged home ownership and provided loans to small banks and mortgage companies. The Glass-Steagall Act of 1932 expanded the credit supply by allowing paper money to serve as partial collateral for Treasury bills—freeing up some $750 million in gold. He signed the Emergency and Relief Construction Act of 1932, which gave $2 billion to state and local governments for public works. He also approved $500 million for the new Reconstruction Finance Corporation (RFC) to make loans to banks, and other needed institutions. Hoover even allowed the RFC to borrow $1.5 billion more a few months later. Hoover signed the Norris-LaGuardia Act of 1932, preventing court injunctions against strikes and picketing. In his mind, Hoover had stretched the power of the presidency in an effort to help the nation.

Despite his best efforts, Hoover was unable to turn the economy around and crop prices continued to fall. Democrats controlled the House after 1930, which ended further efforts by the Republican president. The Farmers Holiday Association began barricading Midwestern highways, stopping shipments of underpriced commodities. The RFC failed at its task. Most of its funds found their way into the hands of large corporations, with only about 10 percent of the funds going to state relief. While Hoover was willing to help American industry and agriculture in their recovery, he was unwilling to sacrifice his principles to help individuals who needed relief. This stance subjected him to the criticism that he was willing to feed farm animals, but not farm children.

While the situation had been bad, it worsened in 1933. The downward spiral triggered by the Crash remained a permanent symbol of our greatest economic catastrophe. By 1933, 25 percent of Americans were unemployed. Wages fell almost by half (down to $31 billion), and farm income fell from $12 billion in 1929 down to $5 billion by 1933. The automobile industry was devastated—its sales fell by 75 percent and construction industries fell from $8.7 billion in 1929 down to $1.4 billion by 1933. Six thousand banks that had had assets of some $4 billion failed and more than 100,000 businesses went bankrupt.

Like the "Alabama" song says:"Somebody told us Wall Street fell, but we were so poor we couldn't tell." The Depression came to the rural areas of the U.S. long before the Crash. While 1929 marks the year that the rest of America joined the fold, southern and midwestern farmers had known suffering since the early 1920s. Of course, industrial poverty is a far more serious event than agricultural scarcity. In hard times, poor farmers were at least able to live off the land. Unemployed factory workers had no means of support when they lost their jobs. In some cities, like Akron and Toledo, unemployment reached as high as 60 to 80 percent. Landlords evicted 200,000 families from their apartments in New York City in 1931. Fights over garbage and restaurant dumpster food became commonplace. Fear became the dominate trait of this generation—fear of losing their jobs (like 100,000 Americans did every week between 1929 and 1932), fear of losing their homes, fear of wage cuts, and fear of being reduced to poverty.

With so many people suffering, Hoover's time as president was limited. By late 1932, Hoover had no plans for helping those who were starving or in need of shelter. Over one hundred cities were without funds to help the homeless. Hoover came to the office of the presidency with great promise. One of the most capable administrators in America at that time, he was called a visionary and a Progressive in an age when there were precious few of either. But now Hoover was discredited. As the election of 1932 approached, the crisis worsened. Hoover never had a chance. In the 1932 presidential election, Franklin Delano Roosevelt won a decisive victory

New Deal for America

It is impossible to fit all of the New Deal into a neat, philosophical package. For one, it was not some carefully planned, coordinated strategy. As FDR himself said, "The country needs, and, unless I mistake its temper, the country demands bold, persistent, *experimentation*. ... Above all, try something." And try things he did.

First Concern—Banking & Finance

One of FDR's immediate concerns had to do with the banking and finance crisis. He had to stop people from withdrawing money from the bank. He had to give people confidence in investing. FDR's first act as president was to declare a national bank "holiday." That is, he closed all the banks in the nation to prevent people from withdrawing their money and, therefore, he kept banks going out of business. Congress immediately passed the Emergency Banking Act, proclaiming that banks would remain closed until March 13, 1933—a week after FDR closed them. Even then, banks could not reopen until they could prove to the Treasury Department that they had sufficient funds to resume normal operations. The key was that on the night before the banks were to reopen, FDR gave the first of his fireside chats over the radio. In his speech, FDR was calm, and reassuring. He asked the American people to have faith in the government, to trust that he would fix the financial problem.

The banks reopened the following morning and stayed open. Few banks closed following FDR's election. The primary reason was a problematic notion called confidence. A week or so later, FDR created the FDIC—the Federal Deposit Insurance Corporation—with the passage of the Glass-Steagall/Banking Act of 1933. The act pledged that the government would guarantee people's bank deposits up to $2,500. Once again, FDR was seeking to reassure the people and, once again, a strong, active government at work restored confidence.

Second Concern—Providing Relief

FDR next turned his attention to providing the nation with relief from the Depression. The Federal Emergency Relief Administration set aside $500 million to address the most immediate suffering of people. These funds went directly to those people who needed them the most, something Hoover would have never done. FDR defended the move, saying, "The test of our progress [as a government] is not whether we add to the abundance of those who have much. It is whether we provide enough for those who have too little."

Then in 1935, FDR secured passage of the monumental Social Security Act. In terms of programs and scope, the Social Security Act did three major things:

1. It created a retirement pension fund for elderly people.
2. It created an unemployment insurance fund to protect those who lost their jobs.
3. It created a plan of disability insurance and provided payments to mothers with dependent children.

To a far greater degree than at any other time in U.S. history, the federal government was actually helping people. Not only was the government acknowledging the social rights of citizens as opposed to decades of emphasis on the economic rights of property owners but the U.S. government actually affirmed that it had a certain amount of responsibility for the well-being of its citizens. This act, more than any other of the period, signaled the creation of an American welfare state. Why? Was it because the government felt sorry for poor people? No. Did government step forward because it wanted to give poor people a break? Again, the answer is no. The government in the 1930s finally admitted what the Populists knew in the 1890s. In a growing, expanding, integrated, market-driven, capitalist economy, individuals were left to the mercy of forces beyond their control. Economic success or failure is only partly the result of one's willingness to work, one's intelligence, or one's ingenuity.

Having bolstered the personal needs of individuals and the economy, FDR turned his attention to creating jobs. He did not want to force companies like Ford to hire more people or to raise wages, nor did he want to foster overproduction. But FDR knew that people needed jobs to support their families and restore confidence in themselves. To bring this about, FDR created the Civilian Conservation Corps (CCC), which hired young men between the ages of 18 and 25 to work on federal work projects. In roughly ten years of existence, the CCC put nearly 3 million young men to work on national parks and national forests. CCC projects included soil conservation, flood control, and disaster relief.

The CCC was so successful that FDR then established the Works Progress Administration (WPA), which was the largest and most comprehensive New Deal Agency, employing millions of people and affecting every locality. Only unemployed people on relief were eligible for most of its jobs. The hourly wages were the prevailing wages in the area, but workers could not work more than twenty to thirty hours a week. About 75 percent of employment and 75 percent of WPA expenditures went to public facilities such as the construction of highways, streets, public buildings, airports, utilities, small dams, sewers, parks, libraries, and recreational fields. The WPA built 650,000 miles of roads, 78,000 bridges, 125,000 buildings, 8,000 parks, 5,900 schools, 13,000 playgrounds, and 700 miles of airport runways. Seven percent of the budget was allocated to arts projects, presenting 225,000 concerts to audiences totaling 150 million, and producing almost 475,000 artworks. Though some 90 percent of WPA projects were directed at unskilled, blue-collar workers, it also took in unemployed, white-collar artists, musicians, actors, and writers in such projects as the Federal Theater Project and the Federal Writers' Project. The key to the success of the CCC and the WPA was that it took people out of the unemployment lines and put them to work for the government. Before it was phased out in 1943, 8.5 million people worked on WPA jobs at one time or another.

Third Concern—Fixing American Business

Naturally FDR had to address the concerns of big industry. Congress passed the National Industrial Recovery Act, which created the National Recovery Administration (NRA). More than 600 codes came out of NRA, and NRA regulations eventually governed everything from car building to making dog food. It sought to create fair labor standards and asked industries to create standards of competition for themselves. These industry councils would hopefully solve some of the issues of overproduction, cutthroat competition, and other problems. The goal was to allow more people to stay in business and keep their workers working. To that affect, Section 7a of the National Industrial Recovery Act guaranteed the right of workers to organize and bargain collectively with employers. Furthering that sentiment, the National Labor

Relations Act, also called the Wagner Act after Sen. Robert Wagner who sponsored it successfully into law. The Wagner Act strengthened the NRA, pledging the federal government's support of the workers' right to unionize.

Another important piece of legislation to help workers was the National Labor Relations Board. The NLRB put government officials into a position to supervise plant elections for unionization. The NLRB also gave the federal government the power to assess penalties on companies that refused to allow union elections, or that refused to allow union members to distribute union literature on company property. The NLRB penalized companies that fired workers for union activity—another old tradition of businesses. Again, it is important to note the contrast from the old days of laissez faire. Now with the Wagner Act, the government had asserted its influence directly into the worker-management relationship.

Sadly, it was not only industrial workers who were suffering during the Depression. To that end, FDR actively tried to provide needed assistance to American farmers. For them, FDR created the Commodity Credit Corporation in October 1933. The idea was to create the sub-treasury system like that of the old Populist Party. Farmers could borrow money from the Commodity Credit Corporation, and would be able to remain in business. FDR also created the Agricultural Adjustment Act to compensate farmers for cutting back on production. Agricultural overproduction was keeping prices depressed and devastating farmers financially. Now farmers were told to go out in the field and plow it under. In return, farmers would be paid for what they did not produce.

Opposing the New Deal

While FDR's New Deal was more successful than any other government effort to end the Depression, it was not without its opponents. Conservatives criticized FDR for his "socialistic tendencies" (when I say socialistic, I mean his creation of a government-planned and -controlled economy). But there were also many people in the 1930s who were critical of FDR for not going far enough, for not involving the government in more areas of society.

FDR believed that capitalism as a whole was a good, sound economic system that had gotten stuck. It needed reform, not rejection. This same sentiment was espoused by the Populists fifty years earlier and taken up by many other leftists. Yet perhaps the most serious challenge to FDR came from the Left (meaning those who would advocate more government involvement). The biggest opponent of FDR was Sen. Huey Long of Louisiana. Huey Long was a one-of-a-kind. The former governor, now senator, of Louisiana, long had built his home state into his personal fiefdom. He had total control over the Louisiana state government. He used his power to attack big business and raise taxes on corporations in order to build schools, roads, and bridges.

Having brought his state into the twentieth century, Long began to turn his attention toward national politics. First as a senator and then as a presidential candidate, Long told Americans he could end the depression (and many people listened to him). Long started speaking about a program he called the Share Our Wealth Society. The idea was to redistribute the wealth in the nation. Long was essentially going to liquidate large fortunes, for instance by taxing income over $1 million by 100 percent, and then redistributing it to common people and the poor. Long promised he could guarantee an annual income for every American family of somewhere between $2,000–2,500. He also pledged to make sure every qualified student in America got a college education.

While some of Long's figures may have been suspect, the impact he had on people was real indeed. More than anything else, Huey Long was a crowd pleaser. You can argue with his accounting, but if you go around telling people that you can get them $2,000–2,500 per year, they are not going to look too hard at how you arrived at that figure. They will be interested. The threat represented by Huey Long was cut short, however, when he was assassinated by a disgruntled political opponent.

While FDR faced opposition from his own party, Republican opposition seemed to be the most successful at capturing public attention. Republicans charged that Roosevelt's government intervention was undermining American individualism, which had flourished throughout American history as they understood it. The Republicans claimed that government handouts were taking way people's incentive and discouraging them from pulling themselves up by their bootstraps. Government welfare, to the Republicans, was bad economic policy in the long run. One New Jersey senator complained that the Social Security program would "take all the romance out of life. We might as well take the child from the nursery, give him a nurse, and protect him from every experience that life affords." FDR and his followers replied that given the depths of the crisis, their government relief measures were the humane thing to do for people who were starving. Other conservatives came together to form the American Liberty League, to oppose New Deal legislation and to "teach the necessity of respect for the rights of person and property." Despite his conservative critics, more people supported

FDR's policies than not. Organized labor especially loved FDR, and why should they not? It was under FDR that the U.S. government pledged its support for the rights of workers to organize and bargain collectively. FDR made the 40-hour week standard, and eliminated child labor.

Instrumental in gaining African-American support for the New Deal was the remarkable Eleanor Roosevelt, Franklin Roosevelt's wife. Eleanor Roosevelt was a powerful public figure during the New Deal. She had her own staff, held her own press conferences, and traveled widely around the country drumming up support for the president's New Deal policies. She appealed to African-Americans by her willingness to defy local segregation ordinances by eating with African-Americans in segregated restaurants. She also encouraged FDR to take stronger steps towards civil rights for African-Americans—steps that FDR did not always take for fear of antagonizing white conservative Southern politicians whose votes he needed. For instance, FDR never support a federal antilynching law.

The Legacy of FDR and the New Deal

FDR's legacy during the Depression was mixed. Some lamented the rise of government spending and government planning in the economy. In the minds of others, he was a hero. As they saw it, FDR had personally saved their home, their family, or their job. In return, they elected him to the presidency an unprecedented four times. During the 1936 election, the Democratic Party re-shuffled into the shape it would take for the next fifty or so years. Working class voters, union voters, women voters, African-American voters, farmers, and newer ethnic voters—all came together to form the Roosevelt Coalition.

Yet FDR's legacy is not without its failures. The Supreme Court had ruled a couple of important parts of the New Deal, particularly the National Industrial Recovery Act and the Agricultural Adjustment Act, to be unconstitutional. Both of these rulings weakened the New Deal's ability to put in economic reforms in two of the nation's most important economic sectors—industry and agriculture. In February 1937, FDR sent to Congress a plan to reorganize the Supreme Court and parts of the lower federal court system. The Court Reform Bill would allow FDR to add a new justice for everyone on the Court over 70 who did not retire. In all, the act would give FDR the chance to add six new Supreme Court justices. Conservatives and Republicans went wild objecting to the Court Reform bill. First, they knew darn well that if FDR had the chance to pick six new Supreme Court justices, conservatives would be shut out completely of an important avenue of dissent—worse, the reform bill was, as they called it, "court packing." FDR was trying to pack the court with more supportive judges. The repercussions are significant, however. Many middle-class Americans joined the conservatives and Republicans in their opposition to FDR. It appeared to many Americans that he was trying to use the power of the government to go too far. It was all right, this part of the middle class reasoned, in 1933 or 1934 when they, too, believed that a national emergency existed. But with recovery (such as it was in early 1937) came a slight return to an older view that did not want an active government the economy and in society.

Another problem with FDR's legacy involved FDR himself. Unemployment numbers in 1937 were still too high, but they had begun to drop. Industrial production had doubled since he took office. Corporate profits were, well, profits once again and not deficits—in 1936, $5 billion worth. Again showing the helter-skelter nature of New Deal policies, FDR, having largely spurred this recovery, turned around and unintentionally undid it by ending several relief programs. Why? FDR never wanted to keep any government program in place any longer than necessary. And by mid 1937, he thought it was safe to roll back the relief programs and the public works programs. As a result, WPA projects were slashed—throwing thousands back out of work (but FDR believed that in a reviving economy they'd soon be back at work in the private sector). Plus, the new Social Security Act (just passed in 1935) had now collected $2 billion in payroll taxes and could provide support in times of need. Yet, the private sector did not move to hire those being let go by WPA projects because, despite the encouraging numbers, business leaders still did not have much confidence in the economic recovery–there is that very important factor of confidence again. Three short months later the steel industry went from operating at 80 percent capacity to only 19 percent capacity. Investors again went on a selling spree on the stock market. Automobile inventories began to stockpile. From Labor Day to the end of 1937, two million people were added to the ranks of the unemployed. As a stopgap, FDR had to plunge government money back into the WPA, the CCC, and other government work programs.

As time progressed, FDR began to lose some middle-class support and Southern Democrats started to drift away (partly because they had no ties to unions, and resented gains for blacks). After 1938, FDR was unable to pass any more significant reform bills. The economy stopped its decline, even though it did not rocket upward. Many historians argue, persuasively, that the New Deal in fact ended in 1938. If not for the start of World War II, there is no certainty FDR's New Deal would have maintained its success. But the war did come, and America had a new responsibility (and markets) to attend to.

Items to Consider

Six reasons for the Bull Market of 1924–29, Black Tuesday, J. P. Morgan, Herbert Hoover, Bonus Army, farm crisis, Emergency and Relief Construction Act (1932), Reconstruction Finance Corporation, election of 1932, FDR, Civilian Conservation Corps, Agricultural Adjustment Act, Dust Bowl

CHAPTER 24

The Second World War and the Greatest Generation

The most fundamental influence in American foreign policy during the 1930s was isolationism. Throughout the history of the U.S., save for the War of 1812 and WWI, the nation had sought to stay out of European affairs. The U.S. by 1900 had staked out Latin America as its sphere of influence and, in return, promised not to poke its nose into European affairs.

The real turning point came in 1898 with the American war with Spain. That war acquired colonies for the U.S. and thrust the nation onto the international stage; however, isolationist sentiment in America remained strong. After WWI, most Americans felt like they had been used by the governments of Western Europe. Americans believed they had been duped into being part of a tremendous slaughter and they wanted nothing to do with future European wars. As a result, the U.S. retreated from the world stage, refused to join the League of Nations, refused to join the newly established world court, and erected substantial trade barriers. But the growing force of Fascism in the 1930s would ultimately force the hand of the United States.

The Rise of German Fascism

So how did the Nazis come to power? Due to the treaty of Versailles, Germany was saddled with a $33 billion debt. Britain, France, and Italy, in the 1920s, recognized how detrimental the war debts had become for Germany and offered to cancel the German war debt if, in return, the U.S. would cancel the $10 billion that those three nations owed to the U.S. for the war. But the Republicans in power said no. The three nations pointed out that the debts should be canceled to fix the American economy, especially since the U.S. was financing its $2.58 billion investment in German rebuilding during the 1920s with the war payments coming to the U.S. from Allied Nations. Still, the U.S. said that a debt is a debt. Then the Depression struck. Hoover issued a one-year moratorium on the debt payments, but when the year was up the Allies still could not resume their payments. The U.S. demanded compensation, but instead the Allies cancelled Germany's debt to them and defaulted on their debts to the U.S., setting off a chain reaction of failure that resulted in financial turmoil. This will become, at first, a major roadblock to financing the European war effort in the 1940s.

The Weimar Germany, 1918–33

At the conclusion of WWI, the German monarchy was overthrown and replaced by a civilian-led republic, whose first task was ending the war and instituting a rebuilding program. During this time, the Allies managed to humiliate the civilian government every chance they could while leaving Army prestige intact. Gen. Hindenburg never signed an armistice or surrendered to the Allied commander Gen. Foch, nor was the war ever carried to German soil. This allowed the

172

German generals to declare that the Army had never really been defeated, but rather was stabbed in the back by civilians. The generals claimed that Jews, Communists, and liberals in the civilian government betrayed Germany from within, forcing a once-great nation to acquiesce to the unpopular war guilt clause in the Versailles Treaty. Then the weak Weimar republican regime was taken over by moderate Socialists. Stigmatized by the defeat, the 1921 reparations bill requiring the repayment of 132 billion gold marks to the Allies did not add to the government's popularity. Mussolini took power in Italy in 1922. Hitler tried to do the same in 1923 with the Munich Beer Hall putsch, but failed and had to wait another ten years. As a result, the Weimar Republic lasted nearly thirteen years longer.

Despite its ability to avert being overthrown, the Weimar Republic faced constant hardships. From 1922–23, inflation devastated the German economy. Sadly, it was caused by the Weimar governments' overprinting of money to pay the war debts rather than raising taxes. Scarcity of important goods led prices to shoot up further, causing an inflationary spiral in nearly every part of the economy. The Germans had no choice but to default on their reparations payments. Nor could they do anything to stop the corresponding French occupation of Ruhr industrial region of Germany in January 1923 to run the German factories and mines themselves. With the support of the Weimar government, German workers refused to work for French. To alleviate the problem, the Weimar leadership printed even more money to re-initiate war debt repayments. Mass overprinting destroyed what little remained in the savings of most common people in Germany. Inflation wiped out the mark, rendering it worthless, and forcing real estate and other goods to skyrocket in value. While common people suffered, speculators were able to make fortunes with the help of big capitalists, whose indebtedness was also wiped out. In the end, the Germans were traumatized by inflation. The Nazis reaped a harvest of the discontent, especially among the middle class, which was forced down into the lower classes, while workers mostly turned toward the Communists.

In August 1923 Gustav Stresemann became chancellor of the Weimar Republic, declared the Ruhr resistance over, and resumed reparations payments. The Right revolted. Hitler declared a coup in November 1923; He convinced Gen. Ludendorff to march on Berlin, as Mussolini had done on Rome a year earlier. Unfortunately for Hitler and the Nazis, the German military broke up the coup and arrested its leaders. Ludendorff was respectfully acquitted, and Hitler was sentence to the minimum term for high treason: five years in solitary confinement. Actually, he spent only eight comfortable months in prison, during which he wrote his great opus, *Mein Kampf,* or My Struggle.

A failed artist from Austria, Adolf Hitler (like Napoleon and Stalin) was an outsider, not German or tall or blond. He found himself in the German Army during WWI, where he served as a corporal. He was then employed as a political education officer and discovered the tiny German Workers' Party. Hitler seized control of the party, and transformed it into a replica of Mussolini's Fascist Storm Troopers, even going so far as to copy their brown shirts from Mussolini's black shirts. Calling themselves the Nationalsozialistische Deutsche Arbeiterpartei (National Socialist German Workers Party), the party was originally just a group focused on the success of Fascism. When Adolf Hitler joined and began speaking to large crowds, the Nazis Party immediately expanded. Seeking out symbols for his new party, Hitler stole the swastika, an ancient Aryan symbol from India. He placed his new symbol on a red background, which represented a future Racial Revolution.

The rise of Hitler and the Nazis Party can be tied directly to Great Depression, which occurred as a result of the U.S. stock market crash of October 1929. During the September 1930 elections, the Nazis rose in the German Reichstag from 12 deputies to 107, the Communists went from 54 to 77. In 1932, Hitler ran for president against old Gen. Hindenburg, who was now eight-four years old, but Hitler failed to attract enough votes and lost. In the elections of July 1932, the Nazis now won 230 seats to become the single largest party in Germany; but then it declined in the November elections to only 196 seats. By 1932, Germany was hit hard again by Depression, with an incredible 43 percent of the workforce unemployed. Hitler began to focus on offering promises of economic salvation to middle and lower middle classes, office workers, artisans, and peasants. He also appealed to the youth by proclaiming them a vital part of his new party, neither Socialist nor capitalist. In 1931, almost 40 percent of the Nazis were under the age of thirty, two-thirds were under age of forty. Fearing a decline in party's membership, Hitler made a pact with the industrialists in January 1933. Surprisingly, he got them to pay for his storm troopers in return for toning down the revolutionary rhetoric of the Nazi Party.

On January 30, 1933, Hindenburg finally conceded to the growing power of the Nazis and appointed Hitler chancellor. The Nazis marched in triumph through Berlin's Brandenburg Gate. In both Italy and Germany, the Fascists had risen to power legally. Once in control, they perverted the constitutional government for their own purposes. Both groups claimed their ascension to power was part of a revolution, but really they enjoyed the collusion of the elected authorities.

The Nazis and Anti-Semitism

Anti-Semitism was central to Hitler's ideology. But why did he single out the Jews? The half-million German Jews represented less than 1 percent of the population in Germany, but they were prominent well beyond their numbers. Active in professions, journalism, arts, and science; identified with big capitalists; they also filled the ranks of the Communists (the political nemesis of the Nazi Party); they were represented by both the Rothschilds (the wealthiest family of Europe) and Karl Marx (the de facto founder of Communism). There is a long history of anti-Semitism in Europe. To most Europeans, the Jews had traditionally been viewed as materialistic, Western, and cosmopolitan—at complete odds with Hitler's "spiritual" nationalist Germans. Thus, Jews were natural outsiders, which made it easy for Hitler to unify the German people against them. Forget being workers, or being exploited by capitalists; Hitler used the Jews to unite all Germans by blood. In his task, Hitler was assisted by religion, since anti-Semitism runs deep within the Christian consciousness, albeit modern anti-Semitism is defined in racial rather than religious terms—Martin Luther would have gladly seen the Jews to convert en masse.

For Hitler, the Jews were a racial "other," even though German Jews looked suspiciously more blond-haired and blue-eyed than Hitler himself. By 1934, Hitler and the Nazis pushed through legislation causing Jewish lawyers, professors, and doctors to lose their jobs. In 1935, the Nuremberg Laws deprived all those with one or more Jewish grandparent of German citizenship, and forbade them from marrying or having sexual relations with the so-called Aryans. Two months later, Jews were expelled from the civil service. By 1938, one-quarter of Germany's Jewish population had emigrated. Those who remained were required to carry special identity papers, making emigration more difficult. Thus, the majority of the German Jewish population remained, still believing themselves to be Germans. Then came *Kristallnacht* on November 9, 1938, the Night of Shattered Glass. In one night, 7,000 Jewish businesses were destroyed, synagogues were burned, and 30,000 Jews were sent to concentration camps. And what did the rest of the Germans think? Few protested against the treatment of the Jews. Hitler was genuinely popular with most Germans in the 1930s.

The Treaty of Versailles and the Coming of War

Germany and the Nazi Party were committed to destruction of the system created by the Treaty of Versailles. They felt that they were the victims of WWI. The defenders of the treaty were the U.S., Britain, and France. Those three nations faced two options. They either had to defend the treaty through the use of military and economic force, or adopt a policy of appeasement. Trying to correct legitimate wrongs perpetrated against Germany, the defenders chose appeasement. In hindsight, appeasement looks like an ill-advised policy. But it was only ill-advised in that the aggressors—Italy, Germany, and the Soviet Union—had unlimited goals. Hindsight is 20/20. In any event, most Americans believed that another European war was unavoidable and they, by and large, wanted to sit this one out. Popular will in America then, made appeasement the policy for the U.S. to follow.

In fact, the war was seen as so inevitable and the American public wanted to stay out so desperately, that Congress passed a series of Neutrality Acts in the 1930s. These acts were designed to keep American financial interests from becoming involved in the war. It was a generally held opinion that it was bankers who had gotten the U.S. into WWI, those merchants of death. Thus, the first Neutrality Act in 1935 issued an arms embargo against all warring nations. The second Neutrality Act prohibited the giving of loans by private sources to foreign governments at war and made it illegal for U.S. citizens to travel into war zones.

Then came *Anschluss* with Austria in March 1938. Hitler's tanks rolled into Austria virtually unopposed. The next day, Austria was incorporated into the German Reich. In London, Foreign Secretary Anthony Eden, the champion of resistance to Fascist aggression, was dropped from Conservative cabinet of Neville Chamberlain less than a month before the Anschluss because the British were shifting toward a policy of appeasement, trying to conciliate the aggressiveness of Hitler and Mussolini. Chamberlain acquiesced to the absorption of Austria into the Reich.

After Anschluss came the dismemberment of Czechoslovakia in September and October 1938. A week after annexing Austria, Hitler began demanding the Sudetenland of Czechoslovakia, a mountainous region where a large population of German-speaking people lived and where Nazi agents had been stirring up trouble, winning the population over to idea of German annexation. Unlike Austria, the French were bound by treaty obligations to defend democratic Czechoslovakia, but in practice it was not prepared to fight an offensive war against the Germans without British support. The British had no such treaty with Czechs, so Chamberlain decided he would personally negotiate with Hitler to avert the threat of war. Chamberlain flew to Hitler's private retreat at Berchtesgaden in mid September, coming away with a formula for self-determination for Sudeten Germans. But Hitler, surprised by British and French acquiescence, now insisted that his troops, massed on the border, must march into the Sudetenland at once. Even Chamberlain refused to give in to this bullying, leaving the French and British with no choice but to prepare for war.

Mussolini came to the rescue, proposing a four-power conference. The meeting was held at Munich on September 30, 1938. In Munich, Chamberlain, French Prime Minister Daladier, and Mussolini agreed to Hitler's demands, with some face-saving clauses added to provide for an occupation in stages and the final delimitation of the frontier by an international commission. Hitler had won, and the Czechs were not even consulted. Chamberlain returned to England promising that he had secured "peace in our time" to a vast crowd that enthusiastically greeted him at the airport. Chamberlain mistakenly saw Hitler as another Bismarck, a man who was simply trying to unite Germans into a national state. The Munich Agreement was, in some sense, treason. Winston Churchill called it a "disaster of the first magnitude."

The Second Czech Crisis followed shortly afterward, in March 1939. With its mountain defenses gone, the Czechs were helpless before the German Army. In March 1939, Hitler marched into the rest of Czechoslovakia, no longer able to justify his aggression with the claim that he only wanted to include Germans in the Reich. The Munich Agreement had been broken in less than six months. Western sentiments finally swung sharply in the opposite direction, toward a policy of resistance. When Hitler announced his next move, to annex the Germans of Danzig and the Polish Corridor, Chamberlain and Daladier pledged military aid to Poland and speeded up their programs for national rearmament. In April 1939, for first time in history, Great Britain initiated a peacetime conscription.

The big question in everyone's mind now was What would Soviet Union do if war broke out? A reluctant Daladier and Chamberlain sent low-ranking diplomats to negotiate with Stalin, who had just dismissed his western-oriented foreign minister, Litvinov, and replaced him with the pro-German Molotov. The western negotiators were reluctant to give Stalin what he wanted, dominance or control of Finland, the Baltic States, and eastern Poland. Thus the German foreign minister, von Ribbentrop, easily secured an agreement with Stalin. Russia and Germany would carve up Poland between them. On August 23, the greatest diplomatic bombshell of the century exploded. The Nazi-Soviet Non-Aggression Pact established a mutual pact of non-aggression between Russia and Germany. The next day, Hitler took Danzig, and at 5 a.m., September 1, 1939, he invaded Poland. On September 3, Britain and France were left with no other option than to declare war; for the moment, Mussolini stayed neutral. The Second World War had begun.

FDR watched it all and did nothing. There was little he could have done, in hindsight. He did, in October 1939, ask Congress to allow arms to be sold via cash and carry to Great Britain. This allowed American industry could sell to the warring states, but not on credit. This, FDR claimed, would protect American neutrality. Congress agreed, and passed the measure in November. The United States went from neutrality to nonbelligerency to a state of undeclared war by fall of 1940. FDR found that he had abdicated in the realm of foreign affairs for far too long.

Events on the battlefield would be significant in pushing the U.S. into the war. After Poland, there was little action except for a shadow war in Northern Europe. The period of the shadow war was shattered by the German blitzkrieg. Standing between the Germans and France was a massive and formidable French battlement known as the Maginot Line. Rather than smash his army against the defensive line, Hitler's Germans did an end run around the French through Belgium and Holland, driving a wedge between the British and the French armies and isolating the British Expeditionary Force at Dunkirk. Hitler withheld his forces for three days, letting the British Expeditionary Force evacuate Dunkirk. Only 325,000 troops managed to leave, abandoning all their war materials behind for the Germans. With the British gone, Hitler turned south against the French, pinning them against their own fortifications. France had no choice but to surrender. Suddenly, all of Europe outside of the U.S.S.R. was either neutral or occupied by the Axis Powers. The impact on U.S. public opinion was tremendous. Prior to that time, only one-fourth of all Americans favored aid to the Allies. After that event, it had increased to four-fifths of all Americans.

When the blitz began, Chamberlain's government fell. It was replaced by a government of national unity, headed by Winston Churchill. Immediately Churchill began to establish a relationship with FDR. Churchill understood that the Americans were necessary to winning the war. Thus, he began to cultivate FDR. Churchill described the military situation to FDR daily. In one of these cables, he thanked the U.S. for its help but pointed out that much of what the U.S. was sending never made it to Britain. German submarines were destroying the transport vessels, and British did not have enough destroyers to fight them. Churchill asked FDR for the fifty dry-docked American destroyers to fight the Germans. In December 1940, FDR agreed to send the destroyers to Churchill in return for an agreement on U.S. bases on British soil. Churchill gave the U.S. the bases for a ninety-nineyear lease in return for the destroyers. FDR justified this deal to Congress by stating it would protect U.S. sea lanes.

In early 1941, Churchill cabled him again and told FDR that Great Britain was about to run out of money and could not purchase U.S. goods. He then asked FDR to help him solve the problem. FDR devised the Lend/Lease Program. In March, FDR introduced a bill for a multibillion-dollar aid program for those nations fighting the Axis Powers. This brought him into confrontation with the isolationists. The measure passed after a bitter struggle in Congress, and $7 billion was appropriated for Britain and the other Allies. This moved the U.S. from neutrality to a position of nonbelligerency. FDR was trying to move carefully (the U.S. budget deficit at that time was only $8 billion). In April of 1941, FDR authorized the Navy to conduct neutrality patrols in the Atlantic to broadcast the position of Axis submarines to the British. He then declared a state of national emergency in May 1941, which gave him nearly complete control of the U.S. economy. He ordered the Army and Navy to occupy Greenland. In July FDR authorized the occupation of Iceland to relieve the British forces already in occupation. In August FDR and Churchill signed the Atlantic Charter, which was a boileddown fourteen points. The purpose of the Atlantic Charter was to demonstrate the solidarity of the two powers.

But the key event that drove the U.S. into war came in September 1941. FDR went to U.S. people on radio and said that an American destroyer had been attacked by a German submarine. He next told them that he had issued a shoot on sight order; a declaration of naval war. In October 1941, the *USS Rueben James* was torpedoed and sunk by a German submarine, with a loss of all 240 hands on board. In November FDR declared that all U.S. merchant vessels would begin carrying goods to Europe. By the winter of 1941/42, the U.S. was in a state of undeclared war with Germany. A war declaration would have followed even without the attack on Pearl Harbor. FDR's role in all of this is debatable: Was he a great leader or was a manipulative coward?

The Road to Pearl Harbor

In the fall of 1937, the Sino-Japanese War erupted. Japan had become increasingly alarmed about the growing strength of the Chinese government and the determination of that government to rid itself of foreign influence in order to re-claim Manchuria, a section of China occupied by Japan. The Japanese Army initiated the war in the hopes that it could establish a buffer zone in Northeastern China to protect Manchuria. Full-scale fighting erupted in September. Signatories of the Nine Power Pact, which included the U.S., had promised in 1921 to protect China if it found itself under attack. China appealed to the Pact members, and all the signatories, save Japan and Italy, met in Brussels. The meeting did not include Germany or the U.S.S.R. After a short meeting, the signatories voted to condemn the Japanese action, but did not impose sanctions. Several weeks later the *USS Haney* was attacked and sunk by the Japanese in the Yangtze River. Two Americans were killed, but there was no public outcry. Japan apologized for the incident and agreed to pay indemnities to the U.S. No groundswell of public opinion rose to support the Chinese military alliance.

The situation remained unchanged until the outbreak of war in September 1939. American planners at that point decided that Fascism in Europe posed a greater threat to American interests than did Japan. As a result, Europe was given primacy. The U.S. would seek victory in Europe, while a hold plan in the Pacific took shape. That policy remained in effect throughout the war. Those who fought in the Pacific Theater had to make do with leftovers, because Allied commanders of the European Theater, Marshall and Eisenhower, got Pacific commanders to go along with the plan.

Up until the Japanese attack on Pearl Harbor, the U.S. and Japan had been close allies. The U.S. provided Japan with 80 percent of its oil and scrap iron. Japan had almost no refining facilities of its own; it had intentionally made itself dependent on the U.S. in that regard. Some Americans called for an embargo due to Japanese aggression, but there was a Japanese-American Treaty that prohibited sanctions without the sanctioning party notifying the other party six months in advance. In September 1939, the U.S. gave notice of possible sanctions to Japan. Many expected that the U.S. would begin squeezing Japan. But the State Department's policy was day-to-day. The German blitzkrieg that led to the surren-der of Belgium, Holland, and France was a great boon to the Japanese. Suddenly, Belgian, Dutch and French colonies were vulnerable to Japan. The islands of the Dutch East Indies were rich in raw materials, and French Indo-China was an important source of foodstuffs. After the fall of France in June 1940, the Germans occupied all of northern France. The southern part of France was led by a puppet government headed by Pétin at Vichy. It was to this government the Japanese issued a demand for French Indo-China.

At that point Hitler was making plans to invade the U.S.S.R., and wanted to cultivate the Japanese to help him in that task. He ordered the Vichy government to surrender French Indo-China. The Japanese occupied the region. The U.S.

responded by constricting the flow of supplies to Japan. The result was the establishment of the Tri-Partite Pact of 1940, among Germany, Italy, and Japan. The military alliance said that if any one of the members was attacked, then the other two must declare war against the attacking power.

Unfortunately, the Tri-Partite Pact seemed to mean different things to different people. To Hitler, the Tri-Partite Pact compelled the Japanese to go to war with the U.S.S.R. But most Americans believed it was really a threat against them. This conception was significant, because it provided America with an overt link between Fascism and Japan. It also seemed to portray Japan as more of a threat than it had been before.

Following the Tri-Partite Pact, the U.S. was in a position to squeeze the Japanese even more. The Japanese premier in 1941 was Konoe. He was a Japanese liberal and wanted to avoid a military conflict with the U.S. That spring Premier Konoe instructed Admiral Nomura, the Japanese ambassador to the United States, to begin discussions with the U.S. ambassador to Japan, Cordell Hull. The Japanese Royal Navy was not infiltrated by uneducated ideologues, as was the Army, and tended to be pro-American.

In March, the U.S. and Japan began discussions. During these discussions, Japan made several proposals: 1) Japan promised to end the war in China, but only if the U.S. supported its posture and only if the U.S. got China to agree to a buffer zone. In return, Japan offered the U.S. a favorable trade treaty. 2) Japan offered to evacuate northern French Indo-China if the U.S. promised not to impose trade sanctions against Japan. 3.) Japan promised to nullify the Tri-Partite Pact if the U.S. cut off its aid to Britain. None of these proposals, of course, were acceptable to the Americans. Hull harangued the Japanese and demanded that Japan immediately evacuate China before any negotiations could take place—legitimate ones, anyway. Talks broke off and some claimed that all chance of a negotiated settlement had ended.

On June 22, 1941, Hitler invaded the U.S.S.R. as part of Operation Barbarossa. Hitler expected Japan to attack into Siberia and confront the U.S.S.R. with a two-front war. But the Japanese had already decided to move southward. The Japanese decision to move south was known by the U.S. almost as soon as it was made. The U.S. knew about it through a little-known surveillance operation called MAGIC, a means by which U.S. intelligence could decipher Japanese military and diplomatic codes. But tragically, MAGIC did not expose information circulating in Japan, only those items that were routed through Washington. Thus, information relevant to the attack on Pearl Harbor was not circulated. In fact, only about six people knew prior to the attack. On July 14, 1941, the U.S. embargoed all trade with Japan and froze Japanese assets in the U.S. These were the most extreme forms of diplomatic pressure, short of war, available.

With the U.S. embargoing them, Japan had only twelve months of supplies to operate with. It had to move forcefully to acquire those needs or try to appease the U.S. Konoe made one last effort at peace. He called for a summit meeting with FDR to resolve the conflict. Hull and the State Department opposed the meeting, mostly because they did not want FDR to give in to Japan. FDR rejected Konoe's request. In August Konoe was replaced, Hideki Tojo became the new prime minister of Japan. Tojo and his cabinet met with Emperor Hirohito on November 5, 1941. Tojo told the Emperor that Japan was going to make a last-ditch effort to get the U.S. to recognize Japanese interests in Asia; otherwise Japan would be forced to declare war. Hirohito acquiesced with silence. Shortly thereafter, an order went out that war with the U.S. was inevitable.

That same day, November 5, a Joint Army-Navy Advisory Board met with FDR. The board warned FDR that the U.S. was incapable of defending its interests in Asia, and told him it was imperative to stall the Japanese for more time. The board also said that if the Japanese moved into Thailand, or farther west, or if it attacked British or American shipping, then the U.S. would have no choice but to go to war. In response, FDR tried to beef up U.S. forces in the Pacific. He sent some national guardsmen to the Philippines and a few B17s to the Pacific, but the military was pessimistic about its ability to defend the Philippines. Throughout November, both sides restated their positions.

On December 6, 1941, the last order to the Japanese embassy was to be prepared to destroy all classified documents. On morning of December 7, a war warning was issued. The Japanese fleet had taken a northern route from the Kuril Islands, somehow going undetected by American defensive forces. Hawaiian air patrols (400 miles out) never spotted a single ship. Early radar operators reported the air attack moments before they hit Pearl Harbor, but the warning went unheeded. The Japanese attack sank or crippled nearly every capital ship the U.S. had in Pearl Harbor. It was a devastating attack, a total tactical triumph for the Japanese. FDR and the nation were caught by surprise. FDR asked a joint session of Congress for a declaration of war the following day, and the U.S. officially entered the Second World War.

Mobilizing for victory was one of the most taxing exercises in American history. The government had to preside over a complete transformation from a civilian to a military economy, it had to raise an army, and it had to assemble the necessary civilian work force. On December 18, 1941, Congress passed the War Powers Act. This gave FDR unprecedented control over the U.S. economy and the conduct of the war. Luckily, the Depression was over. The Gross National Product of America in 1940 was $99.7 billion; by the war's end the GNP would reach $211 billion. Business profits almost doubled and agricultural productivity had increased by one-third. By 1943, the U.S. government was spending $250 million a day on the war economy and some two-thirds of the American economy was focused on the war effort. By the war's end in 1945, the U.S. had turned out 86,000 tanks, 296,000 airplanes, 15 million rifles and machine guns, and 6,500 warships.

The federal bureaucracy grew with the war effort. Government employees increased in number by 400 percent. Taxes financed 50 percent of the U.S. war effort. The Revenue Act of 1942 increased the number of people being taxed from 3.9 million in 1939 to 42.6 million in 1945. Tax collections went from $2.2 billion in 1939 to $35 billion in 1943. War bonds also contributed a great deal. The War Finance Committees, in charge of the loan drives, sold a total of $185.7 billion in securities. This incredible mass selling achievement to help finance the war has not been matched, before or since. By the end of World War II, over 85 million Americans had invested in war bonds, a number unmatched by any other country.

To control war production, FDR established the War Production Board, headed by a former Sears' executive. It awarded defense contracts and helped to allocate scarce resources. The domestic economy was controlled by the Office of Price Administration and Civilian Supply, which allocated domestic resources and tried with varying degrees of success to keep the U.S. price index and economic inflation under control. FDR, however, remained by and large unhappy with the way the economy was managed. He thought there were too many organizations. So in 1942 he created a central planning organization called the Office of War Mobilization, which finally brought some order to the problems of resource allocation.

George C. Marshall, who was FDR's new chief of staff, increased the size of the Army from 200,000 in 1939 to over 8 million by 1945. By the end of the war, the U.S. Armed Forces numbered some 15 million men and women. To raise such a military force, the various draft boards had to register nearly 31 million men between the ages of 18 and 44. Of that group, it ordered physical exams for about one-sixth. Almost half of those examined were rejected for some physical problem, ranging from bad feet to poor vision. More than 700,000 blacks served the nation during the war, mostly in menial positions; this was a special problem in the Navy. Segregation remained firmly in place within the military during the war, from living quarters to blood banks. Despite their isolation, American minorities served with distinction. By war's end, seventeen had won the Congressional Medal of Honor. Gender discrimination was practiced during the war. About 350,000 women served the American war effort in limited fashion, often as medical personnel. About 1,000 women did serve as ferry pilots as members of the WASPs.

The greatest contribution by women, however, was in industry. By 1945 women comprised about 36 percent of the industrial labor force. They still had to face all kinds of discrimination though. In shipyards, for example, the most senior women made about $7 a day, while the most senior man made about $22. The number of women in the workforce dropped severely after the war, but recovered strength in those industries by the late 1940s; especially in terms of young married women.

One unexpected outcome of the war was a loosening of social tensions. Women, organized labor, and African-Americans enjoyed new-found powers. Membership numbers of the NAACP grew by 900 percent during the war. In June of 1941, FDR issued Executive Order 8802 declaring it illegal to discriminate in employment on the basis of race. To police that policy, FDR created the Fair Employment Practices Committee (FEPC). Its success, however, was limited. Of the 8,000 complaints the FEPC received, it only resolved one-third. On another front, in 1942, James Farmer founded the Congress of Racial Equality (CORE), which staged sit-ins and demonstrations, and began organizing African-Americans, setting in motion the shift toward civil rights that would come after the war. In 1944, CORE forced several Washington-area restaurants to serve blacks. When refused service, the CORE members picketed them with signs reading: "Are you for Hitler's way or the American way? Make up your mind."

Life on the home front during WWII was completely different than other wars. Compared to WWI, there was almost no opposition to the war within the U.S. once Congress declared war. The lines between good and evil seemed so clear that most Americans believed they were fighting a just cause. In fact, that is exactly why WWII is often called the Good War. Unemployment was no longer a problem. But the stresses of the war were real. Families lived in constant fear that the Western Union telegram boy would arrive on his bicycle bringing a telegram from the War Department. Rationing was a problem but, in general, the return to prosperity meant life was far better than during the Depression years. People gladly donated to the war effort, everything from clothes to blood to scrap metal. Many planted victory gardens which in the end produced nearly 40 percent of all vegetables grown in the U.S.

There was a strong sense of connection between the home front and the war overseas. Popular culture reinforced that connection. War correspondents like John Hersey (who wrote *A Bell for Adano,* which told the story of how American GIs helped a small Italian town during the war) and Ernie Pyle (who was killed in Pacific) brought the war home to many Americans. Movies like *Wake Island* and *Thirty Seconds over Tokyo* portrayed life in the armed services; other movies and newsreels explained why we fought and what we were fighting for. Movie attendance, in fact, soared to over 100 million people per week during the war. Demand was so high for movies that many theaters operated around the clock.

Media-based propaganda also contributed to the way most Americans viewed the enemy. While Americans were able to separate, intellectually, the good Germans from the bad Germans, the same cannot be said for the Japanese. Thus, the Japanese were hated far more than the Germans ever were. Part of that sentiment is represented in what happened to Japanese-Americans in the U.S. during the war. In California, war paranoia was high after the surprise attack on Pearl Harbor. Residents on the Coast began to demand protection against Japanese spies who many believed were preparing the way for an invasion.

Early in 1942, the War Department, with FDR's approval, developed a relocation plan to remove Japanese-Americans from coastal regions. The War Relocation Authority, led by Milton Eisenhower, brother to Gen. Dwight D. Eisenhower, began to relocate Japanese-Americans living on the West Coast to detention camps in the interior of the country. Despite the fact that no one was ever tried for espionage and there was no proof that any plot had been formed, almost no public official objected to the program. Japanese-Americans were shocked. Almost two-thirds of them were native born (the *Issei,* first-generation immigrants, and *Nisei,* children of Issei who were American citizens). They saw themselves as loyal Americans. They were shocked and outraged by the attack on Pearl Harbor. Yet they did not resist relocation, even when they only were allowed a few days to dispose of their belongings and prepare for transfer. Businesses, which took a lifetime to build, were sold over night, often for only a fraction of their value. The total financial loss to JapaneseAmericans has been estimated at $400 million. In 1988, Congress finally gave an official apology to relocated Japanese-Americans, paying $20,000 to $60,000 in cash to each surviving internee.

Relocation took place in two stages. First, Japanese-Americans were sent to temporary assembly centers, such as the Santa Anita Racetrack in Los Angeles. Here, the internees lived in horse stables for periods ranging from a few days to as long as a few months. Later, the internees were moved far from the Coast to ten permanent camps away in California, Arizona, Utah, Colorado, Wyoming, Idaho, and Arkansas. The camps were all located in hot, dusty places. Eight people were assigned to live in spaces 25 feet by 20 feet. No one had any privacy, and there was no effort made to keep families together. There were a few ways out of the camps. Internees could volunteer to work in agricultural labor, or to go to college, or to enlist in the military. It was one of the most shameful chapters in American history.

From Pearl Harbor to Japan

The Japanese Empire had reached its high tide by 1944. Japan captured Shanghai, the Philippines, and the Dutch East Indies. By late spring of 1943, it moved into Burma and New Guinea, and was in position to threaten India and Australia. All of Europe was either neutral or dominated by the Axis. In 1941 the German Army had driven so deep into the Caucuses Mountains that it had overrun most of European Russia and was in a position to threaten Central Asia. Churchill, FDR, and several other European leaders met to sign a new declaration, a defensive alliance promising to fight on until the Axis Powers were defeated. This was the first American military alliance since the Franco-American agreement of the 1770s.

By 1943, the U.S. and Allied forces were finally able to halt the Axis advance. In the Pacific, the U.S. put together a makeshift fleet and turned back the Japanese war machine at Midway. In Africa, British Gen. Bernard Montgomery turned back Germans forces at El Alamein, despite the brilliant leadership of Germany's Gen. Erwin Rommel. With the defeat of the Germans in Africa in 1943, North Africa became a springboard for the Allies to invade Sicily and Italy. Having stopped the Axis advancement, the Allies called for the first wartime conference, to be held in Casablancam Morocco. The Casablanca Conference was only attended by Churchill and FDR. Stalin declined. The leaders pressed on, laying plans for the invasion of Italy and pledging that their nations would fight until they achieved the unconditional surrender of Germany. Some historians argue that this pledge was a propaganda mistake, but it has to be taken in context. Churchill and FDR deemed it a necessity of the war.

In the summer of 1943, Churchill and FDR met again at what we now call the first Quebec Conference. Here, they discussed the situation in Italy, and FDR privately told Churchill of a project known as the Tube Alloy Program,

America's secret program to build a nuclear weapon. In response to the news, FDR and Churchill signed a secret agreement promising never to use atomic weapons against each other or to use them on a third power without mutual consent. They also agreed to never share their atomic secrets with another power.

By the fall of 1944, MacArthur reclaimed the Philippines. The U.S. destroyed the Japanese carrier fleet at the Battle of Leyte Gulf. From that time on, the Allies had air superiority in both military theaters. In June 1944, the Joint Allied Task Force invaded Normandy. By the end of that year, the Allies were poised to invade Germany. In December, the Germans countered the Allied superiority by launching its last major offensive of the war, the Battle of the Bulge in Belgium. After ten days of success, however, the German Army was stopped and then pushed back. As the Americans entered Germany, what they found shocked the world. Across Occupied Europe, the Germans had erected and placed into operation extermination camps where 6 million Jews and some 6 million Poles, Slavs, Gypsies, homosexuals, and other "undesirables" were executed. The names and horror of these death camps still have a hold on the imagination: places like Buchenwald, Dachau, and Auschwitz. Sadly, the U.S. government had known about them as early as 1942, but did nothing to stop it.

FDR died on April 12, 1945, just before the Germans surrendered. By April 30, Berlin was reduced to rubble. The Soviet Army had reached the outskirts of the city. Fearing capture, Hitler committed suicide. His body was carried outside of the bunker, dumped in a shallow grave along with that of his mistress, Eva Braun, covered with gasoline, and set afire. On May 8, 1944 Germany surrendered.

With the German surrender, the Allied focus turned toward Japan and the Pacific Theater. FDR's vice president, Harry Truman, now president, wanted to end the war with Japan as quickly as possible. Truman had three options to end the War with Japan: He would consider them all before the final surrender was achieved.

1. The first option was a military invasion of the islands of Japan. Plans for an invasion were put under way as soon as Germany surrendered. Troops were moved from Europe to the Pacific Theater. A two-pronged attack was developed. American forces would take Okinawa and Iwo Jima. Another force was gathered in Alaska, so the two forces, one from the north and one from the south, could converge on Japan. D-Day for the final invasion of Japan was tentatively set for September 1945. Conservative estimates said it would to take 1 million men to capture Japan, and the invading force would suffer more than 100,000 casualties.

2. The second option open to Truman was to end the war through negotiation. The chief advocate for this approach was Under Secretary of State Joseph Grew. He pointed out that Japan was defenseless. Japanese resources were depleted, and its military force was in tatters. American and British shipping could shell Japanese cities at will. An incendiary raid on Tokyo killed 100,000 people, and went unopposed. Yet despite America's overwhelming strength, the Japanese were too obstinate to surrender. Anger at Japan's obstinacy, Truman was unwilling to make gesture toward peace. Since Japan initiated the war by attacking Pearl Harbor, Truman felt Japan must take the first step toward peace. Thus, the closest the U.S. got to brokering peace came at the Potsdam Conference, where Truman offered a public invitation for the Japanese to surrender, but he received no response.

3. The final option available to Truman was to find a way to shock the Japanese into surrender. This only became possible after Secretary of War Henry L. Stimson told Truman of the Manhattan Project. On April 25, 1945, Stimson told Truman, "If the problem of the proper use of this weapon can be solved, we will have the opportunity to bring the world into a pattern in which the peace of the world and our civilization can be saved." In response, Truman put Stimson in charge of a team that would investigate options for ending the war using the atomic bomb. The team decided on three possibilities: First, it decided that the U.S. could explode a test blast and notify the Japanese if it worked. This was rejected as unworkable, if for no other reason than the Japanese might not believe the U.S. Second, the team considered the possibility of the U.S. dropping the bomb with warning, but this was rejected because of the 10,000+ American POWs scattered across the Japanese home islands. There was no way to provide a warning explosion without the risk of hitting our own people, especially if we warned the Japanese in advance. And third, the team decided the U.S. could drop an atomic bomb without warning on a military or industrial target in Japan. For Truman, this was the only real option for America to secure the quickest and least destructive surrender possible.

While at the Potsdam Conference from July to August of 1945, Truman received word that U.S. scientists had successfully test exploded an atomic bomb. Truman had them begin construction on a workable weapon, and instructed the Air Force to select one or more targets. On August 6, 1945, the U.S. dropped a single bomb on Hiroshima, instantly killing 80,000 people. It was hoped that the Japanese would surrender after the first attack. Two days later the Soviets declared war on Japan and invaded Manchuria. When the Japanese did not surrender, the U.S. dropped a second bomb on Nagasaki, instantly killing between 80,000 and 85,000 people.

With no options remaining and facing atomic annihilation, Japan surrendered on August 15. The Second World War had come to a conclusion. Defenders of the decision to drop the bomb argued that the U.S. used the weapon only on military grounds. The obstinacy of the Japanese left no choice. If the Allies had invaded Japan, millions of lives would have been lost, rather than a few hundred thousand. But critics of the decision to drop the bomb say the U.S. only did it as a demonstration for the Soviets—a Machiavellian plot of the pre–Cold War. In any case, the most costly war in world history was over. And from its ashes, the U.S. and the Soviet Union emerged as the world superpowers.

While not every aspect of America's participation in the war was noble, the final outcome seemed to justify the means to most Americans. Here we have the greatest nation on Earth fighting evil empires for the goals of democracy and free enterprise. Yet, at the same time the U.S. discriminated against African-Americans, segregating them even in war. The U.S. even interned Japanese-Americans much as we had restricted the movements of American Indians sixty years before. The contradictions were paradoxical, and these paradoxes would become, in the end, significant in the way in which the social and cultural history of the U.S. would unfold in the decades to come.

Items to Consider

War debt cycle, Adolf Hitler, Nuremberg Laws, Neutrality Acts, Anschluss, Lend-Lease, Tri-Partite Pact, D-Day, tube alloy program, Truman's options to end the war with Japan

CHAPTER 25
The Civil Rights Movement

It is difficult to generalize about life for African-Americans in the 1950s. They numbered about 15.8 million in 1950 and 19 million in 1960, essentially composing about 10.6 percent of the U.S. population. Blacks continued to flee the South in large numbers. By 1970, 47 percent of all black people lived outside the South. The reason for this migration was obvious. Within the South, the black population still struggled under Jim Crow laws that restricted access to everything in society, ranging from bathrooms to schools to restaurants to theaters. The situation was compounded by social patterns that reinforced the second-class legal status of African-Americans. Whites never addressed black men as "mister;" instead the used terms like "boy" or "Jack." Whites did not shake hands with blacks or socialize with them in any way. When a black man met a white in public, he was expected to remove his hat, but whites refused to return the favor.

Even at the national level, talented African-Americans continued to face obstacles. There was little demand for black actors. The most famous was probably Sidney Poitier, but he had to accept roles of meek, cheek-turning men. In sports, the New York Yankees waited until 1955 before hiring black baseball player Elston Howard. The Red Sox waited until 1959 (the last team to do so). In 1959, only 15 percent of all major leaguers were African-Americans, but that 15 percent were at the very top of the game. Tennis and golf remained almost exclusively white, despite the greatness of Arthur Ashe and Althea Gibson.

African-Americans in the North faced discrimination in housing at the hands of city planners trying to keep them in ghettos. Black education in the North was greatly underfunded. Staffs were small. Discipline was lax. Often these children came to school hungry, and were forced to read Dick and Jane primers showing happy, middle-class white children running and playing. Most of their school materials were second-hand from wealthier school districts, and there was little effort to serve their needs or interests.

The origins of the Civil Rights Movement lay in the war years. Blacks served the nation with such distinction and other blacks were of such vital use to the national war industry that the hypocritical nature of African-Americans' place in American society would no longer be acceptable for thinking people. After the war, a series of events began to break down the barriers of segregation and political inequality. The first shift came under Harry Truman in 1946. Truman created a Presidential Commission on Civil Rights. The report of that commission outlined the way in which political inequality could be ended in America.

Legal action by the NAACP helped, too. That National Association for the Advancement of Colored People (NAACP) had grown to half a million members after the war. The NAACP conducted voter registration drives and challenged segregation. It initiated various court decisions, which struck down all-white election primaries, racially restrictive housing agreements, and the exclusion of blacks from professional schools.

Adding to this situation was a series of African-American firsts in 1940s, which opened the door to real action in the 1950s. Jackie Robinson broke the color barrier in baseball in 1947. Ralph Bunche won the Nobel Peace Prize in 1950 for arranging an Arab-Israeli truce. And black musicians played important roles, as well. The music of America was jazz, and its best performers were black. Black jazz musicians played to every audience, taking their music from the back room of Harlem speakeasies in the 1920s to the national scene by the 1930s and 1940s.

The Battle for Equality in the South

Since the late 1950s, the NAACP had been chipping away at the legal foundation of segregation. The head of the NAACP's legal defense section was Thurgood Marshall. Marshall's goal was to overturn the much-hated *Plessey v. Ferguson* decision, which provided the legal underpinning for the practice of racial segregation. For a test case, Marshall combined five lawsuits challenging segregation in public schools. The central case of the five suits argued the case of Oliver Brown of Topeka, Kansas. Brown wanted to overturn a state law allowing for segregated schools. The law forced Brown's eight-year-old daughter, Tina, to be bussed to a substandard black school, even though a better white elementary school was only three blocks away. The Supreme Court heard Marshall's arguments on the five cases, grouped together as *Brown v. Board of Education* in December 1952. In his argument, Marshall used sociological and psychological evidence to prove that segregated schools were inherently unequal. It was a brilliant attack on segregation, proving that the policy was equally detrimental to both white and black children. In May 1954, Earl Warren read the Supreme Court's unanimous decision. They agreed with Marshall and declared that all segregation laws were invalid.

But in their decision, the Warren Court only said that segregated schools should be integrated with "all deliberate speed." In later years, arguments over the definition of that phrase would allow some states to drag their feet on integration. Resistance was strong in the South, and there were many ways to work around the Brown decision. One of the most popular was the creation of all-white private academies. Some states refused to implement the federal decisions. In 1956, one hundred and one congressmen of the former Confederate states, led by Strom Thurmond of South Carolina, signed the Southern Manifesto, a document that encouraged their state governments not to comply with the federal law. The federal government also dragged its feet over forcing compliance, as President Eisenhower was privately against the Brown decision, later saying that the appointment of Earl Warren to the Supreme Court was the worst mistake he had ever made.

The federal court, however, was angered by Southern resistance. The first test of federal power in this matter came in Little Rock, Arkansas. Gov. Orval Faubus was facing a tense reelection battle and decided to make resistance to integration his personal crusade. He blatantly and publicly defied a court order to segregate Little Rock schools, going so far as to send the Arkansas National Guard to prevent nine black students from entering Central High School. For three weeks, the guardsmen stood guard and denied the Little Rock Nine entrance to the school. Screaming crowds cheered Faubus, menaced the black students, and beat up two black reporters, all the while chanting, "Two, four, six, eight, we ain't going to integrate."

Eisenhower tried to broker a peaceful solution to integration, but Faubus was unwilling. Suddenly and without warning on Monday, September 23, 1957, Faubus withdrew his troops from the school and left the nine black kids at the mercy of the mob. The mob demanded that the children be turned over to them so they could be lynched, but policemen whisked them away to safety. Eisenhower could wait no longer. He nationalized the Arkansas National Guard and sent in 1,000 paratroopers from the 101st Airborne Division to Little Rock. Central High was integrated at the point of a bayonet.

The nine were admitted to Little Rock Central High under the protection of the U.S. Army, but they were still subjected to a year of physical and verbal abuse by many of the white students. One of the nine, Minni-Jean Brown, was verbally confronted during lunch by a group of male white students in December 1957 in the school cafeteria. In response to their taunts, she dumped a bowl of chili on the boys and was suspended for nine days. After several more incidents, she was suspended for the rest of the school year on February 6, 1958. No action was taken against her persecutors. Faubus was unfazed by the forced integration of Central High. In August 1958, with support from Gov. Faubus and the Arkansas State Legislature, the school board canceled the entire 1959 school year for its three high schools rather than integrate them. Thousands of high school students left the city to attend high schools in other school districts or enrolled in all-white private schools. One year later, additional federal court rulings and the Little Rock Chamber of Commerce pressured the school board to reopen the school system. By the fall of 1959, Little Rock public schools had reopened as an integrated school system.

There had finally been a legal breakthrough. Now it just had to be exploited. But the cause needed a strong leader. And in Martin Luther King Jr. it would find one. Let's look at the incident that brought him national recognition: the Montgomery Bus Boycott.

On December 1, 1955 a Montgomery seamstress and black activist named Rosa Parks was arrested for refusing to give up her seat to a white man. She was charged with violating a local Jim Crow law. Her standing as a member of the

NAACP soon made her plight a national story. The black community responded by turning to King, who had become the pastor of Montgomery Dexter St. Baptist Church the year before at the age of 26. The son of a prominent Atlanta minister, King had received a Bachelor's degree from Morehouse College and a Ph.D. in Theology from Boston University. He embraced the teachings of Mahatma Gandhi; a program of nonviolent passive resistance. After Park's arrest, King endorsed a plan created by a local black women's group to boycott Montgomery's bus system until it was integrated. The bus system in Montgomery depended, in a large measure, on its black customers. African-Americans also depended on the Montgomery bus system, but for the next 381 days they refused to ride the bus. The united black community formed carpools or walked to work—in some cases suffering through serious hardships. Eventually, the bus company was near bankruptcy and downtown stores complained that they were losing business. They begged city leaders to give in to the boycott, but the city would not give in. It was only after the Supreme Court ruled bus segregation unconstitutional in November 1956 that the city finally give in.

The success of this boycott catapulted Martin Luther King to national prominence. He became the de facto leader of the Civil Rights Movement. In 1957, along with the Rev. Ralph Abernathy and other southern black clergy, King created the Southern Christian Leadership Conference (SCLC), based in Atlanta. For African-Americans in the South, the church had long been the moral and social center of their lives. Now that church lent its organizational skills, as well as the talent of its best preachers, to the Civil Rights Movement. The SCLC and the NAACP were the two primary advocacy groups for racial justice. While their victories during the 1950s were limited, they laid the foundation, the organizational groundwork, for the successes of the 1960s. Most important, the struggle for racial equality was now based in the South— the heart of the American system of segregation and disenfranchisement.

But the Civil Rights Movement was not only a movement led entirely from the top. In fact, a large part of its success came from the active resistance of common people. In February 1960, four black freshmen at North Carolina A&T went into the local Woolworth's to sit down at the counter for lunch, something they were forbidden to do by local custom and law. The students asked for coffee and donuts, but were denied service. Undaunted, they sat there the rest of the day waiting to be served. Despite being forced to endure harsh verbal and sometimes physical resistance by local whites, the students returned the next day and the next, eventually filling their ranks with supporters until Woolworth's was filled with sit-in protesters. Facing a strong African-American boycott that would cut into business profits and generate bad publicity, Woolworth's and the Greensboro city leadership gave in to the protesters.

The Greensboro sit-ins triggered a larger sit-in movement, composed of 70,000 black students across the South over the next eighteen months. The largest sit-in was held in Atlanta, where students from Morehouse, Spellman, and Atlanta universities started sit-ins across the city that led to the arrest of more than seventy people the first day. The protest, led by Morehouse undergraduates Julian Bond and Lonnie King, lasted for months and hundreds were sent to jail before it ended. Concerned about loss of profits and bad publicity from an organized and effective boycott, the city's leadership finally gave in during September 1961.

In the election of 1960, the question of Civil Rights ran straight to the heart of every political campaign. The Republican nominee, Vice President Richard M. Nixon, advocated calling for more Civil Rights legislation among Republicans, while his Democratic opponent, John F. Kennedy, had done little with the matter while in the Senate. But during the campaign, Nixon, who had done much for Civil Rights, tried to court Southern whites by downplaying his previous support for the movement. By contrast, JFK spoke out in favor of the Civil Rights Movement and even had his brother Robert intercede when King was arrested at a demonstration in Atlanta. JFK ended up winning 70 percent of the black vote in the U.S., and that allowed him to win crucial battleground states like Texas, Illinois, Michigan, and Pennsylvania. Nevertheless, JFK disappointed much of the Civil Rights Movement leadership by not acting on his victory by promoting the movement. JFK felt his margin of victory had been too narrow, so he did not dare alienate the white South, lest he lose in 1964. Instead, JFK chose to work behind the scenes, appointing Thurgood Marshall to the federal bench and breathing new life into the Civil Rights Division of the Justice Department by making his brother Robert Attorney General of the U.S.

Frustrated by the lack of presidential support they were seeing, James Farmer, the director of the Congress of Racial Equality (CORE), decided in 1961 to launch a series of freedom rides across the South to draw national attention to the problems of segregation. CORE hoped that they would be arrested and beaten, so that those actions would lead to court reviews of Southern laws. Many Southern states had laws that prevented blacks and whites from traveling together across state lines. The first Freedom Ride left Washington, D.C. in early May 1961 bound for Alabama and Mississippi. In Anniston, Alabama a mob attack the bus with rocks and knives. Just outside of town, the tires on the bus went flat and it was firebombed, forcing the passengers out. Outside, the passengers found themselves beset by an angry crowd, that beat the passengers with iron bars and clubs as the bus burned. One rider was killed. Despite this setback, the riders were determined to complete their planned route. As they tried to get back underway in Birmingham, forty whites attacked the Freedom Riders again. Finally, on May 17, CORE gave up the program.

While CORE members decided to cancel the Freedom Rides, others were not so hesitant. The Student Nonviolent Coordinating Committee (SNCC) refused to let mob violence stop the movement. SNCC volunteers, including Robert Moses, Diane Nash, James Bevel, Marion Barry, and SNCC president John Lewis, put themselves at great personal risk by traveling into the Deep South. The new group left Birmingham on a bus to Montgomery on May 20. The bus was attacked in Birmingham by members of the Ku Klux Klan, and a young white rider from Wisconsin, James Zwerg, had his spinal cord severed. The mob beat not only the riders, but also journalists and a Justice Department official sent to observe the events. This attack finally forced the Kennedy Administration to provide federal protection for the Riders to avoid more mob violence.

More than one thousand people eventually took part in the Freedom Rides in the year that followed. Three-fourths of the riders were under age thirty, mostly male and evenly divided between black and white. While they never achieved their ultimate goal of riding unmolested across the South, they did compel the Kennedy administration to get the Interstate Commerce Commission to make such travel legal.

Not every step in the crusade for Civil Rights was successful. In Albany, Georgia, for example, SNCC and NAACP activists tried to integrate public facilities there and win voting rights. Over 1,000 protesters were arrested, so King tried to elevate the Albany struggle into a national crusade. Unlike other cities, the Albany chief of police, Laurie Pritchett, did not beat the protesters. Instead he instructed his officers only to arrest them, knowing that violence in the end would be self-defeating. King was arrested twice, but quickly freed both times. In the end, Civil Rights gains at Albany were minimal. Another failure for the movement came at the University of Mississippi, where a court order allowed James Meredith to register for courses. Gov. Ross Barnett encouraged active resistance to federal authorities, encouraging Mississippi residents to attack the 200 federal marshals at Ole Miss University. When the dust settled, two men were dead and 160 marshals were wounded in the assault; 28 of them had been shot. Meredith eventually attended classes and graduated in 1963, but he faced constant hostility and required federal protection.

In the final months of 1962, King decided to target segregation in Birmingham. It was obvious he needed a victory by that time. The failure in Albany was a challenge to not only his leadership, but the policy of nonviolence. Birmingham was a big test. Among the most segregated cities in the U.S., it had a history of violence and would not be an easy target. Blacks made up 40 percent of the total population, but only 10,000 of the city's 80,000 blacks were registered to vote. SCLC chose to fill the city's jails with protesters, launching boycotts of Birmingham businesses to provoke the chief of police, Bull Connor, into violence. King and hundreds of others were arrested. There he composed his famous *Letter from Birmingham City Jail* on April 16, 1963. The letter is a response to a statement made by eight white Alabama clergymen on April 12, 1963 entitled "A Call for Unity," which agreed that social injustices were taking place but expressed the belief that the battle against racial segregation should be fought solely in the courts and not taken onto the streets. King responded that, without forceful, direct actions like the nonviolence movement, true civil rights could never be achieved. As he put it, "This 'Wait' has almost always meant 'Never.'" King asserted that civil disobedience was not only justified in the face of unjust laws, but it was a "moral responsibility for citizens to disobey unjust laws."

By May 1963, police chief Connor chose to turn up the violence in Birmingham. Police used dogs and water cannons against protesters, creating scenes that were broadcast across the country on national TV. The response was outrage, and it forced the Kennedy administration to consider stronger action against the South. As the violence escalated, Kennedy eventually sent 3,000 troops to Birmingham and made plans to send more. Though the violence temporarily subsided, four black children were killed at the Birmingham Baptist Church when a bomb exploded on September 15, 1963.

By the summer of 1963, it was clear to the Kennedy administration that the time was ripe, given black activism and white support, for sweeping civil rights legislation. It was also obvious that federal intervention was going to be necessary. Ole Miss and Birmingham had proven that. In June 1963, Gov. George Wallace threatened to block the entrance of two black students into the University of Alabama. This action forced JFK and his brother RFK to finally nationalize the Alabama National Guard and order Wallace aside; allowing the two students access. On June 11, 1963, JFK went on national TV and offered his personal endorsement of the Civil Rights Movement, telling the U.S. that America would not be fully free until all its citizens were free. The next week he asked Congress for a law that would ensure voting rights, outlaw public segregation, and bolster federal authority to deny funds to programs that discriminated. After three years of fence-sitting, JFK finally decided to solidly back the movement.

But JFK's proclamation was not going to be enough. A few hours after his speech, a gunman murdered Medgar Evers, the leader of the Mississippi NAACP. In the weeks leading up to his death, Evers found himself the target of a number of threats. On May 28, 1963, a Molotov cocktail was thrown into the carport of his home, and five days before his death, he was nearly run down by a car after he emerged from the Jackson NAACP office. Despite the risks, Evers stepped up civil rights demonstrations in Jackson during the first week of June 1963. A local television station granted Evers time for a short speech, his first in Mississippi, where he outlined the goals of the Jackson movement. Following the speech, threats on Evers' life increased. At approximately 12:40 a.m. on June 12, 1963, Evers pulled into his driveway after returning from an integration meeting where he had conferred with NAACP lawyers. Emerging from his car and carrying NAACP T-shirts that stated "Jim Crow Must Go," Evers was struck in the back with a bullet that ricocheted into his home. He staggered thirty feet before collapsing. He died at the local hospital fifty minutes later. Byron De La Beckwith, a fertilizer salesman and member of both the White Citizens' Council and Ku Klux Klan, was arrested on June 23 for Evers' murder. Not surprisingly, two all-white juries that year deadlocked on De La Beckwith's guilt, allowing him to escape justice. During the course of his first 1964 trial, De La Beckwith was visited by former Mississippi Governor Ross Barnett and onetime Army Major General Edwin A. Walker.

The leaders of the Civil Rights Movement understood the seriousness of the problems in the South. So to pressure Congress, to show the urgency of their cause, to demonstrate their dedication to nonviolence, they organized a march on Washington, D.C. The idea had originated with A. Phillip Randolph, president of the Brotherhood of Sleeping Car Porters, back in 1941. Now, more than twenty years later, Randolph revived the concept and convinced the major Civil Rights Movement leaders to endorse it. JFK originally opposed the march, fearing it might jeopardize support for his civil rights bill in Congress. But as plans for the march solidified, he gave in. Leaders from the SCLC, NAACP, SNCC, the Urban League, and CORE put aside their differences for a time to bring off the event.

Trouble emerged immediately. Not all the civil rights leaders participating in the March were happy with the Kennedy Administration. John Lewis, head of SNCC and later a member of the House of Representatives, who as a Freedom Rider had been beaten numerous times, planned to denounce JFK and RFK as hypocrites for their waffling on the Civil Rights Movement. But Walter Reuther, the leader who was helping pay for the event, along with Randolph, convinced Lewis to change his speech in the interests of liberal harmony.

On August 28, 1963, more than 250,000 people, including 50,000 whites, gathered at the Lincoln Memorial to rally for freedom. Present were people from all walks of life: doctors, teachers, union members, students, clergy, and entertainers. Joan Baez led what became one of the largest singalongs ever with a stirring rendition of *We Shall Overcome*. At the end of the day, MLK gave what is widely regarded as the greatest speech in American history. He combined his conviction with his speaking talents, the principles of the Declaration of Independence, and his fiery Southern Baptist heritage to produce what became one of the most defining moments in American history. Somehow, some way, this stirring interracial unity marked the high water mark of the Civil Rights Movement and it buoyed the spirits of the liberals trying to push the legislation through Congress.

JFK, however, died on the operating table at Parkland Hospital in Dallas on November 22, 1963. Many were unsure what would happen next. His successor was Lyndon Baines Johnson of Texas, a man who had never been much of a friend of civil rights. In fact, Johnson, as one of the most powerful members of Congress, had actively worked against civil rights legislation. But Johnson recognized the stark reality of the situation when he sat in the Oval office. The Democratic Party, which had dominated national affairs since 1932, was about to be thrashed in national politics. The South was becoming increasingly conservative and, thus, Republican. The Southern base that Democrats had been able to depend on for a century was crumbling. Meanwhile, the North was becoming more Democratic. So Johnson tried to turn it around and rescue the Democratic Party. His solution was to embrace the Civil Rights Movement, hoping to ensure a solid Democratic base among African-Americans and Northern and Western liberals. It was a brilliant strategy because it allowed the party to seize new Democratic areas and yet maintain some control over the South simply because there were, for a time, few political alternatives in the South other than the Democratic Party.

Over the long term, Johnson's maneuver forced the Democrats to become more liberal, but it also drove white Southerners into the Republican Party. Nevertheless, LBJ vowed to give the U.S. a civil rights bill much stronger than JFK's plan, had he lived. Johnson used all his political skill to push his bill through Congress mostly unchanged. On

July 2, 1964, LBJ signed the Civil Rights Act of 1964 into law. It was the most significant piece of civil rights legislation passed in the U.S. since Reconstruction. Among its most important points, the Civil Rights Act of 1964:

1. Prohibited discrimination in most places of public accommodation
2. Outlawed discrimination in employment on the basis of race, color, religion, sex, or national origin
3. Authorized the Justice Department to begin lawsuits to desegregate public schools and other facilities
4. Created the Equal Employment Opportunity Commission
5. Gave federal money to assist communities in desegregating their schools

For the Civil Rights Movement, it was a profound victory.

But, in one sense the Civil Rights Act of 1964 was only half the battle. While segregation was now illegal, true political equality only comes with the ability to vote. And throughout the South, the vast majority of African-Americans still could not vote. In the spring of 1964, SNCC launched a program to fix that problem. It was called the Freedom Summer Project. Mississippi was in many ways the toughest challenge for the Civil Rights Movement. It was the poorest, most backward state in the nation and had remained untouched by the struggle. Forty-two percent of the people in that state were black, but fewer than 5 percent of them were registered to vote. The median black family income in Mississippi was $1,500 per year, about one-third of what white families earned. Politically, the state was still controlled by a white planter elite that rigidly maintained the racial system in Mississippi. To combat this situation, the Freedom Summer Project recruited some 900 volunteers, mostly white college students from all over the U.S. to achieve three goals: 1) To aid in voter registration, 2) To teach in "freedom schools," and 3) To help build a Freedom Party as an alternative to the all-white Democratic Party of Mississippi.

The organizers of Freedom Summer, Bob Moses of SNCC and Dave Dennis of CORE, expected violence. And that is precisely why they wanted white volunteers. As Dennis later explained, the death of a white college student would be of more political value than the death of a black college student. Mississippi authorities prepared for the arrival of the Freedom Summer volunteers like they were preparing for an invading army, beefing up local and state police forces.

Neither side had to wait long for trouble to develop. Early in the project, while most volunteers were still training in Ohio, three activists disappeared in Neshoba County, Mississippi after they went to investigate the burning of a black church. Their names were Goodman, Schwerner, and Chaney. Six weeks later, the FBI found their bodies. Goodman and Schwerner had each been shot once, while Chaney (the only black man in the group) was beaten horribly before he was shot three times. Three more Freedom workers died that summer. All in all, 1,000 workers were arrested, 80 were beaten, there were thirty-five shooting incidents, and thirty buildings were bombed.

Freedom Summer marked a change in the Civil Rights Movement. There was a lot of tension within the project between black and white leaders, but Dennis' goal was a success. National attention was riveted on the racism of Mississippi. But the tension within the Freedom Summer Project was indicative of the division within the Civil Rights Movement. The younger factions were growing tired of the limits of nonviolent protests. Many of those youths were becoming sympathetic to the radical and militant language used by an emerging leader in the movement, Malcolm X.

Malcolm X was actually born Malcolm Little in Michigan. A life of petty crime led to his conviction on burglary charges for which he served seven years in prison. While in prison he converted to the Nation of Islam, a version of Islam that championed Black Nationalism, and had been created in Detroit in the 1930s. Malcolm chose to use the surname X to mark the loss of his original African name through slavery. Since the 1950s, Malcolm had acted as the spokesman of the Nation, and the personal spokesman of Elijah Muhammad, leader of the Nation of Islam.

When Malcolm left jail in 1952, he became a tireless speaker for the Nation of Islam. From everywhere, ranging from street corners to college campuses, Malcolm offered a message of self-help and racial solidarity. He urged blacks to take pride in their African heritage and to take any means necessary to free themselves from white oppression. He criticized white people—all white people—as blue-eyed devils who were responsible for the entire world's evil. He opposed integration. Malcolm was actually for segregation, especially the creation of a separate black state. His message of self-help and economic independence played well in the industrial North and the movement by the early 1960s was strong. Malcolm admitted in his own *Autobiography* that his positions were extreme. But he said that the black race in North America had suffered under awful conditions, noting, "[Y]ou show me a black man [in America] who isn't an extremist and I'll show you one in need of psychiatric attention."

Malcolm left the Nation of Islam in 1964, troubled by the paternity suits that surrounded Elijah Muhammad. Having broken with the Nation, Malcolm made a pilgrimage to Mecca where he met Islamic peoples of all colors. He later said that event showed him that blacks and whites could live together peaceably. When he returned to the U.S., Malcolm abandoned his separatist views and founded the Organization of Afro-American Unity. He began to work within the mainstream of the Civil Rights Movement. Malcolm was assassinated on February 21, 1965 by agents of the New Jersey branch of the Nation of Islam. In death, Malcolm became more powerful than in life. Now, Malcolm was a martyr for the idea that became known as Black Power, which stressed self-respect, celebrated African heritage and black culture, and called for black self-sufficiency. More than any other person, Malcolm X was responsible for the more militant nature of the movement after 1965.

In the election of 1964, LBJ defeated Barry Goldwater by a landslide. Goldwater won only his home state of Arizona and five Deep South states. Democrats had firm control of both the House and Senate. This victory promised to lead to more reforms. Movement leaders sought to provoke another confrontation that would, once again, humiliate Washington into passing new laws. King chose Selma, Alabama as his target, a city of some 27,000 about fifty miles west of Montgomery. Of the 15,000 eligible black voters there, less than 1,000 were registered. Back in 1963, local SNCC activists tried to register black voters but they were met by violence at the hands of county sheriff Jim Clark. Sensing that Clark might be another Bull Conner, MLK arrived in Selma in January 1965 just after accepting the Nobel Peace Prize in Oslo.

Once in Selma, King demanded that black activists be allowed to register voters and began to lead daily marches on the courthouse. By early February, Clark had imprisoned more than 3,000 protesters. One black activist was killed and another beaten, but still there was not the national outcry King wanted. So, in early March, SCLC staffers called on black activists to march from Selma to Montgomery where they planned to deliver a list of grievances to Gov. Wallace.

On Sunday, March 7, a group of 600 marchers left Selma for Montgomery. Just outside town, on the Pettis Bridge that spanned the Alabama River, the marchers were met by a group of mounted, heavily armed county and state police. The police ordered the marchers to turn back, but they refused to move. When the marchers did not disperse, they were tear-gassed and billy-clubbed, driven back over the bridge through gas and blood. Fifty were sent to the hospital. This attack, which became known as Bloody Sunday, received extensive coverage on network TV.

Undaunted, King called for a second march on Montgomery. A federal court, though, issued a temporary restraining order against SCLC, telling them not to march. King compromised, infuriating the more militant factions. King promised to lead the march over the bridge, pray, then turn around and go back. Just when it seemed like the Selma movement might fall apart, a gang of white thugs rescued them. They attacked four white Unitarian ministers who had come to Selma to participate in the march. One of them, a minister from Boston, died from multiple skull fractures.

President Johnson was finally forced to act. On March 15, he asked Congress for a voting rights bill. Johnson also persuaded a federal judge to allow the march to proceed and he warned Gov. Wallace not to interfere. On March 21, MLK led 3,000 black and white marchers out of Selma. By the time they reached Montgomery, their numbers had swollen to 30,000.

In August 1965, LBJ signed the Voting Rights Act into law. It did two things:

1. It authorized federal supervision of voter registration in states and counties where fewer than half the voting age residents were registered.
2. It outlawed literacy and other discriminatory tests that had been used to keep blacks from voting.

The Voting Rights Act was fairly successful. By 1968, black registration jumped from 7 percent to 59 percent in Mississippi and from 24 to 57 percent in Alabama. The total number of southern voters grew from 1 million to 3.1 million.

Yet, the victory the civil rights leaders had hoped for was not complete. Poverty, racism, and slums persisted. MLK continued to struggle for civil rights until the day of his assassination in Memphis in 1968, but he was no longer the leader of a united movement at Selma. Many members of the movement were unwilling to wait for nonviolence to succeed, buying into the tenets of Black Power and demanding immediate equality. Perhaps the greatest failure of liberalism in the twentieth century was the belief that once political rights were obtained, economic and social inequality would end as well. It did not happen. Those problems had other causes. And sadly, they persist in America to this day.

Items to Consider

President's Commission on Civil Rights, Thurgood Marshall, *Brown v. Board of Education*, Southern Manifesto, Little Rock Crisis, Montgomery Bus Boycott, SCLC, sit-ins, March on Washington, Civil Rights Act, Freedom Summer Project

CHAPTER 26

Conformity in an Affluent Society & the Rise of Counterculture

The Second World War not only decisively ended the Great Depression, but it created conditions for a productive post-war collaboration among the federal government, private enterprise, and organized labor. The collaboration of these three groups established continued economic growth after the war. The U.S. emerged from the war not only physically unscathed, but also economically strengthened by wartime industrial expansion, which placed the United States at a relative advantage over its allies and its enemies. As economic historian Alan Milward wrote, "The United States emerged in 1945 in an incomparably stronger position economically than in 1941. By 1945 the foundations of the United States' economic domination over the next quarter of a century had been secured … [This] may have been the most influential consequence of the Second World War for the post-war world."

In fact, the U.S. possessed an economy much larger and richer than any other nation in the world, and American leaders were determined to make the United States the center of the postwar world economy. American aid to Europe ($13 billion via the Economic Recovery Program, or Marshall Plan, 1947–51) and Japan ($1.8 billion, 1946–52) furthered this goal, tying the economic reconstruction of West Germany, France, Great Britain, and Japan to American import and export needs.

But it was not only in economic aid that the U.S. showed its domination. In the years immediately following the war, the U.S. successfully turned its massive wartime production toward consumer production. As a result, the GNP more than doubled between 1946 and 1960. The U.S. produced more than two-thirds of the world's manufactured goods by 1960. Americans benefited directly from the economic growth, family incomes doubled between 1949 and 1973, and the U.S. population grew to 151,684,000 people, becoming 6 percent of world population.

Everywhere one looked within the country it appeared that Americans were living the high life. In every measurable way—diet, housing, wages, education, recreation—Americans were living better than their parents and grandparents. In the period between 1945 and 1960, nearly 50 percent of all adults owned homes and 95 percent of all American families owned at least one car. In 1945, car companies sold barely 70,000 new cars. By 1950, the car companies had sold 6 million new cars. Another indicator of economic success could be found in the drastically increased levels of college enrollment, which quadrupled in the period from 1945 to 1970.

By 1950, life in the United States began to return to normal. Soldiers came home and found peacetime jobs. Industry stopped producing war equipment and began to produce goods that made peacetime life pleasant. The American economy was stronger than ever. Some major changes took place in America. Many Americans were dissatisfied with the old way of life. They wanted something better. And many people were earning enough money to look for that better life. There were four major engines of prosperity making this possible in the U.S.

1. The first engine of change was the Baby Boom and the growth of the nuclear family. The United States has always counted its population every ten years as part of the political system. By 1950, there were more than 150 million people in the United States. The population changed immediately after World War II. Suddenly, it appeared as if every family was having babies. Parents were hopeful about the future. There were lots of jobs. And people everywhere felt the need for a family and security after the long, difficult years of the war. So the birth rate increased suddenly. This baby boom increased the U.S. population by 30 percent (40 million) from 1945 to 1960, one of the highest birth rates in history. The average age of marriage dropped for women from 22 in 1900 to 20.3 in 1962, which meant more women were having children that year than ever before. The baby boom resulted in a tremendous growth in the traditional nuclear family. It seemed like every household had two adults, and at least two children. The population spurt created a huge demand for durable household goods and baby-related items, but it also led to the sale of 21 million cars, 20 million refrigerators, and 12 million TVs.

2. The Service Sector Boom: The growth in the population corresponded with a boost in money for families to spend on travel, recreation, education, insurance, and medical services. In 1956, the airlines attracted as many passengers as railroads. Money spent on personal recreation jumped from $11 billion in 1950 to more than $18 billion in 1959. By 1956, service sector jobs—like sales, clerical work, and other white-collar—exceeded the number of manufacturing occupations.

The change in employment reflected the fact that the U.S. was becoming a post-industrial society. Focus was now being placed on technological innovation and labor productivity, not on farming or creating things. Efficiency became the byword of the day, with each company seeking out new and better ways to make things or to sell things or to speed up American life. The best example for this growth can be found in a product called Tupperware. Tupperware was developed in 1945 by Earl Silas Tupper. He developed plastic containers to contain food and keep it airtight. The formerly patented "burping seal" is a famous aspect of Tupperware that distinguished it from competitors.

Tupperware succeeded because he pioneered the direct marketing strategy made by the "Tupperware party." During the early 1950s, Tupperware's sales and popularity exploded, thanks in large part to sales associate Brownie Wise's influence among women who sold Tupperware, and some of the famous "jubilees" celebrating the success of Tupperware ladies at lavish and outlandishly themed parties. It is crucial to understand that Tupperware's success did not come from the labor of men. Tupperware was known, at a time when women came back from working during World War II only to be told to "go back to the kitchen," as a way to empower women and give them a toehold in the postwar business world.

3. The Culture of Consumption: America's burgeoning economy after the war was supported by a desire to buy. Americans bought things like never before, far surpassing the previous record-breaking consumption levels of the 1920s. In some cases, people could buy because they were making higher salaries than previous generations, but it also was due to an increase in private credit. "Buy Now, Pay Later" became the motto of the day. Private installment credit soared for first time in American history, going from $4 billion in 1954 to $43 billion in 1960. Credit was gender specific, and most married women could not get personal credit cards until 1970.

The main reason for the growth of personal credit can be attributed to the emergence of a new industry: the credit card company. Prior to 1950, the only way to get personal credit was by getting a private loan from a bank or by having a personal account at a store. After 1950, personal credit cards emerged to fill this void. It began with Diner's Club in 1950, but there were two other major credit card companies in business by the end of the decade: American Express (1958) and BankAmeriCard (1959, later renamed VISA). With the increase in personal credit came a rise of the nationwide business chains, which meant consumers could go anywhere in America and use credit at the same stores and restaurants.

The nationwide business chain was an important innovation, and it began with Ray Kroc's franchise, McDonald's. Kroc, dubbed the Hamburger King, took over a small-scale McDonald's Corporation franchise in 1955. Six years later, Kroc bought out the McDonald brothers for $2.7 million, stating, "The McDonald brothers were simply not on my wavelength at all … I was obsessed with the idea of making McDonald's the biggest and the best. They were content with what they had; they didn't want to be bothered with more risks and more demands." Kroc quickly built his new company into the most successful fast food operation in the world. He began by standardizing the entire process, so that it could be effectively replicated in any city in any state across the country. Guaranteeing a hamburger fat content below 19 percent and a patty that weighed 1.6 ounces and was 3.875 inches in diameter ensured predictability in all McDonald's outlets, which became one of the keys to the chain's immense popularity. No one was making things for themselves anymore. With people eating out more often, the conformity of standardized products and services gave them a homey feeling, even if they were at a drive-in.

Television played a major role in the growth of the Culture of Consumption. The first TV stations appeared in 1940s, but hundreds existed by 1960. People spent huge amounts of their free time watching TV, and they identified with characters on popular shows. Along with more stations came a growth of the TV advertising industry in 1950s. The first TV advertisement was aired at 2:29 p.m., July 1, 1941 by a New York City NBC affiliate. The Bulova Watch Co. paid $9 for a 20-second spot that aired the before Brooklyn Dodgers–Philadelphia Phillies game. Commercial spots became entrenched in the television format before the year ended. Surprisingly, the first political TV advertisement did not occur until the 1952 presidential election. During the election, the Democrats felt they needed more exposure to get their candidate elected. On a whim, they bought a 30-minute slot for Adlai Stevenson in the middle of the most popular show of the day, *I Love Lucy*. Stevenson introduced himself to the voters, talked about his family, and discussed the Democratic political platform. Political advisers were certain the commercial would be a deciding factor in the election.

The exposure the Democrats got was not what they expected though. Enraged fans sent hate mail to Stevenson and the Democratic Party for interrupting *I Love Lucy*. The Republicans quickly moved to gain their candidate exposure as well, although they learned an important lesson. Commercials pressing voters to support Eisenhower never stretched longer than 20 seconds and they never interrupted a television show, coming only before or afterward. The move worked, and Eisenhower and the Republicans swept the elections.

4. The GI Bills: Helping Returning Veterans: Political leaders recognized that a crucial need at the end of the war would be the re-integration of servicemen into the economy. It was not purely about economics, though, as many in the nation were thankful for the sacrifices made by those who went off to fight the war. Congress responded with the Servicemen's Readjustment Act of 1944. Commonly called the "Bill That Changed America," the Servicemen's Readjustment Act was both good and bad. The core of the act was a desire to set aside money to educate veterans. Since not everyone wanted to go to college, the act allowed for veterans to go either to vocational school or college. Since it was not enough money at first to provide more than tuition and books, the act included a subsistence program called the "52-20 Club." Essentially, the 52-20 Club was Veteran Unemployment Insurance, providing readjustment benefits of $20 a week for up to 52 weeks. The final part of the Servicemen's Readjustment program was the Veterans Preference Act (1944), which gave veterans preferential status when applying for jobs and government services and ensuring they were in more favorable positions than nonveterans. While the G.I. Bill helped returning veterans get back to regular life, it is important to remember that it effectively doubled cost of war.

By far, the most important part of the GI Bill was its educational benefits. Educational benefits in the GI Bill provided four years of full-time tuition or training, along with paying for all fees and books. Another important part was a small stipend given to the veteran while attending school that was added a few years later. Although the stipend was only subsistence pay for dependents, it was often the deciding factor that allowed many veterans take advantage of the program. Of the more than 15 million eligible veterans, about half used the G.I. Bill's educational benefits: 2.2 million went to college or postgraduate study, 3.5 million enrolled in other schooling, 1.4 million got on-the-job training, and 700,000 got farm training. One and a half million students would use the G.I. Bill in 1946 alone.

The G.I. Bill was so successful that Congress followed it up with the Veteran's Administration (VA) benefits. This program increased homeownership by providing veterans with access to loans featuring no money down, low interest rates, and low monthly payments. From 1945 to 1966, one-fifth of all single-family residences in the U.S. were financed by the VA. In California, the VA insured 50 percent of all new mortgages, and 28 percent of all WWII veterans received VA home loans. While the main portion of VA benefits focused on home loans, the program also helped expand entrepreneurial activities by providing a deferred loan of up to $2,000 to start a business. While the amount seems small by today's standards, in the 1950s it was enough to give veterans an additional advantage of access to investment capital, as well as supplemental funds from most states.

The G.I. Bill and its subsidiary programs offered veterans a tremendous amount of help and were beneficial for the economy, but they also had several unexpected results. For one, it created an advantaged class out of the veterans. The G.I. Bill gave veterans an important edge over nonveterans in matters of work, education, and society. The problem with this was that most veterans were white and male, leaving them best prepared for the high-earning, white-collar work of the postwar economy at the expense of other members of society. Another problem emerged when male veterans went to college. Despite efforts to expand enrollment, there were never enough spots to serve everyone seeking an education, which meant increased veteran enrollment came at the expense of women and minorities—two groups who only got access to schools during the war because so many white men were gone. To make room for returning veterans, schools cut female and minority admissions. Cornell University cut female enrollment by 20 percent in 1946 alone. The final problem involved the acceptance of female and minority veterans. Neither group was ever considered full-fledged military personnel by the government. Female veterans were forced to prove independence from a male breadwinner in order to receive full G.I. benefits. Widows fared even worse, getting much poorer benefits than their husband would have received had he lived. Minority male veterans were sanctioned to receive full benefits, but could not use them because minority enrollment dropped so low most could not get into postsecondary schools. As a result, minority and female veterans could not access the many profitable tickets of upward mobility being offered to their white male counterparts.

Creating a Homogenized Society

The increase in wealth and commerce in the U.S. unexpectedly set in motion the homogenization of American society. *Homogenization* is a process whereby every region of the nation is slowly made uniform. Prior to the 1950s, American society was differentiated by distinctive regional characteristics. In some ways it still is, but those divisions slowly began a process of erosion in the 1950s that continues to the present day, leaving the regional divisions within American society far less distinct then they had originally been.

There are several reasons for the homogenization of American society during the 1950s, but it all began with the expansion of highway system. Starting with the Collier-Burns Act in 1947, the federal government instituted a massive transportation construction program, resulting in 12,500 miles of highway projects. Creating a seven-cent per gallon gas tax, the federal government was able to spend $1 million a day on road construction by the late 1950s. In 1956, Congress passed the Interstate Act, which provided federal funds for 90 percent of all new freeways built in the U.S. The expansion of roads had a profound effect on American society. People began to drive their cars everywhere: to work, to entertainment, to visit friends and family, for recreation, and to travel.

Americans loved their cars so much that new industries arose to fulfill their passion, creating a drive-in culture that still dominates the nation. It began with the establishment of the first drive-through McDonald's in 1954, which quickly grew into 228 by 1960. But it went beyond eating in the car; Americans seemed to refuse to exit their automobiles. By 1960, the U.S. had nearly 5,000 drive in movie theaters. Rev. Robert Schuller even went so far as to hold religious services at the Orange Drive-In Theater in California, letting people "Worship as you are in the family car." By the 1960s, a family could travel nearly anywhere in the country and find the same drive-in restaurants and car-based forms of entertainment.

Another important result of the expansion of roadways across the country and the blossoming drive-in culture was a complete redistribution of the American population. It began with white flight to suburbia. With so many veterans enjoying the economic benefits of the G.I. Bill, they used the freedom provided by their cars to escape the racial mixing pot that was the American city. As time progressed, white people moved away from increasingly racial-minority inner-city neighborhoods to white suburbs and exurbs, which they kept racially segregated through neighborhood associations, redlining, mortgage discrimination, and racially restrictive covenants. Population shifts were also about economics, since many people living in the Sunbelt and blacks living in the South migrated North during the period, seeking better opportunities. These shifts in population meant fewer farmers, the growth of agribusiness, and the expansion of the megalopolis.

While transportation was a major boost toward the establishment of a homogeneous culture, an even bigger factor was the growth of television and the mass culture it engendered. The national broadcasting networks stretched from the East Coast to the West Coast by 1951. For the first time in U.S. history, TV allowed a national audience to tune in to the same shows and the same news at nearly the same time. Two-thirds of American households had at least one TV (40 million TV sets) by the mid 1950s. There were more TVs than bathtubs by 1960.

Television shows varied, but family wholesomeness prevailed. The first prime time cartoon show was *Rocky and His Friends* in 1959. The second, *The Flintstones*, began in 1960. Both appealed to children and adults and set off a trend that included *Alvin & the Chipmunks*, *The Jetsons*, and *Mr. Magoo*. *The Andy Griffith Show* and *I Love Lucy* were the epitome of prime-time family television and ran for most of the decade. *The Beverly Hillbillies* heralded the rise of the sitcom. The supernatural and science fiction blended in with many of the popular shows, including *Bewitched*, *The Addams Family*, *My Favorite Martian*, *I Dream of Jeannie*, *Star Trek*, *The Outer Limits*, and *The Twilight Zone*. In the late 60s, humor was revived in a show called *Rowan & Martin's Laugh-In*, where many regular performers and guests became part of a show biz classic.

Although many of these shows seem quaint to us today (or fodder for bad motion pictures), the influence of television on the development of a homogenized American society cannot be understated. The average family watched TV for five hours per week in 1950, but that number had nearly doubled by 1960. Television watching is a highly ritualized behavior, allowing the subject matter consumed through television viewing to set the standards and values for many American homes. Shows like *Leave It to Beaver, The Mickey Mouse Club,* and *I Love Lucy* projected images of the perfect family and wholesomeness, making value teaching an integral part of the entertainment factor. Not everything to be learned on TV was seen as good. Many adults thought shows like *American Bandstand* only appeared to be wholesome, but really introduced young people to new and dangerous forms of music and dancing. It should be no surprise that TV commercial sales quickly surpassed radio advertising revenue once TV began to reach the entire nation. TV allowed companies to advertise to new sections of society, and reach people they never considered before. One successful advertisement could to take an item produced by a small local company and make it into a national consumer product.

While television had its detractors, its influence on the growth of a homogeneous culture had an unexpected result: religious revival. In the years after the war, America started to become an outwardly religious nation for the first time in its history. Weekly church attendance rose from 38 percent to 50 percent during the 1950s, and three-fifths of the country were church members by 1958. Reflecting the growing religiosity in the country, Congress added "Under God" to the Pledge of Allegiance in 1954 and "In God We Trust" became the nation's official motto in 1956. All of this is nice, but the deciding factor was the introduction of religion to TV. Three times a week Billy Graham preached on the various networks stretching across the nation as well as regularly broadcasting at least one several day revival each year. On Sunday mornings, there was a myriad of religious shows, but the most popular was a Catholic variety show featuring Bishop Fulton Sheen.

Although many factors led to the homogenization of American society, the single-most important influence had to be suburbanization. There are many reasons why Americans built suburbs, some (like escapism) were more innocuous than others (racism). Despite people's motivations, the G.I. Bill created a need for more housing in America. But it was not enough to build just any house, Americans needed economical housing. Looking to fulfill the country's need and make a tidy profit; a small design firm came up with the plans for Levittown. Getting its name from its builder, the firm of Levitt & Sons, Inc., four Levittowns were built in different locations as planned communities between 1947 and 1951. The Levittown was the first truly mass-produced suburb and is widely regarded as the archetype for postwar suburbs throughout the country. The mass production of uniform-plan tract housing, the "ranch-style" house as it was called, allowed builders to recreate neighborhoods of the same structural format in any section of the nation.

Americans flocked to these suburban neighborhoods, desiring an escape from urban life. Many new parents moved to homes in the new suburbs, and suburbia became a bastion of uniformity, emphasizing family togetherness and anti-urban sentiment. The word *suburb* comes from the word urban, or having to do with cities. A suburb was sub, or something less than, a city. It was usually created on an empty piece of land just outside a city. A businessman would buy the land and build houses on it. Young families would buy the houses with money they borrowed from local banks.

Life was different in the suburbs. There were all sorts of group activities. Moving to Suburbia brought with it expectations of the suburbanite ideal. Each member of the family had a specific role to fulfill. For women, that role was the Perfect Housewife. A woman's place was believed to be in the home, and she was expected to observe a strictly domestic, "feminine" role. A perfect housewife took care of the domestic chores, emphasized her family as her major source of personal fulfillment, and completely curbed her sexuality. According to an article in *Good Housekeeping,* "A woman with a grade-point average of 'C' was more likely to succeed than women of greater intelligence because she had a greater chance for a lasting marriage & a content family" (May 13, 1955).

Men also had a specific role to play: that of the bread winner. Men had to have a good job to provide for their family, with their manly worth tied directly to the size of their paycheck. The American Dream had become privatized. For men, work, work, and more work was the only way to be a good husband, creating a new workaholic regulated by societal mores. The best example for this phenomenon can be found in the book (and later, a movie) *The Man in the Gray Flannel Suit* (1956). The story follows the life of a heroic WWII captain who comes back from the war and becomes a public relations middle manager at an unnamed broadcasting company. No matter how successful he becomes, his pesky, overly ambitious wife always wants more steaks in the freezer. To quench her insatiable thirst for social advancement (and good meat), the husband learns to maneuver corporate channels, all the while suffering from debilitating flashbacks caused by the shocks and strains he suffered during war duty. Persecuted by his wife and driven by unforgiving societal expectations of manhood, the hapless character cannot even take the time to heal from the trauma of the war, driving himself nearly to the point of breakdown.

With so much emphasis being placed on conformity, perfection, and role fulfillment, it was only a matter of time before a counterculture of anticonformity emerged. It started with the Beat Generation, a term that describes both a group of American writers who came to prominence in the late 1950s and early 1960s and the cultural phenomena they wrote about and inspired. The best works of the Beatniks were Jack Kerouac's *On the Road* (1957), Allen Ginsberg's *Howl* (1956), and William Burroughs' *Naked Lunch* (1959). Regardless of what they were writing about, the Beatniks produced literature of pure experience. They did not follow literary conventions. But most important, their work was filled with their reaction to and condemnation of what they saw as the spiritual bankruptcy and meaninglessness of American life: conformity.

Once the Beatniks opened a door of criticism against the conformity of America's increasingly homogenized society, a flood of social critics arose to follow their lead. The first was Vance Packard, whose two books, *The Hidden Persuaders* (1957) and *The Status Seekers* (1959), detailed the rise of American social stratification and the effect of media manipulation. David Riesman came next. His book *The Lonely Crowd* (1960) proclaimed that Americans had become "other-directed conformists who lack inner resources to lead truly autonomous lives." William Whyte's *The Organization Man* (1958) said that Americans had sold out to corporate life by becoming nation of employees who "take vows of organization life" to become "dominant members of our society." C. Wright Mills was another important critic of the early years. In *The Power Elite* (1956) Mills stated that "The powers of ordinary men are circumscribed by the everyday worlds in which they live, yet even in the rounds of job, family, and neighborhood they often seem driven by forces they can neither understand nor govern." Of all of them, John Kenneth Galbraith was the most negative critic of American conformity. In *An Affluent Society* (1958) he asked two crucial and scathing questions: 1) What kind of society slights investment in schools, parks, and public services while producing ever more goods to fulfill desires created by advertising? 2) Is the spectacle of millions of educated, middle-class women seeking happiness in suburban dream houses a reason for celebration or a waste of precious "womanpower" at a time when the Soviets trumpet the accomplishments of their female scientists, physicians, and engineers? While each of these intellectuals harshly criticized the ills of American homogenization and conformity, they never offered a solution to the problems they addressed. Despite that shortcoming, they did hold the door open for more anticonformity.

With so many critics of American conformity and the push toward homogenization, people began to step forward and demand the right to claim new freedoms within American culture. The loudest and most influential may have been Hugh Hefner's "Male Revolt." Questioning the culture of uniformity, Hefner created a lifestyle that stressed male liberation from the sexual and financial constraints associated with the social ideal of family togetherness that was being espoused in conformity. First with *Playboy* magazine and later with a short lived television variety show called *Playboy's Penthouse* (1959), Hefner actively and unabashedly sexualized the female body and celebrated male bachelorhood (one not dependent on monogamy or even headed toward marriage). It is important to note that Hugh Heffner did not instigate the sexual revolution. It was going to happen with or without him, but he did act as one of its heralds.

There have been significant shifts in social attitudes, behaviors, and institutional regulations surrounding sexuality since Sigmund Freud opened the door to the bedroom. Sexuality throughout the twentieth century has moved closer to the center of public debate than ever before. One hundred years ago the idea of sexual politics would have been unthinkable. For many today the 1960s, which unleashed the so-called sexual revolution, seems more a source of comic relief and tragic nostalgic recirculation than political inspiration. Yet throughout the late 1960s and early 1970s, a combination of student protests, counterculture movements, and medically prescribed contraceptives ushered in a decisive break with the preceding values that prescribed the confinement of women's sexual pleasure within the suburban walls of heterosexual marriage and the regulation of man's sexuality in the public. D. H Lawrence may have shocked an earlier generation with Lady Chatterley's extramarital sexual independence, but it was not until the 1970s that women's sexuality outside marriage became widely accepted.

The sexual revolution in America began with the pioneering work of Dr. Alfred Kinsey. His two reports—*Sexual Behavior in the Human Male* (1948) and *Sexual Behavior in the Human Female* (1953)—challenged traditional beliefs about sexuality. According to Kinsey, human sexual behavior included physical contact and psychological phenomena. This meant that sexual desire, sexual attraction, sexual fantasies, and sexual activities were normal occurrences for a natural and normal sex drive, rather than some conspiracy of the devil or wanton sinfulness. While such talk stirred the fears of many moral leaders, the most controversial aspect of Kinsey's reports was his willingness to discuss sexual topics that had previously been social taboos. Kinsey noted that there were many sexual orientations, he stated that none is dominant, and that sexual activity outside of procreation was both fun and healthy. His openness and frank approach shocked the nation.

With sex becoming a part of the public discussion, the young people of the nation, the same group that got involved with the peace movement and the flourishing counterculture, took to sexual liberation and sexual freedom as an integral part of their politics. This shift in sexuality was possible because a new invention, the Combined Oral Contraceptive Pill. The Pill was invented in 1960, and immediately had an enormous social impact. It gave women unprecedented control over their fertility and did not require special preparation. The most important aspect of the pill was that it did not interfere with spontaneity or sensation. But many people in America had serious problems with the pill: It divorced sex from reproduction, which heightened the debate over the moral and health consequences of premarital sex and female promiscuity.

Armed with the protection of the pill, a new generation of women arose in America. As Helen Gurley Brown's book *Sex and the Single Girl* (1962) openly advocated, women could finally actively pursue the full single life that men had always enjoyed. Women could acquire a career, gain financial independence, accept their looks, and most important, have sex without fear of repercussions. Such advice remains the basis of Brown's magazine, *Cosmopolitan*. But it also became the rallying point for a developing Feminist Movement.

Many women were not happy in the home of 1950s. This was partly a result of the ironies of housework, where women work as slaves to their family and homes for little or no recognition. But it was also because women lacked the ability to have their own identity in the 1950s and 1960s. For women, marriage meant surrendering their assets and wages to their husbands. Even single women had limited access to tools of independence—credit cards, mortgages, and fair wages.

Surprisingly, married women did not get inspiration from places like *Cosmo* or the Pill as one would expect. Those things were for single girls. No, married women got the germ of their inspiration from an inauspicious book called *Dr. Spock's Baby and Child Care* (1946). This book offered a revolutionary message. It told mothers that they actually "know more than you think you do" and urged them to be flexible and affectionate as parents and not to act as a disciplinarian. It renewed their confidence in themselves and began to open their eyes to the inequities they were enduring. Although it took some time for the revolutionary message to take root, it would eventually grow to fruition in Betty Friedan's groundbreaking work *The Feminine Mystique* (1963). Friedan openly attacked popular notion that women could only find fulfillment through childbearing and homemaking. Instead, she called on married women to get back into the workforce and to take their rightful place next to their husband rather than behind him.

With Friedan's call to arms, feminism as a movement went mainstream. Thousands of married women and mothers returned to the workforce in the late 1950s. They protested the deplorable perfectionism of the female form by beauty contests like the Miss America Protest (1968); they burned their bras; they formed the National Organization of Women in 1966 to force Congress to recognize their civil rights and assure them of the equality they deserved; and they secured full control of their bodies and reproduction with *Roe v. Wade* (1973). To put it simply, they finally broke free from the shackles of conformity and societal controls.

As more and more elements of society began to break out of conformity, young people turned their backs on the world their parents had created for them only to form the Counterculture Movement. At its best, Counterculture was a reaction against the conservative social norms of the 1950s, the political conservatism (and perceived social repression) of the Cold War period, and the U.S. government's extensive but destructive military intervention in third-world nations like Vietnam. At its worse, Counterculture was an aimless, pointlessly rebellious, drug-induced cross-country voyage of narcissistic self-indulgence as well as unpatriotic and morally destructive behavior, where the nation's younger generation claimed to be defining itself as a class that aimed to create a new kind of society but really just engaged in free love, abused tremendous amounts of drugs, and listened to some great music.

While it could be all of its extremes, both good and bad, the majority of the counterculture movement sits firmly in the middle. As the 1960s progressed, widespread tensions developed in American society that tended to flow along generational lines regarding certain polarizing issues, like the war in Vietnam, race relations, sexual mores, women's rights, traditional modes of authority, experimentation with psychedelic drugs, and the predominantly materialist interpretation of the American Dream espoused by conformity. New cultural forms emerged, including the pop music of English bands like the Beatles and the Rolling Stones, which rapidly evolved to shape and reflect the youth culture's emphasis on change and a desire for experimentation. The counterculture lifestyle integrated many of the ideals and indulgences of the time: peace, love, harmony, music, mysticism, and religions outside the Judeo-Christian tradition. Pursuits like meditation, yoga, and psychedelic drugs were embraced as routes to expanding one's consciousness.

In 1967 Scott McKenzie's rendition of the song *San Francisco (Be Sure to Wear Flowers in Your Hair)* brought as many as 100,000 young people from all over the world to celebrate San Francisco's Summer of Love in the famed Haight-Ashbury District. San Francisco's flower children, also called Hippies by local newspaper columnist Herb Caen, adopted new styles of dress, experimented with psychedelic drugs, lived communally, and developed a vibrant music scene. When people returned home from The Summer of Love, these styles and behaviors spread quickly from San Francisco and Berkeley to all the major U.S. cities. The counterculture movement had gained momentum and footsoldiers. Some hippies formed communes to live as far outside the established system as possible. This aspect of the counterculture rejected active political engagement with the mainstream and, following the dictates of Dr. Timothy Leary to "Turn on, tune in, and drop out," hoped to change society by dropping out of it altogether. Looking back on his own life prior to 1960 as a Harvard professor, Leary interpreted it to have been that of "an anonymous institutional employee who drove to work each morning in a long line of commuter cars and drove home each night and drank martinis ... just like several million middle-class, liberal, intellectual robots." Now Leary believed life was meant to be experienced, not merely lived.

The hippie ethos posed a considerable impediment to the success of alternative movements growing within counterculture. At the extremes, "doing one's own thing" led to the rejection of values imposed from without and adamant avoidance of other people's expectations. As a result, the individual tended to be isolated, which may or may not have been much of a problem for that individual—but it did threaten collaborative actions or accomplishments. This would become a serious problem for the counterculture movement, and ultimately kept it from achieving serious change.

Opposition to U.S. involvement in the Vietnam War began slowly and in small numbers in 1964 on various college campuses in the United States. This happened during a time of unprecedented student activism reinforced in numbers by the demographically significant baby boomers, but grew to include a wide and varied cross-section of Americans. The growing opposition to the Vietnam War was also partly attributable to greater access to uncensored information compared with previous wars and to extensive television coverage of what ultimately became America's longest combat war up to that time. Likewise, a system of conscription that provided exemptions and deferments more easily claimed by middle- and upper-class registrants—and thus inducted disproportionate numbers of poor, working-class, and minority registrants—drove many young people to the protest movement. By the end of 1967, as U.S. troop casualties mounted and the war ground on with no end in sight, public opinion polls showed that a majority of Americans opposed the war and wanted it to end. As a result, the antiwar movement became a major facet of the counterculture.

The year 1968 was a watershed for the counterculture movement and it was dominated by visual images. Television played an enormous role in bringing the turmoil to the forefront. Every day common Americans witnessed images during the nightly news of soldiers fighting for their lives in the streets of Saigon during the nearly nine-month-long Tet Offensive; or the haunting image of South Vietnamese police chief Gen. Nguyen Ngoc Loan executing Viet Cong captive captain Nguyen Van Le with a pistol; or the month-long occupation of Columbia University's president's office by the radical antiwar group, Students for a Democratic Society, or the assassination of the much-beloved civil rights leader Martin Luther King at 6:01 p.m. on April 4, 1968, followed by riots and continued racial urban unrest; or the televised assassination of presidential candidate Robert F. Kennedy on June 5, 1968; or Walter Cronkite's Vietnam Editorial calling the war unwinnable and a tragic mistake; or the bloody assault by Chicago police on seemingly peaceful students marching in protest of the continuation of the Vietnam War during the Democratic National Convention. While 1968 marked the highest level of action for the counterculture movement, it was also the year when the optimism of the 1960s, with its utopian hippie dreams and hopes of social change for a better future, started to turn sour. Nothing that came after would ever be the same as what had come before. It was a year of deep tragedy, pain, and anger, but also a year of remarkable social upheaval.

There is great irony in the fact that the most difficult year of the counterculture movement was capped by an event that marked its ultimate conclusion. The Woodstock Music and Art Fair was a historic event held at Max Yasgur's 600-acre dairy farm in the rural town of Bethel, New York from August 15 to August 18, 1969. To many, the festival exemplified the counterculture of the 1960s and the "hippie era." Thirty-two of the best-known musicians of the day appeared during the sometimes-rainy weekend, and no attempt to recreate it has been nearly as successful. It certainly is rightfully regarded as one of the greatest moments in music history. But it really represented none of the nonconformist tendencies of the counterculture movement. Woodstock was first and foremost a profit-making venture. It only became a free festival after it became obvious the concert was drawing hundreds of thousands more people than the organizers had prepared for—around 186,000 tickets were sold beforehand and organizers anticipated approximately 200,000 festival goers would turn up. In reality, it was a festival where nearly 500,000 hippies came together to celebrate under the slogan of "Three

Days of Peace and Music." Instead, there was violence, excessive use of drugs and alcohol, and youthful hedonism. And all the while the organizers and their suppliers made huge amounts of money. It was a consumer extravaganza.

After the sellout that was Woodstock, the counterculture movement ambled about with no real direction, becoming not a movement so much as a progression of events. The first has to be the series of terrorist activities staged by the Weather Underground Organization (WUO). A radical Leftist group, the WUO took its name from a line in the Bob Dylan song *Subterranean Homesick Blues* where he said, "You don't need a weatherman to know which way the wind blows." Splintered from Students for a Democratic Society and the Maoist-based Revolutionary Youth Movement, the WUO formed at University of Michigan in the 1960s. During the late 1960s to mid 1970s, they carried out a series of mostly harmless attacks in an attempt to overthrow U.S. government. Their actions mainly consisted of the detonation of a bomb in prominent government buildings shortly after they called in bomb threats to make sure the target building evacuated. While they scared a lot of people and killed a police officer, most Americans ignored the WUO and their cause.

Another major event in the dying gasps of the counterculture movement after Woodstock occurred in Ohio. At Kent State University, a massive demonstration was held to protest the American invasion of Cambodia, which President Richard Nixon had just announced in a televised address on April 30. As the students gathered on Monday, May 4, 1970, members of the Ohio National Guard open fired on the chanting crowd. Four students were killed and nine others wounded, one of whom suffered permanent paralysis. Some of the students who were shot were there for the protest, but others were merely walking nearby or observing the protest at a distance. There was a significant national response to the shootings: hundreds of universities, colleges, high schools, and even middle schools closed throughout the United States due to a student strike of 8 million students, and the event further divided the country along political lines. Photographs of the dead and wounded at Kent State that were distributed in newspapers and periodicals worldwide amplified sentiment against the United States' invasion of Cambodia and the Vietnam War in general. Only five days after the shootings, 100,000 people marched on Washington, D.C. in demonstration against the war and the killing of unarmed student protesters.

The years following the shootings (1970 to 1979) were filled with lawsuits against the State of Ohio filed by families of the victims, in hopes of placing blame on Gov. Rhodes and the Ohio National Guard. Trials were held on both the federal and state levels but all ended in acquittals or were dismissed. There was one civil trial for wrongful death and injury brought by the victims and their families against Gov. Rhodes and the National Guardsmen that eventually led to the students' families being awarded approximately $63,000 per victim, and the defendants agreeing to state for the record that they regretted their actions. With that last act, the counterculture movement came to an end. While fighting ended much earlier than this, the final fall of Vietnam came on the morning of April 29, 1975 with the evacuation from Saigon by helicopter of the last U.S. diplomatic, military, and civilian personnel. The president of South Vietnam was forced to resign, accusing the United States of betrayal. In a TV and radio address, outgoing President Nguyen Van Thieu said his forces had failed to stop the advance of the Vietcong because of a lack of funds promised to him by the Americans. He said, "The United States did not keep its promise to help us fight for freedom and it was in the same fight that the United States lost 50,000 of its young men."

It is difficult to access and understand the culture of dissent that emerged in America as a result of the Countercultural Movement. Perhaps it is best to leave to the words of participant Kurt Vonnegut, "The moral uncertainty of the 1950s, was, at least in part, a response to the dilemma of fighting communism at home without sacrificing the rights and privileges of a democratic republic. The cultures of dissent that flourished in the 1950s and 1960s responded to the peculiar combination of prosperity and anxiety that characterized the decade by opting out—by choosing not to conform to the dictates of mainstream America."

In any case, as the members of the hippie movement grew older and moderated their lives and their views, the 1960s counterculture was to some extent absorbed by the mainstream, leaving a lasting impact on morality, lifestyle, and fashion. While many once-ardent advocates of radical ideas now live in the suburbs and vote Republican, others have held fast to the dream of creating a new kind of American society and they have been joined by fresh streams of younger idealists. Thus the legacy of the counterculture is still being actively contested in debates that are now sometimes framed in terms of a "culture war."

Items to Consider

Affluent Society, G.I. Bill, Betty Friedan, *Playboy*, students and the New Left, SDS, Counterculture, drug culture, 1968, Kent State

CHAPTER 27

The Dawning of the Cold War and the Tragedy of Containment

The First World War began in euphoria and ended with hope that Europe might be remade in a new image. The Second World War began with much less enthusiasm, and made clear what the horrors of modern war could be to everyone involved. When Germany finally collapsed, much of Europe lay in ruins and what remained of the self-image of western civilization was haunted by the reality of Jewish death camps. Everywhere millions were homeless and jobless. Europe, once the proudest place on the face of the earth, now lay impotent. The possibility of a Communist takeover of Europe seemed possible in 1945. The Red Army already controlled much of Eastern Europe. Where the Second World War left off, a new Cold War had begun.

Totalitarianism

In 1949, the great novelist George Orwell satirized Stalinism in his dystopian novel *1984,* which outlined a future where constant warfare would infect the world as the rise of superstates mandated an enemy against which to unify their populations. To many people living at the start of the Cold War, the book seemed to foretell the immediate future. Just after the Fascist threat had been defeated, a new threat emerged for the Western nations, International Communism, at the head of which was Western Europe's one-time ally the Soviet Union. Many political theorists suggested that such threats to liberal democracy were more similar than different, thus Fascism and Communism were lumped together into the threat of totalitarianism, one party-states that fought both democracy and individual liberty, repressing civil rights. To succeed, totalitarian states must eradicate democracy and individual liberty, for the two ideologies cannot coexist. Thus, with the rise of Communist Russia to a position of world power, the western states believed themselves to be locked in a struggle for survival. Russia too, fell under this malaise, and in this misconception, the Cold War was born.

East-West and North-South

The Cold War fear of Communism divided the world into East and West (or Communist vs. the free world of liberal democratic capitalism). But there was another major development taking place, too. A wave of nationalism swept through the former European empires in Asia and Africa. These newly emergent, underdeveloped nations presented a major challenge to the developed democracies of Western Europe. Many of the nations embraced a form of nationalistic Socialism that infuriated U.S. and Western democratic leaders, who were inclined to see Communist threats under every rock. Even if a third-world nation became Socialist or Communist, it did not necessarily mean it was part of the Soviet bloc or took orders directly from Moscow. Yet increasingly, as the Cold War progressed, the answer to that question in the United States was yes, they were under Soviet influence and control.

The Division of Germany

At the Potsdam Conference in August 1945, the Allied Powers decided that Germany at the end of the war was to be divided into four occupation zones. The British, Americans, and French occupied the western portions, and the Soviets took eastern Germany. The intended governing body of Germany was called the Allied Control Council. The commanders-in-chief exercised supreme authority in their respective zones and acted in concert on questions affecting the whole country. Berlin was also divided into four zones, but the city was 110 kilometers into the Soviet zone, which would cause problems during the Cold War. A key item in the occupiers' agenda was denazification. Toward this end, the swastika and other outward symbols of the Nazi regime were banned, and a Provisional Civil Ensign was established as a temporary German flag; the latter remained the official flag of the country (necessary for reasons of international law as German ships had to carry some sort of identifying marker) until East Germany and West Germany came into existence, separately, in 1949. The Soviets also demanded and got reparations of $10 billion dollars from the Germans, though they were not allowed to occupy the Ruhr industrial region of western Germany, as they wished.

Cold War and Containment

In 1946, Churchill announced that an iron curtain divided East and west Europe; by 1947, a weakened Great Britain informed the U.S. that it was unable to stem the Communist tide in the sector allotted to it, the Mediterranean. Fears of Communist insurgent movements in Greece and Turkey prompted President Truman to address a joint session of Congress in March 1947, announcing what came to be called the Truman Doctrine. Essentially, the new policy of the U.S. shifted from relaxed detente to the containment of the spread of Communism wherever it threatened. Truman promised to "support free peoples who are resisting attempted subjugation by armed minorities or by outside pressure." In marked contrast to post WWI isolationism, global interventionism was now the declared U.S. policy. Containment—containing the spread of Communism—was essentially a negative policy that would immediately get the U.S. into trouble in trying to distinguish between foreign intervention and internal national liberation struggles. Containment also meant, as in the case of postwar Greece, that the U.S. would commit itself to supporting right-wing military governments and even tyrannical despots, as long as they were not Communist.

The Marshall Plan

After six years of war, much of Europe was devastated, with millions killed or injured. Fighting had occurred throughout much of the continent, encompassing an area far larger than in the First World War. Sustained aerial bombardment meant that most major cities in Europe had been badly damaged, with industrial production especially hard-hit. Many of the continent's greatest cities, including Warsaw and Berlin, lay in ruins. Others, such as London and Rotterdam, had been severely damaged. The region's economic structure was broken, and millions had been made homeless. Especially damaged were transportation infrastructures such as railways, bridges, and roads. All been heavily targeted by air strikes. By and large, small towns and villages in Western Europe had suffered little damage, but the destruction of transportation networks left them economically isolated. None of these problems could be easily remedied as most nations engaged in the war had exhausted their treasuries in its execution. A similar situation occurred after WWI, with the U.S. retreating into a policy of isolationism and letting Europe work out on its problems on its own, a reaction resulting in the rise of the Fascists and the Second World War. This time Washington was unwilling to repeat those mistakes.

In June 1947, Secretary of State George Marshall announced the European Recovery Program to provide economic aid to the shattered European economies. More commonly called the Marshall Plan; this was the carrot to go along with the stick of military intervention. It was feared that Western European countries might succumb to the lure of Communism, for which the best cure was prosperity. The reconstruction plan was developed at a meeting of the participating European states on July 12, 1947. The Marshall Plan offered the same aid to the Soviet Union and its allies, if they would make political reforms and accept certain outside controls. In fact, America worried that the Soviet Union would take advantage of the plan and, therefore, made the terms deliberately hard for the U.S.S.R. to accept. The plan was in operation for four fiscal years beginning in July 1947. During that period, some $13 billion of economic and technical assistance—equivalent to around $130 billion in 2006—was given to help the recovery of the European countries that had joined in the Organization for Economic Co-Operation and Development.

By the time the Marshall Plan had come to completion, the economy of every participant state, with the exception of Germany, had grown well past pre-war levels. Over the next two decades, Western Europe as a whole would enjoy unprecedented growth and prosperity. The Marshall Plan has also long been seen as one of the first elements of European integration, as it erased tariff trade barriers and set up institutions to coordinate the economy on a continental level. An intended consequence was the systematic adoption of American managerial techniques.

Since Stalin vetoed any aid from reaching Eastern Europe, it all went to rebuild the West, the lion's share going to England and France, with lesser amounts reaching West Germany, Italy, Austria, and the Benelux countries of Belgium, the Netherlands, and Luxembourg. It is important to note how revolutionary this was; before the Marshall Plan, the U.S. had never given any foreign aid. But between 1947 and 1950, the U.S. gave $9.4 billion. Yet there was a stick attached to this carrot: In return for economic aid, the U.S. demanded that Communists not be included in French and Italian governments, and we intervened in their elections to help defeat Communist candidates, who were getting a quarter of the popular vote.

Marshall Plan aid quickly became identified with the Cold War. Extremely successful, it allowed the shaky European economies to recover rapidly and soon helped stabilize the countries politically. One exception to Cold War the pattern was Yugoslavia, where Marshall Tito asked for and got U.S. aid, pulling away from Stalin's orbit despite being Communist. Yugoslavia became the only nonaligned Communist country. Stalin was furious. He expelled Yugoslavia from the Cominform, the new Communist International Organization, in June 1948. Then he clamped down elsewhere in Eastern Europe to guard against the spread of what he called "Titoism."

In reaction to what was perceived as aggressiveness on the part of the Americans, Stalin tried to compel the West to abandon Berlin. In 1948, Stalin closed the road leading to West Berlin, which was located 110 kilometers inside the Soviet occupation zone. The Americans and Allies responded with the Berlin airlift. Every day, 13,000 tons of supplies were flown into the beleaguered West Berlin, a huge effort that Stalin thought impossible. After a year, Stalin finally gave up his plan of securing Berlin. By 1949, the Soviet zone was consolidated into the German Democratic Republic, or DDR. The three western zones, in turn, were consolidated into the German Federal Republic of West Germany, with its capital at Bonn.

In response to Stalin's aggression at Berlin, the U.S. and Western European nations formed the North Atlantic Treaty Organization (NATO) in 1949. NATO linked the U.S. and Canada militarily with the Western European nations in order to forestall the threat of Communist expansion from Eastern Europe. NATO was headquartered in Paris until it was forced it out of France by Charles de Gaulle in the 1960s, when it moved to Brussels, Belgium. As part of NATO, the U.S. nuclear umbrella was offered to shield Europe. The U.S.S.R. responded to the creation of NATO with the Warsaw Pact of 1955, linking the Soviet Union with Eastern Europe. Also in 1949, the Soviets exploded their first atomic bomb, shocking the West. Finally, the Chinese Nationalist government of Chiang Kai-shek fell to the Communists under Mao Tse-tung in 1949. Communism now stretched from Eastern Europe across Asia to the Pacific Ocean.

The Cold War Thaws a Little, Then Begins Anew

Stalin died in 1953, which led to a power struggle in the U.S.S.R. Nikita Khrushchev eventually emerged as the new General Secretary of the Communist Party. At the now-famous 20th Party Congress in 1956, Khrushchev denounced Stalin's cult of personality and his reign of terror. Khrushchev immediately began to dismantle the worst of Stalin's police state, releasing political prisoners from the gulag, closing some Siberian prison camps, and eventually permitting more intellectual freedoms such as the publication in 1962 of Solzhenitsyn's *A Day in the Life of Ivan Denisovich*, which revealed the horrors of Stalinist labor camps.

Although it seemed as if the Cold War was thawing a little, Khrushchev's leadership eventually led to new tensions with the West. He created a number of crises over West Berlin, from which he was forced to back down, but eventually led him to construct the Berlin Wall in 1961 to stop the flow of East German defectors to West Berlin. While the Berlin

Wall fulfilled Churchill's prophecy that an iron curtain had truly descended across Eastern Europe, it did not add to the militarism that existed between the Communists and the West. But the situation would quickly change.

For eleven days in October 1962, the Cuban Missile Crisis, perhaps last great episode of the Cold War, threatened to hurl the world into nuclear war. Khrushchev rashly placed Soviet missiles on bases in his new ally of Cuba (just ninety miles from Miami) not long after Fidel Castro took power through a successful Communist revolution. President Kennedy was advised by his generals to bomb the missile sites, which might easily have led to all-out nuclear war; but he decided to blockade Cuba instead, giving Khrushchev a way out. Khrushchev eventually recognized his recklessness and withdrew the missiles. In return, the U.S. would withdraw its own missiles from Turkey, on the Soviet border. Khrushchev lost face and was ousted from power by the Communist Politburo in 1964, but he was able to retire rather than be killed like many other failed leaders. As a result of the Cuban Missile Crisis, a hotline was opened between the Kremlin and the White House, initiating a new policy of detente, or relaxing of tensions.

One major problem during the Cold War period was the decolonization of former territories held by the European powers before war. The British and French empires began to collapse around the world in the midst of WWII. But after the war ended, these states recognized that the old colonial system was outdated and more trouble than it was worth. This lesson came partly from rising independence movements. Regardless of how the decision arose, even the U.S. was moving to decolonize some of its possessions by the war's end. The Philippines was granted its independence in 1946 (although the U.S. held on to two major naval bases until the 1990s). In like manner, the Dutch granted Indonesia its freedom in 1949. India became independent from Britain in 1947, quickly becoming the world's largest democracy. But Hindu–Muslim conflict resulted in the separation of Pakistan from India by the end of that year.

With successful partitions made in the Koreas and India-Pakistan, a partition would also be tried in Palestine. Zionists had been fighting for the establishment of a Jewish homeland since the 1890s. In 1917, Britain became a protector of that dream with the Balfour Declaration, which stated the position that the British government supported Zionist plans for a national home to be established for the Jewish people within Palestine. After the war, Jews fled Europe for the Holy Lands, often with the support of the British. As the Jewish population increased, so, too, did clashes between Arabs and Jews. Jewish settlers who wanted independence began targeting British bases/garrisons in the area with terrorist actions. As a result, the British pulled out in 1948.

In May 1948, the United Nations agreed to partition Palestine between the Arabs and the Jews, giving Arabs the land that is now the West Bank. The Jews accepted the partition, but the Arabs refused, declaring war against new Jewish state created by the decision. In the war that followed, the Jewish army won a stunning victory, driving many Arabs out of Palestine, although some remained in refugee camps. Surrounded on all sides by Arab nations, Israel became a garrison state, firmly allied to the U.S., which encouraged Arabs to see the U.S. as colonial power in the region. Thus Arab states, like Syria and Egypt, aligned with the Soviets while Iran and Israel remained close to the U.S.

In 1967, the Egyptian President Jamal Abdel Nasser closed the Strait of Tiran to Israeli use, which led to another Arab war with Israel. Egypt's Air Force was quickly destroyed on the ground. The Six-Day War, as it is now known, led Israel to overrun Sinai, to take all of Palestine west of the Jordan River, including Jerusalem, and to take the Golan Heights from Syria. This was a huge defeat for Egypt, Syria, and their Soviet supporters. In 1978, the Sinai was returned to Egypt under the Camp David Accords, but Egyptian President Anwar Sadat was assassinated for offering peace to Israel for its return. Israel chose to keep the Golan Heights and the West Bank. After the SixDay War, the Palestinians formed the Palestinian Liberation Organization (PLO), a terrorist organization fighting to liberate Palestine through what they called the *Intifida*, or people's war—a major part of the tumultuous events occurring in the region in 1980s and 1990s, but that is beyond our discussion.

The Truman Presidency

FDR died on April 12, 1945 while he was in Warm Springs, Georgia. Harry Truman, his vice president, brought a complex personality to the presidency. He alternated between being cocky and being humble. It seems there was a streak of insecurity in Truman—a feeling of self-doubt. Perhaps Truman feared that he was not capable enough to do the job. Or maybe Truman was simply cognizant of the reality that he gained the presidency without being elected. Regardless of the reasoning, the way he handled affairs endeared him to later generations. Truman handled problems in a way that made you feel confident in his decisions.

When Truman became president after FDR's death, Truman assumed leadership in a way that disturbed a many people. He asked Congress to pass a twenty-one-point plan to expand the federal role in U.S. society, including the creation of programs for job protection and adequate housing, medical insurance, and educational benefits for soldiers. Later, Truman added his support for civil rights and called his program the Fair Deal. Truman presidential approval rating was 87 percent when he first assumed the presidency. Within a year, it had dropped to 32 percent and new sayings such as "To err is Truman" entered the political language. What happened to cause such a substantial drop in presidential approval? More than anything else, the change was less Truman's fault than a reaction to the reconversion of a wartime nation back into a peacetime economy and society. Most economic planners felt they could slowly bring the U.S. back to a peacetime economy while the war with Japan played out. But they did not count on the atomic bomb ending the war as quickly as it did, which meant adequate plans were not in place when reconversion actually occurred.

One of the greatest fears was that a Depression might return with the end of war. But it did not happen. Massive unemployment never came, and consumers continued to spend a good deal of money. Those two things, along with the G.I. Bill, pumped a continuous flow of money into the U.S. economy. Reconversion was hardly trouble free, though. The main problem was inflation. During the war, a system of price controls had been established to keep inflation down. Truman was reluctant to ease those restrictions, but when he did in November 1946, prices soared; increasing by 18.2 percent in just a few months. These price increases, along with shortages of food and consumer products, irritated many Americans.

Another problem Truman faced was an increase number of strikes by labor unions. As prices went up and the cost of living soared, labor unions began to demand wage increases. By 1945, there were 14 million union members determined to do something about their loss of income, especially since they were living in a time when business profits were doubling. In 1946 alone, 5 million workers went out on strike, closing factories and mines for a total of 116 million days of lost labor. The labor movement had allied itself with the Democratic Party during the 1930s, but Truman did not care. He thought it was his job to ensure the prosperity of the U.S. economy. Therefore, he nationalized railroads when they were paralyzed by strikes and he asked Congress for legislation allowing him to draft striking workers into the U.S. Army so he could force them to do their jobs. He also seized control of the nation's coal mines to end a strike led by the United Mine Workers of America.

Truman's actions pressured many workers to return to work, but this move infuriated labor leaders. While it did win him some support among those fed up with labor unions, by and large it hurt Truman politically. In the congressional elections of 1946, the Republicans seized on the phrase "Have you had enough of the Alphabet?" (referring to the countless number of New Deal agencies). This tactic allowed them to win majorities in both houses of Congress. That Republican Congress then passed the Taft-Hartley Act of 1947, which gave states the right to enact laws forbidding unions from forcing members of a certain industry to join unions. It also created a cooling-off period of eighty days before a strike could take place and limited political activities by unions. Truman vetoed the bill, winning back a portion of labor's support, but Congress overrode that veto and the bill became law.

All this turmoil erupted in the presidential election of 1948. Truman was the Democratic nominee (with Alben Barkley as his vice president). Truman faced Republican Gov. Thomas Dewey of New York and Earl Warren (governor of California) as the vice president. It looked for all the world like Dewey would win. The Republicans were solidly behind their candidate, while the Democrats were split. Southern Democrats bolted from the party over the issue of civil rights; creating a States Rights Party called the Dixiecrats and nominating South Carolina's Gov. Strom Thurmond as their presidential candidate. Truman ran a strong campaign, though, and was able to defeat Dewey. After the election, Truman tried to implement his Fair Deal, but Republican opposition in Congress and opposition within his own party limited its effectiveness; especially in regard to civil rights.

The event that finally destroyed Truman and the Democrats was the Korean War and the Red Scare. In 1938, the House Committee on Un-American Activities (also known as HUAC) was created to investigate Communist and Fascist subversion in the U.S. In 1947, that committee launched the postwar Red Scare by holding public hearings on Communist infiltration of the film industry. Numerous people in the entertainment industry were called before Congress to testify; many of whom were later blacklisted in Hollywood. By 1954, the *New York Times* estimated that 1,400 radio and TV personalities had lost their jobs. Hollywood reflected the new tension with movies like the *Iron Curtain* (1948), the *Red Menace* (1949), and numerous films in the 1950s *(I Married a Communist, Red Snow, My Son John)*. A new, growing genre, science fiction, also played on anti-Communist emotions with films like *When Worlds Collide* (1951), *The War of the Worlds* (1943), and *Invasion of the Body Snatchers* (1956), all of which depicted good democratic scientists fighting off an alien "other."

At the same time, labor unions began to root out their own Communists. Truman fueled this campaign by requiring labor leaders to take anti-Communist oaths. Phillip Murray, who was president of the Congress of Industrial Organizations (CIO), denounced Commies as skulking cowards and apostles of hate; demanding all of the CIO's unions expel their Communist members. Eleven unions that refused to do so were kicked out. Truman responded to all this hysteria by issuing an executive order authorizing loyalty investigations of federal employees, starting with some 6 million security checks. Many states followed his lead. It was especially difficult in universities. The University of California, Berkeley required 11,000 faculty members to take loyalty oaths and UCLA fired 157 who refused to do so.

In 1948 the anti-Communism crusade broadened. HUAC investigated Alger Hiss, a former New Deal State Department official. Hiss denied any affiliation with the Communists and charges that he had passed on classified information. The HUAC investigation of Hiss was led by Congressman Richard Nixon of California. The investigation culminated with the public release of the Pumpkin Papers (microfilm supposedly hidden in a Maryland pumpkin patch for the Communists to pick up). Later, the microfilm was found only to contain information on New Deal life rafts and fire extinguishers. In any case, Alger Hiss was convicted of lying to Congress and given five years in prison. His conviction is important in that it fueled the fire of anti-Communism.

Beginning in 1950, HUAC's role was, by and large, handed over to a Senate committee led by Sen. Joseph McCarthy of Wisconsin. He claimed to have a list of 205 men in the State Department who were known Communists. McCarthy was able to make, for a time, great political hay out of this claim. Later, when journalists and government officials pushed him to reveal his list, McCarthy reduced the number to 81, then 57. He never actually released a single name. McCarthy used the Red Scare as a political tool, and was able to portray the Democratic Party as soft on Communism. A series of other events lent special credence to his claim. The Korean War broke out in 1950. In 1951 Julius and Ethel Rosenberg were convicted of giving atomic secrets to the Russians. Eventually, McCarthy overreached himself when he claimed in 1954 that he had evidence the Communists had infiltrated the U.S. Army hierarchy. When he could produce no evidence, the Senate censured him in December 1954, ending his tyranny of fear and accusations.

The Tragedy of Containment

When the Second World War ended, most American military commanders believed two major changes had to be made. First, the U.S. had to create an integrated fighting force. The war-time experience of using separate military branches was that very there had been little cooperation among them. Second, it was obvious that new support institutions would be needed if the U.S. were to be successful in the contest with the Soviet Union. Thus, in 1947, Congress passed the National Security Act, creating a Department of Defense (headed by a civilian). It also created the Central Intelligence Agency to gather intelligence on foreign governments. Lastly, it established a National Security Council (NSC) made up of the service secretaries (the Secretary of Defense and the Secretary of State) to advise the president on military and intelligence matters.

Though the reason for creating an integrated force was to enhance cooperation, the Air Force quickly became the dominant branch in protecting the nation's interests around the world. This was best exemplified by the fact that half of the 1949 military budget went to the Air Force. When the Soviets exploded their first atomic bomb in 1949 and it became known they were working on a much more powerful hydrogen bomb, Truman allowed the U.S. military to produce its own H-Bomb, over the objections of some American scientists. Secretary of State Dean Acheson had the NSC draw up a new plan for national defense in 1950. That document became NSC-68. It called for a massive military buildup, including the pursuit of strategic weapons that could be used against the Soviets. The U.S. intended to win the Cold War at all costs.

Unlike the rapidly unfolding events in Europe, the Cold War developed slowly in Asia. The Russians controlled the northeast part of Asia and the Americas held the high ground in the Pacific. Both Japan and its former empire of islands were in the control of the United States. The U.S. acted quickly to consolidate its control over this region by preventing the Russians from having any role in the reconstruction of Japan. The American general in charge of rebuilding Japan, Douglas MacArthur, noted in 1949 that the entire Pacific had become an "Anglo-Saxon lake."

China, however, remained a conundrum. Outside both the influence of the United States and the Soviet Union, the Chinese were plagued by internal war in the years shortly after the Second World War. The civil war that broke out between the Communists, who had been on the run before the Second World War and the forces of Gen. Chiang Kai-shek, came to an abrupt end in 1949 when the Communists under Mao Tse-tung drove the Nationalist forces out of Mainland China. The U.S. did little in the years between 1945 and 1949 to prevent a Communist victory in China, especially as the corruption and mismanagement of resources in the Nationalist armies became known. Yet the U.S. refused to recognize the new government in China, instead recognizing the remaining Nationalists who had fled to Taiwan. For a brief moment, the U.S. could have made a friend out of Mao Tse-tung and altered the progression of Asian history in the twentieth century, but the fear of Communism held sway.

The first major battle between American forces and the Communist world came in Korea. When the Second World War ended in 1945, the Korean peninsula was divided at the thirty-eighth parallel, with the Russians occupying the North and the Americans taking the South, mostly in name only. The U.S. sponsored the rule of Syngman Rhee in the South. By 1949, most Russian and American troops had been withdrawn. In June 1950, the North Korean Army crossed the thirty-eighth parallel and nearly drove the South Koreans and the few American troops into the sea. Kim Il-Sung, the North Korean leader, had gained approval for the invasion from Stalin himself. Stalin and Mao (now a reluctant ally of the Soviets) believed Truman would do nothing, but he responded forcefully and persuaded the United Nations to commit troops to defend South Korea. The U.S. nearly lost the war before it could get involved. But by August 1950 MacArthur led a stunning amphibious landing at Inchon, leading to a disastrous defeat for the North Koreans. Truman's policy changed immediately. No longer was he willing to turn back the invasion; he was committed to unifying the peninsula and kicking out the Communists once and for all. MacArthur drove the North Koreans out of their own country. As they approached the border of China, however, U.S. forces were routed by a flood of Chinese troops crossing the frontier. The American Army was finally able to turn back the Chinese at the thrty-eighth parallel, and there it stabilized for the rest of the war.

The ultimate tragedy of the Containment Doctrine concerns the American experience in Vietnam. Since the Second World War, French forces had been fighting a losing battle to contain Communism in their former third-world Asian colony. As the French ability to contain what they saw as a Communist threat, but what in reality was a nationalist movement, came to an end, the only power capable of preserving the colonial government in South Vietnam was the United States. President Kennedy was reluctant to get involved, yet thoroughly convinced (as many Americans were) that American technology and firepower could win the day.

What became known in the popular mind as Vietnam was really Lyndon B. Johnson's war. Johnson's advisors in 1964 urged an increase in the American presence in Vietnam to give the South Vietnamese government a fighting chance against the Communists. Using an impressive network of trails and tunnels, the North Vietnamese supplied the Vietcong insurgents with all the supplies they needed. To win, the free flow of supplies had to be checked. LBJ did not want to become involved in a major ground war, as it would distract attention and resources from his domestic reforms. But he also understood what happened to Truman for "losing China." Thus, Johnson was determined not to lose Vietnam and decided to escalate the American presence in South Vietnam.

To get broader popular support in America, LBJ needed an incident. He found one in August 1964, when two American destroyers (the *USS C. Turner Joy* and the *USS Maddox*) reported that they had been fired on by North Vietnamese torpedo boats. In reality, no one was ever sure that it actually happened. Even Johnson did not know, but he used the "incident" to ask Congress for permission to expand American involvement. Congress gave it to him willingly. The "Gulf of Tonkin" Resolution gave Johnson the ability to fight an undeclared war. LBJ thus began to bomb North Vietnam. LBJ found himself increasingly isolated from liberals at home. When Arkansas Sen. J. William Fulbright published *The Arrogance of Power*, a criticism of LBJ's foreign policy in 1966, it signaled the growing gap between American liberals (especially the so-called "thinking liberals") and LBJ.

Unfortunately, the bombing plan did not help the South Vietnamese government. It continued to fall apart, and the North Vietnamese continued to send large quantities of supplies to the South. In response, LBJ started "Operation Rolling Thunder" in February 1965, a three-year bombing campaign of the North. Still the flow of goods to the South only increased. In 1964, the North Vietnamese Army (NVA) moved into South Vietnam for the first time. The military situation continued to worsen, and the South Vietnamese Army (ARVN) seemed unable to turn the situation around. LBJ's advisors, especially Secretary of Defense Robert McNamara, pressed LBJ to take the fight to North Vietnam, to bomb the North and put large numbers of American ground troops in the South. By July 1965, American ground troops were finally committed in large numbers. Vietnam was now America's war.

LBJ selected Gen. William Westmoreland to lead American ground troops in Vietnam. His policy was to bleed the NVA dry by producing high body counts through the use of search-and-destroy combat missions, artillery, air power, and B-52 bombers. The air war, however, proved inconclusive at best. Supplies for Communist troops in the South were often carried in tunnels or on bicycles down the Ho Chi Minh Trail. American bombing of North Vietnamese cities did not cripple their primarily agricultural economy, since most of their manufactured goods were being supplied by the Russians and Chinese. Unable to win in the air, LBJ gradually increased the number of ground troops, thinking that a little more effort would break the NVA's back. It never did.

In reality, it was North Vietnam that was fighting the war of attrition, bleeding America dry. Even though the NVA lost far more troops, Ho Chi Minh, the leader of North Vietnam, knew that if he could turn American public opinion against the war, then the American public would force the military to withdraw. In that, the NVA was successful. Many of the troops sent to Vietnam to fight were poor, black, and emotionally unprepared for the kind of guerrilla war they had to fight. Even more important, Americans were horrified by the destruction and death tolls broadcast daily on the evening news.

When Nixon took office in 1969, his main goal was to end the war in such a way that American honor was restored. The man most responsible for bringing about the end of the war was Henry Kissinger, Secretary of State. Nixon slowly reduced the number of ground troops (545,000 in 1969) to cut the number of casualties. In May 1969, he announced a new policy of Vietnamization, whereby the ARVN would be gradually strengthened to the point that it could fight the war on its own. By September 1972, there were only 30,000 American ground troops in South Vietnam. Nixon was not about to quit, though. In 1969, he secretly bombed Cambodia (to take out protected NVA resupply routes) and ordered a new round of massive bombings of North Vietnam. By the end of 1970, the U.S. had dropped more bombs on Vietnam than it had in Europe and the Pacific in WWII. Still, the bombing did little to stem the tide and the ARVN continued to lose the war in the South. Nixon ordered the invasion of Cambodia in April 1970 to ensure that the supply lines were put out of commission. Still, little was accomplished. The NVA remained intact and the invasion only destabilized the Cambodian government, contributing to the rise of a new Cambodian government run by the Communist Khmer Rouge.

The South was on the verge of collapse, so the North launched a massive invasion in March 1972. But Nixon acted quickly and took the war to the North yet again, in an operation code-named Linebacker. The escalation of the war led both sides to the negotiating table and some movement toward peace was found in September 1972. Kissinger, meeting in Paris with North Vietnamese representatives, hammered out a deal, but Nixon rejected it. The result was that both sides left the bargaining table, and Nixon was convinced he had to show the North Vietnamese that he would continue to bomb them until he got the agreement he wanted. On December 18, 1972, Nixon launched operation "Linebacker II," a massive eleven-day bombing campaign of North Vietnam.

Operation Linebacker II brought both sides back to the negotiating table, but the positions remained unchanged. North Vietnam wanted to keep some troops in the South. This time Nixon agreed. In the Paris Peace Accords of January 27, 1973, U.S. involvement in the Vietnam War came to an official end. Within a few months, the North violated the cease-fire agreement and completely overran South Vietnam. By April 1975, Saigon was in North Vietnamese hands. More than 57,000 Americans had been killed, along with maybe as many as 925,000 North Vietnamese soldiers.

American invincibility was shattered, having lost the war to what many regarded as a fourth-rate power. Many liberals regarded the debacle as an example of the failure of the Containment Doctrine and a lesson on the limits of American power. Conservatives argued that the war was lost not in Vietnam, but at home, because we lacked the political, moral, and national will to win. The liberal media and a collection of students had, in this view, torpedoed American efforts to emerge victorious.

The real tragedy of the Cold War was in the promises that were never delivered. The Cold War polarized the world, with the U.S. and U.S.S.R. forcing nations to choose sides in return for empty promises of modernization and equality of sovereignty. But what those nations really got in return was instability and uncertainty. The old colonial system of national domination had merely been replaced by one of ideological colonialism. There would be no neutrals, only those that supported Communism or Democracy. The Cold War created a new race to balance the power between the two ideological sides, and the Third World was trapped in the middle. So while countless American and Russian lives were squandered in undeclared struggles for global domination, millions upon millions suffered the consequences of that struggle in the third-world nations. The Cold War unofficially concluded on June 13, 1990, not through a great battle field victory, but with the official dismantling of the Berlin Wall by the East German military. The Soviet Union would collapse in late 1991, leaving the U.S. the remaining world power and opening up a whole new set of problems for the future.

Items to Consider

HUAC, Pumpkin Papers, Joseph McCarthy, totalitarianism, Iron Curtain, Marshall Plan, Berlin Blockade, NATO, Cuban Missile Crisis, decolonization, National Security Act, Chinese Civil War, Korean War, Vietnamization

Notes for Lectures
1 through 9

A World of Villages, Part 1: The Americas

America Before 1492

Ancient continent

Heavily populated, with advanced cultures

Not virgin land awaiting conquest

Native peoples not a counterbalance to "American" history

To be overcome by overwhelming tide of America

Progress

Technology

Cultural power

Westward expansion

Native America Before 1492

Extensive series of diverse civilizations, dividable into three categories

Decentralized hunter-gatherer groups and subgroups

Complex farming communities

Massive and powerful civilizations

Most wealthy and resource rich

Depend on vast trading networks for survival

Nebraska Grave—Trade goods from east and west coasts

Coming to America

First Americans

30,000 BCE

But misleading: Only a few Asians cross into N.A.

How is this possible?

World's water locked in glacier ice

Exposed land bridges located all over world

SW Asia to islands of Java & Bali

English Channel

Beringia

Definite origins

J. Leitch Wright (*The Only Land They Knew*)

People near Tampa, Florida in 13,000 BCE

The First Americans

Small bands

Hunters following game

Mastodons, bison, woolly rhinos, other animals

What did their world look like?

Teeming with game and abundant food sources

Until 15,000 years ago, NA had same wildlife as Africa and Australia

By 10,500 BCE

Spread from eastern Montana to Tierra del Fuego in southern South America

How did they spread so quickly?

And American Culture

11,000 BCE marks change

Rise of village life worldwide

End of last Ice Age

End of Pleistocene Era

Birth of modern era

1st identifiable culture

Clovis sites (NM town)

Characterized by large stone spear points

Stretch from Alaska, down ice corridor into Canada to far northern plains near Edmonton

Changes in the Land

Massive die-off of megafauna ensues when modern humans appear

Disappear between 15,000 and 11,000 BCE

Ice Age ends, climate and flora change

Why did megafauna dwindle?

Human hunters slaughtered animals

Associated with kill site evidence

Hunters alter landscape with fires and attempts at agriculture

Assisted by climatic changes

The Shift to Agriculture:

A complex process

Most plants useless as food

90% (+?) of biomass (grass, trees, leaves, bark) can't be consumed by humans

Many can't be digested by humans

Others are poisons

What is a good thing to eat?

Must have nutritional value

Be easily adapted to large populations (like nuts)

Must be easily gathered

The Advantages of Agriculture

Allows humans to produce large amounts of necessary calories

One acre of plants can feed between 10–100 times number of people that one acre of land can naturally produce (in terms of game animals) for hunter-gatherer society

Leads to domestication of certain animals

Sheep, cows, pigs, and chickens

But why domesticate?

Animals pull plows, furnish meat, produce milk, and provide fertilizer

Drastically increases caloric production of early agricultural societies

A Result of Food Surpluses

Changed the way societies were structured

Frees up some people to work in the traditional sense of food production

These specialists mostly monarchy and bureaucrats—oversaw food production on increasingly larger scale

The emergence of artisans

Crops/animals provide more than foodstuffs

Manufactured goods like blankets, nets, tools, and ropes made from cotton, flax, hemp, wool, hide, and bone

The Spread of Agriculture

Agricultural communities produce larger populations than hunter-gathers

North of Rio Grande, populations practiced agriculture in limited ways at contact

South of the river, there are several large agriculturally based cultures

Mexico and Central America

The Toltecs first complex agricultural society in Mexico

Agriculture in Mexico grew rapidly

By 2,000 BCE have numerous cities with permanent bureaucracies

Produce great temples and complicated social structures

By 650 CE, Toltec society dominates region

But not through conquest

Support urban environment of 200,000 at today's Mexico City

Elite group of religious and political leaders

Control trading network stretching from South America to Arizona

Around 900 CE, Toltecs expand militarily

Conquer Monte Alban, Teotihuacan, and Mayan centers in Yucatan

The Mayan

Around since 300 CE

Agricultural society supporting large leisure class

Mayan artisans produce fantastic art and jewelry

Intellectuals produce writing, a nearly modern mathematical system, and highly accurate calendars (better than anything in Europe prior to computer)

By 1200 CE, Toltec withdraw to central highlands

Replaced by new group

Aztecs migrate to area by 1325

Founded Tenochtitlan (now Mexico City)

By time of Spanish arrival in 1519, Tenochtitlan supports population of 300,000

The Aztecs

Produce wealth of manufactured goods

Build great pyramids to moon and sun gods (used to sacrifice war captives)

Build complex irrigation system

Have fresh water in city and houses

Markets filled with food and household goods from across Americas

Empire controlled over 5 million people across Mexico

The Peruvians

Andes Mountains, flourish from 900 to 200 BCE

Irrigated soil, produced endless types of potatoes, built great temples

Though earlier group (Chavins) fell to drought, Inka reached height between 1200 and 1400 CE

Aggressively extended borders to span much of western coast of South America

Warrior class dominated culture

Subjects mined great quantities of silver and gold, built immense terraced farms, and domesticated llama

Peruvian Society

Organize complex trade system to allow life in Andes

Three biospheres dominate region:

Coastal zone: catch fish and manufacture

Mountain zone: grow lima beans, potatoes, and squash; home of bureaucracy

Jungle zone: grow corn, peanuts, cotton, and provide wood; hunting

By 1500, capital has 250,000 people

Empire total 8 to 12 million subjects

Indian Cultures of the Eastern U.S.

Semi-Sedentary Tribes

Two major types

Semi-Sedentary/Woodland

Adena/Hopewell/Mississippian

Semi-Sedentary Tribes

Emerge after 1,000 BCE

First found along Ohio and Mississippi rivers

Large numbers of Woodland societies

Gradually spread out as time passes

Cyclically move from place to place

Yearly and seasonal

Focus mainly hunting and gathering

But also cultivate tobacco and corn to supplement foraging

Only domesticate small birds and dogs

Adena culture

Found along Upper Ohio Valley

First mound-building sedentary tribes in NA

Flourish to 200 CE

Eventually replaced by Hopewell, but very similar

Hopewell spread along Ohio and Mississippi river valleys

Build enormous ceremonial burial mounds, and cultivate few food crops

Graves contain materials from Gulf Coast to south, Great Lakes to north, and Rockies to west

After 900 CE, corn brought to NA

Hopewell replaced by Mississippians

Experience serious population increases

Centered at Cahokia

Had population near 40,000

Suddenly collapsed between early to late 1400s

Possibly when natural resources of region reach limits

Overpopulation cause nutritional deficiencies, and diseases (Europeans?)

Despite collapse, Natchez people of south preserve Mississippian culture until destroyed by Europeans

Historical View of Native American Cultures Before European Contact

Estimates of population vary greatly, hotly debated

In 1980s, Kirkpatrick Sale (*Conquest of Paradise*)

Charged Europe, especially Spanish, with 16th c. genocide of Native Americans

Most agree now that Americas had Indian population of 80 to 100 million

600 to 800 languages spoken in western hemisphere

Compared to Europe, Americas had remarkable cultural diversity

Who was where?

Between 4 and 10 million live north of Rio Grande

In 1950s, NA population barely 1 million

Central American and Peru

25 million under empires of Aztecs, Maya, and Inca

Introduction, Part II: The Nature of Africa and Western Europe: 1350–1550

Africa

Hundreds of distinct cultures and languages

On verge of major change by 1400

Like societies of New World

Highly productive agriculture

Stratified complex societies

Political hierarchy

By 1400, sub-Saharan Africa had population at about 20 million

Connected to Asia through Arab traders in east, and to Europe through Portuguese

West African Societies Shared Some Fundamental Qualities

West African Societies Share Some Fundamental Qualities

Use slash-and-burn agriculture

Produce rice, millet, and sorghum

Have strongly bonded extended families

Serve as basis of identity for both individual and community

Matrilineal families

Property and authority pass along female kinship lines

Women make most basic communal decisions

Crop production

Community punishment

Communal distribution of goods and services

Believed in polytheistic universe (animism)

Gods inhabit everyday items

Acts of hunting and planting hold spiritual property

Allow for compromises and agreements between man and god to be worked out on daily basis

Two Advanced Civilizations of West Africa

Ghana

Flourish from 6th to 11th centuries

Vast agricultural, herding, and trading power in region

Wealth dependent on mining of gold and salt

Prosperity attracted invaders

Destroyed by invading armies from North, mostly Muslim

Mali

Ghana taken over by Islamic Songhai (Mali)

Centered at Timbuktu

City becomes major administrative and scholastic center of Islamic world

Mansa Musa

Trade heavily with Europe, India, and China

Practiced advanced agriculture, maintain fishery harvesting on Niger River and Atlantic Ocean, and had immense cattle herds roaming inland grasslands

Songhai expanded by conquering agricultural villages in surrounding grasslands and Sahara

Height of power from 1450 to 1590

Western Europe Before Discovery

Relative backwater, why become so important?

Locked in intense internal competition

Dream of engaging in an external contest with Constantinople and Islamic states

Competition played out along political, social, and economic lines

Meanwhile, a rapid series of changes dating back to 1300 alters everything

Three Forces of Change

Plague

Warfare

Religious Turmoil

1. The Black Death

First strikes in 1348, but many follow

Bubonic plague, or Black Death

Kill 40–45% of European population

Destroy economic and political systems

Make labor scarce

Allow lower classes to gain political power

Worker rebellions scattered across Europe in years after plagues:

Jacqueries (1358)

Wat Tyler's Rebellion (1381)

2. Hundred Years War, 1337–1453

Between English and French, but less than half time spent fighting

Began when King of England Edward III (1327–1377) claimed French throne after French king died without a heir

Fought mostly in France

Ravages western part of country

England suffers little save loss of soldiers and political unrest

Richard II deposed in 1399

War of the Roses

3. Changes in Religion

Religion was the glue of Europe

But Christian Church, centered in Rome, in serious trouble

Plagued by corruption, inflexibility, and lost touch with people

Yet, great triumphs of 13th-century Church:

Crusaders conquer Holy Lands

Missionaries Christianized all of eastern and northern Europe

Moors driven out of Spain

Why Did the Church Decline in the 14th Century?

Competition between kings and popes creates crisis

In 1378, College of Cardinals elects 2 popes (Rome and Avignon)

Later there were 3 popes

People uncertain which pope held keys to salvation

Confusion coincides with black death

Leads some to reject Christianity outright: Heretics!

Others turn to cults of death, devil worshiping, and witchcraft

Also get interest in perversions of faith: the Order of Flagellants

The Rise of Secularism

Doubts over utility of Christianity lead to Renaissance in Florence and other Italian states

Mark by renewed interest in ideas and institutions of Classical world

Greeks and Romans

Later expand to interest in learning fostered by Islamic world

Seen as origins of modern Europe

But all major institutions originate in Middle Ages, or "Dark Ages" and not Renaissance

First Value of the Renaissance

Creates change in attitude

Where secular character of Europe emerged

Before, most important question was what a man ought to do to prepare for afterlife

Human frailty and dangers of life central to old way of thinking

But now life no longer seen by intellectuals as brief preparation for next world

Power of humanity characterized new way of thinking

These two ways of thought interact with one another in interesting ways

Lead to development of modern European or Western culture

A New Way of Thinking

Creating a new society

Before, adults act like big children

Spit, belch, grab food with hands, etc.

Now elites try to be polite and act educated

People believe they can change station and situation in life

Renaissance changed education

People divided into grades or levels

Teach language skills

Encourage social etiquette

Emergence of science

Changing the world

Older Christian thought fatalistic

God's plan dictates everything

Can't make lasting changes in world

Renaissance move people beyond that, especially elites

Begin to think they could create lasting changes in world

But more importantly, they begin to do it

Final Change Came in Politics

Renaissance creates new generation of leaders

Try to make their countries stronger

Want centralized, and more powerful govenment

Niccolo Machiavelli (1513)

Encourage leaders to act like old Romans

Answering the challenge:

Henry VII of England

Louis XI of France

Ferdinand of Aragon and wife Isabella of Castile

Renaissance ends around 1528 after French Army annihilates Rome

But cultural influence lives on

The Protestant Revolt

Before 1517, western Europe led by a single religion, Christian, headed by the pope in Rome

After 1517, the Christian religion split: Catholics and Protestants (the new churches, who split into hundreds of branches eventually, rejected the authority of the pope in Rome)

When Christ and His Saints Slept

Corruption in Church commonplace:

1) Pope Leo X (1513–1521), Medici family, received 500,000 ducats per year from the sale of religious offices

2) In England, Cardinal Thomas Wolsey gave religious offices to family who abused position

3) Ordinary priests and monks use religious authority to extract favors, economic and sexual

Abuses ignited a smoldering anticlericalism in northern Europe

Anger with the Church

Before 1517, complainers either ignored or condemned as heretics

Martin Luther different

German monk

Professor at University of Wittenberg

Publicly challenge church with 95 Theses

Widely reprinted

Condemn church for selling indulgences

The New Vision

Luther says forgiveness only comes from God through grace

Not from church or man for fee

Retribution

Pope Leo X excommunicated him

King Charles I of Spain (also head of Holy Roman Empire) threatened to arrest and punish

Salvation: German princes protect Luther

Sentiment for reform strong in northern German states

Mostly due to widespread hatred of HRE

Germans mad that emperor not speak German

Charles I dispatched armies to reestablish Catholicism and his authority in HRE

Luther Emboldened

Responds with broader attack on Church

Rejects four major Catholic doctrines:

1) The ability to win salvation by good deeds

2) The spiritual authority of the pope

3) The role of priests as mediators between God and the people

4) Luther says Bible was sole authority in matters of faith

Most influential was focus on Bible

Must be interpreted in native languages and digested by believers

Allows for multiple interpretations

Opening the Floodgates

Atmosphere sparked formation of Protestant religions.

Lutheranism, Calvinism, Anglicans

Calvinism—Huldrych Zwingli (Zurich, 1520), John Calvin (Geneva, 1530)

Differ from Luther in two ways:

1) Doctrine of predestination

2) Believed government to be tool of Church

The English Revolt

Henry VIII (1509–1547)

"Defender of the Faith"

Building a Tudor dynasty

Catherine of Aragon

Previously married to his brother Arthur

Daughter of Charles V of Spain

Anne Boleyn

Establishing the Church of England

Not create new doctrine, but some members of Parliament want change

Looks just like Catholic Church, except…

A Kingdom for an Heir

A succession of rulers

Henry dies in 1547

Edward VI dies in 1553 (son of Jane Seymour)

Mary dies in 1558

Elizabeth I (daughter of Anne Boleyn) takes throne in 1558

By Elizabeth's reign, Anglican church completely Protestant

Not radically Protestant

Retain most Catholic symbolism

England now defender of Protestantism, but only by default

Catholicism Strikes Back

Issue not settled

Catholic Church, wounded and splintered, not accept split

Pope pushes emperor to stop Luther and Germans

War ensues, 1560–1648

Catholic Church launches Counter Reformation

Want to reform problems of church

Need to eliminate Protestantism

Council of Trent, 1545

Northern Italy

Reassert Catholic doctrine against Protestant challenge

Expel abusers and end abuses in church

Religious war ensues

War and Inquisitions change nothing, as politics continue to control everything.

If your king or prince became Protestant, you were Protestant. If Catholic, then you were Catholic.

By 1560, divisions final:

Catholic versus Protestant	
France	England
Austria	Netherlands
Spain Portugal	The German States?

The Protestants had nothing compared to power aligned against them

The Catholics could have easily destroyed Protestantism, but they were divided

The wars of religion achieved nothing, but the consequences of failure would be immense for Spain

LECTURE 3

The Spanish Century and the Great Biological Exchange

The Rise of Europe

Changes in Europe reinforce need to colonize and explore

Not quick, occurs slowly

Exploration haphazard

Lots of starts and stops

Not all European nations begin expansion/settlement at same time

Portugal leads early on

Begins exploration, and trans-Atlantic slave trade

Portugal

Nation of 1.5 million

Not likely candidate

So why able to take lead?

Stable politics

Smaller size meant easier to organize and solidify power

Long seafaring tradition

Large fleet of merchant ships

Good location

Henry the Navigator wants water route to Asia

Seeking to break Arab hold on trading

European Arrival in Africa

Portuguese on the move

First to explore African coast

Looking for route to India

Culminates with Vasco da Gama reaching India in 1497

Bartholomeus Diaz

Born in Portugal, 1450

Squire in royal household

In 1481, commanded a vessel in flotilla sent to Gold Coast of Africa

Sail from Lisbon in August 1487

The Voyage of Bartholomeus Diaz

Blown off course by storm

Don't see land for 13 days

Realized at southern tip of Africa

February 1488

Rounds Cape of Good Hope

Want to go to India, but men exhausted and food supply low

Opens sea route to India

Vasco da Gama

Born in Portugal, 1469

Father held position at Court

Expands on work of Diaz

Left Lisbon July 8, 1497

December 1497 pass Cape of Good Hope

January 1498 at mouth of Zambezi

May 20, 1498 reach Calcutta

Returns to Portugal, 1499

Coming to America

Most believe Earth round

Globe mainly land

Atlantic just tiny strip of water

Cristobal Colon seeks western route to Asia

From Genoa

Convinces Spanish to fund exploration

Why Spain?

Reunited after long years fighting to drive out Moors

The Portuguese?

Left early August 1492 with 90 men

Land October 12, 1492 in San Salvador

Columbus in America: One mistake After Another

Seriously, I think the captain is lost…

Where's Pedro?

Is this India?

I dub thee "Indians," but sir we are the Arawak

Mistakes Cuba for Japan, then on to Hispaniola

The Birth of the Spanish Century

Colon "discovered" western hemisphere

Spain claims it all

Must get pope to validate

Treaty of Tordesillas (1494)

Divides world between Spain and Portugal

Rest of Europe left out

Why?

The Spanish Century

16th c. colonization mostly Spanish

Conquistadors hard men

Looking for wealth, plunder, and souls

Defeating Natives not too hard

Germs slay overwhelming percentage

Looking to the Mainland

Control Caribbean by 1511

Rumors of great civilizations to west

Vasco Balboa crosses Panama in 1513

The Fateful Year: 1519

Hernando Cortés

19 nobles and 400 men

Capture Aztec capital

Technology and Conquest

Too much emphasis on technology

Few firearms were relatively useless

Armor and steel only formidable technology

Real secret to success

Horse: strange and fierce

Dogs of war

Variations in warfare

What About the Numbers?

But still, Aztec nation of 20–25 million conquered by roughly 400 guys. How?

Disease?

Smallpox reduces Aztec population to barely 2.5 million by 1570s, 1.6 million by 1618

Spanish win through divide and conquer

Ally with subject peoples

Capture Monteczuma

Conquering the Inka

Francisco Pizarro moves against Inka with only 200 men

Takes Cuzco

Executes emperor Atahualpa

Steals great amount of silver

But half population dead before Pizarro arrives

Why Were the Natives so Vulnerable to Disease?

Lack of domesticated animals

No large domesticated animals in western hemisphere

Llamas, dogs, ducks, and guinea pigs

Most European diseases crossovers

Isolation

Europeans in contact with most of world

Americans in contact with only Americas

The Great Biological Exchange

Principle epidemic occurrences in Latin America 1519-1600

The Effect of Conquest

Radical changes for Africa, Americas, and Europe

Americas?

Epidemic disease destroys American population

Falls from 20–25 million to 1.5 million by 1630 in Central America

Inkas drop from 9 million to 500,000 by 1630

North America?

The Encomienda System

Forced to work plantations and mines

Forced conversion to Christianity

Cultural destruction

Wealth to Europe?

Utility of African slavery?

The Columbian Exchange

What is it?

Wheat and other Eurasian grains; pear, peach, orange, lemon trees, chick peas, grape vines, melons, onions, and radishes to New World

Maize, potatoes, sweet potatoes, tomatoes, peanuts, manioc, cacao, peppers, most beans, and squash to Old

Europeans bring horses, pigs, sheep, goats, burros, and cattle

Europeans also brought wheeled vehicles, and other technological advances

The Good and Bad of the Columbian Exchange

The Good

Arrival of more useful tools

New food sources fuel European population growth

The Bad

Weeds, Rats, and Cats to New World

Gold and Silver fill Spanish treasure houses

Disease: syphilis and other niceties

LECTURE 4
Inflation and Persecution

Background to English Impulse

England slow to colonize New World

Little interest, effort, or encouragement

John Cabot, Newfoundland in 1497

Trading posts and fishing

Significant changes at work in England: Leads to peopling of British North America

Role of European Affairs in English Impulse

Reformation, 1517; Cortés in Mexico, 1521

Events inevitably linked

Cortés makes Spain wealthy nation

Royal fifth

Wealth and monarchy

Philip II (grandson of who?) controls Italy, Spanish Netherlands, and New World

Seen as Catholic Defender

Must restore faith and end Protestant Revolt

Squanders wealth of New World in wars of Old

Dutch fearful: Will Calvinism survive?

Philip and their economic independence

The Wars of Religion

Dominate 16th century

Dutch Revolt ends, 1609

30 Years War, 1618–1648

And England

Elizabeth I supports Dutch

Harasses Spanish with exploration and attacks

What to Do?

Philip knows England must fall

Spanish Armada, 1588

Dutch independence, 1609

Begins 30-year revolution

Thirty Year's War ends 1648

Religious wars complete

Protestantism to survive

Spanish intervention in European domestic affairs curtailed

Spain in decline: 1648–1713

Great wealth wasted in wars

Causes massive inflation and price revolution

Center of power shifts north

Queen Elizabeth 1

1533–1603

Daughter of Henry VIII and Anne Boleyn

Takes power in 1558

De facto defender of european Protestantism

Wants to take advantage of exploration, but how?

English Problems

Cabot's efforts in 1497

England too weak to capitalize?

English fortunes beginning to change, but is it for the better?

Plague declines

Population grows 40% to 5 million

Price revolution:

Population increase plus currency decrease equals inflation

Changes life for most elements of English society

Consequences of Price Revolution in England

Nobility: titled landowners

See profound changes due to fixed rents on estates

Status decline leads to rise of middle class

Prices triple in 16th century

Gentry: landowners, but no title

Smaller estates, better managed

Yeomen:

Family farmers, profitable

Labor fixed

Wheat prices increase greatly

Political Consequences

Middle-class/yeomen have more power, aristocracy less

Viewing the shift in political power: HoC rises while HoL declines

Price revolution changes English system of government

All property owners get voice

Impact on America?

English Peasants and the Price Revolution

Peasants 75% of English population

Change has most dire consequence here

Increased prices lead aristocrats to want better use of land

Wool expensive, so want to participate

Enclosure Acts

Sheep fenced in, peasants driven out

Cotters move to woods or urban centers

Poverty encourages migration to America

Meant protection from poverty and debt

Possibility of land ownership and control of one's life

Mercantilism

Fixed amount of wealth in world

Goal: acquire as much fixed wealth as possible

How?

Maximize exports, minimize imports

Issue of raw materials...

Need for new markets...

Role of markets/colonies

Manufacturing fuels expansion, reinvestment, and dependence

Joint-stock companies

Investor buys in hope for returns

Jamestown, 1607

The English Religious Impulse

Persecution:

Dates to Henry VIII

Characterized by conflict in Church

Catholic/Protestant debate

Who would rule in England?

Leads to Civil War in 1640s and 1688

Reformers want certain changes

Changes in church structure

Want bishops out

Congregational form of Presbyterians

Want changes in church practice:

"Unspotted Lambs of the Lord"

Want "false teachings" to stop

Want to do away with icons and symbolism

Puritan Protest in England

Calling for three main changes

A) Congregational control:

Spiritual and financial control to reside in hands of local churches

B) Priesthood of the individual:

Abolishment of priests

Older Lutheran point about not needing priests as intermediaries

Religious education provided by state?

C) End religious rituals

God does not speak through senses, but through mind

Place importance on reading Bible and concentrating on sermon

Puritan Dilemma

Elizabeth I dies in 1603

James is brought down from Scotland as James I

Believes in Divine Right Monarchy

Hates Puritans and Presbyterians

Tries to drive Puritans out of England

Other separatists leave by choice

Pilgrims go to Holland, then Plymouth in 1620

Charles 1

Persecution increases

Civil War possible

Puritans leave for West

Massachusetts Bay:

Transplant England to New England

Expect to return when Church of England repents

American Puritans as Calvinists:

Sermons/Bible

Predestination

Role of state

Intolerance

So What Factors Led to English Colonization

Economic/religious issues transplanted:

Gives settlements their basic character

Aristocracy in decline:

American settlements led by landowners without title

Growth of merchant class:

Fuels trans-Atlantic economy, migration

Price revolution/Enclosure Acts:

Forces English working class to flee

Calvinism:

Puritans heavily influenced, carry radical Christianity to America

England's First Colony

The Irish Experiment,

1400s to 1600s

Jurisdiction of English crown since 12th century

The view from the top

Irish remain culturally different and inferior

Impressions of Irish creation of those guiding original Anglo-Norman invasion

Entrenched and polarized from 16th to 17th centuries due to reformation

The Irish Problem

The view from the bottom:

Want to retain Gaelic elements of population

Heritage, culture, and tradition

Try to avoid Anglicizing influences

And the heretics?

"An obdurate and dirty people…"

Cromwell (Puritan) believed Irish Catholics in need of taming

Establish comprehensive reform:

Education and persuasion

Reforming the Unwashed

Reform meant religious as well as social improvement

Want to make Ireland Protestant

Make Protestantism official religion

Forceful conversion

Catholics heavily taxed

Restructuring Irish society

Establish English-born, or -related, officials

Irish (Gaelic) landowners lose ⅔ of land

Conscripts, and Scotland

Enclosure movement, and Scottish settlers

Punishing Revolt

Subjugation and indentured servitude

Isolated on plantations or urban areas

Restrict property ownership and government participation

Make second-class members of society in own lands

Limit to laborer or lowest level skilled workers

The Irish response: America?

Coming to America

Sir Francis Drake

The Queen's pirate

Lucrative raids on Caribbean

Capture St. Augustine

Panama

Treasure fleet

Traversed the Straits of Magellan 1577–80

Walter Raleigh

Favor of Queen Elizabeth I

Unofficial commission to harass and interdict Spanish

Forced mercantile expeditions

Depredatory acquisition of exotic goods traded in Europe

Relative failure compared to Drake

Raleigh (and the English) learned three important things:

1) How to organize oceanic voyages

2) How to navigate the open seas

3) How to develop new markets for exotic products

The English Invasion of the Chesapeake

First Attempts at Colonization

1584–1590

Walter Raleigh

Undertook series of explorative voyages and colonizing experiments

Brings first English settlers to NA

Roots of English experience in NA

Firsthand evidence:

Narratives Richard Hakluyt

Drawings of John White

The 1585–86 Colony on Close Examination

Barrier Islands off NC (1585), re-supplied 1586

Goal:

Military outpost

Maritime supply base for Drake to plunder Caribbean and Gulf Stream

The settlers:

Soldiers

Gentlemen

The governor:

Ralph Lane

Experienced military man

Expert in planning fortifications

Colonists to look for, prepare for, and repel Spanish invaders

Spanish threat real

Searching for English base

Spanish mission in VA during 1560s

Depictions of North Carolinians

Early writers depict Natives as part of background or landscape

Just difficulty to be surpassed

Indians owned and occupied lands Europeans invaded

Had developed societies

Provide inroads that enable European settlement

Taught ways of growing crops

Provide new ways of fishing and hunting

Destruction left openings

Getting Along with the Neighbors

Native languages very

Different than Europe, more complex

Short-term relationships

Easy

Mutual curiosity

Natural willingness to learn

Desire to exchange gifts

Admiration conveyed in simple, nonlinguistic terms

Long-term contacts difficult

Occupation causes tensions

Settlers go everywhere, and take anything

Place strains on accustomed patterns of life and thought

Wearing Out the Welcome

Each society expected too much from other

English demand food

Corn, fish, and game

Don't understand fragile cyclical nature of Native economy

Indians at first provide food as expected, then stop when gifts end

Refusal leads to resistance and ambush of settlers

English decide must be repressed (like Irish)

The Wingina example

Ralph Lane killed, but not genocide

First expedition abandoned when Drake returns

Soldiers bored, and demoralized

The Second Time's the Charm, Roanoke 1587

Settlers (mostly family groups) and soldiers

Desire own life near Indian friends

But self-supporting

Not want to impose on hosts

John White

Had friends on Croatoan Island and southern shores of Chesapeake Bay

Most settlers want to move

Sailors refused

Why?

White reluctantly leaves them alone

The Problem with Roanoke?

The Return of White

White to return 1588

Spanish Armada

Roanoke, August 1590

Settlers gone

Settlement dismantled

Spanish ship

Where was the settlement?

"Croatoan"

No crosses, no distress

Death and incorporation

Autumn storms

Sailors, winter

Mystery

And the Next Settlement?

The Next Venture

Newfoundland or Roanoke?

James I

Spanish War, 1588–1604

1580–1600: Raleigh's reports circulating

Virginia Company in 1606

Chesapeake Bay

Algonquians (20,000)

Jamestown

Depart for VA in December 1606

Arrive 4 months later

Plant Jamestown

Early future does not look promising

First settlers

Hostile Natives

Environmental conditions

Starving time, 1609–10

Population numbers:

60/500 (1607)

60/900 (1609)

John Smith, the new governor…

The Tragedy of Early Jamestown

Other examples, 1611

Where are the runaways?

Powhatan refuses to return them

Attacking the Chickahominie

Indians killed, corn cut

Queen captured

Back at Jamestown

English need Indians and corn, destroy both

The Rise of the Tobacco Economy

English relationship with natives poor

Kidnappings, assault, theft

The marriage of Pocahontas in 1614

John Rolfe

Tobacco

Indentured servitude

The Growth of Virginia

By 1620, English exporting 50,000 pounds of tobacco

English merchants saturate their country, move to continent to compete with Dutch

Europe goes mad, but Virginia Company knows productivity limited

Tobacco and Development

Plantations

Must have lots of land

Need access to River

Need wooded areas

Architecture

Big house

Outbuildings

Work buildings

The quarter

Transportation systems

River landings and loading docks

Hogshead tracks to river

No towns of any size

Williamsburg

Norfolk

The Demands of Tobacco

Difficult, labor-intensive crop

Lasts from February through November

Seeds planted in February in beds

From February to March must weed beds

March–April fields plowed and sow grain for food

In June, tobacco transplanted to small, raked dirt hills

Plants tended daily

Cutting begins in August

Then dried through late October to early November

Packed into hogsheads of 500 lbs

The Problem with Tobacco

Depletes soil

Needs constant access to new land

Cannot use fertilizer

Dung and fish change taste

Floods, droughts, worms

Labor intensity 10 times that of other crops

Damn, Where Is My Servant?

Never enough workers

By 1670s, VA exporting 20 million pounds

Tobacco market falls off

Productivity and new lands opened up

Only difference for large producers

Labor in great need, but what can be done?

English not familiar with slavery, suspicious of it

An English labor System…

The Rise of Indentured Servitude

Thousands brought to VA as indentured servants

Why come to Virginia?

Surplus population at home

Many in great poverty

Price revolution/inflation

Forces many into desperate need

A natural way to solve two problems

Planters pay for passage in return for service

Service 3–7 years

Most not treated well, many die before indenture complete

Those who survive mired in poverty, but they have land?

Head Right System

Payment to landholder for workers brought over at their expense

Fifty acres, and tools when finished

1619–24: 4,500 arrive

Yet total population only 1,000?

1640 to 1700:

100,000 new settlers sent

75% of population indentured servants

Population shift causing changes to occur in VA

The arrival of families

No longer depend on Indians, so exclude them and drive them out

Need for another new labor system?

Virginia Survives

War in 1622: Natives attack, kill ⅓ of population

Company bankrupt

Becoming a royal colony

House of Burgesses (1619)

Continues to grow, 10,000 by 1640

Natives reduced to 10,000

By 1670s: 40,000 English, 2,000 Indians (of original 20,000 in 1607)

The Death of Indentured Servitude

Early VA more like frontier town than England

Sense of equality prevails, even though gentry erecting a hard class line to control politics

The tobacco quandary

Staple dependency

Production exhausts soil

Forces opening of western lands

Settlement creates conflict between poor farmers, Natives, and eastern elites

Frustration sets in

Bacon's Rebellion in 1675–76

Forces transition from servitude to slavery

Awash in a Sea of Faith

The Northern Colonies

 Stories of VA and New England differ from start

 Who came to Jamestown?

 Who came to New England?

 Pilgrims

 People with religious reasons to leave England

 Puritan families

The Northern Colony

 VA Company had plans for northern colony

 John Smith hired to explore MA in 1614

 But after 1622, Co. in trouble?

 The Pilgrims

 Scrooby, 1608

 Flee persecution to Holland

 Refuse to conform

 Company gives grant

 Financed in London

 Settlers:

 102 colonists leave in 1620

 $1/3$ were Pilgrims (Separatist Puritans)

The Voyage

 Mayflower departs in September 1620

 See land in November

 Storm drove them farther to north

 Mayflower Compact

 First constitution

John Carver (d. April 1621)

Land at Pawtuxet, and Plymouth Harbor

Half dead by spring

Winter

The Pilgrims Make Friends

Wampanoag (Massasoit)

Tisquantum

Supplies

An old village

Teach planting of corn

Plymouth Colony thrives and quickly grows

Focus on subsistence agriculture

When the Honeymoon Is Over...

Native relations quickly deteriorate

William Bradford

First elected governor

Minister William Brewster

"Savages"

Subhumans

Controlling the masses

Maintaining a Pilgrim colony?

Nonseparatists cannot vote (but must pay taxes)

Calvinist government

Remains separate until 1691

And the Puritans

Puritans soon follow

Create Massachusetts Bay colony

Want to reform Church of England, not to separate

But driven out of England

John Winthrop and Puritans receive patent from VA Company, 1630

Shares for Plymouth already sold to Pilgrims in 1627

"City Upon a Hill"

See selves as being like Israelites

The Puritan Experiment

Salem founded with 400

700 more settle around Boston

The first winter

Caves and tents

200 dead, 100 quit

Discouraged, but not deterred

18,000 in MA Bay by 1642

Why successful so early?

Families instead of individuals

Skilled workers, and leaders

Calvinism powerful tool

Gave purpose, and resolve

Encouraged education, justice, and democracy—within "reason"

A relatively strict society

Many social controls

Small localized settlements and government

Male church members

The Puritan Economy

Centers located at church and town meeting hall

Land ownership supposedly universal and equal

But class concerns emerging

Older families get best lands and larger tracts of land

Subdividing land becoming problematic

Declining soil conditions

Frontier too dangerous, so what can be done?

A More Diversified Economy

Dairy

Shipbuilding

Fishing

Lumber

Crafts

Shipping

All make up 20% of NE economic activity by 1660s

The Benefit of a Good Economy

Advantages

More wealth

Better conditions lead to longer life

Some reaching nearly 60

Leads to population explosion, but why?

Children marry young

Large families (8-13)

More children living to adulthood

New England as a result had labor surplus

No need for slavery, or indentured servitude

Family Dynamics

Patriarchy

Large families, but increasingly less land

Primogeniture

The son who never leaves home

Second sons?

Dowries

Emigration

Four Key Problems for Puritans

1) Religion

Uncertainty

Harsh beliefs

2) Puritan government

Native Americans

Threats to established order

Dissenters

3) What to do with future generations?

4) The influx of non-Puritans

1. Puritan Religion

What did they believe?

Puritans stress idea of Elect, or Saints

Church divided between Saints and everyone else

Who were the elect?

Everyone pious, but still unsure

Nervous, and fearful atmosphere

Can only wait for Millennium

Standards for church membership high and limiting

Puritan World View

World place where religion worked out daily

God and devil, angels and demons, at work in larger world

Belief in signs dictates much about daily life

Cotton Mather and lightning

Interpreters of signs become important

White magic and folk healers

Harsh Religious Views: Wigglesworth's Day of Doom (1662)

2. Puritan Government

Puritans democratic, but not tolerant

Salem minister Roger Williams

Separation of church and state

Relations with Indians

Land acquisition

General Court banished him (1635)

Moves south to create Providence, RI

Portsmouth and Newport emerge by 1644

Parliament gives charter for RI

Dealing with Native Americans

Pequot War (1637)

Pequot's trading with Dutch

Exchanging furs for guns

Winthrop wants their land

Use Indian allies to spread rumors of attack

Narragansetts and Mohegans

Destroying the Pequots

Puritans get land

Uncas gets slaves

And the next war?

King Philip's War 1675–76

Metacom

Not like Puritan attempts to control and manipulate his people

Wampanoag arrests

John Sassamon

Narragansetts

NY and MA attack

Metacom flees west to Iroquois

Puritan's parade his head around colony on pike

Ends Indian resistance in NE

Threatening the Established Order

Anne Hutchinson

Mother of 7

Attacks Puritan definition of salvation

Questions authority of Congregationalist ministers in MA

Threatens domination of male leadership

The Way to Handle Dissent...

Charged with heresy,

convicted of 80 offences

Banished to RI in 1637

Later killed in raid in NY

Ministers say act was God's retribution?

Others dissenters:

Baptists

Quakers (Inner Light)

Angry Puritans

3. Dealing with Future Generations:

Church and Society

The second generation

Those in declension (backsliders) grow more common after first generation

Membership decreases

Puritans become minority by mid-17th c.

Three reasons why?

Scattering: Thomas Hooker left over land issues in 1639, creates CT

Immigration: Success attracts more families, but also many non-Puritans

Covenant: Who can be member?

How can Puritans maintain control of government?

Maintaining Control

Second generation less committed to Puritan way

Children not religious, nor members

Elect fear minority status, so reduce church standards

The Halfway Covenant (1662)

All children of baptized made "half-way" members of church

Being one of the select now hereditary?

Sig: Marks moment most realize journey is permanent

Must create pure society here and now

Does It Matter Who's in Charge?

Puritans and the Millennium

Think it will begin in NE

Evidence for Millennium in England

Archbishop William Laud

Force new prayer book on Presbyters in Scotland

Threatens to send bishops

Led to invasion in 1639

Charles I calls Parliament into session

Asks for money, but refused

Royalists and Parliamentarians

Civil War (1642–46)

The End Is Nigh!

Oliver Cromwell wins

Charles I executed in January 1649

Dictatorship (1653–60)

Restoration (1660)

Charles II seems like anti-Christ to Puritans

The world looks prime for change, but was NE ready?

Puritan Cosmology

World place where religion worked out daily

God and devil, angels and demons, at work in larger world

Belief in signs dictates much about daily life

Falling stars

Cotton Mather and lightning

Protection from the Dark Arts

White magic and folk healers

Astrology

Interprets natural phenomena, movement of planets and stars

Used to determine everything

Planting season

Life decisions (marriage, birth)

Protection from whom?

People who claim natural knowledge threaten religious authority

Labeled undesirables

14 hanged in NE between 1647–62

Usually weak members of society

Witches!!! Everywhere

Salem (1692)

The troupe of actors

Samuel Parris

Tituba

Betty and Abigail

The trial

The courtroom

Cotton Mather

Spectral evidence

175 total arrested, 22 executed

Bridget Bishop

Why Did It Happen?

Boredom of winter

Wheat rust and hysteria

Class tension and the new church

Poor Puritans with unprofitable lands bring charges against wealthy

Everyone against new minister charged

Leaders seeking establishment of Salem Township charged

Part of 17th c. culture

Burnings in Scotland

Hangings in England

Alsace, 5,000

Does This Mean the Party Is Over?

Salem marked end of Calvinist experiment

Backlash against hysteria

Government open afterward

Increasingly democratic, liberal, and rational

Puritanism weakened, so splinters into congregations

An Empire for Slavery: The Origins of American Slavery

The Origins of Slavery

Ancient institution

Greece

Rome

Practiced in Europe, Africa, and Middle East for centuries

Something new about New World slavery

The Portuguese Connection

Portuguese exploit slave trade monopolized by others

First Africans in Portugal 1441

Exploring West Africa

Disease keeps them on coast

Spain takes slavery to West Indies, 1550–1700

The new agricultural system

Take land from Indians

Get labor from Africans

Produce sugar and/or tobacco

The South Atlantic System:

Triangular Trade

Important for 3 reasons:

1) Saps human resources of Africa

2) Sparks Commercial Revolution

3) Stimulates growth of British North America

Origins of the Atlantic System: Rise of the Sugar Economy

    Boom economy of 15th/16th centuries

    European sugar access limited

    Honey

    Beets

    The Asian Trade

    Hey, that cane tastes sweet!

    Europe goes mad about sugar

    By 1900, replaces bread and salt as most-consumed item

Early European Sugar Production:

The Plantation System

Bringing Sugar and Plantations to the Americas

But Aren't Sweets Bad, You Say

    The problem with sugar

    Eat fewer starches

    Sugar offers only simple carbohydrates

    Provide less energy

    Forced to eat more fats/sugar

    Body has less energy

    Health ailments increase

    By 1900, sugar makes up 20% of worldwide calories

The Sugar Economy

    Demands of production

    Tropical climate

    Wet sandy soil

    Requires intense, disposable labor, so need cheap source?

    Columbus introduces sugar cane to Caribbean

    Hispaniola and Indians

    Spanish bring Africans to Caribbean and Brazil

There's Always a Better Way

    Dutch take control of Brazil in 1630s

    Use talent to spread market for sugar

    Why was sugar so popular?

    Tea, coffee, and tobacco all stimulants

    Allow people to work longer and harder

But not taste very good without sugar

Dutch expand operations to Barbados

Let's not Forget the English

By end 17th c., English control most valuable sugar colonies:

Barbados

Jamaica

In 1750, Jamaica has 700 plantations, 105,000 Africans

Sugar Production and Slavery

Complicated, and expensive process

Fertile land and environment

Large supply of manual labor and heavy equipment

Requires huge outlay of capital

Participation dominated by plantation elite

But is it a good investment?

8–10% profits, little risk

French develop Martinique/St. Domingue (Haiti)

Why West Africans?

Region has long history of slavery

Many societies

Community

Family

Fragmented?

Advanced agriculture

Industrial skills

Overpopulation?

The Numbers Question

Africans represent largest immigrant group to Americas until 1850s

Outnumber Europeans, 6–1

Actual numbers uncertain, but hotly debated

Conservative estimates, 10–11 million people

Wild guess, 30–70 million

More likely, 15 million

But for Europeans, it was always about profit

Numbers and Destinations

When do they come?

76% brought to New World between 1701–1810

Where do they go?

½ go to Caribbean

⅓ go to Brazil

10% go to Spanish America

$\frac{1}{20}$ (600,000) go to British North America

Estimated Numbers for the Atlantic Slave Trade

The Demographics of Trade

Predominantly male

⅔ of all people involved

Aged 15–30

Mostly from W. Africa

Wolof

Mandingo

Hausa

Ibo

By 1700, Dutch challenge Portuguese for control of slave trade

Shift trade southeast to Angola

Royal African Company

1672–1752

Holds English monopoly

Founded by Crown

Want piece of the pie

Mercantilism

By 1700, English own 30 slave forts on West African coast

Actual numbers unknown

Company invoices to English Caribbean—90,768 in just 1 year

Stage 1:

Process of Enslavement

Europeans rarely act as slave trappers

Why not?

Powerful nation-states control area

Fear of the unknown

Disease

Then, how were slaves procured?

Warfare

Kidnapping

Territory in danger expands over time

Detailing the Process

Village raids

Marched to slave forts on coast

Long distance, hot, no water, bound

Examined by European traders

Branded on back and/or buttocks

Put into storage

Prepared for journey

Stage 2:

Middle Passage

Named by English sailors

Second leg of enslavement

First moved from coastal forts to ships

It's all about the packing...

Free standing shelves

Six feet by two

Spoon, overcrowded, unsanitary

Loose Vs. Tight Packing

Biggest economic debate of day

Economic philosophers encourage tight packing

Sometimes 600 crammed into 450-person hold

But was tight packing cost effective?

Trip takes anywhere from 3 weeks to 3 months

Enduring the Middle Passage

Locked below deck

Unbearable conditions

Poor food

Screams and the dead

May get exercise, but only in leg irons

Some jump overboard

Safety netting

Survival of the Damned

Lie in own waste

Most contract bed sores

Ship owners give orders to clean

Sailors seldom carried out

Morning cleaning and sharks

Ships abandoned after a few trips

Dysentery

Smallpox

Disease and fevers

Revolts common

Always feared on slave ships

Thus, locked below decks

Stage 3

Arrival in America

Quarantine

Cleaned up for market

Buyers inspection

Sold at auction

Divided up, isolated on plantations

The Cost of Slavery

Misery can't be calculated

Drains human resources

Equal number killed in slave raids

African economy destroyed

Goods only 25% of value of an individuals' production

Thus have 75% loss for per person removed

Africa in the Aftermath of Slavery

In 16th century, Africa independent

Dominated by powerful nation-states

Well developed

By 18th century, Africa…

Depopulated

Mired in political chaos

Stricken by war

Suffering economic disaster

Left easy prey for European nations in 19th c.

Slavery in North America

First Africans in VA in 1619

Few others until after 1660

What was their condition?

British do not recognize chattel slavery

Servants or slaves?

Africans twice as expensive as indentured servants, but serve longer indenture

Was Race a Factor?

The Early Years

Racial situation in colonies not defined

Intermarriage common

Mulatto population growing

Even have a few black slave owners

The life of Anthony Johnson

Jamestown (1621), "Antonio a Negro"

Bennett family servant?

1622 massacre

Commended for "hard labor & known service"

Moved to Eastern Shore in 1640s

Wife, and 4 children—status uncertain

1651, collects 250-acre headright

1653, Johnson plantation burns

Gets tax relief for long residence and faithfulness

Goes to court to reclaim slave

John Casar

Robert and George Parker

The Descendents of Johnson

Anthony Johnson dies 1670

Sons collect headrights

John, 500 acres

Richard, 100 acres

Make sizable fortune with cattle, hogs, and tobacco

Yet, still need patrons?

Forced from colony by 1705 Slave Code

Slavery in America

The West Indies

Sugar and death

Harsh life with many punishments

Massive importation

1708, 42,000 slaves

1708–35, 85,000 imported

1735, 46,000

Where did they all go?

South Carolina

Rice economy

Gang system

Punishments

Stono Rebellion, 1739

Pack of 75

The Chesapeake by 1700

Tobacco easier

Breeding wealth

The Tie That Binds

All NA colonies implicated in African enslavement

West Indies major market for NE

Bread, lumber, fish, and meat

Two economies tightly interwoven

Food for sugar

Sugar for English bills of credit

Or made into molasses and rum

Then traded in Africa for slaves

Middle colonies provide credit to buy slaves and finance slave ships

LECTURE 8

Salutary Neglect, the Great War for the Empire, and the Road to Revolution

North America, 1713

Other Concerns

　　European political history, 1713–50

　　Treaty of Utrecht ends Queen Anne's war in 1713

　　Cold war exists between Britain and France for next 40 years

　　And the American colonies

　　British focused on Europe and German States

　　Reluctant to impose policies on colonies

　　Period of neglect ensues as colonies nurture themselves

　　Fosters self-governance and economic independence

　　Lead colonists to challenge mercantile system

Two Georges and Sir Robert Walpole

　　Hanoverian Kings: George I (1714–27), George II (1727–60)

　　Instill government of relaxed colonial enforcement, mild rule

　　Political philosopher Edmund Burke calls it "salutary neglect"

　　Most identified with Sir Robert Walpole, leader of Whigs in Commons

　　Two Parts:

　　1. Lax enforcement of imperial trade relations

　　2. Seek enhanced freedom for colonists to stimulate imperial commerce

The Government of the Two Georges

Walpole rules through patronage to win support in Parliament

Patronage weakens imperial rule in three ways

Conflicts with American definition of freedom and liberty

Corruption convinces Americans that British oppose political liberty

Patronage weakens royal officials in colonies

Walpole Tries to Perfect Mercantilism in 3 Ways

Support Oglethorpe's plan for GA (1730s)

Refuge for poor and buffer for SC

But contested by Spain

Uses Parliament to keep America dependent

Navigation Acts

Outlaws American manufacturing

Woolens Act (1699), Hat Act (1732), Iron Act (1750)

Get Americans involved in Atlantic System

Carry goods between colonies and Britain

Changes Lead to Mob Rule in Colonies

Colonial Assemblies grow in power

Aristocratic families grow as well

Want control over taxes

Want equality with royal governors

Use mobs to intimidate governors

Power of royal governors in decline

Assemblies refuse to follow orders

Colonials protest Taxes

Prevent enforcement of policies

The Great War for Empire:

The French and Indian War, 1756–63

Before 1750, few Europeans in MS Valley

British rarely moving across Appalachians

Iroquois and French control middle of NA

But Iroquois falling into faction

Gift giving ending in 1740s

Europeans encroaching on Iroquois lands

GW Starts war

An Inauspicious Beginning

VA and PA move into Ohio Country

The Ohio Company

Robert Dinwiddie, governor of VA, 1749

Royal grant of 200,000 acres

George Washington

Massacre of Joseph Coulon de Jumonville

Fort Necessity

British government wants to stop war

Parliament War Hawks too powerful

William Pitt (The Great Commoner)

Lord Halifax (George Montague Bunk, BOT)

Unifying the colonies

Albany Convention, June 1754

Franklin offers Plan of Union

Continental Congress for western affairs

Never created

Colonies too divided

War Rages in the West

1755, Britain finally send troops

Edward Braddock

Marches 1,800 troops to Fort Duquesne

May 1755

Delaware and Shawnee attack

Braddock's force nearly annihilated

Sets off first world war:

Fought in Europe, India, W. Africa, and NA

Things keep getting worse

British defeated all over in next 2 years

Europe, India, Louisburg?

French American offensive (1757)

Attack frontier everywhere

Oswego captured in 3 days

Fort William Henry: 2,000 captives

Pitt Comes to the Rescue

Pitt becomes PM in 1757

Determined, sets forth brilliant plan

Use navy to bottle up French

Attack French overseas colonies

Use Prussian mercenaries in Europe

Send money and best armies to NA

Cultivates American forces

Offers merit promotions

The year of miracles (1758)

General James Wolfe invades Canada

Captures Louisburg and Fort Duquesne

Next takes Nova Scotia and Fort Niagara

On to Quebec

Impregnable fortress of 4,500

Battle of the Plains of Abraham

Defeats Montcalm

Secures Montreal by 1760

The End of an Empire

France forced to peace table, but nothing to negotiate with?

The Treaty of Paris, 1763

The British keep Canada

New France east of MS River

Spanish FL

The Spanish

New France west of MS River

And France's great empire?

Few islands in Atlantic and Caribbean

Fishing rights to Grand Banks

Britain at high tide

Won greatest victory over France

Support in colonies unmatched

First British Empire, 1763

Pontiac's War

Pontiac's Rebellion (1763)

Last act of F&I War

Chief Pontiac of Ottawa

Brother of Delaware Prophet

Led uprising in NY, Great Lakes

Why Revolt?

Indians suffering at hands of British

Lands stolen and limited gifts

Nearly destroy British on western frontier

But Pontiac defeated

British have new respect for Natives

Make fateful decision

Must limit western migration

The Road to Revolution

Britain after 1763

Strongest nation in world

Largest navy

Strongest, best trained army

Largest world empire

But Britain has serious problems:

1. The American colonies

Profited from war

Not participating in empire

Must end western migration

2. Must pay off new war debts

Can't tax England

Need new revenue source

3. Need to reform colonial administration

Establishing Order in the Colonies

Proclamation of 1763

No settlement west of treaty line

Revoke all charters for western lands

Revoke all land titles west of line

Angers colonists

Gives Americans idea they're separate and distinct people

Think British out to control them

Protecting the Colonies

British send 10,000 troops to American frontier

Expensive, so colonies must help out

Why put troops in America?

60,000 French Canadians

Fear another Native revolt

Some politicians fear revolution

See growing independence movement

Troops can't stop, but might stifle

Explaining occupation to colonials?

No real reason for troops

Becomes evident British willing to use force against them

Britain's Financial Crisis

Great War doubles British debt

Reaches £133 million by 1763

New PM (Bute) must pay off debt

But how?

Increase duties on tobacco and sugar

Establish new sales tax on luxuries

Passing expense to consumers

Collecting the new taxes?

Enlarge customs service in America

From 5,000 in 1750 to 11,000 by 1775

But doesn't this raise costs?

Expanding the power of officials

1. Broaden power to confiscate property

2. Give right to search without warrant

3. Establish stiff fines for smugglers

Paying Their Due

Sugar Act of 1764

Ends trade with French islands

Reduce tax on British sugar from 6 to 3 pence

Price below foreign sources

But sugar supply limited

Creates vice-admiralty court to enforce trade

1. No trial by jury

2. British judge

The colonial response

Expect to ignore, but British actually enforce

John Hancock

Furious over act and enforcement

Protests in MA Legislature

Tax to regulate trade okay

But only colonial Legislature can raise revenue tax inside colony

Shift debate from what proper in Empire to what legally constitutional for Parliament

The Stamp Act of 1765

New PM (Grenville) asks Parliament for Stamp Act

Must raise £200,000 to pay for troops

Place small tax on everything printed in colonies

Must use stamped paper sent from England

Expect objections, but what can they do?

Stamp Act includes Quartering Act

Passed at same time

Colonials to provide barracks and food

Violators to be severely punished

Outrage in America

Stamp Act mobs run amuck

Burn effigies of Grenville

Harass customs officials

Revolt rejects British authority

British at loss for what to do next

Americans move protest to the Assembly

MA calls colonial meeting

Stamp Act Congress (NY, October 1766)

9 colonies attend

Pass Stamp Act Resolves

1. Declare Sugar/Stamp acts unconstitutional

2. Say only colony can tax to raise revenue within borders

3. Beg George III to repeal acts, or they will embargo British goods

The British Response

Parliament in chaos

Some call for military intervention

But embargo threat leads merchants to call for repeal

Compromising with the colonies

Repeal Stamp Act

Sugar Act reduced from 3 to 1

But issues Declaratory Act (1766)

Says Parliament *can* legislate for colonies

Charles Townsend becomes PM

Promises to find tax revenue in colonies

The Townshend Acts (1767)

New tax on luxury items

Expected to raise £35,00–40,000

Pay some troop costs

Most pay salaries of royal officials

Includes Revenue Act (1767)

Reorganized customs under board of revenue at Boston

Makes it easier to collect taxes

America responds

See act as threat to colonial independence

Talk of embargo

NY refuses Quartering Act

Townsend passes Restraining Act

NY Assembly suspended until pays

NY gives in, but a line has been crossed

The Embargo (1768)

MA takes lead, February 1768

Boston creates non-importation movement

Send letter to Parliament and other colonies

Call for embargo

Not universal at first, but spreads

Sons of Liberty force compliance

By March 1769, boycott universal

Ending the embargo

MA letter gets to Parliament (1768)

Parliament dissolves MA Legislature

4 Regiments sent to Boston by December 1768

Gage seeks out MA leaders

But British repeal duties

Sparking the Tinder

Boston Massacre

Boston atmosphere poisonous

Citizens harass soldiers

Radicals vow "we will destroy every soldier that dares to put his foot on shore"

Troops moved about to avoid conflict

March 5, 1770

Mob marches on custom house

Sentry calls for support

Capt. Preston arrives with 6 soldiers

Mob assaults soldiers, chaos ensues, shots fired

Mob flees, but 3 dead, 4th dying, 5th fatally wounded

Trial finds soldiers not guilty, peace reigns for 3 years

The Case of the Disappearing Patriot

Paul Revere's Depiction of the Boston Massacre

The Tea Act of 1773

British East India Co. needed serious economic relief

Townshend Act added 3 pence per lb. tax after 1768

EIC cut price below Dutch tea with tax

Still profiting from sale

Angers Patriots

Scheme to make them accept taxes

SoL encourage folks not to drink Tea

The Boston Tea Party

Patriots (Revere, Wm. Molineaux, Thos. Young) board Dartmouth

Dump 342 chests into sea

Destroy 10,000 pounds of tea, or $800,000

Coercive Acts 1774

Crown outraged by Tea Party

Time for concession over

George III forced to act

1. Port Bill

Closes Boston Harbor until pay for tea

2. Government Act

Annuls Massachusetts charter

Town meetings outlawed

3. Quartering Act

Force MA colonists to build barracks or put soldiers in private homes

4. Administration of Justice Act

Royal officials only to be tried in Britain

5. Quebec Act:

Extends Canadian boundary to Ohio River

Establishes Catholicism in Quebec

The First Continental Congress

Committees place call for Continental Congress

Only GA refuses to attend

Remaining 12 mainland colonies there

Philadelphia, 1774

Declaration of Rights and Grievances

Demand repeal of "intolerable acts"

Threaten another embargo

Lord North orders Gage to take action in MA

Lexington and Concord

Patriots Day (April 19, 1775)

Gage ordered to take control of MA

Marches on Concord Arsenal

First shots fired at Lexington

Gage left Boston with 700 men

Wins both engagements

But return march painful

By end of day British: 73 dead, 174 incapacitated, 353 walking wounded

Americans: 49 killed, 39 wounded

Compromise now remote

The Revolution has begun!

The Long March to Boston

The American Revolution

Second Continental Congress

May 1775 in Philadelphia

GA not there at first, but later joins

John Adams has three major issues:

1. Wants Declaration of Independence

2. Need Continental Army established

3. Military to fall under command of one man: GW?

Debate over military shows political limitations of colonies

Colonial leaders distrust standing army (why?)

Prefer militia, but what would be the outcome?

Most more cautious about independence

To vote independence means treason

John Adams barely wins

Battle of Breed's Hill

While Congress debates, war rages in MA

June 17, 1775: Bunker Hill

3,000 British attack Breed's and Bunker hills

British disrespect value of American militia

But three assaults cost the British 1,000 casualties

The Olive Branch Petition

Some still hope for reconciliation

John Dickinson (PA)

Olive Branch Petition

Say colonies loyal to King George

Asks for repeal of "intolerable acts"

George III rejects petition

Declares MA in state of rebellion

Orders it put down

Congress authorizes invasion of Canada as response

Hope to secure 14th colony

Montreal falls, but Quebec holds

Parliament passes Prohibitory Act of 1775

Outlaws all trade with colonies

Americans on Brink of Rebellion

Most still believe themselves British

Process toward declaration slow and cautious

Three groups of people in colonies:

1. Patriots: want independence even through war

2. Loyalists: want to remain loyal to Britain

3. The Middle Half: want to be left alone

Pushing the South to Rebellion

Lord Dunmore

Chased out of Virginia in June

Hoarding powder?

Brands Patriots traitors

Declares martial law

November 1775

Issues proclamation

Pushed fence-sitters into Patriot camp

Josiah Martin, Scottish Highlanders, Moore's Creek Bridge (defeat)

Violence escalates, independence nears

"Tis time to part"

Events still in flux

Enlightenment questioned monarchy

But revolution not inevitable

Single pamphlet tips balance

Thomas Paine

Corset maker

Fired customs agent (cheat)

Professional rabble rouser

Common Sense, January 1776

"Blood and Ashes"

Argument based in biblical themes and geographic absurdity

Rejects monarchy and Parliament

"Tis time to part"

Calls for creation of republic

Over 100,000 purchased by July

Read publicly, widely circulated

The Declaration of Independence, July 4, 1776

Writing the Declaration

Thomas Jefferson

A Summary View of the Rights of British America

Attack coercive acts, mobilized Colonials

Makes Declaration justification for revolt

Blames George III

Says centralized government threatens liberty

The role of Adams and Franklin

Continental Congress evaluate in June 1776

Loyalist members withdraw

Give up floor to Patriots

Approved by margin of 12–1

Only NY held back

John Dickinson refused to sign

No Turning Back

Jefferson and Paine push uncommitted to act

George III effigies burn across colonies

Crucial Act

Broke psychological tie

Shatters British identity

But still must win war, or lives to be lost

GW could be drawn and quartered if caught, instead of first president

Declaration ends colonial squabbling, war only option

Britain uses massive force to crush rebellion

Future looks bleak for Americans

In 1776, defeat of Patriots seemed easy task

Comparing the Contenders

Great Britain

11 million people

Rich economy

Strong military:

48,000 soldiers

Money for more

Largest navy

American Colonies

2.5 million people, 20% slaves

Dependent economy

Weak military:

No navy, militia army

Short terms of service, undisciplined, poor training

The Campaign of 1776

North replaces Gage with Gen. William Howe

Ordered to take NYC Hudson River

The capture of NYC, July 1776

British send 32,000 soldiers

Supported by 30 warships and 10,000 sailors

GW had newly formed untrained army of 18,000

Americans driven out in August 1776

GW retreats to PA

Congress flees Philadelphia for Baltimore

Washington strikes back

Christmas night, 1776

Route Hessians at Trenton

Then take Princeton

Boosts American moral and gives Army confidence in GW as leader

British realize they overextended so retreat to NYC

The British Problem

Lord North not understand Howe

Cannot grasp why rebellion not crushed

Fail to realize would need long-term commitment

Increases taxes to raise money for war

Develop new plan to isolate NE

Seen as home of rebellion

Three-pronged attack converging on Albany

1. Gen. John Burgoyne to come south from Quebec down St. Johns

2. Smaller force of Iroquois to attack from west down Mohawk River Valley

3. Howe provides anvil to crush Americans

Sends force north from NYC

The Revolutionary War in the North, 1775–81

The Campaigns of 1777: A Failure of Leadership

Howe not like plan

Wants to catch Congress at Philadelphia

Heads there from Chesapeake Bay

GW met at Brandywine Creek, but outflanked

September 26, Howe takes Philadelphia

But Revolution continues?

Burgoyne moves south to Albany

Takes Ticonderoga

But force stalls

"Gentleman Johnny"

Horatio Gates

Attacks wagon trail

Blocks lines back to Canada

Traps 6,600 men in wilderness near Saratoga

Mohawk River expedition not coming, where's Howe?

Saratoga: The American Great Victory

With Burgoyne trapped, Americans pour in

October 17, 1777

Burgoyne surrenders

Americans capture 5,000 troops and equipment

More valuable victory than capture of Philadelphia

Victory assures success of diplomats in Paris

Convinces French monarchy that Americans serious and capable

Allows Franklin to secure support and military alliance

Spanish and Dutch follow

The French Alliance

Arranged by Benjamin Franklin

Knows France wants revenge for Great War

French foreign minister Pierre de Beaumarchais (Comte de Vergennes)

Persuades Louis XVI to give secret loans and supply gunpowder

News of Saratoga reaches Paris in December 1777

Treaty of Alliance signed February 6, 1778

France enters war

Will fight until independence secured

Americans to recognize French conquests

Alliance isolates British diplomatically

Puts British militarily on defense

War expands outside colonies

Legitimizes independence movement

Benefits of alliance:

Supplies, money, troops

American Problems in the War

1. Devastation of New Jersey
2. Anxiety in the countryside
3. Paying the bills

Problem 1:

Devastation in New Jersey

One victory, lots of suffering

Armies marching back and forth

Patriots flee British, Loyalists Americans

Whole towns switch sides depending on day

Soldiers loot farms, harass citizens, get drunk

Families live in fear

Problem 2:

Atmosphere of Anxiety

Patriot farmers beat Loyalists, destroy property

Neighborhood squabbling

Committees of Safety

Organized to collect taxes

Supposed to funnel food and clothing to Continental Army

Imposed fines and jail sentences on those nonpatriots

In some communities, neutrality not possible

Problem 3:

Financing a Rebellion

Congress and states cannot tax

Revolution was tax revolt

Congress borrowed and received foreign donations

Funds not even close enough

States create currency: dollar

$260 million issued to pay soldiers and supplies

Supposed to be redeemable in silver or gold, but too much issued and never backed

Congress issued money

Massive circulation causes inflation

In MD, bag of salt cost $1 in 1776, $3,900 in 1778

Leads to food riots

Economic troubles lead some to doubt cause and possibility of success

France and America vs. Britain

Response to French alliance in Britain

War already unpopular

Radicals support Americans

Gentry and aristocracy against taxes

George III outraged

18th c. domino theory

Lord North's seeks negotiated settlement (February 1778)

Parliament to repeal Tea and Prohibitory acts

Must renounce right to tax colonies

Appoint Carlisle Commission to negotiate settlement with Continental Congress

Offer return to system before 1763

But too late!

The War Outside America

France wants to hurt England

Try to retake sugar islands in West Indies

Spain enters war in 1779

Want FL and Gibraltar returned

Americans left alone

British have odds against them, but not lost hope

NE lost, but what value was it?

Southern colonies essential to South Atlantic system

Rich crops of rice and tobacco

So why not cut losses and steal the South?

The Shift to the South

Want to recapture VA, Carolinas, and GA

Strong Loyalist sentiment

Recruit backcountry farmers

Rivalry between Low Country and Easterners

Scotch Highlanders in western NC remain loyal

Racial issue

In 1776, Dunmore offer freedom to runaways

Militarily, slaves valuable commodity

Potential sources of manpower

Must keep men home to protect property

Does it work?

Difficult to estimate

10,000 evacuated after war, but not all

No slave uprising ever occurs

The Southern Campaign

Sir Henry Clinton

Replaced Howe in early 1778

Evacuates Philadelphia

Falls back to NY and prepares to invade South

Who was Clinton?

Raised in colonies

Enlists as officer in English Army

Serves in Europe during French & Indian War

Moving south

December 1778

British land 3,500 at Savannah

By end of 1779, retake all of GA

10,000 troops ready to invade SC

Continental Congress worried

Ask SC to raise 3,500 black troops

Into the Carolinas

British invade in 1780

One victory after another

May, capture Charleston

Clinton resigns

June, Cornwallis takes control

Tries to secure SC countryside

August, Cornwallis routs Horatio Gates at Camden

Southern strategy working

British control SC and GA

Thousands of slaves flee to British

Southern loyalists rally to king

Horatio Gates

Tries to rally support for Battle of Camden

Only 1,200 come to help

Most panic: Drop guns and flee without firing

The Road to Yorktown

Success in South not enough

Dutch/Britain declare war in 1780

French arrive in July 1780

Marquis de Lafayette persuades Louis XVI to commit troops in NA

French arrive with 5,500 at Newport, RI

Under Gen. Comte de Rochambeau

Gates replaced with Nathanael Greene

Divide force into small groups to harass Loyalists

The Tide Finally Rolls Out

British driven from South

Francis Marion (Swamp Fox)

Nathanael Greene

Cowpens, NC January 1781

Cornwallis abandons GA and Carolinas

Spring 1781

Believes Virginia key to future

Gets reinforcements from Clinton in NY

Marches into Tidewater

Benedict Arnold leads VA foray

Little resistance as move up James River

The Battle of Yorktown

Washington marches south

Meets with Rochembeau at York Peninsula

French fleet positioned on coast to prevent British evacuation

Cornwallis trapped

Army of 9,500 outnumbered 2–1

Yorktown, October 19, 1781

British war effort destroyed

"Oh God! It is all over!"

Lord North

No will to raise new army and fight longer

Combined fleets of France and Spain threatening sugar islands

Get no quarter in Europe

No political support at home

War effort collapses

War in NA over except for isolated attacks

Making the Peace

Diplomats argue for 2 years after Yorktown

Begins in Paris, April 1782

French and Spanish stall for time

Want naval victory against Brits and territorial conquest

Americans can't make separate peace

Abandoning our allies

Benjamin Franklin, John Adams, and John Jay

Angered by allies

Fear delay could sacrifice of American interests

Begin secret negotiations

Did we abandon our allies?

The Treaty of Paris (September 3, 1783)

Brits agree to everything

US gets independence

Canada limited to north and west of Great Lakes

US gets land to MS River

No protection for British Indian allies

Only American concessions:

Loyalists get property back and equal treatment/citizenship

Allies make separate peace

France gets Tobago

National debt increased by 400%

Creates financial crisis which sparks revolution 6 years later

Spain gets Florida, but not Gibraltar

North America, 1783

Notes for Lectures 10 through 17

LECTURE 10

The Early Republic: Confederation, Constitution, and the Federalist Nation

Who Will Rule America?

Revolution about home rule

Military victory over British in 1783

But second struggle takes much longer

Fight over nature and character of early Constitution and government

Political theories plus practical politics

Elite vs. commoners?

The Democratic-Republican Impulse

Patriots create state governments based on popular rule

Declaration of Independence:

Power of government depend on consent of governed

Radicals call for democracy

Democratic-Republicanism

All who helped win war should have voice

Popular in NE

Pennsylvania in 1776

End property qualifications in voting and office holding

Extend vote to all taxpayers

PA Constitution

Mandate elementary education for all white males

No imprisonment for debt

John Adams and Democracy

Many alarmed by PA Constitution

Don't believe in democracy

Fear underclass abuse numerical advantage

John Adams

Denounce PA example and democratic governments

Thoughts on Government (April 1776)

Traditional mixed government in republican terms

Three distinct branches:

Like British system except no king

Divided by functions, not social lines

Lawmaking, administering, judging

Divided house (lower and upper)

Ensures check on Democracy

Adams model used for most new state governments

Applying the *Thoughts*

New York example (John Jay)

Mixed government

Bi-cameral legislature

Governor

Appointed judiciary

Property qualifications for voting, office holding

Means only 40% able to vote

South Carolina (1778)

Mixed government with a twist

Restrict participation with high demands on net worth

Governor $450K, senator $90K, assemblyman $45K

Prevents 90% of white males from holding office

Property or Democracy?

Slowly states become more democratic

Two reasons:

1. Most have lower house based on population

Favors western and yeoman farmers

2. Political consciousness of masses intrigued by Revolution

Militia elected officers, so extend to politicians

The changing political landscape

Before war, 85% of assemblymen wealthy (averaging $90,000)

After war, lower houses of NY, NH, NJ controlled by farmers

Dominate in VA, MA, and SC

State capitals move west:

NYC to Albany

Philadelphia to Harrisburg

Charlestown to Columbia

Conservatives maintain control, but barely

Articles of Confederation

November 15, 1777, John Dickinson

States retain powers not given to fed government

Congress center of structure

Each state has 1 vote

No president or supreme court

Makes war and peace

Resolves differences

Borrows or prints money

Problems for the Articles

1. Western land claims

Continental Congress control land issues between states, but not western lands

2. Financial failure

Can't tax

Must beg states for money

3. All 13 had to agree to changes

One state could veto taxes, tariffs

Some Measure of Success

Only success came with Western claims

1. Asserts titles

Government to sell land to pay expenses

2. Ties West to US

An American colonial empire?

Congress control NW Territory

NW Ordinance, 1787 (Jefferson):

Rules dictating pattern of settlement

Establish grid system to survey land

Survey, settle, then build government

Once get 60,000

Write Constitution

Apply for admission

DE 59,000 in 1790

Create 5 states, but no slavery

OH, IN, IL, MI, WI

Shays' Rebellion and the Crisis of 1786

The elusiveness of prosperity

Trade disrupted and markets destroyed

Limited manufacturing base

Merchant fleet destroyed

States have high debts and worthless paper money

NC owed $1.7 million, VA $2.7 million

Farmers in poor shape

No debtor relief and high taxes

Creditors and sheriffs drag farmers into court

1786 angry farmers close courts and release debtors

Resistance grows into full-scale revolt

Led by Daniel Shays (captain in Continental Army)

Shays' Rebellion

Tax protest like Revolution

Governor and merchants raise army

Winter of 1786–87, rioters dispersed

The Constitution of 1787

Shays' Rebellion awakens Nationalists

Confederation too weak to deal with problems

Worry about democracy in state Legislatures

Must protect rights of minority (themselves)

Commerce and borders?

Includes figures like GW and Hamilton

Alexander Hamilton

West Indies merchant's son

Legal training in NYC

Married into rich family

GW's aide

Asks Congress for convention to be held in spring of 1787

Confederation Congress, or Constitutional Convention?

Philadelphia Convention, May 1787

All but RI attend

Many people not there

T. Jefferson and J. Adams in Europe

Patrick Henry refused to go

Who was there?

GW, Franklin, Madison, and Mason

Delegates as group educated

Many trained in law

Experienced in Congress or war

$\frac{1}{3}$ own slaves

No commoners or others

GW chairs

Debates held in secret

James Madison's Virginia Plan

Madison wants Articles abolished to form new government

Need national government rather than collection of states

States have little power

Federal government has power and makes laws for entire nation

The VA Plan offers mixed government thru bicameral legislature

Lower House apportioned on population by vote

Upper House elected by Lower House

President and judges appointed by both

Three ways VA Plan differed from Articles:

1. Based on popular sovereignty, not will of individual states

2. Creates republic based on power coming from individuals, not states

3. Establishes the 3 branches of government

The New Jersey Plan

VA plan controversial

Gives too much power to Congress

Large states like, but NJ, DE, and CT fight

Undermines power because ends 1 Rep. CC

William Patterson offers NJ Plan

Revises Articles

Congress gets new power

Raise money, control commerce, and force states to contribute

Want to preserve balance between states with 1 vote

Large states reject

Convention agree on VA plan for purpose of debate

NY Reps leave

Rest work 6 day/week thru long hot summer of 1787

Try to make everyone happy to ensure ratification

Thus, all participants agree they didn't make *best* Constitution

The Great Compromise

How should states be represented?

CT offers compromise

Senate to have 2 members from each state

HoR based on population determined by census

Some large states have reservations, but give in

Placating those afraid of national government

President elected thru states by creation of electoral college

Senators elected by state Legislatures (would last until 1913)

Federal courts review, and Supreme Court gets final say

The Constitution and Slavery

Only major issue defined by north-south split

Other issues were big state vs. small state

Why not abolition?

Some noise about slave trade

But delegates give in to South, why?

Results in slavery being protected in 3 ways:

1. Fugitive Slave clause

2. 20 year prohibition on abolition of slave trade

3. $3/5$th Compromise

The Final Document

Final document was drastic revision of Articles

Constitution to be supreme law of land

Government gets broad powers over taxation, defense, and trade

State powers severely limited

Franklin knew it was flawed, but best chance for ratification

Ratification

38 of 41 delegates left signed document

Violate law

Constitution go into effect when ratified by 9 of 13

Only way to deal with problem of RI

Ratification

Constitution goes to states (December 1787–June 1788)

First test: MA, December 1787

Strong antifederalist sentiment

Western farmers put up resistance

Shays supporters publicly oppose

Sam Adams and Gov. John Hancock use scare tactics

Narrowly win 187–168

NH ratifies, June 1788

Makes 9

But outcome still uncertain

NY and VA, or nothing

Both still haven't ratified

Federalists promise Bill of Rights

Undermine concern about individual liberty being at risk

Eventually win VA, 89–79

NY follows suit, barely, 30–27

RI pressured into joining in May 1790

The First Government

Ratification led to elections

First Congress

President

Spring of 1789, government moves to NY

Federalists dominate early government

First U.S. Congress

44 (out of 91) had some role in Constitution

Washington (57), President

John Adams, vice president

Hamilton leads Treasury

Bill of Rights enacted, quiets opposition

Origins of the Supreme Court

US court system emerges from legislation

Judiciary Act of 1789

Creates system of federal courts

Supreme Court (6, then 9 justices) created

Reviews appealed state rulings

Power expands over time

John Jay led first course

Chisholm v. GA (1793)

Jay sides with citizens against GA

Undermines idea that state can't be sued without consent

Hylton v. US (1796)

Law declared constitutional

First time Court reviewed act of Congress

Court's main role today

Hamilton's Great Dream

Though some prosperity, many believe US economy needs firm foundation

US debt still high, bankruptcy possible

Tariff of 1789

First way for government to raise revenue

Remain most important source of revenue until 20th c.

Report on Public Credit (1790)

Assumption Plan

US assumes debts of states and pays with interest-bearing bonds

Establish excise tax on liquor

Internal fee for producing something for domestic sale

Trying to encourage foreign investment

Plans to redeem Confederation stock at face value

Speculators hold most of it, including many of Hamilton's friends

Madison outraged

Hamilton buys off VA and MD with placement of capital

A National Bank

The Bank Address (December 1790)

Congress to create Central Banking Authority

Establishes Bank of United States

Public institution, but privately financed

Holds federal government deposit

Treasury's arm of economic policy

Make loans, issue notes, and handle accounts of the country

Service needed to cope with market revolution

Madison and Jefferson believed Bank unconstitutional

Two opposing views

Strict Construction

If not in Constitution, then not possible

Loose Construction

Art. I, Sect. 8: Congress can make all laws necessary and proper

Hamilton favors Loose Construction

GW sign Bank Bill into law

First bank established in Philadelphia

Assisting Manufacturers

Report on Manufactures (December 1791)

Vision of America as industrial civilization

Government should promote industry and protect with tariffs

US tied to Atlantic and Britain via laissez faire capitalism

Mercantilism is dead

Embracing Adam Smith's *Wealth of Nations*, 1776

Controlling Foreign Influences

Citizen Genet

French Ambassador Edmond

Genet arrives in SC, April 1793

Travels US

Stirs pro-French and pro-Republican passions

Attracts large following

Many still hate British and admire Republican France

Conservatives believe pro-French policy will hurt US economy

Washington declares US neutrality in 1793

Angers T. Jefferson and Anti-Federalists

Create democratic societies

Modeled after Jacobin Clubs in Paris

Philadelphia Dinner

Conservative fears

The First Domestic Problem: The Whiskey Rebellion

Uprising in 1794

Farmers angry about Hamilton's excise tax on whiskey

Depend on Whiskey for profits

Upset with wealthy PA land barons

Squatters treated poorly

GW leads 13,000 troops to quash revolt

20 arrested

Charged with treason

The British Blockade

First major problem in foreign affairs

British issue blockade in 1793

No trade with France

In 2 years, seize 250 US ships

John Jay sent to negotiate, fall 1794

The Jay Treaty, 1795

British withdraw from Western lands

Most-favored-nation status

But blockade continues

By 1795, US ends Spanish claims to Southeast

Spain defeated by French, so weak militarily and fiscally

Thomas Pinckney gets Spain to accept boundary at 31st parallel

Opens MS River to American shipping

Gives US complete control over West

The Adams Presidency

Adams wins in 1796

Jefferson second

Election contested

Decided by Congress

Adams as President

Pro-British policy

Condemns French seizure of US ships

Claim French meddling in US domestic affairs

Tries to negotiate with Talleyrand (foreign minister)

Agents (XYZ) demand 250,000 bribe before negotiations begin

Adams sees American honor attacked

Congress cuts off trade and allows seizure of French ships

US officially allied with Britain, 1798–1800

Begins undeclared war with France

Adam's Great Mistakes

Adams under siege from Irish newspapermen living in US

Alien Act of 1798: deportation of foreigners

Naturalization Act: residence requirement increased from 5 to 14 years

Sedition Act: illegal to publish attacks on Congress and government

20 Republican newspaper editors and publishers arrested

Mathew Lyon, VT representative, reelected from prison

Republican Response

First Amendment violated, but Supreme Court in Federalist hands

Madison and Jefferson begin to write

Virginia and Kentucky Resolves (1798)

Declare Alien and Sedition Acts null and void

Say unenforceable within individual states

Establishes Nullification Doctrine

Election of 1800

Debate over Alien & Sedition Act sets stage for election

T. Jefferson points at wrongful imprisonment

Claims to be champion of states' rights

Adams ends war with France

Federalists depict T. Jefferson as Jacobin

The election results

Republicans swept into power

Win both House and Senate

Jefferson and Burr tie at 73

Presidential ballot ties for 35 ballots

The Revolution of 1800

First bloodless transition of power

Federalists fading from national scene

Never again hold presidency

No longer party by 1816

The Agrarian Republic

Revolution of 1800

Thomas Jefferson (1743–1826)

Enlightenment thinker

Seasoned diplomat, politician, and political philosopher

President, 1800–1808

First term

Tries to appease Federalists by naming 3 to cabinet

First president to occupy DC

Stacking the Cards

After 12 years of Federalist presidents, government saturated with Federalists

Dominate administration and Supreme Court

John Marshall, 1801

Last appointment by Adams

The Midnight Appointments

John Adams packs court system with Judiciary Act of 1801

President takes office March

John Adams fills court vacancies just before T. Jefferson takes office

Samuel Chase appointed to Supreme Court

Even lower courts filled

Republicans in Congress outraged

Repeal Judiciary Act

Dismiss Adams' appointees

Try to impeach Samuel Chase

Moderation Rules the Day

Jefferson disturbed by radicals

Calls for moderation

Believed ruling party should control ½ to ⅔ of appointed offices

Only removes 109 of 433 Federalist officeholders in 8 years

Almost ½ from Midnight Appointees

A New Vision of America

T. Jefferson has different vision of America

Government too big and powerful

Refuses to renew Alien & Sedition Acts in 1801

Amends Naturalization Act

Waiting period pushed back to 5 years

Alters Federalist foreign policy

Barbary Pirates

Tunis, Morocco, Tripoli, Algiers

Changes in domestic policy

Abolishes internal taxes

Reduces size of government and Army

Accepts Bank as necessary to health and development of economy

Wants to redirect the American nation

Shifts attention from Eastern bankers and markets to West

Another reason election of 1800 seen as revolutionary

The Agrarian Nation

T. Jefferson wants to create/preserve an agricultural nation

Tries to help Western farmers

Problems in NW

Speculators control land

Due to flaws of the Ordinance

$1/acre minimum

½ townships sold in blocks of 23,000 acres, who can afford that?

Rest sold in 640 acre blocks

Federalist Land Act of 1796

Changed price to $2 to put land with speculators

Republican Congress changes Ordinance

Pass law to help cash-poor yeomen

Reduce minimum size to 320 acres, then 160 (1800)

Allow installment payments up to 4 years (1804)

Problems in Foreign Affairs

T. Jefferson tries to pull away from Europe

Napoleon Bonaparte

1799, takes power in France

Creates French empire

In 1800, gets LA from Spanish

In 1802, restricts US access to New Orleans

Sends Army to restore Haiti, (1791–93)

Wants to establish American empire

T. Jefferson must reconsider pro-French stance

New Orleans crucial to American development

Napoleon ends American traffic down MS

T. Jefferson uncertain, but takes 2 steps:

Robert Livingston tries to buy New Orleans

US minister in Paris

James Monroe sent to Britain to ask for help in case France and US go to war

Former congressman and VA governor

The Louisiana Purchase

French invasion of Haiti falters in 1802

Spirited black resistance, yellow fever

Napoleon stretched thin in Europe

Dealing with Napoleon

Knows if British win Europe, then US will invade Louisiana

Abandons American empire

April 1803

Offers New Orleans and entire Louisiana territory

$15 million (about $180 million today)

Livingstone and Monroe (who joined him in Paris) jump on deal

Doubles size of US

Senate ratifies 26–6

T. Jefferson and the Louisiana Purchase

Size overwhelms him

Has reservations about Loose Construction and Implied Powers

Contradiction between belief and practice

Dreams of Western empire, but also pragmatic

Federalists criticism harsh

Violates Republican principles

Examining the Purchase

In 1803, government knows nothing about LA territory

T. Jefferson wants detailed information on region:

Physical features

Plant and animal life

Indians

The Expedition

Meriwether Lewis (Jefferson's secretary)

William Clark (Army officer)

Aided by Indian guides, French traders and hunters

Travel up Missouri River, cross Rocky Mountains, then head down Columbia River to Pacific Ocean

Problems with the LA Purchase

Although great triumph, the purchase creates problems

Federalists fear Western expansion would diminish political power of NE

Some Federalists begin to talk openly of secession

Approach Alexander Hamilton

But he would not support plan of northern confederacy

The Embryonic Caesar: Aaron Burr

Running against Hamilton for NY governor in 1804

Secessionists offer help

Acceptance angers Alexander Hamilton

Says Burr trying to break up US

Duel kills Hamilton, July 1804

Burr indicted for murder (in NY and NJ)

Aaron Burr, Criminal at Large

Burr completes term as VP early in 1805

Flees west to avoid prosecution

Conspires with Gen. James Wilkinson

US military governor of Louisiana Territory

What were they doing?

Fomenting rebellion in LA

Want to establish separate country with Burr as leader

Wilkinson got cold feet and arrests Burr for treason

The Burr Trial

Chief Justice Marshall presides

Jefferson tries to apply Loose Construction of definition of treason under Constitution

Marshall rejects, insisting on strict interpretation of treason

Burr acquitted

The Crisis of 1805–1811

Napoleonic Wars

Neutrality fails

Both sides, Britain and France, refuse to accept

Claim right to board US merchant ships

Take cargos like 1790s

In 1805, Horatio Nelson defeats French at Trafalgar

British tighten continental blockade

Seize Essex for carrying sugar and molasses from West Indies to France

Threaten profits of American merchants

Revive anti-British sentiment

Impressments

Federalists and Republicans angered by situation

British policy of impressments

Stop and search ships for British deserters

Deserters forced back into service

From 1802–11, Brits take nearly 8,000 men from US ships

Some legitimate

Some mistaken identity

But also taking sailors as needed

Situation erupts in 1807

Leopard attacked US frigate Chesapeake

21 killed/wounded

4 seized as deserters

Many Americans call for war

Jefferson demands apology and monetary damages

British comply

But blockade and impressments continue

Defending American Honor

Merchants up in arms

Jefferson and Secretary of State Madison try to put economic pressure on British

The Embargo Act (1807)

Prohibit ships from leaving US ports until British and French recognize US neutrality

Abysmal failure

Overestimate European need for US trade

Merchants circumvent

Embargo drastically reduces American exports

Drop from $108 million in 1806 down to $22 million in 1808

NE hurt most by embargo

Jefferson attacked from all sides

Federalists say intentionally destroying NE economy

Alarmed when Republican Congress passes Force Act

Want to prevent smuggling between NE and Canada

Gave US customs officials extraordinary powers to seize illegal goods

James Madison: The Second Republican President

Jefferson's second term ends in 1809

Madison obvious choice to replace

Jefferson's Secretary of State

Chief architect of embargo

Wrote Constitution

Advocated Bill of Rights

Congressman and party leader

But not a great diplomat

Acknowledged embargo not working

Repeals in 1809

Enacts Non-Intercourse Act (1809)

Allow US to trade with everyone *but* British and French

Normal commerce not return until respect US neutrality rights

Britain/France ignore

Madison forced to accept Macon's Bill in 1810

Reopened legal trade with both Britain and France

Was War Inevitable?

Relationship with Britain growing tense after 1810

US uneasy

Want to resist, but not want war

How far should US go to avoid war?

If war necessary, which nation would US attack?

The Republican decision

In 1810, Western Republicans (War Hawks) accuse Brits of arming Indians tribes

Was the charge false?

Tecumseh's War

Tecumseh (Shawnee chief)

Want to revive old Western Confederacy of 1790s

Recruits southern tribes

Claim all territory north of OH River belongs to Indians

Want to drive out white settlers

Tenskwatawa

Mixed Christianity with Native American cultural nationalism

Call for holy war

Congress Responds to Tecumseh

Condemn British support of new Western Confederacy

Rush of war fever and nationalism spreads across US

Pushes reluctant James Madison to war

War Hawks

Henry Clay (KY) and John C. Calhoun (SC)

Urge invasion of Spanish FL and British Canada

Sporadic fighting between western settlers and Shawnee breaks out in 1811

Does this mean war?

NW Territory Gov. William Henry Harrison

Defeats Shawnee at Battle of Tippecanoe (1811)

War with Britain

War inevitable now

Frontiersmen and War Hawks

Madison abandons economic strategy

Demands British respect

US sovereignty in West and neutrality rights

British ignore!

Madison asks Congress to declare war

June 1812

Senate divided, 19–13 for war

House concurred 79–49

Causes of the War

Very complex

Traditionally, historians say war over violation of American neutrality rights

But what about the West?

Some believe war really about who would control the West

War furthered regional tensions

NE opposed war

See as unnecessary and undesirable

Federalist merchants condemn

Say Britain source of wealth and major trade partner

War not make sense

Presidential Election of 1812

De Witt Clinton

Federalist candidate

Gets almost all electoral votes from NE

James Madison

Won most support from South and West

Areas where demand for war highest

Madison victory seen as mandate for war

Fighting the War of 1812

Near-disaster for United States

Republican congressmen predict easy victory

War Hawks see Canada as ripe for taking

Republicans and military? State militias?

US get few military victories at first:

Dominates Great Lakes region

Gen. William Henry Harrison attacks British and Indian forces near Detroit

British withdraw

Gen. Tecumseh dead (British made him general in October 1813)

US forces capture and burn Toronto

Problems for the Americans

Invading Canada

Serious lack of manpower

Political problems back home

NE governors and militiamen

Boston refuses to lend money to nation

Some invest in British interests instead

Daniel Webster, Federalist (NH)

Leads rejection of higher taxes for war effort

Discourages enlistment

Prevents drafting of state militiamen

Federalists want nothing at all to do with war

Madison made mistake of leading divided nation into war

Can't seize British Canada

Despite overwhelming military advantage

The Decline Continues

American effort not impressive

By 1814, British control waters off American coast

British sail into Chesapeake Bay

Army storms ashore

Overrun Washington, DC

James and Dolley Madison forced to flee

British officers dine on their dinner

DC burned in retaliation for Toronto

Moved toward Baltimore, but stopped at Fort McHenry

The Red Sticks?

The War in the South

War in South mainly against Indians allied with British

Led by Andrew Jackson

The Creek War

Stirred by rhetoric of Tecumseh and his brother

Divided over what to do about white encroachment

Signing away future

Red Sticks

Align with British and Spanish

In 1813, attack Fort Mims on Alabama River

Slaughter more than 500 Americans and mixed-race Creeks

Gathered for safety

Success in the South?

Andrew Jackson (KY and TN troops) turn to traditional foes of Creeks

Ally US with Cherokees, Choctaws, and Chickasaws

Wage campaign of attrition

Attack and burn Red Stick villages

Most brutal tactics of entire war

Invasion of Florida

Grand strategy of War Hawks

Andrew Jackson wins several battles, but not take entire region

Capture Mobile and Pensacola (1814)

Can't hold either

Battle of New Orleans (1815)

Two weeks after war officially over

Why important?

No guarantee British follow treaty and return region to America

Protection of New Orleans imperative

Makes Jackson into national hero

Opens door to national politics

Salvages US honor in failed war

Ending the War

Treaty of Ghent, Christmas Eve 1814

Restores prewar borders

Evaluating the War of 1812

Poorly conceived

Miserably executed

Nearly causes breakup of US

Thrusts TN slaveholder (Jackson) into national politics

Hartford Convention, late 1814

Reps from 5 NE states meet to discuss grievances

Consider leaving union

Reassert doctrine of nullification

The Federalists After 1812

Federalist lose power

Doomed as political party

Branded as unpatriotic

Hartford Convention

Refusal of Federalists to participate in war

NE unwillingness to support war

Party associated with disloyalty

Republicans say guilty of treason

Party collapses on national level

By 1820, can't even run presidential candidate

An Empire of Slavery in the Old Southwest: Race and Slavery in the U.S.

The Legal Origins of Chattel Slavery

    English had little experience with Institution

    Irish

    Caribbean

    Early on flexibility was key

    At start, race did not mean legal status as slave

    Early documents do not make connection

    So what happened?

English Ideas About Race

    Irish example: Gaelic, Catholics

    Scots: Picts, natural man

    Non-Christians: Muslims and Indians

    Other Europeans

English Ideas of Bondage

    Peonage

    Indentured servitude

    Impressment of sailors

    Prison

    Abusing thy neighbor…

    Imprisonment

Subjugation

Reduction to peasant status

Enslave??

Why Enslave Africans?

Excuses

Tapping into pre-existing system

Knowledge of blackness

Linguistics

Definition: darkest color there is, like night without light. Without hope. Bad or evil.

Blackness and Shakespeare

Othello

Titus Andronicus

The Caribbean: A Trial Ground for North America

West African slaves brought to grow sugar

Arrive as chattel slaves, perhaps a few indentures at first

Price of sugar high, value of slaves low

Leads to poor conditions

Disease, overwork, food, clothes, shelter

Easier to replace than take care of them

Brutality transferred to America

How Did Race Become Equated with a Legal Status?

Two Theories:

1) The Legal Origins of Chattel Slavery in VA

Race came with slavery

VA and MD first to make race equal legal status

Morgan, American slavery, American freedom

Limitations to slave status

No guns

Militia service

Interracial sex

Labor contracts with indentures

Restrict freedom of movement

Virginia Slave Codes

1662: slavery dependent on condition of mother

1667: baptism does not change status

1668: moderate corporal punishment legal

1669: beating deaths of resisting slaves not a felony

1680: no armed slaves, slaves in hiding could be killed

1691: no intermarriage, punishment for interracial children

1705: no punishment or purchase of white indentures

2) The Necessity of a Situation: Asserting Control in the Chesapeake

Law does not equate control

General pattern of oppression and resistance

No forgiveness

Why was American slavery so harsh?

Come from culture where poor oppressed

Religious conflicts end in death

Most minor crimes punished with death

The Natural Progression to Violence

Owners need punishment to maintain control

Branding

Castration

Nose slits

Amputations

Hobbling

Violence depends on size of population

In West Indies and SC, few whites in charge of 25–100 slaves

Whites rule through fear and intimidation

Some Form of Freedom?

In SC, slavery developed from experience of Barbados migrants

Peter Wood's Black Majority

Certainly racial separation, but voluntary at first

Blacks not excluded from trades

Legal status changed as population increased

By 18th century, chattel slaves

Why?

Stono Rebellion

So Which Came First: Race or Slavery

Story of Francis Payne, SC

Begins enslavement in 1637 as "Francisco, a Negroe"

Slave blacksmith for nearly 20 years

1653, negotiates agreement with Jane Eltonhead to buy freedom

1666, buys freedom of family

Wealthy for period, changes name to Frank Paine

Seems a free man, but insidious distinction

Documents identified him as Frank Paine, Negro

Creating an Empire for Slavery:

The Old Southwest

Spread to NA from West Indies, but how does it migrate to AL, MS, LA?

Constitution of 1787

Slave trade ends in 1808

But 250,000 more brought into US

African-American population 1.8 million by 1820

Most involved in rice, tobacco

But economy changing

Sugar in LA, cotton across Southwest

Demand for cotton cloth grows, rapidly alters shape of country

Planters leave coast, headed for Old Southwest

Toward Alabama, Mississippi

Major upheaval for slaves

Forced West, or sold by thousands

With so much change, what was experience of slavery?

A Slave Narrative

The only incident I can remembered which occurred while my mother continued on Mr. Newman's farm, was the appearance one day of my father with his head bloody and his back lacerated. It seemed the overseer had sent my mother away from the other field hands to a retired place, and after trying persuasion in vain, had resorted to force to accomplish a brutal purpose. Her screams aroused my father at his distant work, and running up, he found his wife struggling with the man. Furious at the sight, he sprung upon him like a tiger. In a moment the overseer was down, and, mastered by rage, my father would have killed him but for the entreaties of my mother, and the overseer's own promise that nothing should ever be said of the matter. The promise was kept—like most promises of the cowardly and debased—as long as the danger lasted.

Josiah Henson, 1789–1883

Three Strategies for Surviving Slavery

Flight

Resistance and rebellion

Religion

1. Flight

Runaways

Flight patterns different

Africans run away in groups, recreate African community

Native-born run away as individuals, want freedom

Social practice: Nursing lasts 2.5 years, but one year of Anglo population.

2. Resistance and Rebellion

Naming: planters at first

Biblical or classical themes

Second generations named by slaves

Anglo names

Some African names kept, but meanings lost

After 1750, naming mostly on Western model

Resistance and Rebellion, Cont.

Negative behavior

Sambo: Poor work, slow movement, tools, fake ignorance

Stealing and obstinate hostility

Suicide and murder

Folk culture: spirituals, work songs, Brer Rabbit

Rebellions: Stono (1739), Denmark Vessey (SC, 1822), Gabriel Prosser (VA, 1800), Nat Turner (VA, 1831).

3. Religion

Acculturation produced spiritual holocaust?

Most older African religions lost, save voodoo

Slaves and Christianity

Jon Butler, *Awash in a Sea of Faith*

African American forms of Christianity mostly Old Testament

Whites prefer more New Testament

Different messages

Four Unique Aspects of American Slavery:

Acculturation

Slave culture

The slave family

Plantation life

1) Acculturation

Difficult to know how much they acculturate to white society

Distinctive trends in America, compared to white slavery of Europe

West African music, language, folk tales, religion, art all remain powerful

Slaves never completely acculturated

South a middle ground where both groups are changing

Whites adopt some African practices

Rice milling

Task system

Food (hoe cakes, dumplings)

2) Slave Culture

Unique culture forms to deal with slavery

Form identity of plantation slaves

Acts like glue

Require leisure time to develop

What did slaves do with Sunday time?

Gardens, washing clothes

Also visiting, fishing, games, stories, gambling, drinking

Coping mechanisms

Folk tales

Conjurers

Religion

Voodoo

An Ever Changing Institution

Sylvia Frey and Betty Wood, Come Shouting to Zion

Nature of slavery change by mid-18th c.

Less like murderous Caribbean, more family based

Sex ratios evened out, marriages and children increased

Slave population growth force creation of slave quarters

Fuels development of first American culture

African music, family life, folk tales, religion merge with that of white southerners, creates distinctiveness of southern culture

3) Slave Families

Was black family destroyed by slavery?

Moynihan Report, early 1970s

Family core of slave society

Some owners encourage slave families

Believe promotes stability, produces docility

Some masters punish infidelity

Hugh Davis' lashes

Rarity?

Most masters ignore immorality, some encourage it

Lust of white owners a serious issue

Slave women relatively unprotected, especially if owner/overseer unmarried

Childcare

Masters determine prenatal care

Women work up until birth

Few days off after birth

Nursing routines established for field hands

Children mostly wards of older slaves, siblings

Little care, high mortality rate

Slave childhoods mixed

Speak of wonderful periods, mixed with extreme violence

Parents change character

Five generations of a slave family

4) Plantation Life: In the Fields

75% of all slaves work in fields

55% in cotton

10% in tobacco

10% rice, sugar, hemp

Remainder of slaves in industry or domestic work

The Life of a Field Hand

Rise at dawn, cooked meals, feed animals, in field by sunrise

Work day varied very little during year

Extended hours

Tobacco curing, packing

Cotton ginning sometimes ran till 9 p.m.

Adult slaves expected to pick 150 lbs/day

A White Southern View of Slavery Compared to Free labor?

James Henry Hammond, 1858 Speech Before Congress

"The difference between us is, that our slaves are hired for life and well compensated; there is no starvation, no begging, no want of employment among our people, and not too much employment either. Yours are hired by the day, not cared for, and scantily compensated, which may be proved in the most painful manner, at any hour in any street in any of your large towns. Why, you meet more beggars in one day, in any single street of the city of New York, than you would meet in a lifetime in the whole South."

George Fitzhugh *The Blessings of Slavery,* 1857 Planter and Lawyer, VA

"The Negro slaves of the South are the happiest, and, in some sense, the freest people in the world. The children and the aged and infirm work not at all, and yet have all the comforts and necessaries of life provided for them. They enjoy liberty, because they are oppressed neither by care nor labor. The women do little hard work, and are protected from the despotism of their husbands by their masters. The Negro men and stout boys work, on the average, in good weather, not more than nine hours a day. The balance of their time is spent in perfect abandon."

The White South

64% of white southerners did not own slaves

Three Southern classes:

Poor whites:

30–50% of population

Abject poverty, renters

"Poor white trash"

Yeomen:

Own land

Grew food crops, especially corn, hogs

Sell extra to planters

Planters:

36% of population, but only 2.5% own more than 50 slaves

Dominate southern politics, society

The Plantation Elite in the West

Elites in Old Southwest not like Easterners

Natchez nabobs

Frederick Stanton (444 slaves, 15,000 acres)

Surget's own 93,000 in MS, AR, LA

Worthingtons have over 500 slaves

Natchez richest county in America, 1850

Thomas Taylor's response

Second generation wealth seek land in West

Use rivers for transportation

Isaac Henry Hilliard and Miriam Hilliard, Chicot County, Arkansas

Importance of Social circles

River as highway, alters development

The Abolitionist Response

Abolitionists on rise by 1800

Slavery not going to die

Fight Fugitive Slave Act of 1793, expansion of slavery to the West

Fail with Alabama, Mississippi, Louisiana

But Missouri applies in 1819

James Tallmadge (NY)

Propose ban on importation, gradual emancipation before admission of state

Missouri fights back, House blocks admission

Southerners fight Maine admission in Senate

Sen. Thomas Cobb (GA)

Stalemate follows

Henry Clay and the Future

Henry Clay (KY)

Author of Missouri Compromise

Maine as free state in 1820, Missouri as slave in 1821

Two by two states admitted in future

36–30 in Louisiana territory

Ties together slavery and westward expansion

Thomas Jefferson

"this momentous question, like a fire bell in the night, awakened and filled me with terror."

"as it is, we now have the wolf by the ear, and we can neither hold him, nor safely let him go. Justice is in one scale, and self-preservation in the other."

Missouri Compromise of 1820

The Age of Jackson

The Reign of the Common Man?

1820–44

Industrial Revolution unleashes new political forces as well as economic ones

Republicanism being realized

Individual as public property

Duties and obligations to state

But US becoming democracy

Equality and respect of common man

More participation

Shift occurring

Democracy now byword for increased political participation

Changes in Politics

Due to industrial and market revolution

1. Expanding the right to vote,

1820–29

More people made eligible

Property qualifications fall away in many states

Even poor allowed to vote by 1840s

By 1840, 90% of all white males can vote

States establish direct elections for governor, judges, and president

2. Emergence of professional politicians

Political parties on rise

Politician as profession emerging

Is this in Constitution?

New parties very democratic

Party identity crucial to success for the party

Politics become entertainment

Party affiliations become part of personal identity

New Political Tools

Martin Van Buren (Little Magician), NY

First to use party as governing tool

Applies organizational talents of market revolution to politics

Van Buren depends on 3 innovations:

Party structure, collective leadership, bureaucracy

Manipulate and shape party loyalty

Party newspapers (*Albany Argus*) publish positions, maintain discipline

Also use other tools

Caucus

Political platforms

Changing national scene

State parties grow in power

National parties collapse by 1824

Federalists disappear by 1816

Republicans divided

Five men seek Presidency in 1824

All call themselves Republicans

Election of 1824

The Republican candidates

1. John Quincy Adams (MA)

2. John C. Calhoun (SC)

3. William H. Crawford (GA)

4. Henry Clay (KY)

5. Andrew Jackson (TN)

Election outcome complete surprise

Crawford was favorite, but has stroke

Still wins in GA and VA

Adams has national support

But viewed as NE's candidate

Clay's support limited to OH Valley

Calhoun drops out

Switches to VP race, and throws support to Andrew Jackson

The Electors Vote:

Adams 84, Crawford 41, Clay 37, Jackson 99

No one wins majority, Jackson has 44% of p.v., John Quincy Adams 31%

So who makes decision?

The Corrupt Bargain

Constitution requires HoR decide on 3 individuals

Jackson, Adams, and Crawford

The King Maker

Clay Speaker of House

Controls votes of KY, MO, IL, OH

Thinks Crawford eliminated (personal, health)

Choice either Adams or Jackson

No real choice for Clay

The lesser of two evils

Clay has poor relationship with both

Fought Jackson over taking Florida (1819)

Competes with Clay for same constituency

Fought Adams while negotiating end to War of 1812

Clay fear's Jackson presidency

Clay's choice never goes public

National Intelligencer (Republican) runs ad

Charges corrupt bargain

Says Adams to presidency, Clay as Secretary of State

Clay furious, but it happens that way

The Adams Presidency

Election of 1824 important because:

Destroyed old Democratic-Republican party

Laid foundation of second-party system

Two new parties:

Dems—Jackson, Martin Van Buren, John Calhoun

National Republicans (later Whigs)—Clay, Daniel Webster, JQ Adams

Adams embraces Clay's American System

1. Protective tariff to stimulate manufacturing

2. Internal improvements to stimulates commerce

3. National Bank to provide uniform currency

Other issues of the Adams' presidency

National university

Western exploration

National system of weights

Scientific observatory

Election of 1828

Adams refuses to campaign

"If my country wants my services, then she must ask for them."

Jackson's second campaign gains momentum

Southwestern support

Calhoun (VP)

Crawford's coalition

VA Republicans

Martin Van Buren and NY

Powerful state political organizations, newspapers

Plans first national political campaign

Dirty Politics

Remembering the corrupt bargain

JQ Adams seen as part of government's immorality

Last election stolen?

American girl for Russian tsar?

Andrew Jackson portrayed as pure western farmer

Claim to be heir to Jeffersonian ideals

Jackson vulnerable to immorality charge

Duels and adultery

Rachel married to man in KY

Jackson rescues her, but divorce not complete

Two married in Spanish Natchez, so Rachel a polygamist and Jackson an adulterer

Clay tells Charles Hammond (Cincinnati newspaper) about marriage

Hammond goes public

Jackson shields Rachel, but she finds out, dies in December 1828

Jackson never forgives Clay

Age of the Common Man?

Jackson lost in 1824, but wins in 1828

56% P.V., 68% E.V.

Wins South, West, Northwest

Only NE remained with Adams

Democratizes public office

Spoils system

William Marcy: "to the victor goes the spoils"

Gives government jobs to friends and supporters

Was Jackson the first?

No, Jefferson did it

Trend growing with each president

Pendleton Civil Service Act

Jackson criticized, but only 10% of jobs go to politicos

Sectionalist or Nationalist?

Jackson first national figure since GW

Focus on national leadership rather than sectional compromise

Believed in strong executive

Majority must govern

But country divided by sectionalism?

Congress full of sectional leaders

Let's look at each up close

John C. Calhoun

Intense, dogmatic

War Hawk in 1812

Missouri Compromise makes him Southerner first

Believes South becoming a minority

Sees self as defender of Southern rights

Rigid, "Cast Iron Man"

Daniel Webster

Brooding, physically imposing, stern

Greatest orator of his age

Could thunder or be sentimental

Went to Dartmouth

Lawyer, probusiness

Tied to commercial interests

Supports high tariff, national bank, strong government

But in old age

Henry Clay

Parliamentarian

Senate, 1808–10

Speaker of House (1811–25)

Great storyteller

Western, wants cheap/good transportation

Authors American System

Bank, tariff, internal improvements

Wants to be president, but blocked by Jackson

Opposing Jackson

The Whig party

Most salient belief

Must end Jacksonian tyranny

Favor internal improvements

Want sound economy and prosperity

Want to use government to protect US economy

Lasts to mid 1850s

Jackson, the Executive

(Ab) Using executive power

Vetoes large number of bills

Following old interpretation

Only 12 vetoes by first 6 presidents

Jackson vetoes 10 in first term

Maysville Road Veto of 1830

Federal funds to extend national road 50 miles (spur) into KY

All to be built in KY

Why did Jackson veto?

Acting as national figure

An angry Clay comes out of retirement

Jackson risks support of West

Uses states' rights to win support in West and South

The Peggy Eaton Affair

John Eaton made Secretary of War

Few move permanently to DC

Eaton stays at home of O'Neal

Flounting social code?

The marriage

Eaton wants to marry Peggy

Asks Jackson's permission

Cave dwellers furious

Snub Peggy in social circles

Jackson outraged at cabinet

Remembers attacks on Rachel

Calhoun's wife leads snubs

Jackson launches federal investigation

Convinced Calhoun trying to embarrass him

The Tariff Debate

Tariff of 1816

First major Tariff

Protects NE's economy

Southerners fight tariffs

Mostly affect luxury items

Want free trade

Fear retaliation against cotton

Tariff of 1816 supposed to be temporary

Extended in 1824 and 1828

The Tariff of Abominations, 1828

Passed in return for Northern support of Jackson

Very high rates (⅓ to ½ value of product)

Southerners can't repeal it

Claim it is unconstitutional

South Carolina especially hard hit

Cotton being shipped to Britain for manufactured goods

Develops now-or-never mentality

Nullification Crisis of 1832

Tariff of 1832

Raises taxes on woolens, iron, hemp

SC calls convention

Issue Ordinance of Nullification

Rejects tariff and refuses to collect

Calls up militia and threatens secession

Jackson denounces armed resistance as treason

Begins preparation for war

Issues Force Bill

Keeps other southern states from following

Finding a peaceful solution

Clay meets with Calhoun

Tariff cut back to rate of 1816 by 1842

SC isolated, accepts compromise

Ordinance repealed, but nullify Force Bill

Jackson and Congress ignore it

Most serious threat to Union to date

Postpones Civil War for 30 years

The Bank Issue

Jackson decides to dismantle Clay's American System

Believes it was bad for US

Sees US Bank as worst part

Private/public, chartered in 1816

Charter to expire in 1836

Bank necessary service

Works, but not understood

Gives nation financial stability

Most US money in bank notes (paper) issued by state banks

Rechartering the Bank

Clay and Webster see Bank issue as way to embarrass Jackson

Ask Nicholas Biddle (Bank president) to seek early recharter of US Bank

New charter pushed thru Congress

Jackson vetoes

Calls bank home of privilege and monopoly

Financially backed by British aristocrats

The election of 1832

Jackson's veto of Bank popular

Clay runs on American System and need to recharter the US Bank

Clay loses 219–49

Jackson gets 54% popular vote

Destroying the Second Bank of the US

Jackson orders US Treasury to dismantle Bank

Treasurer refuses

Jackson replaces 3 separate appointees until get what he wants

March 1834

Senate drafts censure

Clay writes it, calls Jackson tyrant

"We are in the midst of a revolution, hitherto bloodless, but rapidly descending towards a total change of the pure republican character of the Government, and the concentration of all power in the hands of one man."

Closing the US Bank

Cuts bank loans to other banks, which leads to string of bankruptcies

Causes recession in 1834

Southern Indian Removal

Large numbers remain in South

Restricted to enclaves

Five Civilized Tribes

Cherokee and Creek (GA, TN, AL)

Chickasaw and Choctaw (MS, AL, TN)

Seminole in Florida

Occupy valuable cotton lands

Jackson committed to removal

Withdraws federal troops from enclaves

Leaves Indians subject to state law

Georgia (1828)

Decide Indians tenants on state land, not a nation

Other states follow

Removing the Indians

Jackson pushes further

Indian Removal Act of 1830

Indians forced to exchanged lands east of MS River for those in West (Indian [Oklahoma] Territory)

Jackson sends agents to negotiate

Nearly 100 removal agreements concluded

But who signs?

Protecting their rights

Cherokee write a constitution

Call themselves nation and claim sovereignty

GA denies right of claim

Appealing Removal

Cherokee appeal to Supreme Court

Cherokee Nation v. Georgia (1831)

Marshall: Indians not independent nation, but "domestic dependent nations."

Worcester v. Georgia (1832).

Marshall: Indian nations represent "distinct political communities, having territorial boundaries, within which their authority is exclusive"

Jackson's response?

The Trail of Tears

Cherokee refuse to move

Repudiate treaties of 1835

May 1838 deadline expires

Only 2,000 of 17,000 left for the West

Van Buren orders Winfield Scott to "move 'em out"

Scott rounds up 15,000

Holds them in government camps called concentration pens

Large numbers die

Others flee

Fall/winter 1838:

Force march 1,200 miles to Oklahoma Territory

11,000 arrived, 4,000 died along way

Only NC Cherokee and Seminoles remain

Yet Another Contested Election...

Election of 1836

Whigs run 3 candidates (no convention)

William Henry Harrison (OH)

Hugh White (TN)

Daniel Webster (NH)

Nearly throw election into HoR

Electoral votes

Van Buren wins 170

Harrison 73

White 26

Webster 14

Anti-Jacksonians lost third straight election

... And Then Financial Crisis in 1837

Van Buren in trouble

Presidency begins w/ panic

Caused by Bank War and problems in Britain

US economy depends on European financial health

Investments in US reduced, crop prices fall, especially cotton

Bank failures begin in NY

Recession lasts until 1843, worst until 1870s

Prices for goods in US fall by 50%

Investment in economy declines by 25%

Canal building falls by 90%

Unemployment reaches almost 10% in 1838, doubled in some coastal cities

An Empire of Reform: Urbanization, Reform Movements, and Abolition

A New Nation

In first 50 years US changed a great deal

Financial, industrial and commercial sectors expand and mature

1775–1825, US develops precapitalist infrastructure

What is capitalism?

Merchants dominate port cities

1775–1825, merchants prosper most

Especially between 1792 and 1815

US experiencing rapid growth: called "Market Revolution"

Dominated by putting out system and urban areas

Great deal of class mobility in US

The Urbanization of America

In 1820, only handful of Americans lived in cities

1820–60, cities grow rapidly

By 1860, urban population nearly triples

Almost 20% of total pop.

Fastest growing areas:

Boston, Philadelphia, NYC, Baltimore, and New Orleans

Grow at rate of about 25% per decade

NYC alone grew 64% from 1820 to 1830

Quickly became commercial center

Expansion of Wealth

    Individual incomes double from 1800 to 1850

    But gap between rich and poor widening

    Late 1840s, top 1% of population owns 40% of US wealth

    Bottom ⅓ owned nearly nothing

    Who were the poor?

    Mostly immigrant families (mainly from Ireland or Germany)

    Workers in unskilled jobs

    No security, poor housing, constantly moving (why?)

Life in Urban American

    Remarkably unsanitary

    No city water supplies, garbage collection, or even sewers

    Wells contaminated by run-off sewer water

    Plagued by epidemic diseases

    Related to sanitation

    Worst: yellow fever, cholera, and typhus

    Problem with basic urban sanitation programs

    Almost all fee-based, so poor can't pay for them

The Distribution of Wealth

    Communities laid out on class basis

    Middle class escape cities to suburbs in 1850s

    Leave behind neighborhoods that quickly became slums

    Five Points

    Worst 19th century slum in New York City

    Populated mostly by free blacks and recent immigrants

    Neighborhood plagued by gangs and thieves of all sorts

    Prostitutes openly work in streets

Entertaining the Masses

    Working-class leisure

    Resemble rough nature of neighborhood life

    Drunken brawls

    Theaters

    Violent and full of vice

    Drunk young men and prostitutes

    Riots against unpopular acts/actors

    By 1830s, middle class and upper class do not attend WC theaters

    Make suburban entertainment

    Can take wives and children

    Other forms of entertainment

The "blackface minstrel" show

Dances, skits, and antiblack comedy

"Zip Coon" (an irresponsible free black)

"Jim Crow"

Show desire to return to pre-industrial world

The "Penny Paper"

New York Sun

Like today's tabloids

Focus on sex, violence, and political scandals

The Changing Nature of Work

Commercial explosion and rise of banks lead to domestic manufacturing

Artisans make furniture, tools, wagons, shoes, and dozens of other items

In NE and Mid-Atlantic states, artisans make comfortable living

Late 1790s, manufactured goods increase in number and market area

Boston cordwainers selling shoes throughout NE

Putting-out system

Recruit and organize households in rural areas to manufacture specific goods

Hire young men to market (hawk) products throughout country

Starts with shoe and boot trade

Establishing the Factory

In 1780s, first factory at Lynn, MA

Families send daughters/wives

Monitor textile machinery

Life at Lynn

Live in company dorms

Shop at company store

Eat at company cafeteria

Expenses deducted from pay

Under constant control of company

In return workers get safe accommodations and education

Most send wages home to family

Some sold into labor by family

Many see it as chance to better themselves and family

The Secret to Success

First American Industrial Revolution

Not technological, but efficient organization

First machines used in textile industry

1780s, merchants build hundreds of small mills along creeks and rivers of NE and Mid-Atlantic

Water-powered machines

Hire workers to comb wool (later cotton) into long strands

Use outwork to spin strands into yarn

Division of labor

Women and children make yarn

Men weave yarn into cloth

Changes in the Economy

Cash replaces barter-exchange

Outwork system means farmers stop producing own food, or make own clothing

Stop bartering surplus agriculture for household necessities

Supply merchants with specialized goods for cash or credit at store

Cash economy not good, has many drawbacks

People work longer and harder:

Make shoes or hats during winter, work farm year round

Loss of independence

Become dependent on part-time wages

No longer working for themselves

Workers more productive, but less self-sufficient

Just Getting By

By 1830s, status of skilled workers declined sharply

Artisans replaced by unskilled workers and machines

Artisans expensive, so replaced with unskilled labor

Started with putting-out system

Unskilled workers easy to manipulate

Need labor union for protection

Focus on wages, work hours and working conditions

Worker protests spill into streets

Increases working-class identity

The Rise of the Union

Unions grow from craft guild system

Philadelphia shoemakers

Form Federated Society of Journeymen Cordwainers (1794)

Press for standard fair wage

Protect against wage cuts

Other trades quickly follow suit

Organized around individual trades

Taking Labor Concerns to Politics

Many laborers unhappy

Face declining incomes, unemployment, and loss of status

Labor theory of value

Price of product should reflect labor required to make it

Income from sale should go to person who made it

Condemn accumulation of wealth by capitalists trying to reduce workers to slavery

The Working Men's Party, 1828

First labor-based political party

Focus on equal taxation, abolition of banks, universal education, separate cemeteries for working men, etc.

Never dominate, but play important role in Philadelphia

Local Unions Go National

National Trades Union, 1834

National union of different trades from Boston to Philadelphia

By 1836 expand West from DC to Cincinnati

Part of strikes for 10-hour day

Get Jackson to establish 10-hour work day for Philly navy yard in 1836

Next turn to changing wages

1836–37, more than 50 union strikes

Succeed with organization and financial support from other unions

Hold out over 2 months

Employers Respond

Employers actively resist, but rarely work together against labor

Develop blacklist in NYC 1836

Refuse to hire workers from Union Trade Society of Journeymen Tailors

Circulate list across city

Use courts to open closed shops

Agreement where employer promises only to hire union workers

Say closed shops violate common law

Win against numerous unions

Carpet weavers union in Thompsonville (CT)

Shoemakers union in Geneva and Hudson (NY)

NYC tailors union

Philly plasterers' union

Union of Journeymen Cordwainers in Boston

The End of the First Labor Union Movement

Panic of 1837 destroys first labor movement

Not return until after Civil War

Nature and character of early union movement debated

Utopian reformist or training ground for the future?

The Urge to Reform?

Response to Industrial Revolution

Dislocations of market

Middle class not like problems of capitalism

Form organizations to help

Often selfishly motivated, but driven to help others

Evangelicalism crucial to reform

Tend toward perfectionism

Charles G. Finney: "as perfect as God"

Characterized by:

Self-discipline

Desire for achievement

Improve your life and that of your neighbor

Hopeful, demanding, but unrealistic

Part of Second Great Awakening of 1830s

Middle Class Women

Trapped in domestic sphere

Duties:

Raise good children: build character and religious world

Run household

Companionate marriage

Economic considerations less important

Participation in reform offers new position in society

Controlling the family

Fewer children

8 in 1800, 4 in 1900

Coitus interruptus, rhythm method, and abstinence

Emergence of abortions

Widely advertised in 1830s

25% of all pregnancies between 1840–60, same as 1990

Sex manuals become popular

No sex after children born

Sex in the Nineteenth Century

Methodist Manual for young brides:

"Nudity, talking about sex, reading stories about sex, viewing photographs and drawings depicting or suggesting sex are the obnoxious habits the male is likely to acquire if permitted. A wise bride will make it the goal never to allow her husband to see her unclothed body, and never allow him to display his unclothed body to her. Sex, when it cannot be prevented, should be practiced only in total darkness.

"Clever wives are ever on the alert for new and better methods of denying and discouraging the amorous overtures of the husband. A good wife should expect to have reduced sexual contacts to once a week by the end of the first year of marriage and to once a month by the end of the fifth year of marriage."

Reforming the Character of Others

Reformers believe in redemption

Focus on basic goodness of society

Think crime, poverty, and prostitution can be prevented

Environment was key

Prisons = Isolation

Asylums = Rural areas

Link between control and reform

Reformers anti-Catholic and anti-immigrant

Focus on issues affecting immigrants

Prostitution, alcohol use, working on Sunday

Try to fix with conversion

Fail due to secular character of US

Early Temperance Crusade

Women take lead in reform

Raise money, send missionaries, and create schools

American Society for Promotion of Temperance

Founded in 1826 by Evangelicals

200,000 by 1835

Focus on dangers of alcohol abuse

Hard-drinking age, but control possible

Mostly Anglo middle class women and Whigs

Target German-Irish men and Democrats

Were they successful?

Prostitution and Moral Reform

The oldest profession

Prevalent in urban east

Reformers try to rescue prostitutes

Provide homes, money, and shelter

But also religion

Get jobs as domestics

Few embrace

Female Moral Reform Society

NYC, 1834

500 societies by 1840

Victorian women talk about issues

Believe it is just about economics

Find jobs and child care for prostitutes

Publish names of Johns

Lobby government to make it a crime for men

Changing Asylums and Prisons

Dorothea Dix

1843, tries to protect insane

Forced to endure horrible conditions

Chained together naked

Beaten and/or caged

What is purpose of prison?

To reform or lock away?

Environment dictates behavior, so must isolate

Sing Sing in New York

Provides inmates with order, discipline, and isolation

Religious Response to Industrial Ills

Many seek isolation from wickedness of industrial world

Evangelical religion of "Burned-over District" fuels reform

Hard times plus Evangelicalism led to apocalyptic religions

Millerites

William Miller

October 22, 1843

"The Great Disappointment"

Spawns Seventh-Day Adventists (returned in spirit, not flesh)

Jehovah's Witnesses, 9 dates between 1874–1984

The Shakers

Anne Lee, 1774

Come from Quakers

Family abandoned for larger spiritual family

No sex

In 1830, 20 Shaker towns, 6,000 people

Today?

The Oneida Community

Takes different approach

Founded by John Humphrey Noyes, 1848

Located in western NY

Shaker family structure with a twist:

"Complex Marriage"

Male continence

Few pregnancies

Doctrine of "Ascending Fellowship"

Noyes greatly criticized

The Abolitionist Movement

American Abolition, 1820–50

Abolitionists make gains, but still not win middle class

Slavery gone in north by 1808

Missouri Compromise (1820) restrict expansion

But not end slavery yet

Only 3 ways to get emancipation

Gradual, with payment to owners

Emancipation via fight or flight

Moral appeals to owners

Two goals of movement

Adopt specific political program and agenda

Must keep slavery out of territories

Recolonization

American Colonization Society, 1817

Upper South politicians want to be like north

Want free blacks out of region

Think them unfit for American republic

Many think repatriation necessary to prevent race war

Blacks 40% population

Henry Clay wants emancipation, but fears racial turmoil

Liberia established in 1830

1,400 relocated

Write Constitution in 1847

But movement fails, why?

Most free blacks do not want to leave

Fomenting Rebellion

Many want to end slavery immediately, so must do so by starting a mass slave revolt

Response supported by blacks and whites

Northern free blacks think slave rebellion necessary

Constitution was obstacle to freedom

Only states can end slavery

William Lloyd Garrison:

Constitution was a "deal with the devil"

Must be destroyed for country to be free

Spreading the word

John Russwurm and Samuel Cornish

Publish *Freedom's Journal,* NY, 1827

First black paper

Attacks slavery and slave south

David Walker's appeal

Says slave rebellions necessary and moral

Goes thru 3 printings

Walker murdered at Abolitionist convention in Philadelphia 1830

Nat Turner's Rebellion, 1831

Religion and Abolition

William Lloyd Garrison

The Liberator, Boston, 1831

Want immediate emancipation

Condemns ACS and slave owners

Attacked Bible and ministers

"I will be harsh as truth and as uncompromising as justice … I am in earnest—I will not equivocate—I will not excuse—I will not retreat a single inch—And I will be Heard."

Theodore D. Weld

More restrained

Publish: *American Slavery As It Is*

Sell 100,000 copies

With Angelina Grimke (SC) research 20,000 southern newspapers

Focus on Slave Punishments

Public treadmill worst:

"one poor girl was she sent there to be flogged, and was according stripped naked and whipped, showed me the deep gashes on her back—I might have laid my whole finger in them—large pieces of flesh had actually been cut out by the torturing lash."

Abolition on Rise

American Anti-Slavery Society

Created by Weld, Garrison and others in 1833

Start mail campaign

Send over 1 million pieces by 1835

Pressure Congress thru public petitions

Spread societies across country

Abolitionist societies

Grow from 200 in 1835 to 500 in 1836 to 2,000 in 1850

By 1850, have 200,000 members

Free blacks, Quakers, evangelicals and transcendentalists like (Emerson, Thoreau)

The South Responds

Defend slavery as positive good

Southern Christians offer new defense of slavery

Focus on biblical slavery

Thornton Stringfellow, Baptist, Culpeper Co. (VA)

Retrenchment

Strengthen slave codes

Gag Rule (1836–44)

Tables antislavery petitions out of Congress

States make Abolitionist mail illegal and ban Abolitionism

GA offers $5,000 reward for Garrison's and Walker's deaths

The Impending Crisis

Manifest Destiny and Western Expansion

March 1845, Democrat James K. Polk (TN) becomes president

Defeats Whig Henry Clay

Elected on platform of Western expansion

Wants to claim two regions:

Oregon Territory

Republic of Texas

Not limit imperial dream to taking two areas

Think US should take CA and NM

But war only way to get it all

Could bring large new territories into US

Would doom reconciliation of regional interests

Scheming Against Our Neighbors

In April, send agent to Mexico

Want to negotiate settlement in TX Revolution

…and possible transfer of CA to US

July 4, 1845

TX formally joins US

Claims Rio Grande as boundary

Polk agrees with TX

Sends Gen. Zachary Taylor with several thousand troops to occupy territory south of Nueces River

Taylor camps near Corpus Christi, just south of Nueces

Taking possession

By October, Taylor doubles force

In November, Polk sends John Slidell to Mexico

Ordered to buy NM, CA, and Rio Grande boundary for as much as $30 million

Clearing the path to war

Mexico refuses to see Slidell

Believe American annexation of TX was illegal

Must hold off Americans to protect Mexican territory

Hope US go to war with Britain and forget SW

Same week, Polk unveils new British policy

Claim British intervention in OR violates Monroe Doctrine

US will drive them from OR and will not let them take CA as compensation for Mexican debts

How to Start a War?

Provoking the Mexicans

January 1846

Polk increases military pressure

Taylor goes to Rio Grande to build fort

Secretary of State James Buchanan sends secret orders to Fremont

Makes base near Sacramento

News of skirmishing on Rio Grande reaches Polk

On 9 May, delivers war message written weeks before

Says Mexico "passed the boundary of the United States, has invaded our territory, and shed American blood upon the American soil."

Congress declares war four days later

Requisitioning the West

The British dilemma

Polk can't fight Mexico and British

Accepts British treaty dividing OR Country at 49th parallel

The Bear Flag State

June 1846, Americans in CA revolt

Unaware of war between US and Mexico

Get help from Fremont's forces

Easily capture Sonoma

Fremont not have formal authority to take CA

Refuses to let rebels fly US flag

Make crude flag displaying bear

Proclaim Bear Flag Republic on July 4, 1846

Becoming an American territory

US naval commander off CA coast

Lands 250 marines in Monterey

No objections against running up US flag

Proclaim CA a US territory

Within weeks, US forces control NM and CA

Crossing the Border

The first invasion force

May 1, Taylor crosses Rio Grande

Two bloody battles ensue

Use artillery to subdue Mexicans

September 25, 1846, capture Monterrey

The second invasion force

December 1846

Col. Alfred Doniphan begins 600-mile march

Goes south from Santa Fe to Chihuahua

Americans victorious on all fronts

Control long line across Mexico

Expect Mexicans to surrender, but don't

Invading the heartland

Gen. Antonio Lopez de Santa Anna

Refuses peace, won't give up any of his country

November 1846, Scott invades Vera Cruz

14,000 troops led by talented West Point officers

Robert E. Lee, George Meade, and P. T. Beauregard

Scott then turns to Mexico City

March 260 miles to seize Mexico City, September 1847

Perceptions of the War at Home

Public happy with outcome

Saw it as war for democracy

The problem with victory

Conscience Whigs

Strong antislavery views

See war as part of proslavery conspiracy

Government has no idea what to do with conquered lands

Mid-term elections, 1846

Whig party at crisis point

Need political issue for next election

Clay's American System failed too often

Should they turn against slavery?

Whigs win Congress

Many become critical of war

Fear new slave states in West will give South too much political power

Angry at rising American war dead

92,000 serve, but 13,000 killed or die of disease

The Wilmot Proviso, August 1846

Disrupting the war effort

Democrats devise most disruptive way to oppose war

David Wilmot (PA congressman)

Propose amendment to military appropriations bill

Prohibits slavery in territory acquired from Mexico

Gathering forces

Proviso quickly becomes rallying point

Especially for those fearing westward expansion of slavery

House of Representatives

Democratic minority joins forces with Whigs

Pass Proviso on several occasions

Proviso killed in Senate

More proslavery interests

The Spoils of War

Polk has to make a decision

Puts interest of Democratic Party first

Backs plan by John C. Calhoun

US gets CA and NM

Rejects all Mexico policy

Endorses Treaty of Guadalupe Hidalgo

Signed February 2, 1848

US pays $15 million

Gets more than ⅓ of Mexico prior to war

Texas north of Rio Grande

New Mexico

California

Congress to pay $3.2 million in claims against Mexican government

Senate quickly ratifies treaty March 1848

The Election of 1848

Polk (D) decides not to seek second term

Democrats turn to Lewis Cass (MI)

Supports expansion policy for slavery

Architect of "Popular Sovereignty"

The Whigs rely on tried-and-true model

Zachary Taylor: war hero and slave owner

The political platform

Parties argue whether Congress had constitutional right to address issue of slavery in territories

Casting the ballot

Voters left to choose between best of two evils

Southerners vote for Taylor (W)

Distrust of northern Democrats

Believe slave owners have same basic interests

Northerners bolt from party to support new party

The Free Soilers

Advocate free labor in West

Nominate disaffected Martin Van Buren

CA and the Compromise of 1850

CA statehood

First battleground for slavery issue

Major destination for western migrants

When gold discovered in 1849 immigration becomes flood

Population increase pressures on Congress and Taylor to admit CA into union

Taylor says determined to admit CA as free state

Settlers draft constitution outlawing slavery

Problem arise when Constitution reaches Congress

Southerners reject admission of free CA

See it as serious threat to their way of life

Slave and free states currently balanced at 15 in HoR

Additional free states put South in minority

Cannot defend its economic and social institutions

The Slavery Problem

War threatened in 1850

Can it be averted?

Henry Clay

Old man

Yet, organizes compromise

The Compromise of 1850

Clay sends compromise package to Senate

Stephen Douglas and Daniel Webster support

John C. Calhoun condemns

Package fails at first

The Douglas strategy

Laws reintroduced as individual measures

All eventually pass

What Was the Compromise?

Five major parts:

Admission of CA as free state

Establishment of TX boundary at modern line

NM and UT territories organized under popular sovereignty

More powerful Fugitive Slave Law

Abolition of slave trade in DC

The problem with the Compromise

No idea how popular sovereignty will work

No mechanism to ensure concept employed

Leaves too many questions unanswered

Could territories have slavery before admitted?

Could slavery be prohibited before admission?

Would northern states accept new invasive Fugitive Slave Law?

What would Supreme Court say?

Seems like Compromise will *cause* more problems than solved

Presidency of Millard Fillmore

Taylor inauguration

Cold, wet, and long

Pneumonia

Taylor's death leaves Millard Fillmore (NY) as president

Taylor cabinet resigned

Only Daniel Webster remained, as he did for Tyler

Trouble for the new president

Begins when he enforced Fugitive Slave Act

Believed in upholding law at all costs

Unpopular in North

The Fugitive Slave Act

Establishing slave courts

Headed by commissioners appointed by government

Slave owners could capture blacks in North

Brought before courts where determined if person was an escaped slave

Why is there a problem with this?

Courts corrupt and incompetent

Accused could not testify on own behalf

No trial by jury

Judges not make sure had right person

Judge had financial incentive:

$10 to convict; $5 if not

Abolitionists

Attack say act violates Bill of Rights

Protests fill northern cities in MA, NY, PA, and OH

Into This Politically Charged Atmosphere Came ...

Harriet Beecher Stowe

Uncle Tom's Cabin

Published March 1852

Dramatized plight of runaway slaves in way that gripped northerners

Polarized issues

Made slavery a major issue in 1852 election

So, what was it about?

The main story

Characters

The Origins of Popular Sovereignty

Future depended on success of Great Compromise

Guaranteed free soil north of 36-30

Southerners block admission of states from region

Allow only IA in 1846, formation of MN Territory

But people pouring into area

Demands something be done

Foremost spokesman Stephen A. Douglas (IL)

Wants to develop West and to be president

Introduces bill to organize NE Territory

A pact with the devil

Douglas needs Southern support to win presidency

Makes two major concessions:

Accepts principle of popular sovereignty

Voids Missouri Compromise's prohibition of slavery in west

Advocates new territories of NE and KS

Believes area to be nonslaveholders

Physical environment not good for slavery

Sealing the Pact

Concessions attract southern support in Congress

Kansas-Nebraska Act passed May 1854

Despite opposition of Northerners

Douglas misreads northern opinion

Repeal of Missouri Compromise viewed as attack on freedom in protected area

Furthers idea of Slave Power Conspiracy

An Anti-Slave Power Party Emerges

Northern Whigs, Anti-NE Dems., and Free Soilers join together in 1854

Form Republican Party

Platform: oppose expansion of slavery into territories

Bleeding Kansas

In 1854 thousands rush into KS

Middle ground of pro-slavery and anti-slavery sentiment

Sen. David R. Atchinson (MO)

Cross into KS and intervene in crucial elections

President Pierce gives preference

March 1855, recognize KS Territorial Legislature

Largely elected by MO residents who crossed border

Legislature makes questioning slavery in KS felony

Aiding fugitive slave made capital offense

Violence soon breaks out

Summer 1856, proslavery gang of 700 destroy Free Soil town of Lawrence

Leads NY abolitionist John Brown to KS

Started more than 20 business ventures in 6 states

Despite failures, very charismatic

Potawatomie Massacre

Responding to sack of Lawrence

Murdered and mutilated 5 proslavery setters in KS

"We must fight fire with fire and strike terror into the hearts of the proslavery people."

Blood for Blood

Potawatomie Massacre starts guerilla war

Nearly 200 killed

Violence even reached halls of Congress

Senator Charles Sumner (MA)

Delivered speech in Senate on "Crimes Against Kansas"

Denounced Pierce, South, and Sen. Andrew P. Butler (SC)

Says Southerners have taken institution of slavery as a mistress

Preston Brooks

Butler's nephew, Member of HoR

Wants to defend uncle's honor

Accosts Sumner at desk while Senate in session

Sumner struggles to stand, rips desk from floor, collapses

For action, HoR censures Brooks

SC return to Congress with over 90% vote

Sumner does not return for 2.5 years after beating

Election of 1856

Violence in KS and Congress dominates election

The Democrats

Advocate popular sovereignty

Believe KA-NE Act good

Nominated James Buchanan (PA)

The Republicans

Count on backlash against violence

Denounce KA-NE Act

Demand government prohibit slavery in territories

Openly attack Slave Power Conspiracy

Nominated John C. Fremont

Many Southerners threaten secession if Fremont wins

Buchanan wins 45% of popular vote

And yet, a Republican victory

Win several large free states

No one expect Republicans to make strong showing

Election showed political realignment

Old second-party system destroyed

New Third-Party system (Democrats and Republicans)

The Case of *Dred Scott v. Sandford* (1857)

Dred Scott

Began 1846 in MO court system

Lived with master in IL and WI Territory

NW Ordinance of 1787 and MO Compromise of 1820 prohibited slavery

Claims residence in territory made him free

March 1857,

2 days after Buchanan inaugurated

Supreme Court makes decision

Little agreement on issues raised by case

Seven members agree on one critical matter

Scott should remain a slave

Chief Justice Roger B. Taney

Says blacks couldn't be US citizen

Scott had no right to sue in federal court

5th Amendment

Prohibits taking property without due process of law

Congress cannot pass law depriving person of slave "property" or give territories powers Congress not possess

Problems with the decision

Most justices southern Democrats

Republican antislavery platform unconstitutional

Seems evidence of Slave Power Conspiracy

The Ordeal of James Buchanan

Buchanan makes more mistakes

Supports proslavery forces in KS

Recommends admission of KS as slave state under Lecompton Constitution

Obtained by voter fraud

Douglas thinks KS admission disastrous

Organize resistance in HoR to defeat KS entrance

KS not enter as free state (1861)

Buchanan's decision catastrophic

President openly sided with South against North

Ends chance of making KS a slave state

Gave Republicans concrete evidence for Slave Power Conspiracy

Broke Democratic party into factions

A New Leader Emerges

Abraham Lincoln

Insignificant local politician

Campaigns for Henry Clay in 1844

Eulogizes Clay in 1852

In 1846, elected to Congress

Opposed KNA because feared it would break Union

The Lincoln-Douglas Debates (1858)

Republicans nominate for Senate against Stephen Douglas (D)

Outline positions in public debates

Lincoln attacks slavery

Morally corrupt institution

Claims Slave Conspiracy controls US government

See it in KNA, Dread Scott, and Buchanan's endorsement of Lecompton Constitution

Douglas defends popular sovereignty

Douglas reelected by narrow margin

Lincoln and Slavery

Prior to Congress, never took stand on slavery

Home region (southern Illinois) known as Little Egypt

Had to avoid issue to build Whig support

Mexican War forced him to take stand

Condemns Polk administration for war

Votes for Wilmot Proviso

So what did Lincoln really think about slavery?

Thinks it was unjust and morally wrong

Recolonization only practical way to solve problem

Lincoln knew Whigs had problem

Must reconcile unpopularity of abolitionism and growing number in party who opposed expansion of slavery

Abolitionists denounced recolonization

John Brown's Raid

While some debate, others take action

October 1859

19 heavily armed men

Try to seize federal arsenal at Harpers Ferry, VA

Want to arm a slave rebellion and create African-American state in South

The government responds

Local militia and US Marines under Robert E. Lee quickly reclaim arsenal

Brown captured, 10 in party killed

Politics as usual

Republicans dismiss Brown as criminal/lunatic

Democrats say plot result of teachings of Republican Party

Crime and Punishment

VA governor charges Brown with treason

State court sentences him to death

Brown hanged

The Next Election

Democrats afraid to lose 1860 election

Increase protections of slavery

Southern Rights Democrats

Moderate party members

Insist party and federal government must commit to protect slavery

Leading spokesmen

Jefferson Davis

Mississippi planter and Mexican war hero

Radical Southern Democrats

Fire-Eaters

Robert B. Rhett (SC) and William L. Yancy (AL)

Demand Douglas and followers must restore international slave trade

Want to drive wedge between N and S

Preparing for the Next Election

Democratic convention meet in Charleston, April 1860

Southerners try to force party to embrace program of Jeff Davis

Call for national protection of slavery in territories

Northern Dems. refuse

Want decision left to popular sovereignty and Supreme Court

The convention decides

Adopts northern platform

Delegates from southern states walk out

Buchanan not re-nominated

Stephen Douglas leading candidate

But opponents deny him ⅔ majority

Convention adjourns with no presidential candidate

The Election of 1860

Two competing conventions

June 1860

Northern Dems. reconvene convention in Baltimore

Stephen Douglas nominated for president

Southern Dems. convene separately in Baltimore

Nominate Buchanan's VP, John C. Breckinridge (KY), as president

Thus, Democrats split into two competing factions

Does this portend secession?

Republicans hold convention

Sensing victory, they nominate Abraham Lincoln

Platform: Free soil in west, but ruled out interference with slavery in South

Deny right of states to secede from Union

The 1860 Election Results

Douglas campaigns nationally

But fighting a losing battle?

Toward end just focus on South

The election results

Lincoln wins uncertain victory

Gets 40% of popular vote

Electoral College

Lincoln 180

Breckinridge 72

Bell 39

Douglas 12

Wins only two states (MO and NJ)

Finishes second with 21% of popular vote

The Road to Disunion

A Clear and Present Danger

Lincoln's election seemed dangerous to South

Thinks slavery morally wrong, fights its extension into territories

No southern votes for Lincoln

What does he owe them?

South outraged, felt loyal

Wants North to follow southern construction

Did Southerners have anything to fear?

Post offices

Slave revolts

How can slavery be protected?

Disunion

Civil War kills more Americans than Vietnam, WWI, WWII, and Spanish-American

But does it have to happen?

Why Disunion?

Compromises won out in 1820, 1833, 1850

Why did it fail this time?

Calhoun, Clay, and Webster dead

Fire-Eaters win day

William L. Yancey, Robert B. Rhett

South Carolina first to break

December 20, 1860 (6 weeks after election)

Moved quickly while public in shock over Lincoln's election

The Birth of Nation

By January 31, 6 cotton states leave

Unionists not have time to stop

Southern militia called up

Meet in Montgomery in February 1861

Confederate States of America

Decide on Constitution, Jeff Davis

Lincoln still not in office

Buchanan refuses to act

Calls secession illegal

Say US can't use force to stop

The Fate of the Upper South

The Upper South

Panic less severe there

AR, DE, KY, MD, MO, NC, TN, VA

Looking in two directions

Pushing the issue

SC demands federal properties turned over to state

Especially Fort Sumter

Buchanan refuses and reinforces garrison

Seeks help from Congress

Sen. John Crittenden (KY)

Crittenden Compromise

1820 line extended to California border

Lincoln and Republican leaders in Congress reject it

Refuse to sacrifice Free Soil agenda

March 4, 1861

Lincoln inaugurated

The speech

Says secession illegal

Slavery must remain in South

States can return to Union

Violence against US an insurrection

Determined to enforce law, and protect federal reservations in South

Leaves choice to South:

Submit to Lincoln's policies or must go to war

Sumter now in need of supply

Lincoln careful

Allows South to take other federal properties

Sumter last, so Lincoln tries to re-supply

Fort Sumter

Davis learns of Lincoln's action on April 8

Confederates welcome it

Know Upper South will come to aid

Violence will push them into CSA

Decide to take fort before troops arrive

P. G. T. Beauregard ordered to take Sumter

Edmund Ruffin fires first shot, April 12, 1861

No one killed, Sumter falls on April 14

April 15, Lincoln calls up 75,000 troops

Sumter outrages North

Stephen Douglas says just before his death: "There are only two sides to the question. Every man must be for the United States or against it. There can be no neutrals in this war, only patriots or traitors."

Lincoln's Dilemma

Lincoln moves to win Upper South

South needs them all

Tried to keep northern 8, hoping war would be short

Northern 8 hold ⅔ of southern population, 75% of industrial capacity, 50% of food/fuel

Robert E. Lee to lead Union army

Advantages of Northern Tier:

Geography

KY has 500 mile border on OH

OH, MS rivers crucial to war effort

MD surrounds Washington, DC

Virginia Takes Sides

April 18, Winfield Scott offers Robert E. Lee command of Union army

Lee resigns declaring: "Save in defense of my native state, I hope never again to draw my sword."

VA militia takes Harpers Ferry and Newport News naval yards

Upper South states of NC, TN, AR quickly follow

But what of the other four?

"West Virginia," Maryland, and Kentucky

Lincoln moved aggressively in West Virginia

May: McClellan invades western VA

By October, 50 western counties join Union

Maryland another matter

Can't let it go

Confederates attack Union troops in Baltimore

Lincoln suspends Constitution

Arrests state legislators, and Baltimore police chief

Kentucky

Controls balance between CSA and Union

Lincoln cautious

In August, Unionist take control of Legislature

Stop flow of mules, horses, food, and whiskey to Lower South

CSA invades capturing Bowling Green and Columbus

KY seeks federal protection

US Grant drives Confederates out Sept.

And Missouri ...

Crucial to control of Western Territories

Lincoln very bold here

The value of St. Louis

River towns key to controlling transportation

Southern Missouri less certain

Full of slave owners, and southern sympathizers

July 1861

Lincoln occupies St. Louis

Drives out Confederates under Claiborne Jackson

Southern Missouri and Northern Arkansas filled with guerrilla fighting

Lincoln now controls 4 of 8 border states, and part of a 5th

States' Rights or Slavery?

July 4, 1861: Lincoln declares war aims

Rebellion must be crushed for the nation to survive

But not sure how to do that in 1861

Is a military victory enough?

Southern society and economy needed to be crushed to destroy slavery

Total war necessary

Alexander Stephens: Confederacy's "cornerstone rests upon the great truth the Negro is not equal to the white man, that slavery—subordination to the superior race—is his natural or normal condition."

War in the East

Two armies not meet until July 1861

Winfield Scott (age 70)

Cautious

Form long-term strategy known as Anaconda Plan

Weaken South thru land/sea blockades until Army strong enough to invade

Public hungry for action, want quick victory

Lincoln afraid longer war lasts more embittered each side becomes

Makes reunion more difficult

July 1861

"Forward to Richmond!"

35,000 partially trained men

General Irvin McDowell

Leave Washington in sweltering heat

Battle of Bull Run (1st Manassas)

25 miles from capital

Northern Army confronts 25,000 raw CSA soldiers

Brigadier Gen. P. G. T. Beauregard

West Point classmate of McDowell

Sightseers, journalists, and politicians expect Sunday picnic outing

Battle sways back and forth

2,300 fresh troops decide day

Turning rout into decisive victory?

Bull Run prophetic

Victory won't be quick or easy for 3 reasons:

Disorganization and confusion of armies show neither had professional military

Sides face severe problems with short-term enlistments

Logistical problems connected with mass armies must be overcome to win

The Little Napoleon

Lincoln replaces McDowell with Gen. George McClellan (34-year-old)

Need commander capable of winning war

McClellan

Army engineer

Scott retired in fall of 1861, McClellan made general in chief of Union armies

Sends short-term militias home

Transforms Army of Potomac into fighting force

McClellan as a commander

Great organizer but not daring battlefield leader

Convinced North must combine military victory with efforts to persuade South to return

Afraid of destroying his army

Want to win by maneuvering rather than fighting

The Peninsular Campaign

By March 1862, Lincoln impatient

Forces McClellan south

Leads army of 130,000 toward Richmond

Wants to capture capital without excessive casualties

Hope CSA would abandon war it couldn't win

By late June, Union army could hear church bells of Richmond

Lee counterattacks

Drives Union forces away

Losses heavy on both sides

Lincoln abandons Peninsula and McClellan

The War in the West

East just 1 of 3 theaters

Middle theater included KY, TN, MS, and AL

Western Theater was MS river and further West

LA, AR, MO, TX, and Great Plains

Native American tribes joined conflict on both sides

MS River crucial due to vital river trade and port of New Orleans

In western theater, Union had 2 strategic objectives:

Domination of KY and eastern TN to control main avenues to South and West

Control of the Mississippi River

If Union forces dominate MS River, splits South in two

Thus, major campaigns sought strategic points along rivers and RRs

The Path to Emancipation

Lincoln must move slowly on Emancipation

Risked several things

Losing allegiance of many Northerners

Offending the border states

Increasing Dems.' chances for political victory

Spring 1862

Lincoln urges Congress to compensate states for "gradual abolishment"

Border-state opposition kills idea

Not believe war's "friction and abrasion" would end slavery

The Deciding Factor

Summer 1862

Lincoln tells cabinet of desire for emancipation

Seward urges delay until North wins decisive military victory

Otherwise, appears urging racial insurrection to compensate for military failures

Lincoln tries to prepare North for shift in war's purpose

Must counteract white racial fears of free blacks

Promotes schemes for establishing free black colonies in Haiti and Panama

Pushing the Decision

August 1862

Horace Greeley attacks Lincoln for not ending slavery

Lincoln links emancipation to military necessity

"If I could save the Union without freeing any slave, I would do it; and if I could save it by freeing all the slaves, I would do it; and if I could do it by freeing some and leaving others alone, I would also do that. What I do about Slavery and the colored race, I do because I believe it helps to save the Union."

Emancipation must happen to…

Save white lives

Preserve democratic process

Win war for Union

September 1862

Union wins at Antietam

Lincoln issues preliminary Proclamation

Return to Union by Jan. 1, 1863, or southern slaves are "forever free"

Knows CSA would reject

Prepares north for "war" necessity

The Final Proclamation

New Years' Day, 1863

Final Proclamation issued

Called "an act of justice, warranted by the Constitution upon military necessity."

War now struggle to free slaves

Judging the Proclamation

Had no immediate impact on slavery

Only affects slaves in unconquered CSA

Ignores slaves in border states

Had tremendous symbolic importance

Blacks gather outside White House to cheer president

Allows for recruitment of black soldiers

Ends foreign support of South by making war about emancipation rather than reunion

The Battle Cry of Freedom

Use of black troops

Thousands offer to serve as soldiers but refused

Forced into menial jobs

Making the decision

As white casualties mount, so did interest in black service on battlefield

Black leaders pressed for black military service

Frederick Douglas

Key to establishing citizenship rights and acceptance

Serving the cause

By war's end 186,000 blacks serve

Represent only 10% of Army

134,000 escaped slaves

The military experience

Highlighted obstacles to racial acceptance

Led by white officers

Viewed as second-class soldiers

Lower pay ($10/month, whites: $13) and poorer food

More menial work, fewer benefits than whites

Finding a Winning Strategy for the North

Ulysses Grant

First objective: Destroy two Confederate armies

Lee's Army of Northern VA

Joe Johnston's Army of TN

Rejects military conventions

Not want great decisive victory like Lee

Initiate campaign of annihilation

Use superior resources to wear down and defeat South

Justify strategy by arguing "now the carnage was to be limited to a single year"

Campaign of annihilation

Focus on destruction of enemy resources fueling war effort

Total warfare

New and shocking idea

Grant "regarded it as humane to both sides to protect the persons of those found at their homes, but to consume everything that could be used to support or supply armies."

Putting the Plan into Operation

Grant must destroy Lee's army

Grant willing to take staggering losses

18,000 in Battle of Wilderness

8,000+ at Spotsylvania

12,000 at Cold Harbor

Union dead replaced with new recruits

Sends Sherman to ravage South

Chase Johnston from TN to Atlanta to Savannah

Want Southerners to "fear and dread" northern Army

Troops told to forage "liberally" from land

Criminal acts punishable by execution

After Lincoln re-elected in 1864, Sherman moves north into Carolinas

April 9, 1865

Lee surrenders at Appomattox

Return home with personal equipment if promise to act peaceably

War essentially over

Winning the War

The North won for the war for three main reasons

Grant's military strategy destroyed the South's manpower and economic resources

As Union armies pushed back borders of CSA, South lost territories essential to war effort

Naval strategy finally paid off once North had enough ships to make blockade work

By 1863, less than ½ of southern blockade runners successful

The End of Days

Lee's surrender signified end, but not really

President Davis called for guerilla resistance on April 4

Guerillas answer call during Reconstruction

Lincoln assassinated on April 14

Secretary of State Seward wounded in knife attack same day

Johnston not surrender to Sherman in NC until April 29

Davis captured May 10 at Irvinsville, GA

Even with complete military defeat, many questions remained unanswered

Reconstruction: The Unfinished Promise

An End to an Era

Lee's surrender at Appomattox not only signals end to war

Really an end to old way of life in South

South lay defenseless in 1865, conquered by superior armies of North

Broken in spirit, but full of contempt for conquerors

Paid high price to preserve, protect, and defend slavery

Much of South lay in ruins

Its industry was smashed

Its plantations lay idle

Its working class, both black and white, suffering from trauma of war

Southern recovery

Takes more than a generation

Southerners shocked by violence and destruction

Unable to explain loss

Turn against African-American population

Blamed blacks for war, and their defeat

Emergence of racism

White Southerners grow increasingly angry as time passes

Makes racial distinctions more rigid

Race provide identity that transcends their material poverty

Regardless of poverty, racial solidarity become source of pride and identity

But white solidarity depends on violence

Reconstructing the South

Planters neither willingly accept emancipation nor oversee process

What would happen after the war was left to Northerners to decide

Reconstructing the South

Began during Civil War

Start with slaves leaving plantations

Wherever Union armies go, slaves sought freedom

Federal government had to reorganize captured Confederate states

First issue: what to do with freedmen

Second: what to do politically with new territory

Lincoln first to deal with issues

Not develop coherent plan

But begin moving toward general Reconstruction policy

"Malice toward none and charity for all"

Felt war about restoring Union, not ending slavery

Emancipation Proclamation only war measure

Seeking full restoration of Union, as fast as possible

Lincoln's Plan for Reconstruction

Started when state fall under federal control

Lincoln appointed military governor

Began process of bringing them back into Union as war continued

The Thirteenth Amendment

June 1864, Lincoln calls for Constitutional ban on slavery

Part of platform in 1864 election

Abolishes and prohibits slavery forever

Passed 1865, and sent to states for ratification

The Ten Percent Plan

$1/_{10}$th of all people who voted in 1860 in state must take oath declaring loyalty to US constitution

Then permitted to form government

By 1864, 3 states (TN, AR, and LA) admitted

But plan hated by some members of Lincoln's own party

Questioning Lincoln's Plan

Many think Lincoln being too lenient on South

Others say he lacks authority to impose Ten Percent Plan anyway

Argue that authority rests Congress

Besides, policy must be tougher

Rejecting Lincoln's plan

Delegates from 4 reconstructed states show up in Congress

Republicans refuse to seat them

Begin to put forward own plan

The Wade-Davis Plan

Republican plan articulated in Wade-Davis Bill of 1864

Unlike Lincoln, Congress not want to move quickly

No state should return to Union during war

Lincoln vetoed

The New Plan

Say ½ of citizens in a state who voted in 1860 had to take loyalty oath before admitted

Oath not more stringent

But had to say never voluntarily aided Confederacy

Means oath-taker could not have participated in Confederate fight

Citizens who serve in any office in Confederate government or in Confederate Army automatically disqualified from voting

Lincoln Responds to Wade-Davis

When bill passed Congress, Lincoln not entirely reject

But not want to be tied down to any one plan so veto

Also claim President should form Reconstruction policy, not Congress

Changing of the guard

In April of 1865 Lincoln assassinated

Andrew Johnson becomes president

Will he continue Lincoln's Plan?

Who Was Andrew Johnson?

Johnson of humble origins

From eastern TN

Never a slave owner

Had considerable hatred for plantation class

He was a vehement racist

Served first in HoR, then Senate

Introduced homestead legislation in 1840s

Military governor of TN (under Lincoln's Ten Percent Plan)Democrat brought on ticket with Lincoln because pro-Unionist

Only time in American history ticket split

Andrew Johnson, President

Becomes president in spring of 1865

War had just ended

Congress out of session

Johnson takes initiative to form own Reconstruction policy

Puts forward own plan

Appoint provisional governors in former Confederate states

Each governor to call for constitutional convention within state

Tasked to write new state constitutions

The Johnson Plan

Johnson attempting to restore Union as quickly as possible

Submission to "King" Andrew

Expressly forbid ex-Confederates and Southerners with over $20,000 in property from participating in conventions

Allows liberal "pardon" policy on an individual basis

Probably too liberal

Many ex-Confederates return to D.C. in fall to retake seats in Congress vacated when states seceded

Included V.P. of Confederacy

Johnson's Plan Sparks Outrage

Return of Confederates to D.C. unacceptable to many Republicans, Vets.

Politics as usual

Republicans need to maintain power nationally

Only sectional party, with no constituency in South

Know that to maintain power must get southern constituency

Other concerns

Want guarantees for protection of black civil liberties

Also need protection for whites sympathetic to Republican party

Division in the Ranks

Republicans divide into two main factions

1. Moderates (the majority)

Accept much of Johnson plan

Want to dispossess Confederates who held office

But establish for special pardons, just as Johnson did

Want basic guarantees for voting rights and civil rights

Some black males should get vote, if prove worthy

Establish education and property qualifications

But would hurt freedmen and poor whites

Southern states had right of refusal

If not accept measures, not get back into Union

Not to be forced into accepting measures

Allowed to suffer consequences of choice

2. The Radical Republicans

Small group of Republicans seeking more severe measures

Thought Union must establish equitable basis for nation to operate

Want vastly restructured South

Must destroy old planter class

Replace with new class of Southerners

Creating a New Nation

To facilitate new system, Radicals want:

To reduce southern states to territories

To impose martial law

To confiscate and redistribute plantations

To eliminate anyone who wouldn't take iron clad loyalty oath from politics

To weaken (if not destroy) old planter class

To build a constituency of blacks and poor whites

Radicals and Freedmen

Led by Thaddeus Stevens,

Charles Sumner

Radicals want basic guarantees for freedmen

Universal suffrage to all men

Voting rights to all men

Equal civil rights for all men

Anything else…

Want federal government to aid in education of blacks

Didn't want South choice of agreement

South should have to accept

Radicals want things to take a long time

Business as Usual

September 1865

Congress back in session

Feel Southerners thumbing noses at spirit of Johnson's plan

On state and local level, planters in power

On national level, former Confederates returned to congressional seats

Johnson pardoned virtually everyone who submitted to him

Incensed most Republicans

Behavior of individual states also a problem

In government

SC refused to repudiate secession in its Constitution

SC, MS, and LA pass black codes

Based on old slave codes

Restrict rights, liberties of freedmen

MS refused to ratify 13th Amendment

In practice

Reports circulate freedmen being forced to work for former masters

Violence toward freedmen rampant

Rejecting Johnson's Plan

In spite of war, not much seemed to have changed

Republicans in Congress think situation unacceptable

Decide to move in different direction

Call for:

Confiscation and redistribution of property

Support for black rights

Punishment of Confederates

Proceed with little support at first

Not even moderates in favor of confiscating rebel plantations and giving blacks land

Moderates believe radical plan too extreme

Moderate Concerns

Wary about implications of radical plan for property rights

Wary of abusing power of federal government

Not sure federal government have authority radicals supposed it did

Fear radical approach rejects their vision of what South should look like after war

Thought it would still be cotton economy

Afraid blacks not grow cotton if given own land

Enacting a New Plan

Despite differences, moderates and radicals want something different than Johnson's plan

Fall of 1865, act together when former Confederates show up in Washington

Congress refused to seat southern representatives

Congress passes series of Reconstruction bills (1866)

Start with Civil Rights Bill

Designed to guarantee some civil rights for blacks

Johnson vetoed, but Congress overrides

Protecting the Plan

Radicals know many Northerners not want to go much further

Afraid Supreme Court might overrule if went too far

To prevent a rollback, embodied new notions as constitutional amendments

Why use amendment?

Cannot be overturned

Applies to all states

Easier than passage in individual states

Step 1: The 14th Amendment

Redefined US citizenship

Everyone born in US a citizen

No state may deprive citizens of privileges of citizenship or due process of law

Enfranchised all males citizens, black and white

Would decrease representation if state not enfranchise blacks

Declare that no person who held office in Confederacy could hold office in United States government

Understanding the 14th Amendment

Written by moderate Republicans

Want to keep southern blacks in South

Also want to maintain their own political power nationally

So sponsor formation of Republican party within South

The question of enforcement

Not clear how much jurisdiction federal government had

So never say states had to accept 14th Amendment

But make it requirement for admittance into Union

Otherwise, state remains territory

Contesting Congressional Reconstruction

Johnson feels 14th Amendment unconstitutional

Tells South not to ratify

TN did anyway, but only southern state that did

Creates conflict between Congress and president

Congress outraged, wants to punish South for transgression

Tension heats up in fall elections 1866

Vehement, bitter campaigning

Yet, Republicans do well at polls

See victory as mandate

By March 1867

Radicals enact series of Reconstruction acts

Known as radical, military, congressional Reconstruction

Put South under military jurisdiction

Not same as territorial status

Step 2 of Radical Reconstruction

Divide South into 5 military districts under control of Union Army

Place military garrisons throughout South

All people not excluded by 14th Amendment to be enrolled to vote

Provided for universal male suffrage, whether white or black

The Freedman's Bureau

Established March 3, 1865

Bureau of Refugees, Freedmen, and Abandoned Land

Offered direct federal aid to citizens on massive scale

First time government had done so

Bureau responsibilities

Distribute food, tools, and medical services

Establish thousands of schools and some colleges for blacks

Negotiate several hundred thousand employment contracts between freedmen and planters

Tried to manage confiscated lands

Often redistribute to blacks

Southern opinion

Hated bureau and its minions

Felt put freedmen's rights over their own

Staffed by opportunists exploiting chaos of postwar South

Limits to Radical Reconstruction

Federal government would only go so far

Difficult to maintain interest of Northerners

Everyone wants to put war into past

Not committed to African-Americans

Had many limits

Enforcement ambiguous, left many loopholes

Voting statutes say cannot deny vote to anyone on basis of color, but could for other reasons

By 1869, 15th Amendment ratified

Specifically enfranchised blacks in North and South

Republican Governments

With help of Radical Plan and military presence, Republicans take control of southern governments

Many blacks elected to office

Carpetbaggers and scalawags

Institute new regimes based on equality, want to provide equal opportunity

But also dominated by corruption

Southerners disgusted, outraged by situation

Three Major Republican Problems

1. Taxation

Too much to pay for

Prewar services, must repair war's destruction, must stimulate industry and need for new ventures like public schools

War destroyed southern tax base

One source gone entirely—slaves

Many destitute and lost former taxable items

Money, livestock, fences, and buildings

Only taxes available: sales, excise, and property

2. Corruption

Many carpetbaggers and black politicians involved

Fraudulent schemes, sell votes, padded expenses

Part of nationwide surge of corruption in an age ruled by "spoilsmen"

Not limited by party, but Dems. pin blame on unqualified blacks and greedy Northerners

3. Party Division

Problems lead Republicans to fracture

Factions form along racial and class lines

Undermines party unity

Southern Redemption

Restoring the status quo

Southerners seek to retake control of South

Establish White Leagues

Kentucky Regulators, KKK, Knights of the White Camellia

Use violence and intimidation

Keep voters from polls

Drive undesirables from office

Redeemer Democrats

Claim to be saviors protecting South from "black domination" and "carpetbag rule"

Use race for voter appeal

Violence and intimidation as political tactic

The Failure of Reconstruction

Radical Reconstruction last only few years

Brought down by fiscal problems, Republican mistakes, racial hostility, and outright terror

Not only political failure though

Had enduring social and economic implications

Failed to alter southern social structure, or distribution of wealth and power

Without land, freedmen at mercy of white landowners

Freedmen have no power armed only with ballot

Was It Possible to Reform the South?

Would have to redistribute southern land

Some say freedom without land just "cheap philanthropy"

North "threw all the Negroes on the world without any way of getting along."

Need careful supervision by Congress, federal government

Require longer attention span by Northerners

War, reconstruction take too long

Other issues prevail

Notes for Lectures 18 through 26

LECTURE 18
The Failure of Southern Agriculture & the Rise of Populism

> ● main point
> ─ sub point
> ＊ sub-sub point

Emergence of Agrarian Radicalism

    Reconstruction transforms southern economy

    Southern economy dependent on 2 crucial elements:

    Rise of black tenancy

    Absorption of white farmers into cotton market

The South and the Nation

    By 1890, more people in cotton than before Civil War

    Creates discontent among farmers in South

    To understand, must place South in national economy

    South assumed something of colonial status

    Engaged in export agriculture

    Dependent on North for manufactured goods

    Produce raw materials for use in industrialized North

    Was there any Southern industry?

    Either extractive or processed agricultural goods and forest products

    Such industries did not develop the South

The Textile Industry

    ● Most important processing industry in South

    Rely on white labor force

    ● Why not use blacks as mill workers?

    Planters control black labor

    Feared that use of blacks in textile mills would threaten plantation system

    Traditionally resist southern industrialization because of this threat

The National Economy

- Important to understand when considering causes of agrarian radicalism in South
- National economy undergoing major stresses
- In 1873, severe depression hit nation

  Part of worldwide depression

  Most serious depression in modern history

  Lasted till end of 19th century

  1873–1878 and 1893–1897 worst periods
- Rural areas hit hardest

  Prices of agricultural commodities drop precipitously

Depression in the Southern Economy

- South hit hardest by drop in cotton prices
- Southern cotton market nearly destroyed
- By early 1890s, price of cotton far less than cost of production
- Depression hard for planters and plain folk
- Poor whites, blacks suffer most
- Tenant farmer (regardless of color) had to pay off landlord and merchants
- Extremely difficult to gain landownership in best of situations, but impossible in this scenario

THE FARMER IS THE MAN

From Depression to Political Discontent

- Several factors lead to political action in South
1 Sad state of economy
2 Poor white farmers spiraling into debt
3 Many lose farms to foreclosure or were close to losing farms
- Leads political discontent to across South
- But limited. Why?

The Problem with Southern Politics

- White southern farmers in political bind
- Most whites were Democrats
- Party controlled by planters, merchants, and industrialists
- Not interested in reform
- Alternative was alignment with Republican Party
- Unthinkable
- Viewed as "black" party
- Party of "radical reconstruction"
- Most whites not willing to join or align with Republicans
- What other options were available?

Matthew A Desorme

Southern Farmers Alliance

- Early 1880s, some whites run as independents
  Rarely won
- Never formed real political organization
- Late 1880s, powerful organization forms in South
- Becomes backbone of largest third-party organization in US
- Started in Texas in 1870s
- Success limited by cattle barons who were fencing in land
- Southern Farmers Alliance
- Between 1886–1888, organization spread to all southern states
- Expanding membership
  2 million whites
  1 million blacks

Forming an Alliance

- Not political at first
- Actually focused on organizing large spectrum of farmers outside politics
- Concentrate of farmer issues
- Particularly try to address financial remedies
- Who were members?
- Limited to whites
- Small farmers, tenants
- Appealed to some planters
- Only people not allowed were merchants, bankers, and speculators

Limited Membership, but Similar Goals

- Blacks not allowed to join SFA
- Form separate, all-black cadres
- Become known as Colored Farmers Alliance (1886)
- What were farmers alliances trying to do?
- Organized at state level, serve local needs
  Farmers needed to sell cotton at better prices
  Want to buy goods without paying inflated credit prices
- Form local cooperatives
  Work out deals with merchants to sell cotton in bulk
  Then buy goods in bulk to reduce costs

The Political Problem

- Farmers Alliance avoids politics at first
- Not want to be side-tracked
- Focus on local issues
- But political involvement become necessity

- Obstacles too inflexible to avoid politics
- What were the obstacles?
- Merchants
    Financing cooperatives

Two Major Problems for Cooperatives

1. Merchants

- Hostile to Farmers Alliance
- Did everything imaginable to undermine them
- Control or heavily influence local political machines
- Make life hard for alliance members
    Separate pricing
    Refusal to do business
    Physical intimidation

2. Financing

- Farmers don't have money to finance
- Pool money locally to develop state cooperatives
- But still massively under funded
- Vulnerable to attack by merchants
- Not easily accessible to membership

Turning to Politics

- Alliance leaders realize must nationalize to accomplish goals
- Convene meeting in 1889
- Join with western farmers alliance
    WFA had about 2,000,000 members
- Develop strategy called Sub Treasury plan
    Quickly becomes centerpiece of program

The Sub Treasury Plan

- Every agricultural county in US to have warehouse
- Farmer exchange cotton crop for credit on 80% of crop at 1% interest
- Warehouse sell crop at best market price
- Supposed to hold cotton off market rather than dump all at once
- To be financed by federal government
- Becomes key issue for two reasons:
- 1) Challenged established credit and marketing structure in economy
    Proposed to reorient way exchange relationships worked
    Discards capitalism for "cooperative" way.
    Planters and merchants especially hostile because ended crop lien system

2) Unavoidably pushed Alliance into politics

Believed could enact Sub Treasury through political action

Problems with Politics

- Political involvement immediately raised question of organization

- Meeting between southern and western branches not united in 1889

- Two sides could not agree on fundamental issues:

- Southern unity concerns

Fearful of party that united blacks and whites

Afraid of reprisals from southern planters

Flew in face of southern racism

Would prevent many Southerners from voting with them

- Western unity concerns

Fearful of being outnumbered by Southerners

Southerners had 3 million members (counting 1 million blacks) while western/midwestern farmers only 2 million

Differing political orientations

Westerners, who more likely Repbulicans, want protective tariffs

Southerners, who mostly Democrats, unilaterally opposed protective tariffs

Working Within the System

- With such differing views, each side returned home to work within their political situation

- Southern alliancemen sided with Dems

- In 1890 elections, some Dems seem to court interests of alliancemen

Those Dems easily swept into office

But not fulfill campaign promises

Too many large planters, merchants, bankers, industrialists in South against policies

Had a lot more influence

The Populist Party

- After 1890, alliancemen discouraged with traditional parties

- One KS group form People's Party in 1890

Members called Populists

Met with success locally

- 1891, western and southern farmers alliancemen again meet

Supposed to discuss uniting, but again failed

- Not until early 1892 does independent party incorporating both western and southern farmers alliances successfully form

But run a number of candidates

Populist Ideology

- Criticize America's concentration of wealth and power

- Age of robber barons

— Mad that some people getting rich at everyone else's expense

— Believe "rich" people not working for a living

Bankers, investors, and speculators

Not really work, just wheeling and dealing in marketplace

— Meanwhile, people doing manual labor getting poorer

Populists believe situation that emerges causes political system corrupted by wealthy

The Populist Program

- Embodied in Populist platform

1) Sub-Treasury System

2) Expanding the money supply

- Want free and unlimited coinage

Coin mintage not regulated by government

Bankers and speculators gave value to currency

- Populists want silver-based coins

Believed it democratizes money supply

Federal control would be more sympathetic to farmers

3) Want government to nationalize transportation and communication

- US only western society where not occur

- Robber barons control and charge discriminatory rates

- Makes it hard for farmers to move products

Populists and Race

- Populist also challenge America in other ways

- Question established idea of race relations

- Try to build coalition between poor whites and blacks in South

- Offers serious threat to planters

- So what was the racial policy of the Populists?

- At best, demand blacks have full civil and political rights

- Want to set a new style in race relations

Blacks must be included

Can no longer be separated into black and white alliances

Denounce lynching and convict leasing system

Combating Racism?

- Racism not disappear, but can't disappear over night

- Qualifying Populists' racial thinking

- Populists always careful to say not support social equality

- Many continue to support white supremacy

- Blacks left in difficult predicament

- Should they support Populists?

Economic reforms better for people who actually own land

But Populists offer more political democracy than Democrats

Racism the deciding factor

Persistence of racism among prominent populists pushes blacks away

Rarely switch where able to build strong Republican organizations

Denounce Populists for not supporting black issues

The First Populist Candidate

Go national in 1892

First presidential candidate

James B. Weaver of Iowa

Received only 8% of popular vote

Lost, but made Populism a national force

First time since 1856 that third party won so many votes in national election

The Demise of the Populists

What defeated the Populists?

Faced widespread fraud

Major problem in South

Democrats stole elections

Democrats also used violence to suppress party

But also got sidetracked

Two issues eventually destroyed the Populists

Fusion

Monetization of silver

What Was Fusion?

Populists successes in 1894 came from tactic of fusing with 1 major party

Agreed on a joint ticket

But fusion had particular problems

Many Democrats and Republicans who "fused" went own way once elected

Required Populists to abandon much of their own platform

The Silver Issue

Western Populists fall under influence of silver mine owners

Became convinced that hope of party lay in single-issue commitment to free and unlimited coinage of silver

Head of party, James B. Weaver, expected both major parties to nominate gold candidates in 1896

Thought action would send disappointed silverites to People's Party standard

The Wizard of Oz

The Republican Candidate

Hold convention first

Nominate William McKinley on first ballot

Congressman 1877–1891

Two-time governor of Ohio

Identified with high protective tariff that bore his name

Platform argued that prosperity depended on tariff protection and gold standard

Thus, McKinley was what Weaver expected: a gold candidate

The Democrat Candidate

Democrats disappoint Weaver

Nominate William Jennings Bryan

Complete surprise

36-year-old congressman from NE

Few saw him as presidential material

So how did Bryan get nominated?

Member of Resolutions Committee (of Democratic convention)

Arranged to give himself closing argument for a silver plank

Gives dramatic speech that swept convention for silver plank

At end, Bryan stretched out his arms as if on a cross, and convention exploded with applause

It ensured his nomination

What Could the Populists Do?

Nomination of silver candidate by Dems left Populist strategy in shambles

Some leaders favored fusion with entire Democratic ticket

Antifusionists were outraged

Dem. V.P. candidate, Arthur Sewall, was East Coast banker and ardent hard money (gold) man

An unwise compromise

Populist convention nominate Bryan as presidential candidate

Populist Tom Watson (GA) to be V.P. running mate

The End of the Populists

Populists absorbed into Democratic Party

Bryan ran as a Democrat/Populist

Only two presidential candidates

Bryan as Democrat/Populist

McKinley as Republican

But three vice presidential candidates

NJ businessman named Hobart as Republican

Sewell as Democrat

Tom Watson as Populist

McKinley won election by handsome margin

LECTURE 19

The Rise of Jim Crow and the African American Experience, From 1877 to the 1920s

Jim Crow and the Solid South

- Populist sought biracial alliance
- Wanted cooperation among poor farmers, regardless of race
- Offered serious threat to southern social system

  Question class advantages of elites

  Question racial caste system of South
- Populism starts process of change
- Brings poor white and black voters together in political alliance
- But they do not have enough time, such a process was slow and painful
- Black voters mostly in Republican Party
- Poor whites Democrats

Responding to the Populist Threat

- Populism collapses in 1896
- Mostly because sold out to free silver
- Also due to violence and intimidation in South
- With Populism gone, Dem. white elites try to end future alliances

  Must eliminate as many poor voters from voting as possible

  Poor disenfranchised in 4 main ways:

  Poll taxes

  Literacy requirements

Property requirements

All-white primaries

Understanding Southern Disenfranchisement

Southern elites claim laws only directed toward blacks

Saw disfranchisement as a way of cleaning up southern politics

15th Amendment supposed to prevent voting restrictions

Southern elite devised specific types of laws to circumvent Amendment

Laws had 3 escape clauses to protect white voters

1 Understanding clause

Voter must recite/explain US Constitution and Declaration of Independence from memory

2 Grandfather clause

If grandfather could legally vote before Civil War, then you can vote

3 Good character clause

Subjective decision made by interviewer

Northern Disfranchisement

Not just southern phenomenon

Many northern states employ similar measures

But want to eliminate different group

Make ability to read English a voting requirement

Difference lies in who being kept from vote

Northerners eliminating immigrant vote

Esp. those from non-English-speaking countries

Italians

Germans

Eastern Europeans

All Jews

The Results of Disfranchisement

1 Led to huge decline in voter turnout

In 1888, number of eligible voters actually voting was about 80%

In 1890, number falls to 60%

By 1910, only 30% voting

Only 5% of blacks voting

But number of white voters dropped too

By 1930s, only 20–30% of eligible white voters cast ballot

2 Republican Party completely eliminated in South

One-party South now led by the Democrats

Democrats remain in exclusive power until passage of Voting Rights Act in 1965

Rise of Jim Crow

- Disenfranchisement quickly followed by social segregation (called Jim Crow)
- Vary among communities and states
- Applies only to racist laws passed after 1890
- Jim Crow came from similar laws passed immediately after Civil War called Black Codes
- Merely transformed codes into Jim Crow laws
- Understanding Jim Crow
- Part of larger national (and worldwide) trend

  But worst in South

- 1870s to 1880s

  Age of racism and new imperialism

  Social Darwinism and racial assumptions it included dominate

- Even hits Supreme Court

  1896, issued *Plessy v. Ferguson*

  Establish "separate but equal" doctrine

  Not overturned until 1954

Segregation

- Key goal of Jim Crow laws
- Had a long history in South
- Slavery itself was a form of segregation

  But segregation of 1890s different

  During slavery, slaves go with owners on train rides or in hotels

  Jim Crow creates separate world

- 1889–1915, Southern states enact Jim Crow laws
- Provide for legal segregation of races
- Includes: schools, railroads, workplaces, hospitals, hotels, taverns, water fountains, even school books

  Applies to all public facilities

Segregation and Travel

"The Black Laws" by Bishop B. W. Arnett

Members [of the Ohio House of Representatives] will be astonished when I tell them that I have traveled in this free country for twenty hours without anything to eat; not because I had no money to pay for it, but because I was colored. Other passengers of a lighter hue had breakfast, dinner and supper. In traveling we are thrown in "jim crow" cars, denied the privilege of buying a berth in the sleeping coach. This monster caste stands at the doors of the theatres and skating rinks, locks the doors of the pews in our fashionable churches, closes the mouths of some of the ministers in their pulpits which prevents the man of color from breaking the bread of life to his fellowmen.

This foe of my race stands at the school house door and separates the children, by reason of color, and denies to those who have a visible admixture of African blood in them the blessings of a graded school and equal privileges … We call upon all friends of Equal Rights to assist us in this struggle to secure the blessings of untrammeled liberty for ourselves and prosperity.

Maintaining Segregation

Racial violence and intimidation

Lynching

1882–1951, 3,437 blacks lynched. Why?

41% felonious assault, 19.2% for rape, 6.1% attempted rape, 4.9% robbery and theft, 1.8% insult to white persons, and 22.7% for miscellaneous offenses or no offense

Why Did Segregation not Happen Earlier Given Southern Racial Views?

1) Most of South rural

Segregation did not make sense in that setting

2) From 1870s to 1880s, planters dominant and opposed segregation

3) Black voting power ensures planters and merchants not support segregation laws

But once voting power gone, no reason not to support

Factors Leading to Segregation

Southern urbanization

Growth of towns and cities creates more situations where blacks and whites would mingle

Merchants and planters unite in 1890s

Agree to disfranchise and segregate black voters

Populist movement contributes to decision

Planters and merchants see group as radical threat

Becomes impetus for southern elites

Must deny blacks and poor whites right to vote

Must separate along lines of race

Segregation ensures races not mingle and learn who true enemies were

3. The Compromise of 1877

Pact made in Congress between Redeemer Democrats and Republicans

Rutherford B. Hayes (R) becomes president

Federal troops pulled from South

Ended Reconstruction in South

Re-establishes dogma of States' Rights

Death sentence for hopes of blacks

Allow restoration of Black Codes as Jim Crow

Offer irrefutable proof southern whites want to keep southern blacks in complete subjugation

Intimidating the Opposition

The end of Reconstruction

Depend on destroying black leadership

Either killed, intimidated, or driven out

Class just as important as race

Southern elites had most to lose

Can't let anyone stand in their way

White politicians who encouraged black political activity also targeted

"Print" Matthews, Copiah County (MS)

Powerful man

Son of slave owner

Sons went to University of Mississippi

Owned biggest general store in Hazelhurst

County evenly divided (5,000 population) between black and white

After Civil War, Print works with Republicans to make transition to freedom easier for blacks in county

In election of 1883, merge supporters into Fusion Independent Party

Includes black Republicans and a few white farmers

Restoring Order in Copiah County

White population responds with campaign of terror

150 armed men roamed the county

Pulled cannon with them

Fired at any blacks they found

Participants include planters and merchants

Beatings and murders keep blacks from voting in 1883 elections

Gang visits cabin of black farmer named Tom Wallis

Friend of Matthews

When he resisted beating, they shot him dead and wounded his wife

Local black church was burned to ground

Most of black population fled homes and forced to hide in woods until election over

Matthews served notice not to go to poll

He told gang to drop dead and went anyway

At voter box, confronted by Democratic thug named Ras Wheeler

Given task of keeping Print from voting

Two argue for moment then Print gave his ballot to an election official

Wheeler reached into wooden box, pulled out a shotgun, and killed Matthews

As the Dust Settles, the Law Steps In...

Next day, Copiah Democratic executive committee met at courthouse

Passes number of resolutions due to Print's murder

Anyone trying to avenge Print's death would find swift retribution

No member of Matthews family was ever allowed to enter politics again

No man of any color would be allowed to organize blacks against whites again

These kinds of events repeated throughout South

In every place, people intimidated into following Democratic Party's lead

By 1890s, thanks to disenfranchisement laws and failure of Populism, blacks lost right to vote in much of South

And poor whites?

The Solid South

- Emerge by turn of 20th century
- Refers to Democrats' domination of southern vote
- Dems. win heavily in South in every presidential election from 1876–1948
- Originates in southern animosity against Republican role in Civil War and Reconstruction
- Maintained by Dems. willingness to accommodate South's Jim Crow laws and racial segregation
- Action always falls under rubric of States' Rights

Who Led the Solid South and What Do They Want?

- Led by merchants and planters
- Work to keep South agricultural

  Lasts through Great Depression
- Only change when WWII forced South to modernize

  Second Reconstruction, this time as Civil Rights Movement, rocks South

  Allows southern blacks to regain freedoms lost at end of 19th c.

Opposing an Abominable Situation

- William Sinclair, Aftermath of Slavery

  1905
- Realized importance of vote for blacks

  Voting let black men be a man in society

  Without the vote, made less than a slave

  "Just a thing, with no control over own destiny"

  Thus, must protect black vote in South
- Points to vulgarities of Senator Benjamin Tillman (SC)

  Advocate murder of 30,000 black men in SC to eliminate black vote

  Publicly boasted he took part in "shooting niggers"

  While in Detroit, claimed he helped murder 7 blacks

  In the Senate chambers, he bragged he didn't know how many blacks he had killed, but said "I got my share"

  Sinclair noted "not one of these unfortunate colored people had committed, or even been charged with, any offense"

  They simply tried to vote, so he gunned them down

"Pitchfork" Ben Tillman and Southern Demagoguery

- Tillman was the prototype politician who used "nigger baiting" for public support
- Holding office

  Governor of SC (1890–94)

  Elected to US Senate from South Carolina in 1894
- Hated SC's 1868 Constitution because drafted by Republicans

  Called Convention in 1895 to adopt a new Constitution

  Of 160 delegates, only 6 were black

  Write new constitution eliminating black vote
- How did Tillman get elected?

—Collapse of southern Populism paved way for rise of demagogues

"Pitchfork Ben" just one of many in south

Wooed poor white votes with agrarian program carrying white supremacist overtones

—Tillman's rhetoric was more inflammatory than his actual policy and positions

Curbs lynching in SC while advocating segregation and disfranchisement

A farmer himself, Tillman spoke for agricultural interests

Directed hostility toward Wall Street, industrial interests, and Northeast

Sought to defend interests of South

Going Beyond Political Discrimination

With political discrimination came economic discrimination

After war, blacks excluded from wide range of jobs

John Mercer Langston

Black lawyer and representative of Freedmen's Bureau

Report after Civil War that ⅓ of black population in NC were skilled craftsmen

10 years later, blacks were completely driven out of those fields

Most tenant farmers/sharecroppers

Found same situation across South

Also noted political problem in South

James Vardamen, Governor of Mississippi

Declared that black people had only 1 role in society: "That of a menial. That is what God designed him for and the white people will see to it that God's design is carried out."

Booker T. Washington

Emerges as leader and spokesman for blacks in America

First for southern blacks, then for all blacks

Who was Washington?

Son of slave

Attends Hampton Institute

Then new teacher training school in Tuskegee

Founds Alabama Normal and Industrial Institute in 1881

Began with 40 students in abandoned shack

Stresses hard work, simple living, healthy diet, cleanliness, and piety

—Best talent was diplomacy in dealing with what he called the "Other Nation"

His name for world of southern whites

Expert at attracting attention of northern capitalists like Andrew Carnegie

Washington and the South

To Washington, South's future lay in entering industrial age and escaping agriculture

Dependence on agriculture caused slavery and Civil War

To be great, South must cast off bonds of agriculture and create industry

Situation offers blacks great opportunity

To succeed, they must master industrial skills

Make themselves vital parts of New (industrial) South

Industrial or practical education at center of his improvements

Science, math, history and literature all valuable

But not as important as training for new tasks that could make black people wealthy and self-sufficient

Thus, students to learn practical artisan and industrial skills

Washington's Secret for Black Success

Getting Black advancement

Based on hard work, thrift, saving and owning property

Not want to keep blacks from succeeding in other areas

Want to improve conditions through practical skills

Want industrial education not to "cramp" the black man, but "because I want to free him."

Building the Tuskegee Institute

Tuskegee taught 33 trade skills

Of institute's 60 buildings, 56 built by students

In one year, manufactured 2 million bricks

Gaining National Prominence

Cotton states and International Exposition in Atlanta, 1893

Washington's speech gets national notoriety

Widely reprinted by white newspapers who agreed with him

Say wisest among "his race understand that the agitation of questions of social equality is the extremist folly, and that progress in the enjoyment of all the privileges will come to us must be the result of severe and constant struggle."

Assures South that immigration not required to become an industrial power

"Cast down your bucket among those people who have, without strikes and labor wars, tilled your fields, cleared your forests, built your railroad and cities. You can be sure in the future, as in the past, that you and your families will be surrounded by the most patient, faithful, law-abiding and unresentful people that the world has seen … with a devotion that no foreigner can approach, ready to lay down our lives, if need be, in defense of yours."

White Southerners have no need to fear that blacks would demand social equality

"In all things that are purely social, we can be as separate as the fingers, yet one as the hand in all things essential to mutual progress."

Black Responses to Washington

Outrage came quickly from many sectors of black community

John Hope

Graduate of Brown University

On faculty at Atlanta Baptist College

Offended by Washington's repeated assurances that blacks did not want social equality

"If we are not striving for social equality, in heaven's name for what are we living? I regard it cowardly and dishonest for any of our men to tell white people or colored people that we are not struggling for equality. Why build a wall to keep me out? I am no wild beast, nor am I an unclean thing."

Others criticized Washington for stressing industrial education over true education

Most prominent was Du Bois

W. E. B. Du Bois

- The successor to Washington
- Grew up in Great Barrington, MA
- In 1885 Du Bois (18) gets scholarship to Fisk University (TN)

  Family did not want him going to South

  Experiences complete culture shock

  Passionate church services and racism
- 1888, graduates from Fisk and wins scholarship to Harvard

  Becomes concerned with "black question"

  At graduation, spoke about Jefferson Davis

  Described Davis as decent and honorable person

  Misled by Teutonic ideals saying it necessary to conquer other peoples to advance civilization
- Teaches at University of Pennsylvania

  Examines predominately black area in Philadelphia

  Found that black crime had risen dramatically since Civil War

  Rising crime rate symptom of larger problem

  Poverty and segregation were destroying black community in America
- Moves to Atlanta University

  Continues to study the problems of black life in urban places

  Still young and idealistic

  Thought problems of race relations simply one of education

  Ignorance and stupidity are the ultimate evils, but they could be ended with education

A Changing Point of View

- But then something unexpected happened
- Du Bois was changed by 1 particular moment in time

  The lynching of Sam Hose, 1899

  Black farmer killed landlord in dispute over wages

  Mob lynched him before arrested

  Knuckles displayed at nearby grocery store
- Realizes scientific detachment impossible

  Turns to journalism to make problems known
- The Transformation of Du Bois
- Slowly recognizes that Black culture had its own "soul"

  Gave inner power and meaning to African-Americans

  Fate of the black soul can't be ignored or absorbed by white America

  Had to be honored for what it was

The Souls of Black Folk (1903)

- Du Bois' greatest work
- Explain what it meant to be black at turn of century
- "The problem of the Twentieth Century is the problem of the color-line"
- Say new men of power in South weren't planters, merchants, or African-Americans

    But poor whites freed from planter dominance by Civil War

    Remade South in their own image, exploiting both planters and blacks
- Du Bois believed true source of distinctive African-American culture lay in religion

    Defined consciousness of black people

    Became creed for black people all around world

Du Bois' View of Black Religion

- Three distinguishing characteristics to Black religion
- 1. Preacher
- 2. Music
- 3. Frenzy of services
- Preacher most unique
- Leader, politician, orator, and idealist
- Devolves from tribal medicine man
- In slavery, preachers heal sick, interpret God's actions, and comfort slaves

    Act as doctor, judge, and priest

    Establishes first true African-American institution—"The Negro Church"

    To Du Bois, blacks must strive to attain preacher role to become leader and teacher of his people
- Religion creates the Black Consciousness
- Black Americans downtrodden, yet have great gift

    See hope and promise of America in ways no white ever could

    Constantly aware of their special place in American history

    Both American and black

    Must struggle to be American, yet not lose their distinctiveness

The South Spawned Two Most Progressive Movements in American History

- 1. Populist Movement
- 2. Civil Rights Movement
- Blacks play prominent roles in both
- But rarely recognized, because the real problem was poverty
- Martin Luther King Jr said it best: "The true enemy of both blacks and whites was poverty. Until both races were free of that condition, nothing would change"

    The message of the Populists clearly echoing 70 years later

Progressivism and the Progressive Movement

A Need for Change

Reform swept America from 1890s to 1917

Everybody wants some form of change

Farmers want better prices and railroad regulation

Urbanites want better city services and better city government

Professionals like social workers and doctors try to improve dangerous and unhealthy conditions where people live and work

Businessmen lobbied for goals they defined as reform

Participants call selves Progressives, while period called Progressive Era

Progressivism not single political movement

Reformers had diverse and often contradictory goals

Progressive Origins

Rooted in Populist and speculative journalism

Mugwumps

Republicans who championed honest government

Adopt reforms of Populists

Want only righteous and educated men to run government

Seen as moderates saddling both sides of issues

Muckrakers

Journalists and literary social critics

Exposed evils of tenement life, city government corruption, industry excesses, etc.

Mugwumps got name from T. Roosevelt

Muckrakers not just throw political mud

Henry D. Lloyd probably the first

Critiqued Standard Oil and other business monopolies

- Jacob Riis

  Danish immigrant who expose NY slums in *How the Other Half Lives* (1890)

- Lincoln Steffens, *The Shame of the Cities* (1904)

  Chronicled organized graft in largest cities

  Publicity led to election of reform-minded mayors in New York, St. Louis, San Francisco, Detroit, and Cleveland

- Ida Tarbell

  Exposed nefarious business practices of corporations

Who Were the Progressives?

- Progressives include 4 key groups:

  1. Middle-class reformers

  Believe science and scientific method should be employed to help urban poor

  Hate partisan politics

  2. Upper-class reformers

  Came from political and social elite

  Seek limited political and economic reform to stabilize American society

  3. WC reformers

  From East, usually immigrants

  Want government to alleviate hardships caused by industrial growth in cities

  Against reformers seeking prohibition and Civil Service reforms

  4. Socialist reformers

  Includes everyone from radical Populists to Unionists to intellectuals

  Want more than reform, they want Revolution!

Progressive Motives

Four Progressive themes

Theme 1: Democracy

- Want government more responsible to people
- Against urban political machines
- Led to creation of direct primary

  1896–1916, nearly every state adopt

  Electors at national conventions must vote for candidates people select

- Call for Initiative and Referendums

  Gave voters right to enact laws directly

- Some 20 states adopt during period

  Some states even begin direct election of senators

  By 1912, 30 states hold senate primaries

  National law with passage of 17th Amendment in 1913

Theme 2: Efficiency

- Progressives depend on "Gospel of Efficiency"
- Frederick Taylor

  Scientific management lays out principles of labor efficiency

  Progressives use to reorganize government agencies and departments

  Discard overlapping and redundant functions
- Get state governments to adopt budget system

  Must create budget for each fiscal year
- Offer 2 ideas for more efficient city government

  1. Commission System:

  Place city in hands of elected committee responsible for sub-areas of government

  Control everything from police to power to sanitation to utilities

  2. City Manager Plan

  Professional urban planner

  Hired to direct efficient functioning of city's municipal government

Theme 3: Regulation

- Must regulate excesses of business, but how?
- Four routes available:

1. Let business work out own destiny under laissez-faire

2. Adopt Socialist program of public ownership

  Only successful on municipal level

  Gas and water Socialism allow cities to own utilities

  But viewed as un-American

3. Government engages in program of trust-busting to destroy monopolies

  Sherman Anti-Trust Act of 1890 perfect tool to combat monopolies

  Think competition would help economy

  Popular at first, but eventually abandoned because competition not return

4. Reform worst abuses of monopolies

  Most viable in long run

  Competition rarely restored after trust broken up

  But who monitors the regulators?

  Regulatory commissions fall under influence of big business

Theme 4: Active Government

- Progressives bring national government into many areas of public service

  1. Build new roads

  Institute national highway system

  2. Expand public education

  Goes from elementary to secondary

  3. Initiate environmental conservation

  Founds national park system

  4. Assists in public health and welfare

Expands sanitation and social services

The Progressives in Action

Helping "public interest" become guiding principle

Government must intervene in society to protect public interests

First impact in cities

Challenge power of urban political machines

Led by powerful bosses

Urban political bosses replace traditional elites

Older leaders move to other opportunities

Irish-American politicians step in with personal form of leadership

Win loyalty of ethnic and working-class voters

Appeal to Catholics, Jews, and different cultures rather than Anglo-Protestants

Controlling the City

Tammany Hall

HQ of NY's political machine

George Washington Plunkitt

Control $12 million payroll

Offer more jobs than Carnegie Steel

Tammany bosses attract supporters by providing needs

Protect workers against accidents, unemployment, and disasters

Intervenes when help needed

Provides food baskets, picnics, parades, and recreation

Meets needs of urban ethnic population to win loyalty

The Trouble with Boss Rule

Made graft and corruption endemic

Expensive way to provide city services

Sells city franchises for public transportation, road construction and public utilities to highest bidder

Raises project costs greatly

Places heavy burden on urban taxpayer

Plunkitt and other bosses call system "honest graft"

Progressives only see corruption

Especially ethnic and class rhetoric of bosses

Determined to change way city governments work

The Galveston Plan

First change in Galveston (TX), 1900

City bosses ineffective in dealing with devastating tidal wave

Next election, people switch to city charter

The Galveston Plan

Turn to city commission form of government

Voters select at-large commissioners

Each administers different part of city government

Makes city administration more professional

Takes it out of hands of bosses

City administrators answer to entire city, not only certain ethnic sections

Citywide elections reduced voting strength of ethnic minorities

Use Civil Service examinations to staff non-elected positions

Makes city services more professional

But tests discriminate against those not from Anglo-Protestant background

State Level Progressives

Robert La Follette

Republican governor of Wisconsin

Elected in 1900

Turned WI into social experiment

Use university-trained experts to administer programs

The "Wisconsin Idea" of government

Want new test of citizenship to be concerned with triumph of "public interest" over private greed

Win passage of direct primary

Shifts nomination of candidates to people, not party

Adopts initiative and referendum laws

Creates regulatory boards for railroads

Increases taxes on businesses and inherited wealth

Creates Workmen's Compensation

IA, CA, IN, and NY elect governors with similar programs

Social Justice and the Purity Crusade

Led by Washington Gladden: "Jesus Christ knew a great deal about organizing society and the application of His law to industrial society will be found to work surprisingly well."

Who was Gladden?

Reform-minded minister

Strong sense of concern for social justice

Wants working-classes to get fair share

But how?

Establish Purity Crusade

Sentiment for social justice motivated by strong religious ideals

Ministers push social gospel movement among liberal Protestants

Program of social reform rooted in New Testament

The Female Progressives

Purity Crusade begins with women

Work to restore morality in public life

General Federation of Women's Clubs

Membership grow from 50,000 in 1898 to over 1 million by 1914

President Sarah Platt Decker

Seeks to improve working conditions for women and children

Others publicize conditions of poor

Jane Addams

Establishes Hull House (Chicago, 1889)

First organized settlement house in America

Monitors living conditions

Provides services like child care, libraries

Teaches classes in housekeeping, cooking, and art

Hull House (and others like it) become crucibles of reform

Getting to the Root of the Problem

Middle-class women staffing settlement houses begin to think wealth sinful

Too many people were poor

Must redistribute wealth of nation

But what can be done?

Form National Child Labor Committee

Lobby states to prohibit labor for children under 14 in factories

Want those under 16 out of mines

Do not want children working nights or for more than 8 hours a day, especially in southern textile mills

By 1916, gets Congress to pass Keating-Owen Child Labor Act

Bans products of child labor from interstate commerce

Destroyed by Supreme Court in 1918

Other women fight against substance abuse

Use of narcotics like opium, morphine, and cocaine grows steadily in 19th century

Drugs widespread and readily available

Doctors often prescribe diluted opium for every ailment

Opium found in many patent medicines

Coca-Cola contained small amounts of cocaine until 1903

By 1900, US had millions of drug addicts

Regulating Narcotics

Emerging health professions help female Progressives regulate drugs

Say widespread drug use harmful

Need professional standards of practice

Professionals should control drug access

Lead to creation of:

American Medical Association (AMA)

American Pharmaceutical Association (APA)

Push Congress for Pure Food and Drug Act

First federal regulation of drugs (1906)

1909, outlaw importation of opium

Harrison Narcotics Act, 1914

Narcotic use restricted to medical purposes

Requires federal registration of all drug manufacturers

Keeps record of all sales and doctor's prescription before drugs dispensed

The Prohibition Movement

Alcohol main target of Purity Crusade

Creation of Anti-Saloon League —

Wants to outlaw sale and manufacture of alcoholic beverages in US

Describes alcohol as socially destructive drug

Really effort to control immigrants

Tries to shut down saloons

Fosters immigrant cultures

Serves as immigrant political centers for ethnic politicians and labor unions

Prohibition

Strongest support comes from evangelical white Southerners

Religion denounced use of alcohol

Most success in South

Serve as tool for social control (over blacks and poor whites)

Based in Baptist and Methodist churches

Persuade ⅔rds of southern counties to go dry by 1907

Get prohibition laws in 6 states by 1909

Webb-Kenyon Act of 1913

States can stop transport of alcohol across state lines

Creates underground economy of bootleggers and moonshiners who supply South with alcohol

Progressivism at the National Level

Theodore Roosevelt first president of 20th century

Successor to William McKinley

Last Gilded Age president

Fresh off laudatory press gathering victory in Cuba

Republican, but independent, reform-minded individual

Typical conservative Progressive

From V.P. to President

Becoming president the easy way

McKinley won second term

Sept. 1901, anarchist Leon Czolgosz shot McKinley at Buffalo RR station

Bought revolver from Sears and Roebuck catalog

➡McKinley dies from operation to remove bullet

Supposedly, dies while holding hand of Mark Hanna and singing *Nearer My God to Thee*

➤ Mark Hanna's worst fears came true

He said, "Now look, that damned cowboy is president of the United States."

The Square Deal

● T. Roosevelt wants to tighten controls on big business

➤ Not trust-busting, just regulating

➤ TR chose targets carefully

Supreme Court ruled manufacturing couldn't be regulated by government

But did not protect RRs

Breaking up Northern Securities

Controls Great Northern and Northern Pacific railroad

Northern Securities Company v. United States (1904)

TR gets Supreme Court to dissolve company

● Taking on Mining Companies

➤ Miner strike in PA

Mine operators refuse to speak to representatives of UMW at conference TR calls at White House

TR threatens to throw George Baer out White House window by seat of his pants

Baer president of Reading RR and mine owner representative

➤ TR had no authority to nationalize mines, but threatens to anyway

Owners cave in, fearing he might nationalize or force strike settlement

Regulating the Economy

● TR enforces Sherman Anti-Trust Act with executive power

➤ Files 25 antitrust suits

➤ Most notable victory comes against beef trust

Swift and Company v. U.S. (1905)

Overturns previous position that manufacturing not interstate commerce

● Other reforms in 1903

➤ Expedition Act (1903) gives priority to antitrust suits in state courts

➤ Creates Department of Commerce (1903) to regulate trade in US

➤ Elkins Act (1903) makes it illegal to take or give railroad rebates

● A modicum of success

➤ TR breaks up Standard Oil in 1911, also American Tobacco Company

➤ TR never gets full regulation he wants

Congress will not pass necessary legislation

So TR uses executive order

Policies build coalition between Republicans and Progressives

Leads to overwhelming victory in election of 1904

TR's Second Term

- TR becomes more aggressive
- Pushed thru Hepburn Act (1906)

  Gave Interstate Commerce Commission power to set maximum RR rates

  Expands powers of ICC to include pipelines, express companies, sleeping-car companies, bridges, and ferries
- *The Jungle* (by Upton Sinclair, 1906)

  Exposes filth of Chicago's meat packing industry

  Meat stored in dark places

  Covered with rats and dried dung

  Supervisors kill rats with poisoned bread

  Rats die, but everything put into grinding hopper together

  Meat packing plants are breeding grounds for TB
- TR reads novel, sends 2 inspectors to confirm Sinclair's work
- Investigation leads to:

  Meat Inspection Act (June 30, 1906)

  Pure Food and Drug Act (June 30, 1906)

Conservation

  Conservation
- Final part of TR's progressive program
- TR unabashed naturalist and big-game hunter
- Determined to halt exploitation of western timber

  Problem since Timber and Stone Act of 1878

  Trying to stimulate settlement of West

  Allowed anyone to buy 160 acres at $2.50 an acre

  Timber companies recruit people to purchase land, then buys it for themselves
- TR as conservationist
- Creates some 50 federal wildlife refuges
- Approves 5 new national parks
- Creates system of national monuments such as Grand Canyon
- Works with Gifford Pinchot, chief of forestry service, to establish 41 state conservation commissions

TR's Successor

- TR can't run for reelection
- Picks successor for next election (1908)
- William Howard Taft selected on first ballot

  From Ohio

  Man of large girth and intelligence

  Once said, "Politics make me sick"
- Taft presidency beset by problems
- Ballinger-Pinchot Controversy (1910)

Richard Ballinger

Secretary of Interior

Opens millions of acres of land to development

Many sites TR ordered protected

Taft agrees with reopening

Say TR exceeded law in protecting sites

Gives coal lands in Alaska to Seattle developers

Worked for them as lawyer

Spiraling Out of Control

When in doubt, follow the money

Land office investigator goes to Pinchot with "evidence" of collusion in land deal

Pinchot goes to Taft, who promptly fires investigator

Pinchot goes public with controversy, so fired by Taft

Ballinger cleared by Congress in 1910

Suspicion so high he forced to resign in 1911

Political effects of Ballinger-Pinchot

Republicans lose House to Democrats

TR off hunting lions, tigers, and bears

Comes home annoyed

Won't openly break with Taft, but supporters want him to sever tie

TR goes on western speaking tour

Outlines new plan under catchy phrase of New Nationalism

1 Program of federal regulatory laws

2 Offers democratic measures like referendum and initiative

3 Seeks to save country from threat of revolution

Bull Moose Party

Destroying the Party

Break comes in 1911

Taft announces antitrust suit against US Steel

TR allows US Steel to acquire coal and iron company in TN

Taft says violates antitrust law so must be broken up

TR says trust-busting old-fashioned

Urged by progressive Republicans to announce candidacy for president

TR announces presidential campaign

Wins many state primaries

But Taft supporters ignore state primaries

Taft faction controls national convention

Taft gets nomination

TR outraged

Creates own political party: The Reform Party

Later called the Bull Moose Party

Calls for progressive Republicans to meet in Chicago

Most figure TR a lost cause and stay home

Election of 1912

3-way Race for presidency

2-man race after Milwaukee incident

TR shot by fanatic

Crowd mobs assassin

TR jumps up, yelling, "Step back, don't harm him"

Not let doctors examine him

Insists on finishing speech

Split Republican ticket allows Wilson to win

Several things to consider about 1912 election:

1 High point for Progressives

All 3 of candidates were reformers

2 Restores Democrats to presidency after years of Republican rule

3 Wilson brings South back into national politics

Many administration appointees from South

4 Changes character of Republican Party

Progressives discredited within Party

When party returns to White House in 1920s, more conservative in nature

World War I: The Great War

Horrors of War

- War in Europe, June 1914
- Slav nationalists murder Austrian archduke Francis Ferdinand in dank town of Sarajevo
- Triggers series of European pacts and alliances
- Plunges Europe into war by end of summer 1914
- Guns of August
- Europeans go to war with smiles on their faces
- Everyone convinced they would be home before Christmas
- America remained neutral
- The contestants
- Allies (Great Britain, France, and their less-than-democratic friend Russia)
- Central powers of Germany and Hapsburg Empire (Austria)

Wilson and American Neutrality

- Wilson says US should have nothing to do with war
- Calls for US to remain neutral in name and deed
- Declaration that US does not have stake in war is blatant lie
- Germany seen as our greatest threat for past 25 years
  - Mostly Anglo-Protestant officials at State department not like Germans
- US moving closer to British
  - Tied by religion, culture, language, and law
  - Wilson admires Britain and its institutions, especially Parliament
  - Publicly remains neutral, but privately Wilson opposes German victory

Supplying the War

- Money draws US into British camp
- War creates enormous demand for US food and war goods
- US trade increases with Allies from $825 million in 1914 to $3.2 billion in 1916

—But Allies run short of money in 1915

US bankers invest heavily in war effort

Give huge loans to Britain and France

Wilson uses Federal Reserve to guarantee loans to protect US economy

By 1917, US bankers loan $2.5 billion to Allies

SS Bryan denounces loans as violation of neutrality

US trade with Central Powers vanishes

Loans to Central Powers amounts to only $300 million

Wilson and the Push for War

TR and Republicans press Wilson to begin military build-up

Wilson hopes US can maintain prestige by remaining neutral

Wants to shape peace after war

Advantages to war

Wilson saw war as way to end European imperialism

Hopes it will open world to free (meaning US) trade

Wilson was a great moralist

Hopes massive death toll would teach Europeans a lesson

Only liberal politics and economic cooperation can prevent these types of disasters in future

Forcing Alliances

Allies and Central Powers try to force US decision

Britain blockades North Sea to keep US from trading with Germany

Wilson does not protest

British blockade via surface ships in rules of "Cruiser Warfare"

Seldom leads to deaths

The German U-boats used to attack ships in British waters

Wilson protests long and loud

Says Germans "violating the rights of neutrals to trade"

Submarines most serious issue between Germany and US

Germans inferior to British at sea

Must use submarines

Subs cannot practice rules of Cruiser Warfare

Results in many neutral deaths

Stopping the Flow of Supplies

To win, Germany must stop Allied supply lines to US

But plays right into hands of Allied propaganda

Britain controlled only surviving telegraph cable to US

They provide US with all war news

US media accepts British story without challenge

Only gets stories of German atrocities

Portrays Germans as "Huns"

Says barbaric and savage monsters murdering babies and raping women

Stories and neutral deaths on ships outraged US public, pushing the US closer toward war

The *Lusitania*

The *Lusitania*

Demonstrates how unrealistic Wilson is

May 1915

German sub sinks British passenger liner off Irish coast

Kills 1,198 passengers, including 128 from US

TR denounces attack as act as piracy

But *Lusitania* carrying rifle cartridges and ammo, other important military cargo

Passengers being used as human shields

Wilson sends strong note to Germany

By 1915, Germans give in to Wilson

Promise not to sink passenger liners

But increase strikes on merchant vessels

Issue boils over in 1916

Allies arm merchant ships

Germany counters with "fire without warning" policy for all merchant vessels

Wilson says either Germany stop sinking merchant and passenger ships or US to enter war

Again surprisingly, Germany gives in

Preparing for War

Though pledged to nonviolence, Wilson secretly building military

Wants US Navy larger than British

Expands Army

Tours country drumming up support

National Defense Act (1916)

$500 million program for military spending

Funding secured by Revenue Act of 1916

First major income and inheritance tax in US since Civil War

Election of 1916

Dominated by question of war or peace

Republicans

Nominate Charles Evans Hughes

Supreme Court Justice

Former governor of New York

Unlike 1912, Republicans united

Offer serious threat to Wilson

Wilson takes advantage of war

⌐Makes himself the "Peace Candidate"

‾ Supporters adopt slogan: "He kept us out of war"

⌒ Wilson and VP candidate Thomas R. Marshall win close victory

∼ Get 277–254 in electoral college

⌐ Smallest margin of victory since 1876

Making Peace

Once reelected, Wilson tries to end war

Tried before, but failed twice

✳Col. Edward House

1 Informally represents Wilson in early 1914

Tries to relieve mounting tensions as Europe plunged into war

US neutrality slipping

Col. House tells Wilson to prepare home front

2 Sent to Europe again in 1915 by Wilson to find some means of mediation

Seeking "peace without victory"

But by 1915, so many dead that each side believes it must win to justify losses

Wilson frustrated by lack of progress

The third attempt, January 1917

Issues address to Congress calling for "peace without victory"

But Germans and Allies refuse to listen

Stalemate and death toll continues to rise

The Zimmerman Telegram

"Let the US come in"

War deadlocked on land

⌐German generals persuade Kaiser to resume unrestricted submarine warfare

⌐ U-boats begin attacking neutrals in war zones

Wilson severs formal relations with Central Powers

⌐Releases Zimmerman telegram to public

Secret German dispatch to Mexico intercepted by British

Note encourages Mexico to attack US if we enter war on the side of the Allies

In return, Germany to help Mexico recover its "lost provinces" of TX, NM, and AZ

The Decision for War

⌐Combination of note, collapse of Russia in East, and sinking of US merchant ships

⌐Late March 1917

Wilson asks Congress for declaration of war

"US must make the world safe for democracy"

⌐April 6, 1917, Congress makes declaration

Organizing for Victory

- First task, financing the war
- Ultimately costs $32 billion
- Most paid for with Liberty Bonds

  New idea launched by government

  Provide largest amount of money for war

  Net $23 bilion in small loans
- Situation in Europe grows desperate
- Russia collapses in East
- British and French troops breaking and depleted
- Britain only has 6 weeks of food left
- U-boats sinking 900,000 tons to floor of Atlantic each month

Organizing the US War Economy

- War Industries Board
- Makes economy run smoothly, produce what needed to win war
- Headed by Bernard Baruch
- Sets production goals
- Controls allocation of raw materials
- Government fixes prices and constrains free trade in return for national security
- Encourages growth of large corporations

  Establishes new idea of corporatism

  Government directs business-sponsored program of central planning and social responsibility
- Controlling food sources
- Herbert Hoover
- Heads Food Administration

  Takes control of agricultural production

  Sets prices for crops and sets levels for production

  Encourages people to sacrifice for war effort

  Sets days when people cannot eat meat or wheat products

Rallying War Support

- Wilson administration creates large propaganda machine to rally support for war
- Committee on Public Information (CPI)
- Headed by journalist George Creel
- Employs 150,000 people
- Distributes over 75 million pieces of pro-war propaganda
- Passions they create soon consume the nation
- Attacks on enemy sound harsh today and xenophobic
- Encourages people to turn in neighbors
- Creates paranoia that leads to postwar Red Scare

Punishing Dissent

Standing against the war

- Socialist Eugene Debs
- Says war being fought to protect interests of elites
- Calls US involvement a "crime against humanity"
- Wins 30+% of vote in cities like Chicago and Buffalo
- Attacking the draft
- La Follette, Idaho Sen. William E. Borah, and others attack draft (passed in June 1917)
- La Follette condemned by faculty of Univ. of WI for giving aid and comfort to enemy
- Randolph Bourne
- Vocalizes intellectual criticism of war
- The State, 1918
- "War is the health of the state."
- Wars cannot exist without state
- Mindless power thrives on war
- War corrupts a nation's moral fabric and especially its intellectuals
- Leads to blind patriotism
- State and government become virtually identical
- Opposition to government considered act of disloyalty to State
- Wilson agrees with Bourne but must quiet him

The War Against Dissent

- Suppressing dissenters
- Wilson deports Socialist immigrants without trials
- Espionage Act of 1917
- Prohibit giving aid or comfort to enemy
- Outlaws "treasonable" publications and controls mail system
- Used to imprison Debs and prevents circulation of Socialist materials
- Movie producer Robert Goldstein gets 10 years in prison

    The Spirit of '76 shows British soldiers attacking American civilians during Revolutionary War

- The Sedition Act of 1918

    Makes it a crime to "utter, print, write or publish any disloyal, profane, scurrilous or abusive language" about military or government

    Government rarely uses

Stomping Out Negative Influences

- Favorite targets of government were radicals and pacifists
- Industrial Workers of the World
- IWW under leadership of Big Bill Haywood

    Rejects leadership of American Socialist Party and American Federation of Laborers

- Began strikes in Washington and Montana for safer working conditions

    Wilson angered by action

Sends troops to end IWW strikes

Arrests 165 IWW men

Haywood forced to flee to Russia

Wilson imprisons 400 conscientious objectors

Upholding Persecution

Supreme Court upholds persecutions

Schenck v. US (1919)

Socialists mailing antidraft stuff to draft-age men

Court rules right to free speech does not apply in times of war

Justice Oliver Wendall Holmes

Says Court can deny free speech when "clear and present danger" exists

Debs v. US (1919)

Debs makes antiwar speech in Canton (OH) June 16, 1918

Says elites cause wars but make working class fight them

Arrested and convicted under wartime Espionage Act

Debs acts as own attorney

Sentenced to 10 years, disenfranchised for life, and loses citizenship

Supreme Court upholds conviction

The Citizen's Leagues

American Protective League

Members carry cards identifying them as agents of Justice Department

Spy on neighbors and harass antiwar activists

Jury dismisses charges against one man who shot persecuted German-American for shouting: "to hell with the United States."

Fear of German threat leads to hysteria

Everything German had to be changed

German measles becomes "liberty measles"

Dachshunds becomes "liberty pups"

Sauerkraut becomes "liberty cabbage"

German-language publications prohibited

Made it illegal to teach German language in school

Numerous attacks across country on German-Americans

The US Enters the War

Wilson runs war by Progressive principles

Creates Selective Service system

Draft some 3 million "doughboys"

Another 2 million volunteer

General John J. Pershing

Commander of American Expeditionary Force (AEF)

- Professional military man
- Believed in West Point, strenuous training, and "professional" army
- Insists on separate military command coordinated with Allies
- US fight as associated power
- Refuses to be member of Allied military force

  Afraid they only want fresh troops to plug depleted reserves
- US arrives on July 4, 1917

  Larger force there by winter/spring of 1918

Military Victory

- Arrival of AEF comes at crucial point
- Turns back German spring offensive
- Launches counterattack and pushes Germans back through Argonne Forest
- 1 million Americans fight along 200-mile front for 47 days
- Germans driven back to own territory for first time in war
- Germans forced to seek cease-fire
- German monarchy falling apart
- Fighting ends at 11 a.m. on Nov. 11, 1918
- Tallying the cost
- 112,432 Americans died

  Half from disease
- The Allied losses

  French lost 1.38 million

  Russia 1.7 million

  Great Britain 947,000

  60,000 lost on first day of Battle of Somme
- The Central Powers

  Germany lost 1.8 million, Austria 1.2 million

  Another 20 million wounded

War to End All Wars

- The "Inquiry"
- Wilson and House establish in 1915
- Think tank that creates Fourteen Points speech and League of Nations
- Wilson's supreme goal to broker effective and lasting peace

Wilson's Fourteen Points

Delivered at Paris Peace Conference on January 8, 1918

1 Returns captured territories to pre-war owner

2 Opens international diplomacy to public view

3 Guarantees absolute navigation of seas outside territorial waters in peace and war

4 Removes economic barriers and establishes free trade among all nations that consent to peace

5 Calls for reduction of national armaments to lowest point needed for domestic safety

6 Colonial claims to consider sovereignty and include interests of populations concerned

7 Calls for creation of League of Nations

Versailles and the League

The Versailles Treaty

- Paris Peace Conference ends in 1919

- Effectively ends WWI

- Everything blamed on Germany that must pay huge war reparations

- Wilson hopes that once League is established, he could fix shortcomings of Treaty

- First 26 articles of Treaty describe League of Nations Covenant

- Explains operational workings of League

- Obliges signers to guarantee political independence

- Must ensure territorial integrity of member nations against outside aggression

- Must consult together to oppose aggression when it occurs

Critical point, which ultimately prevent treaty's ratification by US Senate

Opposing the League in Congress

- Sen. Henry Cabot Lodge led US opposition

- Lodge and Wilson bitter political foes

- But have legitimate difference in views of League

- Lodge believes League could force US to commit economic or military forces to maintain collective security of member nations

- Wilson does not think this would happen

- US would have veto power in League Council

Could prevent League sanctions

League decisions only amount to advice

US not legally bound to League's dictates

League's resolutions only morally "grave and solemn obligation"

Concluding the War

And then nature steps in

Wilson suffers massive stroke in October 1919

Ends possibility of compromise

No accommodation by either side

Treaty voted down in Congress, 34–53

US remains officially at war until June 1921

Pres. Warren Harding approves joint congressional resolution to end war with Central Powers

Later signs separate peace treaty

Resolution and treaty specify:

Although US not party to Versailles Treaty, retains all rights and advantages accorded under its terms, excluding League Covenant

US never joined League of Nations

The Roaring Twenties

The Rise of Materialism

- At every societal level, get relaxation of traditional American values of thrift and sobriety
- People growing attached to acquisition of things

    Still plenty of poverty and social injustice, but middle class caught up in present
- Middle class believes future only will get better
- New trends touch everyone, but especially cities
- Indoor plumbing and electricity commonplace
- Canned foods and mass-produced clothing normal
- If you had cash and credit, you could even get a car
- Why?
- 1919–29, GNP (total value of all goods and services produced in country) increased by 40%
- Wages and salaries increase but not nearly as much
- Cost of living stays relatively stable
- People have more purchasing power, spends like never spent before
- Was anyone bothered by this increased materialism?
- Most content to pay more for better services and goods
- Benefits of technology reaching everyone

    By 1929, 2/3 have electricity

    In 1912, it was only 1/6th

    By 1929, 25% of all families owned an electric vacuum cleaner, 1/5 had electric toasters

    Most also had radios and washing machines

    First time these things available to a majority of population

The Automobile

- Most significant change in availability of cars
- During 20s, car registrations go from 8 million to 23 million
- Mass production and competition drive costs down

    By 1926, a Model T Ford cost just under $300

    Chevy sold for $700

    Model numbers increase to 108 in 1923, more colors
- Industrial workers make $1,300 a year

- Most clerical workers about $2,300
- Cars change American society as nothing else had
- Requires network of roads to be built
- Allows for greater freedom of movement
- Gives kids opportunity to escape parents

    Conservative critics call it house of prostitution on wheels
- Of course, cars create real problems
- In 1921, federal government passes Federal Highway Act

    Gives federal aid for state roads
- In 1923, Bureau of Public Roads plans national highway system
- Auto industry is boon for oil industry

    Shift production from lubrication and illumination to propulsion

Birth of Advertising

- First great decade of advertising
- Materialism influenced by advertising
- Advertising and salesmanship become gospel 1920s
- Packaging and product displays make sciences
- One book by advertising exec Bruce Barton claims Jesus was founder of modern business

    Took 12 men from bottom ranks

    Forged organization that conquered the world
- Advertising trend aided by widespread use of radios
- Stations carry 1000s of commercials daily
- By 1922, 508 commercial radio stations
- By 1929, Americans spent $850 million per year on radio equipment
- NBC charges advertisers $10,000 to sponsor 1-hour-long show

Urbanization

- Pattern of increasing urbanization continues in 1920s
- In 1920, 51% live in urban areas

    First time in America

    Cities like Detroit, Houston, and Birmingham become major industrial centers

    Growth in Atlanta, Minneapolis, and Seattle sparked by major service and retail trades
- The Great Migration
- Part of growth from large-scale migration by African-Americans North

    About 1.5 million blacks move to urban areas
- Quickly squeezed into ghettos in central cities

    Partly due to economics

    Could only afford substandard housing

    Still deal with discrimination and racism

    Some landlords try to keep them out

—First real urban conflict between whites and blacks

Especially when spill into nearby nonblack neighborhoods looking for housing

White Response to Minorities

● General white response to influx of minorities was to pack up and get out

➣ During 20s get massive white flight from city to suburbs

By 50s, trend would greatly increase

● Some major suburbs grow at rates from 5–10 times as fast as central cities

➡ Oak Park and Evanston, Illinois

➤ Burbank and Inglewood, California

● Most become bedroom communities

Have own city services and fight against annexation efforts

Want to stay away from city: crime, dirt, and taxes

The City Tax Problem

Suburban Culture

● Urban and suburban environment create new mass culture

‾ Gives 20s its character

– People go to specialized shops, movie houses, and sporting arenas for fun

◄ Actively embrace fads like crossword puzzles, miniature golf, and marathon dancing

⤶ People go to speakeasies (illegal)

⤴ Wear outlandish clothing (Zoot suits)

– Listen to jazz

● Regardless of where you live, you want to be like city and suburb dwellers

⬅ Yet, ironically, people retain many small-town values

⬋ Urbanites long for simpler times and fewer choices

⬋ Rural past becomes moral anchor

Suburban Life

● Amid changes, get new social values and ways of using time

‾ People divide time into three phases, yet each type of time altered over time

❘ Work

✳ Time at work declines for most people

✳ Work days for industrial workers dropped to 5.5 days

✳ Many clerical workers only there 5 days a week

❷ Family

✳ Family size continues to fall

Birth rates drop noticeably

Birth control more widely practiced

Diaphragms, cervical caps

✳ In 1880, over half women living to 50 had 5 children

By 1920s, falls to just 20 percent

- Divorce rates rise

    1 in every 7.5 in 1920

    1 in 6 by 1929, as high as 2 in 7 in many cities

Changes in the Family

- Labor-saving devices
- For women machines lightened work loads

    Electric irons and washing machines

    Hot water heaters and central heating mean have hot water without coal or wood

- Also have prefabricated items like clothes and preserved foods
- New responsibilities
- Less time on domestic chores means more time elsewhere

    Particularly family shopping and spending family money wisely

- Women also cleaning more

    20s saw new standard of cleanliness introduced

    Companies make cleaning products to play into trend:

    Advocate healthy foods full of vitamins, strong soap, and personal hygiene items like mouth wash

3. Leisure

- Leisure time increased dramatically
- Kids spend more time in school

    By 1929, ⅓ of all high school graduates went to college

- Evening entertainment
- Electric lights changed home life

    People could now stay up at night

    Read, listen to radio programs and ball games

    Go riding in cars or go to movies

- Changes in life expectancy
- Significantly increased

    Average American lifespan went from 54 to 60 from 1920 to 1930

    More rest and better diet

    Advances in medicine

- Medical progress not egalitarian

    Among blacks stillborn and infant mortality rates 50–100 percent higher than whites

    TB rampant in urban settings

    Automobile accidents rise 150 percent

- Increases in aged population

    Number of people over 65 grows 35% from 1920–1930

    Increases lead to first efforts to take care of elderly

    Elderly often in poverty

    By 1933, almost every state providing minimal assistance

Changing Social Values

 As population demographics change, so do social values

Especially middle class

Become more socially liberal

Styles of clothing increasingly gaudy and colorful

More smoking, swearing, and sex

Quasi-intellectual youth believe key to happiness in uninhibited sex life

Based on work of Sigmund Freud, which most never read

Birth control becoming popular

Especially with Margaret Sanger advocating birth control use

Get increased generational conflict

Kids no longer work with parents

Increasingly bond together in social units thru school and sport

Allows people to become intellectually distinct from older generations

Women in the Workplace

Another breakdown of traditional values

Get massive increase in number of women taking jobs outside home

WWI brought women into workplace

By 1930, 10.8 million women hold paying jobs

Women segregated by work

Limited to teachers, nurses, typists, bookkeepers, and office clerks

Wages seldom more than ½ that of men

Why work outside home?

Want to support nation in time of war

Limited number of men to fill jobs

Need to help support family

Want to participate in broad-based consumerism

Feminist groups of period say women going to work to gain independence

Feminists oppose laws restricting number of hours women work

Feel laws limit types of jobs women can do

Also preserves system of sexual separation

Age of Play

 Another aspect of mass culture manifested during 20s

 Americans develop thirst for recreation

In 1919, Americans spend $2.5 billion on leisure activities

By 1929, figure tops $4.3 billion

Manifested in variety of forms

Movies, theater, and sports account for 21% of 1929 figure

Rest taken up by individual recreation

Ranges from participatory sports to hobbies, music, and travel

By 1930, nearly every community has at least one theater

Movie viewers increase from 40 million per week in 1922 to over 100 million per week by 1930

Total population just 120 million, total weekly church attendance barely 60 million

When color and sound added, reinforce realism movies offered

Most popular were mass spectacles

Cecil B. DeMille's *The Ten Commandments* (1923)

Slapstick comedies with stars like Charlie Chaplin and Fatty Arbuckle also popular

Professional Sports

- Spectator sports boomed
- Millions packed arenas to watch college and professional sports
- Gate receipts for college football alone surpassed $21 million by late 20s
- Baseball drew huge followings
- Judge Kennesaw Mountain Landis

   Baseball commissioner during the 1920s

   Rooted out corruption in game, redesigned ball to increase homers
- Boxing, football, and baseball produced major sports heroes
- Jack Dempsey
- Red Grange
- Babe Ruth
- Somehow, Americans seemed able to identify with such figures

Movie Stars

- Identification also found in movies and public realm
- Rudolph Valentino, Gloria Swanson, Douglas Fairbanks

   Filled yearning for romance and adventure
- News media had own heroes
- Floyd Collins trapped in Kentucky cave
- Plethora of flagpole sitters, marathon dancers, and other record seekers

   Charles Lindbergh
- Most notable news hero

   First to fly nonstop solo flight across Atlantic in 1927
- Adulation may reflect guilt Americans felt over relaxed social standards

Caught in the Middle

- During 20s, Americans caught between two value systems
1. Puritan work ethic, sobriety, and restraint

   Prevailed in rural areas, but important cities
2. Personal liberation
- Creates tension pulling artists into new directions
- Prompts experimentation in literature, art, and music
- Desire to protect individual from vices of modern civilization becomes a consistent theme

Literature of the 20s

- Most creative decade in American history

    Cultural climax of modernization

    Peak produced by 50 years of industrial, technological, and social change

- Many literary figures of period appalled by materialism

- Become disillusioned by American society

- Called Lost Generation

- Themes revolve around 2 issues:

    Middle-class Materialism

    Impersonality of modern society

- Many moved to Europe

    Hemingway and poets Ezra Pound and T. S. Eliot

- Others remain in US

    Become bitter critics of isolation of modern man

    William Faulkner and Sinclair Lewis

- The Harlem Renaissance

- Different intellectual trend occurs in Harlem

- Young black writers who reject assimilation into white culture and militantly assert pride in their African heritage

- Realize black Americans have to become participants in American experience

    Need to find ways to express themselves inside a polarized society

    Harlem fostered many gifted writers and singers

- Langston Hughes—best known poet of time

    Florence Mills and Josephine Baker

    Jazz

    Came from Mississippi Delta

    Expression of personal freedom thru emotional rhythms and improvisation

Screening Out the Past

- Movies offer keen insight into customs and values

- Movies from 1920s tell more about time than anything else

- Not only descriptive, but also prescriptive

- Muncie, Indiana

    Weekly attendance at 9 theaters in Muncie equaled 3 times entire city population

    More people attend movies on Sunday than church

    Viewers came from all classes and ethnic groups

- Movies truly mass medium

    Held great figures of period

    D. W. Griffith, Mary Pickford, Douglas Fairbanks, Charlie Chaplin, and Cecil B. DeMille

- Main themes:

    Change from Victorian Age to Modern

    Shattering of old values and replacing with modern ones

How Did People Learn What Modern Values Were?

- Mass production cause higher standard of living, and altered visions of success
  - Now to be successful, had to acquire "things"

    Ranged from homes, cars, clothes, vacuum cleaners, etc.
- Movies taught Americans how to think like this

    Values and dreams reflected in movies
- New America of 20th century America
- Movies not cause change, but added to momentum

    Helped to change morality of western culture

    Build movie houses

    Create stars

    Publishing fan magazines

    Hollywood helped integrate imagery on screen into everyday lives of audience
- Movies work because see ourselves as main characters
- Help screen out older American identity, replace it with exclusively modern one

The 1920s: Politics and Society

- Political trends of period

    Conservatives dominate
- Progressivism does not resurface until Depression
- Presidency controlled by Republicans
- Warren Harding, Calvin Coolidge, and Herbert Hoover
- Seen as men who turned back clock to simpler time before progressivism of Teddy Roosevelt
- Blamed for sticking head into sand

    Ignored needed reforms

    Led US to stock market crash of 1929 and Great Depression
- Republican policies

    Returned to high-tariff policy

    Pay little attention to concentration of power and wealth

    Not sympathetic to Union movement

    General lack of presidential leadership

Political Changes

Innovations in sphere of government's relationship to business community

Mostly result of Herbert Hoover

Brilliant man

Wanted new mercantilism for America

Acting first as Secretary of Commerce, then as President

Thought role of government to help make American economy work

To provide information to people and business

To make business more efficient and profitable

Believed in managed competition

Thought it made national economy profitable and stable

The Election of 1924

President Coolidge

Nominated by Republicans

V.P. Charles G. Dawes

Democrats

Meet in NYC

Knock-drown drag-out fight for nomination

Eventually chose John W. Davis (WV)

Wall Street lawyer

Reject Al Smith and William McAdoo

Charles W. Bryan named V.P. candidate

Progressives

Had no chance to win

Nominate Bob La Follette

Election results

Coolidge won easily

Conservative Davis did so poorly Democrats turn more liberal

Prohibition: The Great Progressive Victory

Origins behind Prohibition complex

Included evangelical Protestantism

Believe that societal evils could be destroyed:

Racial tensions, class conflict, rural distrust of cities and especially immigrants

Short-term origins go back to 1917

Congress prohibits manufacture of alcohol for rest of the war

Grain needed for food

December 1917, Congress adopts 18th Amendment and sends it to states

As long as ¾th states agree, it would outlaw sale or manufacture of "intoxicating liquors"

36 states ratify 18th Amendment by January 1919

Enforcing Prohibition

Enforcement another matter

Too many people drink

Booze cheap, easy to make

Black market for illegal booze develops immediately

Easy to evade law

Federal Prohibition Bureau complete joke until 1928

Easy to bribe low-paid federal enforcement officers

1 in 12 of officers fired for bribery

Smuggling widespread

Bring liquor in via Canada and Caribbean

Some even use industrial alcohol as beverage

Dangerous since bootleggers not remove denaturants

Causes blindness and death

18th Amendment and Volstead Act complete disaster

Not increase respect for law, leads to more corruption

Not increase organized crime, but leads organized criminals to violence

Business depends on law to enforce order, but organized crime can only depend on violence

Why wasn't Prohibition repealed before 1933?

Most people not approved of Prohibition for themselves

But favored it for others

Whites want prohibition for blacks

Urban middle class want for immigrants

Repeal comes when Hoover begins to enforce law

Congress passes 21st Amendment (February 1933)

Repeals 18th

Immigration Restriction

Xenophobia unleashed by WWI triggers move to restrict massive immigration from last 20 years

Motivations numerous:

To some, pure racism

To others, immigrants are radicals who endanger American stability

Others thought immigrants too conservative and would prevent social progress

Unions didn't want them because they would work for cheap wages

Emergency Quota Act (May 1921)

Signed by Warren Harding

Number of aliens of any nationality not to exceed 3% of foreign-born of that nationality counted by Census of 1910

Italian example

1,000 Italian-born counted by Census of 1910

Only 3% (30) Italians could immigrate in any year

Designed to discriminate against immigrants from southern and eastern Europe, but failed

Most immigrants still coming from S+E Europe

The National Origins Act (1924)

Signed by Calvin Coolidge

"America must be kept American"

Ugly and complicated piece of legislation

Each foreign nation had immigration quota equal to 2% of foreign-born of that nation living in US in 1890

Pushing census date from 1910 to 1890 further restricts S and E European immigrants

After 1927, total immigrants allowed per year restricted to 150,000, with sliding percentage scale

New quota system goes into effect in 1929

Quotas

Britain: 65, 721

Germany: 25,957

Scandinavian nations: 7,501

Poland: 6,524

Italy: 5,802

Russia: 2,712

Ironies of law numerous

Does not prohibit immigration from Canada or Mexico

By time start, US in grip of major depression

European immigration stopped

The Ku Klux Klan

Prohibition, immigration restriction, anti-Catholicism, and religious fundamentalism all products of rural and small-town America

- Ku Klux Klan another product of American Conservatism

- From 1922 until 1925, Klan major force in American politics and rural life

- Strongest hate organization in America

- Origins seemingly innocent

- William J. Simmons   Hiram Wesley Evans

  History teacher at Lanier College (GA)

  Romantic man who yearned for Old South

  Never got over Civil War

  Wants to start new fraternal lodge

  What could be better than lodge named after Ku Klux Klan

  Formally founded in 1915

  By 1920, only have few chapters in GA and AL

  Hiram Wesley Evans

  Racist dentist from TX

  Became new Imperial Wizard

  Hire fundraisers and marketing people

  Use modern mass media techniques to recruit members in scheme like pyramid plan

  Each time you recruit member, got share of $10 fee

- Movement spreads across South, then to Midwest and far West

  Rhetoric against blacks and Catholics

  Against immigration, favor prohibition, and frown on sexual immorality

  Fundamentalists play important role in reviving Klan

  Use it as tool against American immorality

The Klan Presence

- Valued 19th c. morality, rural life

- Used modern political tactics (bloc voting), terror, and violence to achieve goals

Burn crosses, but usually furthest they went

   Did turn to violence and murder when needed

Hard to fight because secret organization

Klan eventually turns to politics

First endorses candidates in 1922 TX Democratic primary

Helped to impeach governor of OK in 1923

Moved into both Dems and Reps in Oregon

   Won control over both houses and governorship

The Midwestern Klan

One stronghold in Indiana

Strong support among members of both parties

Klan reaches greatest height but also crumbles as national political movement

D. C. Stephenson

– Leader of Midwest Klan

– Made organization major political force

– Everything changes in 1925

– Discredits entire organization

   At Indianapolis party, met state secretary, got her drunk, and then attacked her on Pullman car bound for Chicago

   Sick over incident, she tries to poison herself

   Moves to hotel and denied medical treatment

   Month later she dies

   IN politicians, tired of Stephenson's influence, arrested him

   Indicted, tried, and sentenced for manslaughter

   Leader sent to prison for crime that violated basic principles of Klan

Klan so discredited it is no longer powerful political force, though hangs on in local areas

The Crash of 1929 & the New Deal

Dawning of a New Era

- The confidence of a nation
- Herbert Hoover elected president in 1928
- Mood of general public optimism and great confidence in US economy

  Hoover's acceptance speech to nomination; "We in America today are nearer to the final triumph over poverty than ever before in the history of any land. The poorhouse is vanishing from among us."

  Hoover becomes president

  Inauguration, proclaims start of New Day in America, one "bright with Hope."

  Cabinet dominated by big business (includes 6 millionaires)

  Lower ranks of government Hoover appoint young professionals

  All agree that scientific methods could solve nation's problems

  Hoover and most Americans overwhelmingly optimistic

- Across country, have widespread belief that individuals responsible for own success

  Unemployment and poverty caused by personal weakness

- Prevailing opinion says business cycle has natural ups/downs

  Thus, government should not tamper with economy

The "Bull Market"

- From 1924 to 1929, stock market growing at fantastic pace
- Bull Market

  When stock prices rising quickly, as opposed to a "Bear Market"

- Why was the market growing?

  Expansion of credit

  Rapid increase in investments

- John Jacob Raskob
- Chief executive of GM

  Head of DNC

- Publishes article in *Ladies Home Journal*

"Everybody Ought to Be Rich"

Says every American could be wealthy by investing as little as $15/week in common stocks and it will grow to $80,000 in 20 years.

Helps create deflated expectation, stock prices skyrocket

Hard to do when average salary ranged between $17–$22 per week, but still reflects nation's optimism

Six Reasons for Growth:

1 Rising stock dividends

Market based in foundation of fresh growth

New investors coming into the market

Many see market as way to "get rich quick"

Only 4 million invest in market at any one time

1,000+ "getting in and getting out" every day

Ensuring lots of cash changes hands, but not stable

2 Increase in personal savings

Wages increase (slowly)

Cost of living remains stable

More have money to save or invest in stock market

3 Easy federal money policy

Credit widely available to anyone who wants to speculate

Interest rates low, whether for automobiles or stock investments

4 Overproduction

After 1925, industry produces more than could be consumed

Business leaders do not scale back production

Anticipate surpluses eventually sold off

Reinvest earnings in industry

New factories, new machinery, more workers

Increases overproduction

5 Lack of federal regulation

Few national guidelines on buying and selling of stock

Corporations make stocks worthless paper with unending printing

Compounded by investors who "buying on the margin" (buying stock on credit)

Building a house of cards

Investors confident stock prices would rise, so could pay off balance, plus interest, with nice profit

Allows them to make money on other people's money

But opportunity for disaster strong

If borrow $50,000 to invest, and price not increase, you lose your money, and bank's

Market filled with money that is not actually there

6 Psychology of consumption

Unquestioning faith in prosperity

Leads people to invest more and consider consequences later

Faith becomes new Gospel of Wealth

But makes Crash far worse when it came

The Crash of 1929

September 1929

Americans put too much confidence in market

Unlike previous century, stock market seen as better indicator of status of American economy

Do not pay attention to health of banks or sales of real estate or consumer goods

Stock prices begin to fluctuate

Initially say just temporary bump in road

Not realize stock prices out of proportion to actual profits

Sales falling, factory construction slows, all while market climbs upward

No one is worried, believes market will take care of itself

Black Thursday

October 24, 1929

One of worst days in American economic history

Investors dumped stocks as quickly as could

Sell, sell, sell; The bull suddenly become a bear

Stunned crowds gather outside frantic NYSE

By noon, leading bankers called to HQ of J. P. Morgan & Co.

To restore faith, convinced to buy $20 million in stocks

By nightfall, market caught its breath

Morgan and bankers save day

October 25, market stabilizes

But when business closes for weekend, people begin to worry

People fear collapse again on next Monday

Everyone decides to sell and cut losses while they could

When Exchange opens on Monday, stage set for disaster

Sell orders resume, swell

Black Tuesday Redux

October 29, 1929

Single most devastating day in history of NYSE

As morning opens, prices fall so far they wipe out all profits made over last year

Destroys little confidence people had left in market

From October 29 to November 13, US economy lost over $30 billion

Same amount US spent during all of WWI

Hoover tries to assure Americans

"The crisis will be over in 60 days"

Prices continue to drop

Hoover optimistic, proclaims 3 months later, "The worst is over without a doubt"

As if on cue, things change

It Just Keeps Getting Worse

- National income falls from $87 billion in 1929 to $75 billion in 1930
- By 1931, down to $59 billion
- Only $42 billion in 1932
- $40 billion by 1933
- Former President Coolidge remarks: "This country is not in good condition"
- Hoover tries not to alarm anyone
- Traditionally these things called "panics"
- He calls it a depression
- America not alone
- All industrialized nations of world suffering
- Germany, Britain, and France owe huge amounts of money to each other and US
- Allies alone owe US $9.5 billion, unable to pay after 1928

Social Problems

- Depression triggered many
- High unemployment
- Breakdown of families
- Fantastic numbers of high school dropouts (2–4 million)
- Hopelessness
- Labor protests
- Seems like US on verge of revolution
- "Hoovervilles" built everywhere
- Empty pockets named "Hoover Flags"
- Newspapers became "Hoover blankets"
- In rural areas, farmers armed with shotguns and rifles march on banks to stop foreclosures
- The "Bonus Expeditionary Force"
- In DC, WWI veterans come to protest for immediate pensions
- In 1932, 20,000 set up tent city, promise to stay until paid
- Hoover panics, sends in Army to break up demonstration and destroy tent city
- Led by future heroes Douglas MacArthur and Dwight D. Eisenhower

Ecological Disaster

- Many farmers devastated by Depression
- Large numbers went into debt to buy machinery and land during 1920s
- Unable to make payments
- Crop prices drop, leaving little hope
- In 1931, it stopped raining on Great Plains
- Montana and Dakota became as arid as Sonora desert

- Temperatures reached 115° in IA
- Farmers watch rich black dirt turned to gray dust
- Then the winds begin to blow
- An ecological disaster
- Farmers moving across Plains stripped region of native grasses
- Used tractors to put millions of acres under cultivation
- Nothing to hold earth, so it literally blows away

The Dust Bowl

- Dust storms officially begin in 1934
- Boiling clouds of dust fill skies
- One storm covered parts of KS, CO, OK, TX, and NM (Dust Bowl)
   Dust obscures noon-day sun; pitch black by 4 pm
   Cattle, blinded by blowing grit, run in circles until they die
   7-year-old boy in KS suffocates in a dust drift
- People lose everything
- Marvin Montgomery
- OK, 1937
- Totaled assets: $53 and a car
- Packs belongings, heads to CA
- In 1940, still in migratory worker camp, barely getting by
- Some 300,000 people migrate to CA
- Abandon at least ⅓ farms in Dust Bowl

Hoover's Response

- Believed president should not admit errors
   Many say Hoover not try to check tide of Crash and Depression, but not true
- Try to stem tide, but only willing to go so far
- Will only compromise laissez faire capitalistic approach to a certain degree
- Hoover enlists power of government to support top of economic structure—Trickle Down economics?
   Late 1931, calls for new public works program of $2.5 billion
   Most expensive to date—included plan for Hoover Dam
   Federal Home Loan Bank Aact of 1932
   Encourage home ownership
   Provide loans to small banks and mortgage companies
   Emergency and Relief Construction Act of 1932
   Gives $2 billion to state and local governments for public works
   Reconstruction Finance Corporation (RFC)
   Approves $500 million (and allowed borrowing of $1.5 billion more) to make loans to banks and other needed institutions
   Norris-LaGuardia Act of 1932
   Prevents court injunctions against strikes and picketing

- Hoover's goal
  - Restore confidence in nation's economy, and stop people from withdrawing savings
  - Keeps biggest banks open to lend money to businesses or new investment opportunities
  - Hopes to create jobs and get ball rolling again

Hoover's Failure

- Despite best efforts, Hoover unable to turn economy around
- Democrats control House after 1930

  Crop prices continue to fall
- Farmers Holiday Association

  Begin barricading Midwestern highways, stopping shipments of underpriced commodities
- Failure of Reconstruction Finance Corporation

  Most funds go to large corporations

  Only about 10% goes to state relief
- Hoover willing to help American industry and agriculture recover

  But unwilling to sacrifice his principles to help common people

  Stance subjects him to criticism he is willing to feed farm animals, but not farm children

1933

Alabama: "Somebody told us Wall Street fell, but we were so poor we couldn't tell."

Downward spiral triggered by Crash remains permanent symbol of our greatest economic catastrophe

By 1933, 25% Americans unemployed

Akron and Toledo reach 60–80%

Wages fall almost by half (down to $31 billion)

Farm income drops $12 bilion in 1929 to just $5 billion by 1933

Automobile industry devastated

Sales fall by 75%

Construction industries fall from $8.7 billion in 1929 to $1.4 billion by 1933

6,000 banks fail; had assets of some $4+ billion

More than 100,000 businesses go bankrupt

Landlords evict 200,000 families in NYC in 1931

Fights over garbage and restaurant dumpster food common

Fear becomes dominant trait of generation

Fear of losing jobs (like 100,000 Americans did *every* week from 1929 to 1932)

Fear of losing their homes

Fear of cuts in wages

Fear of being reduced to poverty

The End of Hoover

By late 1932, Hoover had no plans for helping those starving or in need of shelter

Over 100 cities without funds to help homeless

Hoover came to office with great promise

One of our most capable administrators

Called a visionary and a progressive in an age when precious few of either

But Hoover is now completely discredited

As election of 1932 approaches, crisis worsens

Hoover never had a chance

Election of 1932

FDR campaign and inauguration

Voters presented with clear choice:

Hoover held to limited federal intervention

Dem challenger Franklin Delano Roosevelt

Insists government must play role

Supports direct relief for unemployment

Such aid "must be extended by Government, not as a matter of charity, but as a matter of social duty."

Offers "new deal for the American People"

Never delineates New Deal plan

Committed to use power of government to stop economic crisis paralyzing nation

Voters respond in kind:

FDR gets 22.8 million votes to Hoover's 15.8 million

FDR and the New Deal

Who was FDR?

Born into life of wealth and privilege

Talented son of politically prominent family

Graduated from Harvard, Columbia Law School

Served in NY State Legislature

Appointed Assistant. Secretary of Navy to Woodrow Wilson

Ran for vice president in 1920

Stricken with polio in 1921

1928 wins governor of NY

Then accepts Democratic nomination in November 1932

The New Deal for America

New Deal does not fit into a neat philosophical package

Not carefully planned, coordinated strategy

As FDR says, "The country needs, and, unless I mistake its temper, the country demands bold, persistent, experimentation … Above all, we must try something."

FIRST CONCERN: BANKING and FINANCE

First immediate concern for FDR was banking and finance crisis

He had to stop people from withdrawing money from banks

To do so, he had to give people confidence in investing

National bank holiday

First act as president

Declared national bank "holiday"

Closes all banks in nation to prevent any more runs and, therefore, prevent anymore banks from going out of business

Uses inaugural address to reassure nation

"Let me assert my firm belief that the only thing we have to fear is fear itself—nameless, unreasoning, unjustified terror"

If need be, promises to "ask Congress for the one remaining instrument to meet the crisis—broad executive power to wage a war against the emergency, as great as the power that would be given to me if we in fact invaded a foreign foe"

Emergency Banking Act

Congress proclaims banks to remain closed until March 13, 1933

Week from when FDR closes them

A banks could not reopen until it proves to Treasury Dept. it has sufficient funds to resume normal operations

Restoring Confidence

Key to bank success is restoring confidence

Night before banks reopen, FDR give first fireside chat via radio

Calm, reassuring

"We have provided the machinery to restore our financial system. It is up to you to support and make it work."

Banks open following morning and stay open

Very few banks close after FDR elected

Glass-Steagall Act (Banking Act of 1933)

Week or so later, FDR creates FDIC

Federal Deposit Insurance Corporation

Pledges government to guarantee people's bank deposits up to $2,500

Once again, tryies to reassure people

Demonstrates strong active government at work

Providing Relief

Federal Emergency Relief Administration

Sets $500 million aside for most immediate suffering of people

Funds go directly to those people who need it most

FDR once said, "The test of our progress [as a government] is not whether we add to the abundance of those who have much. It is whether we provide enough for those who have too little."

Social Security Act, 1935

In terms of programs and scope, does 3 key things:

Provides retirement pension fund for elderly people

Establishes Unemployment Insurance fund

Creates Disability Insurance and payments to mothers with dependent children

Changing responsibilities

Social Security changes relationship of state to people

Government acknowledges social rights of citizens (as opposed to decades of emphasis on economic rights of property owners)

Government takes responsibility for people's well-being

Marks beginning of welfare state

Why? Because it feels sorry for poor people? Because it wants to give poor people a break? No!

Government of 1930s finally admits what Populists knew in 1890s

In growing, expanding, integrated, market-driven, capitalist economy, individual at mercy of forces beyond their control

Economic success or failure only partly result of one's willingness to work, one's intelligence, one's ingenuity

Providing Jobs

Next turns attention to creating jobs

Does not want to force companies to hire more people, or raise wages

Does not want to foster overproduction, but provide needed jobs

Civilian Conservation Corps (1933–42)

Hired men between 18 and 25 to work on federal work projects

In roughly 10 years, nearly 3 million work in national parks and national forests

Projects include soil conservation, flood control, disaster relief

Works Progress Administration

Follows same kind of thinking as CCC

Gets people off Unemployment, puts them to work for governmentt

Builds new government buildings, airports, libraries, over 650,000 miles of road, 125,000 buildings, 8,000 parks, hundreds of bridges, 5,900 schools, 1,000 airport runways, 13,000 playgrounds

Also puts unemployed writers and artists (and college professors) to work

Write pamphlets and information books on whole range of topics

Before phased out in 1943, 8.5 million people work for WPA

Helping Industry

FDR had to address concerns of big industry

National Industrial Recovery Act

Creates National Recovery Administration

600+ codes come out of NRA

NRA regulations govern everything from car making to making dog food

Also seeks to create fair labor standards

Industries to create councils

Supposed to establish standards of competition

Wants to solve problems with overproduction, cutthroat competition, etc.

Allows more to stay in business and keep workers working

Section 7a guaranteed right of workers to organize and bargain collectively with employers

National Labor Relations Act (Wagner Act)

Strengthens National Recovery Administration, pledges government support for workers' right to unionize

Create National Labor Relations Board

Puts government officials in position to supervise plant elections for unionization

Gives government power to inflict penalties on companies that:

Refuse to allow union elections

Do not allow union members to distribute union literature on company property

Fires workers for union activity

Government asserts influence directly into worker-management relationship

Helping Farmers

Commodity Credit Corporation

Like subtreasury plan of Populists

Provides money for farmers to borrow

Agricultural Adjustment Act

Compensates farmers for cutting back on production

Overproduction keeps prices depressed and devastates farmers financially

Pays farmers to go out to fields and plow them under

Has mixed results

Government subsidies disaster for tenant farmers and sharecroppers

In South, numbers drop by almost ⅓ from 1930 to 1940

Results in homeless blacks crowding into urban areas

But subsidies help landowners

Accounts for almost ¾ of total farm income in Dakotas for 1934

Ending the New Deal

Opponents

Conservatives criticize FDR for his "socialistic tendencies"

Meaning government-planned economy

Many people in 1930s critical of FDR for not going far enough

Want government involved in more areas

FDR believes capitalism mostly good

Sound economic system that got stuck

Needed reform, not rejection

Huey P. Long of Louisiana

Most serious challenge to FDR from Left

Huey Long

Saying he was interesting does not do him justice

Former governor, now senator from Louisiana

Makes home state into personal fiefdom

Attacks big business, raises taxes on corporations to build schools, roads, bridges

Share Our Wealth Society

Wants to redistribute wealth in country

Plans to essentially liquidate large fortunes by taxing income over $1 million @ 100%

Would redistribute money to less fortunate

Thought would guarantee annual income for every family somewhere between $2,000–2,500

Pledges college education for every qualified student

While Long's figures suspect, impact on people real

People listen to Long

His threat dissipates when assassinated by disgruntled political opponent

Republican Opposition

Republicans say FDR's government intervention undermining American individualism

Government handouts takes people's incentive away, discourages people from helping themselves

Government welfare bad economic policy in long run

NJ senator complains that Social Security would "take all the romance out of life. We might as well take the child from the nursery, give him a nurse, and protect him from every experience that life affords."

FDR and followers reply that given depth of crisis, government relief measures humane thing for starving people

American Liberty League

Conservatives come together to oppose New Deal legislation

Want to "teach the necessity of respect for the rights of person and property"

Eleanor Roosevelt

Instrumental in gaining black support for New Deal

Powerful public figure during New Deal

Has own staff, holds own press conferences

Travels widely across country drumming up support for president and New Deal policies

Gains political support

Appeals to blacks with willingness to defy local segregation ordinances

Eats with African-Americans in segregated restaurants

Encourages FDR to take stronger steps toward Civil Rights

FDR resists for fear of antagonizing white conservative Southern politicians

For example, FDR won't support federal antilynching law

Eleanor's appeal works

Blacks vote overwhelmingly for Democrats

One African-American newspaper editor writes of change:

"My friends, go home and turn Lincoln's picture to the wall. That debt has been paid in full."

The Legacy of the New Deal

FDR's legacy mixed

Some lament rise of government spending and government planning in economy

Others say he was a hero

FDR personally saved their home or their job

In return, they elect him to presidency 4 times

Political legacy

During 1936 election, Democrats re-shuffle party

Shape exists for next 50 or so years

Working class voters, union voters, women voters, African-American voters, farmers, newer ethnic voters

All come together to form Roosevelt Coalition

The Roosevelt Recession

Due to helter-skelter nature of New Deal policies, FDR spurs recovery and unintentionally undoes it

Never keeps government programs in place any longer than necessary

By mid 1937, believes it safe to roll back relief programs and public works programs

Slashing WPA projects put thousands out of work

Private sector does not move to hire WPA workers, despite encouraging numbers

Most business leaders not confident in economic recovery

From Labor Day to end of 1937, 2 million people added to ranks of unemployed

FDR forced to plunge $$ back into WPA, CCC, and other government work programs

After 1938, FDR unable to pass any more significant reform bills

Economy stopped decline, but does not rocket upward

LECTURE 24
The Second World War and the Greatest Generation

Weimar Germany, 1918–33

Stigmatized by defeat of WWI

Signed Versailles Treaty

War Guilt Clause:

Germany responsible for everything

Must pay reparations and dismantle military

Depression hits Germany

Reparations bill for 132 billion gold marks

Government taxes people, overprints money

Massive inflation ensues

People lose everything

France occupies Ruhr Valley to get reparations

Allies humiliating civilian government while leaving Army prestige intact

Military never surrenders or lets war touch German soil

Generals declare Army tricked by civilian government

Forced to accept unpopular war guilt clause and Versailles Treaty

Stabbed in back by civilians—Jews, Communists, and liberals

Taking Advantage of the Situation

Nazis reap harvest of discontent

Reject French occupation of Ruhr and reparations

Claim liberal government abandoning people and Motherland

Munich Beer Hall Putsch

Hitler declares coup in November 1923

Gets Gen. Ludendorff to march on Berlin

Troops broken up and leaders arrested

Ludendorff respectfully acquitted

Hitler sentenced to minimum term (5 years) for high treason

Actually spends 8 comfortable months in prison writing *Mein Kampf* (My Struggle)

Attracting a Following

Germany hit hard by world depression in 1932

43% of workforce idle

Hitler promises economic salvation

Appeals to youth as vital, new party, neither socialist nor capitalist

In 1931, 40% of Nazis under age 30, $\frac{2}{3}$s under 40

January 30, 1933

Hindenburg appoints Hitler chancellor

Nazis march through Brandenburg Gate

Fascists legally in power in Germany

But Nazis must find way to unify Germany?

Anti-Semitism and Krystallnacht

German anti-Semitism

Central to Hitler's ideology

Why single out Jews?

German Jews represent less than 1% of total population

But prominent way beyond numbers

Active in professions, journalism, arts, and science

Identified with big capitalists

For Hitler, Jews represent racial "other"

Uniting against the enemy

Nuremberg Laws 1935

Take citizenship from those with 1 or more Jewish grandparents

Forbidden from marrying or having sex with "Aryans"

By 1938, ¼ German Jews emigrate

Kristallnacht, November 9, 1938, "Night of Shattered Glass"

7,000 Jewish businesses destroyed

Synagogues burned

30,000 Jews sent to concentration camps

Few protest against treatment of Jews

The Policy of Appeasement

Anschluss with Austria (March 1938)

Hitler's tanks roll into Austria w/ no opposition

Austria taken into German Reich

British enact policy of appeasement

Try to conciliate Hitler and Mussolini

Chamberlain accepts absorption of Austria into Reich

Czechoslovakia dismembered September–October 1938

Week after annexing Austria

Hitler demands Sudetenland of Czechoslovakia

Mountainous region populated by Germans

Nazi agents win people to idea of German annexation

And what of Europe?

France treaty bound to defend Czechoslovakia

But not prepared to fight offensive war in practice without British help

Brits have no treaty w/ Czechs, so won't help

The Munich Agreement

Mussolini proposes 4 power conferences at Munich, September 30, 1938

Supposed to discuss German aggression, but just give in to Hitler by allowing occupation of Czech in stages

Czechs never consulted

Chamberlain, Daladier, Hitler and Mussolini

The Allied mistake

Thought Munich Agreement would provide "peace in our time"

Saw Hitler as just Nationalist

Simply trying to unite Germans into national state

Churchill called agreement a "disaster of the first magnitude"

The second Czech Crisis, March 1939

Hitler takes rest of Czechoslovakia

No longer bothers to justify aggression

Hitler annexes Germans in Danzig and Polish corridor

Britain and France pledge military aid to Poland

Munich agreement broken in less than 6 months

The Soviets

Big question was what would the Soviets do if war breaks out?

Allies reluctant to negotiate with Stalin

Stalin demands control in Finland, Baltic states and eastern Poland

Germans agree to carve up Poland

Nazi–Soviet Non-Aggression Pact (August 23, 1939)

Greatest diplomatic bombshell of century

Next day, Hitler takes Danzig

At 5 a.m., September 1, 1939, he invades Poland

War!

September 3, Britain and France declare war

For moment, Mussolini stays neutral

But WW II has begun

Germany Initiates the Blitzkrieg

Germany moves against France

Go around French Maginot Line through Belgium and Holland

Drives wedge between Brits and French

Isolate British Expeditionary Force at Dunkirk

Hitler holds forces 23 days while BEF evacuates Dunkirk

BEF abandons all equipment

Only 325,000 troops manage to leave

Then Nazis pin French against own fortifications

France surrenders

Suddenly all of Europe outside of USSR either neutral or occupied by Axis

Impact on US public opinion great

Prior, only ¼ favored aid

But after, $^4/_5$s favors aid

The US Appraises the Situation

FDR watches Europe, but does nothing

October of '39

Asks Congress to sell arms by Cash and Carry

Lets American industry sell to warring states but not on credit

FDR claims would protect US neutrality

The Lend/Lease Program, March 1941

Churchill says England does not have money to purchase US goods

Asks FDR to solve problem

FDR introduces bill to nations fighting Axis powers

Isolationists angry, but measure passed

$7 billion appropriated for Britain and Allies

Move US from neutrality to non-belligerency

US military stance, 1940–41

Neutrality patrols of Atlantic, April 1940

In July 1940, US occupies Iceland

September 1941, US issues shoot on sight order: Declaration of naval war against Germany

By winter of 1941/42, US at war with Germany

The Road to Pearl Harbor

US and Japan good friends before war

US provides Japan with 80% of its gas and scrap iron

Japan does not even have refining facilities, so totally dependent on US

Fall 1937, Sino-Japanese war erupts

Japan alarmed by growing strength of China

Wants to rid itself of foreign influence and reclaim Manchuria

Hopes to establish buffer zone in NE China to protect Manchuria

Japanese next take advantage of German blitzkrieg

Occupies colonies of Belgium, Holland, and France, 1937–39

Area rich in raw materials

September 1939, US gives Japan notice of sanctions

US slows flow of supplies

Tri-Partite Pact (1940)

Military alliance requires members must be defended by 2 other powers

Hitler believes it compels Japan to go to war with USSR

US sees it as threat against them

Japan and US in Pacific

US–Japan Meeting, 1940

Admiral Nomura, Japanese ambassador, begins discussions with US Secretary of State Cordell Hull

None acceptable

Hull demands Japan leave of China before legitimate negotiations begin

Talks break off

Some claim chance for negotiation is over

Japan Faces Crucial Test

Japan must forcefully acquire supplies or appease US

Spring 1940, Japan seeks meeting with US

Japan makes several proposals:

Promises to end war in China if US get China to agree to buffer zone

In return, Japan gives favorable trade treaty to US

Offers to evacuate northern Indo-China if US promises not end trade sanctions

Promise to nullify Tri-Partite Pact if US cuts off aid to Britain

US rejects proposal

July 1941

Konoe, Premier of Japan asks to meet with FDR to resolve conflict in

US rejects meeting

Military takes control of Japanese government

December 6, 1941

Last order to Japanese embassy

Destroy all classified documents

On morning of December 7, issue war warning

Pearl Harbor

Japanese fleet takes northern route from Kuril Islands

Entirely undetected by US

Hawaii air patrols go 400 miles out, but do not spot anything

Early radar operators report air attack, but ignored

Japanese bombers sink or cripple nearly every capital ship in Pearl Harbor

Devastating attack for US

Tactical triumph for Japan

FDR asks joint session of Congress for war next day

US enters WWII

Pearl Harbor and Declaration of War

The Axis at high tide

Within months, Japan takes Shanghai, Philippines, and Dutch East Indies

By late spring of 1943, takes Burma and New Guinea

Threatening India and Australia

All of Europe either neutral or dominated by Axis

In 1941, Germans drive deep into Caucasus Mountains

Overrun most of European Russia

Threatening Central Asia

Churchill, FDR, and several others sign new declaration

Defensive alliance promising to fight until Axis defeated

First American military alliance since Franco-American agreement of 1770s

The Rush to Defense

Millions try to enlist after attack on Pearl Harbor

Increase Army from 200,000 in 1939 to 8 million by 1945

By war's end, military at 15 million men and women

Draft boards register 31 million men from 18–44 years

Physical exams given to $\frac{1}{6}$th of total

Almost $\frac{1}{2}$ rejected for physical problems ranging from bad feet to poor vision

700,000 blacks serve

Mostly in menial positions; especially in navy

Segregation enforced everywhere from living quarters to blood banks to battlefield

Other minorities never officially segregated

350,000+ women serve in limited capacity

Mostly as medical and office personnel

Nearly 1,000 as ferry pilots while members of WASPs

Staffing War Industries

Greatest contribution by women comes in industry

By 1945, comprise about 36% of industrial labor force

Face all kinds of discrimination

In shipyards, most senior women make about $7 a day; senior men about $22

Out of workforce at end of war but recover strength again by late 1940s; especially young married women

Der Fuhrer's Face

War Propaganda

Propaganda contributes to way Americans view enemy

Everyone could separate good Germans from bad Germans

But unable to do so with Japanese

Hated far more than Germans

Part of sentiment explaining what happened to Japanese-Americans

When Paranoia Takes Control

War paranoia high

CA residents think Japanese spies preparing way for invasion

Early 1942, War Dept. begins relocation plan putting Japanese-Americans in camps

War Relocation Authority

Led by Milton Eisenhower

Two-thirds native born (Nisei, Issei)

Only get few days to prepare for relocation

Must sell or leave everything

Total financial loss estimated at $400 million

Relocation happens in two stages

Sent to temporary assembly centers

Santa Anita racetrack LA where piled into horse stables

Later move to 10 permanent camps away from coasts

Found in CA, AZ, UT, CO, WY, ID, and AR

8 people live in space 25x20 feet

No privacy

Internment

The Allied offensive, 1944

The invasion of Normandy

June 6, 1944

156,000 troops cross English Channel

Combine air attack, naval bombardment, and amphibious assault

The Battle of the Bulge, December 16–26, 1944

Last major German offensive of war

Launch attack on Allies at Belgium

After 10 days, Germans driven back

Invading the Motherland, 1945

Allies immediately find extermination camps

6 million Jews murdered

Some 6 million other Poles, Slavs, Gypsies, homosexuals, and other "undesirables" executed

Buchenwald, Dachau, and Auschwitz

US government aware of situation since 1942

Germany surrenders May 7, 1945

The War Drags On

FDR dies April 12, 1945

V.P. Harry S. Truman takes over

War in the Pacific

Truman has 3 options to end the war with Japan:

Military invasion

Negotiation

Shock Japan into surrender

1. Military invasion

Plans immediately put into action

Troops shifted to Pacific

US develops 2-prong attack

Americans take key islands

Iwo Jima, Feb. 16–March 26, 1945

23,000 casualties out of 70,000 Marines

20,000+ Japanese killed

Okinawa, April 1–June 21, 1945

US: 38,000+ wounded, 12,000 killed or missing

207,000+ Japanese soldiers/civilians dead

Another force gathers in Alaska

Two forces to invade Japan from north and south, September 1945

Believe would take 1 million men to capture Japanese mainland

Expect to suffer over 100,000 casualties

2. Ending the War by Negotiation

Under Secretary of State Joseph C. Grew

Chief advocate for negotiations

Points out Japan defenseless

American and British ships shelling Japanese cities at will

Incendiary raid on Tokyo kills 100,000

Truman remains stubborn

Potsdam Conference, August 2, 1945

Allies gather to decide German surrender

Says to Japan; they must surrender or face "prompt and utter destruction"

Japan refuses

3. Shocking Japan into Submission

Secretary of War Henry Stimson

Told Truman of Manhattan Project at Potsdam

Truman tells Stimson to investigate options for ending war with atomic bomb

Viewed as quickest way to end war

Stimson decides only three possibilities:

Test blast

Rejected as unworkable and forewarns Japan

Dropping bomb after warning first

Reject because of 10,000 American POWs in Japan

Fear Japan would use POWs as shield

Dropping without warning on military-industrial target

Approved

Dropping the Bomb

Dropping the Atomic Bomb

Truman instructs Air Force to select 1 or more targets

August 6, 1945, bomb dropped on Hiroshima—80,000 killed

August 8, Soviets declare war and invade Manchuria

August 9, Nagasaki destroyed—80,000–85,000 killed

Analyzing the Decision

Defenders argue bomb used on military grounds

Critics say bomb only dropped as demonstration for Soviets

It killed only civilians

Changed the world

Japan Surrenders August 15, 1945

No options remaining and facing complete annihilation

Most costly war in world history

From ashes, US and Soviets emerged as world superpowers

Life After the War

WWII painted as greatest nation (and generation) fighting an evil empire to protect democracy and free enterprise

Certainly, some truth in that

But, simultaneously US discriminating against: African-Americans, who were segregated even while fighting for US in war

Japanese-Americans, who were interned in armed camps like POWs

Paradoxes would be, in the end, significant to the way social and cultural history of US unfolds in 1950s, 60s, and 70s

LECTURE 25
The Civil Rights Movement

Race in America

Difficult to generalize about African-Americans in 1950s

About 15.8 million in 1950

19 million in 1960

About 10.6% of population

Fled South in large numbers after 1900

By 1970, 47% of blacks live outside South

In South, blacks struggle under Jim Crow laws

Restricted access to everything from bathrooms to schools

Situation compounded by social patterns reinforcing second-class legal status of blacks

Whites never address black men as "mister," just "boy" or "Jack"

Whites will not shake hands or socialize with blacks in any way

When black men meet whites in public, expected to remove hat

Whites refused to return favor

Segregation

Taking Civil Rights

Origins lay in war years

African-Americans served with distinction

Vital use to war industries

Hypocritical place in society could not be ignored

After war ends, series of events break barriers

Important firsts in sports and entertainment

Truman's Commission on Civil Rights (1946)

Report outlines need to end political inequality

Legal action of NAACP

Conducts voter registration drives and challenges segregation in courts

Various court decisions in North

427

End all-white election primaries, racially restrictive housing agreements, and exclusion of blacks from professional schools

Brown Decision

Battle for equality in the South

NAACP chips away legal foundation of segregation

Thurgood Marshall

Heads NAACP's legal defense section in late 1940s–50s

Wants to overturn *Plessy* decision

Combines 5 lawsuits challenging segregation in public schools

Oliver Brown v. Board of Education of Topeka (1954)

Overturns Kansas school segregation

Brown's 8-year-old daughter Tina bussed to black school although white elementary only 3 blocks away

Supreme Court hears arguments on 5 cases in December 1952

Marshall use sociological and psychological evidence to prove segregated schools inherently unequal

Earl Warren reads Court's unanimous decision

Declares all segregation laws invalid

But only says schools should integrated with "all deliberate speed"

Arguments over definition of phrase allows some states to sandbag integration

Enforcing Brown

Resistance strong in South

Many work around Brown decision

Most create all-white private academies

Virginia closes all schools

Some states refuse to implement federal decisions

Southern Manifesto

In 1956, 101 congressmen from former Confederate states sign

Led by Strom Thurmond

Document encourages state governments not to comply with federal law

Eisenhower privately against Brown decision

Says appointment of Earl Warren worst mistake he ever made

Little Rock

Little Rock Nine

Federal courts get tired of waiting

Little Rock, Arkansas

First test of federal power

Gov. Orval Faubus faces tense reelection battle

Makes resistance to desegregation personal crusade

Defies court order to integrate Little Rock schools

Sends National Guard to prevent 9 black students from entering Central High

Succeeds for 3 weeks

Screaming crowds cheer Faubus, menace students and beat up 2 black reporters

Chant, "two, four, six, eight, we ain't gonna integrate"

Eisenhower tries to work with Faubus, but rejected

Then Faubus suddenly withdraws troops leaving 9 kids at mercy of mob

Forcing Compliance

Eisenhower unable to wait any longer

Nationalizes Arkansas National Guard

Sends in 1,000 paratroopers from 101st Airborne Division

Forcefully integrates Central High at bayonet point

Faubus unfazed

Closes Central High following year

Remains closed till fall of 1959

With legal breakthrough, Civil Rights leaders realize it must be exploited

Civil Rights Movement needs a strong leader

The Montgomery Bus Boycott

Martin Luther King Jr. comes to national prominence due to incident

Montgomery Bus Boycott

December 1, 1955, Montgomery seamstress and black activist Rosa Parks arrested

Refuses to give up seat to white man

Charged with violating local Jim Crow law

Member of NAACP, so plight gets national story

Black community responds by turning to MLK

Becomes pastor of Montgomery's Dexter St. Baptist Church year before at age of 26

Son of prominent Atlanta minister

Received BA from Morehouse College

Ph.D. in Theology from Boston U.

Embraces teachings of Mahatma Gandhi

Program of nonviolent passive resistance

After Park's arrest, MLK endorses plan of local women's group to boycott Montgomery's bus system until integrated

Bus system dependent on blacks, just as they depend on it

For next 381 days, united black community forms carpools or walks to work

Giving In to Demands

Ending the boycott

Bus company near bankruptcy

Downtown stores complain of losing business

City still won't give in

Supreme Court rules bus segregation unconstitutional in November 1956

City gives in

● Southern Christian Leadership Conference (SCLC)

— Created by MLK in 1957 with Rev. Ralph Abernathy and other southern black clergy

— Based in Atlanta

— Church long been moral and social center of life for southern blacks

    Now lends organizational skills and best preachers to Civil Rights Movement

— SCLC and NAACP are two primary advocacy groups for racial justice

    Victories limited in 1960s

    Lay foundation and organizational groundwork for successes

    Move struggle of equality to heart of segregation and disenfranchisement

The Sit-Ins: From Greensboro to Atlanta

    Civil Rights Movement not led entirely from top down

    In February 1960, 4 black freshmen at NC A&T go to Woolworth's to sit at counter for lunch

    Forbidden to blacks by local custom and law

    Ask for coffee and donuts, but denied service

    Return with supporters each day until Woolworth's filled with sit-in protesters

    Eventually Greensboro's leadership gives in

    Strong black boycott cuts into business profits

    Greensboro triggers larger movement of 70,000 students across South over next 18 months

    Largest in Atlanta

    Students from Morehouse, Spellman, and Atlanta universities participate

    Led by Morehouse undergraduates Julian Bond and Lonnie King

    Police arrest of more than 70 on first day

    Lasts for months, hundreds jailed

    City's leadership finally gives in September 1961

    Fears massive loss of profit by organized and effective boycott

The Freedom Rides, 1961

    ● Congress of Racial Equality (CORE)

    — James Farmer, director

    — Launches rides across South to draw national attention

    — Want arrests and violence to get court review of southern laws

    — Southern laws prevent integrated travel across state lines

    ● The first ride

    — Left DC in early May bound for Alabama and Mississippi

    — At Anniston (AL), mob attack flattens tires and firebombs bus

    Passengers beaten with iron bars and clubs

    One rider dies

    — Birmingham

    When rest try to get back under way, 40 whites attack Riders again

    On May 17, CORE gives up program

    ● The Next Ride

Student Nonviolent Coordinating Committee (SNCC)

Leaves Birmingham for Montgomery on May 20

Bus attacked in Birmingham, beating riders, journalists, and Justice Dept. officials

White rider from Wisconsin, James Zwerg, has spinal cord severed

JFK forces Interstate Commerce Commission to legalize interstate travel

Birmingham, 1962–64

MLK targets segregation in Alabama

Wants decisive victory

Birmingham to be big test

Most segregated city in US

Has history of violence, so not easy target

Blacks 40% of population

Only 10,000 of 80,000 blacks registered to vote

SCLC starts movement

Fills city jails with protesters

Launches boycotts of Birmingham businesses

Wants to provoke police chief Bull Connor into violence

King and hundreds of others arrested

MLK composes famous Letter from Birmingham Jail

Outrage Against the South

By May 1963, Connor turns up violence

Police use dogs and water cannons against protesters

Broadcast across country on TV

Americans respond with outrage

JFK must consider stronger action

As violence escalates, sends 3,000 troops to Birmingham

Plans to send more, but violence temporarily subsides

16th Street Baptist Church

Bombing, September 15, 1963

4 black children killed

Riots erupt, leading to deaths of 2 more youths

Kennedy and Civil Rights Movement

By summer of 1963, JFK sees time is ripe for change

With black activism and white support, sweeping Civil Rights legislation possible

But federal intervention necessary

Ole Miss and Birmingham prove that

June 1963, Gov. Wallace threatens to block entrance of 2 black students into Univ. of Alabama

JFK and RFK nationalize Alabama National Guard

Order Wallace to step aside and allow students access

On June 11, JFK goes on national TV

Personally endorses Civil Rights Movement

Tells US freedom not possible until all citizens free

Next week, asks Congress for law protecting voter rights

Outlaws public segregation

Bolsters federal authority to deny funds to discriminating programs

After 3 years of doing nothing, JFK backs Civil Rights Movement solidly

But proclamation not enough

Few hours after speech, gunman murders Medgar Evers

Leader of Mississippi's NAACP

The March on Washington

Civil Rights Movement leaders understand seriousness of Southern situation

Organize march on Washington to pressure Congress, show urgency of cause and demonstrate dedication to nonviolence

Idea originates with A. Phillip Randolph in 1941

President of Brotherhood of Sleeping Car Porters

JFK opposes march

Fears would jeopardize support for Civil Rights bill

But as plans for march become solid, JFK gives in

Leaders from SCLC, NAACP, SNCC, Urban League, and CORE put aside differences to bring event off

Most not happy with JFK administration

John Lewis

Head of SNCC

Freedom rider who was beaten numerous times

Plans to denounce JFK and RFK as waffling hypocrites

But Walter Reuther (UAW leader) and Randolph convince Lewis to change speech in interest of liberal harmony

Free at Last ...

On August 28, 1963

250,000+ people rally at Lincoln Memorial for freedom

Includes 50,000 whites

People from all walks of life: doctors, teachers, union members, students, clergy, and entertainers

Joan Baez leads largest sing-along with stirring rendition of *We Shall Overcome*

Ends when MLK gives best speech in US history

"Let Freedom Ring"

"When we allow freedom to ring, when we let it ring from every village and every hamlet, from every state and every city, we will be able to speed up that day when all God's children, black men and white men, Jews and Gentiles, Protestants and Catholics, will be able to join hands and sing in the words of the old Negro spiritual: "Free at last! Free at last! Thank God Almighty, we are free at last!"

Why was MLK's speech so powerful?

Speaking brilliance of MLK

Creates stirring interracial unity

Marks high point of Civil Rights Movement

Buoyed spirit of liberals trying to push Civil Rights Movement legislation through Congress

Johnson and the New Democratic Party

November 22, 1962, Dallas

JFK dies on operating table at Parkland Hospital that fall

Many unsure what will happen next

Lyndon Baines Johnson (TX) his successor

Not friend of Civil Rights and worked against Civil Rights legislation

But LBJ faced with stark reality as president

Democrats dominate since 1932, but about to be thrashed

South becoming conservative, and thus Republican

Southern base of Democrats crumbling

North solidly Democratic and liberal

LBJ sees chance to rescue Democratic Party

Embraces Civil Rights Movement

Hopes to insure solid Democratic base among blacks and northern and western liberals

Brilliant strategy lets Dems. seize new areas and maintain Southern control

The Civil Rights Act of 1964

LBJ vows to give US a Civil Rights Bill

Must be stronger than JFK's plan

LBJ uses all of his political skills to push bill thru Congress mostly unchanged

In closed-door meeting, convinces southern legislators to read writing on wall

Better to control change, then have no say

July 2, 1964

LBJ signs Civil Rights Act of 1964

Most significant Civil Rights legislation since Reconstruction

Among most important points:

Prohibits discrimination in places of public accommodation

Outlaws discrimination in employment on basis of race, color, religion, sex, or national origin

Authorizes Justice Dept. to begin lawsuits to desegregate public schools and other facilities

Creates Equal Employment Opportunity Commission

Gives federal money to help communities desegregate schools

Freedom Summer

But battle only half complete

Segregation now illegal, but true political equality requires ability to vote

Blacks could not vote in South

Freedom Summer Project

Spring of '64

SNCC launches program to fix voting problem

Mississippi seen as toughest challenge

Poorest and most backward state in nation

Politically controlled by white planter elite who rigidly maintained Mississippi racial system

Remained untouched by Civil Rights struggle

Yet represents 42% of all US blacks

Fewer than 5% could register to vote

Median black family income only $1,500/year

About ⅓ of what white families earn

Freedom Summer Project

Freedom Summer Project recruits 900+ volunteers

Mostly white college students from all over US

Going to Mississippi to:

Aid in voter registration

Teach in "freedom schools"

Help build "freedom party" as alternative to all-white Democratic Party of Mississippi

Expecting Trouble

Bob Moses of SNCC and Dave Dennis of CORE

Organizers expect violence in Mississippi

Precisely why sought white volunteers

As Dennis later explained, "The death of a white college student would be of more political value then the death of a black college student."

Mississippi authorities prepare for Freedom Summer like they would an invading army

Beef up local and state police forces

Not have to wait long for trouble

And Then Comes the Violence

Mississippi Burning

While volunteers still training in Ohio, 3 activists disappear in Neshoba County

Goodman, Schwerner and Chaney

Went to investigate burning of black church

Six weeks later FBI finds bodies

Goodman and Schwerner each shot once

Chaney beaten horribly, then shot 3 times

In all, 1,000 volunteers arrested and 80 beaten

35 shooting incidents and 30 bombings

Violence creates tension within project between black and white leaders

But Dennis' goal successful

National attention riveted on racism of Mississippi

"The times they are a changin'"

Tension within project indicative of division within Civil Rights Movement

Younger factions tired with limits of nonviolent protests

Many youths sympathetic to radical and militant language of Malcolm X

Selma

Civil Rights leaders want to humiliate government into passing new laws

MLK chooses Selma, Alabama as target

Selma

Has 27,000 people

About 50 miles west of Montgomery

Of 15,000 eligible black voters, less than 1,000 registered

Back in 1963, local SNCC activists tried to register black voters

Met by violence at hands of county sheriff Jim Clark

MLK believes Clark might be another Bull Conner

MLK arrives in Selma in January of '65

Just received Nobel Peace Prize in Oslo

Demands right to register voters

Leads daily marches on courthouse

By early February, Clark imprisons more than 3,000 protesters

One black activist killed

Another beaten

But does not get national outcry that MLK needs

Bloody Sunday

Early March, SCLC march from Selma to Montgomery

Plan to deliver list of grievances to Gov. Wallace

Sunday, March 7, 1964

600 marchers leave Selma for Montgomery

At Pettus Bridge met by mounted, heavily armed county and state police

Marchers ordered to turn back, but refuse

Police fire tear gas and attack with clubs

Drive protesters back over bridge through gas and blood

50 hospitalized

Receives extensive coverage on network TV

MLK calls for second march on Montgomery

Federal court issues temporary restraining order telling them not to march

MLK compromises

Promises to lead march over bridge, pray, then turn around and go back

Infuriates more militant factions, who vow not to participate

Selma movement collapsing, but gang of white thugs rescues

Attacks 4 white Unitarian ministers who came for march

One dies from multiple skull fractures

LBJ Forced to Act

March 15, 1964

Asks Congress for a voting rights bill

Persuades federal judge to allow Montgomery march to proceed

Warns Wallace not to interfere

March 21, 1964

MLK leads 3,000 black and white marchers out of Selma

By time reaches Montgomery, number swells to 30,000

Changes in Registration

Voting Rights Act of 1965

August 1965

LBJ signs Voting Rights Act into law

Federal supervision of registration in states and counties where fewer than ½ of voting age residents registered

Outlaws literacy and other discriminatory tests being used to keep blacks from voting

Voting Rights Act fairly successful

By 1968, black registration jumps from 7% to 59% in Mississippi

Goes from 24% to 57% in Alabama

Total southern voters grow from 1 million to 3.1 million

An Incomplete Victory

Poverty, racism, and slums persist

Greatest failure of liberalism in 20th c. is belief that once political rights obtained, economic equality would follow

Did not happen because those problems have other causes

LECTURE 26

Conformity in an Affluent Society & the Rise of Counterculture

An Affluent Society

US turns war production to consumerism

GNP (Gross National Product) more than doubles from 1946 to 1960

US produces ⅔ of world's manufactured goods

Family income doubles from 1949 to 1973

US Population: 151,684,000

6% of world population

Living the High Life

In every measurable way—diet, housing, wages, education, recreation—Americans live better than parents and grandparents

Nearly 50% of adults own homes (1945–60)

95% of families own at least 1 car

1945, car companies sell 70,000 new cars

1950, car companies sell 6 million new cars

College enrollment quadruples (1945–70)

Engines of Prosperity 1: The Baby Boom and Nuclear Family

Baby Boom increases US population by 30% (40 million) between 1945–60

1945–60, one of highest birthrates

Average age of marriage drops for women from 22 in 1900 to 20.3 in 1962

The nuclear family

2 adults, 2+ kids per household

..age demand for durable household goods and baby-related items

21 million cars

20 million refrigerators

12 million TVs

Engines of Prosperity II: The Service Sector Boom

See increased travel, recreation, education, insurance, and medical services

In 1956, airlines attract as many passengers as railroads

Personal recreation jumps from $11 billion in 1950 to more than $18 billion in 1959

By 1956, service sector jobs exceed number of manufacturing occupations

Sales, clerical, and other white-collar occupations

US becoming post-industrial society

Focus on technological innovation and labor productivity

The Tupperware Party

Tupperware developed by Earl Silas Tupper (1945)

Patents "burping seal"

Early 1950s, Tupperware's sales and popularity explode

Women sell product at "jubilees"

Lavish and outlandishly themed parties

Part of women's return "to the kitchen"

Being a Tupperware Girl empowering

Provides toehold in postwar business world

Rallies held to recognize and reward top-selling demonstrators, managers, and distributorships

Engines of Prosperity III: The Culture of Consumption

Buy Now, Pay Later

Installment credit soars for first time

$4 billion in 1954

$43 billion in 1960

Most married women cannot get personal credit cards until 1970

Credit cards emerge to fill void

Diner's Club (1950), American Express (1958), BankAmeriCard (1959, later renamed VISA)

Rise of nationwide business chains

Ray Kroc and the franchise

McDonald's

Works because people eating out more often

Standardization of products and services (again conformity)

No one makes things for themselves

TV and the Culture of Consumption

First TV stations appear in 1940s, but hundreds exist by 1960

Growth of TV advertising industry in 1950s

First TV advertisement

14:29, July 1, 1941, on NYC NBC affiliate

Bulova Watch Co. pays $9 for a 20-second spot

Airs before Brooklyn Dodgers–Philadelphia Phillies game

1952 first presidential election TV ad

Dems buy 30-minute slot for Adlai Stevenson

Sent hate mail for interrupting *I Love Lucy*

Eisenhower wins election with 20-second spot

Engines of Prosperity IV:

Helping Returning Veterans

Servicemen's Readjustment Act of 1944

"The Bill That Changed America"

Effectively doubled cost of war

Set aside money to educate veterans

Vocational or college

The "52-20 club"

Veteran Unemployment Insurance

Provides readjustment benefits of $20 a week up to 52 weeks

The Veterans Preference Act (1944)

Puts veteran in more favorable position than nonveterans

Educational Benefits in the GI Bill

Offers 4 years of full-time tuition or training

Provides stipend while attending school

Subsistence pay for dependents

Pays for fees and books

Of more than 15 million eligible veterans, about half use

2.2 million attend college or postgraduate study

3.5 million enroll in other schooling

1.4 million get on-the-job training

700,000 get farm training

1.5 million students in 1946 alone

Veteran's Administration (VA) Benefits

Increases homeownership

No money down, low monthly payments

1945–66, $\frac{1}{5}$ of all single-family residences financed by GI Bill

In California, FHA and VA insure 50% of new mortgages

28% of WWII veterans use VA home loans

Expanding entrepreneurial activities

GI Bill promise of a loan of up to $2,000 to start business

Gives veterans additional advantage of investment capital

Most states supplement this deferred loan

Unexpected Impact of GI Bill

The advantaged class

GI Bill gives vets edge over nonvets in work, education, and society

Most vets white males

Vets best prepared for high-earning, white-collar work of postwar economy

Male vets at college come at expense of women and minorities

Schools cut admissions for veteran attendance

Cornell University cuts female enrollment by 20% in 1946 alone

Those on the outside

Female vets never considered full-fledged military personnel

Must prove independence from male breadwinner to receive full GI benefits

Widows get poorer benefits than husbands would receive

Women have no access to tickets of upward mobility

Creating a Homogenized Society

Expansion of highway system

Collier-Burns Act, 1947

12,500 miles of highway projects

7 cent gas tax per gallon

$1 million per day spent by late 50s

Interstate Act of 1956

Provides federal funds for 90% of new freeways

Creates drive-in culture

First McDonald's in 1954, 228 by 1960

Nearly 5,000 drive-in theaters by 1960

Rev. Robert Schuller (Orange Drive-In Theater)

"Worship as you are in the family car."

Redistribution of people

White flight to suburbia

Sunbelt and black migration goes North

Fewer farmers—agribusiness

Growth of the megalopolis

Toward Homogeneous Culture

TV and mass culture

Links East and West coasts by 1951

National audience seeing same thing at same time

TV commercial sales surpass radio advertising revenue

$2/3$ of American homes have at least 1 TV (40 million TV sets) by mid 1950s

More TVs than bathtubs by 1960

The influence of TV

Average TV watching time: 5 hours per week

Set standards and values for homes

Shows portray perfect family and wholesomeness

Leave It to Beaver, American Bandstand, Mickey Mouse Club, I Love Lucy

Is it the reality of "real" homes?

Are You Popular? (1955)

Toward Homogeneous Culture: Religious Revival

Becoming a religious nation

Weekly church attendance rises from 38% to 50%

$3/5$ of country are church members by 1958

"Under God" added to pledge of allegiance (1954)

"In God We Trust" nation's official motto (1956)

Religion on TV

Billy Graham and Bishop Fulton Sheen

Religious books dominate bestsellers

Revised standard version of the Bible

Norman Vincent Peale, *Power of Positive Thinking*

"Anybody can do just about anything with himself that he really wants to and makes his mind up to do."

Why a religious revival?

The Cold War

Fear of communism and godlessness

Toward Homogeneous Culture: Suburbanization

Why build suburbs?

GI Bill creates need for more housing

Developing economical housing

Levittown

Mass production of uniform-plan tract housing

"Ranch-style" house

Desire to escape urban life

Suburbia becomes bastion of uniformity

Antithesis of individualism

Emphasizes family togetherness

Center of anti-urban sentiment

Reflects culture of anxiety

Rise of "big four" magazines

Life

Reader's Digest

Look

Saturday Evening Post

Moving to Suburbia

The Suburbanite Ideal

The perfect housewife

Strict domestic "feminine" role

A woman's place is in the home

Emphasizes family as source of individual fulfillment

Restricted sexuality

Good Housekeeping, May 13, 1955

"A woman with a grade-point average of 'C' is more likely to succeed than a women of greater intelligence because she had a greater chance for a lasting marriage and content family."

In 1957 poll found 80% believe people who chose not to marry were sick or immoral

Privatized American Dream

The Man in the Gray Flannel Suit (1956)

Heroic captain becomes public relations middle manager at Broadcasting Company

Pesky, ambitious wife always wants more steaks in freezer

Learns to maneuver corporate channels, but keeps flashing back to trauma of war duty

Good Housewife's guide, *Housekeeping Monthly,* May 13, 1955

The Beat Generation

Jack Kerouac's *On the Road* (1957)

Allen Ginsberg's *Howl* (1956)

William Burroughs' *Naked Lunch* (1959)

Literature of pure experience

Does not follow literary conventions

Reaction to what they think is the spiritual bankruptcy and meaninglessness of American life

The Rise of the Social Critic

Vance Packard's *The Status Seekers* (1959) and *The Hidden Persuaders* (1957)

Describes American social stratification and effect of media manipulation

David Riesman's *The Lonely Crowd* (1950)

Says Americans "other-directed conformists who lack inner resources to lead truly autonomous lives."

William Whyte's *The Organization Man* (1956)

Says Americans sold out to corporate life by becoming nation of employees who "take vows of organization life" to become "dominant members of our society."

C. Wright Mills, *The Power Elite* (1956)

"The powers of ordinary men are circumscribed by the everyday world in which they live, yet even in the rounds of job, family, and neighborhood they often seem driven by forces they can neither understand nor govern."

John Kenneth Galbraith, *The Affluent Society* (1958)

Most negative critic of American conformity

Asks 2 crucial questions:

What kind of society slighted investment in schools, parks, and public services while producing ever more goods to fulfill desires created by advertising?

Was the spectacle of millions of educated middle-class women seeking happiness in suburban dream houses a reason for celebration or a waste of precious "womanpower" at a time when the Soviets trumpeted the accomplishments of their female scientists, physicians, and engineers?

New Freedoms

The "Male Revolt": Sexualizing the female body

The success of *Playboy* magazine

Hugh Hefner

Questions culture of uniformity

Stresses male liberation from sexual and financial restraints associated with ideal of family togetherness

Playboy's Penthouse

Variety show

Ran 5 episodes in 1959

The Sexual Revolution

The Dr. Alfred Kinsey Reports

Sexual Behavior in the Human Male (1948)

Sexual Behavior in the Human Female (1953)

Challenges beliefs about sexuality and discusses taboos

Most controversial: Says there are many sexual orientations, none is dominant

Sexual behavior includes physical contact and psychological phenomena (desire, sexual attraction, fantasy)

The Pill (1960)

Combined oral contraceptive pill

Enormous social impact

Gives women unprecedented control over fertility

Does not require special preparation

Does not interfere with spontaneity or sensation

Divorces sex from reproduction, which heightens debate over moral and health consequences of premarital sex and promiscuity

Helen Gurley Brown's *Sex and the Single Girl* (1962)

Encourages women to actively pursue full single life

Acquire a career, gain financial independence, accept one's looks and have sex

Basis for her magazine *Cosmopolitan*

Perversion for Profit (1955)

The Feminist Movement

Many women not happy at home of 1950s

Ironies of housework

Marriage means surrendering assets and wages to husband

Women have limited access to tools of independence—credit cards, mortgages

Dr. Spock's *Baby and Child Care* (1946)

Revolutionary message

Mothers "know more than you think you do"

Urges parents to be flexible and affectionate, not a disciplinarian

Betty Friedan and *The Feminine Mystique* (1963)

Attacks popular notion that women can only find fulfillment thru childbearing and homemaking

Feminism as a movement

Return to work in late 1950s

Miss America protest (1968)

National Organization of Women (1966)

Bra burning and popular media coverage mid 1960s–1970

Roe v. Wade (1973)

The Equal Rights Amendment

Youth Rebellion and the Teenager

Emergence of youth culture

Result of postwar prosperity and suburban expansion

More teenagers by 1960 than any time prior

Young people have lots of leisure time

Kids no longer help support family

Advertisers recognize teen purchasing power

Get fragmentizing of citizens as consumers

Rock 'n' Roll, a symbol of protests?

Afro-American rhythm & blues crossing over to white teenage consumers

American Bandstand and Elvis Presley

Teen sexuality and juvenile delinquency

Teenage girls get mixed message

Warned of danger of uncontrolled sexuality

Targeted by sexualized images of beauty

Boys with no direction

Rebel Without a Cause, 1955

Counterculture

The Counterculture Movement

Mommas, don't let your babies grow up to be Hippies

Centered at Haight-Ashbury District in San Francisco

Relatively apolitical

Seeking revolutionary freedom rooted in personal liberation from social mores

Living in the commune

The music

LSD guru Timothy Leary

Tune On, Tune In, Drop Out

Calls for explorations in consciousness

America and the Vietnam War

First televised war in US history

Media brought war to dinner table

Death and destruction shown on evening news

Atrocities of war could not be ignored

Hippies as foot soldiers

Antiwar movement (1965–71)

Most significant US movement of its kind

Began with senators criticizing American involvement during summer of 1964

Berkeley Free Speech Movement, 1964

The Teach-In

Antiar Posters

Berkeley Teach-In

The Antiwar Movement

Mass antiwar movement does not appear until summer of 1965

Self-immolation of Buddhist priest, 1965

Teach-ins in spring of 1965

Swept hundreds of campuses

Rallies involve thousands of students

March on Washington (April 17, 1965)

Students for a Democratic Society (SDS)

Largest antiwar demonstration in Washington (25,000 people)

Demonstrations continue that year

Berkeley (15,000), Manhattan (20,000), again in Washington (25,000), New York (300,000–500,000)

By 1968, US casualties mounting and war has no end in sight

Most Americans oppose war and want it to end

Antiwar Demonstrations

1968 as Watershed

Tet Offensive and Vietnam

South Vietnamese police chief Gen. Nguyen Ngoc Loan executing Viet Cong captain Nguyen Van Le

SDS in president's office, Columbia University, 1968

Martin Luther King assassinated

6:01 p.m. on April 4, 1968

Continued racial urban unrest

Robert F. Kennedy assassinated

June 5, 1968

Walter Cronkite's Vietnam Editorial, 1968

Democratic National Convention, Chicago, Aug. 1968

Woodstock, 1969

Weather Underground Organization

US radical Left group

Took name from Bob Dylan song *Subterranean Homesick Blues*

"You don't need a weatherman to know which way the wind blows"

Splintered from SDS and Maoist-based Revolutionary Youth Movement

Form at University of Michigan in 1960s

Carry out series of attacks to overthrow US government, late 60s to mid 70s

Mostly bomb government buildings

Only after calling in bomb-threats to make sure target evacuated

Killed some, wounded others

Patty Hearst, 1970

4 dead in O-hi-O

Kent State University, 1970

Students gather to protest war

National Guardsmen open fire

4 dead and 9 wounded

Mary Brandt

The Vietnamese Girl Wounded by Napalm (by Nick Ut, 1972)

Understanding the Culture of Decency in America

The moral uncertainty of the 1950s was, at least in part, a response to this dilemma of fighting Communism at home without sacrificing the rights and privileges of a democratic republic. The cultures of dissent that flourished in the 1950s and 1960s responded to the peculiar combination of prosperity and anxiety that characterized the decade by opting out—by choosing not to conform to the dictates of mainstream America.

Kurt Vonnegut